MW01383022

Messianic Siddur
Daily Prayers

BOKER LE'YELADIM
(Morning Prayer for Children)

Having awakened from sleep, before any other act, rise from your bed without laziness and, having gathered your thoughts, stand before the All-seeing Elohim (God) and make the Ot Ha-Ts'lav (Sign of the Cross), saying:

Ot Ha-Ts'lav (Sign of the Cross)

In the name of the Father YAHUWAH, and of the Son Yah'shua (Jesus), and of the Ruach HaKodesh (Holy Spirit). Amen.

Blessed be YAHUWAH, always now and for ever, and unto the ages of ages. Amen.

Cheneniy
(Have Mercy on me)

Afterwards, stand in silence for a few moments until all your senses are calmed and your thoughts have laid aside all earthly cares. At that point, begin with the Prayer of the Publican without haste and with heartfelt attentiveness:

O YAHUWAH, have mercy on me, a sinner.

O Yah'shua (Jesus), have mercy on me, a sinner.

O Ruach HaKodesh (Holy Spirit), have mercy on me, a sinner.

Then, continue:

O Adon Yah'shua the Messiah (Lord Jesus Christ), Son of Elohim (God), have mercy on us. Amen.

Glory to You, our Elohim (God); glory to You.

O Melek HaShamayim (Heavenly King), Me'nachem (Comforter), Ruach Ha-Emet (Spirit of Truth), Who are everywhere and fills all things, Treasury of Blessings, and Giver of Life: Come and abide in us, and cleanse us from every impurity, and save our souls, O HaTov (Good One).

El Kadosh (Holy God), Abiyr Kadosh (Holy Mighty), Almavet Kadosh (Holy Immortal One), have mercy on us. *(thrice)*

Glory to the Father YAHUWAH, and to the Son Yah'shua (Jesus), and to the Ruach HaKodesh (Holy Spirit), now and ever, and unto ages of ages. Amen.

O Hashilush HaKodesh (Most Holy Trinity), have mercy on us; Adonai (Lord), cleanse our sins; Adon (Master), pardon our transgressions; Kadosh (Holy One), visit and heal our infirmities for Your Name's sake.

YAHUWAH, have mercy.

Yah'shua (Jesus), have mercy

Ruach HaKodesh (Holy Spirit), have mercy.

Glory to the Father YAHUWAH, and to the Son Yah'shua (Jesus), and to the Ruach HaKodesh (Holy Spirit), now and ever, and unto ages of ages. Amen.

Avinu / Tefillat Talmid
(Our Father / The disciple's prayer)

Avinu (Our Father), Who is in heaven, hallowed be Your Name. Your Kingdom come. Your will be done, on earth as it is in heaven. Give us this day our daily bread; and forgive us our trespasses, as we forgive those who trespass against us; and lead us not into temptation, but deliver us from the Hara (evil one). For Yours is the kingdom, and the power, and the glory, for ever. Amen.

Tefillat Hashilush HaKodesh (Prayer to the Most Holy Trinity)

Having risen from sleep, we fall down before You, O HaTov (Good One), and sing to You, O Abiyr (Mighty One), the angelic song: holy, holy, holy are You, O YAHUWAH Tzeva'ot (Lord of Hosts); through Yah'shua the Messiah (Jesus Christ), have mercy on us.

Glory to the Father YAHUWAH, and to the Son Yah'shua (Jesus), and to the Ruach HaKodesh (Holy Spirit):

Having raised me from my bed and from sleep, O Adonai (my Lord); enlighten my mind and heart, and open my lips, that I may praise You, O Hashilush Hakodesh (Holy Trinity): holy, holy, holy are You, O YAHUWAH Tzeva'ot (Lord of Hosts); through Yah'shua the Messiah (Jesus Christ), have mercy on us.

Now and ever, and unto ages of ages. Amen.

Suddenly the Judge will come, and the deeds of every man shall be revealed; but in the middle of the night we cry with fear: holy, holy, holy are You, O YAHUWAH Tzevas'ot (Lord of Hosts); through Yah'shua the Messiah (Jesus Christ), have mercy on us.

YAHUWAH, have mercy.

Yah'shua (Jesus), have mercy

Ruach HaKodesh (Holy Spirit), have mercy.

Tefillat Hashilush HaKodesh (Prayer to the Holy Trinity)

Having risen from sleep, I thank You, O Hashilush Hakodesh (Holy Trinity), for in the abundance of Your goodness and Your patience, You have not become angry with me for my laziness and sinfulness, nor have You destroyed me together with my iniquities. Instead, in Your usual love for mankind, You have raised me from the gloominess of sleep, that I might rise up early and glorify Your power. Enlighten now the eyes of my mind and open my lips, that I might come to learn Your Torah (Law), understand Your mitzvot (commandments), accomplish Your will, glorify You in heartfelt confession, and praise Your Shem Kodesh (Holy Name), of the Father YAHUWAH, the Son Yah'shua (Jesus), and the Ruach Hakodesh (Holy Spirit), now and ever, and unto ages of ages. Amen.

Come, let us worship YAHUWAH our Elohim (God) and our King.

Come, let us worship and fall down before Messiah (Christ), our King and our Elohim (God).

Come, let us worship and fall down before Messiah (Christ) Himself, our King and our Elohim (God).

YAHUWAH, have mercy.

Yah'shua (Jesus), have mercy

Ruach HaKodesh (Holy Spirit), have mercy.

Yesha'eka Titen Lanu
(Grant Us Your Salvation)

O Adon Yah'shua the Messiah (Lord Jesus Christ), have mercy on us. Amen.

O YAHUWAH, show Your mercy upon us; And grant us Your salvation. Endue Your ministers with righteousness; And make Your chosen people joyful. Give peace, O YAHUWAH, in all the world; For only in You can we live in safety. YAHUWAH, keep this nation under Your care; And guide us in the way of justice and truth. Let Your way be known upon earth; Your saving health among all nations. Let not the needy, YAHUWAH, be forgotten; Nor the hope of the poor be taken away. Create in us clean hearts, O Elohim (God); And sustain us with Your Ruach HaKodesh (Holy Spirit).

O YAHUWAH, save Your people, and bless Your inheritance; Govern them and lift them up for ever. Day by day we magnify You; And we worship Your Shem Kodesh (Holy Name) for ever, world without end. Vouchsafe, YAHUWAH, to keep us this day without sin; YAHUWAH, have mercy upon us. YAHUWAH, let Your mercy be upon us; As our trust is in You. YAHUWAH, in You have I trusted; Let me never be ashamed or confounded. In the name of Yah'shua the Messiah (Jesus Christ). Amen.

Torah Emet
(Law of Truth)

Blessed are You YAHUWAH our Elohim (God), Melek Ha'Olam (King of the universe), the God and the Father of our Lord Yah'shua the Messiah (Jesus Christ), who removes sleep from my eyes, and slumber from my eyelids.

Blessed are You YAHUWAH our Elohim (God), Melek Ha'Olam (King of the universe), the God and the Father of our Lord Yah'shua the Messiah (Jesus Christ), who has given us the Torah Emet (Law of truth), and has planted everlasting life in our midst.

Moses commanded us the Torah (Law) as an inheritance of the congregation of Jacob.

Hear, O Israel: YAHUWAH our Elohim (God), YAHUWAH is One.

Blessed be His name, whose glorious kingdom is for ever and ever.

And you shall love YAHUWAH your Elohim (God) with all your heart, and with all your soul, and with all your might.

And these words which I command you this day shall be upon your heart: and you shall teach them diligently unto your children, and shall talk of them when you sit in your house, and when you walk by the way, and when you lie down, and when you rise up. And you shall bind them for a sign upon your hand, and they shall be for frontlets between your eyes. And you shall write them upon the doorposts of your house and upon your gates. Amen.

O Elohai (my God), guard my tongue from evil, and my lips from speaking guile.

Open my heart to your torah (law), and let my soul pursue your mitzvot (commandments).

Let me fulfill the righteous requirements of your Torah (Law), and sanctify me with Your truth, Your word is Truth, O YAHUWAH.

Let the words of my mouth and the meditation of my heart be acceptable before You, YAHUWAH, my Rock and my Redeemer, in the name of Yah'shua the Messiah (Jesus Christ). Amen.

YAHUWAH, have mercy.

Yah'shua (Jesus), have mercy

Ruach HaKodesh (Holy Spirit), have mercy.

ASERET HIPUCHIM
(THE TEN REVERSALS)
The Beatitudes

Blessed are the poor in spirit, for theirs is the kingdom of heaven.

Blessed are those who mourn, for they shall be comforted.

Blessed are the meek, for they shall inherit the earth.

Blessed are those who hunger and thirst for righteousness, for they shall be filled.

Blessed are the merciful, for they shall obtain mercy.

Blessed are the pure in heart, for they shall see God.

Blessed are the peacemakers, for they shall be called sons of God.

Blessed are those who are persecuted for righteousness' sake, for theirs is the kingdom of heaven.

Blessed are you when they revile and persecute you, and say all kinds of evil against you falsely for My sake. Rejoice and be exceedingly glad, for great is your reward in heaven, for so they persecuted the Navi'iym (prophets) who were before you.

But woe to you who are rich, for you have received your consolation.

Woe to you who are full, for you shall hunger.

Woe to you who laugh now, for you shall mourn and weep.

Woe to you when all men speak well of you, for so did their fathers to the shaker navi'iym (false prophets).

Kitvei HaKodesh (Holy Scriptures)

Hebrews 13:10-17

We have a mizbeach (altar) from which those who serve the tabernacle have no right to eat. For the bodies of those animals, whose blood is brought into the sanctuary by the Kohen Gadol (high priest) for sin, are burned outside the camp. Therefore Yah'shua (Jesus) also, that He might sanctify the people with His own blood, suffered outside the gate. Therefore let us go forth to Him, outside the camp, bearing His reproach. For here we have no continuing city, but we seek the one to come. Therefore by Him let us continually offer the sacrifice of praise to Elohim (God), that is, the fruit of our lips, giving thanks to His name. But do not forget to do good and to share, for with such sacrifices Elohim (God) is well pleased. Obey those who rule over you, and be submissive, for they watch out for your souls, as those who must give account. Let them do so with joy and not with grief, for that would be unprofitable for you.

Ephesians 5:15-21

See then that you walk circumspectly, not as fools but as wise, redeeming the time, because the days are evil. Therefore do not be unwise, but understand what the will of YAHUWAH is. And do not be drunk with wine, in which is dissipation; but be filled with the Spirit, speaking to one another in psalms and hymns and spiritual songs, singing and making melody in your heart to YAHUWAH, giving thanks always for all things to Elohim (God) the Father in the name of our Lord Yah'shua the Messiah (Jesus Christ), submitting to one another in the Yirat Elohim (fear of God).

Colossians 3:22-25

And whatever you do, do it heartily, as to YAHUWAH and not to men, knowing that from YAHUWAH you will receive the reward of the inheritance; for you serve the Lord Messiah (Christ). But he who does wrong will be repaid for what he has done, and there is no partiality.

TEFILLAT BOKER
(Morning Prayers)

After the Boker Le'yeladim (Morning Prayer for Children) and before the Avodah Shacharit (Morning Prayer Service) one says the Teffilat Boker (Morning Prayers).

Ot Ha-Ts'lav (Sign of the Cross)

In the name of the Father YAHUWAH, and of the Son Yah'shua (Jesus), and of the Ruach HaKodesh (Holy Spirit). Amen.

Blessed be YAHUWAH, always now and for ever, and unto the ages of ages. Amen.

At this point, one netilat yadayim (washing of the hands) to ritually wash his hands according to the mitzvot (commandment) Exodus 30:19.

NETILAT YADAYIM
(Hand Washing Blessing)

Blessed are You YAHUWAH our Elohim (God), Melek Ha'Olam (King of the universe), the God and the Father of our Lord Yah'shua the Messiah (Jesus Christ), who has sanctified us with Your commandments, and commanded us about washing the hands. Amen.

MISHPAT SHLOMO
(The Judgment of Solomon)

1. Magnified and praised be Elohim Chayim (the living God): he is, and there is no limit in time unto his being.

2. He is One, and there is no unity like unto his unity; inconceivable is he, and unending is his unity.

3. He has neither bodily form nor substance: we can compare nothing unto him in his holiness.

4. He was before anything that has been created—even the first: but his existence had no beginning.

5. Behold he is Adonei Ha-Olam (the Lord of the universe): to every creature he teaches his greatness and his sovereignty.

6. The rich gift of his ne'vu'a (prophecy) he gave unto the men of his choice, in whom he gloried.

7. There has never yet arisen in Israel a navi (prophet) like unto Moses, one who has beheld his similitude

8. The Torah Emet (Law of truth) Elohim (God) gave unto his people by the hand of his navi (prophet) who was faithful in his house.

9. Elohim (God) will not alter nor change his Torah (Law) to everlasting for any other.

10. He watches and knows our secret thoughts: he beholds the end of a thing before it exists.

11. He bestows loving kindness upon a man according to his work; he gives to the rasha'iym (wicked) evil according to his ra'ah (wickedness).

12. He has sent out His Mashiyach (Anointed One) Yah'shua (Jesus) at the end of days, to redeem them that wait for the end—his salvation.

13. In the abundance of his loving kindness Elohim (God) will quicken the dead. Blessed for evermore be his glorious name. Amen.

ADON OLAM
(Master of the Universe)

He is the Adon Ha-Olam (Lord of the universe), who reigned before any creature yet was formed: At the time when all things were made by his desire, then was his name proclaimed Melek (King). And after all things shall have had an end, he alone, the Ayom (dreaded one), shall reign; Who was, who is, and who will be in glory. And he is One, and there is no second to compare to him, to consort with him: Without beginning, without end: to him belong strength and dominion. And he is Elohai (my God)—my Go'el (Redeemer) lives—and a rock in my travail in time of distress; And he is my banner and my refuge, the portion of my cup on the day when I call. Into his hand I commend my spirit, when I sleep and when I wake: And with my spirit, my body also: YAHUWAH is with me, and I will not fear. Amen.

MODEH ANI
(Upon Arising)

I gratefully thank You, O Melek Chayim Ve'Olam (living and eternal King), for returning my soul within me in compassion, great is Your faithfulness! Blessed are You YAHUWAH our Elohim (God), Melek Ha'Olam (King of the universe), the God and the Father of our Adon Yah'shua the Messiah (Lord Jesus Christ), who returns my soul within me. Amen.

ASHER YATZER
(Who Formed)

Blessed are You YAHUWAH our Elohim (God), Melek Ha'Olam (King of the universe), the God and the Father of our Lord Yah'shua the Messiah (Jesus Christ), who has formed man in wisdom, and created in him many orifices and vessels. It is revealed and known before the throne of Your glory, that if one of these be opened, or one of those be closed, it would be impossible to exist and to stand before You. Blessed are You, YAHUWAH, who heals all flesh and does wondrously. Amen.

BIRKAT HATORAH
(Blessing of the Law)

Blessed are You YAHUWAH our Elohim (God), Melek Ha'Olam (King of the universe), the God and the Father of our Lord Yah'shua the Messiah (Jesus Christ), who has sanctified us by Your commandments, and commanded us to engross ourselves with the words of the Torah (Law).

Make pleasant, therefore, we beseech You, YAHUWAH our Elohim (God), the words of Your Torah (Law) in our mouth and in the mouth of Your people, the house of Israel, so that we with our offspring and the offspring of Your people, the house of Israel, may all know Your name and learn Your Torah (Law). Blessed are You, YAHUWAH, who teaches the Torah (Law) to Your people Israel.

Blessed are You YAHUWAH our Elohim (God), Melek Ha'Olam (King of the universe), the God and the Father of our Lord Yah'shua the Messiah (Jesus Christ), who has chosen us from all nations and given us Your Torah (Law). Blessed are You, YAHUWAH, who gives the Torah (Law). Amen.

BIRKAT KOHANIYM
(Priestly Blessing)

YAHUWAH bless you, and keep you:

YAHUWAH make his face to shine upon you, and be gracious unto you:

YAHUWAH turn his face unto you, and give you peace.

Amen.

Mishnah. Treatise Peah, ch. i.

These are the things which have no fixed measure (by enactment of the Torah (Law)): the corners of the field, the first fruits, the offerings brought on appearing before YAHUWAH at the three festivals, the practice of tzedakah (charity) and the study of the Torah (Law).—These are the things, the fruits of which a man enjoys in this world, while the stock remains for him for the world to come: honoring father and mother, the practice of tzedakah (charity), timely attendance at the house of study morning and evening, hospitality to wayfarers, visiting the sick, dowering the bride, attending the dead to the grave, devotion in prayer, and making peace between man and his fellow; but the study of the Torah (Law) is equal to them all.

ELOHAI NESHAMA
(My Pure Soul)

O Elohai (my God), the soul which you gave me is pure; You did create it, You did form it, You did breathe it into me; You preserve it within me; and You will take it from me, but will restore it unto me hereafter. So long as the soul is within me, I will give thanks unto You, YAHUWAH Elohai (my God) and God of my fathers, Sovereign of all works, Lord of all souls! Blessed are You YAHUWAH our Elohim (God), Melek Ha'Olam (King of the universe), the God and the Father of our Lord Yah'shua the Messiah (Jesus Christ), who restores souls unto dead bodies. Amen.

DEREKH HA-YAH'SHUA
(The blessing for Salvation in the Messiah)

Blessed are You, YAHUWAH our God, Melek Ha'Olam (King of the universe), Who gave to us the way of salvation through Yah'shua the Messiah (Jesus Christ), blessed be He. Amen.

MELEKH HAMELEKIM
(Praising the King of Kings)

Blessed are You YAHUWAH our Elohim (God), Melek Ha'Olam (King of the universe), the God and the Father of our Lord Yah'shua the Messiah (Jesus Christ), a King to be praised in adoration. Amen.

YIRDAT YAHUWAH
(The Fear of YAHUWAH)

The fear of YAHUWAH is the beginning of wisdom: a good understanding have all they that do his commandments: his praise endures for ever. Blessed be the name of his glorious kingdom, for ever and ever. Amen and Amen. Blessed are You YAHUWAH our Elohim (God), Melek Ha'Olam (King of the universe), the God and the Father of our Lord Yah'shua the Messiah (Jesus Christ), who gave himself for us, that he might redeem us from every transgression of the law, and purify for himself his own special people, zealous of good works. Amen.

BIRCHOT HASHACHAR
(Morning Blessings)

Blessed are You YAHUWAH our Elohim (God), Melek Ha'Olam (King of the universe), the God and the Father of our Lord Yah'shua the Messiah (Jesus Christ), who has given the heart understanding to distinguish between day and night. Amen.

Blessed are You YAHUWAH our Elohim (God), Melek Ha'Olam (King of the universe), the God and the Father of our Lord Yah'shua the Messiah (Jesus Christ), Who has made me in His image. Amen.

Blessed are You YAHUWAH our Elohim (God), Melek Ha'Olam (King of the universe), the God and the Father of our Lord Yah'shua the Messiah (Jesus Christ), not made me a heathen. Amen.

Blessed are You YAHUWAH our Elohim (God), Melek Ha'Olam (King of the universe), the God and the Father of our Lord Yah'shua the Messiah (Jesus Christ), who has not made me a bondman. Amen.

Men say:—

Blessed are You YAHUWAH our Elohim (God), Melek Ha'Olam (King of the universe), the God and the Father of our Lord Yah'shua the Messiah (Jesus Christ), who has not made me a woman. Amen.

Women say:—

Blessed are You YAHUWAH our Elohim (God), Melek Ha'Olam (King of the universe), the God and the Father of our Lord Yah'shua the Messiah (Jesus Christ), who has made me according to Your will. Amen.

Blessed are You YAHUWAH our Elohim (God), Melek Ha'Olam (King of the universe), the God and the Father of our Lord Yah'shua the Messiah (Jesus Christ), Who heals the sick. Amen.

Blessed are You YAHUWAH our Elohim (God), Melek Ha'Olam (King of the universe), the God and the Father of our Lord Yah'shua the Messiah (Jesus Christ), who opens the eyes of the blind.Amen.

Blessed are You YAHUWAH our Elohim (God), Melek Ha'Olam (King of the universe), the God and the Father of our Lord Yah'shua the Messiah (Jesus Christ), who clothes the naked. Amen.

Blessed are You YAHUWAH our Elohim (God), Melek Ha'Olam (King of the universe), the God and the Father of our Lord Yah'shua the Messiah (Jesus Christ), who looses them that are bound. Amen.

Blessed are You YAHUWAH our Elohim (God), Melek Ha'Olam (King of the universe), the God and the Father of our Lord Yah'shua the Messiah (Jesus Christ), who raises up them that are bowed down. Amen.

Blessed are You YAHUWAH our Elohim (God), Melek Ha'Olam (King of the universe), the God and the Father of our Lord Yah'shua the Messiah (Jesus Christ), who spreads forth the earth above the waters. Amen.

Blessed are You YAHUWAH our Elohim (God), Melek Ha'Olam (King of the universe), the God and the Father of our Lord Yah'shua the Messiah (Jesus Christ), who has supplied my every want. Amen.

Blessed are You YAHUWAH our Elohim (God), Melek Ha'Olam (King of the universe), the God and the Father of our Lord Yah'shua the Messiah (Jesus Christ), who has made firm the steps of man. Amen.

Blessed are You YAHUWAH our Elohim (God), Melek Ha'Olam (King of the universe), the God and the Father of our Lord Yah'shua the Messiah (Jesus Christ), who girds Israel with might. Amen.

Blessed are You YAHUWAH our Elohim (God), Melek Ha'Olam (King of the universe), the God and the Father of our Lord Yah'shua the Messiah (Jesus Christ), who crowns Israel with glory. Amen.

Blessed are You YAHUWAH our Elohim (God), Melek Ha'Olam (King of the universe), the God and the Father of our Lord Yah'shua the Messiah (Jesus Christ), who gives strength to the weary. Amen.

Blessed are You YAHUWAH our Elohim (God), Melek Ha'Olam (King of the universe), the God and the Father of our Lord Yah'shua the Messiah (Jesus Christ), who removes sleep from my eyes and slumber from mine eyelids. Amen.

Blessed are You YAHUWAH our Elohim (God), Melek Ha'Olam (King of the universe), the God and the Father of our Lord Yah'shua the Messiah (Jesus Christ), both now and ever and unto the ages of ages. Amen and Amen.

YETZAR HARA
(Evil Inclination)

May it be Your will, YAHUWAH our God and God of our fathers, in the name of Yah'shua the Messiah (Jesus Christ), to make us familiar with Your Torah (Law), and to make us cleave to Your mitzvot (commandments), O lead us not into the power of sin, or of transgression or iniquity, or of temptation, or of scorn: let not the yetzar hara (evil inclination) have sway over us: keep us far from a bad man and a bad companion: make us cleave to the yetzar hatov (good inclination) and to good works: subdue our inclination so that it may submit itself unto You; and let us obtain this day, and every day, grace, favor and mercy in Your eyes, and in the eyes of all who behold us; and bestow loving kindnesses upon us. Blessed are You, YAHUWAH, who bestows loving kindnesses upon Your people Israel.

May it be Your will, YAHUWAH Elohai (my God) and God of my fathers, in the name of Yah'shua the Messiah (Jesus Christ), to deliver me this day, and every day, from arrogant men and from arrogance, from a bad mar, from a bad companion and from a bad neighbor, and from any mishap, and from the adversary that destroys; from a hard judgment, and from a hard opponent, whether he be a son of the covenant or be not a son or the covenant. Amen.

SHACHARIT
(Morning Prayers)

MA TOVU
(Prayer on Entering the Synagogue)

On entering the Bet Knesset (Synagogue) say the following:—

As for me, in the abundance of your loving kindness will I come into your house: I will worship toward Your holy temple in the fear of You.

Into the Bet Elohim (house of God) we will walk with the throng.

How goodly are your tents, O Jacob, your dwelling places, O Israel! As for me, in the abundance of Your loving kindness will I come into Your house: I will worship toward Your holy temple in the fear of You. YAHUWAH, I love the habitation of Your house, and the place where Your glory dwells. As for me, I will worship and bow down: I will bend the knee before YAHUWAH, my Maker. And as for me, may my prayer unto You, O YAHUWAH, be in an acceptable time: O Elohim (God), in the abundance of Your loving kindness, answer me in the truth of Your salvation. Amen.

L'OLAM YEHEI ADAM
(Always Should a Man Revere God)

At all times let a man fear Elohim (God) as well in private as in public, acknowledge the truth, and speak the truth in his heart; and let him rise early and say:

Sovereign of all worlds! Not because of our righteous acts do we lay our supplications before You, but because of Your abundant mercies. What are we? What is our life? What is our piety? What our righteousness? What our helpfulness? What our strength? What our might? What shall we say before You, YAHUWAH our Elohim (God) and God of our fathers? Are not all the mighty men as nought before You, the men of renown as though they had not been, the wise as if without knowledge, and the men of understanding as if without discernment? For most of their works are void, and the days of their lives are vanity before You, and the pre-eminence of man over the beast is nought, for all is vanity.

Nevertheless we are Your people, the children of Your covenant, the children of Abraham, Your friend, to whom You did swear on Mount Moriah; the seed of Isaac, his only son, who was bound upon the altar, the congregation of Jacob, Your first born son, whose name You did call Israel and Jeshurun by reason of the love wherewith You did love him, and the joy wherewith You did rejoice in him.

It is, therefore, our duty to thank, praise and glorify You, to bless, to sanctify and to offer praise and thanksgiving unto Your name, through Yah'shua the Messiah (Jesus Christ). Happy are we! How goodly is our portion, and how pleasant is our lot, and how beautiful our heritage! Happy are we who, early and late, morning and evening, twice every day, declare:

Hear, O Israel: YAHUWAH our Elohim (God), YAHUWAH is One. Blessed be His name, whose glorious kingdom is forever and ever. Amen.

ATAH HU
(You are the Same)

You was the same before the world was created; You have been the same since the world has been created; You are the same in this world, and You will be the same in the world to come. Sanctify Your name upon them that sanctify it, yes, sanctify Your name throughout Your world; and through Your salvation let our horn be exalted and raised on high. Blessed are You, YAHUWAH, who sanctifies Your name among the many.

You are YAHUWAH our Elohim (God) in heaven and on earth, and in the highest heaven of heavens. Truely You are the first and You are the last, and beside You there is no El (God). O gather them that hope for You from the four corners of the earth. Let all the inhabitants of the world perceive and know that You are Elohim (God), You alone, over all the kingdoms of the earth. You have made the heavens and the earth, the sea and all that is therein; and which among all the works of Your hands, whether among those above or among those beneath, can say unto You, What are You doing? Our Father who is in heaven, deal kindly with us for the sake of Your great name by which we are called; and fulfil unto us, YAHUWAH our Elohim (God), that which is written, At that time will I bring you in, and at that time will I gather you; for I will make you a name and a praise among all the peoples of the earth, when I bring back your captivity before your eyes, says YAHUWAH. In the name of Yah'shua the Messiah (Jesus Christ). Amen.

MINCHA
(Offerings)

Numbers 28:1–8

And YAHUWAH spoke unto Moses, saying, Command the children of Israel, and say unto them, My oblation, my food for my offerings made by fire, of a sweet savor unto me, shall you observe to offer unto me in its due season. And you shall say unto them, This is the offering made by fire which you shall offer unto YAHUWAH; he-lambs of the first year without blemish, two day by day, for a continual burnt offering. The one lamb shall you offer in the morning, and the other lamb shall you offer at evening; and the tenth part of an ephah of fine flour for a meal offering, mingled with the fourth part of an hin of beaten oil. It is a continual burnt offering, which was ordained in mount Sinai for a sweet savor, an offering made by fire unto YAHUWAH. And the drink offering thereof shall be the fourth part of a hin for the one lamb: in the holy place shall you pour out a drink offering of strong drink unto YAHUWAH. And the other lamb shall you offer at evening: as the meal offering of the morning, and as the drink offering thereof, you shall offer it, an offering made by fire, of a sweet savor unto YAHUWAH.

Leviticus 1:11

And he shall slay it on the side of the altar northward before YAHUWAH: and Aaron's sons, the priests, shall sprinkle its blood upon the altar round about.

On Sabbath the following is added:—

Numbers 28:9-10

And on the sabbath day two he-lambs of the first year without blemish, and two tenth parts of an ephah of fine flour for a meal offering, mingled with oil, and the drink offering thereof: this is the burnt offering of every sabbath, beside the continual burnt offering, and the drink offering thereof.

On New Moon the following is added:—

Numbers 28:11–15

And in the beginnings of your months you shall offer a burnt offering unto YAHUWAH; two young bullocks, and one ram, seven he-lambs of the first year without blemish; and three tenth parts of an ephah of fine flour for a meal offering, mingled with oil, for each bullock; and two tenth parts of fine flour for a meal offering, mingled with oil, for the one ram; and a several tenth part of fine flour mingled with oil for a meal offering unto every lamb; for a burnt offering of a sweet savor, an offering made by fire unto YAHUWAH. And their drink offerings shall be half an hin of wine for a bullock, and the third part of an hin for the ram, and the fourth part of an hin for a lamb: this is the burnt offering of every month throughout the months of the year. And one he-goat for a sin offering unto YAHUWAH; it shall be offered beside the continual burnt offering, and the drink offering thereof.

Psalms 20

May YAHUWAH answer you in the day of trouble; May the name of the God of Jacob defend you; May He send you help from the sanctuary, and strengthen you out of Zion; May He remember all your offerings, and accept your Olat (burnt offerings). Selah.

May He grant you according to your heart's desire, and fulfill all your purpose. We will rejoice in your salvation, and in the name of our Elohim (God) we will set up our banners! May YAHUWAH fulfill all your petitions.

Now I know that YAHUWAH saves His Mashiyach (anointed); He will answer him from His holy heaven with the saving strength of His right hand. Some trust in chariots, and some in horses; But we will remember the name of YAHUWAH our Elohim (God). They have bowed down and fallen; But we have risen and stand upright. Save, YAHUWAH! May the King answer us when we call.

Psalms 50

El Elohim (The mighty God), even YAHUWAH, has spoken, and called the earth from the rising of the sun unto the going down of the same. Out of Zion, the perfection of beauty, Elohim (God) has shined. Our Elohim (God) shall come, and shall not keep silence: a fire shall devour before him, and it shall be very tempestuous round about him. He shall call to the heavens from above, and to the earth, that he may judge his people. Gather my saints together unto me; those that have made a covenant with me by sacrifice. And the heavens shall declare his righteousness: for Elohim (God) is judge himself. Selah.

Hear, O my people, and I will speak; O Israel, and I will testify against You: I am Elohim (God), even your Elohim (God). I will not reprove you for your sacrifices or your burnt offerings, to have been continually before me. I will take no bullock out of your house, nor he goats out of your folds. For every beast of the forest is mine, and the cattle upon a thousand hills. I know all the fowls of the mountains: and the wild beasts of the field are mine. If I were hungry, I would not tell you: for the world is mine, and the fulness thereof. Will I eat the flesh of bulls, or drink the blood of goats?

Offer unto Elohim (God) thanksgiving; and pay your vows unto the most High: And call upon me in the day of trouble: I will deliver you, and you shall glorify me.

But unto the wicked YAHUWAH says, What have you to do to declare my statutes, or that you should take my covenant in your mouth? Seeing you hate instruction, and cast my words behind you. When you saw a thief, then you consented with him, and have been partaker with adulterers. You give your mouth to evil, and your tongue frames deceit. You sit and speak against your brother; you slander your own mother's son. These things have you done, and I kept silence; you thought that I was altogether such an one as yourself: but I will reprove you, and set them in order before your eyes.

Now consider this, you that forget YAHUWAH, lest I tear you in pieces, and there be none to deliver. Whoso offers praise glorifies me: and to him that orders his conversation aright will I show the salvation of YAHUWAH.

Psalms 89:24-37

But My faithfulness and My mercy shall be with him, and in My name his horn shall be exalted. Also I will set his hand over the sea, and his right hand over the rivers. He shall cry to Me, 'You are my Father, Elohai (my God), and the rock of my salvation.' Also I will make him My firstborn, the highest of the kings of the earth. My mercy I will keep for him forever, and My covenant shall stand firm with him. His seed also I will make to endure forever, and his throne as the days of heaven.

"If his sons forsake My Torah (law) And do not walk in My Mishpat (judgments), If they break My Chukot (statutes) and do not keep My Mitzvot (commandments), Then I will punish their transgression with the rod, and their iniquity with stripes. Nevertheless My lovingkindness I will not utterly take from him, nor allow My faithfulness to fail. My covenant I will not break, nor alter the word that has gone out of My lips. Once I have sworn by My holiness; I will not lie to David: His seed shall endure forever, and his throne as the sun before Me; It shall be established forever like the moon, even like the faithful witness in the sky." Selah.

Donning Tallit (Prayer Shawl)

Before putting on the Tallit, say the following:—

I am here enwrapping myself in this tasseled garment, in fulfilment of the command of my Borei (Creator), as it is written in the Torah (Law), They shall make them a tassel upon the corners of their garments throughout their generations. And even as I cover myself with the Tallit in this world, so may my soul deserve to be clothed with a beauteous spiritual robe in the world to come, in the garden of Eden. Amen.

On putting on the Tallit, say:—

Blessed are You YAHUWAH our Elohim (God), Melek Ha'Olam (King of the universe), the God and the Father of our Lord Yah'shua the Messiah (Jesus Christ), who has sanctified us by Your commandments, and has commanded us to enwrap ourselves in the tasseled garment.

How precious is Your loving kindness, O Elohim (God)! And the children of men take refuge under the shadow of Your

31

wings. They sate themselves with the fatness of Your house; and You give them to drink of the river of Your pleasures. For with You is the fountain of life: in Your light do we see light. O continue Your loving kindness unto them that know You, and Your righteousness to the upright in heart. Amen.

Donning Tefilin

Meditation before laying the Tefillin.

I am here intent upon the act of laying the Tefillin, in fulfilment of the command of my Creator, who has commanded us to lay the Tefillin, as it is written in the Torah (Law), And You shall bind them for a sign upon Your hand, and they shall be for frontlets between Your eyes. Within these Tefillin are placed four sections of the Torah (Law), that declare the absolute unity of Elohim (God), and that remind us of the miracles and wonders which he wrought for us when he brought us forth from Egypt, even he who has power over the highest and the lowest to deal with them according to his will. He has commanded us to lay the Tefillin upon the hand as a memorial of his outstretched arm; opposite the heart, to indicate the duty of subjecting the longings and designs of our heart to his service, blessed be he; and upon the head over against the brain, thereby teaching that the mind, whose seat is in the brain, together with all senses and faculties, is to be subjected to his service, blessed be he. May the effect of the precept thus observed be to extend to me long life with sacred influences and holy thoughts, free from every approach, even in imagination, to sin and iniquity. May the yetzar hara (evil inclination) not mislead or entice us, but may we be led to serve YAHUWAH as it is in our hearts to do. In the name of Yah'shua the Messiah (Jesus Christ). Amen.

On placing the Tefillah on the arm, say:—

Blessed are You YAHUWAH our Elohim (God), Melek Ha'Olam (King of the universe), the God and the Father of our Lord Yah'shua the Messiah (Jesus Christ), who has sanctified us by Your commandments, and has commanded us to lay the Tefillin.

On placing the Tefillah on the forehead, say:—

Blessed are You YAHUWAH our Elohim (God), Melek Ha'Olam (King of the universe), the God and the Father of our Lord Yah'shua the Messiah (Jesus Christ), who has sanctified us by Your commandments, and has given us command concerning the precept of the Tefillin.

Blessed be His name, whose glorious kingdom is for ever and ever.

The Retsuah is placed thrice round the middle finger, and the following is said:—

And I will betroth you unto me for ever; yea, I will betroth you unto me in righteousness, and in judgment, and in loving kindness, and in mercy: I will betroth you to me in faithfulness; and you shall know YAHUWAH.

HOSHIENU

Save us YAHUWAH our Elohim (God), and gather us from among the nations, to thank the Name of Your holiness, and to glory in Your praise. Blessed is YAHUWAH, the God of Israel, from this world to the world to come, and let all the people say Amen! Hallelu-Yah. Blessed is YAHUWAH from Zion, the One Who dwells in Jerusalem, Hallelu-Yah. Blessed is YAHUWAH Elohim, the God of Israel, Who alone does wondrous things. And Whose glorious Name is blessed forever, and Whose glory fills all the earth, amen and amen.

On New Moon, Psalm 104 is read

Bless YAHUWAH, O my soul: YAHUWAH Elohai (my God), You are very great; You have robed in splendor and majesty. He covers himself with light as with a garment; he stretches out the heavens like a curtain: he lays the beams of his upper chambers in the waters; he makes the clouds his chariot; he walks upon the wings of the wind. He makes winds his messengers; his ministers flaming fire: he founded the earth upon its bases, that it might not be moved for ever. You covered it with the deep as with a vesture; the waters stood above the mountains. At Your rebuke they fled; at the voice of Your thunder they hasted away. The mountains rose, the valleys sank unto the place which You had founded for them. You have set a bound that they may not pass over; that they turn not again to cover the earth. He sends forth springs into the valleys; they run among the mountains. They give drink to every beast of the plain; the wild asses quench their thirst. By them the birds of the heaven have their dwelling, they utter their voice from among the branches. He gives drink to the mountains from his upper chambers: the earth is satisfied with the fruit of Your works. He causes grass to grow for the cattle, and herbs for the service of man; that he may bring forth bread from the earth; and wine that makes glad the heart of man, and oil to make his face to shine, and bread that strengthens man's heart. The trees of YAHUWAH are satisfied; the cedars of Lebanon which he has planted; where the birds make their nests: as for the stork, the fir trees are her house. The high mountains are for the wild goats; the rocks are a refuge for the conies. He made the moon for seasons: the sun knows its going down. You make darkness, and it is night; wherein all the beasts of the forest do move.

The young lions roar after their prey, and seek their food from God. The sun arises, they get them away, and lay them down in their dens. Man goes forth unto his work and to his labor until the evening How manifold are Your works, YAHUWAH! In wisdom have You made them all: the earth is full of Your possessions. Yonder is the sea, great and of wide extern therein are moving things innumerable, living creatures both small and great. There the ships make their course; there is leviathan whom You have formed to sport therein. These all wait upon You, that You may give them their food in due season. You give unto them, they gather; You open Your hand, they are satisfied with good. You hide Your face, they are confounded; You gather in their breath, they die, and return to their dust. You send forth Your Spirit, they are created; and You renew the face of the ground. Let the glory of YAHUWAH endure for ever; let YAHUWAH rejoice in his works. He looks on the earth, and it trembles; he touches the mountains, and they smoke. I will sing unto YAHUWAH as long as I live; I will sing praise to my God while I have my being. May my meditation be sweet unto him: as for me, I will rejoice in YAHUWAH. Sinners shall be consumed out of the earth, and the wicked shall be no more. Bless YAHUWAH, O my soul: Hallelu-Yah.

Ana Be'choach

Release all those in captivity, we beseech You, Almighty One whose power sets us free. Accept the singing of all Your people Who praise and glorify You alone. Preserve those Who seek Your unity, guard them like the pupil of the eye. Bless and purify them and always grant them Your compassionate righteousness. Invincible and Mighty One, with the abundance of Your goodness, watch over Your people. O Exalted One, turn to Your people Who remember Your holiness. Turn to us and hear our prayers, You Who know all hidden things. Blessed is the Name of His glorious realm for ever and ever. Amen.

Baruch Sheamar
(Blessed be He)

Blessed be he who spoke, and the world existed: blessed be he: blessed be he who was the maker of the world in the beginning: blessed be he who speaks and does: blessed be he who decrees and performs: blessed be he who has mercy upon the earth: blessed be he who has mercy upon his creatures: blessed be he who pays a good reward to them that fear him: blessed be he who lives for ever, and endures to eternity: blessed be he who redeems and delivers: blessed be his name.— Blessed are You YAHUWAH our Elohim (God), Melek Ha'Olam (King of the universe), the God and the Father of our Lord Yah'shua the Messiah (Jesus Christ),: O God and merciful Father, praised by the mouth of Your people, lauded and glorified by the tongue of Your loving ones and Your servants. We also will praise You, O YAHUWAH our Elohim (God), with the songs of David Your servant; with praises and psalms we will magnify, laud and glorify You, and we will make mention of Your name, and proclaim You our King, O our Elohim (God), You the only one, the life of all worlds. O King, praised and glorified be Your great name for ever and ever. Blessed are You, YAHUWAH, a King extolled with praises. Amen.

Katzi Kaddish
(Half Sanctification)

Praised be Your name for ever, O our King, the great and holy God and King, in heaven and on earth; for unto You, O YAHUWAH our Elohim (God), and God of our fathers, song

36

and praise are becoming, hymn and psalm, strength and dominion, victory, greatness and might, renown and glory, holiness and sovereignty, blessings and thanksgivings from henceforth even for ever. Blessed are You, O YAHUWAH, God and King, great in praises, God of thanksgivings, Lord of wonders, who makes choice of song and psalm, O King and God, the life of all worlds.

Magnified and sanctified be his great name in the world which he has created according to his will. May he establish his kingdom during your life and during your days, and during the life of all the house of Israel, even speedily and at a near time, and say, Amen.

Let his great name be blessed for ever and to all eternity. Blessed, praised and glorified, exalted, extolled and honored, magnified and lauded be the name of the Holy One, blessed be he; though he be high above all the blessings and hymns, praises and consolations, which are uttered in the world; and say, Amen.

Blessed, praised, glorified, exalted and extolled be the name of the supreme King of kings, the Kadosh (Holy One), blessed be he, who is the first and the last, and beside him there is no God. Extol him that rides upon the heavens by his name Yah, and rejoice before him. His name is exalted above all blessing and praise. Blessed be His name, whose glorious kingdom is for ever and ever. Let the name of YAHUWAH be blessed from this time forth and for evermore.

B'rchu
(Call to Prayer)

Reader.—Bless YAHUWAH who is to be blessed.

Cong. and Reader.—Blessed is YAHUWAH who is to be blessed for ever and ever.

Yatser Or
(Who Formed the Lights)

Blessed are You YAHUWAH our Elohim (God), Melek Ha'Olam (King of the universe), the God and the Father of our Lord Yah'shua the Messiah (Jesus Christ), who forms the light and creates darkness, who makes peace and creates all things:

Who in mercy gives light to the earth and to them that dwell thereon, and in Your goodness renews the creation every day continually. How manifold are Your works, O YAHUWAH! In wisdom have You made them all: the earth is full of Your possessions. O King, who alone was exalted from aforetime, praised, glorified and extolled from days of old; O El Olam (everlasting God), in Your abundant mercies, have mercy upon us, YAHUWAH our strength, Rock of our stronghold. Shield of our salvation, the Stronghold of ours!

The blessed God, great in knowledge, prepared and formed the rays of the sun: it was a boon he produced as a glory to his name: he set the luminaries round about his strength. The chiefs of his hosts are holy beings that exalt the Shaddai (Almighty), and continually declare the glory of God and his holiness. Be blessed, YAHUWAH our Elohim (God), for the excellency of Your handiwork, and for the bright luminaries which You have made: they shall glorify You for ever. In Yah'shua's (Jesus') name. Amen.

Borei Kol
(Creator of All Things)

All shall thank You, and all shall praise You, and all shall say, There is none holy like YAHUWAH. All shall extol You for ever, Borei (Creator) of all things, O Elohim (God) who openes every day the doors of the gates of the East, and cleaves the windows of the firmament, bringing forth the sun from his place, and the moon from her dwelling, giving light to the whole world and to its inhabitants whom You created by Your attribute of mercy. In mercy You give light to the earth and to them that dwell thereon, and in Your goodness renew the creation every day continually; O Melek (King), who alone was exalted from aforetime, praised, glorified and extolled from days of old. O El Olam (everlasting God), in Your abundant mercies, have mercy upon us, YAHUWAH of our strength, Rock of our stronghold, Shield of our salvation, Stronghold of ours! There is none to be compared unto You, neither is there any beside You; there is none but You: who is like unto You? There is none to be compared unto You, YAHUWAH our Elohim (God), in this world, neither is there any beside You, O our King, for the life of the world to come; there is none but You, O our Redeemer, for the days of the Messiah; neither is there any like unto You. O our Saviour, for the resurrection of the dead.

Elohim Al Kol
(God over All)

YAHUWAH, God over all works, blessed is he, and ever to be blessed by the mouth of everything that has breath. His greatness and goodness fills the universe; knowledge and understanding surround him: he is exalted above the holy Chayot and is adorned in glory above the celestial chariot: purity and rectitude are before his throne, lovingkindness and tender mercy before his glory. The gerem shmeimi (luminaries) are good which our Elohim (God) has created:

39

he formed them with knowledge, understanding and discernment; he gave them might and power to rule in the midst of the world. They are full of lustre, and they radiate brightness: beautiful is their lustre throughout all the world. They rejoice in their going forth, and are glad in their returning; they perform with awe the will of their Master. Glory and honor they render unto his name, exultation and rejoicing at the remembrance of his sovereignty. He called unto the sun, and it shined forth in light: he looked, and ordained the figure of the moon. All the hosts on high render praise unto him, the Seraphim, the Ophanim and the holy Chayot ascribing glory and greatness. Amen.

Titbarach
(Be blessed)

Be blessed, O our Rock, our King and Redeemer, Creator of holy beings, praised be Your name for ever, O our King; Creator of ruchot hasheret (ministering spirits), all of whom stand in the heights of the universe, and proclaim with awe in unison aloud the words of Elohim Chayim (the living God) and Melek Olam (everlasting King). All of them are beloved, pure and mighty; and all of them in dread and awe do the will of their Adon (Master); and all of them open their mouths in holiness and purity, with song and psalm, while they bless and praise, glorify and reverence, sanctify and ascribe sovereignty to—

The name of the Melek Elohi (Divine King), the great, mighty and dreaded One, holy is he; and they all take upon themselves the yoke of the kingdom of heaven one from the other, and give sanction to one another to hallow their Borei (Creator): in tranquil joy of spirit, with pure speech and holy melody they all respond in unison, and exclaim with awe:

Holy, holy, holy is YAHUWAH Tzeva'ot (the Lord of hosts): the whole earth is full of his glory.

And the Ophanim and the holy Chayot with a noise of great rushing, upraising themselves towards the Seraphim, thus over against them offer praise and say:

Blessed be the glory of YAHUWAH from his place.

To the El Baruch (blessed God) they offer pleasant melodies; to the Melek (King), the ever-enduring Elohim Chayim (Living God), they utter hymns and make their praises heard; for he alone performs mighty deeds, and makes new things; he is the Adon Milchanot (Lord of battles); he sows righteousness, causes salvation to spring forth, creates remedies, and is revered in praises. He is the Adon Mopetiym (Lord of wonders), who in his goodness renews the creation every day continually; as it is said, O give thanks to him that makes great lights, for his loving kindness endures for ever. O cause a new light to shine upon Zion, and may we all be worthy soon to enjoy its brightness. Blessed are You, YAHUWAH, Creator of the luminaries. In Yah'shua's (Jesus') name. Amen.

Ahava Rabba
(Abundant Love)

With abounding love have You loved us, YAHUWAH our Elohim (God), with great and exceeding pity have You pitied us. O our Father, our King, for our fathers' sake, who trusted in You, and whom You did teach the statutes of life, be also gracious unto us and teach us. O our Father, merciful Father, ever compassionate, have mercy upon us; O put it into our hearts to understand and to discern, to mark, learn and teach, to heed, to do and to fulfil in love all the words of instruction in Your Torah (Law). Enlighten our eyes in Your Torah (Law), and let our hearts cleave to Your mitzvot (commandments), and unite our hearts to love and fear Your name, so that we be never put to shame. Because we have trusted in Your holy, great and revered name, we shall rejoice and be glad in Your salvation. O bring us in peace from the four corners of the earth, and make us go upright to our land; for You are a God who works salvation. You have chosen us from all peoples and tongues, and have brought us near unto Your great name for ever in faithfulness, that we might in love give thanks unto You and proclaim Your unity. Blessed are You, YAHUWAH, who has chosen Your people Israel in love. Amen.

Yishtabach
(Praised Forever)

Praised be Your name for ever, O our King, the great and El Kadosh Ve'Melek (holy God and King), in heaven and on earth; for unto You, YAHUWAH our Elohim (God), and God of our fathers, song and praise are becoming, hymn and psalm, strength and dominion, victory, greatness and might, renown and glory, holiness and sovereignty, blessings and thanksgivings from henceforth even for ever. Blessed are You, YAHUWAH, El Melek (God and King), great in praises, El Todah (God of thanksgivings), Adon Mopetiym (Lord of wonders), who makes choice of song and psalm, O Melek Ve'Elohim (King and God), the life of all worlds. Amen.

Hari'shonah L'kol HaMitzvot
(The First Commandment of All)

And one of the Soferiym (scribes) came, and having heard them reasoning together, and perceiving that he had answered them well, asked him, Which is the first mitzvah (commandment) of all? And Yah'shua (Jesus) answered him,

"The first of all the mitzvot (commandments) is, Hear, O Israel; YAHUWAH our Elohim (God), YAHUWAH is one: And You shall love YAHUWAH your Elohim (God) with all your heart, and with all your soul, and with all your mind, and with all your strength: this is the first mitzvah (commandment). And the second is this, You shall love your neighbour as yourself. There is no other mitzvah (commandment) greater than these. And on these two mitzvot (commandments) hang all the torah (law) and the navi'iym (prophets).

Tochecha
(Admonition)

Therefore through Him (Yah'shua) let us continually offer the sacrifice of praise to YAHUWAH, that is, the fruit of our lips, giving thanks to His name. But do not forget to do good and to share, for with such sacrifices Elohim (God) is well pleased. *(Hebrews 13:15-16)*

Therefore do not be unwise, but understand what the will of YAHUWAH is. And do not be drunk with wine, in which is dissipation; but be filled with the Spirit, speaking to one another in psalms and hymns and spiritual songs, singing and making melody in your heart to YAHUWAH, giving thanks always for all things to God the Father in the name of our Lord Yah'shua the Messiah (Jesus Christ), submitting to one another in the fear of Elohim (God). *(Ephesians 5:17-21)*

And, Be anxious for nothing, but in everything by prayer and supplication, with thanksgiving, let your requests be made known to God; and the peace of God, which surpasses all understanding, will guard your hearts and minds through Yah'shua the Messiah (Jesus Christ). *(Philippians 4:6-7)*

SHEMA

Shema (Hear)
Deut. 6:4-9

Hear, O Israel: YAHUWAH our Elohim (God), YAHUWAH is One.

Blessed be His name, whose glorious kingdom is for ever and ever.

And You shall love YAHUWAH your Elohim (God) with all your heart, and with all your soul, and with all your might. And these words, which I command you this day, shall be upon your heart: and you shall teach them diligently unto your children, and shall talk of them when you sit in your house, and when you walk by the way, and when you lie down, and when you rise up. And you shall bind them for a sign upon your hand, and they shall be for frontlets between your eyes. And you shall write them upon the door posts of your house, and upon your gates.

Vehaya (If You Will)
Deut. 11:13-21

And it shall come to pass, if you will hearken diligently unto my mitzvot (commandments) which I command you this day, to love YAHUWAH your Elohim (God), and to serve him with all your heart and with all your soul, that I will give the rain of your land in its season, the former rain and the latter rain, that you may gather in your corn, and your wine, and your oil. And I will give grass in your field for your cattle, and your shall eat and be satisfied. Take heed to yourselves, lest your heart be deceived, and you turn aside, and serve other gods, and worship them; and the anger of YAHUWAH be kindled against you, and he shut up the heaven, that there be no rain, and that the land yield not her fruit; and you perish quickly from off the good land which YAHUWAH gives you. Therefore shall you lay up these my words in your heart and in your soul; and you shall bind them for a sign upon your hand, and they shall be for frontlets between your eyes. And you shall teach them to your children, talking of them when you sit in your house, and when you walk by the way, and when you lie down, and when you rise up. And you shall write them upon the door posts of your house, and upon your gates: that your days may be multiplied, and the days of your children, upon the land which YAHUWAH swore unto your fathers to give them, as the days of the heavens above the earth.

Vayomer (The Lord Said)
Numbers 15:37-41

And YAHUWAH spoke unto Moses, saying, Speak unto the children of Israel, and bid them that they make them a Tzitzit (tassel) upon the corners of their garments throughout their generations, and that they put upon the Tzitzit (tassel) of each corner a cord of blue: and it shall be unto you for a Tzitzit (tassel), that you may look upon it, and remember all the mitzvot (commandments) of YAHUWAH, and do them; and that you go not about after your own heart and your own eyes, after which you use to go astray: that you may remember and do all my mitzvot (commandments), and be holy unto your Elohim (God). I am YAHUWAH your Elohim (God), who brought you out of the land of Egypt, to be your Elohim (God): I am YAHUWAH your Elohim (God).

Ahava (Love)
Leviticus 19:18

AND YOU WILL love your neighbor as yourself. I am YAHUWAH. *(There is no other mitzvot (commandments) greater than these.)* For circumcision is nothing and uncircumcision is nothing, but keeping the mitzvot Elohim (commandments of God). He that loves his neighbor has fulfilled the torah (law). The end of the mitzvah (commandment) is love from a pure heart, and a good conscience, and faith without hypocrisy. By this we know, that we love the children of Elohim (God), when we love Elohim (God) and we keep his mitzvah (commandments). And this is the love of Elohim (God), that we keep his mitzvot (commandments), and his mitzvot (commandments) are not a burden.

Emet...
(True...)

True and firm, established and enduring, right and faithful, beloved and precious, desirable and pleasant, revered and mighty, well-ordered and acceptable, good and beautiful is this Your word unto us for ever and ever. It is true, the El Olam (God of the universe) is our Melek (King), the Rock of Jacob, the Shield of our salvation: thoughout all generations He endures and His name endures; His throne is established, and His kingdom and His faithfulness endures for ever. His words also lives and endures; they are faithful and desirable for ever and to all eternity, as for our fathers so also for us, our children, our generations, and for all the generations of the seed of Israel His servants. Amen.

Al Horishonim
(Upon the Generations)

For the first and for the last ages Your word is good and endures for ever and ever; it is true and trustworthy, a statute which shall not pass away. True it is that You are indeed YAHUWAH our Elohim (God), and the God of our fathers, the God and the Father of our Lord Yah'shua the Messiah (Jesus Christ), our King, our fathers' King, our Redeemer, the Redeemer of our fathers, our Maker, the Rock of our salvation; our Deliverer and Rescuer from everlasting, such is Your name; there is no El (God) beside You. Amen.

Ezras Avoteinu
(Helper of Our Forefathers)

You have been the help of our fathers from of old, a Shield and Saviour to their children after them in every generation: in the heights of the universe is your habitation, and Your judgments and Your righteousness reach to the furthest ends of the earth. Happy is the man who hearkens unto Your mitzvot (commandments), and lays up Your Torah (Law) and Your word in his heart. True it is that You are indeed the Lord of Your people, and a Melek Gibor (mighty King) to plead their cause. True it is that You are indeed the first and You are the last, and beside You we have no King, Redeemer and Saviour. From Egypt You did redeem us, YAHUWAH our Elohim (God), and from the house of bondmen You did deliver us; all their first born You did slay, but Your first-born You did redeem; You did divide the Red Sea, and drown the proud; but You made the beloved to pass through, while the waters covered their adversaries, not one of whom was left. Wherefore the beloved praised and extolled Elohim (God), and offered hymns, songs, praises, blessings and thanksgivings to the Melek Ve'Elohim (King and God), who lives and endures; who is high and exalted, great and revered; who brings low the haughty, and raises up the lowly, leads forth the prisoners, delivers the meek, helps the poor, and answers his people when they cry unto him; even praises to El Elyon (the God Most High), blessed is he, and ever to be blessed. Moses and the children of Israel sang a song unto You with great joy, saying, all of them,

Who is like unto You, YAHUWAH, among the mighty ones? Who is like unto You, glorious in holiness revered in praises, doing marvels?

With a new song the redeemed people offered praise unto Your name at the sea shore: they all gave thanks in unison, and proclaimed Your sovereignty, and said,

YAHUWAH shall reign for ever and ever.

O Rock of Israel, arise to the help of Your people and of Israel, and deliver, according to Your promise, Judah and Israel. Our Redeemer, YAHUWAH Tzava'ot (Lord of Hosts) is his name, the Kadosh (Holy One) of Israel. Blessed are You, YAHUWAH, who has redeemed Israel.

Gorem'lanu
(Cause Us)

Cause us, YAHUWAH our Elohim (God), to lie down in peace, and raise us up, O our King, unto life. Spread over us the tabernacle of your peace; direct us aright through your own good counsel; save us for Your name's sake; be a shield around us; remove from us every enemy, pestilence, sword, famine and sorrow; remove also the adversary from before us and from behind us. O shelter us beneath the shadow of your wings; for you, O Elohim (God), are our Apotropos (Guardian) and our Go'el (Deliverer); yes, You, O Elohim (God), are a gracious and merciful King; and guard our going out and our coming in unto life and unto peace from this time forth and for evermore. Blessed are you, YAHUWAH, who guards your people (Israel) for ever. Amen.

Kaddish Yatom
(Mourners Kaddish)

Reader.—Magnified and sanctified be his great name in the world which he has created according to his will. May he establish his kingdom during your life and during your days, and during the life of all the house of Israel, even speedily and at a near time, and say, Amen.

Cong. and Reader.—Let his great name be blessed for ever and to all eternity.

Reader.—Blessed, praised and glorified, exalted, extolled and honored, magnified and lauded be the name of the Kadosh (Holy One), blessed be he; though he be high above all the blessings and hymns, praises and consolations, which are uttered in the world; and say, Amen.

AMIDA (Standing) SHEMONEH ESREH (Eighteen Prayers)

YAHUWAH, open my lips, and my mouth will declare Your praise.

Avot
(Fathers)

Blessed are You YAHUWAH our Elohim (God), Melek Ha'Olam (King of the universe), the God and the Father of our Lord Yah'shua the Messiah (Jesus Christ), and God of our fathers, God of Abraham, God of Isaac, God of Jacob, God of Sarah, God of Rebecca, God of Rachel, and the God of Leah the great, mighty and revered Elohim (God), the El Elyon (God most high), who bestows loving kindnesses, and possesses all things; who rememberes the pious deeds of the patriarchs, and in love will bring a redeemer to their children's children for Your name's sake. Remember us unto life, O King, who delights in life, and inscribe us in the book of life, for Your own sake, O Elohim Chayim (living God). O King, Helper, Saviour and Shield. Blessed are You, YAHUWAH, the Shield of Abraham. You, YAHUWAH, are mighty for ever, You quicken the dead, You are mighty to save, You cause the wind to blow and the rain to fall.

Gevurot
(Gods Might)

You sustain the living with loving kindness, quicken the dead with great mercy, support the falling, heal the sick, loose the bound, and keep Your faith to them that sleep in the dust. Who is like unto You, Lord of mighty acts, and who resembles You, O King, who kills and quickens, and causes salvation to spring forth? Who is like unto You, Father of mercy, who in mercy remembers Your creatures unto life? Yes, faithful are You to quicken the dead. Blessed are You, YAHUWAH, who quickens the dead.

Kedushat HaShem
(Holiness of Gods Name)

You are holy, and Your name is holy, and holy ones praise You daily. (Selah.) Blessed are You, YAHUWAH, the El Kadosh Ve'Melek (holy God and King). We will sanctify Your name in the world even as they sanctify it in the highest heavens, as it is written by the hand of Your navi (prophet): And they called one unto the other and said, Holy, holy, holy is YAHUWAH Tzeva'ot (the Lord of hosts): the whole earth is full of his glory. Those over against them say, Blessed be the glory of YAHUWAH from his place. And in Your Holy Words it is written, saying, YAHUWAH shall reign for ever, Your Elohim (God), O Zion, unto all generations. Hallelu Yah (Praise the Lord).

Unto all generations we will declare Your greatness, and to all eternity we will proclaim Your holiness, and Your praise, O our Elohim (God), shall not depart from our mouth for ever, for You are a great and holy God and King. Blessed are You, YAHUWAH, the El Kadosh Ve'Melek (holy God and King).

Da'at
(Knowledge)

You favor man with knowledge, and teach mortals understanding. You have favored us with a knowledge of Your Torah (Law), and have taught us to perform the statutes of Your will. O favor us with knowledge, understanding and discernment from You. Be gracious to us; a mind of understanding and intellect is from You. Blessed are You, YAHUWAH, Who favors us with knowledge.

Teshuva
(Repentance)

Cause us to return, O our Father, unto Your Torah (Law); draw us near, O our King, to serve You, and bring us back in perfect repentance unto Your presence. Blessed are You, YAHUWAH, who delights in repentance.

Selichot
(Forgiveness)

Forgive us, O our Father, for we have sinned; pardon us, O our King, for we have transgressed; for You do pardon and forgive. Blessed are You, YAHUWAH, who are gracious, and does abundantly forgive.

Geulah
(Redemption)

Look upon our affliction and plead our cause, and redeem us speedily for Your name's sake; for You are a mighty Redeemer. Blessed are You, YAHUWAH, the Redeemer of Israel. Blessed are You, YAHUWAH, who answers in time of trouble.

Refuah
(Healing)

Heal us, O YAHUWAH, and we shall be healed; save us and we shall be saved; for You are our praise. Vouchsafe a perfect healing to all our wounds; for You, Melek Shaddai (almighty King), are a faithful and merciful Physician. Blessed are You, YAHUWAH, who heals the sick of Your people Israel. May it be Your will, YAHUWAH our Elohim (God), the God and the

Father of our Lord Yah'shua the Messiah (Jesus Christ), and the God of our forefathers, that You quickly send *refuah sh'lemah* (complete healing) from heaven, *refuah ruchani* (spiritual healing) and *refuah gufani* (physical healing) to Your servant *(name)* among the other patients of Your people and Israel. In the Name of Yah'shua the Messiah (Jesus Christ).

Birkat Hashanim
(Prosperity)

Bless for us, YAHUWAH our Elohim (God), this year and its crops. Grant us a blessing on the earth. Satisfy us from Your bounty and bless our year like other good years. Blessed are You, YAHUWAH, Who blesses the years.

Kibbutz Galuyot
(Ingathering of Exiles)

Sound the great shofar for our freedom and raise the banner to gather our exiles, and gather us from the four corners of the earth. Blessed are You, YAHUWAH, who gathers the scattered of Your people Israel.

Birkat HaDim
(Restoration of Justice)

Restore our judges as at the first, and our counsellors as at the beginning; remove from us grief and suffering; reign over us, YAHUWAH, You alone, in lovingkindness and tender mercy, and justify us in judgment. Bestow Your Spirit upon the rulers of all lands; guide them that they may govern justly. Then shall love and compassion be enthroned among us.

Blessed are You YAHUWAH, the Melek Ha-Mishpat (King of Judgment), who loves righteousness and justice.

Al Hatzadikim
(Source of Righteousness)

For the righteous and faithful of all humankind, for all who join themselves to your people, for all who put their trust in YAHUWAH our Elohim (God) and Yah'shua the Messiah (Jesus Christ), the Son of the Father, and for all honest men and women, we ask Your favor. Grant that we may be always numbered among them. Blessed are You, YAHUWAH, staff and support of the righteous.

Tsaddikim
(Righteous Ones)

Towards the righteous and the pious, towards the elders of Your people the house of Israel, towards the remnant of their scribes, towards the proselytes of righteousness, and towards us also may Your tender mercies be stirred, YAHUWAH our Elohim (God); grant a good reward unto all who faithfully trust in Your name; set our portion with them for ever, so that we may not be put to shame; for we have trusted in You. Blessed are You, YAHUWAH, the stay and trust of the righteous.

Binyan Yerushalayim
(Rebuilding of Jerusalem)

And to Jerusalem, Your city, return in mercy, and dwell therein as You have spoken; rebuild it soon in our days as an everlasting building, and speedily set up therein the throne of David. Blessed are You, YAHUWAH, who rebuilds Jerusalem.

Malkhut Beit David
(Kingdom of David)

Speedily cause the Seed of David Your servant to flourish, and let his horn be exalted by Your salvation, because we wait for Your salvation all the day. Blessed are You, YAHUWAH, who causes the horn of salvation to flourish.

Kabbalat Tefillah
(Acceptance of Prayer)

Hear our voice, YAHUWAH our Elohim (God); spare us and have mercy upon us, and accept our prayer in mercy and favor; for You are Elohim (God) who hearkens unto prayers and supplications: from Your presence, O our King, turn us not away empty; for You hearken in mercy to the prayer of Your people Israel. Blessed are You, YAHUWAH, who hearkens unto prayer.

Avodah
(Worship)

Accept, YAHUWAH our Elohim (God), Your people Israel and their prayer; restore the service to the oracle of Your house; receive in love and favor both the fire-offerings of Israel and their prayer; and may the service of your people Israel be ever acceptable unto You. Even as it written, My House shall be a house of prayer; and again, My house shall be called a house of prayer for all people.

On New Moon and the Intermediate Days of Passover and Tabernacles the following is added:—

Our God and God of our fathers! May our remembrance rise, come and be accepted before You, with the remembrance of our fathers, of Yah'shua the Messiah (Jesus Christ) the son of David Your servant, of Jerusalem Your holy city, and of all Your people the house of Israel, bringing deliverance and well-being, grace, loving kindness and mercy, life and peace on this day of

On Passover—

the Feast of Unleavened Bread.

On New Moon say—

the New Moon.

On Tabernacles—

the Feast of Tabernacles.

Remember us, YAHUWAH our Elohim (God), thereon for our well-being; be mindful of us for blessing, and save us unto life: by Your promise of salvation and mercy, spare us and be gracious unto us; have mercy upon us and save us; for our eyes are bent upon You, because You are a gracious and merciful God and King.

And let our eyes behold Your return in mercy to Zion. Blessed are You, YAHUWAH, who restores Your divine presence unto Zion.

Hodah
(Thanksgiving)

We give thanks unto You, for You are YAHUWAH our Elohim (God), the God and the Father of our Lord Yah'shua the

Messiah (Jesus Christ), and the God of our fathers, for ever and ever; You are the Rock of our lives, the Shield of our salvation through every generation. We will give thanks unto You and declare Your praise for our lives

We give thanks unto You, for You are YAHUWAH our Elohim (God), the God and the Father of our Lord Yah'shua the Messiah (Jesus Christ); the God of our fathers, the God of all flesh, our Borei (Creator) and the Borei (Creator) of all things in the beginning. Blessings and thanksgivings be to Your great and holy name, because You have kept us in life and have preserved us: so may You continue to keep us in life and to preserve us. O gather our exiles to Your holy courts to observe Your statutes, to do Your will, and to serve You with a perfect heart; seeing that we give thanks unto You. Blessed be Elohim (God) to whom thanksgivings are due.

Which are committed unto Your hand, and for our souls which are in Your charge, and for Your miracles, which are daily with us, and for Your wonders and Your benefits, which are wrought at all times, evening, morning and at noon. O You who are all-good, whose mercies fail not; You, Merciful One, whose lovingkindnesses never cease, we have ever hoped in You.

On Chanukah and Purim the following is added:—

We thank You also for the miracles, for the redemption, for the mighty deeds and saving acts, wrought by You, as well as for the wars which You did wage for our fathers in days of old, at this season.

On Chanukah.

In the days of the Hasmonean, Mattathias son of Johanan, the Kohen Gadol (High Priest), and his sons, when the iniquitous power of Greece rose up against Your people Israel to make them forgetful of Your Torah (Law), and to force them to transgress the statutes of Your will, then did You in Your abundant mercy rise up for them in the time of their trouble; You did plead their cause, You did judge their suit, You did avenge their wrong; You delivered the strong into the hands of the weak, the many into the hands of the few, the impure into the hands of the pure, the wicked into the hands of the righteous, and the arrogant into the hands of them that occupied themselves with Your Torah (Law): for Yourself You did make a great and holy name in Your world, and for Your people Israel You did work a great deliverance and redemption as at this day. And thereupon Your children came into the oracle of Your house, cleansed Your temple, purified Your sanctuary, kindled lights in Your holy courts, and appointed these eight days of Chanukah in order to give thanks and praises unto Your great name.

On Purim.

In the days of Mordecai and Esther, in Shushan the capital, when the wicked Haman rose up against them, and sought to destroy, to slay and make to perish all the Jews, both young and old, little children and women, on one day, on the thirteenth day of the twelfth month, which is the month Adar, and to take the spoil of them for a prey,—then did You in Your abundant mercy bring his counsel to nought, did frustrate his design, and return his recompense upon his own head; and they hanged him and his sons upon the gallows.

For all these things Your name, O our King, shall be continually blessed and exalted for ever and ever.

During the Ten Days of Penitence say:—

58

O inscribe all the children of Your covenant for a happy life.

And everything that lives shall give thanks unto You for ever, and shall praise Your name in truth, O Elohim (God), our salvation and our help. Blessed are You, YAHUWAH, whose name is All-good, and unto whom it is becoming to give thanks.

Birkat Kohanim
(Priestly Blessing)

Our God and God of our fathers, in the name of Yah'shua the Messiah (Jesus Christ), bless us with the three-fold blessing of Your Torah (Law) written by the hand of Moses Your servant, which was spoken by Aaron and his sons, the koheniym (priests), Your holy people, as it is said,

YAHUWAH bless You, and keep You:
YAHUWAH make his face to shine upon You, and be gracious unto You:
YAHUWAH turn his face unto You, and give You peace.

Sim Shalom
(Grant Peace)

Grant peace, welfare, blessing, grace, loving kindness and mercy unto us and unto all Israel, Your people. Bless us, O our Father, even all of us together, with the light of Your countenance for by the light of Your countenance You have given us, YAHUWAH our Elohim (God), the Law of life, lovingkindness and righteousness, blessing, mercy, life and peace; and may it be good in Your sight to bless Your people Israel at all times and in every hour with Your peace.

During the Ten Days of Penitence say:—

In the book of life, blessing, peace and good sustenance may we be remembered and inscribed before You, we and all Your people the house of Israel, for a happy life and for peace. Blessed are You, YAHUWAH, who makes peace.

Blessed are You, YAHUWAH, who blesses Your people Israel with peace.

ELOHAI NETSOR
(My God Please Keep)

O Elohai (my God)! Guard my tongue from evil and my lips from speaking guile; and to such as curse me let my soul be dumb, yes, let my soul be unto all as the dust. Open my heart to Your Torah (Law), and let my soul pursue Your mitzvot (commandments). If any design evil against me, speedily make their counsil of none effect, and frustrate their designs. Do it for the sake of Your name, do it for the sake of Your right hand, do it for the sake of Your holiness, do it for the sake of Your Torah (Law), do it for the sake of the name of Your Holy child Yah'shua the Messiah (Jesus Christ). In order that Your beloved ones may be delivered, O save with Your right hand, and answer me. Let the words of my mouth and the meditation of my heart be acceptable before You, YAHUWAH, my Rock and my Redeemer. He who makes peace in his high places, may he make peace for us and for all Israel, and say, Amen.

Kaddish
(Sanctification)

Reader and Cong.— YAHUWAH, God of Israel, turn from Your fierce wrath, and repent of the evil against Your people.

Cong.—Look from heaven and see how we have become a scorn and a derision among the nations; we are accounted as sheep brought to the slaughter, to be slain and destroyed, or to be smitten and reproached.

Cong. and Reader.—Yet, despite all this, we have not forgotten Your name: we beseech You, forget us not.

Cong.—Strangers say, There is no hope or expectancy for you. Be gracious unto a people that trust in Your name. O You who are most pure, bring our salvation near. We are weary, and no rest is granted us. Let Your tender mercies subdue Your anger from us.

Cong. and Reader.—We beseech You, turn from Your wrath, and have mercy upon the treasured people whom You havet chosen.

Cong.— YAHUWAH, spare us in Your tender mercies, and give us not into the hands of the cruel. Wherefore should the nations say, Where now is their God? For Your own sake deal kindly with us, and delay not.

Cong. and Reader.—We beseech You, turn from Your wrath, and have mercy upon the treasured people whom You have chosen.

Cong.—Hear our voice, and be gracious, and forsake us not in the hand of our enemies to blot out our name; remember what You have sworn to our fathers, I will multiply your seed as the stars of heaven: and now we are left a few out of many.

Cong. and Reader.—Yet, despite all this, we have not forgotten Your name: we beseech You, forget us not.

Cong.—Help us, O Elohim (God) of our salvation, for the sake of the glory of Your name; and deliver us, and pardon our sins for Your name's sake.

Cong. and Reader.— YAHUWAH our Elohim (God), God of Israel, turn from Your fierce wrath, and repent of the evil against Your people.

YOM KOL
(Every Day)

Every day I will give thanks to You, and praise Your name forever, yes, for ever and ever. YAHUWAH, You have been our refuge from generation to generation. I said, YAHUWAH have mercy upon me, heal my soul, for I have sinned against You. YAHUWAH, I flee unto You for refuge, teach me to do Your will, for You are Elohai (my God). For with You is the fountain of life, and in Your light shall we see light. Continue Your mercy upon those that know You. Vouchsafe, YAHUWAH, to keep us this day without sin. Blessed are You, YAHUWAH, the God and the Father of our Lord Yah'shua the Messiah (Jesus Christ), and the God of our fathers, and praised and glorified is Your name for evermore. Amen.

SHELICHIYM HA'EMUNA
(The Apostles Creed)

I believe in YAHUWAH our Elohim (God), the Avi Shaddai (Father almighty), Bore (Creator) of heaven and earth, and in Yah'shua the Messiah (Jesus Christ), his only-begotten Son, our Adon (Lord), who was conceived by the Ruach HaKodesh (Holy Spirit), born of the Virgin Miriam (Mary), suffered under Pontius Pilate, was crucified, died and was buried; he descended into hell; on the third day he rose again from the dead; he ascended into heaven, and is seated at the right hand of Elohim (God) the Avi SHaddai (Father almighty); from there he will come to judge the living and the dead. I believe in the Ruach HaKodesh (Holy Spirit), the holy (set apart) Apostolic Universal Church, the Chavarut Ha-Kadoshiym (communion of saints), the forgiveness of sins, the resurrection of the body, and life everlasting. Amen.

ALEINU
(OUR DUTY)

It is our duty to praise YAHUWAH, the Lord of all things, to ascribe greatness to him who formed the world in the beginning, since he has not made us like the nations of other lands, and has not placed us like other families of the earth, since he has not assigned unto us a portion as unto them, nor a lot as unto all their multitude. For we bend the knee and offer worship and thanks before the supreme King of kings, the Kadosh (Holy One), blessed be he, who stretched forth the heavens and laid the foundations of the earth, the seat of whose glory is in the heavens above, and the abode of whose might is in the loftiest heights. He is our Elohim (God); there is none else, in truth he is our King; there is none besides him; as it is written in his Torah (Law), And You shall know this day, and lay it to your heart, that YAHUWAH he is Elohim (God) in heaven above and upon the earth beneath: there is none else.

We therefore hope in You, YAHUWAH our Elohim (God), that we may speedily behold the glory of Your might, when You will remove the abominations from the earth, and the giliyliym (idols) will be utterly cut off, when the world will be perfected under the kingdom of the Shaddai (Almighty), and all the children of flesh will call upon Your name, when You will turn unto Yourself all the wicked of the earth. Let all the inhabitants of the world perceive and know that unto You every knee must bow, every tongue must swear. Before You, YAHUWAH our Elohim (God), let them bow and fall; and unto Your glorious name let them give honor; let them all accept the yoke of Your kingdom, and do You reign over them speedily, and for ever and ever. For the kingdom is Yours, and to all eternity You will reign in glory; as it is written in Your Law, YAHUWAH shall reign for ever and ever. And it is said, And YAHUWAH shall be king over all the earth: in that day shall YAHUWAH be One, and his name One. Amen.

Yom Rishon (1st Day) Sunday

Hodu (Give Thanks)
1 Chronicles 16:8-36

O give thanks unto YAHUWAH, call upon his name; make known his doings among the peoples. Sing unto him, sing praises unto him; tell of all his marvellous works. Glory in his Shem Kadosh (holy name): let the heart of them rejoice that seek YAHUWAH. Search for YAHUWAH and his strength; seek his face evermore. Remember his marvellous works that he has done: his wonders, and the judgments of his mouth; O you seed of Israel, his servant, you children of Jacob, his chosen ones. He is YAHUWAH our Elohim (God): his judgments are in all the earth. Remember his covenant for ever, the word which he commanded to a thousand generations; (the covenant) which he made with Abraham, and his oath unto Isaac; and confirmed the same unto Jacob for a statute, to Israel for an everlasting covenant: saying, Unto you will I give the land of Canaan, as the lot of your inheritance: when you were but a few men in number; yea, few, and sojourners in it; and they went about from nation to nation, and from one kingdom to another people. He suffered no man to oppress them; yes, he rebuked kings for their sakes; (saying), Touch not mine mashiyachiym (anointed ones), and do my navi'iym (prophets) no harm. Sing unto YAHUWAH, all the earth; proclaim his salvation from day to day. Recount his glory among the nations, his marvels among all the peoples. For great is YAHUWAH, and greatly to be praised: he is to be feared above all gods. For all the gods of the peoples are things of nought; but YAHUWAH made the heavens. Grandeur and majesty are before him: strength and gladness are in his place. Give unto YAHUWAH, you families of the peoples, give unto YAHUWAH glory and strength. Give unto YAHUWAH the glory due unto his name: take an offering, and come before him: worship YAHUWAH in the beauty of holiness. Tremble before him all the earth; the world also is set firm, that it cannot be moved. Let the heavens rejoice, and let the earth be glad; and let them say among the nations, YAHUWAH reigns. Let the sea roar, and the fulness thereof; let the plain exult, and all that is therein. Then shall the trees of the forest exult before YAHUWAH, for he comes to judge the earth. O give thanks unto YAHUWAH; for he is good: for his loving kindness endures forever. And say, Save us, O God of our salvation, and gather us and deliver us from the nations, to give thanks unto your holy name, and to triumph in Your praise. Blessed be YAHUWAH, the Elohei Yisra'el (God of Israel), from everlasting even to everlasting. And all the people said, Amen, and praised YAHUWAH.

Lislo'ach Resha
(He Forgives Iniquity)

And he, being merciful, forgives iniquity and destroys not: yes, many a time he turns his anger away and does not stir up all his wrath. Withhold not Your tender mercies from us, YAHUWAH: let Your lovingkindness and Your truth continually preserve us. Save us, YAHUWAH our Elohim (God), and gather us from amongst the nations, to give thanks unto Your holy name, and to triumph in Your praise. If You should mark iniquities, YAHUWAH, who could stand? But there is forgiveness with You, that You may be feared.

Not according to our sins will You deal with us, nor requite us according to our iniquities. If our iniquities testify against us, work, YAHUWAH, for Your name's sake, for the sake of the name of Yah'shua (Jesus), the Son of the Father. In His name and by the faith that is in His name. Remember, YAHUWAH, Your tender mercies and Your lovingkindnesses; for they have been ever of old.

May YAHUWAH answer us in the day of trouble, the name of the God of Jacob set us up on high. Save, YAHUWAH: may the King answer us on the day when we call. Our Father, our King, be gracious unto us and answer us, for we have no good works of our own; deal with us in charity for Your name's sake. YAHUWAH our Elohim (God), hearken to the voice of our supplications, and remember unto us the covenant of our fathers, and save us for Your name's sake.

And now, YAHUWAH our Elohim (God), that has brought Your people forth out of the land of Egypt with a mighty hand, and has made You a name as at this day; we have sinned, we have done wickedly. YAHUWAH, according to all Your righteous acts, let Your anger and Your fury, I pray You, be turned away from Your city Jerusalem, Your holy mountain; because for our sins and for the iniquities of our fathers, Jerusalem and Your people are become a reproach to all that are round about us. Now therefore, hearken, O our Elohim (God), unto the prayer of Your servant and to his supplications, and cause Your face to shine upon us, for YAHUWAH's sake.

Incline Your ear, O Elohai (my God), and hear; open Your eyes, and behold our desolations, and the city which is called by Your name: for we do not lay our supplications before You because of our righteous acts, but because of Your abundant mercies. YAHUWAH, hear; YAHUWAH forgive; YAHUWAH, hearken and do; defer not; for Your own sake, O Elohai (my God), because Your city and Your people are called by Your name O our Father. Merciful Father, show us a sign for good, and gather our scattered ones from the four corners of the earth. Let all the nations perceive and know that You are YAHUWAH our Elohim (God).

And now, YAHUWAH, You are our Father; we are the clay, and You are our potter, yes, we are all the work of Your hand. Save us for Your name's sake, our Rock, our King, and our Redeemer. Spare Your people, YAHUWAH, and give not Your inheritance over to reproach, that the nations should make a by-word of them. Wherefore should they say among the peoples, Where is their God? We know that we have sinned, and there is none to stand up in our behalf; let Your great name stand for our defence in time of trouble. We know that we have no good works of our own; deal with us in charity for Your name's sake. As a father has mercy upon his children, so, YAHUWAH, have mercy upon us, and save us for Your name's sake. Have pity upon Your people; have mercy upon Your inheritance; spare, we pray You, according to the abundance of Your tender mercies; be gracious unto us and answer us, for charity is Yours, YAHUWAH; You do wondrous things at all times.

Look, we beseech You, and speedily have mercy upon Your people for Your name's sake in Your abundant mercies. YAHUWAH our Elohim (God), spare and be merciful; save the sheep of Your pasture; let not wrath rule over us, for our eyes are bent upon You; save us for Your name's sake. Have mercy upon us for the sake of Your covenant; look, and answer us in time of trouble, for salvation is Yours, YAHUWAH. Our hope is in You, O God of forgiveness. We beseech You, forgive, O good and forgiving God, for You are a gracious and merciful God and King.

We beseech You, O gracious and merciful King, remember and give heed to the Covenant between the Pieces (with Abraham), let the binding (upon the altar) of (Isaac) an only son appear before You, and remember the sacrifice of your only begotten Son Yah'shua the Messiah (Jesus Christ), to the welfare of Israel. Our Father, our King, be gracious unto us and answer us, for we are called by Your great name. You who do wondrous things at all times, deal with us according to Your lovingkindness. O gracious and merciful Being, look, and answer us in time of trouble, for salvation is Yours, YAHUWAH. Our Father, our King, our Refuge, deal not with us according to the evil of our doings; remember, YAHUWAH, Your tender mercies and Your lovingkindnesses; save us according to Your abundant goodness, and have pity upon us, we beseech You, for we have no other God beside You, our Rock.

Forsake us not, YAHUWAH our Elohim (God), be not far from us; for our soul is shrunken by reason of the sword and captivity and pestilence and plague, and of every trouble and sorrow. Deliver us, for we hope in You; put us not to shame, YAHUWAH our Elohim (God); make Your countenance to shine upon us; remember unto us the covenant of our fathers, and save us for Your name's sake. Look upon our troubles, and hear the voice of our prayer, for You hear the prayer of every mouth.

Merciful and gracious Elohim (God)! Have mercy upon us and upon all Your works, for there is none like unto You, YAHUWAH our Elohim (God). We beseech You, forgive our transgressions, O our Father, our King, our Rock and our Redeemer, O Elohim Chayim Olam (living and everlasting God), mighty in strength, loving and good to all Your works; for You are YAHUWAH our Elohim (God). O Elohim (God), who are slow to anger and full of mercy, deal with us according to the abundance of Your tender mercies, and save us for Your name's sake. Hear our prayer, O our King, and deliver us from the hand of our enemies; hear our prayer, O

69

our King, and deliver us from all trouble and sorrow. You are our Father, our King, and we are called by Your name; desert us not. Forsake us not, our Father, and cast us not off, O our Creator, and forget us not, O our Maker, for You are a gracious and merciful El Ve'Melek (God and King).

There is none gracious and merciful like You, YAHUWAH our Elohim (God); there is none like You, O Elohim (God), slow to anger and abounding in lovingkindness and truth. Save us in Your abundant mercies; from fierceness and rage deliver us. Remember Your servants, Abraham, Isaac and Jacob; look not unto our stubbornness and our wickedness and our sin. Turn from Your fierce anger, and repent of the evil against Your people. Remove from us the stroke of death, for You are merciful, for such is Your way, showing lovingkindness freely throughout all generations. Spare Your people, YAHUWAH, and deliver us from Your wrath, and remove from us the stroke of the plague, and harsh decrees, for You are the Guardian of Israel. Unto You, YAHUWAH, belongs righteousness, but unto us confusion of face. How may we complain? What can we say, what can we speak, or how can we justify ourselves? We will search our ways and try them, and turn again to You; for Your right hand is stretched out to receive the penitent. Save, we beseech You, YAHUWAH; we beseech You, YAHUWAH, send prosperity. We beseech You, YAHUWAH, answer us on the day when we call. For You, YAHUWAH, we wait; for You, YAHUWAH, we hope; in You, YAHUWAH, we trust; be not silent, nor let us be oppressed; for the nations say, Their hope is lost. Let every knee and all that is lofty bow down to You alone.

O You, who opens Your hand to repentance, to receive transgressors and sinners, our soul is sore vexed through the greatness of our grief; forget us not for ever; arise and save us, for we trust in You. Our Father, our King, though we be without righteousness and good deeds, remember unto us the covenant of our fathers, and the testimony we bear every day that YAHUWAH is One. Look upon our affliction, for many are our griefs and the sorrows of our heart. Have pity upon us, YAHUWAH, in the land of our captivity, and pour not out Your wrath upon us, for we are Your people, the children of Your covenant. O Elohim (God), look upon our sunken glory among the nations, and the abomination in which we are held as of utter defilement. How long shall Your strength remain in captivity, and Your glory in the hand of the foe? Arouse Your might and Your zeal against Your enemies, that they may be put to shame and broken down in their might. O let not our travail seem little in Your sight. Let Your tender mercies speedily come to meet us in the day of our trouble; and if not for our sake, do it for Youre own sake, and destroy not the remembrance of our remnant; but be gracious unto a people, who in constant love proclaim the unity of Your name twice every day, saying, Hear, O Israel: YAHUWAH our Elohim (God), YAHUWAH is One.

And David said unto Gad, I am troubled exceedingly; let us fall, I pray You, into the hand of YAHUWAH, for his mercies are many; but let me not fall into the hand of man.

O You who are merciful and gracious, I have sinned before You. YAHUWAH, full of mercy, have mercy upon me and receive my supplications.

Psalm 1

1 Blessed is the man who walks not in the counsel of the rasha'iym (ungodly), nor stands in the path of chata'iym (sinners), nor sits in the seat of the letsiym (mockers); 2 But his delight is in the Torah YAHUWAH (Law of the Lord), and in His torah (law) he meditates day and night. 3 He shall be

like a tree planted by the rivers of water, that brings forth its fruit in its season, whose leaf also shall not wither; and whatever he does shall prosper. 4 The rasha'iym (ungodly) are not so, but are like the chaff which the wind drives away. 5 Therefore the rasha'iym (ungodly) shall not stand in the judgment, nor chata'iym (sinners) in the adat tsadiyk'iym (congregation of the righteous). 6 For YAHUWAH knows the way of the tsadiyk'iym (righteous), but the way of the rasha'iym (ungodly) shall perish.

Psalm 2

1 Why do the Goyim (nations, heathens) rage, and the people plot a vain thing? 2 The melakiym (kings) of the earth set themselves, and the rozaniym (rulers) take counsel together, against YAHUWAH and against His Mashiyach (Anointed), saying, 3 "Let us break Their bonds in pieces and cast away Their cords from us." 4 He who sits in the heavens shall laugh; Adonai (The Lord) shall hold them in derision. 5 Then He shall speak to them in His wrath, and distress them in His deep displeasure: 6 "Yet I have set My Melek (King On) My holy hill of Zion." 7 "I will declare the decree: YAHUWAH has said to Me, 'You are My Son, today I have begotten You. 8 Ask of Me, and I will give You the nations for Your inheritance, and the ends of the earth for Your possession. 9 You shall break them with a rod of iron; You shall dash them to pieces like a potter's vessel.'" 10 Now therefore, be wise, O melakiym (kings); Be instructed, you shoftiym (judges) of the earth. 11 Serve YAHUWAH with fear, and rejoice with trembling. 12 Kiss the Son, lest He be angry, and you perish in the way, when His wrath is kindled but a little. Blessed are all those who put their trust in Him.

Psalm 3

1 A Psalm of David when he fled from Absalom his son. YAHUWAH, how they have increased who trouble me! Many are they who rise up against me. 2 Many are they who say of me, "There is no help for him in Elohim (God)." Selah. 3 But You, YAHUWAH, are a shield for me, My glory and the One who lifts up my head. 4 I cried to YAHUWAH with my voice, and He heard me from His holy hill. Selah. 5 I lay down and slept; I awoke, for YAHUWAH sustained me. 6 I will not be afraid of ten thousands of people who have set themselves against me all around. 7 Arise, YAHUWAH; Save me, O my Elohim (God)! For You have struck all my oyev'iym (enemies) on the cheekbone; You have broken the teeth of the rasha'iym (ungodly). 8 Salvation belongs to YAHUWAH. Your blessing is upon Your people. Selah.

Psalm 4

1 To the Chief Musician. With stringed instruments. A Psalm of David. Hear me when I call, O Elohim (God) of my righteousness! You have relieved me in my distress; Have mercy on me, and hear my prayer. 2 How long, O you sons of men, Will you turn my glory to shame? How long will you love worthlessness (emptiness) and seek falsehood (a lie)? Selah. 3 But know that YAHUWAH has set apart for Himself him who is chasiyd (godly); YAHUWAH will hear when I call to Him. 4 Be angry, and do not sin. Meditate within your heart on your bed, and be still. Selah. 5 Offer the sacrifices of righteousness, and put your trust in YAHUWAH. 6 There are many who say, "Who will show us any good?" YAHUWAH, lift up the light of Your countenance upon us. 7 You have put gladness in my heart, more than in the season that their grain and wine increased. 8 I will both lie down in peace, and sleep; for You alone, YAHUWAH, make me dwell in safety.

Psalm 5

1 To the Chief Musician. With flutes. A Psalm of David. Give ear to my words, YAHUWAH, consider my meditation. 2 Give heed to the voice of my cry, My Melek (King) and Elohai (my God), for to You I will pray. 3 My voice You shall hear in the morning, YAHUWAH; In the morning I will direct it to You, and I will look up. 4 For You are not an El (God) who takes pleasure in resha (wickedness), nor shall ra (evil) dwell with You. 5 The hola'liym (foolish, boastful) shall not stand in Your sight; You hate all polei aven (workers of iniquity). 6 You shall destroy those who speak kazav (falsehood, lies); YAHUWAH abhors the iysh damiym U'mirmah (bloodthirsty and deceitful man). 7 But as for me, I will come into Your house in the multitude of Your mercy; In fear of You I will worship toward Your holy temple. 8 Lead me, YAHUWAH, in Your tsedakah (righteousness) because of my enemies; make Your way straight before my face. 9 For there is no faithfulness in their mouth; Their inward part is destruction; Their throat is an open tomb; They flatter with their tongue. 10 Pronounce them guilty, O Elohim (God)! Let them fall by their own counsels; Cast them out in the multitude of their pesha'iym (transgressions), For they have rebelled against You. 11 But let all those rejoice who put their chasah (trust) in You; Let them ever shout for joy, because You defend them; Let those also who love Your name be joyful in You. 12 For You, YAHUWAH, will bless the tsadiyk (righteous); With favor You will surround him as with a shield.

Psalm 6

1 To the Chief Musician. With stringed instruments. On an eight-stringed harp. A Psalm of David. YAHUWAH, rebuke me not in Your anger, nor chasten me in Your hot displeasure. 2 Have mercy on me, YAHUWAH, for I am weak; YAHUWAH,

heal me, for my bones are troubled. 3 My soul also is greatly troubled; But You, YAHUWAH—how long? 4 Return, YAHUWAH, deliver me! Oh, save me for Your mercies' sake! 5 For in mavet (death) there is no remembrance of You; In Sheol (Hades, the grave, the underworld) who will give You thanks? 6 I am weary with my groaning; All night I make my bed swim; I drench my couch with my tears. 7 My eye wastes away because of grief; It grows old because of all my enemies. 8 Depart from me, all you polei aven (workers of iniquity); for YAHUWAH has heard the voice of my weeping. 9 YAHUWAH has heard my supplication; YAHUWAH will receive my prayer. 10 Let all my oyev'iym (enemies) be ashamed and greatly troubled; Let them turn back and be ashamed suddenly.

Psalm 7

1 A Meditation of David, which he sang to YAHUWAH concerning the words of Cush, a Benjamite. YAHUWAH Elohai (Lord my God), in You I put my chasah (trust); Save me from all those who persecute me; And deliver me, 2 Lest they tear me like a lion, rending me in pieces, while there is none to deliver. 3 YAHUWAH Elohai (Lord my God), if I have done this: If there is avel (iniquity) in my hands, 4 If I have repaid ra (evil) to him who was at peace with me, or have plundered my enemy without cause, 5 Let the enemy pursue me and overtake me; Yes, let him trample my life to the earth, and lay my honor in the dust. Selah. 6 Arise, YAHUWAH, in Your anger; Lift Yourself up because of the rage of my enemies; Rise up for me to the judgment You have commanded! 7 So the congregation of the peoples shall surround You; For their sakes, therefore, return on high. 8 YAHUWAH shall judge the peoples; Judge me, YAHUWAH, according to my tsedekah (righteousness), and according to my integrity within me. 9 Oh, let the ra (evil) of the rasha'iym (wicked) come to an end,

but establish the tsadiyk (righteous, just); For the Elohim Tsadiyk (righteous God) tests the hearts and reigns. 10 My defense is of Elohim (God), Who saves the yishrei lev (upright in heart). 11 Elohim (God) is a just judge, and El (God) is angry with the rasha'iym (wicked) every day. 12 If he does not turn back, He will sharpen His sword; He bends His bow and makes it ready. 13 He also prepares for Himself keliy mavet (instruments of death); He makes His arrows into fiery shafts. 14 Behold, the wicked brings forth aven (iniquity); 15 Yes, he conceives trouble and brings forth sheker (falsehood, lies). He made a pit and dug it out, and has fallen into the ditch which he made. 16 His trouble shall return upon his own head, and his violent dealing shall come down on his own crown. 17 I will praise YAHUWAH according to His tsedekah (righteousness), and will sing praise to the name of YAHUWAH Elyon (Lord Most High).

Psalm 8

1 To the Chief Musician. On the instrument of Gath. A Psalm of David. YAHUWAH, our Adonai (Lord), how excellent is Your name in all the earth, Who have set Your glory above the heavens! 2 Out of the mouth of babes and nursing infants You have ordained strength, because of Your enemies, that You may silence the oyev (enemy) and the nakam (avenger). 3 When I consider Your heavens, the work of Your fingers, the moon and the stars, which You have ordained, 4 what is man that You are mindful of him, and the Ben Adam (Son of Man) that You visit him? 5 For You have made him a little lower than the elohim (gods, i.e. angels), and You have crowned him with glory and honor. 6 You have made him to have dominion over the works of Your hands; You have put all things under his feet, 7 all sheep and oxen, even the beasts of the field, 8 the birds of the air, and the fish of the sea that pass through

the paths of the seas. 9 YAHUWAH, our Adonai (Lord), How excellent is Your name in all the earth!

Psalm 9

1 To the Chief Musician. To the tune of "Death of the Son." A Psalm of David. I will praise You, YAHUWAH, with my whole heart; I will tell of all Your marvelous works. 2 I will be glad and rejoice in You; I will sing praise to Your name, O Elyon (Most High). 3 When my oyev'iym (enemies) turn back, they shall fall and perish at Your presence. 4 For You have maintained my right and my cause; You sat on the throne judging in tsedekah (righteousness). 5 You have rebuked the Goyim (nations, heathens), You have destroyed the rasha (wicked); You have blotted out their name forever and ever. 6 O oyev (enemy), destructions are finished forever! And you have destroyed cities; Even their memory has perished. 7 But YAHUWAH shall endure forever; He has prepared His throne for mishpat (judgment). 8 He shall judge the world in tsedekah (righteousness), and He shall administer yadiyn (judgment) for the peoples in meyshar'iym (uprightness). 9 YAHUWAH also will be a refuge for the oppressed, a refuge in times of trouble. 10 And those who know Your name will put their trust in You; For You, YAHUWAH, have not forsaken those who seek You. 11 Sing praises to YAHUWAH, who dwells in Zion! Declare His deeds among the people. 12 When He doresh damiym (avenges blood), He remembers them; He does not forget the cry of the humble. 13 Have mercy on me, YAHUWAH! Consider my trouble from those who hate me, You who lift me up from the sha'ariym mavet (gates of death), 14 That I may tell of all Your praise in the gates of the daughter of Zion. I will rejoice in Your salvation. 15 The Goyim (nations) have sunk down in the pit which they made; In the net which they hid, their own foot is caught. 16 YAHUWAH is known by the judgment He executes; The rasha

(wicked) is snared in the work of his own hands. Haggaion (a Meditation). Selah. 17 The rasha'iym (wicked) shall be turned into Sheol (Hages, the grave, underworld), and all the Goyim (nations) that forget Elohim (God). 18 For the evyon (needy) shall not always be forgotten; The expectation of the aniyiym (poor) shall not perish forever. 19 Arise, YAHUWAH, Do not let man prevail; Let the Goy (heathen) be judged in Your sight. 20 Put them in fear, YAHUWAH, that the Goyim (nations) may know themselves to be but men. Selah.

Psalm 10

1 Why do You stand afar off, YAHUWAH? Why do You hide in times of trouble? 2 The rasha (wicked) in his ga'avah (pride) persecutes the aniy (poor); Let them be caught in the plots which they have devised. 3 For the rasha (wicked) boasts of his heart's desire; He blesses the betsa (greedy, covetous) and renounces YAHUWAH. 4 The rasha (wicked) in his proud countenance does not seek Elohim (God); Elohim (God) is in none of his thoughts. 5 His ways are always prospering; Your mishpat'iym (judgments) are far above, out of his sight; As for all his enemies, he sneers at them. 6 He has said in his heart, "I shall not be moved; I shall never be in adversity." 7 His mouth is full of alah (cursing) and mirmot (deceit) and tok (oppression); Under his tongue is amal (trouble) and aven (iniquity). 8 He sits in the lurking places of the villages; In the secret places he murders the innocent; His eyes are secretly fixed on the nakiy (helpless, innocent). 9 He lies in wait secretly, as a lion in his den; He lies in wait to catch the aniy (poor); He catches the aniy (poor) when he draws him into his net. 10 So he crouches, he lies low, that the chelekah (helpless, unfortunate person) may fall by his strength. 11 He has said in his heart, "El (God) has forgotten; He hides His face; He will never see." 12 Arise, YAHUWAH! O El (God), lift up Your hand! Do not forget the anav'iym (humble). 13 Why

do the rasha (wicked) renounce Elohim (God)? He has said in his heart, "You will not require an account." 14 But You have seen, for You observe trouble and grief, to repay it by Your hand. The chelekah (helpless) commits himself to You; You are the helper of the yatom (fatherless, orphan). 15 Break the arm of the rasha (wicked) and the ra (evil man); Seek out his resha (wickedness) until You find none. 16 YAHUWAH is Melek (King) forever and ever; The Goyim (nations, heathens, Gentiles) have perished out of His land. 17 YAHUWAH, You have heard the desire of the anav'iym (humble); You will prepare their heart; You will cause Your ear to hear, 18 to do justice to the yatom (fatherless, orphan) and the dak (oppressed, afflicted), That the man of the earth may oppress no more.

Yom Sheni (2nd Day) Monday

Psalms 40:6-8

Zevach (Sacrifice) and Minchah (offering) You did not desire; My ears You have opened. Olah (Burnt offering) and Chata'ah (sin offering) You did not require. Then I said, "Behold, I come; In the scroll of the book it is written of me. I delight to do Your will, O Elohai (my God), And Your Torah (law) is within my heart."

Psalms 51:15-19

YAHUWAH, open my lips, and my mouth shall show forth Your praise. For You do not desire zevach (sacrifice), or else I would give it; You do not delight in olah (burnt offering). The Zevach Elohim (sacrifices of God) are a ruach nishbarah (broken spirit), A lev nishbar ve'nidkeh (broken and a contrite heart), These, O Elohim (God), You will not despise. Do good in Your good pleasure to Zion; Build the walls of Jerusalem. Then You shall be pleased with the zevach tsedek (sacrifices of righteousness), With olah (burnt offering) and kaliyl (whole burnt offering); Then they shall offer bulls on Your mizbeach (altar).

ROM'MU YAHUWAH ELOHEINU (Exalt the Lord our God)

Exalt YAHUWAH our Elohim (God), and worship at his footstool; holy is he. Exalt YAHUWAH our Elohim (God), aim worship at his holy mount; for YAHUWAH our Elohim (God) is Kadosh (holy). And he, being merciful, forgives iniquity, and destroys not: yea, many a time he turns his anger away, and does not stir up all his wrath. Withhold not Your tender mercies from me, O YAHUWAH: let Your loving kindness and Your truth continually preserve me. Remember, O YAHUWAH, Your tender mercies and Your loving kindnesses; for they have been ever of old. Ascribe strength unto Elohim (God): his majesty is over Israel, and his strength is in the skies. O ELohim (God), You are to be feared out of Your holy places: the El (God) of Israel he gives strength and power unto his people. Blessed be Elohim (God). O El (God) of vengeance, YAHUWAH, O El (God) of vengeance, shine forth. Lift up Yourself, O judge of the earth: render to the proud their desert. Salvation belongs unto YAHUWAH: Your blessing be upon Your people. (Selah.) YAHUWAH Tzeva'ot (Lord of Hosts) is with us; the El (God) of Jacob is our stronghold. (Selah). O YAHUWAH Tzeva'ot (Lord of Hosts), happy is the man that trusts in You. Save, YAHUWAH: may the King answer us on the day when we call. Save Your people, and bless Your inheritance: feed them, and carry them for ever. Our soul waits for YAHUWAH: he is our help and our shield. For our heart shall rejoice in him, because we have trusted in his Shem Kadosh (holy name). Let Your loving kindness, O YAHUWAH, be upon us, according as we have hoped for You. Show us Your loving kindness, O YAHUWAH, and grant us Your salvation. Rise up for our help and set us free for Your loving kindness' sake. I am YAHUWAH your Elohim (God), who brought You up out of the land of Egypt: open wide your mouth and I will fill it. Happy is the people that is in such a case: happy is the people whose Elohim (God) is YAHUWAH. And as for me, I have trusted in Your loving kindness; my heart shall be glad in Your salvation: I will sing unto YAHUWAH, because he has dealt bountifully with me. In the name of Yah'shua the Messiah (Jesus Christ). Amen.

As For Us

As for us, we know not what to do; but our eyes are upon You. Remember, YAHUWAH, Your tender mercies and Your lovingkindnesses; for they have been ever of old. Let Your lovingkindness, YAHUWAH, be upon us, according as we have waited for You. Remember not against us the iniquities of our ancestors: let Your tender mercies speedily come to meet us; for we are brought very low. Be gracious unto us, YAHUWAH, be gracious unto us; for we are sated to the full with contempt. In wrath remember to be merciful. For he knows our frame; he remembers that we are dust. Help us, O Elohei Yish'enu (God of our salvation), for the sake of the glory of Your name; and deliver us, and pardon our sins, for Your name's sake. In Yah'shua's (Jesus') Name. Amen.

Psalm 11

1 To the Chief Musician. A Psalm of David. In YAHUWAH I put my chasah (trust); How can you say to my soul, "Flee as a bird to your mountain?" 2 For look! The rasha'iym (wicked) bend their bow, they make ready their arrow on the string, that they may shoot secretly at the yishrei lev (upright in heart). 3 If the foundations are destroyed, what can the tsadiyk (righteous) do? 4 YAHUWAH is in His holy temple, YAHUWAH's throne is in heaven; His eyes behold, His eyelids test the banei Adam (sons of men). 5 YAHUWAH tests the tsadiyk (righteous), but the rasha (wicked) and the ohev chamas (one who loves violence) His soul hates. 6 Upon the rasha'iym (wicked) He will rain coals; Fire and brimstone and a burning wind shall be the portion of their cup. 7 For YAHUWAH is tsadiyk (righteous), He loves tsedakah (righteousness); His countenance beholds the yashar (upright).

Psalm 12

1 To the Chief Musician. On an eight-stringed harp. A Psalm of David. Help, YAHUWAH, for the chasiyd (godly man) ceases! For the amuniym (faithful) disappear from among the benei adam (sons of men). 2 They speak idly everyone with his neighbor; with flattering lips and a double heart they speak. 3 May YAHUWAH cut off all flattering lips, and the tongue that speaks proud things, 4 Who have said, "With our tongue we will prevail; Our lips are our own; Who is lord over us?" 5 "For the oppression of the aniy'iym (poor), for the sighing of the evyon'iym (needy), Now I will arise," says YAHUWAH; "I will set him in the safety for which he yearns." 6 The words of YAHUWAH are pure words, like silver tried in a furnace of earth, purified seven times. 7 You shall keep them, YAHUWAH, You shall preserve them from this generation forever. 8 The rasha'iym (wicked) prowl on every side, when vileness is exalted among the benei adam (sons of men).

Psalm 13

1 To the Chief Musician. A Psalm of David. How long, YAHUWAH? Will You forget me forever? How long will You hide Your face from me? How long shall I take counsel in my soul, having sorrow in my heart daily? 2 How long will my oyev (enemy) be exalted over me? 3 Consider and hear me, YAHUWAH Elohai (Lord my God); Enlighten my eyes, lest I sleep the sleep of mavet (death); 4 Lest my oyev (enemy) say, "I have prevailed against him;" Lest those who trouble me rejoice when I am moved. 5 But I have trusted in Your mercy; My heart shall rejoice in Your salvation. 6 I will sing to YAHUWAH, because He has dealt bountifully with me.

Psalm 14

1 To the Chief Musician. A Psalm of David. The naval (fool) has said in his heart, "There is no Elohim (God)." They are corrupt, They have done ta'av (abominable works), there is none who does good. 2 YAHUWAH looks down from heaven upon the children of men, to see if there are any who understand, who seek Elohim (God). 3 They have all turned aside, they have together become corrupt; There is none who does good, No, not one. 4 Have all the polei aven (workers of iniquity) no knowledge, who eat up my people as they eat bread, and do not call on YAHUWAH? 5 There they are in great fear, for Elohim (God) is with the generation of the tsadiyk (righteous). 6 You shame the counsel of the aniy (poor), but YAHUWAH is his refuge. 7 Oh, that the salvation of Israel would come out of Zion! When YAHUWAH brings back the captivity of His people, let Jacob rejoice and Israel be glad.

Psalm 15

1 A Psalm of David. YAHUWAH, who may abide in Your Ohel (tabernacle)? Who may dwell in Your har kodesh (holy hill)? 2 He who halak tamiym (walks uprightly), and po'el tsedek (works righteousness), and speaks the truth in his heart; He who does not ragal (backbite) with his tongue, nor does ra'ah (evil) to his neighbor, nor does he take up a cherfah (reproach) against his friend; 4 In whose eyes a ma'as (rejected / vile person) is despised, But he honors those who fear YAHUWAH; He who swears to his own hurt and does not change; He who does not put out his money at usury, nor does he take a bribe against the innocent. He who does these things shall never be moved.

Psalm 16

1 A Michtam of David. Preserve me, O El (God), for in You I put my trust. 2 O my soul, you have said to YAHUWAH, "You are Adonai (my Lord), my goodness is nothing apart from You." 3 As for the kadoshiym (holy ones, saints, set apart ones) who are on the earth, "They are the addiyr'iym (excellent ones), in whom is all my delight." 4 Their sorrows shall be multiplied who hasten after another god; Their nesek'iym (drink offerings, libations) of blood I will not offer, nor take up their names on my lips. 5 YAHUWAH, You are the portion of my inheritance and my cup; You maintain my lot. 6 The lines have fallen to me in pleasant places; Yes, I have a good inheritance. 7 I will bless YAHUWAH who has given me counsel; My heart also instructs me in the night seasons. 8 I have set YAHUWAH always before me; Because He is at my right hand I shall not be moved. 9 Therefore my heart is glad, and my glory rejoices; My flesh also will rest in hope. 10 For You will not leave my soul in Sheol (Hades, the grave, the underworld), nor will You allow Your Chasiyd (Holy One) to see corruption. 11 You will show me the path of life; In Your presence is fullness of joy; At Your right hand are pleasures forevermore.

Psalm 17

1 A Prayer of David. Hear a just cause, YAHUWAH, Attend to my cry; Give ear to my prayer which is not from deceitful lips. 2 Let my vindication come from Your presence; Let Your eyes look on the things that are upright. 3 You have tested my heart; You have visited me in the night; You have tried me and have found nothing; I have purposed that my mouth shall not transgress. 4 Concerning the works of men, By the word of Your lips, I have kept away from the paths of the Periyts (destroyer, violent one, robber). 5 Uphold my steps in Your

paths, That my footsteps may not slip. 6 I have called upon You, for You will hear me, O El (God); Incline Your ear to me, and hear my speech. 7 Show Your marvelous lovingkindness by Your right hand, O You who save those who trust in You from those who rise up against them. 8 Keep me as the apple of Your eye; Hide me under the shadow of Your wings, 9 From the rasha'iym (wicked) who oppress me, from my oyev nephesh (enemies of my soul) who surround me. 10 They have closed up their fat hearts; With their mouths they speak proudly. 11 They have now surrounded us in our steps; They have set their eyes, crouching down to the earth, 12 As a lion is eager to tear his prey, and like a young lion lurking in secret places. 13 Arise, YAHUWAH, confront him, cast him down; Deliver my life from the rasha (wicked) with Your sword, 14 With Your hand from men, YAHUWAH, from men of the world who have their portion in this life, and whose belly You fill with Your hidden treasure. They are satisfied with children, and leave the rest of their possession for their babes. 15 As for me, I will see Your face in tsedek (righteousness); I shall be satisfied when I awake in Your likeness.

Psalm 18

1 To the Chief Musician. A Psalm of David the servant of YAHUWAH, who spoke to YAHUWAH the words of this song on the day that YAHUWAH delivered him from the hand of all his enemies and from the hand of Saul. And he said: I will love You, YAHUWAH, my strength. 2 YAHUWAH is my rock and my fortress and my deliverer; My El (God), my strength, in whom I will trust; My shield and the horn of my salvation, my stronghold. 3 I will call upon YAHUWAH, who is worthy to be praised; So shall I be saved from my enemies. 4 The chevel mavet (pangs of death) surrounded me, and the floods of Beliya'al (Belial - worthlessness; a name of Satan, the enemy;

an evil spirit) made me afraid. 5 The sorrows of Sheol (Hades, the grave, the underworld) surrounded me; The mokesh mavet (snares of death) confronted me. 6 In my distress I called upon YAHUWAH, and cried out to Elohai (my God); He heard my voice from His temple, and my cry came before Him, even to His ears. 7 Then the earth shook and trembled; The foundations of the hills also quaked and were shaken, because He was angry. 8 Smoke went up from His nostrils, and devouring fire from His mouth; Coals were kindled by it. 9 He bowed the heavens also, and came down with darkness under His feet. 10 And He rode upon a cherub, and flew; He flew upon the wings of the wind. 11 He made darkness His secret place; His canopy around Him was cheshkah mayim (dark waters) and thick clouds of the skies. 12 From the brightness before Him, His thick clouds passed with hailstones and coals of fire. 13 YAHUWAH thundered from heaven, and Elyon (the Most High) uttered His voice, Hailstones and coals of fire. 14 He sent out His arrows and scattered the foe, lightnings in abundance, and He vanquished them. 15 Then the channels of the sea were seen, the foundations of the world were uncovered at Your rebuke, YAHUWAH, at the blast of the breath of Your nostrils. 16 He sent from above, He took me; He drew me out of many waters. 17 He delivered me from my strong enemy, from those who hated me, for they were too strong for me. 18 They confronted me in the day of my calamity, but YAHUWAH was my support. 19 He also brought me out into a broad place; He delivered me because He delighted in me. 20 YAHUWAH rewarded me according to my tsedekah (righteousness); According to the cleanness of my hands He has recompensed me. 21 For I have kept the ways of YAHUWAH, and have not wickedly departed from my Elohim (God). 22 For all His mishpatiym (judgments) were before me, and I did not put away His chukkot (statutes) from me. 23 I was also tamiym (blameless) before Him, and I kept myself from my avon (iniquity). 24 Therefore YAHUWAH has recompensed me according to my tsedekah (righteousness), according to the cleanness of my hands in His sight. 25 With the chaciyd (godly) You will show Yourself chesed (merciful); With a tamiym (blameless) man You will show Yourself tamam (complete); 26 With the barar (pure) You will show Yourself barar (pure); And with the ikkesh (devious, twisted, perverse, distorted) You will show Yourself patal (twisted). 27 For You will save the aniy (poor, afflicted, humble) people, but will bring down haughty looks. 28 For You will light my lamp; YAHUWAH Elohai (my God) will enlighten my darkness. 29 For by You I can run against a troop, by Elohai (my God) I can leap over a wall. 30 As for El (God), His way is perfect; The word of YAHUWAH is proven; He is a shield to all who trust in Him. 31 For who is Eloah (God), except YAHUWAH? And who is a rock, except our Elohim (God)? 32 It is El (God) who arms me with strength, and makes my way perfect. 33 He makes my feet like the feet of deer, and sets me on my high places. 34 He teaches my hands to make war, so that my arms can bend a bow of bronze. 35 You have also given me the shield of Your salvation; Your right hand has held me up, Your gentleness has made me great. 36 You enlarged my path under me, so my feet did not slip. 37 I have pursued my enemies and overtaken them; Neither did I turn back again till they were destroyed. 38 I have wounded them, so that they could not rise; They have fallen under my feet. 39 For You have armed me with strength for the battle; You have subdued under me those who rose up against me. 40 You have also given me the necks of my enemies, so that I destroyed those who hated me. 41 They cried out, but there was none to save; Even to YAHUWAH, but He did not answer them. 42 Then I beat them as fine as the dust before the wind; I cast them out like dirt in the streets. 43 You have delivered me from the strivings of the people; You have made me the head of the goyim (nations, Gentiles); A people I have not known shall serve me. 44 As soon as they hear of me they obey me; The Bnei Nekar (sons of foreigners) submit to me. 45 The Bnei Nekar (sons of foreigners) shall fade away, and come frightened from their hideouts. 46 YAHUWAH lives! Blessed be my Rock! Let the Elohim (God) of my salvation be exalted. 47 It is El (God) who avenges me, and subdues the peoples under me; 48 He delivers me from my oyev'iym (enemies). You also lift me up above those who rise against me; You have delivered me from the iysh chamas (violent man). 49 Therefore I will give thanks to You, YAHUWAH, among the Goyim (Gentiles), and sing praises to Your name. 50 Great deliverance He gives to His king, And shows mercy to His mashiyach (anointed), To David and his seed forevermore.

Psalm 19

1 To the Chief Musician. A Psalm of David. The heavens declare the glory of El (God); And the firmament shows His handiwork. 2 Day unto day utters speech, and night unto night reveals knowledge. 3 There is no speech nor language where their voice is not heard. 4 Their line has gone out through all the earth, and their words to the end of the world. In them He has set a tabernacle for the sun, 5 Which is like a chatan (bridegroom) coming out of his chamber, and rejoices like a strong man to run its race. 6 Its rising is from one end of heaven, and its circuit to the other end; and there is nothing hidden from its heat. 7 The torat (laws) of YAHUWAH is perfect, converting the soul; The edut (testimony) of YAHUWAH is sure, making wise the simple; 8 The piqudiym (precepts) of YAHUWAH are right, rejoicing the heart; The mitzvot (commandments) of YAHUWAH is pure, enlightening the eyes; 9 The fear of YAHUWAH is clean, enduring forever; The mishpatiym (judgments) of YAHUWAH are true and righteous altogether. 10 More to be desired are they than

gold, Yea, than much fine gold; Sweeter also than honey and the honeycomb. 11 Moreover by them Your servant is warned, and in keeping them there is great reward. 12 Who can understand his errors? Cleanse me from secret faults. 13 Keep back Your servant also from zediym (presumtiousness, presumptuous sins); Let them not have dominion over me. Then I shall be tamam (complete), and I shall be innocent of great transgression. 14 Let the words of my mouth and the meditation of my heart be acceptable in Your sight, YAHUWAH, my strength and my Redeemer.

Yom Shlishi (3rd Day) Tuesday

Psalms 54

Save me, O Elohim (God), by Your name, And vindicate me by Your strength. Hear my prayer, O Elohim (God); Give ear to the words of my mouth. For strangers have risen up against me, and oppressors have sought after my life; They have not set Elohim (God) before them. Selah.

Behold, Elohim (God) is my helper; YAHUWAH is with those who uphold my life. He will repay my enemies for their evil. Cut them off in Your truth. I will freely sacrifice unto You; I will praise Your name, O YAHUWAH, for it is good. For He has delivered me out of all trouble; And my eye has seen its desire upon my enemies.

Psalms 107:20-22

He sent His word and healed them, and delivered them from their destructions. Oh, that men would give thanks to YAHUWAH for His goodness, and for His wonderful works to the children of men! Let them sacrifice the sacrifices of thanksgiving, and declare His works with rejoicing.

Yehi Chavod (May the Glory)

Let the glory of YAHUWAH endure for ever; let YAHUWAH rejoice in his works. Let the name of YAHUWAH be blessed from this time forth and for evermore. From the rising of the sun unto the going down of the same YAHUWAH's Name is to be praised. YAHUWAH is high above all nations, and his glory above the heavens. Your name, YAHUWAH, endures for ever; Your memorial, YAHUWAH, throughout all generations. YAHUWAH has established his throne in the heavens; and his kingdom rules over all. Let the heavens rejoice, and let the earth be glad; and let them say among the nations, YAHUWAH reigns. YAHUWAH reigns; YAHUWAH has reigned; YAHUWAH shall reign for ever and ever. YAHUWAH is King for ever and ever; the nations are perished out of his land. YAHUWAH has frustrated the design of the nations; he has foiled the thoughts of the peoples. Many are the thoughts in a man's heart; but the council of YAHUWAH, that shall stand. The council of YAHUWAH stands fast for ever, the thoughts of his heart to all generations. For he spoke, and it was; he commanded, and it stood fast. For YAHUWAH has chosen Zion; he has desired it for his habitation. For YAHUWAH has chosen Jacob unto himself, Israel for his peculiar treasure. For YAHUWAH will not cast off his people, neither will he forsake his inheritance. And he, being merciful, forgives iniquity, and destroys not: yes, many a time he turns his anger away, and does not stir up all his wrath. Save, YAHUWAH: may the King answer us on the day when we call. In Yah'shua's (Jesus') name. Amen.

SLOW TO ANGER

O Elohim (God), slow to anger and abounding in lovingkindness and truth, rebuke us not in Your anger. Have pity upon Your people, YAHUWAH, and save us from all evil. We have sinned against You, YAHUWAH: forgive, we beseech You, according to the abundance of Your tender mercies, O Elohim (God).

O Elohim (God), slow to anger and abounding in lovingkindness and truth, hide not Your face from us. Have pity upon Israel, Your people, and deliver us from all ra (evil).

We have sinned against You, YAHUWAH; forgive, we beseech You, according to the abundance of Your tender mercies, O Elohim (God). In Yah'shua's (Jesus') name. Amen.

Psalm 20

1 To the Chief Musician. A Psalm of David. May YAHUWAH answer you in the day of trouble; May the name of the Elohim (God) of Jacob defend you; 2 May He send you help from the sanctuary, and strengthen you out of Zion; 3 May He remember all your Minchot (offerings), and accept your Olat (burnt sacrifices). Selah. 4 May He grant you according to your heart's desire, and fulfill all your purpose. 5 We will rejoice in your salvation, and in the name of our Elohim (God) we will set up our banners! May YAHUWAH fulfill all your petitions. 6 Now I know that YAHUWAH saves His Mashiyach (anointed); He will answer him from His holy heaven with the saving strength of His right hand. 7 Some trust in chariots, and some in horses; But we will remember the name of YAHUWAH our Elohim (God). 8 They have bowed down and fallen; But we have risen and stand upright. 9 Save, YAHUWAH! May the King answer us when we call.

Psalm 21

1 To the Chief Musician. A Psalm of David. The king shall have joy in Your strength, YAHUWAH; And in Your salvation how greatly shall he rejoice! 2 You have given him his heart's desire, and have not withheld the request of his lips. Selah. 3 For You meet him with the blessings of goodness; You set a crown of pure gold upon his head. 4 He asked life from You, and You gave it to him— Length of days forever and ever. 5 His glory is great in Your salvation; Honor and majesty You have placed upon him. 6 For You have made him most blessed forever; You have made him exceedingly glad with

Your presence. 7 For the king trusts in YAHUWAH, and through the mercy of Elyon (the Most High) he shall not be moved. 8 Your hand will find all Your enemies; Your right hand will find those who hate You. 9 You shall make them as a fiery oven in the time of Your anger; YAHUWAH shall swallow them up in His wrath, and the fire shall devour them. 10 Their offspring You shall destroy from the earth, and their seed from among the sons of men. 11 For they intended evil against You; They devised a plot which they are not able to perform. 12 Therefore You will make them turn their back; You will make ready Your arrows on Your string toward their faces. 13 Be exalted, YAHUWAH, in Your own strength! We will sing and praise Your power.

Psalm 22

1 To the Chief Musician. Set to "The Deer of the Dawn." A Psalm of David. Eli (My God), Eli (My God), why have You forsaken Me? Why are You so far from helping Me, and from the words of My groaning? 2 Elohai (My God), I cry in the daytime, but You do not hear; And in the night season, and am not silent. 3 But You are holy, Enthroned in the praises of Israel. 4 Our fathers trusted in You; They trusted, and You delivered them. 5 They cried to You, and were delivered; They trusted in You, and were not ashamed. 6 But I am a worm, and no man; A reproach of men, and despised by the people.7 All those who see Me ridicule Me; They shoot out the lip, they shake the head, saying, 8 "He trusted in YAHUWAH, let Him rescue Him; Let Him deliver Him, since He delights in Him!" 9 But You are He who took Me out of the womb; You made Me trust while on My mother's breasts. 10 I was cast upon You from birth. From My mother's womb You have been Eliy (my God). 11 Be not far from Me, for trouble is near; For there is none to help. 12 Many bulls have surrounded Me; Strong bulls of Bashan have encircled Me. 13 They gape at Me

with their mouths, like a raging and roaring lion. 14 I am poured out like water, and all My bones are out of joint; My heart is like wax; It has melted within Me. 15 My strength is dried up like a potsherd, and My tongue clings to My jaws; You have brought Me to the dust of death. 16 For dogs have surrounded Me; The adat me're'iym (congregation of the wicked) has enclosed Me. They pierced My hands and My feet; 17 I can count all My bones. They look and stare at Me. 18 They divide My garments among them, and for My clothing they cast lots. 19 But You, YAHUWAH, do not be far from Me; O My Strength, hasten to help Me! 20 Deliver Me from the sword, my precious life from the power of the dog. 21 Save Me from the lion's mouth and from the horns of the re'emiym (unicorn)! You have answered Me. 22 I will declare Your name to My brethren; In the midst of the kahal (assembly) I will praise You. 23 You who fear YAHUWAH, praise Him! All you seed of Jacob, glorify Him, and fear Him, all you seed of Israel! 24 For He has not despised nor abhorred the enut (affliction) of the aniy (afflicted); Nor has He hidden His face from Him; But when He cried to Him, He heard. 25 My praise shall be of You in the kahal rav (great assembly); I will pay My neder'iym (vows) before those who fear Him. 26 The anaviym (humble, poor) shall eat and be satisfied; Those who seek Him will praise YAHUWAH. Let your heart live forever! 27 All the ends of the world shall remember and turn to YAHUWAH, and all the families of the Goyim (nations, Gentiles) shall worship before You. 28 For the kingdom is YAHUWAH's, and He rules over the Goyim (nations, Gentiles). 29 All the prosperous of the earth shall eat and worship; All those who go down to the dust shall bow before Him, even he who cannot keep himself alive. 30 A posterity shall serve Him. It will be recounted to Adonai (the Lord) to the next generation, 31 They will come and declare His tsedakah (righteousness) to a people who will be born, that He has done this.

Psalm 23

1 A Psalm of David. YAHUWAH is my Ro'iy (shepherd); I shall not want. 2 He makes me to lie down in green pastures; He leads me beside the still waters. 3 He restores my soul; He leads me in the paths of tsedek (righteousness) for His name's sake. 4 Yea, though I walk through the valley of the tsalmavet (shadow of death), I will fear no ra (evil); for You are with me; Your rod and Your staff, they comfort me. 5 You prepare a table before me in the presence of my enemies; You anoint my head with oil; My cup runs over. 6 Surely goodness and mercy shall follow me all the days of my life; And I will dwell in the house of YAHUWAH forever.

Psalm 24

1 A Psalm of David. The earth is YAHUWAH's, and all its fullness, the world and those who dwell therein. 2 For He has founded it upon the seas, and established it upon the waters. 3 Who may ascend into the hill of YAHUWAH? Or who may stand in His holy place? 4 He who has naqiy kapayim (clean hands) and a bar levav (pure heart), who has not lifted up his soul to an idol, nor sworn deceitfully. 5 He shall receive blessing from YAHUWAH, and tsedakah (righteousness) from the Elohim (God) of his salvation. 6 This is Jacob, the generation of those who seek Him, Who seek Your face. Selah. 7 Lift up your heads, O you gates! And be lifted up, you everlasting doors! And the Melek Ha-Kavod (King of glory) shall come in. 8 Who is this Melek Ha-Kavod (King of glory)? YAHUWAH strong and mighty, YAHUWAH mighty in battle. 9 Lift up your heads, O you gates! Lift up, you everlasting doors! And the Melek Ha-Kavod (King of glory) shall come in. 10 Who is this Melek Ha-Kavod (King of glory)? YAHUWAH Tzeva'ot (the Lord of Hosts), He is the Melek Ha-Kavod (King of glory). Selah.

Psalm 25

1 A Psalm of David. To You, YAHUWAH, I lift up my soul. 2 O Elohai (my God), I trust in You; Let me not be ashamed; Let not my enemies triumph over me. 3 Indeed, let no one who waits on You be ashamed; Let those be ashamed who deal treacherously without cause. 4 Show me Your ways, YAHUWAH; Teach me Your paths. 5 Lead me in Your truth and teach me, for You are the Elohim (God) of my salvation; On You I wait all the day. 6 Remember, YAHUWAH, Your tender mercies and Your lovingkindnesses, for they are from of old. 7 Do not remember the sins of my youth, nor my transgressions; According to Your mercy remember me, for Your goodness' sake, YAHUWAH. 8 Good and upright is YAHUWAH; Therefore He teaches sinners in the way. 9 The humble He guides in justice, and the humble He teaches His way. 10 All the paths of YAHUWAH are mercy and truth, to such as keep His covenant and His testimonies. 11 For Your name's sake, YAHUWAH, pardon my avon (iniquity), for it is great. 12 Who is the man that fears YAHUWAH? Him shall He teach in the way He chooses. 13 He himself shall dwell in prosperity, and his seed shall inherit the earth. 14 The secret of YAHUWAH is with those who fear Him, and He will show them His covenant. 15 My eyes are ever toward YAHUWAH, for He shall pluck my feet out of the net. 16 Turn Yourself to me, and have mercy on me, for I am desolate and afflicted. 17 The troubles of my heart have enlarged; Bring me out of my distresses! 18 Look on my affliction and my pain, and forgive all my sins. 19 Consider my enemies, for they are many; And they hate me with cruel hatred. 20 Keep my soul, and deliver me; Let me not be ashamed, for I put my trust in You. 21 Let integrity and uprightness preserve me, for I wait for You. 22 Redeem Israel, O Elohim (God), Out of all their troubles!

Psalm 26

1 A Psalm of David. Vindicate me, YAHUWAH, For I have walked in my integrity. I have also trusted in YAHUWAH; I shall not slip. 2 Examine me, YAHUWAH, and prove me; Try my mind and my heart. 3 For Your lovingkindness is before my eyes, and I have walked in Your truth. 4 I have not sat with matei shav (false/vain persons), nor will I go in with dissemblers. 5 I have hated the kehal me'ra'iym (assembly of evildoers), and will not sit with the rasha'iym (wicked). 6 I will wash my hands in innocence; So I will go about Your mizbeach (altar), YAHUWAH, 7 That I may proclaim with the voice of thanksgiving, and tell of all Your wondrous works. 8 YAHUWAH, I have loved the habitation of Your house, and the place where Your glory dwells. 9 Do not gather my soul with chata'iym (sinners), nor my life with anshei damiym (bloodthirsty men), 10 In whose hands is an zimah (evil plan), and whose right hand is full of shochad (bribes). 11 But as for me, I will walk in my integrity; Redeem me and be merciful to me. 12 My foot stands in an even place; In the makhel'iym (congregations) I will bless YAHUWAH.

Psalm 27

1 A Psalm of David. YAHUWAH is my light and my salvation; Whom shall I fear? YAHUWAH is the strength of my life; Of whom shall I be afraid? 2 When the me'ra'iym (wicked) came against me to eat up my flesh, my tsar'iym (foes) and oyev'iym (enemies), they stumbled and fell. 3 Though an machaneh (army) may encamp against me, my heart shall not fear; Though war may rise against me, In this I will be confident. 4 One thing I have desired of YAHUWAH, that will I seek: That I may dwell in the Bet YAHUWAH (house of the Lord) all the days of my life, to behold the beauty of YAHUWAH, and to inquire in His temple. 5 For in the time of

trouble He shall hide me in His pavilion; In the secret place of His tabernacle He shall hide me; He shall set me high upon a rock. 6 And now my head shall be lifted up above my oyev'iym (enemies) all around me; Therefore I will offer Zivchei Teru'ah (sacrifices of joy [blowing the trumpet]) in His tabernacle; I will sing, yes, I will sing praises to YAHUWAH. 7 Hear, YAHUWAH, when I cry with my voice! Have mercy also upon me, and answer me. 8 When You said, "Seek My face," My heart said to You, "Your face, YAHUWAH, I will seek." 9 Do not hide Your face from me; Do not turn Your servant away in anger; You have been my help; Do not leave me nor forsake me, O Elohim (God) of my salvation. 10 When my father and my mother forsake me, then YAHUWAH will take care of me. 11 Teach me Your way, YAHUWAH, and lead me in a smooth path, because of my enemies. 12 Do not deliver me to the will of my adversaries; For edei sheker (false witnesses) have risen against me, and such as breathe out violence. 13 I would have lost heart, unless I had believedthat I would see the goodness of YAHUWAH In the land of the living. 14 Wait on YAHUWAH; Be of good courage, and He shall strengthen your heart; Wait, I say, on YAHUWAH!

Yom Re'vi'i (4th Day) Wednesday

Baruch Hashem Le'olam (Blessed is His Name Forever)

Blessed be YAHUWAH for evermore. Amen, and Amen. Blessed be YAHUWAH out of Zion, who dwells in Jerusalem. Praise YAHUWAH. Blessed be YAHUWAH our Elohim (God), the God of Israel, who alone does wondrous things: and blessed be his glorious name for ever; and let the whole earth be filled with his glory. Amen, and Amen.

LET YOUR MERCY

YAHUWAH, let Your mercy be upon us, as we have set our hope in You. Blessed are You, YAHUWAH: teach me Your statutes. Blessed are You, O Master: make me to understand Your mitzvot (commandments). Blessed are You, O Kadosh (Holy One): enlighten me with Your statutes. YAHUWAH, Your mercy endures for ever: O despise not the works of Your hands. To You belongs praise, to You belongs hymns, to You belongs glory. To the Father YAHUWAH, and to the Son Yah'shua (Jesus), and to the Ruach HaKodesh (Holy Spirit), now and ever, and unto ages of ages. Amen.

Psalm 28

1 A Psalm of David. To You I will cry, YAHUWAH my Rock: Do not be silent to me, lest, if You are silent to me, I become like those who go down to the pit. 2 Hear the voice of my supplications when I cry to You, when I lift up my hands toward Your holy sanctuary. 3 Do not take me away with the

rasha'iym (wicked) and with the polei aven (workers of iniquity), who speak peace to their neighbors, but ra'ah (evil) is in their hearts. 4 Give them according to their po'al'iym (deeds), and according to the roa (badness, evil) of their endeavors; Give them according to the ma'aseh yadeyhem (work of their hands); Render to them what they deserve. 5 Because they do not regard the works of YAHUWAH, nor the operation of His hands, He shall destroy them and not build them up. 6 Blessed be YAHUWAH, because He has heard the voice of my supplications! 7 YAHUWAH is my strength and my shield; My heart trusted in Him, and I am helped; Therefore my heart greatly rejoices, and with my song I will praise Him. 8 YAHUWAH is their strength, and He is the saving refuge of His mashiyach (anointed). 9 Save Your people, and bless Your inheritance; Ro'eh (Shepherd) them also, And bear them up forever.

Psalm 29

1 A Psalm of David. Give unto YAHUWAH, you bnei eliym (sons of the gods), give unto YAHUWAH glory and strength. 2 Give unto YAHUWAH the glory due to His name; Worship YAHUWAH in the beauty of holiness. 3 The voice of YAHUWAH is over the waters; The El (God) of glory thunders; YAHUWAH is over many waters. 4 The voice of YAHUWAH is powerful; The voice of YAHUWAH is full of majesty. 5 The voice of YAHUWAH breaks the cedars, yes, YAHUWAH splinters the cedars of Lebanon. 6 He makes them also skip like a calf, Lebanon and Sirion like a young re'emiym (unicorn). 7 The voice of YAHUWAH divides the flames of fire. 8 The voice of YAHUWAH shakes the wilderness; YAHUWAH shakes the Wilderness of Kadesh. 9 The voice of YAHUWAH makes the deer give birth, and strips the forests bare; And in His temple everyone says, "Glory!" 10 YAHUWAH sat enthroned at the Flood, and YAHUWAH sits as Melek (King)

forever. 11 YAHUWAH will give strength to His people; YAHUWAH will bless His people with shalom (peace).

Psalm 30

1 A Psalm. A Song at the dedication of the house of David. I will extol You, YAHUWAH, for You have lifted me up, and have not let my foes rejoice over me. 2 YAHUWAH Elohai (my God), I cried out to You, and You healed me. 3 YAHUWAH, You brought my soul up from Sheol (Hades, the grave, the underworld); You have kept me alive, that I should not go down to the pit. 4 Sing praise to YAHUWAH, His chasiyd (godly ones), and give thanks at the remembrance of His Shem Kadosh (holy name). 5 For His anger is but for a moment, His favor is for life; Weeping may endure for a night, but joy comes in the morning. 6 Now in my prosperity I said, "I shall never be moved." 7 YAHUWAH, by Your favor You have made my mountain stand strong; You hid Your face, and I was troubled. 8 I cried out to You, YAHUWAH; And to YAHUWAH I made supplication: 9 "What profit is there in my blood, When I go down to shachat (the pit, destruction, corruption)? Will the dust praise You? Will it declare Your truth? 10 Hear, YAHUWAH, and have mercy on me; YAHUWAH, be my helper!" 11 You have turned for me my mispade (mourning) into machol (dancing); You have put off my sak (sackcloth) and clothed me with simchah (gladness), 12 To the end that my glory may sing praise to You and not be silent. YAHUWAH Elohai (my God), I will give thanks to You forever.

Psalm 31

1 To the Chief Musician. A Psalm of David. In You, YAHUWAH, I put my chasah (trust); Let me never be boshah (ashamed, disconnected); Deliver me in Your tsedakah (righteousness).

2 Bow down Your ear to me, deliver me speedily; Be my rock of refuge, a fortress of defense to save me. 3 For You are my rock and my fortress; Therefore, for Your name's sake, lead me and guide me. 4 Pull me out of the net which they have secretly laid for me, for You are my strength. 5 Into Your hand I commit my spirit; You have redeemed me, O YAHUWAH, the El Emet (god of truth). 6 I have hated those who regard empty lies; But I trust in YAHUWAH. 7 I will be glad and rejoice in Your mercy, for You have considered my trouble; You have known my soul in adversities, 8 And have not shut me up into the hand of the oyev (enemy); You have set my feet in a wide place. 9 Have mercy on me, YAHUWAH, for I am in trouble; My eye wastes away with grief, Yes, my soul and my body! 10 For my life is spent with grief, and my years with sighing; My strength fails because of my iniquity, and my bones waste away. 11 I am a reproach among all my tsarar (foe), but especially among my neighbors, and am repulsive to my acquaintances; Those who see me outside flee from me. 12 I am forgotten like a dead man, out of mind; I am like a broken vessel. 13 For I hear the slander of many; Fear is on every side; While they take counsel together against me, they scheme to take away my life. 14 But as for me, I trust in You, YAHUWAH; I say, "You are Elohai (my God)." 15 My times are in Your hand; Deliver me from the hand of my oyev'iym (enemies), and from those who persecute me. 16 Make Your face shine upon Your servant; Save me for Your mercies' sake. 17 Do not let me be ashamed, YAHUWAH, for I have called upon You; Let the wicked be ashamed; Let them be silent in Sheol (Hades, the grave, the underworld). 18 Let the lying lips be put to silence, which speak insolent things proudly and contemptuously against the tsadiyk (righteous). 19 Oh, how great is Your goodness, which You have laid up for those who fear You, Which You have prepared for those who trust in You In the presence of the sons of men! 20 You shall hide them in the secret place of Your presence from the plots of man; You

shall keep them secretly in a pavilion from the strife of tongues. 21 Blessed be YAHUWAH, for He has shown me His marvelous kindness in a strong city! 22 For I said in my haste, "I am cut off from before Your eyes"; Nevertheless You heard the voice of my supplications when I cried out to You. 23 Oh, love YAHUWAH, all His chasiyd (godly ones)! For YAHUWAH preserves the faithful, and fully repays the proud person. 24 Be of good courage, and He shall strengthen your heart, all you who hope in YAHUWAH.

Psalm 32

1 A Psalm of David. A Contemplation. Blessed is he whose pesha (transgression) is forgiven, whose chata'ah (sin) is covered. 2 Blessed is the man to whom YAHUWAH does not impute avon (iniquity), and in whose spirit there is no remiyah (deceit, slackness). 3 When I kept silent, my bones grew old through my groaning all the day long. 4 For day and night Your hand was heavy upon me; My vitality was turned into the drought of summer. Selah. 5 I acknowledged my sin to You, and my avon (iniquity) I have not hidden. I said, "I will Odeh (confess) my pesha (transgressions) to YAHUWAH," And You forgave the avon (iniquity) of my chata'ah (sin). Selah. 6 For this cause everyone who is chasiyd (godly) shall pray to You in a time when You may be found; Surely in a shetef mayim raviym (flood of great waters) they shall not come near him. 7 You are my hiding place; You shall preserve me from trouble; You shall surround me with ranei palet (songs/shouts of deliverance). Selah. 8 I will instruct you and teach you in the way you should go; I will guide you with My eye. 9 Do not be like the horse or like the mule, which have no understanding, which must be harnessed with bit and bridle, else they will not come near you. 10 Many mak'oviym (sorrows, pains, afflictions) shall be to the rasha (wicked); But he who batach (trusts, is bold) in YAHUWAH, mercy shall

surround him. 11 Be glad in YAHUWAH and rejoice, you tsadiykiym (righteous); And shout for joy, all you yashariym lev (upright in heart)!

Psalm 33

1 Rejoice in YAHUWAH, O you tsadiykiym (righteous)! For praise from the yashariym (upright) is beautiful. 2 Praise YAHUWAH with the harp; Make melody to Him with an instrument of ten strings. 3 Sing to Him a new song; Play skillfully with a shout of joy. 4 For the word of YAHUWAH is right, and all His work is done in truth. 5 He loves tsedakah (righteousness) and mishpat (judgment); The earth is full of the goodness of YAHUWAH. 6 By the word of YAHUWAH the heavens were made, and all the host of them by the breath of His mouth. 7 He gathers the waters of the sea together as a heap; He lays up the deep in storehouses. 8 Let all the earth fear YAHUWAH; Let all the inhabitants of the world stand in awe of Him. 9 For He spoke, and it was done; He commanded, and it stood fast. 10 YAHUWAH brings the counsel of the Goyim (nations, Gentiles) to nothing; He makes the plans of the peoples of no effect. 11 The counsel of YAHUWAH stands forever, the plans of His heart to all generations. 12 Blessed is the Goy (nation, Gentile) whose Elohim (God) is YAHUWAH, the people He has chosen as His own inheritance. 13 YAHUWAH looks from heaven; He sees all the sons of men. 14 From the place of His dwelling He looks on all the inhabitants of the earth; 15 He fashions their hearts individually; He considers all their works. 16 No melek (king) is saved by the multitude of an army; A Gibor (mighty man) is not delivered by great strength. 17 A horse is a vain hope for safety; Neither shall it deliver any by its great strength. 18 Behold, the eye of YAHUWAH is on those who fear Him, on those who hope in His mercy, 19 To deliver their soul from mavet (death), and to keep them alive in famine. 20 Our soul waits for YAHUWAH;

He is our help and our shield. 21 For our heart shall rejoice in Him, Because we have trusted in His Shem Kadosh (holy name). 22 Let Your mercy, YAHUWAH, be upon us, Just as we hope in You.

Psalm 34

1 A Psalm of David when he pretended madness before Abimelech, who drove him away, and he departed. I will bless YAHUWAH at all times; His praise shall continually be in my mouth. 2 My soul shall make its boast in YAHUWAH; The humble shall hear of it and be glad. 3 Oh, magnify YAHUWAH with me, and let us exalt His name together. 4 I sought YAHUWAH, and He heard me, and delivered me from all my fears. 5 They looked to Him and were radiant, and their faces were not ashamed. 6 This aniy (poor/humble/afflicted man) cried out, and YAHUWAH heard him, and saved him out of all his troubles. 7 The Mal'ak YAHUWAH (Angel of the Existing One) encamps all around those who fear Him, and delivers them. 8 Oh, taste and see that YAHUWAH is good; Blessed is the man who trusts in Him! 9 Oh, fear YAHUWAH, you His kadoshiym (holy ones, saints, set apart ones)! There is no want to those who fear Him. 10 The young lions lack and suffer hunger; But those who seek YAHUWAH shall not lack any good thing. 11 Come, you children, listen to me; I will teach you the fear of YAHUWAH. 12 Who is the man who desires life, and loves many days, that he may see good? 13 Keep your tongue from ra (evil), and your lips from speaking mirmah (deceit). 14 Depart from ra (evil) and do tov (good); Seek shalom (peace) and pursue it. 15 The eyes of YAHUWAH are on the tsadiykiym (righteous), and His ears are open to their cry. 16 The face of YAHUWAH is against those who do ra (evil), to cut off the remembrance of them from the earth. 17 The tsadiykiym (righteous) cry out, and YAHUWAH hears, and delivers them out of all their troubles. 18 YAHUWAH is

near to those who have a shavar lev (broken heart), and saves such as have a dakka ruach (contrite spirit). 19 Many are the ra'ot (evils, afflictions) of the tsadiyk (righteous), but YAHUWAH delivers him out of them all. 20 He guards all his bones; Not one of them is broken. 21 Ra'ah (Evil) shall slay the rasha (wicked), and those who hate the tsadiyk (righteous) shall be asham (guilty, condemned, desolate). 22 YAHUWAH redeems the soul of His servants, and none of those who chasiym (trust) in Him shall be asham (guilty, condemned, desolate).

Yom Chamishi (Fifth Day) Thursday

Psalms 141

YAHUWAH, I cry out to You; Make haste to me! Give ear to my voice when I cry out to You. Let my tefillat (prayers) be set before You as ketoret (incense), the lifting up of my hands as the minchat erev (evening sacrifice). Set a guard, O YAHUWAH, over my mouth; Keep watch over the door of my lips. Do not incline my heart to any davar ra (evil thing), to practice alilot resha (wicked works) with men who polei aven (work iniquity); And do not let me eat of their man'am (delicacies). Let the tsadiyk (righteous) strike me; It shall be a kindness. And let him rebuke me; It shall be as excellent oil; Let my head not refuse it.

For still my tefillah (prayer) is against the ra'ot (evil's, deeds of the wicked). Their shoftiym (judges) are overthrown by the sides of the cliff, and they hear my words, for they are sweet. Our bones are scattered at the mouth of She'ol (Hades, the grave, the underworld), as when one plows and breaks up the earth. But my eyes are upon You, O YAHUWAH Adonai; In You I take refuge; Do not leave my soul destitute. Keep me from the snares they have laid for me, and from the traps of the polei aven (workers of iniquity). Let the rasha'iym (wicked) fall into their own nets, while I escape safely.

Vayevareh David
(And David Blessed)
1 Chron. 39:10–13

And David blessed YAHUWAH in the presence of all the kehila (congregation): and David said, Blessed are You, YAHUWAH, the El (God) of Israel our father, from everlasting to everlasting. Yours, YAHUWAH, is the greatness, and the power, and the glory, and the victory, and the majesty: for all that is in the heaven and in the earth is Yours; Yours, YAHUWAH, is the malchut (kingdom), and the supremacy as head over all. Riches and honor come of You, and You rule over all; and in Your hand are might and power; and in Your hand it is to make great, and to give strength unto all. Now, therefore, our Elohim (God), we give thanks unto You, and praise Your glorious Name.

Psalm 35

1 A Psalm of David. Plead my cause, YAHUWAH, with those who strive with me; Fight against those who fight against me. 2 Take hold of shield and buckler, and stand up for my help. 3 Also draw out the spear, and stop those who pursue me. Say to my soul, "I am your salvation." 4 Let those be put to shame and brought to dishonor who seek after my life; Let those be turned back and brought to confusion who plot my hurt. 5 Let them be like chaff before the wind, and let the Mal'ak YAHUWAH (Angel of the Existing One) chase them. 6 Let their way be dark and slippery, and let the Mal'ak YAHUWAH (Angel of the Existing One) pursue them. 7 For without cause they have hidden their net for me in a pit, which they have dug without cause for my life. 8 Let destruction come upon him unexpectedly, and let his net that he has hidden catch himself; Into that very destruction let him fall. 9 And my soul

shall be joyful in YAHUWAH; It shall rejoice in His salvation. 10 All my bones shall say, "YAHUWAH, who is like You, delivering the aniy (poor, afflicted, humble) from him who is too strong for him, Yes, the aniy (poor, afflicted, humble) and the evyon (needy) from him who plunders him?" 11 Fierce witnesses rise up; They ask me things that I do not know. 12 They reward me ra (evil) for tov (good), to the sorrow of my soul. 13 But as for me, when they were chalah (sick, diseased), My clothing was sackcloth; I humbled myself with fasting; And my tefilla (prayer) would return to my own heart. 14 I paced about as though he were my friend or brother; I bowed down heavily, as one who mourns for his mother. 15 But in my adversity they rejoiced and gathered together; Nekiym (Abjects,Attackers) gathered against me, and I did not know it; They tore at me and did not cease; 16 With chanef la'egei (ungodly mockers) at feasts they gnashed at me with their teeth. 17 Adonai (My Lord), how long will You look on? Rescue my soul from their destructions, My precious life from the lions. 18 I will give You thanks in the kahal rav (great assembly); I will praise You among many people. 19 Let them not rejoice over me who are wrongfully my oyev'iym (enemies); Nor let them wink with the eye who hate me without a cause. 20 For they do not speak peace, but they devise deceitful matters against the quiet ones in the land. 21 They also opened their mouth wide against me, and said, "Aha, aha! Our eyes have seen it." 22 This You have seen, YAHUWAH; Do not keep silence. O Adonai (my Lord), do not be far from me. 23 Stir up Yourself, and awake to my vindication, to my cause, Elohai (my God) and Adonai (my Lord). 24 Vindicate me, YAHUWAH Elohai (Lord my God), according to Your tsedekah (righteousness); And let them not rejoice over me. 25 Let them not say in their hearts, "Ah, so we would have it!" Let them not say, "We have swallowed him up." 26 Let them be ashamed and brought to mutual confusion who rejoice at my hurt; Let them be clothed with shame and dishonor who exalt themselves against me. 27 Let them shout for joy and be glad, who favor my righteous cause; And let them say continually, "Let YAHUWAH be magnified, who has pleasure in the prosperity of His servant." 28 And my tongue shall speak of Your tsedekah (righteousness) and of Your praise all the day long.

Psalm 36

1 To the Chief Musician. A Psalm of David the servant of YAHUWAH. An oracle within my heart concerning the pasha (transgression) of the rasha (wicked): There is no fear of Elohim (God) before his eyes. 2 For he flatters himself in his own eyes, when he finds out his avon (iniquity) and when he sane (hates). 3 The words of his mouth are aven (wickedness) and mirmah (deceit); He has ceased to be wise and to do tov (good). 4 He devises aven (wickedness) on his bed; He sets himself in a way that is not tov (good); He does not abhor ra (evil). 5 Your mercy, YAHUWAH, is in the heavens; Your emunah (faithfulness) reaches to the clouds. 6 Your tsedakah (righteousness) is like the great mountains; Your mishpat'iym (judgments) are a great deep; YAHUWAH, You preserve man and beast. 7 How precious is Your lovingkindness, O Elohim (God)! Therefore the children of men put their trust under the shadow of Your wings. 8 They are abundantly satisfied with the fullness of Your house, and You give them drink from the river of Your pleasures. 9 For with You is the fountain of life; In Your light we see light. 10 Oh, continue Your lovingkindness to those who know You, and Your tsedakah (righteousness) to the yashar lev (upright in heart). 11 Let not the foot of ga'avah (pride) come against me, and let not the hand of the rasha'iym (wicked) drive me away. 12 There the polei aven (workers of iniquity) have fallen; They have been cast down and are not able to rise.

Psalm 37

1 A Psalm of David. Do not fret because of ra'iym (evildoers), Nor be envious of the oseh avlah (workers of iniquity). 2 For they shall soon be cut down like the grass, and wither as the green herb. 3 Batach (Trust, be bold) in YAHUWAH, and do tov (good); Dwell in the land, and feed on His emunah (faithfulness). 4 Delight yourself also in YAHUWAH, and He shall give you the desires of your heart. 5 Commit your way to YAHUWAH, batach (trust, be bold) also in Him, and He shall bring it to pass. 6 He shall bring forth your tsedekah (righteousness) as the light, and your mishpat (judgment) as the noonday. 7 Rest in YAHUWAH, and wait patiently for Him; Do not fret because of him who prospers in his way, because of the man who brings mezimot (wicked schemes) to pass. 8 Cease from anger, and forsake wrath; Do not fret—it only causes harm. 9 For ra'iym (evildoers) shall be cut off; But those who wait on YAHUWAH, they shall inherit the earth. 10 For yet a little while and the rasha (wicked) shall be no more; Indeed, you will look carefully for his place, but it shall be no more. 11 But the meek shall inherit the earth, and shall delight themselves in the rov shalom (abundance of peace). 12 The rasha (wicked) plots against the tsadiyk (righteous), and gnashes at him with his teeth. 13 Adonai (The Lord) laughs at him, for He sees that his day is coming. 14 The rasha'iym (wicked) have drawn the sword and have bent their bow, to cast down the aniy (poor) and evyon (needy), to slay those who are of a yashar derek (upright way). 15 Their sword shall enter their own heart, and their bows shall be broken. 16 A little that a tsadiyk (righteous man) has is better than the riches of many rasha'iym (wicked). 17 For the arms of the rasha'iym (wicked) shall be broken, but YAHUWAH upholds the tsadiykiym (righteous). 18 YAHUWAH knows the days of the tamiymim (blameless, upright), and their

inheritance shall be forever. 19 They shall not be ashamed in the evil time, and in the days of famine they shall be satisfied. 20 But the rasha'iym (wicked) shall perish; And the oyev'iym YAHUWAH (enemies of the Lord), like the splendor of the meadows, shall vanish. Into smoke they shall vanish away. 21 The rasha (wicked) borrows and does not repay, but the tsadiyk (righteous) shows mercy and gives. 22 For those blessed by Him shall inherit the earth, but those cursed by Him shall be cut off. 23 The steps of a geber (warrior, good man) are ordered by YAHUWAH, and He delights in his way. 24 Though he fall, he shall not be utterly cast down; For YAHUWAH upholds him with His hand. 25 I have been young, and now am old; Yet I have not seen the tsadiyk (righteous) forsaken, nor his seed begging bread. 26 He is ever merciful, and lends; And his seed are blessed. 27 Depart from ra (evil), and do tov (good); And dwell forevermore. 28 For YAHUWAH loves mishpat (judgment, justice), and does not forsake His chaciyd'iym (godly ones); They are preserved forever, but the seed of the rasha'iym (wicked) shall be cut off. 29 The tsadiyk'iym (righteous) shall inherit the land, and dwell in it forever. 30 The mouth of the tsadiyk (righteous) speaks cholmah (wisdom), and his tongue talks of mishpat (judgment). 31 The torah (law) of his Elohim (God) is in his heart; None of his steps shall slide. 32 The rasha (wicked) watches the tsadiyk (righteous), and seeks to slay him. 33 YAHUWAH will not leave him in his hand, nor condemn him when he is judged. 34 Wait on YAHUWAH, and keep His way, and He shall exalt you to inherit the land; When the rasha'iym (wicked) are cut off, you shall see it. 35 I have seen the rasha (wicked) in great power, and spreading himself like a native green tree. 36 Yet he passed away, and behold, he was no more; Indeed I sought him, but he could not be found. 37 Mark the tam (blameless man), and observe the yashar (upright); For the future of that man is shalom (peace). 38 But the pasha'iym (transgressors, rebels) shall be destroyed together; The future of the rasha'iym (wicked) shall be cut off. 39 But the salvation of the tsadiyk'iym (righteous) is from YAHUWAH; He is their strength in the time of trouble. 40 And YAHUWAH shall help them and deliver them; He shall deliver them from the rasha'iym (wicked), and save them, because they trust in Him.

Psalm 38

1 A Psalm of David. To bring to remembrance. YAHUWAH, do not rebuke me in Your wrath, nor chasten me in Your hot displeasure! 2 For Your arrows pierce me deeply, and Your hand presses me down. 3 There is no soundness in my flesh because of Your anger, nor any shalom (peace, health) in my bones because of my chattat (sin; punishment for sin). 4 For my avonot (iniquities; punishment for iniquity) have gone over my head; Like a heavy burden they are too heavy for me. 5 My chavurot (wounds) are foul and festering because of my ivelet (foolishness, folly). 6 I am troubled, I am bowed down greatly; I go mourning all the day long. 7 For my loins are full of inflammation, and there is no soundness in my flesh. 8 I am feeble and severely broken; I groan because of the turmoil of my heart. 9 Adonai (Lord), all my desire is before You; And my sighing is not hidden from You. 10 My heart pants, my strength fails me; As for the light of my eyes, it also has gone from me. 11 My loved ones and my friends stand aloof from my nega (plague, disease), and my relatives stand afar off. 12 Those also who seek my life lay snares for me; Those who seek my hurt speak of destruction, and plan deception all the day long. 13 But I, like a deaf man, do not hear; And I am like a mute who does not open his mouth. 14 Thus I am like a man who does not hear, and in whose mouth is no response. 15 For in You, YAHUWAH, I hope; You will hear, O Adonai Elohai (Lord my God). 16 For I said, "Hear me, lest they rejoice over me, lest, when my foot slips, they exalt themselves against

me." 17 For I am ready to fall, and my sorrow is continually before me. 18 For I will declare my avon (iniquity; punishment for iniquity); I will be in anguish over my chattat (sin, punishment for sin). 19 But my oyev'iym (enemies) are vigorous, and they are strong; And those who hate me wrongfully have multiplied. 20 Those also who render ra (evil) for tov (good), they are my satan (adversaries), because I follow what is tov (good). 21 Do not forsake me, YAHUWAH; O Elohai (my God), be not far from me! 22 Make haste to help me, Adonai (Lord), my salvation!

Psalm 39

1 To the Chief Musician. To Jeduthun. A Psalm of David. I said, "I will guard my ways, lest I chata (sin) with my tongue; I will restrain my mouth with a muzzle, while the rasha (wicked) are before me." 2 I was mute with silence, I held my peace even from tov (good); And my sorrow was stirred up. 3 My heart was hot within me; While I was musing, the fire burned. Then I spoke with my tongue: 4 "YAHUWAH, make me to know my end, and what is the measure of my days, that I may know how frail I am. 5 Indeed, You have made my days as handbreadths, and my age is as nothing before You; Certainly every man at his best state is but vapor. Selah. 6 Surely every man walks about like a shadow; Surely they busy themselves in vain; He heaps up riches, and does not know who will gather them. 7 "And now, Adonai (Lord), what do I wait for? My hope is in You. 8 Deliver me from all my pesha'iym (transgressions); Do not make me the reproach of the nabal (foolish, stupid, vile). 9 I was mute, I did not open my mouth, Because it was You who did it. 10 Remove Your nega (plague) from me; I am consumed by the blow of Your hand. 11 When with rebukes You correct man for avon (iniquity), You make his chamad (beauty, delight) melt away like a moth; Surely every man is vapor. Selah. 12 "Hear my tefillat (prayer),

YAHUWAH, and give ear to my cry; Do not be silent at my tears; For I am a stranger with You, a sojourner, as all my fathers were. 13 Remove Your gaze from me, that I may regain strength, before I go away and am no more."

Yom Shishi (Sixth Day) Friday

Proverbs 15:8-9, 26-29

The zevach rasha'iym (sacrifice of the wicked) is a to'evat (abomination) to YAHUWAH, but the tefillat yashar'iym (prayer of the upright) is His delight. The derek rasha (way of the wicked) is a to'evat (abomination) to YAHUWAH, but He loves him who follows tsedakah (righteousness).

The machashavot ra (thoughts of the wicked) are an to'evat (abomination) to YAHUWAH, but the words of the tahoriym (pure) are pleasant. He who is greedy for gain troubles his own house, but he who hates bribes will live. The heart of the tsadiyk (righteous) studies how to answer, but the mouth of the rasha'iym (wicked) pours forth ra'ot (evil). YAHUWAH is far from the rasha'iym (wicked), but He hears the tefillat (prayer) of the tsadiyk'iym (righteous).

Proverbs 21:3, 27

To do tsedakah (righteousness) and mishpat (judgment, justice) is more acceptable to YAHUWAH than zevach (sacrifice). The zevach rasha'iym (sacrifice of the wicked) is a to'evah (abomination); How much more when he brings it with zimah (wicked intent)!

Nehemiah 8:10

Then he said unto them, Go your way, eat the fat, and drink the sweet, and send portions unto them for whom nothing is prepared: for this day is holy unto YAHUWAH: neither be sorry; for the chedvah (joy, gladness) of YAHUWAH is your ma'oz (strength, protection).

Attah Hu YAHUWAH Lavadekah (Thou art the Lord, Even Thou alone) Nehemiah 9:6-11

You are YAHUWAH, even You alone; You have made the heavens, the heaven of heavens, and all their host, the earth and all things that are therein, the seas and all that is in them, and You give life to them all; and the host of heaven worship You. You are YAHUWAH, the Elohim (God), who did choose Abram, and brought him forth out of Ur of the Chaldees, and gave him the name of Abraham: and found his heart faithful before You:

And You made a covenant with him to give the land of the Canaanite, the Hittite, the Amorite, and the Perizzite, and the Jebusite, and the Girgashite, even to give it unto his seed, and have performed Your words; for You are righteous. And You saw the affliction of our fathers in Egypt, and heard their cry by the Red Sea; and showed Otot (signs) and mofet'iym (wonders) upon Pharaoh, and on all his servants, and on all the people of his land; for You knew that they dealt arrogantly against them; and did make You a name, as it is this day. And You did divide the sea before them, so that they went through the midst of the sea on dry land; and their pursuers You did cast into the depths, as a stone into the mayim aziym (mighty waters).

Apotropos
(Guardian)

O Guardian of Israel, guard the remnant of Israel, and suffer not Israel to perish, who say, Hear O Israel.

O Guardian of an only nation, guard the remnant of an only nation, and suffer not an only nation to perish, who proclaim the unity of Your name, saying, YAHUWAH our Elohim (God), YAHUWAH is One.

O Guardian of a holy nation, guard the remnant of a holy nation, and suffer not a holy nation to perish, who thrice repeat the three-fold sanctification unto the Kadosh (Holy One).

O You who are propitiated by prayers for mercy, and are conciliated by supplications, be propitious and reconciled to an afflicted generation; for there is none that helps.

Our Father, our King, be gracious unto us, and answer us, for we have no good works of our own; deal with us in charity and lovingkindness, and save us.

Have mercy upon us YAHUWAH, who at the name of Yah'shua (Jesus) bow our knees and confess with our tongues that Yah'shua the Messiah (Jesus Christ) is Lord, to the glory of Elohim (God) the Father.

Psalm 40

1 To the Chief Musician. A Psalm of David. I waited patiently for YAHUWAH; And He inclined to me, and heard my cry. 2 He also brought me up out of a horrible pit, out of the miry clay, and set my feet upon a rock, and established my steps. 3 He

has put a new song in my mouth— Praise to our Elohim (God); Many will see it and fear, and will trust in YAHUWAH. 4 Blessed is that man who makes YAHUWAH his mivtach (trust, confidence), and does not respect the rahaviym (proud, defiant), nor such as turn aside to kazav (falsehood, lies). 5 Many, YAHUWAH Elohai (my God), are Your wonderful works which You have done; And Your thoughts toward us cannot be recounted to You in order; If I would declare and speak of them, they are more than can be numbered. 6 Zevach (Sacrifice) and Minchah (offering) You did not desire; My ears You have opened. Olah (Burnt offering) and Chata'ah (sin offering) You did not require. 7 Then I said, "Behold, I come; In the scroll of the book it is written of me. 8 I delight to do Your will, O Elohai (my God), and Your torah (law) is within my heart." 9 I have basar tsedek (preached righteousness) in the kahal rav (great assembly); Indeed, I do not restrain my lips, YAHUWAH, You Yourself know. 10 I have not hidden Your tsedakah (righteousness) within my heart; I have declared Your emunah (faithfulness) and Your teshuv'ah (salvation); I have not concealed Your chesed (mercy, lovingkindness) and Your emet (truth) from the kahal rav (great assembly). 11 Do not withhold Your rachamiym (tender mercies) from me, YAHUWAH; Let Your chesed (lovingkindness) and Your emet (truth) continually preserve me. 12 For innumerable ra'ot (evils) have surrounded me; My avonot (iniquities; punishment for iniquity) have overtaken me, so that I am not able to look up; They are more than the hairs of my head; Therefore my heart fails me. 13 Be pleased, YAHUWAH, to deliver me; YAHUWAH, make haste to help me! 14 Let them be ashamed and brought to mutual confusion who seek to destroy my life; Let them be driven backward and brought to dishonor who wish me ra (evil). 15 Let them be confounded because of their shame, who say to me, "Aha, aha!" 16 Let all those who seek You rejoice and be glad in You; Let such as love Your salvation say continually, "YAHUWAH be magnified!" 17 But I am aniy (poor) and evyon (needy); Yet YAHUWAH thinks upon me. You are my help and my deliverer; Do not delay, O Elohai (my God).

Psalm 41

1 To the Chief Musician. A Psalm of David. Blessed is he who considers the dal (poor, weak, lowly); YAHUWAH will deliver him in time of trouble. 2 YAHUWAH will preserve him and keep him chai (alive), and he will be blessed on the earth; You will not deliver him to the will of his oyev'iym (enemies). 3 YAHUWAH will strengthen him on his eres devai (bed of illness / languishing); You will sustain him in his choliy (sickness). 4 I said, "YAHUWAH, be merciful to me; Rafa'ah nafshiy (Heal my soul), for I have chatat (sinned) against You." 5 My oyev'iym (enemies) speak ra (evil) of me: "When will he die, and his name perish?" 6 And if he comes to see me, he speaks shav (lies, emptiness, falsehood); His heart gathers aven (iniquity, wickedness) to itself; When he goes out, he tells it. 7 All who hate me whisper together against me; Against me they devise my hurt. 8 "A Devar Beliya'al (thing of Belial - worthlessness; a name of Satan, the enemy; an evil spirit)," they say, "clings to him. And now that he lies down, he will rise up no more." 9 Even my own Shalom (peace, familiar friend) in whom I trusted, who ate my bread, has lifted up his heel against me. 10 But You, YAHUWAH, be merciful to me, and raise me up, that I may repay them. 11 By this I know that You are well pleased with me, because my oyev'iym (enemy) does not triumph over me. 12 As for me, You uphold me in my tom (integrity), and set me before Your face forever. 13 Blessed be YAHUWAH, the Elohim (God) of Israel from everlasting to everlasting! Amen and Amen.

Psalm 42

1 To the Chief Musician. A Contemplation of the sons of Korah. As the deer pants for the water brooks, so pants my soul for You, O Elohim (God). 2 My soul thirsts for Elohim (God), for the El Chai (living God). When shall I come and appear before Elohim (God)? 3 My tears have been my food day and night, while they continually say to me, "Where is your Elohim (God)?" 4 When I remember these things, I pour out my soul within me. For I used to go with the multitude; I went with them to the Bet Elohim (house of God), with the voice of rinah (cries of joy) and todah (praise, thanksgiving), with a multitude that kept a chagag (pilgrim feast). 5 Why are you cast down, O my soul? And why are you disquieted within me? Hope in Elohim (God), for I shall yet praise Him for the help of His countenance. 6 Elohai (my God), my soul is cast down within me; Therefore I will remember You from the land of the Jordan, and from the heights of Hermon, from the Hill Mizar. 7 Deep calls unto deep at the noise of Your tsinur'iym (waterspouts); All Your waves and billows have gone over me. 8 YAHUWAH will command Hischesed (lovingkindness, mercy) in the yomam (daytime), and in the lai'lah (night) His shiyr (song) shall be with me; A tefilla (prayer) to the El Chayai (God of my life). 9 I will say to El (God) my Rock, "Why have You forgotten me? Why do I go mourning because of the lachats oyev (oppression of the enemy)?" 10 As with a breaking of my bones, My tsarar'iym (enemies) reproach me, while they say to me all day long, "Where is your Elohim (God)?" 11 Why are you cast down, O my soul? And why are you disquieted within me? Hope in Elohim (God); For I shall yet praise Him, the help of my countenance and my Elohim (God).

Psalm 43

1 Vindicate me, O Elohim (God), and plead my cause against an goy lo-chasiyd (ungodly nation); Oh, deliver me from the iysh mirmah ve'avlah (deceitful and unjust man)! 2 For You are the Elohim (God) of my strength; Why do You cast me off? Why do I go mourning because of the lachats oyev (oppression of the enemy)? 3 Oh, send out Your light and Your truth! Let them lead me; Let them bring me to Your Har Kadasha (holy hill) and to Your mishkan (tabernacle). 4 Then I will go to the mizbeach Elohim (altar of God), To El (God) my exceeding joy; And on the harp I will praise You, O Elohim Elohai (God my God). 5 Why are you cast down, O my soul? And why are you disquieted within me? Hope in Elohim (God); For I shall yet praise Him, the yeshu'ot panai (salvation of my countenance) and my Elohim (God).

Psalm 44

1 To the Chief Musician. A Contemplationa of the sons of Korah. We have heard with our ears, O Elohim (God), our fathers have told us, the deeds You did in their days, in days of old: 2 You drove out the Goyim (nations) with Your hand, but them You planted; You afflicted the peoples, and cast them out. 3 For they did not gain possession of the land by their own sword, nor did their own arm save them; But it was Your right hand, Your arm, and the light of Your countenance, because You favored them. 4 You are my King, O Elohim (God); Command victories for Jacob. 5 Through You we will push down our tsar'iym (enemies); Through Your name we will trample those who rise up against us. 6 For I will not trust in my bow, nor shall my sword save me. 7 But You have saved us from our tsar'iym (enemies), and have put to shame those who hated us. 8 In Elohim (God) we boast all day long, and praise Your name forever. Selah. 9 But You have cast us

off and put us to shame, and You do not go out with our armies. 10 You make us turn back from the tsar (enemy), and those who hate us have taken spoil for themselves. 11 You have given us up like sheep intended for food, and have scattered us among the Goyim (nations). 12 You sell Your people for next to nothing, and are not enriched by selling them. 13 You make us a reproach to our neighbors, a scorn and a derision to those all around us. 14 You make us a byword among the Goyim (nations), a shaking of the head among the peoples. 15 My dishonor is continually before me, and the shame of my face has covered me, 16 Because of the voice of him who charef (reproaches) and gadaf (reviles, blasphemes), because of the oyev (enemy) and the nakam (avenger). 17 All this has come upon us; But we have not forgotten You, nor have we dealt falsely with Your covenant. 18 Our heart has not turned back, nor have our steps departed from Your way; 19 But You have severely broken us in the place of taniym (dragons), and covered us with the tsalmavet (shadow of death). 20 If we had forgotten the name of our Elohim (God), or stretched out our hands to an el zar (strange god), 21 Would not Elohim (God) search this out? For He knows the ta'alumot lev (secrets of the heart). 22 Yet for Your sake we are killed all day long; We are accounted as sheep for the slaughter. 23 Awake! Why do You sleep, O Adonai (Lord)? Arise! Do not cast us off forever. 24 Why do You hide Your face, and forget our oniy (affliction, poverty) and our lachats (oppression)? 25 For our soul is bowed down to the dust; Our body clings to the ground. 26 Arise for our help, and redeem us for Your mercies' sake.

Psalm 45

1 To the Chief Musician. Set to "The Lilies." A Contemplation of the sons of Korah. A Song of Love. My heart is overflowing with a davar tov (good thing); I recite my composition

concerning the Melek (King); My tongue is the pen of a ready writer. 2 You are fairer than the sons of men; Grace is poured upon Your lips; Therefore Elohim (God) has blessed You forever. 3 Gird Your sword upon Your thigh, O Gibor (Mighty One), with Your glory and Your majesty. 4 And in Your majesty ride prosperously because of emet (truth), anvah (humility), and tsedek (righteousness); And Your right hand shall teach You nora'ot (awesome things). 5 Your arrows are sharp in the heart of the oyev'iym ha-Melek (King's enemies); The peoples fall under You. 6 Your throne, O Elohim (God), is forever and ever; A shevet miyshor (scepter of uprightness) is the shevet malchuteka (scepter of Your kingdom). 7 You love tsedek (righteousness) and hate resha (wickedness); Therefore Elohim (God), Your Elohim (God), has anointed You With the shemen sason (oil of gladness) more than Your companions. 8 All Your garments are scented with myrrh and aloes and cassia, out of the ivory palaces, by which they have made You glad. 9 Kings' daughters are among Your honorable women; At Your right hand stands the Shegal (Queen) in gold from Ophir. 10 Listen, O daughter, consider and incline your ear; Forget your own people also, and your father's house; 11 So the Melek (King) will greatly desire your beauty; Because He is your Adon (Lord), worship Him. 12 And the daughter of Tyre will come with a gift; The noble among the people will seek your face (figuratively: favor). 13 The royal daughter is all glorious within the palace; Her clothing is woven with gold. 14 She shall be brought to the Melek (King) in robes of many colors; The betulot (virgins), her companions who follow her, shall be brought to You. 15 With simchah (gladness) and giyl (rejoicing) they shall be brought; They shall enter the King's palace. 16 Instead of Your fathers shall be Your children, whom You shall make Sariym (princes) in all the earth. 17 I will make Your name to be remembered in all generations; Therefore the people shall praise You forever and ever.

Psalm 46

1 To the Chief Musician. A Psalm of the sons of Korah. A Song for Alamoth. Elohim (God) is our refuge and strength, A very present help in trouble. 2 Therefore we will not fear, Even though the earth be removed, and though the mountains be carried into the midst of the sea; 3 Though its waters roar and be troubled, though the mountains shake with its swelling. Selah. 4 There is a river whose streams shall make glad the city of Elohim (God), the kadosh (holy place) of the Mishkan (tabernacle) of Elyon (the Most High). 5 Elohim (God) is in the midst of her, she shall not be moved; Elohim (God) shall help her, just at the break of dawn. 6 The nations raged, the kingdoms were moved; He uttered His voice, the earth melted. 7 YAHUWAH Tzeva'ot (the Lord of Hosts) is with us; The El (God) of Jacob is our refuge. Selah. 8 Come, behold the works of YAHUWAH, Who has made desolations in the earth. 9 He makes wars cease to the end of the earth; He breaks the bow and cuts the spear in two; He burns the chariot in the fire. 10 Be still, and know that I am Elohim (God); I will be exalted among the Goyim (nations, Gentiles), I will be exalted in the earth! 11 YAHUWAH Tzeva'ot (the Lord of Hosts) is with us; The Elohim (God) of Jacob is our refuge. Selah.

Psalm 47

1 To the Chief Musician. A Psalm of the sons of Korah. Oh, clap your hands, all you peoples! Shout to Elohim (God) with the voice of triumph! 2 For YAHUWAH Elyon (Most High) is awesome; He is a Melek Gadol (great King) over all the earth. 3 He will subdue the peoples under us, and the le'umiym (nations) under our feet. 4 He will choose our inheritance for us, the excellence of Jacob whom He loves. Selah. 5 Elohim (God) has gone up with a shout, YAHUWAH with the sound of a shofar (rams horn). 6 Sing praises to Elohim (God), sing

praises! Sing praises to our Melek (King), sing praises! 7 For Elohim (God) is the Melek (King) of all the earth; Sing praises with understanding. 8 Elohim (God) reigns over the Goyim (Gentiles); Elohim (God) sits on His holy throne. 9 The princes of the people have gathered together, the people of the Elohim (God) of Abraham. For the shields of the earth belong to Elohim (God); He is greatly exalted.

Psalm 48

1 A Song. A Psalm of the sons of Korah. Great is YAHUWAH, and greatly to be praised in the city of our Elohim (God), In His Har Kedoshat (holy mountain). 2 Beautiful in elevation, the joy of the whole earth, is Mount Zion on the sides of the north, the city of the Melek Rav (great King). 3 Elohim (God) is in her palaces; He is known as her refuge. 4 For behold, the kings assembled, they passed by together. 5 They saw it, and so they marveled; They were troubled, they hastened away. 6 Fear took hold of them there, and pain, as of a woman in birth pangs, 7 As when You break the ships of Tarshish with an east wind. As we have heard, so we have seen in the city of YAHUWAH Tzeva'ot (the Lord of Hosts), in the city of our Elohim (God): Elohim (God) will establish it forever. Selah. 9 We have thought, O Elohim (God), on Your chesed (lovingkindness, mercy), in the midst of Your Heykal (temple). 10 According to Your name, O Elohim (God), so is Your praise to the ends of the earth; Your right hand is full of tsedek (righteousness). 11 Let Mount Zion rejoice, let the daughters of Judah be glad, because of Your mishpatiym (judgments). 12 Walk about Zion, and go all around her. Count her towers; 13 Mark well her bulwarks; Consider her palaces; That you may tell it to the generation following. 14 For this is Elohim (God), our Elohim (God) forever and ever; He will be our guide even to death.

Yom Shabbat (7th Day - Sabbath) Saturday

Ecclesiastes 5:1-7

Walk prudently when you go to the Bet Elohim (house of God); and draw near to hear rather than to give the kesiyl'iym zevach (sacrifice of fools), for they do not know that they do ra (evil). Do not be rash with your mouth, and let not your heart utter anything hastily before Elohim (God). For Elohim (God) is in heaven, and you on earth; Therefore let your words be few. For a chalom (dream) comes through much activity, and a kesiyl's (fool's) voice is known by his many words. When you make a neder (vow) to Elohim (God), do not delay to pay it; For He has no pleasure in kesiyl'iym (fools). Pay what you have nadar (vowed). Better not to nadar (make a vow) than to nadar (make a vow) and not pay. Do not let your mouth cause your flesh to chata (sin), nor say before the Mal'ak (Angel) that it was an error. Why should Elohim (God) be angry at your excuse and destroy the work of your hands? For in the multitude of chalomot (dreams) and many words there is also vanity. But fear Elohim (God).

Ecclesiastes 12:13-14

Let us hear the conclusion of the whole matter: Fear Elohim (God), and keep his mitzvot (commandments): for this is the whole duty of man. For Elohim (God) shall bring every work into mishpat (judgment), with every secret thing, whether it be good, or whether it be ra (evil).

Vayosha (Saved)
Exod. 14:30–15:18

Thus YAHUWAH saved Israel that day out of the hand of the Egyptians; and Israel saw the Egyptians dead upon the sea shore. And Israel saw the great power which YAHUWAH put forth against the Egyptians, and the people feared YAHUWAH: and they believed in YAHUWAH, and in Moses his servant.

Then sang Moses and the children of Israel this song unto YAHUWAH, and spoke, saying: I will sing unto YAHUWAH, for he has been highly exalted: the horse and his rider has he thrown into the sea. YAHUWAH is my strength and song, and he is become my salvation: this is Elohai (my God), and I will glorify him; my father's Elohim (God), and I will exalt him. YAHUWAH is a man of war: YAHUWAH is his name. Pharaoh's chariots and his host has he cast into the sea: and his chosen captains are sunk in the Red Sea. The floods cover them: they went down into the depths like a stone. Your right hand, YAHUWAH, that is glorious in power, Your right hand, YAHUWAH, dashes in pieces the enemy. And in the greatness of Your majesty You overthrow them that rise up against You: You send forth Your wrath, it consums them as stubble. And with the blast of Your nostrils the waters were piled up, the streams stood upright as an heap; the floods were congealed in the heart of the sea. The enemy said, I will pursue, I will overtake, I will divide the spoil: my lust shall be satisfied upon them; I will draw my sword, my hand shall destroy them. You did blow with Your wind, the sea covered them: they sank as lead in the mighty waters. Who is like unto You, YAHUWAH, amongst the mighty ones: who is like unto You, glorious in holiness, revered in praises, doing marvels? You stretched out Your right hand, the earth swallowed them.

You in Your lovingkindness have led the people which You have redeemed: You have guided them in Your strength to Your holy habitation. The peoples have heard it; they tremble: pangs have taken hold of the inhabitants of Philistia. Then were the dukes of Edom confounded; the mighty men of Moab, trembling takes hold of them: all the inhabitants of Canaan are melted away. Terror and dread falls upon them: by the greatness of Your arm they are as still as a stone; till Your people pass over, YAHUWAH, till the people pass over, which You have acquired. You will bring them in, and plan them in the mountain of Your inheritance, the place, YAHUWAH, which You have made for You to dwell in, the sanctuary, O Lord, which Your hands have established. YAHUWAH shall reign for ever and ever. YAHUWAH shall reign for ever and ever.

For the kingdom is YAHUWAH's: and he is ruler over the nations. And saviors shall come up on mount Zion to judge the mount of Esau; and the kingdom shall be YAHUWAH's. And YAHUWAH shall be King over all the earth: in that day shall YAHUWAH be One, and his name One. And in Your Law it is written, saying, Hear, O Israel: YAHUWAH our God, YAHUWAH is One.

Avoneinu
(Our Father)

Our Father, our King! we have sinned before You.

Our Father, our King! we have no king but You.

Our Father, our King! deal with us for the sake of Your name.

Our Father, our King! let a happy year begin for us.

Our Father, our King! nullify all evil decrees against us.

Our Father, our King! nullify the designs of those that hate us.

Our Father, our King! make the counsGod of our enemies of none effect.

Our Father, our King! rid us of every oppressor and adversary.

Our Father, our King! close the mouths of our adversaries and accusers.

Our Father, our King! of pestilence and the sword, of famine, captivity and destruction, rid the children of Your covenant.

Our Father, our King! withhold the plague from Your inheritance.

Our Father, our King! forgive and pardon all our iniquities.

Our Father, our King! blot out our transgressions, and make them pass away from before Your eyes.

Our Father, our King! erase in Your abundant mercies all the records of our guilt.

Our Father, our King! bring us back in perfect repentance unto You.

Our Father, our King! send a perfect healing to the sick of Your people.

Our Father, our King! rend the evil judgment decreed against us.

Our Father, our King! let Your remembrance of us be for good.

Our Father, our King! inscribe us in the book of happy life.

Our Father, our King! inscribe us in the book of redemption and salvation.

Our Father, our King! inscribe us in the book of maintenance and sustenance.

Our Father, our King! inscribe us in the book of merit.

Our Father, our King! inscribe us in the book of forgiveness and pardon.

Our Father, our King! let salvation soon spring forth for us.

Our Father, our King! exalt the horn of Israel, Your people.

Our Father, our King! exalt the horn of Your anointed.

Our Father, our King! fill our hands with Your blessings.

Our Father, our King! fill our storehouses with plenty.

Our Father, our King! hear our voice, spare us, and have mercy upon us.

Our Father, our King! receive our prayer in mercy and in favor.

Our Father, our King! open the gates of heaven unto our prayer.

Our Father, our King! we pray You, turn us not back empty from Your presence.

Our Father, our King! remember that we are but dust.

Our Father; our King! let this hour be an hour of mercy and a time of favor with You.

Our Father, our King! have compassion upon us and upon our children and our infants.

Our Father, our King! do this for the sake of them that were slain for Your holy name.

Our Father, our King! do it for the sake of them that were slaughtered for Your Unity.

Our Father, our King! do it for the sake of them that went through fire and water for the sanctification of Your name.

Our Father, our King! avenge before our eyes he blood of Your servants that has been shed.

Our Father, our King! do it for your sake, if not for ours.

Our Father, our King! do it for Your sake, and save us.

Our Father, our King! do it for the sake of Your abundant mercies.

Our Father, our King! do it for the sake of Your great, mighty and revered name by which we are called.

Our Father, our King! be gracious unto us and answer us, for we have no good works of our own; deal with us in charity and kindness, and save us.

Psalm 49

1 To the Chief Musician. A Psalm of the sons of Korah. Hear this, all amiym (peoples); Give ear, all yoshebei chaled

(inhabitants of the world), 2 Both bnei adam (sons of humans) and bnei iysh (sons of man), ashiyr (rich) and evyon (poor) together. 3 My mouth shall speak chokmah (wisdom), and the hagut (meditation) of my heart shall give tevunot (understanding). 4 I will incline my ear to mashal (proverb, parable); I will disclose my chiydah (dark saying, riddle, puzzle) on the harp. 5 Why should I fear in the yom ra (days of evil), when the avon (iniquity) at my heels surrounds me? 6 Those who batach (trust) in their chayil (wealth) and halal (boast) in the multitude of their asheram (riches), 7 None of them can by any means redeem his brother, nor give to Elohim (God) a ransom for him. 8 For the redemption of their souls is costly, and it shall cease forever. 9 That he should continue to live eternally, and not see corruption. 10 For he sees chakamiym (wise men) die; Likewise the kesiyl (fool) and the ba'ar (brutish, stupid, senseless person) perish, and leave their chayil (wealth) to others. 11 Their inner thought is that their houses will last forever, their dwelling places to all generations; They call their lands after their own names. 12 Nevertheless man, though in honor, does not remain; He is like the beasts that perish. 13 This is the way of those who are kesel (stupid, folly), and of their achar'iym (posterity) who approve their sayings. Selah. 14 Like sheep they are laid in Sheol (Hades, the grave, the underworld); Mavet (Death) shall feed on them; The yashar'iym (upright) shall have dominion over them in the morning; And their beauty shall be consumed in Sheol (Hades, the grave, the underworld), far from their dwelling. 15 But Elohim (God) will redeem my soul from the power of Sheol (Hades, the grave, the underworld), for He shall receive me. Selah. 16 Do not be afraid when one becomes ashar (rich), when the glory of his house is increased; 17 For when he dies he shall carry nothing away; His glory shall not descend after him. 18 Though while he lives he blesses himself (for men will praise you when you do well for yourself), 19 He shall go to the generation of his fathers; They shall never see light. 20 A man who is in honor, yet does not understand, is like the beasts that perish.

Psalm 50

1 A Psalm of Asaph. El Elohim (Mighty God), YAHUWAH, has spoken and called the earth from the rising of the sun to its going down. 2 Out of Zion, the perfection of beauty, Elohim (God) will shine forth. 3 Our Elohim (God) shall come, and shall not keep silent; A fire shall devour before Him, and it shall be very tempestuous all around Him. 4 He shall call to the heavens from above, and to the earth, that He may judge His people: 5 "Gather My chasiyd'iym (godly ones) together to Me, those who have made a covenant with Me by zevach (sacrifice)." 6 Let the heavens declare His tsedakah (righteousness), for Elohim (God) Himself is shofet (Judge). Selah. 7 "Hear, O My people, and I will speak, O Israel, and I will testify against you; I am Elohim (God), your Elohim (God)! 8 I will not rebuke you for your zevachiym (sacrifices) or your olot (burnt offerings), which are continually before Me. 9 I will not take a bull from your house, nor goats out of your folds. 10 For every beast of the forest is Mine, and the cattle on a thousand hills. 11 I know all the birds of the mountains, and the wild beasts of the field are Mine. 12 "If I were hungry, I would not tell you; For the world is Mine, and all its fullness. 13 Will I eat the flesh of bulls, or drink the blood of goats? 14 Offer to Elohim (God) todah (thanksgiving), and pay your neder'iym (vows) to Elyon (the Most High). 15 Call upon Me in the day of trouble; I will deliver you, and you shall glorify Me." 16 But to the rasha (wicked), Elohim (God) says: "What right have you to declare My chukot (statutes), or take My brit (covenant) in your mouth, 17 Seeing you hate musar (instruction) and cast My davar (words) behind you? 18 When you saw a ganav (thief), you ratsah (consented, were pleased, accepted) with him, and

have been a chelek (partaker) with na'afiym (adulterers). 19 You give your mouth to ra (evil), and your tongue frames mirmah (deceit). 20 You sit and speak against your brother; You dofiy (slander, blemish, find fault with) your own mother's son. 21 These things you have done, and I kept silent; You thought that I was altogether like you; But I will rebuke you, and set them in order before your eyes. 22 "Now consider this, you who forget Eloah (God), lest I tear you in pieces, and there be none to deliver: 23 Whoever zavach todah (offers thanksgiving) glorifies Me; And to him who orders his conduct aright I will show the salvation of Elohim (God)."

Psalm 51

1 To the Chief Musician. A Psalm of David when Nathan the navi (prophet) went to him, after he had gone in to Bathsheba. Have mercy upon me, O Elohim (God), according to Your chesed (lovingkindness, mercy); According to the multitude of Your racham'iym (tender mercies), blot out my pesha'iym (transgressions). 2 Wash me thoroughly from my avon (iniquity; punishment for sin), and cleanse me from my chatat (sin; punishment for sin). 3 For I acknowledge my pesha'iym (transgressions), and my chatat (sin; punishment for sin) is always before me. 4 Against You, You only, have I chata (sinned), and done this ra (evil) in Your sight; That You may be found tsadak (just) when You speak, and zakah (blameless, pure, clean) when You judge. 5 Behold, I was brought forth in avon (iniquity), and in chet (sin) my mother conceived me. 6 Behold, You desire emet (truth) in the inward parts, and in the hidden part You will make me to know chokmah (wisdom). 7 Purge me with hyssop, and I shall be taher (clean); Wash me, and I shall be whiter than snow. 8 Make me hear sason (joy) and simchah (gladness), that the bones You have broken may rejoice. 9 Hide Your face from

my chet (sins), and blot out all my avonot (iniquities). 10 Create in me a lev tahor (clean heart), O Elohim (God), and renew a ruach nakon (steadfast spirit) within me. 11 Do not cast me away from Your presence, and do not take Your Ruach Kodesh (Holy Spirit) from me. 12 Restore to me the sason (joy) of Your yesha (salvation), and uphold me by Your ruach nadiyv (generous Spirit). 13 Then I will teach posh'iym (transgressors) Your derek (ways), and chataiym (sinners) shall be converted to You. 14 Deliver me from the guilt of bloodshed, O Elohim (God), the Elohim (God) of my teshuv'ah (salvation), and my tongue shall sing aloud of Your tsedakah (righteousness). 15 Adonai (Lord), open my lips, and my mouth shall show forth Your tehilah (praise). 16 For You do not desire zevach (sacrifice), or else I would give it; You do not delight in Olah (burnt offering). 17 The Zevach Elohim (sacrifices of God) are a ruach nishbarah (broken spirit), a lev nishbar ve'nidkeh (broken and a contrite heart); These, O Elohim (God), You will not despise. 18 Do good in Your good pleasure to Zion; Build the walls of Jerusalem. 19 Then You shall be pleased with the zivchei tsedek (sacrifices of righteousness), with Olah (burnt offering) and Kaliyl (whole burnt offering); Then they shall offer bulls on Your mizbeach (altar).

Psalm 52

1 To the Chief Musician. A Contemplation of David when Doeg the Edomite went and told Saul, and said to him, "David has gone to the house of Ahimelech." Why do you boast in ra (evil), O gibor (mighty man)? The chesed(mercy, goodness) of El (God) endures continually. 2 Your tongue devises havah (destruction), like a sharp razor, working deceitfully. 3 You love ra (evil) more than tov (good), sheker (lying) rather than speaking tsedek (righteousness). Selah. 4 You ahava (love) all divrei bala (devouring words), You lashon mirmah (deceitful

tongue). 5 El (God) shall likewise destroy you forever; He shall take you away, and pluck you out of your dwelling place, and uproot you from the land of the chayim (living). Selah. 6 The tsadiykiym (righteous) also shall see and fear, and shall laugh at him, saying, 7 "Here is the man who did not make Elohim (God) his ma'oz (strength, protection), but batach (trusted) in the rov osher (abundance of his riches), and strengthened himself in his havot (destruction,wickedness)." 8 But I am like a green olive tree in the Bet Elohim (house of God); I trust in the chesed Elohim (mercy of God) forever and ever. 9 I will praise You forever, because You have done it; And in the presence of Your chasiyd'iym (godly ones) I will wait on Your name, for it is tov (good).

Psalm 53

1 To the Chief Musician. Set to "Mahalat." A Contemplation of David. The nabal (fool) has said in his heart, "There is no Elohim (God)." They are shachat (corrupt, destroyed), and have done ta'av avel (abominable iniquity); There is none who does tov (good). 2 Elohim (God) looks down from heaven upon the children of men, to see if there are any who understand, who seek Elohim (God). 3 Every one of them has turned aside; They have together become alach (filthy); There is none who does tov (good), no, not one. 4 Have the polei aven (workers of iniquity) no knowledge, who eat up my people as they eat bread, and do not call upon Elohim (God)? 5 There they are in great fear where no fear was, for Elohim (God) has scattered the bones of him who encamps against you; You have put them to shame, because Elohim (God) has despised them. 6 Oh, that the salvation of Israel would come out of Zion! When Elohim (God) brings back the captivity of His people, let Jacob rejoice and Israel be glad.

Psalm 54

1 To the Chief Musician. With stringed instruments. A Contemplation of David when the Ziphites went and said to Saul, "Is David not hiding with us?" Save me, O Elohim (God), by Your name, and vindicate me by Your strength. 2 Hear my tefillah (prayer), O Elohim (God); Give ear to the words of my mouth. 3 For strangers have risen up against me, and oppressors have sought after my life; They have not set Elohim (God) before them. Selah. 4 Behold, Elohim (God) is my helper; Adonai (The Lord) is with those who uphold my life. 5 He will repay my sharar'iym (enemies) for their ra (evil). Cut them off in Your emet (truth). 6 I will nedavah zevach (freely sacrifice) to You; I will praise Your name, YAHUWAH, for it is tov (good). 7 For He has delivered me out of all trouble; And my eye has seen its desire upon my oyev'iym (enemies).

Psalm 55

1 To the Chief Musician. With stringed instruments. A Contemplation of David. Give ear to my tefilat (prayer), O Elohim (God), and do not hide Yourself from my supplication. 2 Attend to me, and hear me; I am restless in my complaint, and moan noisily, 3 Because of the voice of the oyev (enemy), because of the akat rasha (oppression of the wicked); For they bring down trouble upon me, and in wrath they hate me. 4 My heart is severely pained within me, and the eymot mavet (terrors of death) have fallen upon me. 5 Fearfulness and trembling have come upon me, and horror has overwhelmed me. 6 So I said, "Oh, that I had wings like a dove! I would fly away and be at rest. 7 Indeed, I would wander far off, and remain in the wilderness. Selah. 8 I would hasten my escape from the windy storm and tempest." 9 Destroy, Adonai (Lord), and divide their tongues, for I have

seen violence and strife in the city. 10 Day and night they go around it on its walls; aven (Iniquity) and amal (trouble) are also in the midst of it. 11 Havah (Destruction, calamity) is in its midst; tok (Oppression) and mirmah (deceit) do not depart from its streets. 12 For it is not an oyev (enemy) who reproaches me; Then I could bear it. Nor is it one who hates me who has exalted himself against me; Then I could hide from him. 13 But it was you, a man my equal, My companion and my acquaintance. 14 We took sweet counsel together, and walked to the Bet Elohim (house of God) in the throng. 15 Let mavet (death) seize them; Let them go down alive into Sheol (Hades, the grave, the underworld), for ra'ot (wickedness) is in their dwellings and among them. 16 As for me, I will call upon Elohim (God), and YAHUWAH shall save me. 17 Erev (Evening) and boker (morning) and at tsohariym (noon) I will siyach (speak, talk), and ehameh (cry aloud), and He shall hear my voice. 18 He has redeemed my soul in shalom (peace) from the battle that was against me, for there were many against me. 19 El (God) will hear, and afflict them, even He who abides from of old. Selah. Because they do not chaliyfot (change), therefore they do not fear Elohim (God). 20 He has put forth his hands against those who were at shalom (peace) with him; He has broken his covenant. 21 The words of his mouth were smoother than butter, but kerav (war, hostile encounter) was in his heart; His words were softer than oil, yet they were drawn swords. 22 Cast your yehav (burden, lot –what is given) on YAHUWAH, and He shall sustain you; He shall never permit the tsadiyk (righteous) to be moved. 23 But You, O Elohim (God), shall bring them down to the be'er shachat (pit of destruction); Anshei damiym uv'mirmah (Bloodthirsty and deceitful men) shall not live out half their days; But I will batach (trust, be bold) in You.

MINCHA
(Afternoon Prayers)

Ot Ha-Ts'lav (Sign of the Cross)

In the name of the Father YAHUWAH, and of the Son Yah'shua (Jesus), and of the Ruach HaKodesh (Holy Spirit). Amen.

Blessed be YAHUWAH, always now and for ever, and unto the ages of ages. Amen.

Avinu / Tefillat Talmid
(Our Father / The disciple's prayer)

Avinu (Our Father), Who is in heaven, hallowed be Your Name. Your Kingdom come. Your will be done, on earth as it is in heaven. Give us this day our daily bread; and forgive us our trespasses, as we forgive those who trespass against us; and lead us not into temptation, but deliver us from the Hara (evil one). For Yours is the kingdom, and the power, and the glory, for ever. Amen.

SHELICHIYM HA'EMUNA
(The Apostles Creed)

I believe in YAHUWAH our Elohim (God), the Avi Shaddai (Father almighty), Bore (Creator) of heaven and earth, and in Yah'shua the Messiah (Jesus Christ), his only-begotten Son, our Adon (Lord), who was conceived by the Ruach HaKodesh (Holy Spirit), born of the Virgin Miriam (Mary), suffered under Pontius Pilate, was crucified, died and was buried; he descended into hell; on the third day he rose again from the dead; he ascended into heaven, and is seated at the right hand of Elohim (God) the Avi SHaddai (Father almighty); from there he will come to judge the living and the dead. I believe in the Ruach HaKodesh (Holy Spirit), the holy (set apart) Apostolic Universal Church, the Chavarut Ha-Kadoshiym (communion of saints), the forgiveness of sins, the resurrection of the body, and life everlasting. Amen.

Ana Be'choach

Release all those in captivity, we beseech You, Shaddai (Almighty One) whose power sets us free. Accept the singing of all Your people Who praise and glorify You alone. Preserve those Who seek Your unity, guard them like the pupil of the eye. Bless and purify them and always grant them Your compassionate righteousness. Invincible and Abiyr (Mighty One), with the abundance of Your goodness, watch over Your people. O Me'romam (Exalted One), turn to Your people Who remember Your kedusha (holiness). Turn to us and hear our tefillot (prayers), You Who know all hidden things. Blessed is the Name of His glorious kingdom for ever and ever. Amen.

Katzi Kaddish
(Half Sanctification)

Reader.—Magnified and sanctified be his great name in the world which he has created according to his will. May he establish his kingdom during your life and during your days, and during the life of all the house of Israel, even speedily and at a near time, and say, Amen.

Cong. and Reader.—Let his great name be blessed for ever and to all eternity.

Reader.—Blessed, praised and glorified, exalted, extolled and honored, magnified and lauded be the name of the Kadosh

(Holy One), blessed be he; though he be high above all the blessings and hymns, praises and consolations, which are uttered in the world; and say, Amen.

AMIDA (Standing) SHEMONEH ESREH (Eighteen Prayers)

The following prayer (Amidah) to "as in ancient years," is to be said standing.

YAHUWAH, open my lips, and my mouth will declare Your praise.

Avot
(Fathers)

Blessed are You YAHUWAH our Elohim (God), Melek Ha'Olam (King of the universe), the God and the Father of our Lord Yah'shua the Messiah (Jesus Christ), and God of our fathers, God of Abraham, God of Isaac, God of Jacob, God of Sarah, God of Rebecca, God of Rachel, and the God of Leah the great, mighty and revered Elohim (God), the El Elyon (God most high), who bestows loving kindnesses, and possesses all things; who rememberes the pious deeds of the patriarchs, and in love will bring a redeemer to their children's children for Your name's sake. Remember us unto life, O King, who delights in life, and inscribe us in the book of life, for Your own sake, O Elohim Chayim (living God). O King, Helper, Saviour and Shield. Blessed are You, YAHUWAH, the Shield of Abraham. You, YAHUWAH, are mighty for ever, You quicken the dead, You are mighty to save, You cause the wind to blow and the rain to fall.

Gevurot
(Gods Might)

You sustain the living with loving kindness, quicken the dead with great mercy, support the falling, heal the sick, loose the bound, and keep Your faith to them that sleep in the dust. Who is like unto You, Lord of mighty acts, and who resembles You, O King, who kills and quickens, and causes salvation to spring forth? Who is like unto You, Father of mercy, who in mercy remembers Your creatures unto life? Yes, faithful are You to quicken the dead. Blessed are You, YAHUWAH, who quickens the dead.

Kedushat HaShem
(Holiness of Gods Name)

You are holy, and Your name is holy, and holy ones praise You daily. (Selah.) Blessed are You, YAHUWAH, the El Kadosh Ve'Melek (holy God and King). We will sanctify Your name in the world even as they sanctify it in the highest heavens, as it is written by the hand of Your navi (prophet): And they called one unto the other and said, Holy, holy, holy is YAHUWAH Tzeva'ot (the Lord of hosts): the whole earth is full of his glory. Those over against them say, Blessed be the glory of YAHUWAH from his place. And in Your Holy Words it is written, saying, YAHUWAH shall reign for ever, Your Elohim (God), O Zion, unto all generations. Hallelu Yah (Praise the Lord).

Unto all generations we will declare Your greatness, and to all eternity we will proclaim Your holiness, and Your praise, O our Elohim (God), shall not depart from our mouth for ever, for You are a great and holy God and King. Blessed are You, YAHUWAH, the El Kadosh Ve'Melek (holy God and King).

Da'at
(Knowledge)

You favor man with knowledge, and teach mortals understanding. You have favored us with a knowledge of Your Torah (Law), and have taught us to perform the statutes of Your will. O favor us with knowledge, understanding and discernment from You. Be gracious to us; a mind of understanding and intellect is from You. Blessed are You, YAHUWAH, Who favors us with knowledge.

Teshuva
(Repentance)

Cause us to return, O our Father, unto Your Torah (Law); draw us near, O our King, to serve You, and bring us back in perfect repentance unto Your presence. Blessed are You, YAHUWAH, who delights in repentance.

Selichot
(Forgiveness)

Forgive us, O our Father, for we have sinned; pardon us, O our King, for we have transgressed; for You do pardon and forgive. Blessed are You, YAHUWAH, who are gracious, and does abundantly forgive.

Geulah
(Redemption)

Look upon our affliction and plead our cause, and redeem us speedily for Your name's sake; for You are a mighty Redeemer. Blessed are You, YAHUWAH, the Redeemer of

Israel. Blessed are You, YAHUWAH, who answers in time of trouble.

Refuah
(Healing)

Heal us, O YAHUWAH, and we shall be healed; save us and we shall be saved; for You are our praise. Vouchsafe a perfect healing to all our wounds; for You, Melek Shaddai (almighty King), are a faithful and merciful Physician. Blessed are You, YAHUWAH, who heals the sick of Your people Israel. May it be Your will, YAHUWAH our Elohim (God), the God and the Father of our Lord Yah'shua the Messiah (Jesus Christ), and the God of our forefathers, that You quickly send *refuah sh'lemah* (complete healing) from heaven, *refuah ruchani* (spiritual healing) and *refuah gufani* (physical healing) to Your servant *(name)* among the other patients of Your people and Israel. In the Name of Yah'shua the Messiah (Jesus Christ).

Birkat Hashanim
(Prosperity)

Bless for us, YAHUWAH our Elohim (God), this year and its crops. Grant us a blessing on the earth. Satisfy us from Your bounty and bless our year like other good years. Blessed are You, YAHUWAH, Who blesses the years.

Kibbutz Galuyot
(Ingathering of Exiles)

Sound the great shofar for our freedom and raise the banner to gather our exiles, and gather us from the four corners of the earth. Blessed are You, YAHUWAH, who gathers the scattered of Your people Israel.

Birkat HaDim
(Restoration of Justice)

Restore our judges as at the first, and our counsellors as at the beginning; remove from us grief and suffering; reign over us, YAHUWAH, You alone, in lovingkindness and tender mercy, and justify us in judgment. Bestow Your Spirit upon the rulers of all lands; guide them that they may govern justly. Then shall love and compassion be enthroned among us. Blessed are You YAHUWAH, the Melek Ha-Mishpat (King of Judgment), who loves righteousness and justice.

Al Hatzadikim
(Source of Righteousness)

For the righteous and faithful of all humankind, for all who join themselves to your people, for all who put their trust in YAHUWAH our Elohim (God) and Yah'shua the Messiah (Jesus Christ), the Son of the Father, and for all honest men and women, we ask Your favor. Grant that we may be always numbered among them. Blessed are You, YAHUWAH, staff and support of the righteous.

Tsaddikim
(Righteous Ones)

Towards the righteous and the pious, towards the elders of Your people the house of Israel, towards the remnant of their scribes, towards the proselytes of righteousness, and towards us also may Your tender mercies be stirred, YAHUWAH our Elohim (God); grant a good reward unto all who faithfully trust in Your name; set our portion with them for ever, so that we may not be put to shame; for we have trusted in You. Blessed are You, YAHUWAH, the stay and trust of the righteous.

Binyan Yerushalayim
(Rebuilding of Jerusalem)

And to Jerusalem, Your city, return in mercy, and dwell therein as You have spoken; rebuild it soon in our days as an everlasting building, and speedily set up therein the throne of David. Blessed are You, YAHUWAH, who rebuilds Jerusalem.

Malkhut Beit David
(Kingdom of David)

Speedily cause the Seed of David Your servant to flourish, and let his horn be exalted by Your salvation, because we wait for Your salvation all the day. Blessed are You, YAHUWAH, who causes the horn of salvation to flourish.

Kabbalat Tefillah
(Acceptance of Prayer)

Hear our voice, YAHUWAH our Elohim (God); spare us and have mercy upon us, and accept our prayer in mercy and favor; for You are Elohim (God) who hearkens unto prayers and supplications: from Your presence, O our King, turn us not away empty; for You hearken in mercy to the prayer of Your people Israel. Blessed are You, YAHUWAH, who hearkens unto prayer.

Avodah
(Worship)

Accept, YAHUWAH our Elohim (God), Your people Israel and their prayer; restore the service to the oracle of Your house; receive in love and favor both the fire-offerings of Israel and their prayer; and may the service of your people Israel be ever acceptable unto You. Even as it written, My House shall be a house of prayer; and again, My house shall be called a house of prayer for all people.

On New Moon and the Intermediate Days of Passover and Tabernacles the following is added:—

Our God and God of our fathers! May our remembrance rise, come and be accepted before You, with the remembrance of our fathers, of Yah'shua the Messiah (Jesus Christ) the son of David Your servant, of Jerusalem Your holy city, and of all Your people the house of Israel, bringing deliverance and well-being, grace, loving kindness and mercy, life and peace on this day of

On Passover—

the Feast of Unleavened Bread.

On New Moon say—

the New Moon.

On Tabernacles—

the Feast of Tabernacles.

Remember us, YAHUWAH our Elohim (God), thereon for our well-being; be mindful of us for blessing, and save us unto life: by Your promise of salvation and mercy, spare us and be gracious unto us; have mercy upon us and save us; for our eyes are bent upon You, because You are a gracious and merciful God and King.

And let our eyes behold Your return in mercy to Zion. Blessed are You, YAHUWAH, who restores Your divine presence unto Zion.

Hodah
(Thanksgiving)

We give thanks unto You, for You are YAHUWAH our Elohim (God), the God and the Father of our Lord Yah'shua the Messiah (Jesus Christ), and the God of our fathers, for ever and ever; You are the Rock of our lives, the Shield of our salvation through every generation. We will give thanks unto You and declare Your praise for our lives

We give thanks unto You, for You are YAHUWAH our Elohim (God), the God and the Father of our Lord Yah'shua the Messiah (Jesus Christ); the God of our fathers, the God of all flesh, our Borei (Creator) and the Borei (Creator) of all things in the beginning. Blessings and thanksgivings be to Your great and holy name, because You have kept us in life and have preserved us: so may You continue to keep us in life and to preserve us. O gather our exiles to Your holy courts to observe Your statutes, to do Your will, and to serve You with a perfect heart; seeing that we give thanks unto You. Blessed be Elohim (God) to whom thanksgivings are due.

Which are committed unto Your hand, and for our souls which are in Your charge, and for Your miracles, which are daily with us, and for Your wonders and Your benefits, which are wrought at all times, evening, morning and at noon. O You who are all-good, whose mercies fail not; You, Merciful One, whose lovingkindnesses never cease, we have ever hoped in You.

On Chanukah and Purim the following is added:—

We thank You also for the miracles, for the redemption, for the mighty deeds and saving acts, wrought by You, as well as for the wars which You did wage for our fathers in days of old, at this season.

On Chanukah.

In the days of the Hasmonean, Mattathias son of Johanan, the Kohen Gadol (High Priest), and his sons, when the iniquitous power of Greece rose up against Your people Israel to make them forgetful of Your Torah (Law), and to force them to transgress the statutes of Your will, then did You in Your abundant mercy rise up for them in the time of their trouble; You did plead their cause, You did judge their suit, You did avenge their wrong; You delivered the strong into the hands of the weak, the many into the hands of the few, the impure into the hands of the pure, the wicked into the hands of the righteous, and the arrogant into the hands of them that occupied themselves with Your Torah (Law): for Yourself You did make a great and holy name in Your world, and for Your people Israel You did work a great deliverance and redemption as at this day. And thereupon Your children came into the oracle of Your house, cleansed Your temple, purified Your sanctuary, kindled lights in Your holy courts, and appointed these eight days of Chanukah in order to give thanks and praises unto Your great name.

On Purim.

In the days of Mordecai and Esther, in Shushan the capital, when the wicked Haman rose up against them, and sought to destroy, to slay and make to perish all the Jews, both young and old, little children and women, on one day, on the thirteenth day of the twelfth month, which is the month Adar, and to take the spoil of them for a prey,—then did You in Your abundant mercy bring his counsel to nought, did frustrate his design, and return his recompense upon his own head; and they hanged him and his sons upon the gallows.

For all these things Your name, O our King, shall be continually blessed and exalted for ever and ever.

During the Ten Days of Penitence say:—

O inscribe all the children of Your covenant for a happy life.

And everything that lives shall give thanks unto You for ever, and shall praise Your name in truth, O Elohim (God), our salvation and our help. Blessed are You, YAHUWAH, whose name is All-good, and unto whom it is becoming to give thanks.

Birkat Kohanim
(Priestly Blessing)

Our God and God of our fathers, in the name of Yah'shua the Messiah (Jesus Christ), bless us with the three-fold blessing of Your Torah (Law) written by the hand of Moses Your servant, which was spoken by Aaron and his sons, the koheniym (priests), Your holy people, as it is said,

YAHUWAH bless You, and keep You:
YAHUWAH make his face to shine upon You, and be gracious

unto You:

YAHUWAH turn his face unto You, and give You peace.

Sim Shalom
(Grant Peace)

Grant peace, welfare, blessing, grace, loving kindness and mercy unto us and unto all Israel, Your people. Bless us, O our Father, even all of us together, with the light of Your countenance for by the light of Your countenance You have given us, YAHUWAH our Elohim (God), the Law of life, lovingkindness and righteousness, blessing, mercy, life and peace; and may it be good in Your sight to bless Your people Israel at all times and in every hour with Your peace.

During the Ten Days of Penitence say:—

In the book of life, blessing, peace and good sustenance may we be remembered and inscribed before You, we and all Your people the house of Israel, for a happy life and for peace. Blessed are You, YAHUWAH, who makes peace.

Blessed are You, YAHUWAH, who blesses Your people Israel with peace.

ELOHAI NETSOR
(My God Please Keep)

O Elohai (my God)! Guard my tongue from evil and my lips from speaking guile; and to such as curse me let my soul be dumb, yes, let my soul be unto all as the dust. Open my heart to Your Torah (Law), and let my soul pursue Your mitzvot (commandments). If any design evil against me, speedily make their counsil of none effect, and frustrate their designs. Do it for the sake of Your name, do it for the sake of Your right hand, do it for the sake of Your holiness, do it for the sake of Your Torah (Law), do it for the sake of the name of Your Holy child Yah'shua the Messiah (Jesus Christ). In order that Your beloved ones may be delivered, O save with Your right hand, and answer me. Let the words of my mouth and the meditation of my heart be acceptable before You, YAHUWAH, my Rock and my Redeemer. He who makes peace in his high places, may he make peace for us and for all Israel, and say, Amen.

Kaddish
(Sanctification)

Reader and Cong.— YAHUWAH, God of Israel, turn from Your fierce wrath, and repent of the evil against Your people.

Cong.—Look from heaven and see how we have become a scorn and a derision among the nations; we are accounted as sheep brought to the slaughter, to be slain and destroyed, or to be smitten and reproached.

Cong. and Reader.—Yet, despite all this, we have not forgotten Your name: we beseech You, forget us not.

Cong.—Strangers say, There is no hope or expectancy for you. Be gracious unto a people that trust in Your name. O You who are most pure, bring our salvation near. We are weary, and no rest is granted us. Let Your tender mercies subdue Your anger from us.

Cong. and Reader.—We beseech You, turn from Your wrath, and have mercy upon the treasured people whom You havet chosen.

Cong.— YAHUWAH, spare us in Your tender mercies, and give us not into the hands of the cruel. Wherefore should the nations say, Where now is their God? For Your own sake deal kindly with us, and delay not.

Cong. and Reader.—We beseech You, turn from Your wrath, and have mercy upon the treasured people whom You have chosen.

Cong.—Hear our voice, and be gracious, and forsake us not in the hand of our enemies to blot out our name; remember what You have sworn to our fathers, I will multiply your seed as the stars of heaven: and now we are left a few out of many.

Cong. and Reader.—Yet, despite all this, we have not forgotten Your name: we beseech You, forget us not.

Cong.—Help us, O Elohim (God) of our salvation, for the sake of the glory of Your name; and deliver us, and pardon our sins for Your name's sake.

Cong. and Reader.— YAHUWAH our Elohim (God), God of Israel, turn from Your fierce wrath, and repent of the evil against Your people.

Yom Rishon (1ˢᵗ Day) Sunday

Psalm 56

1 To the Chief Musician. Set to "The Silent Dove in Distant Lands." A Michtam of David when the Philistines captured him in Gath. Be merciful to me, Elohim (God), for man would swallow me up; Fighting all day he oppresses me. 2 My sharar'iym (enemies) would hound me all day, for there are many who fight against me maron (on high). 3 Whenever I am afraid, I will batach (trust, be bold) in You. 4 In Elohim (God) (I will praise His word), in Elohim (God) I have put my batach (trust); I will not fear. What can flesh do to me? 5 All day they davar atsav (twist my words); All their machashavah (thoughts) are against me for ra (evil). 6 They gather together, they hide, they mark my steps, when they lie in wait for my life. 7 Shall they escape by aven (iniquity)? In anger cast down the peoples, O Elohim (God)! 8 You number my wanderings; Put my tears into Your bottle; Are they not in Your book? 9 When I cry out to You, then my oyev'iym (enemies) will turn back; This I know, because Elohim (God) is for me. 10 In Elohim (God) (I will praise His word), in YAHUWAH (I will praise His word), 11 In Elohim (God) I have put my batach (trust); I will not be afraid. What can adam (man, mankind, humans) do to me? 12 Nederiym (Vows) made to You are binding upon me, O Elohim (God); I will render praises to You, 13 For You have delivered my soul from mavet (death). Have You not kept my feet from falling, that I may walk before Elohim (God) in the light of the chayim (living)?

Psalm 57

1 To the Chief Musician. Set to "Do Not Destroy." A Michtam of David when he fled from Saul into the cave. Be merciful to me, O Elohim (God), be merciful to me! For my soul chasah (trusts) in You; And in the shadow of Your wings I will make my refuge, until these havot (calamities, destructions) have passed by. 2 I will cry out to Elohim Elyon (God Most High), to El (God) who performs all things for me. 3 He shall send from heaven and save me; He reproaches the one who would swallow me up. Selah. Elohim (God) shall send forth His chesed (mercy) and His emet (truth). 4 My soul is among lions; I lie among the sons of men who are set on fire, whose teeth are spears and arrows, and their tongue a sharp sword. 5 Be exalted, O Elohim (God), above the heavens; Let Your glory be above all the earth. 6 They have prepared a net for my steps; My soul is bowed down; They have dug a pit before me; Into the midst of it they themselves have fallen. Selah. 7 My heart is steadfast, O Elohim (God), my heart is steadfast; I will sing and give praise. 8 Awake, my glory! Awake, lute and harp! I will awaken the shachar (dawn). 9 I will praise You, Adonai (Lord), among the peoples; I will sing to You among the umiym (nations). 10 For Your chesed (mercy) reaches unto the heavens, and Your emet (truth) unto the clouds. 11 Be exalted, O Elohim (God), above the heavens; Let Your glory be above all the earth.

Psalm 58

1 To the Chief Musician. Set to "Do Not Destroy." A Michtam of David. Do you indeed speak tsedek (righteousness), you elem (silent ones)? Do you judge meshariym (uprightly, in equity), you bnei adam (sons of men)? 2 No, in heart you work ovlot (unrighteousness, injustice); You weigh out the chamas (violence) of your hands in the earth. 3 The rasha'iym

(wicked) are estranged from the womb; They go astray as soon as they are born, speaking kazav (lies, falsehood). 4 Their chemat (poison; rage, indignation, hot displeasure) is like the chemat nachash (poison of a serpent); They are like the peten cheresh (deaf cobra) that stops its ear, 5 Which will not heed the voice of lachashiym (charmers), chover chavariym (Charming) ever so skillfully. 6 Break their shen'iym (teeth) in their mouth, O Elohim (God)! Break out the malta'ot (fangs, great teath) of the kephiyr (young lions), YAHUWAH! 7 Let them flow away as waters which run continually; When he bends his bow, let his arrows be as if cut in pieces. 8 Let them be like a snail which melts away as it goes, like a stillborn child of a woman, that they may not see the sun. 9 Before your pots can feel the burning thorns, He shall take them away as with a whirlwind, as in His living and burning wrath. 10 The tsadiyk (righteous) shall rejoice when he sees the vengeance; He shall wash his feet in the blood of the rasha (wicked), 11 So that men will say, "Surely there is a reward for the tsadiyk (righteous); Surely He is Elohim (God) who judges in the earth."

Psalm 59

1 To the Chief Musician. Set to "Do Not Destroy." A Michtam of David when Saul sent men, and they watched the house in order to kill him. Deliver me from my enemies, Elohai (my God); Defend me from those who rise up against me. 2 Deliver me from the polei aven (workers of iniquity), and save me from anshei damiym (bloodthirsty men). 3 For look, they lie in wait for my life; The aziym (mighty, fierce) gather against me, not for my pasha (transgression) nor for my chatat (sin), YAHUWAH. 4 They run and prepare themselves through no avon (iniquity, fault) of mine. Awake to help me, and behold! 5 You therefore, O YAHUWAH, Elohim tseva'ot (the god of hosts), the Elohim (God) of Israel, awake to punish all the

Goyim (nations, Gentiles); Do not chanan (be gracious, be merciful, show favor/pity) to any bog'dei aven (wicked transgressors). Selah. 6 At evening they return, they growl like a kelev (dog), and go all around the city. 7 Indeed, they belch with their mouth; Swords are in their lips; For they say, "Who hears?" 8 But You, YAHUWAH, shall laugh at them; You shall have all the Goyim (nations, Gentile) in derision. 9 I will wait for You, O You his Strength; For Elohim (God) is my defense. 10 Elohim (God) of my mercy shall come to meet me; Elohim (God) shall let me see my desire on my sharar'iym (enemies). 11 Do not slay them, lest my people forget; Scatter them by Your power, and bring them down, Adonai (Lord) our shield. 12 For the chatat (sin) of their mouth and the words of their lips, let them even be taken in their ga'on (pride, exaltation), and for the alah (cursing) and kachash (lying, deception) which they speak. 13 Consume them in wrath, consume them, that they may not be; And let them know that Elohim (God) rules in Jacob to the ends of the earth. Selah. 14 And at evening they return, they growl like a kelev (dog), and go all around the city. 15 They wander up and down for food, and complain if they are not satisfied. 16 But I will sing of Your power; Yes, I will sing aloud of Your chesed (mercy) in the morning; For You have been my defense and refuge in the day of my trouble. 17 To You, O my Strength, I will sing praises; For Elohim (God) is my defense, Elohim (God) of my chesed (mercy).

Psalm 60

1 To the Chief Musician. Set to "Lily of the Testimony." A Michtam of David. For teaching. When he fought against Mesopotamia and Syria of Zobah, and Joab returned and killed twelve thousand Edomites in the Valley of Salt.

Elohim (God), You have cast us off; You have broken us down; You have been displeased; Oh, restore us again! 2 You have made the earth tremble; You have broken it; Heal its breaches, for it is shaking. 3 You have shown Your people hard things; You have made us drink the yayin tar'elah (wine of confusion). 4 You have given a banner to those who fear You, that it may be displayed because of the emet (truth). Selah. 5 That Your beloved may be delivered, save with Your right hand, and hear me. 6 Elohim (God) has spoken in His kadosh (holiness): "I will rejoice; I will divide Shechem and measure out the Valley of Succoth. 7 Gilead is Mine, and Manasseh is Mine; Ephraim also is the helmet for My head; Judah is My lawgiver. 8 Moab is My washpot; Over Edom I will cast My shoe; Philistia, shout in triumph because of Me." 9 Who will bring me to the strong city? Who will lead me to Edom? 10 Is it not You, Elohim (God), who cast us off? And You, Elohim (God), who did not go out with our armies? 11 Give us help from trouble, for the help of man is useless. 12 Through Elohim (God) we will do valiantly, for it is He who shall tread down our tsariym (enemies).

Psalm 61

1 To the Chief Musician. On a stringed instrument. A Psalm of David. Hear my cry, O Elohim (God); Attend to my tefilat (prayer). 2 From the end of the earth I will cry to You, when my heart is overwhelmed; Lead me to the rock that is higher than I. 3 For You have been a shelter for me, a strong tower from the oyev (enemy). 4 I will abide in Your Ohel (tent, tabernacle) forever; I will trust in the shelter of Your wings. Selah. 5 For You, Elohim (God), have heard my neder'iym (vows); You have given me the heritage of those who fear Your name. 6 You will prolong the king's life, His years as many generations. 7 He shall abide before Elohim (God) forever. Oh, prepare chesed (mercy) and emet (truth), which

may preserve him! 8 So I will sing praise to Your name forever, that I may daily perform my neder'iym (vows).

Psalm 62

1 To the Chief Musician. To Jeduthun. A Psalm of David. Truly my soul silently waits for Elohim (God); From Him comes my yeshua (salvation). 2 He only is my rock and my salvation; He is my defense; I shall not be greatly moved. 3 How long will you attack a man? You shall be slain, all of you, like a leaning wall and a tottering fence. 4 They only consult to cast him down from his high position; They delight in kazav (lies); They bless with their mouth, But they curse inwardly. Selah. 5 My soul, wait silently for Elohim (God) alone, for my expectation is from Him. 6 He only is my rock and my yeshua (salvation); He is my defense; I shall not be moved. 7 In Elohim (God) is my yesha (salvation) and my kavod (glory); The rock of my strength, And my refuge, is in Elohim (God). 8 Batach (Trust, be bold) in Him at all times, you people; Pour out your heart before Him; Elohim (God) is a refuge for us. Selah. 9 Surely bnei adam (sons of mankind/humans) are a hevel (vapor), bnei iysh (sons of man) are a kazav (lie, falsehood); If they are weighed on the scales, they are altogether lighter than vapor. 10 Do not batach (trust, be bold) in oshek (oppression, gain by extortion), nor haval (become vain) in gazel (robbery); If chayil (riches) increase, do not set your heart on them. 11 Elohim (God) has spoken once, twice I have heard this: That oz (power, might, streangth) belongs to Elohim (God). 12 Also to You, Adonai (Lord), belongs chesed (mercy); For You render to each one according to his work.

Psalm 63

1 A Psalm of David when he was in the wilderness of Judah. O Elohim (God), You are my El (God); Early will I seek You; My soul thirsts for You; My flesh longs for You in a dry and thirsty land where there is no mayim (water). 2 So I have looked for You in the kodesh (holy place, sanctuary), to see Your oz (power) and Your kavod (glory). 3 Because Your chesed (mercy, lovingkindness) is better than chayim (life), My lips shall praise You. 4 Thus I will bless You while I live; I will lift up my hands in Your name. 5 My soul shall be satisfied as with marrow and fatness, and my mouth shall praise You with joyful lips. 6 When I remember You on my bed, I eha'geh (meditate) on You in the night watches. 7 Because You have been my ezra (help), therefore in the shadow of Your wings I will rejoice. 8 My soul follows close behind You; Your right hand upholds me. 9 But those who seek my life, to destroy it, shall go into the lower parts of the earth. 10 They shall fall by the sword; They shall be a portion for shu'aliym (foxes, jackals). 11 But the Melek (king) shall samach (rejoice) in Elohim (God); Everyone who shava (swears) by Him shall halel (glory); But the mouth of those who speak sheker (lies) shall be stopped.

Psalm 64

1 To the Chief Musician. A Psalm of David. Hear my voice, O Elohim (God), in my siyach (meditation, complaint); Preserve my life from fear of the oyev (enemy). 2 Hide me from the secret plots of the ra'iym (wicked, evil ones), from the regesh (insurrection, rebellion) of the polei aven (workers of iniquity), 3 Who sharpen their tongue like a sword, And bend their bows to shoot their arrows—bitter words, 4 That they may shoot in secret at the tam (blameless, perfect); Suddenly they shoot at him and do not fear. 5 They encourage

themselves in an davar ra (evil matter, evil thing); They talk of laying snares secretly; They say, "Who will see them?" 6 They devise ovlot (unrighteousness, iniquities): "We have perfected a shrewd scheme." Both the inward thought and the heart of man are deep. 7 But Elohim (God) shall shoot at them with an arrow; Suddenly they shall be wounded. 8 So He will make them stumble over their own tongue; All who see them shall flee away. 9 All men shall fear, and shall declare the work of Elohim (God); For they shall wisely consider His doing. 10 The tsadiyk (righteous) shall be glad in YAHUWAH, and chasah (trust) in Him. And all the yashar lev (upright in heart) shall glory.

Psalm 65

1 To the Chief Musician. A Psalm of David. A Song. Praise is awaiting You, O Elohim (God), in Zion; And to You the neder (vow) shall be performed. 2 O You who hear tefila (prayer), to You all flesh will come. 3 Avonot divrei (Iniquitous works) prevail against me; As for our pasha (transgressions), You will provide kapara (atonement) for them. 4 Blessed is the man You choose, and cause to approach You, that he may dwell in Your courts. We shall be satisfied with the goodness of Your house, of Your Kadosh Heykal (holy temple). 5 By nora'ot (awesome deeds) in tsedek (righteousness) You will answer us, O Elohim (God) of our salvation, You who are the confidence of all the ends of the earth, and of the far-off seas; 6 Who established the mountains by His strength, being clothed with gevurah (mighty power); 7 You who still the noise of the seas, the noise of their waves, and the tumult of the peoples. 8 They also who dwell in the farthest parts are afraid of Your Otot (signs); You make the outgoings of the morning and evening rejoice. 9 You visit the earth and water it, You greatly enrich it; The river of Elohim (God) is full of water; You provide their grain, for so You have prepared it.

10 You water its ridges abundantly, You settle its furrows; You make it soft with showers, You bless its growth. 11 You crown the year with Your goodness, and Your paths drip with abundance. 12 They drop on the pastures of the wilderness, and the little hills rejoice on every side. 13 The pastures are clothed with flocks; The valleys also are covered with grain; They shout for joy, they also sing.

Yom Sheni (2nd Day) Monday

Psalm 66

1 To the Chief Musician. A Song. A Psalm. Make a joyful shout to Elohim (God), all the earth! 2 Sing out the honor of His name; Make His praise glorious. 3 Say to Elohim (God), "How awesome are Your works! Through the greatness of Your oz (power) Your oyev'iym (enemies) shall submit themselves to You. 4 All the earth shall worship You and sing praises to You; They shall sing praises to Your name." Selah. 5 Come and see the miph'a lot Elohim (works of God); He is awesome in His doing toward the bnei adam (sons of mankind). 6 He turned the sea into dry land; They went through the river on foot. There we will rejoice in Him. 7 He rules by His gevurah (mighty power) forever; His eyes observe the Goyim (nations, Gentiles); Do not let the rebellious exalt themselves. Selah. 8 Oh, bless our Elohim (God), you peoples! And make the voice of His praise to be heard, 9 Who keeps our soul among the chayim (living), and does not allow our feet to be moved. 10 For You, O Elohim (God), have tested us; You have refined us as silver is refined. 11 You brought us into the net; You laid mu'akah (affliction, distress) on our backs. 12 You have caused men to ride over our heads; We went through fire and through water; But You brought us out to rich fulfillment. 13 I will go into Your house with Olot (burnt offerings); I will pay You my neder'iym (vows), 14 Which my lips have uttered and my mouth has spoken when I was in trouble. 15 I will offer You Olot (burnt offerings) of fat animals, with the sweet aroma of rams; I will offer bulls with goats. Selah. 16 Come and hear, all you who fear Elohim (God), and I will declare what He has done for my soul. 17 I cried to Him with my

mouth, and He was extolled with my tongue. 18 If I regard Aven (iniquity, wickedness) in my heart, Adonai (The Lord) will not hear. 19 But certainly Elohim (God) has heard me; He has attended to the voice of my tefilah (prayer). 20 Blessed be Elohim (God), who has not turned away my tefilah (prayer), nor His chesed (mercy) from me!

Psalm 67

1 To the Chief Musician. On stringed instruments. A Psalm. A Song. Elohim (God) be merciful to us and bless us, and cause His face to shine upon us, Selah. 2 That Your way may be known on earth, Your salvation among all Goyim (Gentiles, nations). 3 Let the peoples praise You, O Elohim (God); Let all the peoples praise You. 4 Oh, let the leumiym (nations) be glad and sing for joy! For You shall judge the people miyshor (righteously), and govern the le'umiym (nations) on earth. Selah. 5 Let the peoples praise You, O Elohim (God); Let all the peoples praise You. 6 Then the earth shall yield her increase; Elohim (God), our own Elohim (God), shall bless us. 7 Elohim (God) shall bless us, and all the ends of the earth shall fear Him.

Psalm 68

1 To the Chief Musician. A Psalm of David. A Song. Let Elohim (God) arise, let His oyev'iym (enemies) be scattered; Let those also who hate Him flee before Him. 2 As smoke is driven away, so drive them away; As wax melts before the fire, so let the rasha'iym (wicked) perish at the presence of Elohim (God). 3 But let the tsadakiym (righteous) be glad; Let them rejoice before Elohim (God); Yes, let them rejoice exceedingly. 4 Sing to Elohim (God), sing praises to His name; Extol Him who rides on the clouds, by His name YAH, and rejoice before Him. 5 An avi (father) of the yatom'iym

(fatherless, orphans), a dayan (judge, defender) of almanot (widows), is Elohim (God) in His ma'on kadosh (holy habitation). 6 Elohim (God) sets the yachiyd'iym (solitary) in bayit (houses, families); He brings out the asiyr'iym (those who are bound, prisoners, captives) into kosharah (prosperity); But the sarar'iym (rebellious, stubborn) dwell in a tsechiychah (dry land). 7 O Elohim (God), when You went out before Your people, when You marched through the wilderness, Selah. 8 The earth shook; The heavens also dropped rain at the presence of Elohim (God); Sinai itself was moved at the presence of Elohim (God), the Elohim (God) of Israel. 9 You, O Elohim (God), sent a plentiful rain, whereby You confirmed Your inheritance, when it was weary. 10 Your congregation dwelt in it; You, O Elohim (God), provided from Your tovat (goodness) for the aniy (poor). 11 Adonai (The Lord) gave the omer (word); Great was the company of those who proclaimed it: 12 "Kings of armies flee, they flee, and she who remains at home divides the spoil. 13 Though you lie down among the sheepfolds, You will be like the wings of a dove covered with silver, and her feathers with yellow gold." 14 When the Shaddai (Almighty) scattered kings in it, it was white as snow in Zalmon. 15 A mountain of Elohim (God) is the mountain of Bashan; A mountain of many peaks is the mountain of Bashan. 16 Why do you fume with envy, you mountains of many peaks? This is the mountain which Elohim (God) desires to dwell in; Yes, YAHUWAH will dwell in it forever. 17 The chariots of Elohim (God) are twenty thousand, Even thousands of thousands; Adonai (the Lord) is among them as in Sinai, in the Kodesh (Holy Place). 18 You have aliyah (ascended) on marom (high), You have led sheviy (captivity) shavah (captive); You have received matanot (gifts) among men, even from the sorar'iym (rebellious, stubborn), That Yah Elohim (the Lord God) might dwell there. 19 Blessed be Adonai (the Lord), who daily loads us with benefits, the El yeshu'at (God of our salvation)! Selah. 20 Our

El (God) is the El Mosha'ot (God of salvation); And to YAHUWAH Adonai (the Lord) belong escapes from mavet (death). 21 But Elohim (God) will wound the head of His oyev'iym (enemies), the hairy scalp of the one who still goes on in his asham (guiltiness, trespasses, offences). 22 Adonai (the Lord) said, "I will bring back from Bashan, I will bring them back from the depths of the sea, 23 That your foot may crush them in blood, and the tongues of your kelev'iym (dogs) may have their portion from your oyev'iym (enemies)." 24 They have seen Your procession, O Elohim (God), the procession of Eli (my God), Malki (my King), into the Kodesh (Holy Place, sanctuary). 25 The shariym (singers) went before, the noganiym (players on instruments) followed after; Among them were the maidens playing timbrels. 26 Bless Elohim (God) in the makhelot (congregations), YAHUWAH, from the fountain of Israel. 27 There is little Benjamin, their leader, the princes of Judah and their company, the princes of Zebulun and the princes of Naphtali. 28 Your Elohim (God) has commanded your strength; Strengthen, O Elohim (God), what You have done for us. 29 Because of Your Heykal (Temple) at Jerusalem, Melekiym (Kings) will bring presents to You. 30 Rebuke the chayat (living things) of the reeds, the herd of bulls with the calves of the peoples, till everyone submits himself with pieces of silver. Scatter the peoples who delight in war. 31 Envoys will come out of Egypt; Ethiopia will quickly stretch out her hands to Elohim (God). 32 Sing to Elohim (God), you kingdoms of the earth; Oh, sing praises to Adonai (the Lord), Selah. 33 To Him who rides on the heaven of heavens, which were of old! Indeed, He sends out His voice, a mighty voice. 34 Ascribe strength to Elohim (God); His excellence is over Israel, and His strength is in the clouds. 35 O Elohim (God), You are more awesome than Your Mikdash'iym (holy places). The Elohim (God) of Israel is He who gives strength and power to His people. Blessed be Elohim (God)!

Psalm 69

1 To the Chief Musician. Set to "The Lilies." A Psalm of David. Save me, O Elohim (God)! For the waters have come in unto my soul. 2 I sink in deep mire, where there is no standing; I have come into deep waters, where the floods overflow me. 3 I am weary with my crying; My throat is dry; My eyes fail while I wait for Elohai (my God). 4 Those who hate me without a cause are more than the hairs of my head; They are mighty who would destroy me, being my oyev'iym sheker (enemies wrongfully); Though I have stolen nothing, I still must restore it. 5 O Elohim (God), You know my ivelet (foolishness, folly); And my ashmot (sins, guilt, wrong doing) are not hidden from You. 6 Let not those who wait for You, O Adonai YAHUWAH Tseva'ot (Lord GOD of hosts), be ashamed because of me; Let not those who seek You be confounded because of me, O Elohim (God) of Israel. 7 Because for Your sake I have borne reproach; Shame has covered my face. 8 I have become a stranger to my brothers, and an alien to my mother's children; 9 Because zeal for Your house has eaten me up, and the reproaches of those who reproach You have fallen on me. 10 When I wept and chastened my soul with fasting, that became my reproach. 11 I also made sackcloth my garment; I became a byword to them. 12 Those who sit in the gate speak against me, and I am the song of the drunkards. 13 But as for me, my tefillah (prayer) is to You, YAHUWAH, in the acceptable time; O Elohim (God), in the multitude of Your chesed (mercy), hear me in the emet (truth) of Your yesha (salvation). 14 Deliver me out of the mire, and let me not sink; Let me be delivered from those who hate me, and out of the deep waters. 15 Let not the floodwater overflow me, nor let the deep swallow me up; And let not the pit shut its mouth on me. 16 Hear me, YAHUWAH, for Your chesed (mercy, lovingkindness) is tov (good); Turn

to me according to the multitude of Your racham'iym (tender mercies). 17 And do not hide Your face from Your eved (servant), for I am in trouble; Hear me speedily. 18 Draw near to my soul, and redeem it; Deliver me because of my oyev'iym (enemies). 19 You know my reproach, my shame, and my dishonor; My tsarar'iym (adversaries) are all before You. 20 Reproach has broken my heart, and I am full of heaviness; I looked for someone to take pity, but there was none; And for comforters, but I found none. 21 They also gave me gall for my food, and for my thirst they gave me vinegar to drink. 22 Let their table become a snare before them, and their well-being a trap. 23 Let their eyes be darkened, so that they do not see; And make their loins shake continually. 24 Pour out Your indignation upon them, and let Your wrathful anger take hold of them. 25 Let their dwelling place be desolate; Let no one live in their tents. 26 For they persecute the ones You have struck, and talk of the grief of those You have wounded. 27 Add avon (iniquity, punishment for iniquity) to their avon (iniquity, punishment for iniquity), and let them not come into Your tsedakah (righteousness). 28 Let them be blotted out of the Sefer Chayim (book of the living), and not be written with the tsadiykiym (righteous). 29 But I am aniy (poor) and ka'av (sorrowful); Let Your yeshua (salvation), O Elohim (God), set me up on high. 30 I will praise the name of Elohim (God) with a shiyr (song), and will magnify Him with todah (thanksgiving). 31 This also shall please YAHUWAH better than an ox or bull, which has horns and hooves. 32 The humble shall see this and be glad; And you who seek Elohim (God), your hearts shall live. 33 For YAHUWAH hears the evyon'iym (poor, needy), and does not despise His asiyr'iym (prisoners). 34 Let heaven and earth praise Him, the seas and everything that moves in them. 35 For Elohim (God) will save Zion and build the cities of Judah, that they may dwell there and possess it. 36 Also, the seed of His servants shall inherit it, and those who love His name shall dwell in it.

Psalm 70

1 To the Chief Musician. A Psalm of David. To bring to remembrance. Make haste, O Elohim (God), to deliver me! Make haste to help me, YAHUWAH! 2 Let them be ashamed and confounded who seek my life; Let them be turned back and confused who desire my hurt. 3 Let them be turned back because of their shame, who say, "Aha, aha!" 4 Let all those who seek You rejoice and be glad in You; And let those who love Your yeshua (salvation) say continually, "Let Elohim (God) be magnified!" 5 But I am aniy (poor) and evyon (needy); Make haste to me, O Elohim (God)! You are my help and my deliverer; YAHUWAH, do not delay.

Psalm 71

1 In You, YAHUWAH, I put my chasah (trust); Let me never be put to shame. 2 Deliver me in Your tsedakah (righteousness), and cause me to escape; Incline Your ear to me, and save me. 3 Be my strong refuge, to which I may resort continually; You have given the commandment to save me, for You are my rock and my fortress. 4 Deliver me, O Elohai (my God), out of the hand of the rasha (wicked), out of the hand of the avel (unrighteous) and chomets (cruel man). 5 For You are my tikvah (hope), O Adonai YAHUWAH (Lord GOD); You are my mibtach (trust, confidence) from my youth. 6 By You I have been upheld from birth; You are He who took me out of my mother's womb. My praise shall be continually of You. 7 I have become as a wonder to many, but You are my strong refuge. 8 Let my mouth be filled with Your praise and with Your glory all the day. 9 Do not cast me off in the time of old age; Do not forsake me when my strength fails. 10 For my oyev'iym (enemies) speak against me; And those who lie in wait for my life take counsel together, 11 Saying, "Elohim (God) has forsaken him; Pursue and take him, for there is

none to deliver him." 12 O Elohim (God), do not be far from me; O Elohai (my God), make haste to help me! 13 Let them be confounded and consumed who act as satan (adversaries) of my life; Let them be covered with reproach and dishonor who seek my hurt. 14 But I will hope continually, and will praise You yet more and more. 15 My mouth shall tell of Your tsedakah (righteousness) and Your teshuv'ah (salvation) all the day, for I do not know their limits. 16 I will go in the strength of Adonai YAHUWAH (the Lord GOD); I will make mention of Your tsedakah (righteousness), of Yours only. 17 O Elohim (God), You have taught me from my youth; And to this day I declare Your wondrous works. 18 Now also when I am old and grayheaded, O Elohim (God), do not forsake me, until I declare Your strength to this generation, Your power to everyone who is to come. 19 Also Your tsedakah (righteousness), O Elohim (God), is very high, You who have done great things; O Elohim (God), who is like You? 20 You, who have shown me great and severe troubles, shall chayeniy (quicken me, make me alive) again, and bring me up again from the depths of the earth. 21 You shall increase my greatness, and comfort me on every side. 22 Also with the lute I will praise You; And Your emet (truth), O Elohai (my God)! To You I will sing with the harp, O Kadosh (Holy One) of Israel. 23My lips shall greatly rejoice when I sing to You, and my soul, which You have redeemed. 24 My tongue also shall talk of Your tsedakah (righteousness) all the day long; For they are confounded, for they are brought to shame who seek my hurt.

Yom Shlishi (3ʳᵈ Day) Tuesday

Psalm 72

1 A Psalm of Solomon. Give the melek (king) Your mishpatiym (judgments), O Elohim (God), and Your tsedakah (righteousness) to the king's Son. 2 He will judge Your people with tsedek (righteousness), and Your aniy'iym (poor) with mishpat (judgment, justice). 3 The mountains will bring shalom (peace) to the people, and the little hills, by tsedakah (righteousness). 4 He will bring justice to the aniy (poor) of the people; He will save the children of the evyon (needy), and will break in pieces the oshek (oppressor). 5 They shall fear You as long as the sun and moon endure, throughout all generations. 6 He shall come down like rain upon the grass before mowing, like showers that water the earth. 7 In His days the tsadiyk (righteous) shall flourish, and rov sahalom (abundance of peace), until the moon is no more. 8 He shall have dominion also from sea to sea, and from the River to the ends of the earth. 9 The tsiyim (desert demons) will bow before Him, and His oyev'iym (enemies) will lick the dust. 10 The kings of Tarshish and of the isles will bring presents; The kings of Sheba and Seba will offer gifts. 11 Yes, all melekiym (kings) shall fall down before Him; All goyim (gentiles, nations) shall serve Him. 12 For He will deliver the evyon (needy) when he cries, the aniy (poor) also, and him who has no helper. 13 He will spare the dal (weak, poor) and evyon (needy), and will save the souls of the evyoniym (needy). 14 He will redeem their life from tok (oppression) and chamas (violence); And precious shall be their blood in His sight. 15 And He shall live; And the gold of Sheba will be given to Him; Tefillah (Prayer) also will be made for Him continually, and

daily He shall be praised. 16 There will be an abundance of grain in the earth, on the top of the mountains; Its fruit shall wave like Lebanon; And those of the city shall flourish like grass of the earth. 17 His name shall endure forever; His name shall continue as long as the sun. And men shall be blessed in Him; All goyim (gentiles, nations) shall call Him blessed. 18 Blessed be YAHUWAH Elohim (the Existing God), the Elohim (God) of Israel, who only does wondrous things! 19 And blessed be His glorious name forever! And let the whole earth be filled with His glory. Amen and Amen. 20 The tefilot (prayers) of David the son of Jesse are ended.

Psalm 73

1 A Psalm of Asaph. Truly Elohim (God) is good to Israel, to such as are pure in heart. 2 But as for me, my feet had almost stumbled; My steps had nearly slipped. 3 For I was envious of the boastful, when I saw the shalom (peace, prosperity) of the rasha'iym (wicked). 4 For there are no pangs in their mavet (death), but their strength is firm. 5 They are not in trouble as other men, nor are they naga (plagued) like other men. 6 Therefore ga'avah (pride) serves as their necklace; Chamas (Violence) covers them like a garment. 7 Their eyes bulge with abundance; They have more than heart could wish. 8 They scoff and speak ra (evil, wickedly) concerning oshek (oppression); They speak marom (loftily). 9 They set their mouth against the heavens, and their tongue walks through the earth. 10 Therefore his people return here, and waters of a full cup are drained by them. 11 And they say, "How does El (God) know? And is there knowledge in Elyon (the Most High)?" 12 Behold, these are the rasha'iym (wicked, ungodly), Who are always at ease; They increase in chayil (riches). 13 Surely I have cleansed my heart in vain, and washed my hands in nikkayon (innocence). 14 For all day long I have been naguva (plagued), And tokechah (chastened) every

morning. 15 If I had said, "I will speak thus," Behold, I would have been untrue to the generation of Your children. 16 When I thought how to understand this, it was too painful for me. 17 Until I went into the mikdash El (sanctuary of God); Then I understood their end. 18 Surely You set them in slippery places; You cast them down to destruction. 19 Oh, how they are brought to desolation, as in a moment! They are utterly consumed with bahalot (terrors). 20 As a chalom (dream) when one awakes, so, Adonai (Lord), when You awake, You shall despise their image. 21 Thus my heart was grieved, and I was vexed in my mind. 22 I was so ba'ar (foolish, stupid, brutish) and lo-eda (ignorant); I was like a beast before You. 23 Nevertheless I am continually with You; You hold me by my right hand. 24 You will guide me with Your counsel, and afterward receive me to glory. 25 Whom have I in heaven but You? And there is none upon earth that I desire besides You. 26 My flesh and my heart fail; But Elohim (God) is the strength of my heart and my portion forever. 27 For indeed, those who are rachek (far from) You shall perish; You have destroyed all those who go zoneh (whoring) from you. 28 But it is good for me to draw near to Elohim (God); I have put my machaseh (trust, refuge, shelter) in Adonai YAHUWAH (the Lord GOD), that I may declare all Your works.

Psalm 74

1 A Contemplation of Asaph. O Elohim (God), why have You cast us off forever? Why does Your anger smoke against the sheep of Your pasture? 2 Remember Your adat (congregation), which You have purchased of old, the tribe of Your inheritance, which You have redeemed. This Mount Zion where You have dwelt. 3 Lift up Your feet to the perpetual desolations. The oyev (enemy) has done ra (evil) to everything in the kodesh (holy place, sanctuary). 4 Your tsarariym (adversaries) roar in the midst of Your moed'iym

(meeting places); They set up their banners for otot (signs). 5 They seem like men who lift up axes among the thick trees. 6 And now they break down its carved work, all at once, with axes and hammers. 7 They have set fire to Your Mikdash (sanctuary); They have defiled the mishkan (dwelling place) of Your name to the ground. 8 They said in their hearts, "Let us destroy them altogether." They have burned up all the moed'iym (meeting places) of El (God) in the land. 9 We do not see our otot (signs); There is no longer any navi (prophet); Nor is there any among us who knows how long. 10 O Elohim (God), how long will the tsar (adversary) reproach? Will the oyev (enemy) blaspheme Your name forever? 11 Why do You withdraw Your hand, even Your right hand? Take it out of Your bosom and destroy them. 12 For Elohim (God) is my Melek (King) from of old, working salvation in the midst of the earth. 13 You divided the sea by Your strength; You broke the heads of the taniynim (dragons) in the mayim (waters). 14 You broke the heads of Livyatan (Leviathan) in pieces, and gave him as food to the people, le'tsiyiym (to the desert demons). 15 You broke open the fountain and the flood; You dried up mighty rivers. 16 The day is Yours, the night also is Yours; You have prepared the light and the sun. 17 You have set all the borders of the earth; You have made summer and winter. 18 Remember this, that the oyev (enemy) has reproached, YAHUWAH, and that an 'am-nabal (foolish people) has blasphemed Your name. 19 Oh, do not deliver the soul of Your turtledove to the chayat (living things)! Do not forget the life of Your aniy'iym (poor) forever. 20 Have respect to the covenant; For the machshak'iym (dark places) of the earth are full of the na'ot chamas (habitations of cruelty / violence). 21 Oh, do not let the dak (oppressed) return ashamed! Let the aniy (poor) and evyon (needy) praise Your name. 22 Arise, O Elohim (God), plead Your own cause; Remember how the nabal (foolish man) reproaches You daily. 23 Do not forget the voice of Your tsarar'iym (enemies); The tumult of those who rise up against You increases continually.

Psalm 75

1 To the Chief Musician. Set to "Do Not Destroy." A Psalm of Asaph. A Song. We give thanks to You, O Elohim (God), we give thanks! For Your wondrous works declare that Your name is near. 2 "When I choose the moed (proper time), I will judge meyshariym (uprightly, in equity). 3 The earth and all its inhabitants are dissolved; I set up its pillars firmly. Selah. 4 "I said to the boastful, 'Do not deal boastfully,' and to the rasha'iym (wicked), 'Do not lift up the horn. 5 Do not lift up your horn on high; Do not speak with a stiff neck.'" 6 For exaltation comes neither from the east nor from the west nor from the south. 7 But Elohim (God) is the shofet (Judge): He puts down one, and exalts another. 8 For in the hand of YAHUWAH there is a cup, and the wine is red; It is fully mixed, and He pours it out; Surely its dregs shall all the rasha (wicked) of the earth drain and drink down. 9 But I will declare forever, I will sing praises to the Elohim (God) of Jacob. 10 "All the horns of the rasha'iym (wicked) I will also cut off, but the horns of the tsadiyk (righteous) shall be exalted."

Psalm 76

1 To the Chief Musician. On stringed instruments. A Psalm of Asaph. A Song. In Judah Elohim (God) is known; His name is great in Israel. 2 In Salem also is His tabernacle, and His dwelling place in Zion. 3 There He broke the arrows of the bow, the shield and sword of battle. Selah. 4 You are more glorious and excellent than the mountains of prey. 5 The abbiyrei lev (stouthearted) were plundered; They have sunk into their sleep; And none of the anshei chayil (mighty men)

have found the use of their hands. 6 At Your rebuke, O Elohim (God) of Jacob, both the chariot and horse were cast into a dead sleep. 7 You, Yourself, are to be feared; And who may stand in Your presence when once You are angry? 8 You caused diyn (judgment) to be heard from heaven; The earth feared and was still, 9 When Elohim (God) arose to mishpat (judgment), to deliver all the anav (meek, humble) of the earth. Selah. 10 Surely the chemat adam (wrath of man) shall praise You; With the remainder of chemat (wrath) You shall gird Yourself. 11 Nadar'iym (Make vows) to YAHUWAH your Elohim (God), and pay them; Let all who are around Him bring presents to Him who ought to be feared. 12 He shall cut off the ruach nagiyd'iym (spirit of princes); He is awesome to the kings of the earth.

Psalm 77

1 To the Chief Musician. To Jeduthun. A Psalm of Asaph. I cried out to Elohim (God) with my voice; To Elohim (God) with my voice; And He gave ear to me. 2 In the day of my tsarah (trouble) I sought Adonai (the Lord); My hand was stretched out in the night without ceasing; My soul refused to be comforted. 3 I remembered Elohim (God), and was troubled; I complained, and my spirit was overwhelmed. Selah. 4 You hold my eyelids open; I am so troubled that I cannot speak. 5 I have considered the days of old, the years of ancient times. 6 I call to remembrance my song in the night; I meditate within my heart, and my spirit makes diligent search. 7 Will Adonai (the Lord) cast off forever? And will He be favorable no more? 8 Has His mercy ceased forever? Has His promise failed forevermore? 9 Has El (God) forgotten to be chanot (gracious)? Has He in anger shut up His rachamiym (tender mercies)? Selah. 10 And I said, "This is my anguish; But I will remember the years of the right hand of Elyon (the Most High)." 11 I will remember the works of Yah; Surely I

will remember Your wonders of old. 12 I will also meditate on all Your work, and talk of Your deeds. 13 Your way, O Elohim (God), is in the Kodesh (Holy place, sanctuary); Who is so great an el (god) as our Elohim (God)? 14 You are the El (God) who does pele (wonders); You have declared Your strength among the peoples. 15 You have with Your arm redeemed Your people, the sons of Jacob and Joseph. Selah. 16 The mayim (waters) saw You, O Elohim (God); The mayim (waters) saw You, they were afraid; The tehomot (depths) also trembled. 17 The clouds poured out water; The skies sent out a sound; Your arrows also flashed about. 18 The voice of Your thunder was in the whirlwind; The lightnings lit up the world; The earth trembled and shook. 19 Your way was in the sea, Your path in the mayim rabiym (great waters), and Your footsteps were not known. 20 You led Your people like a flock by the hand of Moses and Aaron.

Yom Re'vi'i (4ᵗʰ Day) Wednesday

Psalm 78

1 A Contemplationa of Asaph. Give ear, O my people, to my torah (law); Incline your ears to the words of my mouth. 2 I will open my mouth in a mashal (parable); I will utter chiydot (dark sayings) of old, 3 Which we have heard and known, and our fathers have told us. 4 We will not hide them from their children, telling to the generation to come the praises of YAHUWAH, and His strength and His wonderful works that He has done. 5 For He established a testimony in Jacob, and appointed a torah (law) in Israel, which He commanded our fathers, that they should make them known to their children; 6 That the generation to come might know them, the children who would be born, that they may arise and declare them to their children, 7 That they may set their hope in Elohim (God), and not forget the works of El (God), but keep His mitzvot (commandments); 8 And may not be like their fathers, a sorer (stubborn) and moreh (rebellious) generation, a generation that did not set its heart aright, and whose spirit was not faithful to El (God). 9 The children of Ephraim, being armed and carrying bows, turned back in the day of battle. 10 They did not keep the covenant of Elohim (God); They refused to walk in His torah (law), 11 And forgot His works and His wonders that He had shown them. 12 Marvelous things He did in the sight of their fathers, in the land of Egypt, in the field of Zoan. 13 He divided the sea and caused them to pass through; And He made the waters stand up like a heap. 14 In the daytime also He led them with the cloud, and all the night with a light of fire. 15 He split the rocks in the wilderness, and gave them drink in abundance

like the depths. 16 He also brought streams out of the rock, and caused waters to run down like rivers. 17 But they chata (sinned) even more against Him by rebelling against Elyon (the Most High) in the wilderness. 18 And they tested El (God) in their heart by asking for the food of their fancy. 19 Yes, they spoke against Elohim (God): They said, "Can El (God) prepare a table in the wilderness? 20 Behold, He struck the rock, So that the waters gushed out, and the streams overflowed. Can He give bread also? Can He provide meat for His people?"

21 Therefore YAHUWAH heard this and was furious; So a fire was kindled against Jacob, and anger also came up against Israel, 22 Because they did not believe in Elohim (God), and did not batach (trust) in His yeshua (salvation). 23 Yet He had commanded the clouds above, and opened the doors of heaven, 24 Had rained down manna on them to eat, and given them of the dagan shamayim (grain of heaven). 25 Men ate the food of the Abiriym (mighty ones, angels); He sent them food to the full. 26 He caused an east wind to blow in the heavens; And by His power He brought in the south wind. 27 He also rained meat on them like the dust, feathered fowl like the sand of the seas; 28 And He let them fall in the midst of their camp, all around their dwellings. 29 So they ate and were well filled, for He gave them their own desire. 30 They were not deprived of their craving; But while their food was still in their mouths, 31 The wrath of Elohim (God) came against them, and slew the stoutest of them, and struck down the choice men of Israel. 32 In spite of this they still chatat (sinned), and did not believe in His wondrous works.

33 Therefore their days He consumed in hevel (vanity, futility), and their years in fear. 34 When He slew them, then they sought Him; And they returned and sought earnestly for El (God). 35 Then they remembered that Elohim (God) was

their rock, and El Elyon (God Most High) their Redeemer. 36 Nevertheless they flattered Him with their mouth, and they lied to Him with their tongue; 37 For their heart was not steadfast with Him, nor were they faithful in His covenant.

38 But He, being rachum (full of compassion), forgave their avon (iniquity), and did not destroy them. Yes, many a time He turned His anger away, and did not stir up all His wrath; 39 For He remembered that they were but flesh, a breath that passes away and does not come again. 40 How often they provoked Him in the wilderness, and grieved Him in the desert! 41 Yes, again and again they tempted El (God), and tavah (limited) the Kadosh (Holy One) of Israel. 42 They did not remember His power: The day when He redeemed them from the tsar (adversary), 43 When He worked His otot (signs) in Egypt, and His mofet'iym (wonders) in the field of Zoan; 44 Turned their rivers into blood, and their streams, that they could not drink. 45 He sent swarms of flies among them, which devoured them, and frogs, which destroyed them. 46 He also gave their crops to the caterpillar, and their labor to the locust. 47 He destroyed their vines with hail, and their sycamore trees with frost. 48 He also gave up their cattle to the hail, and their flocks to fiery lightning. 49 He cast on them the fierceness of His anger, wrath, indignation, and trouble, by sending Mal'ak Ra'iym (evil angels) among them.

50 He made a path for His anger; He did not spare their soul from mavet (death), but gave their life over to dever (plague), 51 And destroyed all the firstborn in Egypt, the first of their strength in the tents of Ham. 52 But He made His own people go forth like sheep, and guided them in the wilderness like a flock; 53 And He led them on safely, so that they did not fear; But the sea overwhelmed their oyev'iym (enemies). 54 And He brought them to the gevul kadosh (border of his Holy Place), this mountain which His right hand had acquired. 55

He also drove out the goyim (gentiles, heathen, nations) before them, allotted them an inheritance by line, and made the tribes of Israel dwell in their tents.

56 Yet they nasah (tested) and marah (provoked) Elohim Elyon (God Most High), and did not keep His edot (testimonies), 57 But turned back and acted bagad (unfaithfully) like their fathers; They were turned aside like a deceitful bow. 58 For they provoked Him to anger with their bamot (high places), and moved Him to jealousy with their pesiyl'im (carved images). 59 When Elohim (God) heard this, He was furious, and greatly abhorred Israel, 60 So that He forsook the mishkan (tabernacle) of Shiloh, the Ohel (tent) He had placed among men, 61 And delivered His strength into captivity, and His glory into the enemy's hand. 62 He also gave His people over to the sword, and was furious with His inheritance. 63 The fire consumed their young men, and their maidens were not given in marriage. 64 Their Koheniym (Priests) fell by the sword, and their amanot (widows) made no lamentation. 65 Then Adonai (the Lord) awoke as from sleep, like a gibor (mighty man) who shouts because of wine. 66 And He beat back His tsariym (adversaries); He put them to a perpetual reproach. 67 Moreover He rejected the tent of Joseph, and did not choose the tribe of Ephraim, 68 But chose the tribe of Judah, Mount Zion which He loved. 69 And He built His mikdash (sanctuary) like the heights, like the earth which He has established forever.

70 He also chose David His servant, and took him from the sheepfolds; 71 From following the ewes that had young He brought him, to shepherd Jacob His people, and Israel His inheritance. 72 So he shepherded them according to the integrity of his heart, and guided them by the skillfulness of his hands.

Psalm 79

1 A Psalm of Asaph. O Elohim (God), the goyim (gentiles, nations, heathens) have come into Your inheritance; Your kodesh (holy place / temple) they have defiled; They have laid Jerusalem in heaps. 2 The dead bodies of Your servants they have given as food for the birds of the heavens, the flesh of Your chasiyd'iym (godly ones) to the beasts of the earth. 3 Their blood they have shed like water all around Jerusalem, and there was no one to bury them. 4 We have become a reproach to our neighbors, a scorn and derision to those who are around us. 5 How long, YAHUWAH? Will You be angry forever? Will Your jealousy burn like fire? 6 Pour out Your wrath on the goyim (nations, gentiles, heathens) that do not know You, and on the kingdoms that do not call on Your name. 7 For they have devoured Jacob, and laid waste his dwelling place. 8 Oh, do not remember avonot rishoniym (former iniquities) against us! Let Your rachamiym (tender mercies) come speedily to meet us, for we have been brought very low. 9 Help us, O Elohim (God) of our salvation, for the glory of Your name; And deliver us, and provide atonement for our sins, for Your name's sake! 10 Why should the nations say, "Where is their Elohim (God)?" Let there be known among the goyim (nations, gentiles, heathens) in our sight the avenging of the blood of Your servants which has been shed. 11 Let the groaning of the asiyr (prisoner) come before You; According to the greatness of Your power preserve those who are bnei temuthah (sons of death); 12 And return to our neighbors sevenfold into their bosom their reproach with which they have reproached You, O Adonai (Lord). 13 So we, Your people and sheep of Your pasture, will give You thanks forever; We will show forth Your praise to all generations.

Psalm 80

1 To the Chief Musician. Set to "The Lilies." A Testimonyb of Asaph. A Psalm. Give ear, O Shepherd of Israel, You who lead Joseph like a flock; You who dwell between the cherubim, shine forth! 2 Before Ephraim, Benjamin, and Manasseh, Stir up Your strength, and come and save us! 3 Restore us, O Elohim (God); Cause Your face to shine, and we shall be saved! 4 O YAHUWAH, Elohim Tseva'ot (God of hosts), how long will You be angry against the tefilat (prayer) of Your people? 5 You have fed them with the bread of tears, and given them tears to drink in great measure. 6 You have made us a strife to our neighbors, and our oyev'iym (enemies) laugh among themselves. 7 Restore us, O Elohim Tseva'ot (God of hosts); Cause Your face to shine, and we shall be saved! 8 You have brought a vine out of Egypt; You have cast out the goyim (nations, gentiles, heathens), and planted it. 9 You prepared room for it, and caused it to take deep root, and it filled the land. 10 The hills were covered with its shadow, and the mighty cedars with its boughs. 11 She sent out her boughs to the Sea, and her branches to the River. 12 Why have You broken down her hedges, so that all who pass by the way pluck her fruit? 13 The boar out of the woods uproots it, and the wild beast of the field devours it. 14 Return, we beseech You, O Elohim Tseva'ot (God of hosts); Look down from heaven and see, and visit this vine, 15 And the vineyard which Your right hand has planted, and the branch that You made strong for Yourself. 16 It is burned with fire, it is cut down; They perish at the rebuke of Your countenance. 17 Let Your hand be upon the man of Your right hand, upon the son of man whom You made strong for Yourself. 18 Then we will not turn back from You; Techaya (Quicken us, make us alive), and we will call upon Your name. 19 Restore us, O

YAHUWAH, Elohim Tseva'ot (God of hosts); Cause Your face to shine, and we shall be saved!

Psalm 81

1 To the Chief Musician. On an instrument of Gath.a A Psalm of Asaph. Sing aloud to Elohim (God) our strength; Make a joyful shout to the Elohim (God) of Jacob. 2 Raise a song and strike the timbrel, the pleasant harp with the lute. 3 Blow the shofar (rams horn) at the time of the Chodesh (New Moon), at the kese (full moon), on our yom chag (solemn feast day). 4 For this is a chol (statute) for Israel, a mishpat (judgment) of the Elohim (God) of Jacob. 5 This He established in Joseph as a edut (testimony), when He went throughout the land of Egypt, Where I heard a language I did not understand. 6 "I removed his shoulder from the burden; His hands were freed from the baskets. 7 You called in trouble, and I delivered you; I answered you in the secret place of thunder; I tested you at the waters of Meribah. Selah. 8 "Hear, O My people, and I will admonish you! O Israel, if you will listen to Me! 9 There shall be no El Zar (strange god) among you; Nor shall you worship any El Nekar (foreign god). 10 I am YAHUWAH your Elohim (God), who brought you out of the land of Egypt; Open your mouth wide, and I will fill it. 11 "But My people would not heed My voice, and Israel would have none of Me. 12 So I gave them over to their own sheriyrut lev (stubborn heart), to walk in their own mo'etsah (counsels). 13 "Oh, that My people would listen to Me, that Israel would halakah (walk) in My derek (ways)! 14 I would soon subdue their oyev'iym (enemies), and turn My hand against their tsariym (adversaries). 15 The haters of YAHUWAH would pretend submission to Him, but their fate would endure forever. 16 He would have fed them also with the finest of wheat; And with honey from the rock I would have satisfied you."

Yom Chamishi (Fifth Day) Thursday

Psalm 82

1 A Psalm of Asaph. Elohim (God) stands in the Adat El (congregation of God); He judges among the Elohim (gods). 2 How long will you shofet avel (judge unjustly), and show partiality to the rasha'iym (wicked)? Selah. 3 Shafat (Defend) the dal (poor, lowly) and yatom (fatherless, orphan); Do tsedakah (righteousness, justice) to the aniy (afflicted, poor) and rash (needy). 4 Palat (Deliver) the dal (poor, lowly) and evyon (needy); Free them from the hand of the rasha'iym (wicked). 5 They do not know, nor do they understand; They walk about in chashekah (darkness; figuratively: misery); All the foundations of the earth are unstable. 6 I said, "You are Elohim (gods), and all of you are children of Elyon (the Most High). 7 But you shall die like men, and fall like one of the sariym (princes)." 8 Arise, O Elohim (God), judge the earth; For You shall inherit all the goyim (nations, gentiles, heathens).

Psalm 83

1 A Song. A Psalm of Asaph. Do not keep silent, O Elohim (God)! Do not hold Your peace, and do not be still, O El (God)! 2 For behold, Your oyev'iym (enemies) make a tumult; And those who hate You have lifted up their head. 3 They have taken crafty counsel against Your people, and consulted together against Your tsafaniym (hidden ones). 4 They have said, "Come, and let us cut them off from being a goy (nation), that the name of Israel may be remembered no more." 5 For they have consulted together with one consent; They form a confederacy against You: 6 The tents of Edom and the

Ishmaelites; Moab and the Hagrites; 7 Gebal, Ammon, and Amalek; Philistia with the inhabitants of Tyre; 8 Assyria also has joined with them; They have helped the children of Lot. Selah. 9 Deal with them as with Midian, as with Sisera, as with Jabin at the Brook Kishon, 10 Who perished at En Dor, who became as refuse on the earth. 11 Make their nadiyv'iym (nobles) like Oreb and like Zeeb, yes, all their nesiyk'iym (princes) like Zebah and Zalmunna, 12 Who said, "Let us take for ourselves the pastures of Elohim (God) for a possession." 13 O Elohai (my God), make them like the galgal (whirling dust), like the chaff before the wind! 14 As the fire burns the woods, and as the flame sets the mountains on fire, 15 So pursue them with Your tempest, and frighten them with Your storm. 16 Fill their faces with shame, that they may seek Your name, YAHUWAH. 17 Let them be confounded and dismayed forever; Yes, let them be put to shame and perish, 18 That they may know that You, whose name alone is YAHUWAH, are Elyon (the Most High) over all the earth.

Psalm 84

1 To the Chief Musician. On an instrument of Gath. A Psalm of the sons of Korah. How lovely is Your Mishkan (tabernacle), O YAHUWAH Tzeva'ot (Lord of Hosts)! 2 My soul longs, yes, even faints for the chatser'iym (courts) of YAHUWAH; My heart and my flesh cry out for the El Chai (living God). 3 Even the sparrow has found a home, and the swallow a nest for herself, where she may lay her young, even Your mizbechot (altars), O YAHUWAH Tzeva'ot (Lord of Hosts), My Melek (King) and Elohai (my God). 4 Blessed are those who dwell in Your house; They will still be praising You. Selah. 5 Blessed is the man whose strength is in You, whose heart is set on pilgrimage. 6 As they pass through the Valley of Baca, they make it a spring; The rain also covers it with pools. 7 They go from strength to strength; Each one appears before Elohim

(God) in Zion. 8 O YAHUWAH, Elohim Tseva'ot (God of hosts), hear my tefillat (prayer); Give ear, O Elohim (God) of Jacob! Selah. 9 Elohim (God), behold our shield, and look upon the face of Your Mashiyach (anointed). 10 For a day in Your courts is better than a thousand. I would rather be a safaf (doorkeeper) in the Bet Elohai (house of my God) than dwell in the oheliym resha (tents of wickedness). 11 For YAHUWAH Elohim (the Existing God) is a sun and shield; YAHUWAH will give grace and glory; No good thing will He withhold from those who halakah tamiym (walk uprightly / in perfection). 12 O YAHUWAH Tzeva'ot (Lord of Hosts), Blessed is the man who trusts in You!

Psalm 85

1 To the Chief Musician. A Psalm of the sons of Korah. YAHUWAH, You have been favorable to Your land; You have brought back the captivity of Jacob. 2 You have forgiven the avon (iniquity) of Your people; You have covered all their chatat (sin). Selah. 3 You have taken away all Your wrath; You have turned from the fierceness of Your anger. 4 Restore us, O Elohim (God) of our salvation, and cause Your anger toward us to cease. 5 Will You be angry with us forever? Will You prolong Your anger to all generations? 6 Will You not techayah (quicken us, revive us, make us alive) again, that Your people may rejoice in You? 7 Show us Your chesed (mercy), YAHUWAH, and grant us Your salvation. 8 I will hear what El YAHUWAH (God the Lord) will speak, for He will speak shalom (peace) to His people and to His chasiyd'iym (godly ones); But let them not turn back to kislah (folly, stupidity). 9 Surely His salvation is near to those who fear Him, that glory may dwell in our land. 10 Chesed (Mercy) and Emet (truth) have met together; Tsedek (Righteousness) and shalom (peace) have kissed. 11 Emet (Truth) shall spring out of the earth, and tsedek (righteousness) shall look down from

189

heaven. 12 Yes, YAHUWAH will give what is tov (good); And our land will yield its increase. 13 Tsedek (Righteousness) will go before Him, and shall make His footsteps our pathway.

Psalm 86

1 A Prayer of David. Bow down Your ear, YAHUWAH, hear me; For I am aniy (poor) and evyon (needy). 2 Preserve my life, for I am chasiyd (godly); You are Elohai (my God); Save Your servant who batach (trusts, is bold) in You! 3 Be merciful to me, O Adonai (Lord), for I cry to You all day long. 4 Rejoice the soul of Your servant, for to You, Adonai (Lord), I lift up my soul. 5 For You, Adonai (Lord), are tov (good), and sallach (ready to forgive), and rav-chesed (abundant in mercy) to all those who call upon You. 6 Give ear, YAHUWAH, to my tefillah (prayer); and attend to the voice of my tachanun (supplications). 7 In the day of my trouble I will call upon You, for You will answer me. 8 Among the elohim (gods) there is none like You, O Adonai (Lord); Nor are there any works like Your works. 9 All goyim (nations) whom You have made shall come and worship before You, O Adonai (Lord), and shall glorify Your name. 10 For You are great, and do wondrous things; You alone are Elohim (God). 11 Teach me Your way, YAHUWAH; I will halak (walk) in Your emet (truth); Unite my heart to fear Your name. 12 I will praise You, O Adonai Elohai (Lord my God), with all my heart, and I will glorify Your name forevermore. 13 For great is Your chesed (mercy) toward me, and You have delivered my soul from the depths of Sheol (Hades, the grave, the underworld). 14 O Elohim (God), the zediym (presumptuous, proud) have risen against me, and a mob of ariyts'iym (violent men) have sought my soul, and have not set You before them. 15 But You, Adonai (Lord), are an El (God) full of rachum (compassion), and chanun (gracious), erek-apayim (longsuffering) and rav-chesed (abundant in mercy) and emet

(truth). 16 Oh, turn to me, and have mercy on me! Give Your strength to Your servant, and save the son of Your maidservant. 17 Show me an ot (sign) for tov (good), that those who hate me may see it and be ashamed, because You, YAHUWAH, have helped me and comforted me.

Psalm 87

1 A Psalm of the sons of Korah. A Song. His foundation is in the holy mountains. 2 YAHUWAH loves the gates of Zion more than all the dwellings of Jacob. 3 Glorious things are spoken of you, O city of Elohim (God)! Selah. 4 "I will make mention of Rahab (a water demon) and Babel (Babylon) to those who know Me; Behold, O Philistia and Tyre, with Ethiopia: 'This one was born there.'" 5 And of Zion it will be said, "This one and that one were born in her; And Elyon (the Most High) Himself shall establish her." 6 YAHUWAH will record, when He registers the peoples: "This one was born there." Selah. 7 Both the shariym (singers) and the chole'liym (players on instruments) say, "All my ma'yaniym (springs) are in you."

Psalm 88

1 A Song. A Psalm of the sons of Korah. To the Chief Musician. Set to "Mahalath Leannoth." A Contemplation of Heman the Ezrahite. YAHUWAH, Elohim (God) of my salvation, I have cried out day and night before You. 2 Let my tefillah (prayer) come before You; Incline Your ear to my cry. 3 For my soul is full of troubles, and my soul draws near to Sheol (Hades, the grave, the underworld). 4 I am counted with those who go down to the pit; I am like a man who has no strength, 5 Chofdhiy (Adrift) among the metiym (dead), like the slain who lie in the kever (grave), whom You remember no more, and who are cut off from Your hand. 6 You have laid me in the lowest pit, in machashakiym (darkness), in the metsolah

(depths, the deep, deep sea). 7 Your wrath lies heavy upon me, And You have afflicted me with all Your waves. Selah. 8 You have put away my acquaintances far from me; You have made me a to'evah (abomination) to them; I am shut up, and I cannot get out; 9 My eye wastes away because of oniy (affliction). YAHUWAH, I have called daily upon You; I have stretched out my hands to You. 10 Will You work pele (wonders) for the metiym (dead)? Shall the rapha'iym (spirits of the dead; ghosts, shades, disembodied spirits) arise and praise You? Selah. 11 Shall Your chesed (mercy, lovingkindness) be declared in the kever (grave)? Or Your emunah (faithfulness) in the place of Aboddon (destruction)? 12 Shall Your pele (wonders) be known in the choshek (dark)? And Your tsedakah (righteousness) in the land of neshiyah (forgetfulness)? 13 But to You I have cried out, YAHUWAH, and in the morning my tefillah (prayer) comes before You. 14 YAHUWAH, why do You cast off my soul? Why do You hide Your face from me? 15 I have been aniy (afflicted) and ready to die from my youth; I suffer Your eymah (dread); I am distraught. 16 Your fierce wrath has gone over me; Your bi'uthiym (terrors) have cut me off. 17 They came around me all day long like mayim (water); They engulfed me altogether. 18 Loved one and friend You have put far from me, and my acquaintances into darkness.

Yom Shishi (Sixth Day) Friday

Psalm 89

1 A Contemplationa of Ethan the Ezrahite. I will sing of the hesed (mercies) of YAHUWAH forever; With my mouth will I make known Your emunah (faithfulness) to all generations. 2 For I have said, "Chesed (Mercy) shall be built up forever; Your emuna (faithfulness) You shall establish in the very heavens." 3 "I have made a covenant with My bachiyr (chosen, elect), I have sworn to My servant David: 4 'Your seed I will establish forever, And build up your throne to all generations.'" Selah. 5 And the heavens will praise Your pele (wonders), O YAHUWAH; Your emunah (faithfulness) also in the kehal (assembly) of the kadoshiym (holy ones, saints, set apart ones). 6 For who in the heavens can be compared to YAHUWAH? Who among the bnei eliym (sons of the gods) can be likened to YAHUWAH? 7 El (God) is greatly to be feared in the sod (assembly) of the kadoshiym (holy ones, saints, set apart ones), and to be held in reverence by all those around Him. 8 O YAHUWAH, Elohim Tseva'ot (God of hosts), who is chasiyn (mighty) like You, O YAH? Your emunah (faithfulness) also surrounds You. 9 You rule the raging of the sea; When its waves rise, You still them. 10 You have broken Rahab (a water demon, sea monster) in pieces, as one who is slain; You have scattered Your oyev'iym (enemies) with Your mighty arm. 11 The heavens are Yours, the earth also is Yours; The world and all its fullness, You have founded them. 12 The north and the south, You have created them; Tabor and Hermon rejoice in Your name. 13 You have a mighty arm; Strong is Your hand, and high is Your right hand.

193

14 Tsedek (Righteousness) and mishpat (judgment) are the foundation of Your throne; Chesed (Mercy) and emet (truth) go before Your face. 15 Blessed are the people who know the teru'ah (joyful sound)! They walk, YAHUWAH, in the light of Your countenance. 16 In Your name they rejoice all day long, and in Your tsedakah (righteousness) they are exalted. 17 For You are the glory of their strength, and in Your favor our horn is exalted. 18 For our shield belongs to YAHUWAH, and our Melek (king) to the Kadosh (Holy One) of Israel.

19 Then You spoke in a vision to Your chasiyd (Godly one), and said: "I have given help to one who is gibor (mighty); I have exalted one chosen from the people. 20 I have found My servant David; With My shemen kadosh (holy oil) I have anointed him, 21 With whom My hand shall be established; Also My arm shall strengthen him. 22 The oyev (enemy) shall not outwit him, nor the ben avlah (son of unrighteousness, wickedness) afflict him. 23 I will beat down his foes before his face, and nagaf (plague, strike, smite) those who hate him. 24 "But My emunah (faithfulness) and My chesed (mercy) shall be with him, and in My name his horn shall be exalted. 25 Also I will set his hand over the sea, And his right hand over the rivers. 26 He shall cry to Me, 'You are my Father, Eli (My God), and the rock of my salvation.' 27 Also I will make him My bekor (firstborn), the highest of the melakiym (kings) of the earth. 28 My chesed (mercy) I will keep for him forever, and My brit (covenant) shall stand firm with him. 29 His seed also I will make to endure forever, and his throne as the days of heaven.

30 "If his baniym (sons, children) forsake My torah (law) and do not walk in My mishpatiym (judgments), 31 If they break My chuqot (statutes) and do not keep My mitzvot (commandments), 32 Then I will punish their pesha'iym

(transgression) with the shevet (rod), and their avon (iniquity) with nega'iym (stripes, plagues, diseases).

33 Nevertheless My chesed (mercy, lovingkindness) I will not utterly take from him, nor allow My emunah (faithfulness) to fail. 34 My brit (covenant) I will not break, nor alter the word that has gone out of My lips. 35 Once I have sworn by My kodesh (holiness); I will not lie to David: 36 His seed shall endure forever, and his throne as the sun before Me; 37 It shall be established forever like the moon, even like the ed-ne'eman (faithful witness) in the sky." Selah.

38 But You have cast off and abhorred, You have been furious with Your mashiyach (anointed). 39 You have renounced the covenant of Your servant; You have profaned his crown by casting it to the ground. 40 You have broken down all his hedges; You have brought his strongholds to ruin. 41 All who pass by the way plunder him; He is a reproach to his neighbors. 42 You have exalted the right hand of his adversaries; You have made all his tsariym (adversaries) rejoice. 43 You have also turned back the edge of his sword, and have not sustained him in the battle. 44 You have made his glory cease, and cast his throne down to the ground. 45 The days of his youth You have shortened; You have covered him with shame. Selah.

46 How long, YAHUWAH? Will You hide Yourself forever? Will Your wrath burn like fire? 47 Remember how short my time is; For what futility have You created all the children of men? 48 What man can live and not see death? Can he deliver his life from the power of Sheol (Hades, the grave, the underworld)? Selah. 49 Adonai (Lord), where are Your former chesed'iym (mercies, lovingkindnesses), Which You swore to David in Your emunah (faithfulness)? 50 Remember, Adonai (Lord), the reproach of Your servants; How I bear in

195

my bosom the reproach of all the many peoples, 51 With which Your oyev'iym (enemies) have reproached, YAHUWAH, with which they have reproached the footsteps of Your mashiyach (anointed). 52 Blessed be YAHUWAH forevermore! Amen and Amen.

Psalm 90

1 A Prayer of Moses the man of Elohim (God). Adonai (Lord), You have been our dwelling place in all generations. 2 Before the mountains were brought forth, or ever You had formed the earth and the world, even from everlasting to everlasting, You are El (God). 3 You turn man to dakka (destruction), and say, "Return, O children of men." 4 For a thousand years in Your sight are like yesterday when it is past, and like a watch in the night. 5 You carry them away like a flood; They are like a sleep. In the morning they are like grass which grows up: 6 In the morning it flourishes and grows up; In the evening it is cut down and withers. 7 For we have been consumed by Your anger, and by Your wrath we are terrified. 8 You have set our avonot (iniquities) before You, our alum (secrets; secret sins) in the light of Your countenance. 9 For all our days have passed away in Your wrath; We finish our years like a sigh. 10 The days of our lives are seventy years; And if by reason of strength they are eighty years, yet their boast is only labor and sorrow; For it is soon cut off, and we fly away. 11 Who knows the power of Your anger? For as the fear of You, so is Your wrath. 12 So teach us to number our days, that we may gain a levav chokmah (heart of wisdom). 13 Return, YAHUWAH! How long? And have compassion on Your servants. 14 Oh, satisfy us early with Your chesed (mercy), that we may rejoice and be glad all our days! 15 Make us glad according to the days in which You have afflicted us, the years in which we have seen ra'ah (evil). 16 Let Your work appear to Your servants, and Your glory to their children. 17 And let

the beauty of YAHUWAH our Elohim (God) be upon us, and establish the work of our hands for us; Yes, establish the work of our hands.

Psalm 91

1 He who dwells in the seter (secret place) of Elyon (the Most High) shall abide under the Tsel Shaddai (shadow of the Almighty). 2 I will say of YAHUWAH, "He is my refuge and my fortress; Elohai (My God), in Him I will batach (trust, be bold in)." 3 Surely He shall deliver you from the pach (snare; figuratively: calamity) and the yakush (fowler, trapper, bait layer) and from the dever havot (pestilence's destruction). 4 He shall cover you with His evrat (feathers), and under His kanaf'iym (wings) you shall take refuge; His emet (truth) shall be your shield and buckler. 5 You shall not be afraid of the pachad (terror) by laila (night), nor of the chets (arrow) that flies by yomam (day), 6 Nor of the dever (pestilence) that walks in ophel (darkness, gloom; spiritual unreceptivity, calamity), nor of the ketev (destruction, destroying, ruin) that lays waste at tsohariym (noonday). 7 A thousand may fall at your side, and ten thousand at your right hand; But it shall not come near you. 8 Only with your eyes shall you look, and see the shilumat rasha'iym (reward of the wicked). 9 Because you have made YAHUWAH, who is my refuge, even Elyon (the Most High), your dwelling place, 10 No ra'ah (evil) shall befall you, nor shall any nega (plague) come near your ohel (tent, dwelling); 11 For He shall give His Mal'akiym (angels) charge over you, to keep you in all your derek (ways). 12 In their hands they shall bear you up, lest you dash your foot against a stone. 13 You shall tread upon the shachal (fierce lion) and the taniyn (dragon), the kephiyr (young lion) and the pethen (cobra) you shall trample underfoot. 14 "Because he has set his love upon Me, therefore I will deliver him; I will set him on high, because he has known My name. 15 He shall call

upon Me, and I will answer him; I will be with him in trouble; I will deliver him and honor him. 16 With long life I will satisfy him, And show him My yeshua (salvation)."

Psalm 92

1 A Psalm. A Song for the Yom Ha'Shabbat (Sabbath day). It is good to give hoda (thanks) to YAHUWAH, and to sing zamar (praises) to Your name, O Elyon (Most High); 2 To declare Your chesed (mercy, lovingkindness) in the boker (morning), and Your emunah (faithfulness) every leylot (night), 3 On an instrument of ten strings, on the lute, and on the harp, with harmonious sound. 4 For You, YAHUWAH, have made me glad through Your work; I will triumph in the works of Your hands. 5 YAHUWAH, how great are Your works! Your machashavah (thoughts) are very deep. 6 An iysh ba'ar (brutish, senseless, or stupid man) does not know, nor does a keciyl (fool) understand this. 7 When the rasha'iym (wicked) spring up like grass, and when all the polei aven (workers of iniquity) flourish, it is that they may be destroyed forever. 8 But You, YAHUWAH, are marom (on high) forevermore. 9 For behold, Your oyev'iym (enemies), YAHUWAH, for behold, Your oyev'iym (enemies) shall perish; All the polri aven (workers of iniquity) shall be scattered. 10 But my horn You have exalted like a re'iym (unicorn); I have been shemen ra'anan (anointed with fresh oil). 11 My eye also has seen my desire on my shur'iym (enemies; watcher's); My ears hear my desire on the re'iym (wicked, evil) who rise up against me. 12 The tsadiyk (righteous) shall flourish like a palm tree, he shall grow like a cedar in Lebanon. 13 Those who are planted in the Bet YAHUWAH (house of the Lord) shall flourish in the courts of our Elohim (God). 14 They shall still bear fruit in old age; They shall be fresh and flourishing, 15 To declare that YAHUWAH is yashar (upright); He is my rock, and there is no ave'latah (unrighteousness) in Him.

Psalm 93

1 YAHUWAH reigns, He is clothed with majesty; YAHUWAH is clothed, He has girded Himself with strength. Surely the world is established, so that it cannot be moved. 2 Your throne is established from of old; You are from everlasting. 3 The floods have lifted up, YAHUWAH, the floods have lifted up their voice; The floods lift up their waves. 4 YAHUWAH on high is Abiyr (mightier) than the noise of mayim rabiym (many waters), than the mighty waves of the sea. 5 Your edot (testimonies) are very sure; Kodesh (Holiness) adorns Your house, YAHUWAH, forever.

Psalm 94

1 O YAHUWAH, El Nekamot (God of vengeance), O El (God), to whom nekamot (vengeance) belongs, shine forth! 2 Rise up, O Sjofet (Judge) of the earth; Render a gemul (reward) to the ge'iym (proud, arrogant). 3 YAHUWAH, how long will the rasha'iym (wicked), how long will the rasha'iym (wicked) triumph? 4 They utter speech, and speak atak (insolent things); All the polei aven (workers of iniquity) boast in themselves. 5 They break in pieces Your people, YAHUWAH, and afflict Your heritage. 6 They slay the almanah (widow) and the ger (stranger), and ratsach (murder) the yatom (fatherless, orphan). 7 Yet they say, "YAH does not see, nor does the Elohim (God) of Jacob understand." 8 Understand, you ba'ariym (stupid, senseless, brutish) among the people; And you kesiyl'iym (fools, stupid), when will you be sakal (wise)? 9 He who planted the ear, shall He not hear? He who formed the eye, shall He not see? 10 He who yasar (chastises) the goyim (nations, heathen, gentiles), shall He not yakach (correct), He who teaches man da'at (knowledge)? 11 YAHUWAH knows the machashavot adam (thoughts of man), that they are hevel (vanity, futile). 12 Blessed is the man

whom You yasar (chasten), O Yah, and teach out of Your torah (law), 13 That You may give him rest from the yomei ra (days of evil), until the pit is dug for the rasha (wicked). 14 For YAHUWAH will not cast off His people, nor will He forsake His inheritance. 15 But mishpat (judgment) will return to tsedek (righteousness), and all the yashar lev (upright in heart) will follow it. 16 Who will rise up for me against the re'iym (evildoers)? Who will stand up for me against the polei aven (workers of iniquity)? 17 Unless YAHUWAH had been my help, My soul would soon have settled in dumah (silence). 18 If I say, "My foot slips," Your chesed (mercy), YAHUWAH, will hold me up. 19 In the multitude of my sar'aph (anxieties) within me, Your comforts delight my soul. 20 Shall the kise havot (throne of wickedness), which devises amal alei chok (evil by law), have chavar (fellowship) with You? 21 They gather together against the soul of the tsadiyk (righteous), and condemn dam nakiy (innocent blood). 22 But YAHUWAH has been my defense, and my Elohim (God) the rock of my refuge. 23 He has brought on them their own aven (iniquity), and shall tsamat (cut them off, put an end to them) in their own ra (evil, wickedness); YAHUWAH our Elohim (God) shall tsamat (cut them off, put an end to them).

Psalm 95

1 Oh come, let us sing to YAHUWAH! Let us shout joyfully to the Rock of our salvation. 2 Let us come before His presence with thanksgiving; Let us shout joyfully to Him with psalms. 3 For YAHUWAH is the El Gadol (great God), and the Melek Gadol (great King) above all elohim (gods). 4 In His hand are the mechkar;iym (deep places) of the earth; The heights of the hills are His also. 5 The sea is His, for He made it; And His hands formed the dry land. 6 Oh come, let us worship and bow down; Let us kneel before YAHUWAH our Maker. 7 For He is our Elohim (God), and we are the people of His pasture,

and the sheep of His hand. Today, if you will hear His voice: 8 "Do not harden your hearts, as in the meriybah (rebellion), as in the day of masah (trial, temptation) in the wilderness, 9 When your fathers nasah (tested, tried) Me; They bachan (proved, tried) Me, though they saw My work. 10 For forty years I was grieved with that generation, and said, 'It is a people who go astray in their hearts, and they do not know My derek'iym (ways).' 11 So I swore in My wrath, 'They shall not enter My rest.'"

Yom Shabbat (7ᵗʰ Day - Sabbath) Saturday

Psalm 96

1 Oh, sing to YAHUWAH a new song! Sing to YAHUWAH, all the earth. 2 Sing to YAHUWAH, bless His name; Proclaim the good news of His salvation from day to day. 3 Declare His glory among the goyim (nations, gentiles), His wonders among all peoples. 4 For YAHUWAH is great and greatly to be praised; He is to be feared above all elohim (gods). 5 For all the elohim (gods) of the peoples are eliliym (idols), but YAHUWAH made the heavens. 6 Honor and majesty are before Him; Strength and beauty are in His mikdash (sanctuary). 7 Give to YAHUWAH, O families of the peoples, give to YAHUWAH glory and strength. 8 Give to YAHUWAH the glory due His name; Bring a minchah (offering), and come into His courts. 9 Oh, worship YAHUWAH in the hadarat kodesh (beauty / adornment of holiness)! Chiyl (Tremble, dance as in whirling) before Him, all the earth. 10 Say among the goyim (nations, gentiles), "YAHUWAH reigns; The world also is firmly established, it shall not be moved; He shall judge the peoples meyshar'iym (righteously, in equity)." 11 Let the heavens rejoice, and let the earth be glad; Let the sea roar, and all its fullness; 12 Let the field be joyful, and all that is in it. Then all the trees of the trees will rejoice before YAHUWAH. 13 For He is coming, for He is coming to judge the earth. He shall judge the world with tsedek (righteousness), and the peoples with His emunah (faithfulness).

Psalm 97

1 YAHUWAH reigns; Let the earth rejoice; Let the multitude of isles be glad! 2 Anan (Clouds) and araphel (thick darkness) surround Him; Tsedek (Righteousness) and mishpat (judgment) are the foundation of His throne. 3 A fire goes before Him, and burns up His tsar'iym (adversaries) round about. 4His lightnings light the world; The earth sees and trembles. 5 The mountains melt like wax at the presence of YAHUWAH, at the presence of the Adon (Lord) of the whole earth. 6 The heavens declare His tsedek (righteousness), and all the peoples see His glory. 7 Let all be put to shame who serve pesel (carved images), who boast of eliliym (idols). Worship Him, all you elohim (gods). 8 Zion hears and is glad, and the daughters of Judah rejoice because of Your mishpatiym (judgments), YAHUWAH. 9 For You, YAHUWAH, are Elyon (most high) above all the earth; You are exalted far above all elohim (gods). 10 You who love YAHUWAH, hate ra (evil)! He preserves the souls of His kadoshiym (holy ones, saints, set apart ones); He delivers them out of the hand of the rasha'iym (wicked). 11 Light is sown for the tsadiyk (righteous), and gladness for the yashar lev (upright in heart). 12 Rejoice in YAHUWAH, you tsadiykiym (righteous), and give thanks at the remembrance of His Kadosh (holiness).

Psalm 98

1 A Psalm. Oh, sing to YAHUWAH a new song! For He has done marvelous things; His right hand and His holy arm have gained Him the victory. 2 YAHUWAH has made known His yeshua (salvation); His tsedakah (righteousness) He has revealed in the sight of the goyim (nations, gentiles). 3 He has remembered His chesed (mercy) and His emunah (faithfulness) to the house of Israel; All the ends of the earth have seen the yeshu'at (salvation) of our Elohim (God). 4 Shout joyfully to YAHUWAH, all the earth; Break forth in song, rejoice, and sing praises. 5 Sing to YAHUWAH with the harp,

with the harp and the sound of a psalm, 6 With trumpets and the sound of a shofar (rams horn); Shout joyfully before YAHUWAH, the Melek (King). 7 Let the sea roar, and all its fullness, the world and those who dwell in it; 8 Let the rivers clap their hands; Let the hills be joyful together before YAHUWAH, 9 For He is coming to judge the earth. With tsedek (righteousness) He shall judge the world, and the peoples with meyshariym (equity).

Psalm 99

1 YAHUWAH reigns; Let the peoples tremble! He dwells between the cherubim; Let the earth be moved! 2 YAHUWAH is great in Zion, and He is high above all the peoples. 3 Let them praise Your great and awesome name— He is kadosh (holy). 4 The King's strength also loves mishpat (judgment); You have established meyshariym (equity); You have executed mishpat (judgment) and tsedakah (righteousness) in Jacob. 5 Exalt YAHUWAH our Elohim (God), and worship at His footstool—He is kadosh (holy). 6 Moses and Aaron were among His Koheniym (Priests), and Samuel was among those who called upon His name; They called upon YAHUWAH, and He answered them. 7 He spoke to them in the amud anan (pillar of the cloud); They kept His edot (testimonies) and the chok (ordinance) He gave them. 8 You answered them, YAHUWAH our Elohim (God); You were to them El Nose (God-Who-Forgives), though You took vengeance on their deeds. 9 Exalt YAHUWAH our Elohim (God), and worship at His holy hill; For YAHUWAH our Elohim (God) is kadosh (holy).

Psalm 100

1 A Psalm of Thanksgiving. Make a joyful shout to YAHUWAH, all you lands! 2 Serve YAHUWAH with simchah (gladness);

Come before His presence with renanah (singing, triumphing, ringing cry). 3 Know that YAHUWAH, He is Elohim (God); It is He who has made us, and not we ourselves; We are His people and the sheep of His pasture. 4 Enter into His gates with todah (thanksgiving), and into His courts with tehillah (praise, a hymn of praise). Be thankful to Him, and bless His name. 5 For YAHUWAH is good; His chesed (mercy) is everlasting, and His emunah (faithfulness) endures to all generations.

Psalm 101

1 A Psalm of David. I will sing of chesed (mercy) and mishpat (judgment); To You, YAHUWAH, I will zamerah (sing praises). 2 I will Askiylah (behave wisely) in a derek tamiym (perfect way). Oh, when will You come to me? I will walk within my house with a tam levav (perfect heart). 3 I will set no devar beliya'al (thing of Belial: worthlessness; a name of Satan, the enemy; an evil spirit) before my eyes; I hate the work of those who setiym (fall away, turn aside); It shall not cling to me. 4 A levav ikesh (perverse heart) shall depart from me; I will not know ra (evil, wickedness). 5 Whoever lashon baseter (secretly slanders) his neighbor, him I will tsamat (destroy, cut off, put an end to); The one who has a gevah eynayim (haughty look) and a rachav levav (proud heart), him I will not endure. 6 My eyes shall be on the faithful of the land, that they may dwell with me; He who walks in a derek tamiym (perfect way), he shall serve me. 7 He who oseh remiyah (works deceit, slackingly) shall not dwell within my house; He who tells shekeriym (lies) shall not continue in my presence. 8 Early I will destroy all the rasha (wicked) of the land, that I may cut off all the polei aven (workers of iniquity) from the city of YAHUWAH.

Psalm 102

1 A tefillah le'aniy (Prayer of the afflicted), when he is overwhelmed and pours out his complaint before YAHUWAH. Hear my tefillah (prayer), YAHUWAH, and let my shav'ah (cry, cry for help) come to You. 2 Do not hide Your face from me in the day of my trouble; Incline Your ear to me; In the day that I call, answer me speedily. 3 For my days are consumed like smoke, and my bones are burned like a hearth. 4 My heart is stricken and withered like grass, so that I forget to eat my bread. 5 Because of the sound of my groaning my bones cling to my skin. 6 I am like a pelican of the wilderness; I am like an owl of the desert. 7 I lie awake, and am like a sparrow alone on the housetop. 8 My oyev'iym (enemies) reproach me all day long; Those who deride me swear an oath against me. 9 For I have eaten ashes like bread, and mingled my drink with weeping, 10 Because of Your indignation and Your wrath; For You have lifted me up and cast me away. 11 My days are like a shadow that lengthens, and I wither away like grass. 12 But You, YAHUWAH, shall endure forever, and the remembrance of Your name to all generations. 13 You will arise and have racham (compassion, mercy) on Zion; For the time to favor her, yes, the set time, has come. 14 For Your servants take pleasure in her stones, and show favor to her dust. 15 So the goyim (nations, gentiles, heathens) shall fear the name of YAHUWAH, and all the kings of the earth Your glory. 16 For YAHUWAH shall build up Zion; He shall appear in His glory. 17 He shall regard the tefilat (prayers) of the ar'ar (destitute), and shall not despise their tefilat (prayers). 18 This will be written for the generation to come, that a people yet to be created may praise Yah. 19 For He looked down from the height of His kadosh (holy place, sanctuary); From heaven YAHUWAH viewed the earth, 20 To hear the groaning of the

206

asiyr (prisoner), to release the bnei temuthah (sons of death), 21 To declare the name of YAHUWAH in Zion, and His praise in Jerusalem, 22 When the peoples are gathered together, and the kingdoms, to serve YAHUWAH. 23 He weakened my strength in the way; He shortened my days. 24 I said, "O Eli (my God), do not take me away in the midst of my days; Your years are throughout all generations. 25 Of old You laid the foundation of the earth, And the heavens are the work of Your hands. 26 They will perish, but You will endure; Yes, they will all grow old like a garment; Like a cloak You will change them, and they will be changed. 27 But You are the same, and Your years will have no end. 28 The children of Your servants will continue, and their seed will be established before You."

Psalm 103

1 A Psalm of David. Bless YAHUWAH, O my soul; And all that is within me, bless His holy name! 2 Bless YAHUWAH, O my soul, and forget not all His gemuliym (benefits): 3 Who forgives all your avoniym (iniquities), who rofe (heals) all your tachalu (diseases), 4 Who redeems your chai (life) from shachat (destruction), Who crowns you with chesed (mercy, lovingkindness) and rachamiym (tender mercies), 5 Who satisfies your mouth with tov (good things), so that your youth is renewed like the nesher (eagle's). 6 YAHUWAH executes tsedakah (righteousness) and mishpatiym (judgment) for all who are ashuk'iym (oppressed). 7 He made known His ways to Moses, His acts to the children of Israel. 8 YAHUWAH is rachum (merciful, full of compassion) and chanun (gracious), erek apayim (slow to anger), and rav chesed (abounding in mercy). 9 He will not always strive with us, nor will He keep His anger forever. 10 He has not dealt with us according to our chatat (sins), nor punished us according to our avonot (iniquities). 11 For as the heavens are high above the earth, so great is His chesed (mercy)

toward those who fear Him; 12 As far as the east is from the west, so far has He removed our pesha'iym (transgressions) from us. 13 As a father pities his children, so YAHUWAH pities those who fear Him. 14 For He knows our frame; He remembers that we are dust. 15 As for man, his days are like grass; As a flower of the field, so he flourishes. 16 For the wind passes over it, and it is gone, and its place remembers it no more. 17 But the chesed (mercy) of YAHUWAH is from everlasting to everlasting on those who fear Him, and His tsedakah (righteousness) to children's children, 18 To such as keep His covenant, and to those who remember His pikudiym (precepts) to do them. 19 YAHUWAH has established His throne in heaven, and His kingdom rules over all. 20 Bless YAHUWAH, you His Mal'akiym (angels), Who excel in strength, who do His word, heeding the voice of His word. 21 Bless YAHUWAH, all you His hosts, you sheret'iym (ministers) of His, who do His pleasure. 22 Bless YAHUWAH, all His works, in all places of His dominion. Bless YAHUWAH, O my soul!

MA'ARIV
EVENING SERVICE FOR
WEEKDAYS
AND THE TERMINATION OF
THE SABBATH

Ot Ha-Ts'lav (Sign of the Cross)

In the name of the Father YAHUWAH, and of the Son Yah'shua (Jesus), and of the Ruach HaKodesh (Holy Spirit). Amen.

Blessed be YAHUWAH, always now and for ever, and unto the ages of ages. Amen.

Baraku YAHUWAH (Bless the Lord) Psalm 134

A Song of Degrees.—Behold, bless YAHUWAH, all you servants of YAHUWAH, who stand in the house of YAHUWAH in the night seasons. Lift up your hands towards the sanctuary, and bless YAUWAH. YAHUWAH bless you out of Zion; even he that made heaven and earth.

YAHUWAH Tzeva'ot (Lord of Hosts) is with us; the El (God) of Jacob is our stronghold. (Selah.)

To be said three times.

O YAHUWAH Tzeva'ot (Lord of Hosts), happy is the man that trusts in You.

To be said three times.

Save, YAHUWAH: may the King answer us on the day when we call.

To be said three times.

Katzi Kaddish
(Half Sanctification)

Reader.—Magnified and sanctified be his great name in the world which he has created according to his will. May he establish his kingdom during your life and during your days, and during the life of all the house of Israel, even speedily and at a near time, and say, Amen.

Cong. and Reader.—Let his great name be blessed for ever and to all eternity.

Reader.—Blessed, praised and glorified, exalted, extolled and honored, magnified and lauded be the name of the Kadosh (Holy One), blessed be he; though he be high above all the blessings and hymns, praises and consolations, which are uttered in the world; and say, Amen.

HE FORGIVES

And he being merciful, forgives iniquity, and destroys not: yes, many a time he turns his anger away, and does not stir up all his wrath. Save, YAHUWAH, may the King answer us on the day when we call. In Yah'shua's (Jesus') Name.

Congregation in an undertone - Blessed, praised, glorified, exalted and extolled be the name of the supreme Melek Melakiym (King of kings), the Kadosh (Holy One), blessed be he, who is the first and the last, and beside him there is no El (God). Exalt him that rides upon the heavens by his name Yah, and rejoice before him. His name is exalted above all blessing and praise. Blessed be His name, whose glorious kingdom is for ever and ever. Let the name of YAHUWAH be blessed from this time forth and for evermore. Amen.

BARCHU
(Call to Prayer)

Reader.—Bless YAHUWAH who is blessed.

Cong. and Reader.—Blessed is YAHUWAH who is blessed for ever and ever.

MA'ARIV NESHEPH
(Evening Twilight)

Blessed are You YAHUWAH our Elohim (God), Melek Ha-Olam (King of the universe), the God and the Father of our Lord Yah'shua the Messiah (Jesus Christ), who at Your word brings on the evening twilight, with wisdom opens the gates of the heavens, and with understanding changes times and varies the seasons, and arranges the stars in their watches in the sky, according to Your will. You create day and night; You roll away the light from before the darkness, and the darkness from before the light; You make the day to pass and the night to approach, and divide the day from the night, YAHUWAH Tzeva'ot (Lord of armies) is Your name; a Elohim (God) living and enduring continually, may You reign over us for ever and ever. Blessed are You, YAHUWAH, who brings on the evening twilight.

Ahavat Olam
(Everlasting Love)

With everlasting love You have loved the house of Israel, Your people; a Torah (Law) and mitzvot (commandments), chukkiym (statutes) and mishpatiym (judgments) have You taught us. Therefore, YAHUWAH our Elohim (God), when we lie down and when we rise up we will meditate on Your chukot (statutes): yea, we will rejoice in the words of Your Torah (Law) and in Your mitzvot (commandments) for ever; for they are our life and the length of our days, and we will meditate on them day and night. And may You never take away Your love from us. Blessed are You, YAHUWAH, who loves Your people Israel.

Yishtabach
(Praised Forever)

Praised be Your name for ever, O our King, the great and holy God and King, in heaven and on earth; for unto You, YAHUWAH our Elohim (God), and El (God) of our fathers, the God and the Father of our Lord Yah'shua the Messiah (Jesus Christ), song and praise are becoming, hymn and psalm, strength and dominion, victory, greatness and might, renown and glory, holiness and sovereignty, blessings and thanksgivings from henceforth even for ever. Blessed are You, YAHUWAH, God and King, great in praises, God of thanksgivings, Lord of wonders, who makes choice of song and psalm, O King and God, the life of all worlds. Amen.

Hari'shonah L'kol HaMitzvot
(The First Commandment of All)

And one of the scribes came, and having heard them reasoning together, and perceiving that he had answered them well, asked him, Which is the first mitzvah (commandment) of all? And Yah'shua (Jesus) answered him, "The first of all the mitzvot (commandments) is, Hear, O Israel; YAHUWAH our Elohim (God), YAHUWAH is one: And You shall love YAHUWAH your Elohim (God) with all your heart, and with all your soul, and with all your mind, and with all your strength: this is the first mitzvah (commandment). And the second is this, You shall love your neighbour as yourself. There is no other mitzvah (commandment) greater than these. And on these two mitzvot (commandments) hang all the torah (law) and the navi'iym (prophets).

Tochecha
(Admonition)

Therefore through Him (Yah'shua) let us continually offer the sacrifice of praise to YAHUWAH, that is, the fruit of our lips, giving thanks to His name. But do not forget to do good and to share, for with such sacrifices Elohim (God) is well pleased. *(Hebrews 13:15-16)*

Therefore do not be unwise, but understand what the will of YAHUWAH is. And do not be drunk with wine, in which is dissipation; but be filled with the Spirit, speaking to one another in psalms and hymns and spiritual songs, singing and making melody in your heart to YAHUWAH, giving thanks always for all things to God the Father in the name of our Lord Yah'shua the Messiah (Jesus Christ), submitting to one another in the fear of Elohim (God). *(Ephesians 5:17-21)*

And, Be anxious for nothing, but in everything by prayer and supplication, with thanksgiving, let your requests be made known to God; and the peace of God, which surpasses all understanding, will guard your hearts and minds through Yah'shua the Messiah (Jesus Christ). *(Philippians 4:6-7)*

SHEMA

Shema (Hear)
Deut. 6:4-9

Hear, O Israel: YAHUWAH our Elohim (God), YAHUWAH is One.

Blessed be His name, whose glorious kingdom is for ever and ever.

And You shall love YAHUWAH your Elohim (God) with all your heart, and with all your soul, and with all your might. And these words, which I command you this day, shall be upon your heart: and you shall teach them diligently unto your children, and shall talk of them when you sit in your house, and when you walk by the way, and when you lie down, and when you rise up. And you shall bind them for a sign upon your hand, and they shall be for frontlets between your eyes. And you shall write them upon the door posts of your house, and upon your gates.

Vehaya (If You Will)
Deut. 11:13-21

And it shall come to pass, if you will hearken diligently unto my mitzvot (commandments) which I command you this day, to love YAHUWAH your Elohim (God), and to serve him with all your heart and with all your soul, that I will give the rain of your land in its season, the former rain and the latter rain, that you may gather in your corn, and your wine, and your oil. And I will give grass in your field for your cattle, and your shall eat and be satisfied. Take heed to yourselves, lest your heart be deceived, and you turn aside, and serve other gods, and worship them; and the anger of YAHUWAH be kindled against you, and he shut up the heaven, that there be no rain, and that the land yield not her fruit; and you perish quickly from off the good land which YAHUWAH gives you. Therefore shall you lay up these my words in your heart and in your soul; and you shall bind them for a sign upon your hand, and they shall be for frontlets between your eyes. And you shall teach them to your children, talking of them when you sit in your house, and when you walk by the way, and when you lie down, and when you rise up. And you shall write them upon the door posts of your house, and upon your gates: that your days may be multiplied, and the days of your children, upon the land which YAHUWAH swore unto your fathers to give them, as the days of the heavens above the earth.

Vayomer (The Lord Said)
Numbers 15:37-41

And YAHUWAH spoke unto Moses, saying, Speak unto the children of Israel, and bid them that they make them a Tzitzit (tassel) upon the corners of their garments throughout their generations, and that they put upon the Tzitzit (tassel) of each corner a cord of blue: and it shall be unto you for a Tzitzit (tassel), that you may look upon it, and remember all the mitzvot (commandments) of YAHUWAH, and do them; and that you go not about after your own heart and your own eyes, after which you use to go astray: that you may remember and do all my mitzvot (commandments), and be holy unto your Elohim (God). I am YAHUWAH your Elohim (God), who brought you out of the land of Egypt, to be your Elohim (God): I am YAHUWAH your Elohim (God).

Ahava (Love)
Leviticus 19:18

AND YOU WILL love your neighbor as yourself. I am YAHUWAH. *(There is no other mitzvot (commandments) greater than these.)* For circumcision is nothing and uncircumcision is nothing, but keeping the mitzvot Elohim (commandments of God). He that loves his neighbor has fulfilled the torah (law). The end of the mitzvah (commandment) is love from a pure heart, and a good conscience, and faith without hypocrisy. By this we know, that we love the children of Elohim (God), when we love Elohim (God) and we keep his mitzvah (commandments). And this is the love of Elohim (God), that we keep his mitzvot (commandments), and his mitzvot (commandments) are not a burden.

EMET...
(True...)

True and trustworthy is all this, and it is established with us that he is YAHUWAH our God, and there is none beside him, and that We, Israel, are his people. It is he who redeemed us from the hand of kings, even our King, who delivered us from the grasp of all the terrible ones; the God, who on our behalf dealt out punishment to our adversaries, and requited all the enemies of our soul; who does great things past finding out, yea, and wonders without number; who holds our soul in life, and has not suffered our feet to be moved; who made us tread upon the high places of our enemies, and exalted our horn over all them that hated us; who wrought for us miracles and vengeance upon Pharaoh, signs and wonders in the land of the children of Ham; who in his wrath smote all the first-born of Egypt, and brought forth his people Israel from among them to everlasting freedom; who made his children pass between the divisions of the Red Sea, who sank their pursuers and their enemies in the depths. Then his children beheld his might. They praised and gave thanks unto his name and willingly accepted his sovereignty. Moses and the children of Israel sang a song unto You with great joy, saying, all of them,

Who is like unto You, YAHUWAH, among the mighty ones? Who is like unto You, glorious in holiness, revered in praises, doing wonders?

Your children beheld Your sovereign power, as You did cleave the sea before Moses: they exclaimed, This is my God! and said, YAHUWAH shall reign for ever and ever.

And it is said, For YAHUWAH has delivered Jacob, and redeemed him from the hand of him that was stronger than he. Blessed are You, YAHUWAH, who hass redeemed Israel.

Gorem'lanu
(Cause Us)

Cause us, YAHUWAH our Elohim (God), to lie down in peace, and raise us up, O our King, unto life. Spread over us the tabernacle of your peace; direct us aright through your own good counsel; save us for Your name's sake; be a shield around us; remove from us every enemy, pestilence, sword, famine and sorrow; remove also the adversary from before us and from behind us. O shelter us beneath the shadow of your wings; for you, O God, are our Guardian and our Deliverer;

217

yes, You, O Elohim (God), are a gracious and merciful King; and guard our going out and our coming in unto life and unto peace from this time forth and for evermore. Blessed are you, YAHUWAH, who guards your people (Israel) for ever. Amen.

BARUKH YAHUWAH
(Blessed be the Lord)

Blessed be YAHUWAH for evermore. Amen and Amen. Blessed be YAHUWAH out of Zion, who dwells in Jerusalem. Hallelu-Yah. Blessed be YAHUWAH God, the God of Israel, who alone does wondrous things: and blessed be his glorious name for ever; and let the whole earth be filled with his glory. Amen and Amen. Let the glory of YAHUWAH endure for ever; let YAHUWAH rejoice in his works. Let the name of YAHUWAH be blessed from this time forth and for evermore. For YAHUWAH will not forsake his people for his great name's sake; because it has pleased him to make you a people unto himself. And when all the people saw it, they fell on their faces: and they said, YAHUWAH, he is God; YAHUWAH, he is God. And YAHUWAH shall be King over all the earth: in that day shall YAHUWAH be One, and his name One. Let your lovingkindness, YAHUWAH, be upon us, according as we have hoped for you. Save us, O God of our salvation, and gather us and deliver us from the nations, to give thanks unto your holy name, and to triumph in your praise. All nations whom you have made shall come and worship before you, YAHUWAH; and they shall glorify your name: for you are great and do marvellous things; you are God alone. But we are your people and the sheep of your pasture; we will give thanks unto you for ever: we will recount your praise to all generations.

Blessed be YAHUWAH by day; blessed be YAHUWAH by night; blessed be YAHUWAH when we lie down; blessed be YAHUWAH when we rise up. For in your hand are the souls of the living and the dead, as it is said, In his hand is the soul of every living thing, and the spirit of all human flesh. Into your hand I commend my spirit; you have redeemed me, YAHUWAH God of truth. Our God who are in heaven, assert the unity of your name, and establish your kingdom continually, and reign over us for ever and ever.

May our eyes behold, our hearts rejoice, and our souls be glad in your true salvation, when it shall be said unto Zion, Your God reigns. YAHUWAH reigns; YAHUWAH has reigned; YAHUWAH shall reign for ever and ever: for the kingdom is yours, and to everlasting you will reign in glory; for we have no king but you. Blessed are you, YAHUWAH, the King, who constantly in his glory will reign over us and over all his works for ever and ever. Amen.

KATZI KADDISH
(Half Sanctification)

Reader.—Magnified and sanctified be his great name in the world which he has created according to his will. May he establish his kingdom during your life and during your days, and during the life of all the house of Israel, even speedily and at a near time, and say, Amen.

Cong. and Reader.—Let his great name be blessed for ever and to all eternity.

Reader.—Blessed, praised and glorified, exalted, extolled and honored, magnified and lauded be the name of the Holy One, blessed be he; though he be high above all the blessings and hymns, praises and consolations, which are uttered in the world; and say, Amen.

True and Firm

True and firm, established and enduring, right and faithful, beloved and precious, desirable and pleasant, revered and mighty, well-ordered and acceptable, good and beautiful is this Your word unto us for ever and ever. It is true, the God of the universe is our King, the Rock of Jacob, the Shield of our salvation: thoughout all generations He endures and His name endures; His throne is established, and His kingdom and His faithfulness endures for ever. His words also lives and endures; they are faithful and desirable for ever and to all eternity, as for our fathers so also for us, our children, our generations, and for all the generations of the seed of Israel His servants.

Al Horishonim
(Upon the Generations)

For the first and for the last ages Your word is good and endures for ever and ever; it is true and trustworthy, a statute which shall not pass away. True it is that You are indeed YAHUWAH our Elohim (God), the God and the Father of our Lord Yah'shua the Messiah (Jesus Christ), and the God of our fathers, our King, our fathers' King, our Redeemer, the Redeemer of our fathers, our Maker, the Rock of our salvation; our Deliverer and Rescuer from everlasting, such is Your name; there is no God beside You.

Ezras Avoseinu
(Helper of Our Forefathers)

You have been the help of our fathers from of old, a Shield and Saviour to their children after them in every generation: in the heights of the universe is your habitation, and Your mishpatiym (judgments) and Your tsedakah (righteousness) reach to the furthest ends of the earth. Happy is the man who hearkens unto Your mitzvot (commandments), and lays up Your Torah (Law) and Your word in his heart. True it is that You are indeed the Lord of Your people, and a mighty King to plead their cause. True it is that You are indeed the first and You are the last, and beside You we have no King, Redeemer and Saviour. From Egypt You did redeem us, YAHUWAH our Elohim (God), and from the house of bondmen You did deliver us; all their first born You did slay, but Your first-born You did redeem; You did divide the Red Sea, and drown the proud; but You made the beloved to pass through, while the waters covered their adversaries, not one of whom was left. Wherefore the beloved praised and extolled God, and offered hymns, songs, praises, blessings and thanksgivings to the King and God, who lives and endures; who is high and exalted, great and revered; who brings low the haughty, and raises up the lowly, leads forth the prisoners, delivers the meek, helps the poor, and answers his people when they cry unto him; even praises to El Elyon (God Most High), blessed is he, and ever to be blessed. Moses and the children of Israel sang a song unto You with great joy, saying, all of them,

Who is like unto You, YAHUWAH, among the mighty ones? Who is like unto You, glorious in holiness revered in praises, doing marvels?

With a new song the redeemed people offered praise unto Your name at the sea shore: they all gave thanks in unison, and proclaimed Your sovereignty, and said,

YAHUWAH shall reign for ever and ever.

O Rock of Israel, arise to the help of Your people and of Israel, and deliver, according to Your promise, Judah and Israel. Our

Redeemer, YAHUWAH Tzava'ot (Lord of Hosts) is his name, the Kadosh (Holy One) of Israel. Blessed are You, YAHUWAH, who has redeemed Israel.

AMIDA (Standing) SHEMONEH ESREH (Eighteen Prayers)

The following prayer (Amidah) to "as in ancient years," is to be said standing.

YAHUWAH, open my lips, and my mouth will declare Your praise.

Avot (Fathers)

Blessed are You YAHUWAH our Elohim (God), Melek Ha'Olam (King of the universe), the God and the Father of our Lord Yah'shua the Messiah (Jesus Christ), and God of our fathers, God of Abraham, God of Isaac, God of Jacob, God of Sarah, God of Rebecca, God of Rachel, and the God of Leah the great, mighty and revered Elohim (God), the El Elyon (God most high), who bestows loving kindnesses, and possesses all things; who rememberes the pious deeds of the patriarchs, and in love will bring a redeemer to their children's children for Your name's sake. Remember us unto life, O King, who delights in life, and inscribe us in the book of life, for Your own sake, O Elohim Chayim (living God). O King, Helper, Saviour and Shield. Blessed are You, YAHUWAH, the Shield of Abraham. You, YAHUWAH, are mighty for ever, You quicken the dead, You are mighty to save, You cause the wind to blow and the rain to fall.

Gevurot
(Gods Might)

You sustain the living with loving kindness, quicken the dead with great mercy, support the falling, heal the sick, loose the bound, and keep Your faith to them that sleep in the dust. Who is like unto You, Lord of mighty acts, and who resembles You, O King, who kills and quickens, and causes salvation to spring forth? Who is like unto You, Father of mercy, who in mercy remembers Your creatures unto life? Yes, faithful are You to quicken the dead. Blessed are You, YAHUWAH, who quickens the dead.

Kedushat HaShem
(Holiness of Gods Name)

You are holy, and Your name is holy, and holy ones praise You daily. (Selah.) Blessed are You, YAHUWAH, the El Kadosh Ve'Melek (holy God and King). We will sanctify Your name in the world even as they sanctify it in the highest heavens, as it is written by the hand of Your navi (prophet): And they called one unto the other and said, Holy, holy, holy is YAHUWAH Tzeva'ot (the Lord of hosts): the whole earth is full of his glory. Those over against them say, Blessed be the glory of YAHUWAH from his place. And in Your Holy Words it is written, saying, YAHUWAH shall reign for ever, Your Elohim (God), O Zion, unto all generations. Hallelu Yah (Praise the Lord).

Unto all generations we will declare Your greatness, and to all eternity we will proclaim Your holiness, and Your praise, O our Elohim (God), shall not depart from our mouth for ever, for You are a great and holy God and King. Blessed are You, YAHUWAH, the El Kadosh Ve'Melek (holy God and King).

Da'at
(Knowledge)

You favor man with knowledge, and teach mortals understanding. You have favored us with a knowledge of Your Torah (Law), and have taught us to perform the statutes of Your will. O favor us with knowledge, understanding and discernment from You. Be gracious to us; a mind of understanding and intellect is from You. Blessed are You, YAHUWAH, Who favors us with knowledge.

Teshuva
(Repentance)

Cause us to return, O our Father, unto Your Torah (Law); draw us near, O our King, to serve You, and bring us back in perfect repentance unto Your presence. Blessed are You, YAHUWAH, who delights in repentance.

Selichot
(Forgiveness)

Forgive us, O our Father, for we have sinned; pardon us, O our King, for we have transgressed; for You do pardon and forgive. Blessed are You, YAHUWAH, who are gracious, and does abundantly forgive.

Geulah
(Redemption)

Look upon our affliction and plead our cause, and redeem us speedily for Your name's sake; for You are a mighty Redeemer. Blessed are You, YAHUWAH, the Redeemer of

Israel. Blessed are You, YAHUWAH, who answers in time of trouble.

Refuah
(Healing)

Heal us, O YAHUWAH, and we shall be healed; save us and we shall be saved; for You are our praise. Vouchsafe a perfect healing to all our wounds; for You, Melek Shaddai (almighty King), are a faithful and merciful Physician. Blessed are You, YAHUWAH, who heals the sick of Your people Israel. May it be Your will, YAHUWAH our Elohim (God), the God and the Father of our Lord Yah'shua the Messiah (Jesus Christ), and the God of our forefathers, that You quickly send *refuah sh'lemah* (complete healing) from heaven, *refuah ruchani* (spiritual healing) and *refuah gufani* (physical healing) to Your servant *(name)* among the other patients of Your people and Israel. In the Name of Yah'shua the Messiah (Jesus Christ).

Birkat Hashanim
(Prosperity)

Bless for us, YAHUWAH our Elohim (God), this year and its crops. Grant us a blessing on the earth. Satisfy us from Your bounty and bless our year like other good years. Blessed are You, YAHUWAH, Who blesses the years.

Kibbutz Galuyot
(Ingathering of Exiles)

Sound the great shofar for our freedom and raise the banner to gather our exiles, and gather us from the four corners of the earth. Blessed are You, YAHUWAH, who gathers the scattered of Your people Israel.

Birkat HaDim
(Restoration of Justice)

Restore our judges as at the first, and our counsellors as at the beginning; remove from us grief and suffering; reign over us, YAHUWAH, You alone, in lovingkindness and tender mercy, and justify us in judgment. Bestow Your Spirit upon the rulers of all lands; guide them that they may govern justly. Then shall love and compassion be enthroned among us. Blessed are You YAHUWAH, the Melek Ha-Mishpat (King of Judgment), who loves righteousness and justice.

Al Hatzadikim
(Source of Righteousness)

For the righteous and faithful of all humankind, for all who join themselves to your people, for all who put their trust in YAHUWAH our Elohim (God) and Yah'shua the Messiah (Jesus Christ), the Son of the Father, and for all honest men and women, we ask Your favor. Grant that we may be always numbered among them. Blessed are You, YAHUWAH, staff and support of the righteous.

Tsaddikim
(Righteous Ones)

Towards the righteous and the pious, towards the elders of Your people the house of Israel, towards the remnant of their scribes, towards the proselytes of righteousness, and towards us also may Your tender mercies be stirred, YAHUWAH our Elohim (God); grant a good reward unto all who faithfully trust in Your name; set our portion with them for ever, so that we may not be put to shame; for we have trusted in You. Blessed are You, YAHUWAH, the stay and trust of the righteous.

Binyan Yerushalayim
(Rebuilding of Jerusalem)

And to Jerusalem, Your city, return in mercy, and dwell therein as You have spoken; rebuild it soon in our days as an everlasting building, and speedily set up therein the throne of David. Blessed are You, YAHUWAH, who rebuilds Jerusalem.

Malkhut Beit David
(Kingdom of David)

Speedily cause the Seed of David Your servant to flourish, and let his horn be exalted by Your salvation, because we wait for Your salvation all the day. Blessed are You, YAHUWAH, who causes the horn of salvation to flourish.

Kabbalat Tefillah
(Acceptance of Prayer)

Hear our voice, YAHUWAH our Elohim (God); spare us and have mercy upon us, and accept our prayer in mercy and favor; for You are Elohim (God) who hearkens unto prayers and supplications: from Your presence, O our King, turn us not away empty; for You hearken in mercy to the prayer of Your people Israel. Blessed are You, YAHUWAH, who hearkens unto prayer.

Avodah
(Worship)

Accept, YAHUWAH our Elohim (God), Your people Israel and their prayer; restore the service to the oracle of Your house; receive in love and favor both the fire-offerings of Israel and their prayer; and may the service of your people Israel be ever acceptable unto You. Even as it written, My House shall be a house of prayer; and again, My house shall be called a house of prayer for all people.

On New Moon and the Intermediate Days of Passover and Tabernacles the following is added:—

Our God and God of our fathers! May our remembrance rise, come and be accepted before You, with the remembrance of our fathers, of Yah'shua the Messiah (Jesus Christ) the son of David Your servant, of Jerusalem Your holy city, and of all Your people the house of Israel, bringing deliverance and well-being, grace, loving kindness and mercy, life and peace on this day of

On Passover—

the Feast of Unleavened Bread.

On New Moon say—

the New Moon.

On Tabernacles—

the Feast of Tabernacles.

Remember us, YAHUWAH our Elohim (God), thereon for our well-being; be mindful of us for blessing, and save us unto life: by Your promise of salvation and mercy, spare us and be gracious unto us; have mercy upon us and save us; for our eyes are bent upon You, because You are a gracious and merciful God and King.

And let our eyes behold Your return in mercy to Zion. Blessed are You, YAHUWAH, who restores Your divine presence unto Zion.

Hodah
(Thanksgiving)

We give thanks unto You, for You are YAHUWAH our Elohim (God), the God and the Father of our Lord Yah'shua the Messiah (Jesus Christ), and the God of our fathers, for ever and ever; You are the Rock of our lives, the Shield of our salvation through every generation. We will give thanks unto You and declare Your praise for our lives

We give thanks unto You, for You are YAHUWAH our Elohim (God), the God and the Father of our Lord Yah'shua the Messiah (Jesus Christ); the God of our fathers, the God of all flesh, our Borei (Creator) and the Borei (Creator) of all things in the beginning. Blessings and thanksgivings be to Your great and holy name, because You have kept us in life and have preserved us: so may You continue to keep us in life and to preserve us. O gather our exiles to Your holy courts to observe Your statutes, to do Your will, and to serve You with a perfect heart; seeing that we give thanks unto You. Blessed be Elohim (God) to whom thanksgivings are due.

Which are committed unto Your hand, and for our souls which are in Your charge, and for Your miracles, which are daily with us, and for Your wonders and Your benefits, which are wrought at all times, evening, morning and at noon. O You who are all-good, whose mercies fail not; You, Merciful One, whose lovingkindnesses never cease, we have ever hoped in You.

On Chanukah and Purim the following is added:—

We thank You also for the miracles, for the redemption, for the mighty deeds and saving acts, wrought by You, as well as for the wars which You did wage for our fathers in days of old, at this season.

On Chanukah.

In the days of the Hasmonean, Mattathias son of Johanan, the Kohen Gadol (High Priest), and his sons, when the iniquitous power of Greece rose up against Your people Israel to make them forgetful of Your Torah (Law), and to force them to transgress the statutes of Your will, then did You in Your abundant mercy rise up for them in the time of their trouble; You did plead their cause, You did judge their suit, You did avenge their wrong; You delivered the strong into the hands of the weak, the many into the hands of the few, the impure into the hands of the pure, the wicked into the hands of the righteous, and the arrogant into the hands of them that occupied themselves with Your Torah (Law): for Yourself You did make a great and holy name in Your world, and for Your people Israel You did work a great deliverance and redemption as at this day. And thereupon Your children came into the oracle of Your house, cleansed Your temple, purified Your sanctuary, kindled lights in Your holy courts, and appointed these eight days of Chanukah in order to give thanks and praises unto Your great name.

On Purim.

In the days of Mordecai and Esther, in Shushan the capital, when the wicked Haman rose up against them, and sought to destroy, to slay and make to perish all the Jews, both young and old, little children and women, on one day, on the thirteenth day of the twelfth month, which is the month Adar, and to take the spoil of them for a prey,—then did You in Your abundant mercy bring his counsel to nought, did frustrate his design, and return his recompense upon his own head; and they hanged him and his sons upon the gallows.

For all these things Your name, O our King, shall be continually blessed and exalted for ever and ever.

During the Ten Days of Penitence say:—

O inscribe all the children of Your covenant for a happy life.

And everything that lives shall give thanks unto You for ever, and shall praise Your name in truth, O Elohim (God), our salvation and our help. Blessed are You, YAHUWAH, whose name is All-good, and unto whom it is becoming to give thanks.

Birkat Kohanim
(Priestly Blessing)

Our God and God of our fathers, in the name of Yah'shua the Messiah (Jesus Christ), bless us with the three-fold blessing of Your Torah (Law) written by the hand of Moses Your servant, which was spoken by Aaron and his sons, the koheniym (priests), Your holy people, as it is said,

YAHUWAH bless You, and keep You:
YAHUWAH make his face to shine upon You, and be gracious

unto You:
YAHUWAH turn his face unto You, and give You peace.

Sim Shalom
(Grant Peace)

Grant peace, welfare, blessing, grace, loving kindness and mercy unto us and unto all Israel, Your people. Bless us, O our Father, even all of us together, with the light of Your countenance for by the light of Your countenance You have given us, YAHUWAH our Elohim (God), the Law of life, lovingkindness and righteousness, blessing, mercy, life and peace; and may it be good in Your sight to bless Your people Israel at all times and in every hour with Your peace.

During the Ten Days of Penitence say:—

In the book of life, blessing, peace and good sustenance may we be remembered and inscribed before You, we and all Your people the house of Israel, for a happy life and for peace. Blessed are You, YAHUWAH, who makes peace.

Blessed are You, YAHUWAH, who blesses Your people Israel with peace.

ELOHAI NETSOR
(My God Please Keep)

O Elohai (my God)! Guard my tongue from evil and my lips from speaking guile; and to such as curse me let my soul be dumb, yes, let my soul be unto all as the dust. Open my heart to Your Torah (Law), and let my soul pursue Your mitzvot (commandments). If any design evil against me, speedily make their counsil of none effect, and frustrate their designs. Do it for the sake of Your name, do it for the sake of Your right

232

hand, do it for the sake of Your holiness, do it for the sake of Your Torah (Law), do it for the sake of the name of Your Holy child Yah'shua the Messiah (Jesus Christ). In order that Your beloved ones may be delivered, O save with Your right hand, and answer me. Let the words of my mouth and the meditation of my heart be acceptable before You, YAHUWAH, my Rock and my Redeemer. He who makes peace in his high places, may he make peace for us and for all Israel, and say, Amen.

Kaddish
(Sanctification)

Reader and Cong.— YAHUWAH, God of Israel, turn from Your fierce wrath, and repent of the evil against Your people.

Cong.—Look from heaven and see how we have become a scorn and a derision among the nations; we are accounted as sheep brought to the slaughter, to be slain and destroyed, or to be smitten and reproached.

Cong. and Reader.—Yet, despite all this, we have not forgotten Your name: we beseech You, forget us not.

Cong.—Strangers say, There is no hope or expectancy for you. Be gracious unto a people that trust in Your name. O You who are most pure, bring our salvation near. We are weary, and no rest is granted us. Let Your tender mercies subdue Your anger from us.

Cong. and Reader.—We beseech You, turn from Your wrath, and have mercy upon the treasured people whom You havet chosen.

Cong.— YAHUWAH, spare us in Your tender mercies, and give us not into the hands of the cruel. Wherefore should the nations say, Where now is their God? For Your own sake deal kindly with us, and delay not.

Cong. and Reader.—We beseech You, turn from Your wrath, and have mercy upon the treasured people whom You have chosen.

Cong.—Hear our voice, and be gracious, and forsake us not in the hand of our enemies to blot out our name; remember what You have sworn to our fathers, I will multiply your seed as the stars of heaven: and now we are left a few out of many.

Cong. and Reader.—Yet, despite all this, we have not forgotten Your name: we beseech You, forget us not.

Cong.—Help us, O Elohim (God) of our salvation, for the sake of the glory of Your name; and deliver us, and pardon our sins for Your name's sake.

Cong. and Reader.— YAHUWAH our Elohim (God), God of Israel, turn from Your fierce wrath, and repent of the evil against Your people.

ALEINU
(OUR DUTY)

It is our duty to praise YAHUWAH, the Lord of all things, to ascribe greatness to him who formed the world in the beginning, since he has not made us like the nations of other lands, and has not placed us like other families of the earth, since he has not assigned unto us a portion as unto them, nor a lot as unto all their multitude. For we bend the knee and offer worship and thanks before the supreme Melek

Melakiym (King of kings), the Kadosh (Holy One), blessed be he, who stretched forth the heavens and laid the foundations of the earth, the seat of whose glory is in the heavens above, and the abode of whose might is in the loftiest heights. He is our El (God); there is none else, in truth he is our Melek (King); there is none besides him; as it is written in his Torah (Law), and You shall know this day, and lay it to your heart, that YAHUWAH he is Elohim (God) in heaven above and upon the earth beneath: there is none else.

We therefore hope in You, YAHUWAH our Elohim (God), that we may speedily behold the glory of Your might, when You will remove the abominations from the earth, and the idols will be utterly cut off, when the world will be perfected under the kingdom of the Shaddai (Almighty), and all the children of flesh will call upon Your name, when You will turn unto Yourself all the rasha'iym (wicked) of the earth. Let all the inhabitants of the world perceive and know that unto You every knee must bow, every tongue must swear. Before You, YAHUWAH our Elohim (God), let them bow and fall; and unto Your glorious name let them give honor; let them all accept the yoke of Your kingdom, and do You reign over them speedily, and for ever and ever. For the kingdom is Yours, and to all eternity You will reign in glory; as it is written in Your Law, YAHUWAH shall reign for ever and ever. And it is said, And YAHUWAH shall be king over all the earth: in that day shall YAHUWAH be One, and his name One. Amen.

KOL LAILAH
Every Night

Every night I will give thanks unto You, and praise Your name forever, yes, for ever and ever. YAHUWAH, You have been our refuge from generation to generation. I said, YAHUWAH have mercy upon me, heal my soul, for I have sinned against You.

YAHUWAH, I flee unto You for refuge, teach me to do Your will, for You are Elohai (my God). For with You is the fountain of life, and in Your light shall we see light. Continue Your mercy upon those that know You. Vouchsafe, YAHUWAH, to keep us this night without sin. Blessed are You, YAHUWAH, God of our fathers, and praised and glorified is Your name for ever. Amen.

Let Your Mercy

YAHUWAH, let Your mercy be upon us, as we have set our hope on You. Blessed are You, YAHUWAH: teach me Your chukot (statutes). Blessed are You, O Master: make me to understand Your mitzvot (commandments). Blessed are You, O Kadosh (Holy One): enlighten me with Your mishpatiym (judgements). YAHUWAH, Your chesed (mercy) endures for ever: O despise not the works of Your hands. To You belongs praise, to You belongs hymns, to You belongs glory. To the Father YAHUWAH, and to the Son Yah'shua (Jesus), and to the Ruach HaKodesh (Holy Spirit), now and ever, and unto the ages of ages. Amen.

SHELICHIYM HA'EMUNA
(The Apostles Creed)

I believe in YAHUWAH our Elohim (God), the Avi Shaddai (Father almighty), Bore (Creator) of heaven and earth, and in Yah'shua the Messiah (Jesus Christ), his only-begotten Son, our Adon (Lord), who was conceived by the Ruach HaKodesh (Holy Spirit), born of the Virgin Miriam (Mary), suffered under Pontius Pilate, was crucified, died and was buried; he descended into hell; on the third day he rose again from the dead; he ascended into heaven, and is seated at the right hand of Elohim (God) the Avi SHaddai (Father almighty); from there he will come to judge the living and the dead. I believe in the Ruach HaKodesh (Holy Spirit), the holy (set apart) Apostolic Universal Church, the Chavarut Ha-Kadoshiym (communion of saints), the forgiveness of sins, the resurrection of the body, and life everlasting. Amen.

Ma'ariv Avarim
(Who brings on Evening)

Blessed are you YAHUWAH our Elohim (God), Melek Ha-Olam (King of the Universe), the God and the Father of our Lord Yah'shua the Messiah (Jesus Christ), who forms the light and creates darkness, who makes peace and creates everything; who in mercy gives light to the earth and to those who dwell upon it, and in Your goodness renews day by day, and continually, the works of creation. Blessed be YAHUWAH our Elohim (God) for the glory of His handiworks, and for the light-giving lights which He has made for his praise, Selah! Blessed be YAHUWAH who formed the lights!"

Yom Rishon (1ˢᵗ Day) Sunday

Psalm 104

1 Bless YAHUWAH, O my soul! YAHUWAH Elohai (my God), You are very great: You are clothed with honor and majesty, 2 Who cover Yourself with light as with a garment, Who stretch out the heavens like a curtain. 3 He lays the beams of His upper chambers in the waters, Who makes the clouds His chariot, Who walks on the wings of the wind, 4 Who makes His Mal'akiym (angels) Ruchot (spirits), His sharatiym (ministers) a eish lohet (flame of fire). 5 You who laid the foundations of the earth, so that it should not be moved forever, 6 You covered it with the deep as with a garment; The waters stood above the mountains. 7 At Your rebuke they fled; At the voice of Your thunder they hastened away. 8 They went up over the mountains; They went down into the valleys, to the place which You founded for them. 9 You have set a boundary that they may not pass over, that they may not return to cover the earth. 10 He sends the springs into the valleys; They flow among the hills. 11 They give drink to every beast of the field; The wild donkeys quench their thirst. 12 By them the birds of the heavens have their home; They sing among the branches. 13 He waters the hills from His upper chambers; The earth is satisfied with the fruit of Your works. 14 He causes the grass to grow for the cattle, and vegetation for the service of man, that he may bring forth food from the earth, 15 And yayin (wine) that makes glad the heart of man, shemen (oil) to make his face shine, and lechem (bread) which strengthens man's heart. 16 The trees of YAHUWAH are full of sap, the cedars of Lebanon which He planted, 17 Where the birds make their nests; The stork has

her home in the fir trees. 18 The high hills are for the wild goats; The cliffs are a refuge for the rock badgers. 19 He appointed the moon for seasons; The sun knows its going down. 20 You make darkness, and it is night, in which all the beasts of the forest creep about. 21 The young lions roar after their prey, and seek their food from El (God). 22 When the sun rises, they gather together and lie down in their dens. 23 Man goes out to his work and to his labor until the evening. 24 YAHUWAH, how manifold are Your works! In wisdom You have made them all. The earth is full of Your possessions; 25 This great and wide sea, in which are innumerable teeming things, chayot (living things) both small and great. 26 There the ships sail about; There is that Livyatan (Leviathan) which You have made to play there. 27 These all wait for You, that You may give them their food in due season. 28 What You give them they gather in; You open Your hand, they are filled with good. 29 You hide Your face, they are troubled; You take away their breath, they die and return to their dust. 30 You send forth Your Ruach (Spirit), they are created; And You renew the face of the earth. 31 May the glory of YAHUWAH endure forever; May YAHUWAH rejoice in His works. 32 He looks on the earth, and it trembles; He touches the hills, and they smoke. 33 I will sing to YAHUWAH as long as I live; I will sing praise to Elohai (my God) while I have my being. 34 May my meditation be sweet to Him; I will be glad in YAHUWAH. 35 May chataiym (sinners) be consumed from the earth, and the rasha'iym (wicked) be no more. Bless YAHUWAH, O my soul! Halelu Yah (Praise YAHUWAH)!

Psalm 105

1 Oh, give thanks to YAHUWAH! Call upon His name; Make known His deeds among the peoples! 2 Sing to Him, sing psalms to Him; Talk of all His wondrous works! 3 Glory in His Shem Kadosh (holy name); Let the hearts of those rejoice who

seek YAHUWAH! 4 Seek YAHUWAH and His strength; Seek His face evermore! 5 Remember His marvelous works which He has done, His mophet'iym (wonders), and the mishpatiym (judgments) of His mouth, 6 O seed of Abraham His servant, You children of Jacob, His Bachiyr'iym (chosen ones)! 7 He is YAHUWAH our Elohim (God); His mishpatiym (judgments) are in all the earth. 8 He remembers His covenant forever, the word which He commanded, for a thousand generations, 9 The covenant which He made with Abraham, and His oath to Isaac, 10 And confirmed it to Jacob for a chok (statute), to Israel as a brit olam (everlasting covenant), 11 Saying, "To you I will give the land of Canaan as the allotment of your inheritance," 12 When they were few in number, Indeed very few, and strangers in it. 13 When they went from one nation to another, from one kingdom to another people, 14 He permitted no one to do them wrong; Yes, He rebuked melakiym (kings) for their sakes, 15 Saying, "Do not touch My mashiyach'iym (anointed ones), and do My navi'iym (prophets) no harm." 16 Moreover He called for a ra'av (famine) in the land; He destroyed all the provision of bread. 17 He sent a man before them, Joseph, who was sold as a slave. 18 They hurt his feet with fetters, he was laid in irons. 19 Until the time that his word came to pass, the word of YAHUWAH tested him. 20 The king sent and released him, the ruler of the people let him go free. 21 He made him lord of his house, and ruler of all his possessions, 22 To bind his princes at his pleasure, and teach his elders wisdom. 23 Israel also came into Egypt, and Jacob dwelt in the land of Ham. 24 He increased His people greatly, and made them stronger than their tsar'iym (adversaries). 25 He turned their heart to hate His people, to deal craftily with His servants. 26 He sent Moses His servant, And Aaron whom He had chosen. 27 They performed His Otot (signs) among them, and mophet'iym (wonders) in the land of Ham. 28 He sent choshek (darkness), and made it chashak (dark); And they did not rebel against

His word. 29 He turned their waters into blood, and killed their fish. 30 Their land abounded with frogs, even in the chambers of their kings. 31 He spoke, and there came swarms of flies, and lice in all their territory. 32 He gave them hail for rain, and flaming fire in their land. 33 He struck their vines also, and their fig trees, and splintered the trees of their territory. 34 He spoke, and locusts came, young locusts without number, 35 And ate up all the vegetation in their land, and devoured the fruit of their ground. 36 He also destroyed all the firstborn in their land, the first of all their strength. 37 He also brought them out with silver and gold, and there was none feeble among His tribes. 38 Egypt was glad when they departed, for the fear of them had fallen upon them. 39 He spread a cloud for a covering, and fire to give light in the night. 40 The people asked, and He brought quail, and satisfied them with the bread of heaven. 41 He opened the rock, and water gushed out; It ran in the dry places like a river. 42 For He remembered His holy promise, and Abraham His servant. 43 He brought out His people with joy, His Bachiyr'iym (chosen ones) with gladness. 44 He gave them the lands of the goyim (Gentiles, heathens), and they inherited the labor of the leumiym (nations), 45 That they might observe His chuqot (statutes) and keep His torot (laws). Halelu-Yah (Praise YAHUWAH)!

Psalm 106

1 Halelu-Yah (Praise the Lord)! Oh, give thanks to YAHUWAH, for He is good! For His chesed (mercy) endures forever. 2 Who can utter the gevurot (mighty acts) of YAHUWAH? Who can declare all His praise? 3 Blessed are those who keep mishpat (judgment), and he who does tsedakah (righteousness) at all times! 4 Remember me, YAHUWAH, with the favor You have toward Your people. Oh, visit me with Your salvation, 5 That I may see the benefit of Your

bachiyr'iym (chosen ones), that I may rejoice in the gladness of Your goy (nation), that I may glory with Your inheritance. 6 We have chata'iym (sinned) with our fathers, we have aviyniym (committed iniquity), we have done rasha'iym (wickedly). 7 Our fathers in Egypt did not understand Your pele (wonders); They did not remember the rav chesediym (multitude of Your mercies), but rebelled by the sea—the Red Sea. 8 Nevertheless He saved them for His name's sake, that He might make His gevurat (mighty power) known. 9 He rebuked the Red Sea also, and it dried up; So He led them through the depths, as through the wilderness. 10 He saved them from the hand of him who hated them, and redeemed them from the yad oyev (hand of the enemy). 11 The waters covered their tsariym (adversaries); There was not one of them left. 12 Then they believed His words; They sang His praise. 13 They soon forgot His works; They did not wait for His counsel, 14 But lusted exceedingly in the wilderness, And tested El (God) in the desert. 15 And He gave them their request, but sent leanness into their soul. 16 When they envied Moses in the camp, and Aaron the Kadosh (saint, Holy one) of YAHUWAH, 17 The earth opened up and swallowed Dathan, and covered the faction of Abiram. 18 A fire was kindled in their company; The flame burned up the rasha'iym (wicked). 19 They made a calf in Horeb, and worshiped the masekah (molded image). 20 Thus they changed their glory into the image of an ox that eats grass. 21 They forgot El (God) their Savior, Who had done gadolot (great things) in Egypt, 22 Nipla'ot (Wondrous works) in the land of Ham, nora'ot (awesome things) by the Red Sea. 23 Therefore He said that He would destroy them, had not Moses His chosen one stood before Him in the breach, to turn away His wrath, lest He destroy them. 24 Then they despised the pleasant land; They did not believe His word, 25 But ragan (complained) in their tents, and did not heed the voice of YAHUWAH. 26 Therefore He raised His hand in an oath against them, to overthrow them in the wilderness, 27 To overthrow their seed among the goyim (nations, gentiles), and to scatter them in the lands. 28 They joined themselves also to Baal of Peor, and ate zivchei metiym (sacrifices made to the dead). 29 Thus they provoked Him to anger with their deeds, and the magephah (plague) broke out among them. 30 Then Phinehas stood up and intervened, and the magephah (plague) was stopped. 31 And that was accounted to him for tsedakah (righteousness) to all generations forevermore. 32 They angered Him also at the mey meribah (waters of strife), so that it went ill with Moses on account of them; 33 Because they rebelled against His Ruach (Spirit), so that he spoke rashly with his lips. 34 They did not destroy the peoples, concerning whom YAHUWAH had commanded them, 35 But they mingled with the goyim (Gentiles, nations) and learned their ma'aseh'iym (works); 36 They served their atsabim (idols), which became a snare to them. 37 They even zavach (sacrificed) their sons and their daughters to shediym (demons), 38 And shed dam nakiy (innocent blood), the blood of their sons and daughters, whom they zavach (sacrificed) to the atsabim (idols) of Canaan; and the land was polluted with blood. 39 Thus they were defiled by their own works, and played the zonah (harlot) by their own deeds. 40 Therefore the wrath of YAHUWAH was kindled against His people, so that He abhorred His own inheritance. 41 And He gave them into the hand of the goyim (Gentiles), and those who hated them ruled over them. 42 Their oyev'iym (enemies) also oppressed them, and they were brought into subjection under their hand. 43 Many times He delivered them; But they marah (rebelled) in their etsah (counsel), and were makak (brought low) for their avon (iniquity). 44 Nevertheless He regarded their affliction, when He heard their cry; 45 And for their sake He remembered His covenant, and relented according to the rav chesediym (multitude of His mercies). 46 He also made them to be pitied by all those

243

who carried them away captive. 47 Save us, YAHUWAH our Elohim (God), and gather us from among the goyim (Gentiles, nations), to give thanks to Your Shem Kadosh (holy name), to triumph in Your praise. 48 Blessed be YAHUWAH, the Elohim (God) of Israel from everlasting to everlasting! And let all the people say, "Amen!" Halelu-Yah (Praise the Lord)!

Yom Sheni (2nd Day) Monday

Psalm 107

1 Oh, give thanks to YAHUWAH, for He is good! For His chesed (mercy) endures forever. 2 Let the redeemed of YAHUWAH say so, whom He has redeemed from the hand of the tsar (adversary), 3 And gathered out of the lands, from the east and from the west, from the north and from the south. 4 They wandered in the wilderness in a desolate way; They found no city to dwell in. 5 Hungry and thirsty, their soul fainted in them. 6 Then they cried out to YAHUWAH in their batsar (trouble), and He delivered them out of their metsukah (distresses). 7 And He led them forth by the right way, that they might go to a city for a dwelling place. 8 Oh, that men would give thanks to YAHUWAH for His chesed (mercy, goodness), and for His nipla'ot (wonderful works) to the children of men!

9 For He satisfies the longing soul, and fills the hungry soul with tov (goodness). 10 Those who sat in choshek (darkness) and in the tsalmavet (shadow of death), asiyr (bound) in oniy (affliction) and barzel (irons); 11 Because they rebelled against the words of El (God), and despised the counsel of Elyon (the Most High), 12 Therefore He brought down their heart with labor; They fell down, and there was none to help. 13 Then they cried out to YAHUWAH in their batsar (trouble), nd He saved them out of their metsukah (distresses). 14 He brought them out of choshek (darkness) and the tsalmavet (shadow of death), and broke their moser'iym (chains) in pieces. 15 Oh, that men would give thanks to YAHUWAH for His chesed (mercy, goodness), and for His nipla'ot (wonderful works) to the children of men!

245

16 For He has broken the gates of bronze, and cut the bars of iron in two. 17 Eviyl'iym (Fools), because of their pesha'iym (transgression), and because of their avonot (iniquities), are yit'anu (afflicted). 18 Their soul abhors all manner of food, and they drew near to the sha'arei mavet (gates of death). 19 Then they cried out to YAHUWAH in their batsar (trouble), and He saved them out of their metsukah (distresses). 20 He sent His davar (word) and healed them, and delivered them from their shechit'iym (destructions; pit). 21 Oh, that men would give thanks to YAHUWAH for His chesed (mercy, goodness), and for His nipla'ot (wonderful works) to the children of men! 22 Let them zabach (sacrifice) the zevach todah (sacrifices of thanksgiving), and declare His works with rejoicing.

23 Those who go down to the sea in ships, who do business on great waters, 24 They see the works of YAHUWAH, and His wonders in the deep. 25For He commands and raises the stormy wind, Which lifts up the waves of the sea. 26 They mount up to the heavens, they go down again to the depths; Their soul melts because of trouble. 27 They reel to and fro, and stagger like a drunken man, and are at their wits' end. 28 Then they cry out to YAHUWAH in their batsar (trouble), and He brings them out of their metsukah (distresses). 29 He calms the storm, so that its waves are still. 30 Then they are glad because they are quiet; So He guides them to their desired haven. 31 Oh, that men would give thanks to YAHUWAH for His chesed (mercy, goodness), and for His nipla'ot (wonderful works) to the children of men! 32 Let them exalt Him also in the kehal am (assembly of the people), and praise Him in the moshav zeken'iym (company of the elders).

33He turns rivers into a wilderness, and the watersprings into dry ground; 34 A fruitful land into barrenness, for the ra'at (wickedness) of those who dwell in it. 35 He turns a wilderness into pools of water, and dry land into watersprings. 36 There He makes the hungry dwell, that they may establish a city for a dwelling place, 37 And sow fields and plant vineyards, that they may yield a fruitful harvest. 38 He also blesses them, and they multiply greatly; And He does not let their cattle decrease. 39 When they are diminished and brought low through otser (oppression), ra'ah (affliction, evil), and yagon (sorrow), 40 He pours buz (contempt) on nadiyv'iym (nobles, princes), and causes them to wander in the wilderness where there is no way; 41 Yet He sets the evyon (needy) on high, far from oniy (affliction), and makes their families like a flock. 42 The yashar'iym (upright) see it and rejoice, and all avlah (unrighteousness) stops its mouth. 43 Whoever is chakam (wise) will observe these things, and they will understand the chesed (mercy, lovingkindness) of YAHUWAH.

Psalm 108

1 A Song. A Psalm of David. O Elohim (God), my heart is steadfast; I will sing and give praise, even with my glory. 2 Awake, lute and harp! I will awaken the dawn. 3 I will praise You, YAHUWAH, among the peoples, and I will sing praises to You among the umiym (nations). 4 For Your chesed (mercy) is great above the heavens, and Your emet (truth) reaches to the clouds. 5 Be exalted, O Elohim (God), above the heavens, and Your glory above all the earth; 6 That Your yediyd (beloved) may be delivered, save with Your right hand, and hear me. 7 Elohim (God) has spoken in His kadosh (holiness): "I will rejoice; I will divide Shechem and measure out the Valley of Succoth. 8 Gilead is Mine; Manasseh is Mine; Ephraim also is the helmet for My head; Judah is My lawgiver. 9 Moab is My washpot; Over Edom I will cast My shoe; Over Philistia I will triumph." 10 Who will bring me into the strong

city? Who will lead me to Edom? 11 Is it not You, O Elohim (God), who cast us off? And You, O Elohim (God), who did not go out with our armies? 12 Give us help from trouble, for the teshu'ah adam (help of man) is shav (useless). 13 Through Elohim (God) we will do valiantly, for it is He who shall tread down our tsar'iym (adversaries).

Psalm 109

1 To the Chief Musician. A Psalm of David. Do not keep silent, O Elohim (God) of my praise! 2 For the mouth of the rasha (wicked) and the mouth of the mirmah (deceitful) have opened against me; They have spoken against me with a lashon sheker (lying tongue). 3 They have also surrounded me with words of hatred, and fought against me without a cause. 4 In return for my ahava (love) they are my satanei (accusers, opposers), but I give myself to tefillah (prayer). 5 Thus they have rewarded me ra (evil) for tov (good), and sinah (hatred) for my ahava (love). 6 Set a rasha (wicked man) over him, and let Satan (the devil) stand at his right hand. 7 When he is shafat (judged), let him yetse rasha (go to the wicked), and let his tefillot (prayer) become chata'ah (sin). 8 Let his days be few, and let another take his pekudah (office). 9 Let his children be yatomiym (fatherless, orphans), and his wife an almanah (widow). 10 Let his children continually be vagabonds, and beg; Let them seek their bread also from their desolate places. 11 Let the nosheh (creditor) seize all that he has, and let zar'iym (strangers) plunder his labor. 12 Let there be none to extend chesed (mercy) to him, nor let there be any to favor his yatom'iym (fatherless children). 13 Let his posterity be cut off, and in the generation following let their name be blotted out. 14 Let the avon (iniquity) of his fathers be remembered before YAHUWAH, and let not the chatat (sin) of his mother be blotted out. 15 Let them be continually before YAHUWAH, that He may cut

off the memory of them from the earth; 16 Because he did not zakar asot chesed (remember to show mercy), but radaph iysh aniy va'evyon (persecuted the poor and needy man), that he might even slay the nik'eh levav (broken in heart). 17 As he loved kelalah (cursing, execration), so let it come to him; As he did not delight in berakah (blessing), so let it be far from him. 18 As he clothed himself with kelalah (cursing) as with his garment, so let it enter his kerev (bowels) like mayim (water), and like shemen (oil) into his etsem'ot (bones). 19 Let it be to him like the garment which covers him, and for a belt with which he girds himself continually. 20 Let this be YAHUWAH's pe'ulat (reward) to sotanei (my accusers), and to those who devariym ra (speak evil) against my person.

21 But You, O YAHUWAH Adonai (GOD the Lord), deal with me for Your name's sake; Because Your chesed (mercy) is tov (good), deliver me. 22 For I am aniy (poor) and evyon (needy), and my heart is wounded within me. 23 I am gone like a shadow when it lengthens; I am shaken off like a locust. 24 My knees are weak through tsom (fasting), and my flesh is feeble from lack of shemen (fatness). 25 I also have become a reproach to them; When they look at me, they shake their heads. 26 Help me, YAHUWAH my Elohim (God)! Oh, save me according to Your chesed (mercy), 27 That they may know that this is Your hand; That You, YAHUWAH, have done it! 28 Let them kalal (curse), but You barak (bless); When they arise, let them be ashamed, but let Your servant rejoice. 29 Let satanei (my accusers) be clothed with boshet (shame), and let them cover themselves with their own kelimah (disgrace) as with a mantle. 30 I will greatly praise YAHUWAH with my mouth; Yes, I will praise Him among the multitude. 31 For He shall stand at the right hand of the evyon (needy), to save him from those who condemn him.

Psalm 110

1 A Psalm of David. YAHUWAH said to Adonai (my Lord), "Sit at My right hand, till I make Your oyev'iym (enemies) Your footstool." 2 YAHUWAH shall send the rod of Your strength out of Zion. Rule in the midst of Your oyev'iym (enemies)! 3 Your people shall be nedavot (volunteers, willing) in the day of Your chayil (power); In the hadrei Kodesh (beauties of holiness), from the womb of the morning, You have the dew of Your youth. 4 YAHUWAH has sworn and will not relent, "You are a Kohen le'olam (Priest forever) al-dibratiy Malkiy-Tsedek (according to the order of Melchizedek [the King of Righteousness])." 5 Adonai (the Lord) is at Your right hand; He shall execute kings in the day of His wrath. 6 He shall judge among the goyim (nations, gentiles), He shall fill the places with geviyot (dead bodies), He shall execute the heads of many countries. 7 He shall drink of the brook by the wayside; Therefore He shall lift up the head.

Psalm 111

1 Halelu-Yah (Praise YAHUWAH)! I will praise YAHUWAH with my whole heart, in the sod-yashariym (assembly of the upright) and in the edah (congregation). 2 The ma'aseh (works) of YAHUWAH are Gadol'iym (great), darash'iym (sought, studied, investigated) by all who have pleasure in them. 3 His work is honorable and glorious, and His tsedakah (righteousness) endures forever. 4 He has made His wonderful works to be remembered; YAHUWAH is chanun (gracious) and rachum (full of compassion). 5 He has given food to those who fear Him; He will ever be mindful of His covenant. 6 He has declared to His people the power of His works, in giving them the heritage of the goyim (nations, gentiles, heathens). 7 The works of His hands are emet (truth) and mishpat (judgment); All His pikudiym (precepts) are

sure. 8 They stand fast forever and ever, and are done in emet (truth(and yashar (uprightness). 9 He has sent redemption to His people; He has commanded His covenant forever: Kadosh (Holy) and Nora (awesome) is His Shem (name). 10 The fear of YAHUWAH is the beginning of chokmah (wisdom); A good understanding have all those who do His mitzvot (commandments). His praise endures forever.

Psalm 112

1 Halelu-Yah (Praise YAHUWAH)! Blessed is the man who fears YAHUWAH, who delights greatly in His mitzvot (commandments). 2 His seed will be mighty on earth; The generation of the yashariym (upright) will be blessed. 3 Wealth and riches will be in his house, and his tsedakah (righteousness) endures forever. 4 Unto the yashar'iym (upright) there arises light in the darkness; He is chanun (gracious), and rachum (full of compassion), and tsadiyk (righteous). 5 A tov iysh (good man) chonen (deals graciously, shows favor) and malveh (lends); He will guide his affairs with discretion. 6 Surely he will never be shaken; The tsadiyk (righteous) will be in zeker olam (everlasting remembrance). 7 He will not be afraid shemu'ah ra'ah (of evil tidings); His heart is steadfast, batach (trusting, being bold) in YAHUWAH. 8 His heart is established; He will not be afraid, until he sees his desire upon his tsar'iym (enemies). 9 He has dispersed abroad, He has given to the evyon'iym (needy); His tsedakah (righteousness) endures forever; His horn will be exalted with honor. 10 The rasha (wicked) will see it and be grieved; He will gnash his teeth and melt away; The ta'avot rasha'iym (desire of the wicked) shall perish.

Yom Shlishi (3rd Day) Tuesday

Psalm 113

1 Halelu-Yah (Praise the Lord)! Praise, O servants of YAHUWAH, Praise the name of YAHUWAH! 2 Blessed be the name of YAHUWAH from this time forth and forevermore! 3 From the rising of the sun to its going down YAHUWAH's name is to be praised. 4 YAHUWAH is high above all goyim (nations), His glory above the heavens. 5 Who is like YAHUWAH our Elohim (God), Who dwells on high, 6 Who humbles Himself to behold the things that are in the heavens and in the earth? 7 He raises the dal (poor, lowly) out of the dust, and lifts the evyon (needy) out of the ash heap, 8 That He may seat him with princes, with the princes of His people. 9 He grants the akaret (barren woman) a home, like a joyful mother of children. Halelu-Yah (Praise the Lord)!

Psalm 114

1 When Israel went out of Egypt, the house of Jacob from a people of strange language, 2 Judah became His kadosh (holy place, sanctuary), and Israel His dominion. 3 The sea saw it and fled; Jordan turned back. 4 The mountains skipped like rams, the little hills like lambs. 5 What ails you, O sea, that you fled? O Jordan, that you turned back? 6 O mountains, that you skipped like rams? O little hills, like lambs? 7 Tremble, O earth, at the presence of Adon (the Lord), at the presence of the Eloah (God) of Jacob, 8 Who turned the rock into a pool of water, the flint into a fountain of waters.

Psalm 115

1 Not unto us, YAHUWAH, not unto us, but to Your name give glory, because of Your chesed (mercy), because of Your emet (truth). 2 Why should the goyim (Gentiles, heathens) say, "So where is their Elohim (God)?" 3 But our Elohim (God) is in heaven; He does whatever He pleases. 4 Their atsabiym (idols) are silver and gold, the work of men's hands. 5 They have mouths, but they do not speak; Eyes they have, but they do not see; 6 They have ears, but they do not hear; Noses they have, but they do not smell; 7 They have hands, but they do not handle; Feet they have, but they do not walk; Nor do they mutter through their throat. 8 Those who make them are like them; So is everyone who trusts in them. 9 O Israel, trust in YAHUWAH; He is their help and their shield. 10 O house of Aaron, batach (trust) in YAHUWAH; He is their help and their shield. 11 You who fear YAHUWAH, batach (trust) in YAHUWAH; He is their help and their shield. 12 YAHUWAH has been mindful of us; He will bless us; He will bless the house of Israel; He will bless the house of Aaron. 13 He will bless those who fear YAHUWAH, both small and great. 14 May YAHUWAH give you increase more and more, you and your children. 15 May you be blessed by YAHUWAH, who made heaven and earth. 16 The heaven, even the heavens, are YAHUWAH's; But the earth He has given to the children of men. 17 The metiym (dead) do not praise Yah, nor any who go down into dumah (silence). 18 But we will bless Yah, from this time forth and forevermore. Halelu-Yah (Praise the Lord)!

Psalm 116

1 I love YAHUWAH, because He has heard my voice and my supplications. 2 Because He has inclined His ear to me, therefore I will call upon Him as long as I live. 3 The chevlei

mavet (pains of death) surrounded me, and the pangs of Sheol (Hades, the grave, the underworld) laid hold of me; I found tsarah (trouble) and yagon (sorrow). 4 Then I called upon the name of YAHUWAH: "YAHUWAH, I implore You, deliver my soul!" 5 Chanun (Gracious) is YAHUWAH, and tsadiyk (righteous); Yes, our Elohim (God) is racham (merciful). 6 YAHUWAH preserves the simple; I was brought low, and He saved me. 7 Return to your rest, O my soul, for YAHUWAH has dealt bountifully with you. 8 For You have delivered my soul from mavet (death), my eyes from tears, and my feet from falling. 9 I will walk before YAHUWAH in the artsot hachayim (land of the living). 10 I believed, therefore I spoke, "I am aniy me'od (greatly afflicted)." 11 I said in my haste, "All men are kozev (liars)." 12 What shall I render to YAHUWAH for all His tagmuwl'iym (benefits) toward me? 13 I will take up the Kos Yeshu'ot (cup of salvation), and call upon the name of YAHUWAH. 14 I will pay my neder'iym (vows) to YAHUWAH now in the presence of all His people. 15 Precious in the sight of YAHUWAH is the mavet (death) of His kadoshiym (holy ones, saints, set apart ones). 16 YAHUWAH, truly I am Your servant; I am Your servant, the son of Your maidservant; You have loosed my bonds. 17 I will offer to You the zevavh todah (sacrifice of thanksgiving), and will call upon the name of YAHUWAH. 18 I will pay my neder'iym (vows) to YAHUWAH now in the presence of all His people, 19 In the courts of YAHUWAH's house, in the midst of you, O Jerusalem. Halelu-Yah (Praise the Lord)!

Psalm 117

1 Praise YAHUWAH, all you goyim (Gentiles, nations)! Laud Him, all you peoples! 2 For His chesed (mercy) is great toward us, and the emet (truth) of YAHUWAH endures forever. Halelu-Yah (Praise the Lord)!

Psalm 118

1 Oh, give thanks to YAHUWAH, for He is tov (good)! For His chesed (mercy) endures forever. 2 Let Israel now say, "His chesed (mercy) endures forever." 3 Let the house of Aaron now say, "His chesed (mercy) endures forever." 4 Let those who fear YAHUWAH now say, "His chesed (mercy) endures forever." 5 I called on Yah in metsar (distress); And Yah answered me and set me in a broad place. 6 YAHUWAH is on my side; I will not fear. What can man do to me? 7 YAHUWAH is for me among those who help me; Therefore I shall see my desire on those who hate me. 8 It is better to chasah (trust, hope) in YAHUWAH than to put batach (trust, confidence) in adam (man, human beings, mankind). 9 It is better to chasah (trust, hope) in YAHUWAH than to put batach (trust, confidence) in princes. 10 All goyim (nations) surrounded me, but in the name of YAHUWAH I will destroy them. 11 They surrounded me, Yes, they surrounded me; But in the name of YAHUWAH I will destroy them. 12 They surrounded me like bees; They were quenched like a fire of thorns; For in the name of YAHUWAH I will destroy them. 13 You pushed me violently, that I might fall, but YAHUWAH helped me. 14 Yah is my strength and song, and He has become my yeshua (salvation). 15 The voice of rejoicing and salvation is in the tents of the tsadiykiym (righteous); The right hand of YAHUWAH does valiantly. 16 The right hand of YAHUWAH is exalted; The right hand of YAHUWAH does valiantly. 17 I shall not die, but live, and declare the works of Yah. 18 Yah has chastened me severely, but He has not given me over to mavet (death). 19 Open to me the sha'arei tsedek (gates of righteousness); I will go through them, and I will praise Yah. 20 This is the Sha'ar la'YAHUWAH (gate of the Lord), through which the tsadiykiym (righteous) shall enter. 21 I will praise You, for You have answered me, and have become my yeshua

(salvation). 22 The stone which the builders rejected has become the chief cornerstone. 23 This was YAHUWAH's doing; It is marvelous in our eyes. 24 This is the day YAHUWAH has made; We will rejoice and be glad in it. 25 Save now, I pray, YAHUWAH; YAHUWAH, I pray, send now tsaleach (prosperity). 26 Blessed is he who comes in the name of YAHUWAH! We have blessed you from the house of YAHUWAH. 27 El (God) is YAHUWAH, and He has given us light; Bind the sacrifice with cords to the horns of the altar. 28 You are Eli (my God), and I will praise You; You are Elohai (my God), I will exalt You. 29 Oh, give thanks to YAHUWAH, for He is good! For His chesed (mercy) endures forever.

Yom Re'vi'i (4ᵗʰ Day) Wednesday

Psalm 119

ALEPH

1 Blessed are the tamiym'iym derek (undefiled in the way), who walk in the Torah YAHUWAH (Law of the Lord)! 2 Blessed are those who keep His edot (testimonies), who seek Him with the kol-lev (whole heart)! 3 They also do no avlah (unrighteousness, iniquity); They derek halakah (walk in His ways). 4 You have commanded us to shamar (keep) Your pikkudiym (precepts) me'od (diligently). 5 Oh, that my ways were directed to keep Your chukot (statutes)! 6 Then I would not be ashamed, when I look into all Your mitzvot (commandments). 7 I will praise You with yosher levav (uprightness of heart), when I learn Your mishpatiym tsedek (righteous judgments). 8 I will keep Your chukot (statutes); Oh, do not forsake me utterly!

BETH

9 How can a young man zakah (cleanse) his orach (way of living)? By taking heed according to Your davar (word). 10 With my kol levav (whole heart) I have sought You; Oh, let me not wander from Your mitzvot (commandments)! 11 Your word I have hidden in my heart, that I might not chata (sin) against You. 12 Blessed are You, YAHUWAH! Teach me Your chukot (statutes). 13 With my lips I have declared all the mishpat'iym (judgments) of Your mouth. 14 I have rejoiced in the derek (way) of Your edot (testimonies), as much as in all riches. 15 I will siyach (meditate) on Your pikudiym

(precepts), and nabat (contemplate) Your orachot (ways of life). 16 I will delight myself in Your chukot (statutes); I will not forget Your davar (word).

GIMEL

17 Deal bountifully with Your servant, that I may chayah (live) and keep Your davar (word). 18 Open my eyes, that I may see nipla'ot (wondrous things) from Your torah (law). 19 I am a ger (stranger) in the earth; Do not hide Your mitzvot (commandments) from me. 20 My soul breaks with longing for Your mishpatiym (judgments) at all times. 21 You rebuke the zediym (proud, presumptuous, arrogant, insolent) - the arur'iym (cursed), who stray from Your mitzvot (commandments). 22 Remove from me cherphah (reproach) and buz (contempt), for I have kept Your edot (testimonies). 23 Sar'iym (Princes) also sit and speak against me, but Your servant siyach (meditates) on Your chuk'iym (statutes). 24 Your edot (testimonies) also are my sha'shua (delight, enjoyment) and my counselors.

DALETH

25 My soul clings to the dust; Chayeniy (Quicken me, give me life) according to Your word. 26 I have declared my ways, and You answered me; Teach me Your chukot (statutes). 27 Make me understand the derek pikudiym (way of Your precepts); So shall I siyach (meditate) on Your nipla'ot (wonderful works). 28 My soul melts from heaviness; Strengthen me according to Your word. 29 Remove from me the derek sheker (way of lying), and grant me Your torah (law) graciously. 30 I have chosen the derek emunah (way of faith); Your mishpatiym (judgments) I have laid before me. 31 I cling to Your edot (testimonies); YAHUWAH, do not put me to

shame! 32 I will run the course of Your mitzvot (commandments), for You shall enlarge my heart.

HE

33 Teach me, YAHUWAH, the derek chukiym (way of Your statutes), and I shall keep it to the end. 34 Give me understanding, and I shall keep Your torah (law); Indeed, I shall observe it with my kol-lev (whole heart). 35 Make me walk in the path of Your mitzvot (commandments), for I delight in it. 36 Incline my heart to Your edot (testimonies), and not to betsa (covetousness). 37 Turn away my einiym (eyes) from looking at shav (emptiness, vanity, falsehood, worthless things), and derek chayeniy (quicken me in Your way). 38 Establish Your imrah (word, speech) to Your servant, who is devoted to Your fear. 39 Turn away my reproach which I dread, for Your mishpatiym toviym (judgments are good). 40 Behold, I long for Your pikudiym (precepts); Chayeniy (Quicken me) in Your tsedakah (righteousness).

WAW

41 Let Your chesediym (mercies) come also to me, YAHUWAH; Your teshu'at (salvation) according to Your imrah (word). 42 So shall I have an answer for him who reproaches me, for I batach (trust) in Your davar (word). 43 And take not the devar emet (word of truth) utterly out of my mouth, for I have hoped in Your mishpatiym (judgments). 44 So shall I keep Your torah (law) continually, forever and ever. 45 And I will halakah ba'rachavah (walk at liberty), for I seek Your pikudiym (precepts). 46 I will speak of Your edot (testimonies) also before melekiym (kings), and will not be ashamed. 47 And I will delight myself in Your mitzvot (commandments), which I ahava (love). 48 My hands also I

will lift up to Your mitzvot (commandments), which I ahava (love), and I will siyach (meditate) on Your chukot (statutes).

ZAYIN

49 Remember the word to Your servant, upon which You have caused me to hope. 50 This is my comfort in my oniy (affliction), for Your imrah (word) has chiyateniy (quickened me, given me life). 51 The zediym (proud) have me in great derision, yet I do not turn aside from Your torah (law). 52 I remembered Your mishpatiym (judgments) of old, YAHUWAH, and have comforted myself. 53 Zal'aphah (Indignation) has taken hold of me because of the rasha'iym (wicked), who azav (forsake, loose, leave behind, depart from) Your torah (law). 54 Your chukot (statutes) have been my songs in the house of my pilgrimage. 55 I remember Your name in the night, YAHUWAH, and I keep Your torah (law). 56 This has become mine, because I kept Your pikkudiym (precepts).

HETH

57 You are my portion, YAHUWAH; I have said that I would keep Your devariym (words). 58 I entreated Your favor with my whole heart; Be merciful to me according to Your word. 59 I thought about my ways, and turned my feet to Your edot (testimonies). 60 I made haste, and did not delay to keep Your mitzvot (commandments). 61 The chevel rasha'iym (cords of the wicked) have bound me, but I have not forgotten Your torah (law). 62 At chatsot (midnight) I will rise to give thanks to You, because of Your mishpatiym tsedek (righteous judgments). 63 I am a companion of all who fear You, and of those who keep Your pikudiym (precepts). 64 The earth, YAHUWAH, is full of Your chesed (mercy); Teach me Your chukidiym (statutes).

TETH

65 You have dealt well with Your servant, YAHUWAH, according to Your word. 66 Teach me good ta'am (judgment) and da'at (knowledge), for I believe Your mitzvot (commandments). 67 Before I was oniy (afflicted) I shagag (went astray), but now I keep Your imrah (word). 68 You are tov (good), and do tov (good); Teach me Your chukot (statutes). 69 The zediym (proud, presumpuous) have forged a sheker (lie) against me, but I will keep Your pikudiym (precepts) with my whole heart. 70 Their heart is as fat as grease, but I delight in Your torah (law). 71 It is good for me that I have been oniy (afflicted), that I may learn Your chuqiym (statutes). 72 The torah (law) of Your mouth is better to me than thousands of coins of gold and silver.

YOD

73 Your hands have made me and fashioned me; Give me understanding, that I may learn Your mitzvot (commandments). 74 Those who fear You will be glad when they see me, because I have hoped in Your word. 75 I know, YAHUWAH, that Your mishpatiym (judgments) are tsedek (righteous), and that in emunah (faithfulness) You have afflicted me. 76 Let, I pray, Your chesed (mercy) be for my comfort, according to Your word to Your servant. 77 Let Your racham (tender mercies) come to me, that I may live; For Your torah (law) is my delight. 78 Let the zediym (proud, presumpuous) be ashamed, for they treated me wrongfully with sheker (falsehood, lie); But I will siyach (meditate) on Your pikudiym (precepts). 79 Let those who fear You turn to me, those who know Your edot (testimonies). 80 Let my heart be blameless regarding Your chukot (statutes), that I may not be ashamed.

KAPH

81 My soul faints for Your salvation, but I hope in Your word. 82 My eyes fail from searching Your imrah (word), Saying, "When will You comfort me?" 83 For I have become like a wineskin in smoke, yet I do not forget Your Chukot (statutes). 84 How many are the days of Your servant? When will You execute mishpat (judgment) on those who persecute me? 85 The zediym (proud, presumptuous) have dug pits for me, which is not according to Your torah (law). 86 All Your mitzvot (commandments) are emunah (faithful); They persecute me wrongfully; Help me! 87 They almost made an end of me on earth, but I did not forsake Your pikudiym (precepts). 88 Chineniy (Quicken me, Give me life) according to Your chesed (mercy, lovingkindness), so that I may keep the edot (testimony) of Your mouth.

LAMED

89 Forever, YAHUWAH, your word is settled in heaven. 90 Your emunah (faithfulness) endures to all generations; You established the earth, and it abides. 91 They continue this day according to Your mishpatiym (judgments), for all are Your servants. 92 Unless Your torah (law) had been my sha'shua (delight), I would then have perished in my oniy (affliction). 93 I will never forget Your pikudiym (precepts), for by them You have chineniy (quickened me, given me life). 94 I am Yours, save me; For I have sought Your pikudiym (precepts). 95 The rasha'iym (wicked) wait for me to destroy me, but I will consider Your edot (testimonies). 96 I have seen the consummation of all perfection, but Your mitzvah (commandment) is exceedingly broad.

MEM

97 Oh, how I love Your torah (law)! It is my siyach (meditation) all the day. 98 You, through Your mitzvot (commandments), make me wiser than my oyev'iym (enemies); For they are ever with me. 99 I have more understanding than all my teachers, for Your edot (testimonies) are my siyach (meditation). 100 I understand more than the zekeniym (elders, ancients), because I keep Your pikudiym (precepts). 101 I have restrained my feet from every orach ra (evil way), that I may keep Your word. 102 I have not departed from Your mishpatiym (judgments), for You Yourself have taught me. 103 How sweet are Your words to my taste, sweeter than honey to my mouth! 104 Through Your pikudiym (precepts) I get understanding; Therefore I hate every orach sheker (false way).

NUN

105 Your word is a lamp to my feet and a light to my path. 106 I have sworn and confirmed That I will keep Your mishpatiym tsedek (righteous judgments). 107 I am oniy (afflicted) very much; Chayeniy (Quicken me, give me life), YAHUWAH, according to Your davar (word). 108 Accept, I pray, the nedavah (freewill offerings) of my mouth, YAHUWAH, and teach me Your mishpatiym (judgments). 109 My life is continually in my hand, Yet I do not forget Your torah (law). 110 The rasha'iym (wicked) have laid a snare for me, yet I have not strayed from Your pikudiym (precepts). 111 Your edot (testimonies) I have taken as a heritage forever, for they are the rejoicing of my heart. 112 I have inclined my heart to perform Your chukot (statutes) forever, to the very end.

SAMEK

113 I hate the Se'ephiym (double-minded, half-hearted), but I love Your torah (law). 114 You are my hiding place and my shield; I hope in Your word. 115 Depart from me, you re'iym (evildoers), for I will keep the mitzvot (commandments) of Elohai (my God)! 116 Uphold me according to Your word, that I may live; And do not let me be ashamed of my hope. 117 Hold me up, and I shall be safe, and I shall observe Your chukat (statutes) continually. 118 You reject all those who stray from Your chukat (statutes), for their tormah (deceitfulness, treachery) is sheker (a lie, falsehood). 119 You put away all the rasha (wicked) of the earth like dross; Therefore I love Your edot (testimonies). 120 My flesh trembles for fear of You, and I am afraid of Your mishpatiym (judgments).

AYIN

121 I have done mishpat (judgment) and tsedek (righteousness); Do not leave me to my ashak (oppressors). 122 Be surety for Your servant for good; Do not let the proud oppress me. 123 My eyes fail from seeking Your salvation and Your imrah tsedek (righteous word). 124 Deal with Your servant according to Your chesed (mercy), and teach me Your chukot (statutes). 125 I am Your servant; Give me understanding, that I may know Your edot (testimonies). 126 It is time for You to act, YAHUWAH, for they have made Your torah (law) void. 127 Therefore I love Your mitzvot (commandments) more than gold, yes, than fine gold! 128 Therefore all Your pikudiym (precepts) concerning all things I consider to be right; I hate every orach sheker (false way).

PE

129 Your edot (testimonies) are wonderful; Therefore my soul keeps them. 130 The entrance of Your words gives light; It gives understanding to the simple. 131 I opened my mouth and panted, for I longed for Your mitzvot (commandments). 132 Look upon me and be chanan (merciful, gracious) to me, as Your custom is toward those who love Your name. 133 Direct my steps by Your word, and let no aven (iniquity) have dominion over me. 134 Redeem me from the oppression of man, that I may keep Your pikudiym (precepts). 135 Make Your face shine upon Your servant, and teach me Your chukot (statutes). 136 Rivers of water run down from my eyes, because men do not keep Your torah (law).

TSADDE

137 Tsadiyk (Righteous) are You, YAHUWAH, and yashar (upright) are Your mishpatiym (judgments). 138 Your edot (testimonies), which You have commanded, are tsedek (righteous) and very emunah (faithful). 139 My zeal has consumed me, because my tsar'iym (adversaries) have forgotten Your words. 140 Your word is very pure; Therefore Your servant loves it. 141 I am small and despised, yet I do not forget Your pikudiym (precepts). 142 Your tsedakah (righteousness) is an tsedek olam (everlasting righteousness), and Your torah (law) is emet (truth). 143 Tsar (Trouble) and matsok (anguish) have overtaken me, yet Your mitzvot (commandments) are my sha'shua (delights). 144 The tsedek (righteousness) of Your edot (testimonies) is everlasting; Give me understanding, and I shall live.

QOPH

145 I cry out with my whole heart; Hear me, YAHUWAH! I will keep Your chukat (statutes). 146 I cry out to You; Save me, and I will keep Your edot (testimonies). 147 I rise before the dawning of the morning, and cry for help; I hope in Your word. 148 My eyes are awake through the night watches, that I may siyach (meditate) on Your word. 149 Hear my voice according to Your chesed (mercy); YAHUWAH, chayeniy (quicken me) according to Your mishpatiym (judgments). 150 They draw near who follow after zimah (mischief, wickedness); They are far from Your torah (law). 151 You are near, YAHUWAH, and all Your mitzvot (commandments) are emet (truth). 152 Concerning Your edot (testimonies), I have known of old that You have founded them forever.

RESH

153 Consider my aniy (affliction) and deliver me, for I do not forget Your torah (law). 154 Plead my cause and redeem me; chayeniy (Quicken me) according to Your word. 155 Salvation is far from the rasha'iym (wicked), for they do not seek Your chukat (statutes). 156 Great are Your rachamiym (tender mercies), YAHUWAH; chayeniy (quicken me) according to Your mishpatiym (judgments). 157 Many are my radaph (persecutors) and my tsar'iym (enemies), Yet I do not turn from Your edot (testimonies). 158 I see the bagadiym (transgressions), and am disgusted, because they do not keep Your word. 159 Consider how I love Your pikudiym (precepts); Chayeniy (Quicken me), YAHUWAH, according to Your chesed (mercy). 160 The entirety of Your davar (word) is emet (truth), and every one of Your mishpat tsedek (righteous judgments) endures forever.

SHIN

161 Princes persecute me without a cause, but my heart stands in awe of Your word. 162 I rejoice at Your word as one who finds great treasure. 163 I hate and abhor sheker (lying), but I love Your torah (law). 164 Seven times a day I praise You, because of Your mishpatiym tsedek (righteous judgments). 165 Shalom Rav (Great peace) have those who love Your torah (law), and nothing causes them to stumble. 166 YAHUWAH, I hope for Your salvation, and I do Your mitzvot (commandments). 167 My soul keeps Your edot (testimonies), and I love them exceedingly. 168 I keep Your pikudiym (precepts) and Your edot (testimonies), for all my ways are before You.

TAU

169 Let my cry come before You, YAHUWAH; Give me understanding according to Your word. 170 Let my supplication come before You; Deliver me according to Your word. 171 My lips shall utter praise, for You teach me Your chukot (statutes). 172 My tongue shall speak of Your word, for all Your mitzvot (commandments) are tsedek (righteousness). 173 Let Your hand become my help, for I have chosen Your pikudiym (precepts). 174 I long for Your salvation, YAHUWAH, and Your torah (law) is my delight. 175 Let my soul live, and it shall praise You; And let Your mishpatiym (judgments) help me. 176 I have gone astray like a lost sheep; Seek Your servant, for I do not forget Your mitzvot (commandments).

Yom Chamishi (Fifth Day) Thursday

Psalm 120

1 A Song of Ascents. In my distress I cried to YAHUWAH, And He heard me. 2 Deliver my soul, YAHUWAH, from safa sheker (lying lips) and from a lashon remiyah (deceitful tongue). 3 What shall be given to you, or what shall be done to you, you lashon remiyah (deceitful tongue)? 4 Sharp arrows of the warrior, with coals of the broom tree! 5 Woe is me, that I dwell in Meshech, that I dwell among the tents of Kedar! 6 My soul has dwelt too long with one who hates shalom (peace). 7 I am for shalom (peace); But when I speak, they are for war.

Psalm 121

1 A Song of Ascents. I will lift up my eyes to the hills, from whence comes my help? 2 My help comes from YAHUWAH, Who made heaven and earth. 3 He will not allow your foot to be moved; He who keeps you will not slumber. 4 Behold, He who keeps Israel shall neither slumber nor sleep. 5 YAHUWAH is your keeper; YAHUWAH is your shade at your right hand. 6 The sun shall not strike you by day, nor the moon by night. 7 YAHUWAH shall preserve you from all ra (evil); He shall preserve your soul. 8 YAHUWAH shall preserve your going out and your coming in from this time forth, and even forevermore.

Psalm 122

1 A Song of Ascents. Of David. I was glad when they said to me, "Let us go into the house of YAHUWAH." 2 Our feet have been standing within your gates, O Jerusalem! 3 Jerusalem is

built as a city that is compact together, 4 Where the tribes go up, the tribes of Yah, to the Testimony of Israel, to give thanks to the name of YAHUWAH. 5 For thrones are set there for mishpat (judgment), the thrones of the house of David. 6 Pray for the shalom (peace) of Jerusalem: "May they prosper who love you. 7 Shalom (Peace) be within your walls, prosperity within your palaces." 8 For the sake of my brethren and companions, I will now say, "Shalom (Peace) be within you." 9 Because of the house of YAHUWAH our Elohim (God) I will seek your tov (good).

Psalm 123

1 A Song of Ascents. Unto You I lift up my eyes, O You who dwell in the heavens. 2 Behold, as the eyes of servants look to the hand of their masters, as the eyes of a maid to the hand of her mistress, so our eyes look to YAHUWAH our Elohim (God), until He has chanan (mercy, pity) on us. 3 Have chanan (mercy, pity) on us, YAHUWAH, have chanan (mercy, pity) on us! For we are exceedingly filled with contempt. 4 Our soul is exceedingly filled with the scorn of those who are at ease, with the contempt of the proud.

Psalm 124

1 A Song of Ascents. Of David. "If it had not been YAHUWAH who was on our side," Let Israel now say:2 "If it had not been YAHUWAH who was on our side, when men rose up against us, 3 Then they would have swallowed us alive, when their wrath was kindled against us; 4 Then the waters would have overwhelmed us, the stream would have gone over our soul; 5 Then the swollen waters would have gone over our soul." 6 Blessed be YAHUWAH, Who has not given us as prey to their teeth. 7 Our soul has escaped as a bird from the snare of the fowlers; The snare is broken, and we have escaped. 8 Our

help is in the name of YAHUWAH, Who made heaven and earth.

Psalm 125

1 A Song of Ascents. Those who batach (trust, is bold in) in YAHUWAH are like Mount Zion, which cannot be moved, but abides forever. 2 As the mountains surround Jerusalem, so YAHUWAH surrounds His people from this time forth and forever. 3 For the shebet ha-resha (scepter of wickedness) shall not rest on the land allotted to the tsadiykiym (righteous), lest the tsadiykiym (righteous) reach out their hands to avalatah (iniquity). 4 Do tov (good), YAHUWAH, to those who are toviym (good), and to those who are yashariym lev (upright in their hearts). 5 As for such as turn aside to their akalkal'ot (crooked way), YAHUWAH shall lead them away with the polei aven (workers of iniquity). Shalom (Peace) be upon Israel!

Psalm 126

1 A Song of Ascents. When YAHUWAH brought back the captivity of Zion, we were like those who dream. 2 Then our mouth was filled with laughter, and our tongue with singing. Then they said among the goyim (nations, gentiles), "YAHUWAH has done great things for them." 3 YAHUWAH has done great things for us, and we are glad. 4 Bring back our captivity, YAHUWAH, as the streams in the South. 5 Those who sow in tears shall reap in joy. 6 He who continually goes forth weeping, bearing seed for sowing, shall doubtless come again with rejoicing, bringing his sheaves with him.

Psalm 127

1 A Song of Ascents. Of Solomon. Unless YAHUWAH builds the house, they labor in vain who build it; Unless YAHUWAH guards the city, the watchman stays awake in vain. 2 It is vain for you to rise up early, to sit up late, to eat the lechem ha'atsabiym (bread of sorrows); For so He gives His beloved sleep. 3 Behold, children are a heritage from YAHUWAH, the fruit of the womb is a reward. 4 Like arrows in the hand of a warrior, so are the children of one's youth. 5 Happy is the man who has his quiver full of them; They shall not be ashamed, but shall speak with their enemies in the gate.

Psalm 128

1 A Song of Ascents. Blessed is every one who fears YAHUWAH, who walks in His ways. 2 When you eat the labor of your hands, you shall be happy, and it shall be well with you. 3 Your wife shall be like a fruitful vine in the very heart of your house, your children like olive plants all around your table. 4 Behold, thus shall the man be blessed who fears YAHUWAH. 5 YAHUWAH bless you out of Zion, and may you see the good of Jerusalem all the days of your life. 6 Yes, may you see your children's children. Shalom (Peace) be upon Israel!

Psalm 129

1 Song of Ascents. "Many a time they have afflicted me from my youth," Let Israel now say - 2 "Many a time they have afflicted me from my youth; Yet they have not prevailed against me. 3 The plowers plowed on my back; They made their furrows long." 4 YAHUWAH is tsadiyk (righteous); He has cut in pieces the avot rasha'iym (cords of the wicked). 5 Let all those who hate Zion be put to shame and turned back.

271

6 Let them be as the grass on the housetops, which withers before it grows up, 7 With which the reaper does not fill his hand, nor he who binds sheaves, his arms. 8 Neither let those who pass by them say, "The blessing of YAHUWAH be upon you; We bless you in the name of YAHUWAH!"

Psalm 130

1 A Song of Ascents. Out of the depths I have cried to You, YAHUWAH; 2 Adonai (Lord), hear my voice! Let Your ears be attentive to the voice of my supplications. 3 If You, Yah, should mark avonot (iniquities), O Adonai (Lord), who could stand? 4 But there is forgiveness with You, that You may be feared. 5 I wait for YAHUWAH, my soul waits, and in His word I do hope. 6 My soul waits for Adonai (the Lord) more than those who watch for the morning; Yes, more than those who watch for the morning. 7 O Israel, hope in YAHUWAH; For with YAHUWAH there is chesed (mercy), and with Him is abundant redemption. 8 And He shall redeem Israel from all his avonot (iniquities).

Psalm 131

1 A Song of Ascents. Of David. YAHUWAH, my heart is not gavah (haughty), nor my eyes ramu (lofty). Neither do I concern myself with gadol'ot (great matters), nor with things too profound for me. 2 Surely I have calmed and quieted my soul, like a weaned child with his mother; Like a weaned child is my soul within me. 3 O Israel, hope in YAHUWAH from this time forth and forever.

Psalm 132

1 A Song of Ascents. YAHUWAH, remember David and all his afflictions; 2 How he swore to YAHUWAH, and vowed to the

Abiyr (Mighty One) of Jacob: 3 "Surely I will not go into the chamber of my house, or go up to the comfort of my bed; 4 I will not give sleep to my eyes or slumber to my eyelids, 5 Until I find a place for YAHUWAH, a dwelling place for the Abiyr (Mighty One) of Jacob." 6 Behold, we heard of it in Ephrathah; We found it in the fields of the woods. 7 Let us go into His mishkan (tabernacle); Let us worship at His footstool. 8 Arise, YAHUWAH, to Your resting place, You and the ark of Your strength. 9 Let Your Koheniym (Priests) be clothed with tsedek (righteousness), and let Your kadoshiym (holy ones, saints, set apart ones) shout for joy. 10 For Your servant David's sake, do not turn away the face of Your Mashiyach (Anointed). 11 YAHUWAH has sworn in truth to David; He will not turn from it: "I will set upon your throne the fruit of your body. 12 If your sons will keep My brit (covenant) and My edot (testimony) which I shall teach them, their sons also shall sit upon your throne forevermore." 13 For YAHUWAH has chosen Zion; He has desired it for His dwelling place: 14 "This is My resting place forever; Here I will dwell, for I have desired it. 15 I will abundantly bless her provision; I will satisfy her evyon (needy) with bread. 16 I will also clothe her Koheniym (Priests) with salvation, and her kadoshiym (holy ones, saints, set apart ones) shall shout aloud for joy. 17 There I will make the horn of David grow; I will prepare a lamp for My Mashiyach (Anointed). 18 His oyev'iym (enemies) I will clothe with shame, but upon Himself His crown shall flourish."

Yom Shishi (Sixth Day) Friday

Psalm 133

1 A Song of Ascents. Of David. Behold, how good and how pleasant it is for brethren to dwell together in unity! 2 It is like the precious shemen (oil) upon the head, running down on the beard, the beard of Aaron, running down on the edge of his garments. 3 It is like the dew of Hermon, descending upon the mountains of Zion; For there YAHUWAH commanded the blessing— Chayim ad-Ha'Olam (Life for evermore).

Psalm 134

1 A Song of Ascents.Behold, bless YAHUWAH, all you servants of YAHUWAH, who by night stand in the house of YAHUWAH! 2 Lift up your hands in the Kodesh (holy place, sanctuary), and bless YAHUWAH. 3 YAHUWAH who made heaven and earth bless you from Zion!

Psalm 135

1 Halelu-Yah (Praise the Lord)! Praise the name of YAHUWAH; Praise Him, O you servants of YAHUWAH! 2 You who stand in the house of YAHUWAH, in the courts of the house of our Elohim (God), Halelu-Yah (Praise the Lord), for YAHUWAH is good; Sing praises to His name, for it is pleasant. 4 For Yah has chosen Jacob for Himself, Israel for His special treasure. 5 For I know that YAHUWAH is great, and our Adonai (Lord) is above all elohim (gods). 6 Whatever YAHUWAH pleases He does, in heaven and in earth, in the seas and in all deep places. 7 He causes the vapors to ascend

from the ends of the earth; He makes lightning for the rain; He brings the wind out of His treasuries. 8 He destroyed the firstborn of Egypt, both of man and beast.9 He sent otot (signs) and mophet'iym (wonders) into the midst of you, O Egypt, upon Pharaoh and all his servants. 10 He defeated many goyim (nations) and slew melekiym atsumiym (mighty kings)—11 Sihon king of the Amorites, Og king of Bashan, and all the kingdoms of Canaan— 12 And gave their land as a heritage, a heritage to Israel His people. 13 Your name, YAHUWAH, endures forever, Your fame, YAHUWAH, throughout all generations. 14 For YAHUWAH will judge His people, and He will have compassion on His servants. 15 The atsabiym (idols) of the goyim (nations) are silver and gold, the work of men's hands. 16 They have mouths, but they do not speak; Eyes they have, but they do not see; 17 They have ears, but they do not hear; Nor is there any breath in their mouths. 18 Those who make them are like them; So is everyone who trusts in them. 19 Bless YAHUWAH, O house of Israel! Bless YAHUWAH, O house of Aaron! 20 Bless YAHUWAH, O house of Levi! You who fear YAHUWAH, bless YAHUWAH! 21 Blessed be YAHUWAH out of Zion, Who dwells in Jerusalem! Halelu-Yah (Praise the Lord)!

Psalm 136

1 Oh, give thanks to YAHUWAH, for He is tov (good)! For His chesed le'olam (mercy endures forever). 2 Oh, give thanks to Elohei Ha'Elohim (the God of gods)! For His chesed le'olam (mercy endures forever). 3 Oh, give thanks to the Adonei Ha'Adoniym (Lord of lords)! For His chesed le'olam (mercy endures forever): 4 To Him who alone does nipla'ot gedolot (great wonders), for His chesed le'olam (mercy endures forever); 5 To Him who by wisdom made the heavens, for His chesed le'olam (mercy endures forever); 6 To Him who laid out the earth above the waters, for His chesed le'olam (mercy

endures forever); 7 To Him who made great lights, for His chesed le'olam (mercy endures forever); 8 The sun to rule by day, for His chesed le'olam (mercy endures forever); 9 The moon and stars to rule by night, for His chesed le'olam (mercy endures forever). 10 To Him who struck Egypt in their firstborn, for His chesed le'olam (mercy endures forever); 11 And brought out Israel from among them, for His chesed le'olam (mercy endures forever); 12 With a strong hand, and with an outstretched arm, for His chesed le'olam (mercy endures forever); 13 To Him who divided the Red Sea in two, for His chesed le'olam (mercy endures forever); 14 And made Israel pass through the midst of it, for His chesed le'olam (mercy endures forever); 15 But overthrew Pharaoh and his army in the Red Sea, for His chesed le'olam (mercy endures forever); 16 To Him who led His people through the wilderness, for His chesed le'olam (mercy endures forever); 17 To Him who struck down great kings, for His chesed le'olam (mercy endures forever); 18 And slew famous kings, for His chesed le'olam (mercy endures forever); 19 Sihon king of the Amorites, for His chesed le'olam (mercy endures forever); 20 And Og king of Bashan, for His chesed le'olam (mercy endures forever); 21 And gave their land as a heritage, for His chesed le'olam (mercy endures forever); 22 A heritage to Israel His servant, for His chesed le'olam (mercy endures forever). 23 Who remembered us in our lowly state, for His chesed le'olam (mercy endures forever); 24 And rescued us from our enemies, for His chesed le'olam (mercy endures forever); 25 Who gives food to all flesh, for His chesed le'olam (mercy endures forever). 26 Oh, give thanks to the Elohim (God) of heaven! For His chesed le'olam (mercy endures forever).

Psalm 137

1 By the rivers of Babylon, there we sat down, yea, we wept when we remembered Zion. 2 We hung our harps upon the willows in the midst of it. 3 For there those who carried us away captive asked of us a song, and those who plundered us requested mirth, saying, "Sing us one of the songs of Zion!" 4 How shall we sing YAHUWAH's song in a foreign land? 5 If I forget you, O Jerusalem, let my right hand forget its skill! 6 If I do not remember you, let my tongue cling to the roof of my mouth; If I do not exalt Jerusalem above my chief joy. 7 Remember, YAHUWAH, against the sons of Edom the day of Jerusalem, Who said, "Raze it, raze it, to its very foundation!" 8 O daughter of Babylon, who are to be destroyed, happy the one who repays you as you have served us! 9 Happy the one who takes and dashes your little ones against the rock!

Psalm 138

1 A Psalm of David. I will praise You with my whole heart; Before the elohim (gods) I will sing praises to You. 2 I will worship toward Your heykal kodesh (holy temple), and praise Your name for Your chesed (mercy) and Your emet (truth); For You have magnified Your word above all Your name. 3 In the day when I cried out, You answered me, and made me bold with strength in my soul. 4 All the kings of the earth shall praise You, YAHUWAH, when they hear the words of Your mouth. 5 Yes, they shall sing of the ways of YAHUWAH, for great is the glory of YAHUWAH. 6 Though YAHUWAH is on high, yet He regards the shaphal (lowly, humble); But the gavah (proud) He knows from afar. 7 Though I walk in the midst of tsarah (trouble), You will chayeniy (quicken me, give me life); You will stretch out Your hand against the wrath of my oyev'iym (enemies), and Your right hand will save me. 8 YAHUWAH will perfect that which

concerns me; Your chesed (mercy), YAHUWAH, endures forever; Do not forsake the works of Your hands.

Psalm 139

1 For the Chief Musician. A Psalm of David. YAHUWAH, You have searched me and known me. 2 You know my sitting down and my rising up; You understand my thought afar off. 3 You comprehend my path and my lying down, and are acquainted with all my ways. 4 For there is not a word on my tongue, but behold, YAHUWAH, You know it altogether. 5 You have hedged me behind and before, and laid Your hand upon me. 6 Such knowledge is too wonderful for me; It is high, I cannot attain it. 7 Where can I go from Your Ruach (Spirit)? Or where can I flee from Your presence? 8 If I ascend into heaven, You are there; If I make my bed in Sheol (Hades, the grave, the underworld), behold, You are there. 9 If I take the wings of the morning, and dwell in the uttermost parts of the sea, 10 Even there Your hand shall lead me, and Your right hand shall hold me. 11 If I say, "Surely the darkness shall fall on me," Even the night shall be light about me; 12 Indeed, the darkness shall not hide from You, but the night shines as the day; The darkness and the light are both alike to You. 13 For You formed my inward parts; You covered me in my mother's womb. 14 I will praise You, for I am fearfully and wonderfully made; Marvelous are Your works, and that my soul knows very well. 15 My frame was not hidden from You, when I was made in secret, and skillfully wrought in the lowest parts of the earth. 16 Your eyes saw my substance, being yet unformed. And in Your book they all were written, the days fashioned for me, when as yet there were none of them. 17 How precious also are Your thoughts to me, O El (God)! How great is the sum of them! 18 If I should count them, they would be more in number than the sand; When I awake, I am still with You. 19 Oh, that You would slay the rasha (wicked),

O Eloah (God)! Depart from me, therefore, you bloodthirsty men. 20 For they speak against You mezimah (wickedly); Your ar'iym (foes, enemies) take Your name in vain. 21 Do I not hate them, YAHUWAH, who hate You? And do I not loathe those who rise up against You? 22 I hate them with perfect hatred; I count them my oyev'iym (enemies). 23 Search me, O El (God), and know my heart; Try me, and know my sar'aph'iym (anxieties); 24 And see if there is any derek otsev (wicked way) in me, and lead me in the way everlasting.

Psalm 140

1 To the Chief Musician. A Psalm of David. Deliver me, YAHUWAH, from an adam ra (evil man); Preserve me from iysh chamas (violent men), 2 Who plan ra'ot (evil things) in their hearts; They continually gather together for war. 3 They sharpen their tongues like a nachash (serpent); The chemat akshub (poison ofasps) is under their lips. Selah. 4 Keep me, YAHUWAH, from the hands of the rasha (wicked); Preserve me from iysh chamas'iym (violent men), who have purposed to make my steps stumble. 5 The ge'iym (proud) have hidden a snare for me, and cords; They have spread a net by the wayside; They have set traps for me. Selah. 6 I said to YAHUWAH: "You are Eli (my God); Hear the voice of my supplications, YAHUWAH. 7 O YAHUWAH Adonai (GOD the Lord), the strength of my salvation, You have covered my head in the day of battle. 8 Do not grant, YAHUWAH, the ma'avay rasha (desires of the wicked); Do not further his zamam (wicked scheme, evil plans), lest they be exalted. Selah. 9 "As for the head of those who surround me, let the amal (mischief) of their lips cover them; 10 Let burning coals fall upon them; Let them be cast into the fire, into deep pits, that they rise not up again. 11 Let not an iysh lashon (man's tongue) be established in the earth; Let ra (evil) hunt the iysh chamas (violent man) to overthrow him." 12 I know that

YAHUWAH will maintain the cause of the aniy (afflicted), and mishpat (judgment) for the evyon'iym (poor). 13 Surely the tsadiyk'iym (righteous) shall give thanks to Your name; The yashar'iym (upright) shall dwell in Your presence.

Psalm 141

1 A Psalm of David. YAHUWAH, I cry out to You; Make haste to me! Give ear to my voice when I cry out to You. 2 Let my tefillat (prayer) be set before You as ketoret (incense), the lifting up of my hands as the minchat erev (evening sacrifice). 3 Set a guard, YAHUWAH, over my mouth; Keep watch over the door of my lips. 4 Do not incline my heart to any davar ra (evil thing), to practice alilot ba'resha (wicked works) with men who polei aven (work iniquity); And do not let me eat of their man'amiym (delicacies, dainties). 5 Let the tsadiyk (righteous) strike me; It shall be chesed (mercy, a kindness). And let him rebuke me; It shall be as excellent oil; Let my head not refuse it. For still my tefillat (prayer) is against the ra'ot (deeds of the wicked). 6 Their judges are overthrown by the sides of the cliff, and they hear my words, for they are sweet. 7 Our bones are scattered at the mouth of Sheol (Hades, the grave, the underworld), as when one plows and breaks up the earth. 8 But my eyes are upon You, O YAHUWAH Adonai (GOD the Lord); In You I take refuge; Do not leave my soul destitute. 9 Keep me from the snares they have laid for me, and from the traps of the polei aven (workers of iniquity). 10 Let the rasha'iym (wicked) fall into their own nets, while I escape safely.

Yom Shabbat (7ᵗʰ Day - Sabbath) Saturday

Psalm 142

1 A Contemplation of David. A Prayer when he was in the cave. I cry out to YAHUWAH with my voice; With my voice to YAHUWAH I make my supplication. 2 I pour out my siyach (meditation, complaint) before Him; I declare before Him my tsarah (trouble). 3 When my spirit was overwhelmed within me, then You knew my path. In the way in which I walk they have secretly set a snare for me. 4 Look on my right hand and see, for there is no one who acknowledges me; Refuge has failed me; No one cares for my soul. 5 I cried out to You, YAHUWAH: I said, "You are my refuge, My portion in the land of the chayim (living). 6 Attend to my cry, for I am brought very low; Deliver me from my radaph'iym (persecutors), for they are stronger than I. 7 Bring my soul out of masger (prison), that I may praise Your name; The tsadiykiym (righteous) shall surround me, for You shall deal bountifully with me."

Psalm 143

1 A Psalm of David. Hear my tefillat (prayer), YAHUWAH, give ear to my tachanun (supplications)! In Your emunah (faithfulness) answer me, and in Your tsedakah (righteousness). 2 Do not enter into mishpat (judgment) with Your servant, for in Your sight no one chai (living) is tsadak (righteous). 3 For the oyev (enemy) has radaph (persecuted) my soul; He has crushed my chai (life) to the ground; He has made me dwell in machshak (darkness), like those who have

long been met (dead). 4 Therefore my spirit is overwhelmed within me; My heart within me is distressed. 5 I remember the days of old; I hagah (muse) on all Your works; I siyach (meditate) on the work of Your hands. 6 I spread out my hands to You; My soul longs for You like a thirsty land. Selah. 7 Answer me speedily, YAHUWAH; My spirit fails! Do not hide Your face from me, lest I be like those who go down into the pit. 8 Cause me to hear Your chesed (mercy, lovingkindness) in the morning, for in You do I batach (trust); Cause me to know the way in which I should walk, for I lift up my soul to You. 9 Deliver me, YAHUWAH, from my oyev'iym (enemies); In You I take shelter. 10 Teach me to do Your will, for You are Elohai (my God); Your Ruach (Spirit) is tov (good). Lead me in the land of miyshor (uprightness). 11 Chayeniy (Quicken me, give me life), YAHUWAH, for Your name's sake! For Your tsedakah's (righteousness') sake bring my soul out of tsarah (trouble). 12 In Your chesed (mercy) cut off my oyev'iym (enemies), and destroy all those who tsarar (afflict) my soul; For I am Your servant.

Psalm 144

1 A Psalm of David. Blessed be YAHUWAH my Rock, Who trains my hands for war, and my fingers for battle. 2 My chesed (mercy, lovingkindness) and my fortress, my high tower and my deliverer, my shield and the One in whom I take refuge, Who subdues my people under me. 3 YAHUWAH, what is man, that You take knowledge of him? Or the son of man, that You are mindful of him? 4 Man is like a breath; His days are like a passing shadow. 5 Bow down Your heavens, YAHUWAH, and come down; Touch the mountains, and they shall smoke. 6 Flash forth lightning and scatter them; Shoot out Your arrows and destroy them. 7 Stretch out Your hand from above; Rescue me and deliver me out of great waters, from the hand of the bnei nekar (sons of foreigners), 8 Whose

mouth speaks shav (emptiness, vanity), and whose right hand is a right hand of sheker (falsehood, lies). 9 I will sing a new song to You, O Elohim (God); On a harp of ten strings I will sing praises to You, 10 The One who gives salvation to kings, Who delivers David His servant from the deadly sword. 11 Rescue me and deliver me from the hand of bnei nekar (sons of foreigners), whose mouth speaks shav (emptiness, vanity), and whose right hand is a right hand of sheker (falsehood, lies); 12 That our sons may be as plants grown up in their youth; That our daughters may be as pillars, sculptured in palace style; 13 That our barns may be full, supplying all kinds of produce; That our sheep may bring forth thousands and ten thousands in our fields; 14 That our oxen may be well laden; That there be no breaking in or going out; That there be no outcry in our streets. 15 Happy are the people who are in such a state; Happy are the people whose Elohim (God) is YAHUWAH!

Psalm 145

1 A Praise of David. I will extol You, Elohai (my God), O Melek (King); And I will bless Your name forever and ever. 2 Every day I will bless You, and I will praise Your name forever and ever. 3 Great is YAHUWAH, and greatly to be praised; And His greatness is unsearchable. 4 One generation shall praise Your works to another, and shall declare Your gevurot (mighty acts). 5 I will siyach (meditate) on the glorious splendor of Your majesty, and on Your nipla'ot (wondrous works). 6 Men shall speak of the might of Your awesome acts, and I will declare Your greatness. 7 They shall utter the memory of Your rav toviym (great goodness), and shall sing of Your tsedakah (righteousness). 8 YAHUWAH is chanun (gracious) and rachum (full of compassion), erek apayim (slow to anger) and gadol chesed (great in mercy). 9 YAHUWAH is tov (good) to all, and His rachamiym (tender mercies) are over all His

works. 10 All Your works shall praise You, YAHUWAH, and Your kadoshiym (holy ones, saints, set apart ones) shall bless You. 11 They shall speak of the glory of Your kingdom, and talk of Your gevurah (power), 12 To make known to the sons of men His gevurot (mighty acts), and the glorious majesty of His kingdom. 13 Your kingdom is an everlasting kingdom, and Your dominion endures throughout all generations. 14 YAHUWAH upholds all who fall, and raises up all who are bowed down. 15 The eyes of all look expectantly to You, and You give them their food in due season. 16 You open Your hand And satisfy the desire of every living thing. 17 YAHUWAH is tsadiyk (righteous) in all His ways, chasiyd (holy, godly) in all His works. 18 YAHUWAH is near to all who call upon Him, to all who call upon Him in emet (truth). 19 He will fulfill the desire of those who fear Him; He also will hear their cry and save them. 20 YAHUWAH preserves all who love Him, But all the rasha'iym (wicked) He will destroy. 21 My mouth shall speak the praise of YAHUWAH, and all flesh shall bless His Shem Kadosh (holy name) forever and ever.

Psalm 146

1 Halelu-Yah (Praise the Lord)! Praise YAHUWAH, O my soul! 2 While I live I will praise YAHUWAH; I will sing praises to Elohai (my God) while I have my being. 3 Do not put your batach (trust) in nadiyv'iym (nobles), nor in a ben adam (son of man), in whom there is no help. 4 His spirit departs, he returns to his earth; In that very day his plans perish. 5 Happy is he who has the El (God) of Jacob for his help, whose hope is in YAHUWAH his Elohim (God), 6 Who made heaven and earth, the sea, and all that is in them; Who keeps emet (truth) forever, 7 Who executes mishpat (judgment) for the ashak'iym (oppressed), Who gives food to the hungry. YAHUWAH matiyr (looses; gives freedom to) the asar'iym (prisoners). 8 YAHUWAH opens the eyes of the blind;

YAHUWAH raises those who are bowed down; YAHUWAH loves the tsadiyk'iym (righteous). 9 YAHUWAH shomer (keeps) the geriym (strangers); He relieves the yatom (fatherless, orphan) and almanah (widow); But the derek rasha'iym (way of the wicked) He turns upside down. 10 YAHUWAH shall reign forever; Your Elohim (God), O Zion, to all generations. Halelu-Yah (Praise the Lord)!

Psalm 147

1 Halelu-Yah (Praise the Lord)! For it is good to sing praises to our Elohim (God); For it is pleasant, and praise is beautiful. 2 YAHUWAH builds up Jerusalem; He gathers together the dachah (outcasts) of Israel. 3 He rofey (heals) the shavar-lev (brokenhearted) and binds up their wounds. 4 He counts the number of the stars; He calls them all by name. 5 Great is our Adon (Lord), and rav koach (mighty in power); His understanding is infinite. 6 YAHUWAH lifts up the anav'iym (humble); He casts the rasha'iym (wicked) down to the ground. 7 Sing to YAHUWAH with thanksgiving; Sing praises on the harp to our Elohim (God), 8 Who covers the heavens with clouds, Who prepares rain for the earth, Who makes grass to grow on the mountains. 9 He gives to the beast its food, and to the young ravens that cry. 10 He does not delight in the strength of the horse; He takes no pleasure in the legs of a man. 11 YAHUWAH takes pleasure in those who fear Him, in those who yachal chesed (hope in His mercy). 12 Praise YAHUWAH, O Jerusalem! Praise your Elohim (God), O Zion! 13 For He has strengthened the bars of your gates; He has blessed your children within you. 14 He makes shalom (peace) in your borders, and fills you with the finest wheat. 15 He sends out His command to the earth; His word runs very swiftly. 16 He gives snow like wool; He scatters the frost like ashes; 17 He casts out His hail like morsels; Who can stand before His cold? 18 He sends out His word and melts

them; He causes His wind to blow, and the waters flow. 19 He declares His word to Jacob, His chukot (statutes) and His mishpatiym (judgments) to Israel. 20 He has not dealt thus with any goy (nation); And as for His mishpatiym (judgments), they have not known them. Halelu-Yah (Praise the Lord)!

Psalm 148

1 Halelu-Yah (Praise the Lord)! Praise YAHUWAH from the heavens; Praise Him in the heights! 2 Praise Him, all His Mal'akiym (angels); Praise Him, all His tseva'ot (hosts, armies)! 3 Praise Him, sun and moon; Praise Him, all you stars of light! 4 Praise Him, you heavens of heavens, and you waters above the heavens! 5 Let them praise the name of YAHUWAH, for He commanded and they were created. 6 He also established them forever and ever; He made a decree which shall not pass away. 7 Praise YAHUWAH from the earth, you great taniyn'iym (dragons) and all tehom'ot (the depths); 8 Fire and hail, snow and clouds; Stormy wind, fulfilling His word; 9 Mountains and all hills; Fruitful trees and all cedars; 10 Beasts and all cattle; Creeping things and flying fowl; 11 Kings of the earth and all peoples; Princes and all judges of the earth; 12 Both young men and maidens; Old men and children. 13 Let them praise the name of YAHUWAH, For His name alone is exalted; His glory is above the earth and heaven. 14 And He has exalted the horn of His people, The praise of all His kadoshiym (holy ones, saints, set apart ones); Of the children of Israel, a people near to Him. Halelu-Yah (Praise the Lord)!

Psalm 149

1 Halelu-Yah (Praise the Lord)! Sing to YAHUWAH a new song, and His praise in the assembly of kadoshiym (holy ones,

saints, set apart ones). 2 Let Israel rejoice in their Maker; Let the children of Zion be joyful in their Melek (King). 3 Let them praise His name with the dance; Let them sing praises to Him with the timbrel and harp. 4 For YAHUWAH takes pleasure in His people; He will beautify the avaniym (humble, meek) with yshu'ah (salvation). 5 Let the kadoshiym (holy ones, saints, set apart ones) be joyful in glory; Let them sing aloud on their beds. 6 Let the high praises of El (God) be in their mouth, and a two-edged sword in their hand, 7 To execute nekamah (vengeance) on the goyim (nations, gentiles, heathen), and tokechot (punishments) on the umiym (peoples); 8 To asar (bind) their melek'iym (kings) with zikiym (chains), and their kavod'iym (nobles, great ones, glorious ones) with kevel barzel (fetters of iron); 9 To asot (execute) on them the mishpat ketuv (written judgment); This hadar (honor, ornament, majesty, glory) have all His kadoshiym (holy ones, saints, set apart ones). Halelu-Yah (Praise the Lord)!

Psalm 150

1 Halelu-Yah (Praise the Lord)! Praise El (God) in His kadosh (holy place, sanctuary); Praise Him in His mighty firmament! 2 Praise Him for His gevurot (mighty acts); Praise Him according to His rov godel (excellent greatness)! 3 Praise Him with the sound of the shofar (rams horn); Praise Him with the lute and harp! 4 Praise Him with the timbrel and dance; Praise Him with stringed instruments and flutes! 5 Praise Him with loud cymbals; Praise Him with clashing cymbals! 6 Let everything that has breath praise Yah. Halelu-Yah (Praise the Lord)!

Psalm 151

This psalm is ascribed to David as his own composition (though it is outside the number), after he had fought in single combat with Goliath. 1 I was small among my brothers, and the youngest in my Father's house; I tended my Father's sheep. 2 My hands made a harp; my fingers fashioned a lyre. 3 And who will tell my Adon (Lord)? YAHUWAH himself; it is he who hears. 4 It was he who sent his messenger and took me from my Father's sheep, and anointed me with his anointing oil. 5 My brothers were handsome and tall, but YAHUWAH was not pleased with them. 6 I went out to meet the Philistine, and he cursed me by his Eliliym (idols). 7 But I drew his own sword; I beheaded him, and took away disgrace from the people of Israel.

BEDTIME SHEMA
(Said Before Retiring for the Night)

Night Prayer for Young Children

Blessed are you YAHUWAH our Elohim (God), Melek Ha-Olam (King of the Universe), the God and the Father of our Lord Yah'shua the Messiah (Jesus Christ), who makes the bands of sleep to fall upon my eyes, and slumber upon my eyelids.

May it be Your will, YAHUWAH Elohai (my God) and El (God) of my fathers, to suffer me to lie down in shalom (peace), and to let me rise up again in shalom (peace).

Hear, O Israel: YAHUWAH our Elohim (God), YAHUWAH is One. Blessed be His name, whose glorious kingdom is for ever and ever.

And You shall love YAHUWAH your Elohim (God) with all Your heart, and with all Your soul, and with all Your might. And these words which I command you this day will be upon your heart: and you will teach them diligently unto your children, and you will talk of them when you sit in your house, and when you walk by the way, and when you lie down, and when you rise up. And you will bind them for a sign upon your hand, and they shall be for frontlets between your eyes. And you will write them upon the doorposts of your house and upon your gates.

Blessed be YAHUWAH by day; blessed be YAHUWAH by night. Blessed be YAHUWAH when we lie down; blessed be YAHUWAH when we rise up.

Behold, he that guards Israel will neither slumber nor sleep.

Into Your hand I commend my spirit: you have redeemed me, YAHUWAH, the El Emet (God of truth).

For Your salvation I hope, YAHUWAH.

In the name of Yah'shua the Messiah (Jesus Christ). Amen.

PRAYERS FOR ADULTS
BEFORE RETIRING TO REST AT NIGHT

Adon Ha-Olam (Master of the universe), I hereby forgive anyone who has angered or vexed me, or sinned against me, either physically or financially, against my honor or anything else that is mine, whether by speech, or by deeds. May no man be punished on my account. May it be Your will, YAHUWAH, my Elohim (God) and God of my fathers, the God and the Father of our Lord Yah'shua the Messiah (Jesus Christ), that I shall sin no more, nor repeat my sins, neither shall I again anger You nor do what is wrong in Your eyes. The sins I have committed, erase in Your abounding chesed'iym (mercies), but not through affliction, suffering and severe illness, nor by me'anot (tormentors), or shediym (demons), or ruchot ha'tumah (unclean spirits), or chalom bahalot (nightmares), but by the shed blood of Yah'shua the Messiah (Jesus Christ). May the words of my mouth and the siyach lev (meditation of my heart) be acceptable before You, YAHUWAH my strength and my Redeemer.

Blessed are ou, YAHUWAH our Elohim (God), Melek Ha-Olam (King of the universe), the God and the Father of our Lord Yah'shua the Messiah (Jesus Christ), who makes the bands of sleep to fall upon my eyes, and slumber upon my eyelids.

May it be Your will, YAHUWAH Elohai (my God) and God of my fathers, the God and the Father of our Lord Yah'shua the Messiah (Jesus Christ), to suffer me to lie down in shalom (peace) and to let me rise up again in shalom (peace). Let not my thoughts trouble me, nor chalom ra (evil dreams), nor me'kushat ra (evil fancies), but let my rest be perfect before You. O lighten my eyes, lest I sleep the sleep of mavet (death), for it is You who gives light to the apple of the eye.

Blessed are You, YAHUWAH, who gives light to the whole world in Your glory.

O Elohim (God), Melek Ne'eman (faithful King).

Hear, O Israel: YAHUWAH our Elohim (God), YAHUWAH is One.

Blessed be His name, whose glorious kingdom is for ever and ever.

And you shall love YAHUWAH your Elohim (God) with all your heart, and with all your soul, and with all your might. And these words, which I command you this day, will be upon your heart: and you will teach them diligently unto your children, and will talk of them when you sit in your house, and when you walk by the way, and when you lie down, and when you rise up. And you will bind them for a sign upon your hand, and they will be for frontlets between your eyes. And you will write them upon the doorposts of our house, and upon your gates.

And let the pleasantness of YAHUWAH our Elohim (God) be upon us: and establish the work of our hands upon us; yes, the work of our hands establish it. In the Name of Yah'shua the Messiah (Jesus Christ). Amen.

Cause Us to Lie Down

Cause us, YAHUWAH our Elohim (God), to lie down in Shalom (peace), and raise us up, O our Melek (King), unto chai (life). Spread over us the Heykal (tabernacle) of Your shalom (peace); direct us aright through Your own good counsel; save us for Your name's sake; be a shield about us; remove from us every oyev (enemy), dever (pestilence), cherev (sword), ra'av (famine) and yagon (sorrow); remove also the yariv (adversary) from before us and from behind us. O shelter us beneath the shadow of Your wings; for You, O Elohim (God), are our Guardian and our Deliverer; yes, You, O Elohim (God), are a gracious and merciful King; and guard our going out and our coming in unto life and unto shalom (peace) from this time forth and for evermore.

Blessed be YAHUWAH by day; blessed be YAHUWAH by night; blessed be YAHUWAH when we lie down; blessed be YAHUWAH when we rise up. For in Your hand are the souls of the living and the dead, as it is said, In his hand is the soul of every living thing, and the spirit of all human flesh. Into Your hand I commend my spirit; You have redeemed me, YAHUWAH, El Emet (God of truth). Our Elohim (God) who is in heaven, assert the unity of Your name, and establish Your kingdom continually, and reign over us for ever and ever.

May our eyes behold, our hearts rejoice, and our souls be glad in Your true salvation, when it shall be said unto Zion, Your El (God) reigns. YAHUWAH reigns; YAHUWAH has reigned; YAHUWAH shall reign for ever and ever: for the kingdom is Yours, and to everlasting You will reign in glory; for we have no king but You.

The Mal'ak (angel) who has redeemed me from all evil bless the lads; and let my name be named on them, and the name of my fathers Abraham and Isaac; and let them grow into a multitude in the midst of the earth. And he said, If you will diligently hearken to the voice of YAHUWAH Your Elohim (God), and will do that which is right in his eyes, and will give ear to his mitzvot (commandments), and keep all his chukot (statutes), I will put none of the diseases upon You, which I have put upon the Egyptians; for I am YAHUWAH that heals you. And Adonai (My Lord) said unto Satan (the adversary), YAHUWAH rebuke you, O Satan (adversary); yes, YAHUWAH that has chosen Jerusalem rebuke You. Is not this a brand plucked out of the fire? Behold the bed of Solomon: sixty mighty men are about it, of the mighty men of Israel: they all handle the sword, expert in war; every man has his sword upon his thigh, because of fear in the night.

YAHUWAH bless you, and keep you:

YAHUWAH make his face to shine upon you, and be gracious unto you:

YAHUWAH turn his face unto you, and give you peace.

To be said three times:—

Behold, he that guards Israel will neither slumber nor sleep.

To be said three times:—

For Your salvation I hope, YAHUWAH.

I hope, YAHUWAH, for Your salvation.

YAHUWAH, for Your salvation I hope.

To be said three times:—

In the name of YAHUWAH, the God of Israel, and in the name of Yah'shua the Messiah (Jesus Christ), the Son of the Father,

may Myka'el (Michael) be at my right hand;

Gavriy'el (Gabriel) at my left;

before me, Uriy'el (Uriel);

behind me, Rapha'el (Raphael);

with in me the Ruach HaKodesh (Holy Spirit)

and above my head the Shekinah Ha-Elohim (divine presence of God).

Psalm 128

A Song of Degrees.—Happy is every one that fears YAHUWAH, that walks in his ways. When you shall eat the labor of our hands, happy shall you be, and it shall be well with you. Your wife shall be as a fruitful vine, in the recesses of your house: your children like olive plants, round about your table. Behold thus shall the man be blessed that fears YAHUWAH. May YAHUWAH bless you out of Zion: may you see the good of Jerusalem all the days of your life. Yes, may you see your children's children. Shalom (Peace) be upon Israel.

To be said three times:—

Stand in awe, and sin not: commune with your own heart upon your bed, and be still. (Selah.)

He is Adon Ha-Olam (Lord of the universe), who reigned ere any creature yet was formed: At the time when all things were made by his desire, then was his name proclaimed King. And after all things shall have had an end, he alone, the dreaded one, shall reign; Who was, who is, and who will be in glory. And he is One, and there is no second to compare to him, to consort with him: Without beginning, without end; to him belong strength and dominion. And he is Elohai (my God), my Redeemer lives, and a rock in my travail in time of distress; And he is my banner and my refuge, the portion of my cup on the day when I call. Into his hand I commend my spirit, when I sleep and when I wake; And with my spirit, my body also: YAHUWAH is with me, and I will not fear. Amen.

Our Elohim (God) and El (God) of my father's, may our tefillat (prayers) come before you, and do not turn away from our supplications. You know the mysteries of the universe and a hidden secrets of every living soul. You search out all our innermost thoughts, and probe our minds and our hearts. Nothing is hidden from you, nothing is concealed from your site. And so, may it be your will YAHUWAH our Elohim (God) and El (God) of our fathers, to have mercy on us and forgive us all our sins, and grant us atonement through the shed Blood of Your Kadosh Mashiyach (Holy Anointed One), Yah'shua (Jesus), who forgive all our iniquities and to forgive and pardon us for all our transgressions.

Abba Father, we implore you, in the name of Yah'shua (Jesus), to release us from bondage. Accept our prayers, strengthen us and purify us, Awsome One, the Abiyr (Mighty One), we beseech you, guard as the apple of Your eye those who seek your salvation. Bless us, cleanse us, bestow upon us forever your merciful righteousness.

Powerful, Kadosh (Holy One), in your abounding goodness, guide Your people. Only and Exalted One, turn to those who are mindful of your holiness. Accept our supplications and hear or cry.

In the Name of Yah'shua (Jesus), I call upon the power of YAHUWAH to protect, and encourage and strengthen the intimate bond of love between myself and my beloved. May YAHUWAH grant all the desires of our hearts, fulfill all our purposes, and all our petitions.

May YAHUWAH hear from heaven, answer quickly all our requests and save us in the day of trouble. In the name of Yah'shua (Jesus) defend us and send help from heaven to deliver us from bondage, from our enemies, and from poverty. In the name of Yah'shua (Jesus) we pray. Amen.

ORDER OF READING THE LAW

The following to "as of old," forms part of the Avodah (Service) when Tefillat (Prayers) are said with a Kehila (Congregation) on Mondays and Thursdays, and also, with the exception of "May it be the will," etc., to "Amen," on Sabbath Afternoons, New Moon, the Intermediate Days of Passover and Tabernacles, and on Fast Days (Mornings and Afternoons).

The Ark is Opened

Reader and Cong.—And it came to pass, when the ark set forward, that Moses said, Rise up, O YAHUWAH, and Your enemies shall be scattered, and they that hate You shall flee before You. For out of Zion shall go forth the Torah (Law), and the word of YAHUWAH from Jerusalem.

Blessed be he who in his holiness gave the Torah (Law) to his people Israel.

The Reader takes the Scroll of the Law, and says:—

Magnify YAHUWAH with me, and let us exalt his name together.

Reader and Cong.—Yours, O YAHUWAH, is the greatness, and the power, and the glory, and the victory, and the majesty: for all that is in the heaven and in the earth is Yours; Yours, O YAHUWAH, is the kingdom, and the supremacy as head over all. Exalt YAHUWAH our Elohim (God), and worship at his footstool: holy is he. Exalt YAHUWAH our Elohim (God), and worship at his holy mount; for YAHUWAH our Elohim (God) is Kadosh (holy).

May the Father of mercy have mercy upon a people that have been borne by him. May he remember the covenant with the patriarchs, deliver our souls from evil hours, check the yetzar hara (evil inclination) in them that have been carried by him, grant us of his grace an everlasting deliverance, and in the attribute of his goodness fulfil our desires by salvation and mercy.

The Scroll of the Law is placed upon the desk. The Reader unrolls it, and says the following:—

And may his kingdom be soon revealed and made visible unto us, and may he be gracious unto our remnant and unto the remnant of his people, the house of Israel, granting them grace, kindness, mercy and favor; and let us say, Amen. Ascribe, all of you, greatness unto our Elohim (God), and render honor to the Torah (Law).

Here the Reader names the Person who is to be called to the Reading of the Law.

Blessed be he, who in his holiness gave the Torah (Law) unto his people Israel. The Law of YAHUWAH is perfect, restoring the soul: the testimony of YAHUWAH is faithful, making wise the simple. The precepts of YAHUWAH are right, rejoicing the heart: the commandment of YAHUWAH is pure, enlightening the eyes. YAHUWAH will give strength unto his people: YAHUWAH will bless his people with peace. As for Elohim (God), his way is perfect: the word of YAHUWAH is tried: he is a shield unto all them that trust in him.

Cong. and Reader.—And you that cleave unto YAHUWAH your Elohim (God) are alive every one of you this day.

Those who are called to the Reading of the Law say the following Blessing:—

Bless YAHUWAH who is to be blessed.

Cong.—Blessed be YAHUWAH, who is to be blessed for ever and ever.

The Response of the Congregation is repeated and the Blessing continued:—

Blessed are You YAHUWAH our Elohim (God), King of the universe, the God and the Father of our Lord Yah'shua the Messiah (Jesus Christ), who has chosen us from all peoples, and has given us Your Torah (Law). Blessed are You, YAHUWAH, who gives the Torah (Law).

After the Reading of a Section of the Law, the following Blessing is said:—

Blessed are You YAHUWAH our Elohim (God), King of the universe, the God and the Father of our Lord Yah'shua the Messiah (Jesus Christ), who has given us the Torah (Law) of truth, and has planted everlasting life in our midst. Blessed are You, YAHUWAH, who gives the Torah (Law).

Persons who have been in peril of their lives, during journeys by sea or land, in captivity or sickness, upon their deliverance or recovery say the following, after the conclusion of the last Blessing:—

Blessed are You YAHUWAH our Elohim (God), King of the universe, the God and the Father of our Lord Yah'shua the Messiah (Jesus Christ), who vouchsafes benefits unto the undeserving, who has also vouchsafed all good unto me.

The Congregation respond:—

He who has vouchsafed all good unto you, may he vouchsafe all good unto you for ever.

After the Reading of the Law, the Scroll is held up, and the Congregation say the following:–

And this is the Law which Moses set before the children of Israel, according to the commandment of YAHUWAH by the hand of Moses. It is a tree of life to them that grasp it, and of them that uphold it every one is rendered happy. Its ways are ways of pleasantness, and all its paths are peace. Length of days is in its right hand; in its left hand are riches and honor. It pleased YAHUWAH, for his righteousness' sake, to magnify the Law and to make it honorable.

On those Mondays and Thursdays when the Prayers, are said, the Reader adds the following, previous to the Scroll of the Law being returned to the Ark:——

May it be the will of our Father who is in heaven to have mercy upon us and upon our remnant, and to keep destruction and the plague from us and from all his people, the house of Israel; and let us say, Amen.

May it be the will of our Father who is in heaven to preserve among us the wise men of Israel; them, their wives, their sons and daughters, their disciples and the disciples of their disciples in all the places of their habitation; and let us say, Amen.

May it be the will of our Father who is in heaven that good tidings of salvation and comfort may be heard and published, and that he may gather our banished ones from the four corners of the earth; and let us say, Amen.

As for our brethren, the whole house of Israel, such of them as are given over to trouble or captivity, whether they abide on the sea or on the dry land,—may the All-present have mercy upon them, and bring them forth from trouble to enlargement, from darkness to light, and from subjection to redemption, now speedily and at a near time; and let us say, Amen.

On returning the Scroll of the Law to the Ark, the Reader says:—

Let them praise the name of YAHUWAH; for his name alone is exalted:

Congregation.—His majesty is above the earth and heaven; and he has lifted up a horn for his people, to the praise of all his loving ones, even of the children of Israel, the people near unto him. Hallelu Yah (Praise the Lord).

PSALM 24

The earth is YAHUWAH's and the fulness thereof; the world, and they that dwell therein. For it is he that has founded it upon the seas, and established it upon the floods. Who may ascend the mountain of YAHUWAH? And who may stand in his holy place? He that has clean hands and a pure heart; who has not set his desire upon vanity, and has not sworn deceitfully. He shall receive a blessing from YAHUWAH, and righteousness from the God of his salvation. This is the generation of them that seek after him, that seek Your face, O God of Jacob! (Selah.) Lift up your heads, O you gates; and be lifted up, you everlasting doors, that the King of glory may come in. Who, then, is the King of glory? YAHUWAH strong and mighty. YAHUWAH mighty in battle. Lift up your heads, O you gates; yea, lift them up, you everlasting doors, that the

King of glory may come in. Who, then, is the King of glory? YAHUWAH Tzeva'ot (the Lord of Hosts), he is the King of glory. (Selah.)

While the Scroll of the Law is being placed in the Ark, the following to "as of old" is said:—

And when it rested, he said, Return, YAHUWAH, unto the ten thousands of the thousands of Israel. Arise, YAHUWAH, unto Your resting place; You, and the ark of Your strength. Let Your koheniym (priests) be clothed with righteousness; and let Your loving ones shout for joy. For the sake of David Your servant, turn not away the face of Your anointed. For I give you good doctrine; forsake you not my Torah (Law). It is a tree of life to them that grasp it, and of them that uphold it every one is rendered happy. Its ways are ways of pleasantness, and all its paths are peace. Turn us unto You, YAHUWAH, and we shall return: renew our days as of old.

YA'ANKA YAHUWAH
(The Lord Answer You)
Psalm 20

YAHUWAH answer you in the day of trouble; the name of the God of Jacob set you up on high; send you help from the sanctuary, and uphold you out of Zion; remember all your offerings, and accept your burnt sacrifice (Selah); grant you your heart's desire, and fulfil all your purpose. We will exult in your salvation, and in the name of our God we will set up our banners: YAHUWAH fulfil all your petitions. Now I know that YAHUWAH saves his anointed; he will answer him from his holy heaven with the mighty saving acts of his right hand. Some trust in chariots and some in horses: but we will make mention of the name of YAHUWAH our God. They are bowed down and fallen: but we are risen and stand upright. Save, YAHUWAH: may the King answer us on the day when we call.

A REDEEMER SALL COME TO ZION

And a redeemer shall come to Zion and to them that turn from transgression in Jacob, says YAHUWAH. And as for me, this is my covenant with them, says YAHUWAH: my spirit that is upon You, and my words which I have put in Your mouth, shall not depart out of Your mouth, nor out of the mouth of Your seed, nor out of the mouth of Your seed's seed, says YAHUWAH, from henceforth and for ever.

But You are Holy, O You that dwells amid the praises of Israel. And one cried unto another, and said, Holy, holy, holy is YAHUWAH Tzeva'at: the whole earth is full of his glory. And they receive sanction the one from the other, and say, Holy in the highest heavens, the place of his divine abode; holy upon earth, the work of his might; holy for ever and to all eternity is YAHUWAH of hosts; the whole earth is full of the radiance of his glory. Then a wind lifted me up, and I heard behind me the voice of a great rushing (saying), Blessed be the glory of YAHUWAH from his place. Then a wind lifted me up, and I heard behind me the voice of a great rushing, of those who uttered praises, and said, Blessed be the glory of YAHUWAH from the region of his divine abode. YAHUWAH shall reign for ever and ever. The kingdom of YAHUWAH endures for ever and to all eternity. YAHUWAH, the God of Abraham, of Isaac and of Israel, our fathers, keep this for ever in the imagination of the thoughts of the heart of Your people, and direct their heart unto You. And he, being merciful, forgives iniquity and destroys not: yes, many a time he turns his anger away, and does not stir up all his wrath.

For You, YAHUWAH, are good and forgiving, and abounding in lovingkindness to all them that call upon You. Your righteousness is an everlasting righteousness, and Your Word is truth. You will show truth to Jacob and lovingkindness to Abraham, according as You have sworn unto our fathers from the days of old.

Blessed be YAHUWAH day by day; if one burdens us, God is our salvation. (Selah.) YAHUWAH Tzeva'ot is with us; the God of Jacob is our stronghold. (Selah.) YAHUWAH Tzeva'ot, happy is the man that trusts in You. Save, YAHUWAH: may the King answer us on the day when we call. Blessed is our God, who has created us for his glory, and has separated us from them that go astray, and has given us the Law of truth and planted everlasting life in our midst. May he open our heart unto his Law, and place his love and fear within our hearts, that we may do his will and serve him with a perfect heart, that we may not labor in vain, nor bring forth for confusion.

May it be Your will, YAHUWAH our God and God of our fathers, in the name of Yah'shua the Messiah (Jesus Christ), that we may keep Your statutes in this world, and be worthy to live to witness and inherit happiness and blessing in these days of the Messiah and in the life of the world to come. To the end that my glory may sing praise unto You, and not be silent: YAHUWAH my God, I will give thanks unto You for ever. Blessed is the man that trusts in YAHUWAH, and whose trust YAHUWAH is. Trust in YAHUWAH for ever; for in Yah YAHUWAH is an everlasting rock.

And they that know Your name will put their trust in You; for You have not forsaken them that seek You, YAHUWAH. It pleased YAHUWAH, for his righteousness' sake, to magnify the Law and to make it honorable.

HALF KADDISH

And now, I pray You, let the power of the Lord be great, according as You have spoken. Remember, YAHUWAH, Your tender mercies and Your loving kindness; for they have been ever of old.

Reader.—Magnified and sanctified be his great name in the world which he has created according to his will. May he establish his kingdom during your life and during your days, and during the life of all the house of Israel, even speedily and at a near time, and say, Amen.

Cong. and Reader.—Let his great name be blessed for ever and to all eternity.

Reader.—Blessed, praised and glorified, exalted, extolled and honored, magnified and lauded be the name of the Holy One, blessed be he; though he be high above all the blessings and hymns, praises and consolations, which are uttered in the world; and say, Amen.

Cong.—Accept our prayer in mercy and in favor.

Reader.—May the prayers and supplications of all Israel be accepted by their Father who is in heaven; and say, Amen.

Cong.—Let the name of YAHUWAH be blessed from this time forth and for evermore.

Reader.—May there be abundant peace from heaven, and life for us and for all Israel; and say, Amen.

Cong.—My help is from YAHUWAH, who made heaven and earth.

Reader.—He who makes peace in his high places, may he make peace for us and for all Israel; and say, Amen.

THE GENERAL THANKSGIVING

YAHUWAH El Shaddai (Lord God Almighty), Father of all mercies, we Your unworthy servants do give You most humble and hearty thanks for all Your goodness and loving-kindness to us and to all men. We bless You for our creation, preservation, and all the blessings of this life; but above all for Your inestimable love in the redemption of the world by our Lord Yah'shua the Messiah (Jesus Christ), for the means of grace, and for the hope of glory. And, we beseech You, give us that due sense of all Your mercies, that our hearts may be unfeignedly thankful; and that we show forth Your praise, not only with our lips, but in our lives, by giving up our selves to Your service, and by walking before You in holiness and righteousness all our days; through Yah'shua the Messiah (Jesus Christ) our Lord, to whom, with You and the Ruach HaKodesh (Holy Spirit), be all honor and glory, world without end. Amen.

YAHUWAH El Shaddai (God Almighty), who has given us grace at this time with one accord to make our common supplication unto You, and has promised through Your well-beloved Son that when two or three are gathered together in his Name You will be in the midst of them: Fulfill now, Adonai (my Lord), the desires and petitions of Your servants as may be best for us; granting us in this world knowledge of Your truth, and in the world to come life everlasting. Amen.

The Officiant may then conclude with one of the following

The grace of the Lord Yah'shua the Messiah (Jesus Christ), and the love of YAHUWAH, and the fellowship of the Ruach HaKodesh (Holy Spirit), be with us all evermore. *Amen.*

May the God of hope fill us with all joy and peace in believing through the power of the Ruach HaKodesh (Holy Spirit). *Amen.*

Glory to God whose power, working in us, can do infinitely more than we can ask or imagine: Glory to him from generation to generation in the Church, and in Yah'shua the Messiah (Jesus Christ) for ever and ever. *Amen. Ephesians 3:20*

PRAYER FOR OUR LEADERSHIP

Father I thank you that our Pastors/Rabbis are faithful (Ps 31:23) and that You preserve them (Ps.21:23). That they abound with blessings (Prov. 28:20), and do not grow weary in well doing. (Gal 6:9). That You who began a good work in them will perfect it. (Phil1:6). They are Your workmanship created in Yah'shua the Messiah (Jesus Christ) (Eph 2:10) and equipped in every good thing to do Your will (Heb 13:21). Work in them that which is well pleasing in Your sight. (Heb. 13:21).

Let all grace, abound toward them, have sufficiency in all things and an abundance for every good work. (2 Cor. 9:8). Because they have sowed bountifully, they will reap bountifully, (2 Cor 9:6) and whether they plant or water, Father, You give the increase (1 Cor. 3:6). I pray that they continually triumph in Messiah (2 Cor 2:14) diffusing the fragrance of His knowledge in every place. (2 Cor. 2:14). That all blessings come upon them and overtake them because they obey the voice of YAHUWAH.(Deut. 28:2).

Instruct them and teach them in the way they should go (Ps 32:8). Reveal the deeper things of YAHUWAH by Your Ruach HaKodesh. (1 Cor 9:10). Let them be vessels of honor, sanctified and useful for the Master prepared for every good work (2 Tim. 2:21). Shepherding the flock willingly, eagerly, and being an example to them (1 Pet 5:2).

Their speech and preaching is in demonstration of the Ruach HaKodesh and power (1 Cor 2:4) and they are instant in and out of season to teach the Word of YAHUWAH (2 Tim. 4:2).

Every place the soles of their feet tread upon has been given to them (Josh 1:3). They are strong and of good courage, for You YAHUWAH go with them. (Deut. 31:6). They wait upon You and You strengthen them in their heart (Ps. 27:14).

Help them set in order things that are lacking and appoint Elders in every city (Titus 1:5)

We tear down the strongholds over the Bema (2 Cor 10:4) and we lift our Pastors/Rabbis up and cover them with the blood of Yah'shua (Jesus) (Heb. 12:24). Sickness and disease shall in no way come near them (Deut 28) for they are redeemed from the curse of the law (Gal 3:13). No weapon formed against them shall prosper and every tongue rising against them shall be shown to be in the wrong. (Isa 54:17).

Father, let the gifts and anointing on their lives come forth (1 Cor 12:11). Birth the things you have spoken to them in their hearts (Luke 1:45) as they continually give themselves to prayer and the ministry of the Word. (Acts 6:4). In the name of Yah'shua the Messiah (Jesus Christ). Amen.

PRAYER FOR SUSTENANCE

My help is from YAHUWAH, who made heaven and earth. Cast Your burden upon YAHUWAH, and he shall sustain You. Mark the perfect man, and behold the upright; for the latter end of that man is peace.

Trust in YAHUWAH, and do good; dwell in the land, and feed upon faithfulness. Behold, God is my salvation; I will trust and will not be afraid: for Yah YAHUWAH is my strength and song, and he is become my salvation. O Sovereign of the universe, in Your holy words it is written, saying, He that trusts in YAHUWAH, lovingkindness shall compass him about; and it is written, And You give life to them all. YAHUWAH, God of truth, vouchsafe blessing and prosperity upon all the work of my hands, for I trust in You that You will so bless me through my occupation and calling, that I may be enabled to support myself and the members of my household with ease and not with pain, by lawful and not by forbidden means, unto life and peace. In me also let the scripture be fulfilled, Cast Your burden upon YAHUWAH, and he shall sustain You. In the name of Yah'shua the Messiah (Jesus Christ). Amen!

TRAVELLERS PRAYER

May it be Your will, YAHUWAH, My God and God of my fathers, in the name of Yah'shua the Messiah (Jesus Christ), to lead me, to direct my steps, and to support me in peace. Lead me in life, tranquil and serene, until I arrive at where I am going. Deliver me from every enemy, ambush and hurt that I might encounter on the way and from all afflictions that visit and trouble the world. Bless the work of my hands. Let me receive divine grace and those loving acts of kindness and mercy in Your eyes and in the eyes of all those I encounter. Listen to the voice of my appeal, for you are a God who responds to prayerful supplication. Blessed are you, YAHUWAH, who responds to prayer.

Kaddish to be said after reading Lessons from the Works of the Rabbis:-

Reader.—Magnified and sanctified be his great name In the world which he has created according to his will. May he establish his kingdom during your life and during your days, and during the life of all the house of Israel, even speedily and at a near time, and say, Amen.

Cong. and Reader.—Let his great name be blessed for ever and to all eternity.

Reader.—Blessed, praised and glorified, exalted, extolled and honored; magnified and lauded be the name of the Holy One, blessed be he; though he be high above all the blessings and hymns, praises and consolations, which are uttered in the world; and say, Amen.

Unto Israel, and unto the Rabbis, and unto their disciples, and unto all the disciples of their disciples, and unto all who engage in the study of the Law, in this or in any other place, unto them and unto you be abundant peace, grace, loving kindness, mercy, long life, ample sustenance and salvation from the Father who is in heaven, and say, Amen.

Cong.—Let the name of YAHUWAH be blessed from this time forth and for evermore.

Reader.—May there be abundant peace from heaven, and a happy life for us and for all Israel; and say, Amen.

Cong.—My help is from YAHUWAH, who made heaven and earth.

Reader.—He who makes peace in his high places, may he in his mercy make peace for us and for all Israel; and say, Amen.

The following Kaddish is said by a Mourner.

And now, I pray You, let the power of YAHUWAH be great, according as You have spoken. Remember, YAHUWAH, Your tender mercies and Your loving kindnesses; for they have been ever of old.

Mourner.—Magnified and sanctified be his great name in the world which he has created according to his will. May he establish his kingdom during your life and during your days, and during the life of all the house of Israel, even speedily and at a near time, and say, Amen.

Cong. and Mourner.—Let his great name be blessed for ever and to all eternity.

Mourner.—Blessed, praised and glorified, exalted, extolled and honored, magnified and lauded be the name of the Holy One, blessed be he; though he be high above all the blessings and hymns, praises and consolations, which are uttered in the world; and say, Amen.

Cong.—Let the name of YAHUWAH be blessed from this time forth and for evermore.

Mourner.—May there be abundant peace from heaven, and life for us and for all Israel; and say, Amen.

Cong.—My help is from YAHUWAH, who made heaven and earth.

Mourner.—He who makes peace in his high places, may he make peace for us and for all Israel; and say, Amen.

PRAYER FOR THOSE WHO HAVE DIED

YAHUWAH full of mercy who dwells on high, grant perfect rest on the wings of Your Shekinah (Divine Presence). In the lofty heights of the holy and pure, who shine as the brightness of the heavens to the soul of *(Name)* who has gone to his eternal rest as all his family and friends pray for the elevation of his soul. His resting place shall be in the Garden of Eden. Therefore, the Master of mercy will care for him under the protection of His wings for all time and bind his soul in the bond of everlasting life. Elohim (God) is his inheritance and he will rest in peace and let us say, Amen.

May the All Merciful One shelter him under the cover of His wings forever, and bind his soul in the bond of life. The Shekinah is his heritage. May he rest in his resting place in peace. May his name be found in the Lamb's Book of Life, and let us say, Amen.

THIRTEEN PRINCIPLES OF THE FAITH

1. I believe with perfect faith that the Creator, blessed be his name, is the Author and Guide of everything that has been created, and that he alone has made, does make, and will make all things.

2. I believe with perfect faith that the Creator, blessed be his name, is a Unity, and that there is no unity in any manner like unto his, and that he alone is our God, who was, is, and will be.

3. I believe with perfect faith that the Creator, blessed be his name, is not a body, and that he is free from all the accidents of matter, and that he has not any form whatsoever.

4. I believe with perfect faith that the Creator, blessed be his name, is the first and the last.

5. I believe with perfect faith that to the Creator, blessed be his name, and to him alone, it is right to pray, and that it is not right to pray to any being besides him.

6. I believe with perfect faith that all the words of the prophets are true.

7. I believe with perfect faith that the prophecy of Moses our teacher, peace be unto him, was true, and that he was the chief of the prophets, both of those that preceded and of those that followed him.

8. I believe with perfect faith that the whole Law, now in our possession, is the same that was given to Moses our teacher, peace be unto him.

9. I believe with perfect faith that this Law will not be changed, and that there will never be any other law from the Creator, blessed be his name.

10. I believe with perfect faith that the Creator, blessed be his name, knows every deed of the children of men, and all their thoughts, as it is said, It is he that fashioneth the hearts of them all, that giveth heed to all their deeds.

11. I believe with perfect faith that the Creator, blessed be his name, rewards those that keep his commandments, and punishes those that transgress them.

12. I believe with perfect faith in the coming of the Messiah, and, though he tarry, I will wait daily for his coming.

13. I believe with perfect faith that there will be a resurrection of the dead at the time when it shall please the Creator, blessed be his name, and exalted be the remembrance of him for ever and ever.

For your salvation I hope, O Lord! I hope, O Lord, for your salvation! O Lord, for your salvation I hope!

THE TEN COMMANDMENTS

Exodus 20:1–17

And God spoke all these words, saying.

1. I am YAHUWAH your God, who brought you out of the land of Egypt, out of the house of bondage.

2. You shall have no other gods before me. You shall not make unto you a graven image; nor the form of anything that is in heaven above, or that is in the earth beneath, or that is in the water under the earth; you shall not bow down yourself unto them, nor serve them: for I YAHUWAH Your God am a jealous God, visiting the iniquity of the fathers upon the children, upon the third and upon the fourth generation, unto them that hate me: and shewing loving kindness to the thousandth generation, unto them that love me and keep my commandments.

3. You shall not take the name of YAHUWAH your God in vain; for YAHUWAH will not hold him guiltless that takes his name in vain.

4. Remember the sabbath day to keep it holy. Six days shall you labor, and do all your work: but the seventh day is a sabbath unto YAHUWAH your God: in it you shall not do any work, you, nor your son, nor your daughter, your manservant, nor your maidservant, nor your cattle, nor your stranger that is within your gates: for in six days YAHUWAH made heaven and earth, the sea and all that is therein, and rested on the seventh day: wherefore YAHUWAH blessed the sabbath day and hallowed it.

5. Honor your father and your mother: that your days may be long upon the land which YAHUWAH your God gives you.

6. You shall not murder.

7. You shall not commit adultery.

8. You shall not steal.

9. You shall not bear false witness against your neighbor.

10. You shall not covet your neighbor's house, you shall not covet your neighbor's wife, nor his manservant nor his maidservant, nor his ox, nor his ass, nor any thing that is your neighbor's.

PSALMS FOR THE DAYS OF THE WEEK

Psalm for the First Day of the Week (Sunday).

This is the First Day of the Week on which the Levites in the Temple used to say:—

PSALM 24

A Psalm of David: The earth is YAHUWAH's, and the fullness thereof; the world, and they that dwell therein. For it is he that has founded it upon the seas, and established it upon the floods. Who may ascend the mountain of YAHUWAH? And who may stand in his holy place? He that has clean hands and a pure heart; who has not set his desire upon vanity, and has not sworn deceitfully. He shall receive a blessing from YAHUWAH, and righteousness from the God of his salvation. This is the generation of them that seek after him, that seek Your face, (O God of) Jacob! (Selah.) Lift up your heads, O you gates; and be lifted up, you everlasting doors, that the King of glory may come in. Who, then, is the King of glory? YAHUWAH strong and mighty, YAHUWAH mighty in battle. Lift up your heads, O you gates; yes, lift them up, you everlasting doors, that the King of glory may come in. Who, then, is the King of glory? YAHUWAH Tzava'ot, he is the King of glory. (Selah.)

Psalm for the Second Day of the Week (Monday)

This is the Second Day of the Week on which the Levites in the Temple used to say:—

PSALM 48

A Song; a Psalm of the Sons of Korah. Great is YAHUWAH, and highly to be praised, in the city of our God, in his holy mountain. Beautiful in elevation, the joy of the whole earth is mount Zion, at the sides of the north, the city of the great king. God has made himself known in her palaces as a stronghold. For, lo, the kings met each other, they passed on together. They saw it; then were they amazed; they were confounded, they hasted away. Trembling took hold of them there; pangs as of a woman in travail. With an east wind You did break the ships of Tarshish. As we have heard, so have we seen in the city of YAHUWAH of hosts, in the city of our God: God will establish it for ever. (Selah.) We thought of Your lovingkindness, O God, in the midst of Your temple. As is Your name, O God, so is Your renown unto the ends of the earth; Your right hand is full of righteousness. Let mount Zion rejoice, let the daughters of Judah be glad, because of Your judgments. Compass Zion and go round about her: count the towers thereof. Mark well her rampart, traverse her palaces; that you may tell a later generation, that this God is our God for ever and ever: he will be our guide even unto death.

Psalm for the Third Day of the Week (Tuesday)

This is the Third Day of the Week, on which the Levites in the Temple used to say:—

Psalm 82

A Psalm of Asaph. God stands in the congregation of the mighty; he judges among the judges. How long will you judge unjustly, and respect the persons of the wicked? (Selah.) Judge the lowly and fatherless: do justice to the afflicted and destitute. Rescue the lowly and needy: deliver them out of the hand of the wicked. They know not, neither do they understand; they walk about in darkness: all the foundations of the earth are moved. I said, You are gods, and all of you sons of Elyon (the Most High). Nevertheless you shall die like men, and fall like one of the princes. Arise, O God, judge the earth: for You shall possess all the nations.

Psalm for the Fourth Day of the Week (Wednesday)

This is the Fourth Day of the Week, on which the Levites in the Temple used to say:—

Psalm 94

O God of vengeance, YAHUWAH, O God of vengeance, shine forth. Lift up Yourself, You judge of the earth: render to the proud their desert. YAHUWAH, how long shall the wicked, how long shall the wicked triumph? They prate, they speak arrogantly: all the workers of iniquity are boastful. They crush Your people, YAHUWAH, and afflict Your heritage. They slay the widow and the stranger, and murder the fatherless. And they say, YAHUWAH will not see, neither will the God of Jacob give heed. Give heed, you brutish among the people: and you fools, when will you be wise? He that planted the ear, shall he not hear? He that formed the eye, shall he not see? He that chastens the nations, shall not he punish, even he that teaches man knowledge? YAHUWAH knows the thoughts of men, that they are vanity. Happy is the man whom You chasten, YAH, and teaches out of Your Law; that You may give him rest from the days of evil, until the pit be digged for the wicked. For YAHUWAH will not cast off his people, neither will he forsake his inheritance. For judgment shall return unto righteousness: and all the upright in heart shall follow it. Who will rise up for me against the evil-doers, who will stand up for me against the workers of iniquity? Unless YAHUWAH had been my help, my soul had soon dwelt in silence. When I say, My foot slips, Your lovingkindness, YAHUWAH, holds me up. In the multitude of my thoughts within me, Your comforts delight my soul. Has the tribunal of destruction fellowship with You, which frames mischief by statute? They gather themselves together against the soul of the righteous, and condemn the innocent blood. But YAHUWAH is become my stronghold; and my God the rock of my refuge. And he brings back upon them their own iniquity, and for their evil shall cut them off; YAHUWAH our God shall cut them off. O come, let us exult before YAHUWAH: let us shout for joy to the rock of our salvation.

Psalm for the Fifth Day of the Week (Thursday)

This is the Fifth Day of the Week, on which the Levites in the Temple used to say:—

Psalm 81

To the Chief Musician. Set to the Gittith. A Psalm of Asaph. Exult aloud unto God our strength: shout for joy unto the God of Jacob. Raise the song, and strike the timbrel, the pleasant lyre with the harp. Blow the Shofar on the new moon, at the beginning of the month, for our day of festival. For it is a statute of Israel, a decree of the God of Jacob. He appointed it in Joseph for a testimony, when he went forth over the land of Egypt: where I heard a language that I knew not. I removed his shoulder from the burden: his hands were freed from the basket. You called in trouble and I delivered you; I answered you in the secret place of thunder, I proved you at the waters of Meribah. (Selah.) Hear, O my people, and I will testify against you: O Israel, if you will hearken unto me. There shall be no strange god in you; neither shall you worship any foreign god. I am YAHUWAH your God, who brought you out of the land of Egypt: open wide your mouth, and I will fill it. But my people hearkened not to my voice; and Israel was not willing towards me. So I let them go in the stubbornness of their heart, that they might walk in their own counsels. O that my people would hearken unto me, that Israel would walk in my ways. I would soon subdue their enemies, and turn my hand against their adversaries. The haters of YAHUWAH should submit themselves unto him; so that their time might endure for ever. He would feed them also with the fat of wheat: and with honey out of the rock would I satisfy you.

Psalm for the Sixth Day of the Week (Friday)

This is the Sixth Day of the Week, on which the Levites in the Temple used to say:—

Psalm 93

YAHUWAH reigns; he has robed him in majesty; YAHUWAH has robed him, yes, he has girded himself with strength: the world also is set firm, that it cannot be moved. Your throne is set firm from of old: You are from everlasting. The streams have lifted up, YAHUWAH, the streams have lifted up their voice; the streams lift up their roaring. Then the voices of many waters, mighty waters, breakers of the sea, more mighty is YAHUWAH on high. Your testimonies are very faithful: holiness becomes Your house, YAHUWAH, for evermore.

AVODAH RAPHE
(Service For Healing)

The Rabbi/Kohen (Priest) begins by saying:

In the name of the Father YAHUWAH, and of the Son Yah'shua (Jesus), and of the Ruach HaKodesh (Holy Spirit). Amen.

The Rabbi/Kohen (Priest) follows by saying:

19 And when the blast of the shofar (ram's Horn) sounded long and became louder and louder, Moses spoke, and Elohim (God) answered him by voice. (Exodus 19:19-20)

20 "Wherever you hear the sound of the shofar (ram's horn), rally to us there. Our Elohim (God) will fight for us." (Nehemiah 4:20)

8 The sons of Aaron, the koheniym (priests), shall blow the chatsotserot (trumpets); and these shall be to you as an chukat olam (ordinance forever) throughout your generations. 9 "When you go to milchamah (war) in your land against the tsar (enemy) who tsarar (oppresses) you, then you shall sound an rua (alarm) with the chatsotserot (trumpets), and you will be remembered before YAHUWAH your Elohim (God), and you will be saved from your oyev'iym (enemies). 10 Also in the day of your simchah (gladness), in your moed'iym (appointed times), and at the beginning of your chodesh'iym (months), you shall blow the chatsotserot (trumpets) over your olot (burnt offerings) and over the zevach shelem'iym (sacrifices of your peace offerings); and they shall be a zikaron (memorial) for you before your Elohim (God): I am YAHUWAH your Elohim (God)." (Numbers 10:7-10)

14 And when Judah looked back, behold, the battle was before and behind: and they cried unto YAHUWAH, and the koheniym (priests) sounded with chatsotserot (trumpets). (2 Chronicles 13:14)

12 And they entered into a brit (covenant) to darash (seek) YAHUWAH the Elohim (God) of their fathers with all their heart and with all their soul; 13 That whosoever would not darash (seek) YAHUWAH the Elohim (God) of Israel should be put to death, whether small or great, whether man or woman. 14 And they swore unto YAHUWAH with a loud voice, and with teru'ah (shouting), and with chatsotserot (trumpets), and with shofar'ot (ram's horns). 15 And all Judah rejoiced at the shevu'ah (oath): for they had shava (sworn) with kol-levav (all their heart), and sought him with their kol-ratson (whole desire); and he was found of them: and YAHUWAH gave them rest round about. (2 Chronicles 15:12-15)

The Rabbi/Kohen (priest) says the following blessing over the shofar:

Blessed are You YAHUWAH our Elohim (God),elek Ha-Olam (King of the Universe), the God and the Father of our Lord Yah'shua the Messiah (Jesus Christ), Who sanctified us withHis mitzvot (commandments), and commanded us concerning the shofar.

The Rabbi/Kohen then blows the shofar and says:

The circle is now made whole and sacred.

The Rabbi/Kohen (Priest) begins the service by pronouncing Shalom (peace):

PRIEST: Shalom (Peace) be with you, this house, and all who live here.

PEOPLE: YAHUWAH, have mercy on us.

Yah'shua (Jesus), have mercy on us.

Ruach HaKodesh (Holy Spirit), have mercy on us.

The Rabbi/Kohen (Priest) then continues:

PRIEST: O Adon Yah'shua the Messiah (Lord Jesus Christ), Son of Elohim (God), have mercy on us. Amen.

PRIEST: Blessed is the Kingdom of the Father, and of the Son, ✠ and of the Ruach HaKodesh (Holy Spirit): now and ever, and unto ages of ages. Amen.

Glory to You, our Elohim (God); glory to You.

O Melek HaShamayim (Heavenly King), Me'nachem (Comforter), Ruach Ha-Emet (Spirit of Truth), Who are everywhere and fills all things, Gizbarut Ha-Berachat (Treasury of Blessings), and Noten Ha-Chayim (Giver of Life): Come and abide in us, and cleanse us from every impurity, and save our souls, O HaTov (Good One).

PEOPLE: ✠ El Kadosh (Holy God), Abiyr Kadosh (Holy Mighty), Almavet Kadosh (Holy Immortal One), have mercy on us.

✠ El Kadosh (Holy God), Abiyr Kadosh (Holy Mighty), Almavet Kadosh (Holy Immortal One), have mercy on us.

✠ El Kadosh (Holy God), Abiyr Kadosh (Holy Mighty), Almavet Kadosh (Holy Immortal One), have mercy on us.

✠ Glory to the Father YAHUWAH, and to the Son Yah'shua (Jesus), and to the Ruach HaKodesh (Holy Spirit), now and ever, and unto ages of ages. Amen.

O Hashilush HaKodesh (Most Holy Trinity), have mercy on us; Adonai (Lord), cleanse our sins; Adon (Master), pardon our transgressions; Kadosh (Holy One), visit and heal our infirmities for Your Name's sake.

YAHUWAH, have mercy on us.

Yah'shua (Jesus), have mercy on us.

Ruach HaKodesh (Holy Spirit), have mercy on us.

✠ Glory to the Father YAHUWAH, and to the Son Yah'shua (Jesus), and to the Ruach HaKodesh (Holy Spirit), now and ever, and unto ages of ages. Amen.

Avinu / Tefillat Talmid (Our Father / The disciple's prayer)

ALL: Avinu (Our Father), Who is in heaven, hallowed be Your Name. Your Kingdom come. Your will be done, on earth as it is in heaven. Give us this day our daily bread; and forgive us our trespasses, as we forgive those who trespass against us; and lead us not into temptation, but deliver us from the Hara (evil one).

PRIEST: For Yours is the kingdom, and the power, and the glory, of the Father, and of the Son, ✠ and of the Ruach HaKodesh (Holy Spirit): now and ever, and unto ages of ages.

PEOPLE: Amen.

YAHUWAH, have mercy on us.

Yah'shua (Jesus), have mercy on us.

Ruach HaKodesh (Holy Spirit), have mercy on us.

✠ Glory to the Father YAHUWAH, and to the Son Yah'shua (Jesus), and to the Ruach HaKodesh (Holy Spirit), now and ever, and unto ages of ages. Amen.

Oh come, let us worship and bow down; Let us kneel before YAHUWAH our Maker. For He is our Elohim (God), and we are the people of His pasture, and the sheep of His hand. (Psalms 95:6-7)

Psalm 143

1 A Psalm of David. Hear my tefillat (prayer), YAHUWAH, give ear to my tachanun (supplications)! In Your emunah (faithfulness) answer me, and in Your tsedakah (righteousness). 2 Do not enter into mishpat (judgment) with Your servant, for in Your sight no one chai (living) is tsadak (righteous). 3 For the oyev (enemy) has radaph (persecuted) my soul; He has crushed my chai (life) to the ground; He has made me dwell in machshak (darkness), like those who have long been met (dead). 4 Therefore my spirit is overwhelmed within me; My heart within me is distressed. 5 I remember the days of old; I hagah (muse) on all Your works; I siyach (meditate) on the work of Your hands. 6 I spread out my hands to You; My soul longs for You like a thirsty land. Selah. 7 Answer me speedily, YAHUWAH; My spirit fails! Do not hide Your face from me, lest I be like those who go down into the pit. 8 Cause me to hear Your chesed (mercy, lovingkindness) in the morning, for in You do I batach (trust); Cause me to know the way in which I should walk, for I lift up my soul to You. 9 Deliver me, YAHUWAH, from my oyev'iym (enemies); In You I take shelter. 10 Teach me to do Your will, for You are

Elohai (my God); Your Ruach (Spirit) is tov (good). Lead me in the land of miyshor (uprightness). 11 Chayeniy (Quicken me, give me life), YAHUWAH, for Your name's sake! For Your tsedakah's (righteousness') sake bring my soul out of tsarah (trouble). 12 In Your chesed (mercy) cut off my oyev'iym (enemies), and destroy all those who tsarar (afflict) my soul; For I am Your servant.

THE LITTLE LITANY

DEACON: Again and again in shalom (peace) let us pray to YAHUWAH.

PEOPLE: YAHUWAH, have mercy.

DEACON: Lord Yah'shua the Messiah (Jesus Christ), Son of David, have mercy on us.

PEOPLE: Yah'shua (Jesus), have mercy.

DEACON: Help us; save us; have mercy on us; and keep us, O Elohim (God), by Your grace.

PEOPLE: Ruach HaKodesh (Holy Spirit), have mercy.

DEACON: Calling to remembrance our Adon (Lord) and Moshiya (Savior), Yah'shua the Messiah (Jesus Christ), our Melek (King) and Kohen Gadol (High Priest), let us commend ourselves and each other, and all our life unto Messiah (Christ) our Elohim (God).

PEOPLE: To You, O Adonai (Lord).

PRIEST: For You are an El Rachum (merciful God) and love mankind, and unto You we give glory, to the Father YAHUWAH and to the Son Yah'shua (Jesus) ✠ and to the

Ruach HaKodesh (Holy Spirit): now and ever, and unto ages of ages.

PEOPLE: Amen.

Canticle 1

CHOIR: Halleluyah, Halleluyah, Halleluyah,

Verse: "O YAHUWAH, rebuke me not in Your anger, or discipline me in Your wrath."

Halleluyah, Halleluyah, Halleluyah,

Verse: "Have mercy on me, O YAHUWAH, for I am weak."

Halleluyah, Halleluyah, Halleluyah,

Canticle 2

Have mercy on us, O YAHUWAH, have mercy on us; for, deprived of all defense, we chata'iym (sinners) offer this supplication unto You.

Adonai (Lord), have mercy on us.

✠ Glory to the Father YAHUWAH, and to the Son Yah'shua (Jesus), and to the Ruach HaKodesh (Holy Spirit),

Have mercy on us, O YAHUWAH, for in You we trust; do not be exceedingly angry with us, nor remember our iniquities. But even now, look favorably upon us, as the compassionate one; and deliver us from our enemies; for You are our Elohim (God), and we are Your people; we are the work of Your hands, and we call upon Your name.

Now and ever, and unto ages of ages. Amen.

Open to us, O Blessed Adonai (Lord), the door of compassion. Setting our hope in you, we will not go astray. Through you, may we be delivered from all adverse circumstances, for You are the salvation of the Messianic people.

Psalm 51

1 To the Chief Musician. A Psalm of David when Nathan the navi (prophet) went to him, after he had gone in to Bathsheba. Have mercy upon me, O Elohim (God), according to Your chesed (lovingkindness, mercy); According to the multitude of Your racham'iym (tender mercies), blot out my pesha'iym (transgressions). 2 Wash me thoroughly from my avon (iniquity; punishment for sin), and cleanse me from my chatat (sin; punishment for sin). 3 For I acknowledge my pesha'iym (transgressions), and my chatat (sin; punishment for sin) is always before me. 4 Against You, You only, have I chata (sinned), and done this ra (evil) in Your sight; That You may be found tsadak (just) when You speak, and zakah (blameless, pure, clean) when You judge. 5 Behold, I was brought forth in avon (iniquity), and in chet (sin) my mother conceived me. 6 Behold, You desire emet (truth) in the inward parts, and in the hidden part You will make me to know chokmah (wisdom). 7 Purge me with hyssop, and I shall be taher (clean); Wash me, and I shall be whiter than snow. 8 Make me hear sason (joy) and simchah (gladness), that the bones You have broken may rejoice. 9 Hide Your face from my chet (sins), and blot out all my avonot (iniquities). 10 Create in me a lev tahor (clean heart), O Elohim (God), and renew a ruach nakon (steadfast spirit) within me. 11 Do not cast me away from Your presence, and do not take Your Ruach Kodesh (Holy Spirit) from me. 12 Restore to me the sason (joy) of Your yesha (salvation), and uphold me by Your

ruach nadiyv (generous Spirit). 13 Then I will teach posh'iym (transgressors) Your derek (ways), and chataiym (sinners) shall be converted to You. 14 Deliver me from the guilt of bloodshed, O Elohim (God), the Elohim (God) of my teshuv'ah (salvation), and my tongue shall sing aloud of Your tsedakah (righteousness). 15 Adonai (Lord), open my lips, and my mouth shall show forth Your tehilah (praise). 16 For You do not desire zevach (sacrifice), or else I would give it; You do not delight in Olah (burnt offering). 17 The Zevach Elohim (sacrifices of God) are a ruach nishbarah (broken spirit), a lev nishbar ve'nidkeh (broken and a contrite heart); These, O Elohim (God), You will not despise. 18 Do good in Your good pleasure to Zion; Build the walls of Jerusalem. 19 Then You shall be pleased with the zivchei tsedek (sacrifices of righteousness), with Olah (burnt offering) and Kaliyl (whole burnt offering); Then they shall offer bulls on Your mizbeach (altar).

THE CANON
FIRST ODE

CHOIR: When Israel of old had passed through the Red Sea's depth with dry feet, through the stretching forth of Moses' hand in the form of a Cross, they overthrew the Amelekites in the wilderness.

O Master, You always make the souls and bodies of mortals glad with the shemen racham (oil of compassion), protecting the faithful by shemen (oil): Have compassion, now, through shemen (oil), on those who approach You.

O Adonai Yah'shua the Messiah (Lord Jesus Christ), have mercy upon Your servants.

O Master, the whole earth is filled with Your chesed (mercy): Therefore, we, who are mystically anointed with the Shemen HaKodesh (Holy Oil) today, implore You with faith to bestow on us Your incomprehensible mercy.

✠ Glory to the Father YAHUWAH, and to the Son Yah'shua (Jesus), and to the Ruach HaKodesh (Holy Spirit),

Having compassion on Your sick servants, O lover of mankind, You have commanded Your disciples to perform Your Mishchah Kodesh (holy anointing) on them. By Your seal have mercy on us all through their tefillat (prayers).

Now and ever, and unto ages of ages. Amen.

O only pure one, Yam Shalom (sea of peace), overflowing in riches; by Your constant intercession with Elohim (God), deliver Your servants from illnesses and afflictions, so that we may unceasingly magnify You.

SECOND ODE

O Messiah (Christ), Your Church rejoices in You crying aloud: You are my strength, the Lord is my fortress, and my refuge.

O Messiah (Christ), You alone are marvelous and merciful to the faithful; grant from on high Your grace unto those who are grievously and gravely ill.

O Lord Messiah (Christ), have mercy upon Your servants.

O Lord, by Your dispensation You once showed forth an olive branch to be the ending of the flood: Save Your afflicted people by Your mercy.

✠ Glory to the Father YAHUWAH, and to the Son Yah'shua (Jesus), and to the Ruach HaKodesh (Holy Spirit),

O Messiah (Christ), in Your mercy, with the torch of divine light, make glad those who faithfully and eagerly now seek Your chesed (mercy) through this Mishchat HaKodesh (Holy Anointing).

Now and ever, and unto ages of ages. Amen.

Favorably look down from on high, O God and Father of our Lord Yah'shua the Messiah (Jesus Christ), and by our prayers save those who are bitterly afflicted with severe suffering.

SESSIONAL HYMN 1

O merciful one, what a divine river of mercy You are! What a boundless source of great compassion You are! Show forth the divine streams of Your mercy, and heal all mankind. Gush forth abundantly the fountains of wonders; for ever turning to You with fervor, we implore Your grace.

SESSIONAL HYMN 2

Rophe (Physician) and Ozer (Helper) of those who are suffering, O Go'el (Deliverer) and Moshiya (Savior) of the sick, O Master and Lord of all, heal Your sick servants, have compassion and mercy on those who have fallen into grave sins, and deliver them from their transgressions, so that they may glorify Your divine power.

THIRD ODE

Beholding You, O Sun of righteousness, uplifted on the Cross, the Church gloriously stands crying, as it is proper: O Lord, Glory to Your might.

O Savior who emptied Yourself in grace and purified the world, You are like an imperishable chrism; with Your divine pledge, have compassion and mercy on those whose wounded flesh will be annointed.

O Lord Messiah (Christ), have mercy on Your servants.

Having now signed the bodily senses of Your servants with the seal of the joy of Your mercy, O Master, render them inviolate and impenetrable to all adverse powers.

✠ Glory to the Father YAHUWAH, and to the Son Yah'shua (Jesus), and to the Ruach HaKodesh (Holy Spirit),

You have commanded the chasiyd'iym koheniym (godly priests) to summon the sick, that by their tefillat (prayers), and anointing with the Shemen HaKodesh (Holy Oil) they might be healed. By Your chesed (mercy), O lover of mankind, save those who are sick.

Now and ever, and unto ages of ages. Amen.

O YAHUWAH Elohai (my God), my steadfast shelter and my protector, my haven and fortress, my ladder of ascent into heaven and bulwark, have compassion and mercy on us who have sought refuge in You alone.

FOURTH ODE

Being the Light, O Adonai (my Lord), You became a light to the World, a Holy Light that delivers from the darkness of ignorance those who in faith sing praises to You.

O Good and Merciful One, You are the depth of mercy. By Your Shemen HaKodesh (Holy Oil), have mercy, on the sick, for You love mankind.

O Lord Messiah (Christ), have mercy on Your servants.

O Messih (Christ), by the seal of Your divine imprint, You have sanctified both our souls and bodies in an inexpressible manner from on high. Heal us all by Your hand.

✠ Glory to the Father YAHUWAH, and to the Son Yah'shua (Jesus), and to the Ruach HaKodesh (Holy Spirit).

Most gracious Lord, through Your ineffable love, You did accept the anointing with myrrh by the harlot, have compassion on Your servants.

Now and ever, and unto ages of ages. Amen.

O all-praised and all-gracious Adonai have mercy on those now to be anointed with shemen HaKodesh (Holy Oil), and save Your servants.

FIFTH ODE

O YAHUWAH, with a voice of todah (thanksgiving), I offer a zevach (sacrifice) to You. The Church cries aloud to You, for she has been purified from the blood of evil ones by the Blood which, for mercy's sake, gushed from Your side.

O Lover of mankind, You have shown through shemen (oil) the Mishchah (anointing) for Melekiym (Kings), and by Your seal performed it at the hands of kohen'iym Gadil'iym (High priests): By Your compassion save also those who endure suffering.

O Lord Messiah (Christ), have mercy on Your servants.

Let no bitter shediym (demons) lay hold on those who participate in godly anointment and whose senses are touched with it; and surround them, O Savior, with the protection of Your Glory.

✠ Glory to the Father YAHUWAH, and to the Son Yah'shua (Jesus), and to the Ruach HaKodesh (Holy Spirit).

O Savior and Lover of mankind, stretch forth Your hand from on High, and consecrate this shemen (Oil), and bestow it on Your servants for healing and relief from all their maladies.

Now and ever, and unto ages of ages. Amen.

O Lord Yah'shua (Jesus), You have manifested yourself a fruitful olive-tree. In your name, and by the faith that is in your name, the world is seen to be filled with mercy. Therefore, by Your touch, save the sick through Your mercy.

O Compassionate One, You are the fountain of mercy and supremely good. Deliver from every affliction those who with fervent faith fall down before Your inexpressible mercy. Put an end to their illnesses, bestowing on them Your divine grace from on High.

SIXTH ODE

The Children of Abraham in the Persian furnace, fired by love of godliness, rather than by the flame, cried aloud: Blessed are You, O YAHUWAH, in the Tabernacle of Your Glory.

O only Moshiya (Savior) and Elohim (God), in Your mercy and compassions, You heal both the passions of the soul and the afflictions of the body: Heal those who are suffering illnesses.

O Lord Messiah (Christ), have mercy on Your servants.

When the heads of all are anointed with the Oil of Unction, grant with it, O Adonai, by the abundance of Your mercy the joy of gladness and salvation, to those who are asking for Your mercy.

✠ Glory to the Father YAHUWAH, and to the Son Yah'shua (Jesus), and to the Ruach HaKodesh (Holy Spirit).

O savior, Your seal, by the tefillat (prayers) of the koheniym (priests), is a sword against shediym (demons) and a fire that destroys the passions of the soul. Therefore, we who have received healing praise You in faith.

Now and ever, and unto ages of ages. Amen.

In a divine manner, You were conceived in the womb, O Son of the Father, the One who holds fast all things in the hollow of his hand; and ineffably You have given him a body. Relieve the suffering of the sick, we implore You.

SEVENTH ODE

When Daniel stretched forth his hand, he stopped the gaping mouths of the Lions in the pit. The Holy young men being zealous in their piety girded themselves with virtues and quenched the raging fire as they cried aloud: "O all works of YAHUWAH, praise YAHUWAH."

Have mercy on all, O Savior, according to Your great and divine mercy, for this figure was mystically foreshadowed for us. We administer anointing by the Shemen HaKodesh (Holy Oil) for those who are suffering. Heal them all by Your power.

O Lord Messiah (Christ), have mercy on Your servants.

In the streams of Your mercy, O compassionate Lord, and through anointing by the koheniym (priests), wash away the sorrow, the wounds and the attacks, of those who are afflicted by the intensity of illness, so that by Your cleansing they may obtain bodily health and strength.

✠ Glory to the Father YAHUWAH, and to the Son (Yah'shua (Jesus), and to the Ruach HaKodesh (Holy Spirit).

The mark of divine help and the shemen sason (oil of gladness) will come down from on high upon us who are marked by it. O Master, do not withhold Your mercy, neither despise those who with faith ceaselessly cry aloud: "O all works of YAHUWAH, praise YAHUWAH."

Now and ever, and unto ages of ages. Amen.

NINTH ODE

Look down from heaven, O merciful One, and show forth Your mercy on all mankind. Grant now Your help and Your strength to those who draw near to You through Divine Unction administered by Your koheniym (priests), O Lover of mankind.

O Lord Messiah (Christ), have mercy on Your servants.

O most benevolent Savior, let us rejoice at beholding the shemen chasiyd (godly Oil). By Your divine condescension You imparted it to the participants as a sign of sacred cleansing.

✠ Glory to the Father YAHUWAH, and to the Son (Yah'shua (Jesus), and to the Ruach HaKodesh (Holy Spirit).

O Savior, have mercy and compassion upon Your servants; deliver their souls and bodies from terrible sufferings and pains; rescue them from the arrows of the evil one, healing them by Your Divine Grace, inasmuch as You are a merciful Lord.

Now and ever, and unto ages of ages. Amen.

As You receive the praises and petitions of Your servants, O Adonai, by our prayers deliver from bitter afflictions and sufferings those who through us flee to Your divine protection.

THE LITTLE LITANY

DEACON: Again and again in shalom (peace) let us pray to YAHUWAH.

PEOPLE: YAHUWAH, have mercy.

DEACON: Lord Yah'shua the Messiah (Jesus Christ), Son of David, have mercy on us.

PEOPLE: Yah'shua (Jesus), have mercy.

DEACON: Help us; save us; have mercy on us; and keep us, O Elohim (God), by Your grace.

PEOPLE: Ruach HaKodesh (Holy Spirit), have mercy.

DEACON: Calling to remembrance our Adon (Lord) and Moshiya (Savior), Yah'shua the Messiah (Jesus Christ), our Melek (King) and Kohen Gadol (High Priest), let us commend ourselves and each other, and all our life unto Messiah (Christ) our Elohim (God).

PEOPLE: To You, O Adonai (Lord).

PRIEST: For You are an El Rachum (merciful God) and love mankind, and unto You we give glory, to the Father YAHUWAH and to the Son Yah'shua (Jesus) ✠ and to the Ruach HaKodesh (Holy Spirit): now and ever, and unto ages of ages.

PEOPLE: Amen.

THE PETITION

In mercy, O Good One, look down favorably upon our petitions; for we have come together in Your holy temple (this place), to anoint with Shemen HaKodesh (Holy Oil) Your sick servants.

THE PRAISES

Let everything that has breath praise YAHUWAH! Praise YAHUWAH from the heavens: praise him in the heights! To You, O Elohim (God), is due our song.

Praise him all his mal'akiym (angels); praise him all his hosts! To You, O Elohim (God), is due our song.

The Praises are sung along with the following verses:

Verse: To execute on them the judgment decreed. This is glory to all his faithful ones.

O lover of mankind, easy to reconcile, through Your apostles, You have given Your grace: heal with Your Shemen HaKodesh (Holy Oil) the wounds and illnesses of all mankind. Therefore, O compassionate One, sanctify those who now with faith approach Your Shemen HaKodesh (holy Oil): have mercy on them, cleanse them from every infirmity, and make them worthy of Your imperishable bliss.

Verse: Praise Elohim (God) in his sanctuary; praise him in his firmament of his power.

Look down from heaven, O incomprehensible, compassionate and Loving Elohim (God); and by Your invisible hand, mark our senses with Your seal. To those who with faith run to You seeking forgiveness of their sins, grant healing of soul and body by Your Shemen HaKodesh (Holy Oil), so that they may with fervent desire glorify Your kingdom.

Verse: Praise him for his mighty deeds; praise him according to his surpassing greatness!

Anointed with Your mercy, and by the touch of Your koheniym (priests), O Lover of mankind, sanctify from on high Your servants; and deliver them from their illnesses. O Savior, purify and wash out the blemish of their souls, and rescue them from evil plots. Comfort their pains, and drive away adverse circumstances. Utterly destroy their afflictions, for You are a merciful and a compassionate Lord.

✠ Glory to the Father YAHUWAH, and to the Son Yah'shua (Jesus), and to the Ruach HaKodesh (Holy Spirit): Now and ever, and unto ages of ages. Amen.

O Most pure palace of the King, I implore You, O greatly honored one: cleanse my mind, which is stained by every sin, and make it a pleasant dwelling place for the supremely divine Hashilush HaKodesh (Trinity), that I, Your worthless servant, being saved, may glorify Your dominion and Your boundless mercy.

PRIEST: It is good to give thanks to YAHUWAH, to sing praises to Your name, O Elyon (Most High); to declare Your mercy in the morning, and Your truthfulness every night.

PEOPLE: ✠ El Kadosh (Holy God), Abiyr Kadosh (Holy Mighty), Almavet Kadosh (Holy Immortal One), have mercy on us.

✠ El Kadosh (Holy God), Abiyr Kadosh (Holy Mighty), Almavet Kadosh (Holy Immortal One), have mercy on us.

✠ El Kadosh (Holy God), Abiyr Kadosh (Holy Mighty), Almavet Kadosh (Holy Immortal One), have mercy on us.

✠ Glory to the Father YAHUWAH, and to the Son Yah'shua (Jesus), and to the Ruach HaKodesh (Holy Spirit), now and ever, and unto ages of ages. Amen.

O Hashilush HaKodesh (Most Holy Trinity), have mercy on us; Adonai (Lord), cleanse our sins; Adon (Master), pardon our transgressions; Kadosh (Holy One), visit and heal our infirmities for Your Name's sake.

YAHUWAH, have mercy.

Yah'shua (Jesus), have mercy

Ruach HaKodesh (Holy Spirit), have mercy.

✠ Glory to the Father YAHUWAH, and to the Son Yah'shua (Jesus), and to the Ruach HaKodesh (Holy Spirit), now and ever, and unto ages of ages. Amen.

Avinu / Tefillat Talmid (Our Father / The disciple's prayer)

Avinu (Our Father), Who is in heaven, hallowed be Your Name. Your Kingdom come. Your will be done, on earth as it is in heaven. Give us this day our daily bread; and forgive us our trespasses, as we forgive those who trespass against us; and lead us not into temptation, but deliver us from the Hara (evil one).

PRIEST: For Yours is the kingdom, and the power, and the glory, of the Father, and of the Son, ✠ and of the Holy Spirit: now and ever, and unto ages of ages."

PEOPLE: Amen.

Canticle

You, who are alone the speedy helper, O Messiah (Christ), grant Your favor from on high upon Your suffering servants. Deliver them from their infirmities and their sufferings. Raise them up to praise and glorify You ceaselessly, O only Lover of mankind.

THE LITANY OF PEACE

DEACON: In shalom (peace) let us pray to Adonai (the Lord).

CHOIR: Adonai (Lord), have mercy.

DEACON: For the peace from above, and for the salvation of our souls, let us pray to Adonai (the Lord).

CHOIR: Adonai (Lord), have mercy.

DEACON: For the peace of the whole world; for the good estate of the holy churches of Elohim (God), and for the union of all men, let us pray to Adonai (the Lord).

CHOIR: Adonai (Lord), have mercy.

DEACON: For this holy House, and for those who with faith, reverence, and fear of Elohim (God) enter therein, let us pray to Adonai (the Lord).

CHOIR: Adonai (Lord), have mercy.

DEACON: For our Bishop, for the venerable priesthood, the diaconate in Messiah (Christ), for all the clergy and the people, let us pray to Adonai (the Lord).

CHOIR: Adonai (Lord), have mercy.

DEACON: For the President of the United States and all civil authorities, and for our armed forces everywhere, let us pray to Adonai (the Lord).

CHOIR: Adonai (Lord), have mercy.

DEACON: For this city, and for every city and land, and for the faithful who dwell therein, let us pray to Adonai (the Lord).

CHOIR: Adonai (Lord), have mercy.

DEACON: For the people here present, awaiting the grace of the Ruach HaKodesh (Holy Spirit), let us pray to Adonai (the Lord).

CHOIR: Adonai (Lord), have mercy.

DEACON: That this shemen (oil) may be blessed with the visitation, majesty and power of the Ruach HaKodesh (Holy Spirit), let us pray to Adonai (the Lord).

CHOIR: Adonai (Lord), have mercy.

DEACON: For the servants of Elohim (God) who have come to this holy mystery that Elohim (God) will visit them and that the grace of the Ruach HaKodesh (Holy Spirit) will come upon them, let us pray to Adonai (the Lord).

CHOIR: Adonai (Lord), have mercy.

DEACON: For our deliverance from all tribulation, wrath, danger, and necessity, let us pray to Adonai (the Lord).

CHOIR: Adonai (Lord), have mercy.

DEACON: Help us; save us; have mercy on us; and keep us, O Elohim (God), by Your grace.

CHOIR: Adonai (Lord), have mercy.

DEACON: Calling to remembrance our Lord and Savior Yah'shua the Messiah (Jesus Christ), let us commend ourselves and each other, and all our life unto Messiah (Christ) our Elohim (God).

CHOIR: To You, O Adonai (Lord).

PRIEST: For unto You are due all glory, honor, and worship: to the Father YAHUWAH and to the Son Yah'shua (Jesus) ✠ and to the Ruach HaKodesh (Holy Spirit): now and ever, and unto ages of ages.

CHOIR: Amen.

DEACON: Let us pray to Adonai (the Lord).

PEOPLE: Adonai (Lord), have mercy.

THE PRAYER OF THE SHEMEN (OIL)

PRIEST: O YAHUWAH, through Your mercies and compassions heal the disorders of our souls and bodies. O Master, consecrate this shemen (oil) that it may heal and deliver those who are anointed with it from every sinful passion, every bodily illness, every defilement of flesh and spirit, and every infliction; and that in this Oil may Your most Holy Name be glorified: of the Father YAHUWAH, and of the Son Yah'shua (Jesus), ✠ and of the Ruach HaKodesh (Holy Spirit): now and ever, and unto ages of ages. Amen.

THE PEOPLE SING THE FOLLOWING HYMN:

O YAHUWAH, You alone are the speedy helper, grant Your favor from on high upon Your suffering servants. Deliver them from their infirmities and their sufferings. Raise them up to praise and glorify You ceaselessly, O only Lover of mankind, through Yah'shua the Messiah (Jesus Christ).

Spiritually blind, I come to You, O Messiah (Christ), as did the man blind from his birth, crying in repentance to You: You are the truly bright light of those who are in darkness.

349

O Adonai (Lord), as You did raise up the paralytic, by Your divine authority raise up my soul, which is dreadfully paralyzed by my dishonest deeds, so that being saved, I may cry to You: O Compassionate Messiah (Christ), glory to Your dominion.

O righteous James, as a disciple of the Lord, you received the Gospel; as a martyr you possess the unperverted truth, as a brother of the Lord you have boldness, and as a Hierarch you have the power of intercession. Implore Messiah (Christ) our Elohim (God) that he may save our souls.

PRAYER OF ST. MICHAEL THE ARCHANGEL

Kadosh Miyka'el Sar-Mal'ak (St. Michael the Archangel), defend us in battle, be our protection against the wickedness and snares of the devil. May Elohim (God) rebuke him, we humbly pray; and do you, O Prince of the heavenly host, by the power of Elohim (God), cast into hell Satan and all the ruchot ra'ah (evil spirits) who prowl about the world seeking the ruin of souls. Amen.

O blessed Kadosh Miyka'el Sar-Mal'ak (St. Michael the Archangel), come to our aid as you did come to the aid of Daniy'el Ha'Navi (Daniel the Prophet), when the Prince of the Kingdom of Persia, that is Satan, withstood the Mal'ak (angel) for twenty one days. Remove from us every ruchot ra'ah (evil spirit), every shediym (demon) and every ruach chalah (spirit of infirmity); along with every ruach machshil (hindering spirit) that would hinder, prevent, or stop our healing from coming quickly, speedily, even this day as we cry out to our Elohim (God), YAHUWAH, in the name of Yah'shua the Messiah (Jesus Christ), his only-begotten son, grant us your help, O mighty prince of the heavenly host.

PRAYER TO ST. RAPHAEL THE ARCHANGEL

Kadosh Rapha'el Sar-Mal'ak (St. Raphael the Archangel), come to our aid this day, even as you came to the aid of Tobit, when you drove away and bound the shed (demon) asmodeus. Now we humbly ask of you, drive away and bind every ruach ra'ah (evil spirit) and ruach ha'tumah (unclean spirit), so that we may receive complete healing this day, in the Name of Yah'shua the Messiah (Jesus Christ).

PRAYER TO ST. GABRIEL THE ARCHANGEL

Kadosh Gavriy'el Sar-Mal'ak (St. Gabriel the Archangel), come to our aid this day as we call upon your help. As you did appear to Daniy'el Ha'Navi (Daniel the prophet) and gave him skill and understanding, so grant unto us also skill and understanding in the wisdom and mysteries of Messiah (Christ). Grant unto us skill and understanding in the gift of healing and in discerning of spirits, so that we may do the will of Elohim (God) and work the work of Messiah Yah'shua (Christ Jesus) and destroy the works of the devil, because for this reason he did come. In the name of Yah'shua the Messiah (Jesus Christ) we pray.

THE FIRST EPISTLE READING

DEACON: Let us be attentive.

READER: Let Your mercy, O YAHUWAH, be upon us, even as we hope in You, Rejoice in the Lord, O tsadiykiym (righteous).

DEACON: Wisdom.

READER: The lesson from the Epistle of James.

DEACON: Let us be attentive.

James 5:10-16

READER: Brethren, take the nani'iym (prophets) who spoke in the name of YAHUWAH as an example of suffering and patience. Indeed we call them blessed who showed endurance. You have heard of the perseverance of Job and seen the accomplishment of YAHUWAH: that YAHUWAH is very compassionate and merciful. Above all, my Brethren, do not swear, either by heaven or by earth or with any other oath. Let your "Yes" be "Yes" and your "No" "No" so that you may not fall under condemnation. Is anyone among you suffering? He should pray. Is anyone cheerful? He should sing hymns of praise. Is anyone among you sick? He should call for the elders of the church and have them pray over him anointing him with oil in the name of the Lord. The prayer of faith will heal the sick, and the Lord will raise him up. And if he has committed sins, he will be forgiven. Confess your trespasses to one another, and pray for one another so that you may be healed. The prayer of the righteous has a powerful effect.

PRIEST: Shalom (Peace) be to you who has read.

PEOPLE: Halleluyah, Halleluyah, Halleluyah

THE FIRST GOSPEL READING

DEACON: Wisdom. Let us attend, let us hear the Holy Gospel.

PRIEST: Shalom (Peace) be to all.

PEOPLE: And to your Spirit.

PRIEST: The reading from the Holy Gospel according to Saint Luke.

PEOPLE: Glory to You, O YAHUWAH, Glory to You.

DEACON: Let us attend.

Luke 10:25-37

DEACON: At that time, a lawyer stood up to put Yah'shua (Jesus) to the test saying, "Teacher, what shall I do to inherit eternal life?" Yah'shua (Jesus) said to him, "What is written in the Torah (law)? What do you read?" And the lawyer answered, "'You shall love YAHUWAH your Elohim (God) with all your heart, and with all your soul, and with all your strength, and with all your mind, and your neighbor as yourself.'" And Yah'shua (Jesus) said to him, "You have answered right; do this and you will live."

But the lawyer, desiring to justify himself, said to Yah'shua (Jesus), "And who is my neighbor?" Yah'shua (Jesus) replied, "A man was going down from Jerusalem to Jericho, and he fell among robbers, who stripped him and beat him, and departed, leaving him half dead. Now by chance a kohen (priest) was going down that road. And when he saw him, he passed by on the other side. So likewise a Levite, when he came to the place and saw him, passed by on the other side. But a Samaritan came to where he was. And when he saw him, he had compassion, and went to him and bound up his wounds, pouring on shemen (oil) and yayin (wine); and he set him on his own beast, and brought him to an inn, and took care of him. And the next day, he took out two denarii and gave them to the innkeeper saying, 'Take care of him; and whatever more you spend, I will repay you when I come back.'

Which of these three do you think proved neighbor to the man who fell among the robbers?" The lawyer said," The one who showed mercy on him." And Yah'shua (Jesus) said to him, "Go and do likewise."

PEOPLE: Glory to You, O YAHUWAH, Glory to You.

DEACON: Have mercy on us, O Elohim (God), according to Your great goodness, we pray You, hearken, and have mercy.

PEOPLE: YAHUWAH, have mercy.

PEOPLE: Yah'shua (Jesus), have mercy.

PEOPLE: Ruach HaKodesh (Holy Spirit), have mercy.

DEACON: Again we pray for mercy, life, peace, health, salvation, visitation, remission and forgiveness of the sins of the servants of Elohim (God), all devout Messianic Yahudiym (Jews) and Christians who live and dwell in this community.

PEOPLE: YAHUWAH, have mercy.

PEOPLE: Yah'shua (Jesus), have mercy.

PEOPLE: Ruach HaKodesh (Holy Spirit), have mercy.

PRIEST: For You are an El Racham (merciful God) and love mankind, and unto You we give Glory: to the Father YAHUWAH, and to the Son Yah'shua (Jesus), ✠ and to the Ruach HaKodesh (Holy Spirit), now and ever and unto ages of ages.

PEOPLE: Amen.

THE FIRST PRAYER

DEACON: Let us pray to YAHUWAH.

PEOPLE: YAHUWAH, have mercy.

PRIEST: O YAHUWAH, Kodesh HaKadashiym (Holy of Holies), eternal without beginning, You have sent forth Your Only-begotten Son Yah'shua the Messiah (Jesus Christ) to heal every illness and every sickness of our souls and bodies: Send down now Your Ruach HaKodesh (Holy Spirit), and consecrate this Shemen (Oil). Make it to be for Your anointed servants the deliverance from their sins, for inheritance of the Kingdom of heaven. For You are a great and marvelous Elohim (God), steadfast in Your covenant and Your mercy for those who love You. You deliver them from their sins through Your holy Son, Yah'shua the Messiah (Jesus Christ). You give us a new birth from our sins. You open the eyes that are blind, and restore the fallen. You love the tsadiyk'iym (righteous) and show mercy to chata'iym (sinners). You renew us who sit in choshek (darkness) and the araphel tsalmavet (dark shadow of death). You say to those in bondage: "Go free," and to those who sit in choshek (darkness): "Uncover your eyes." For the knowledge of Your Only-Begotten Son has shone in our hearts, since for our sake he appeared on earth, and lived with mankind. To all who received him, he gave power to become children of Elohim (God), granting us adoption through the washing of rebirth and freeing us from participation in the oppression of the devil. Since it was not his pleasure that we should be cleansed by blood, but by shemen ha'kodesh (Holy Oil), he gave us the imprint of his Cross, so that we might become the flock of Messiah (Christ), a Kehunah Malchuto (Royal Priesthood), a Goy Kodesh (Holy Nation); he purified us by mayim (water) and sanctified us by the Ruach HaKodesh (Holy Spirit). O Master and Lord, grant us grace in this ministry, as You gave to Your servant Moses and to Samuel Your beloved and to John Your chosen one and to all those who in every generation were pleasing unto you. In like manner, make us servants of the Brit Chadasha (New Covenant) of Your Son, through this Shemen (Oil), which You have secured through the precious Blood of Your Messiah (Christ). Thus putting away earthly desires, we may be dead to sin and alive to tsedakah (righteousness), putting on our Lord Yah'shua the Messiah (Jesus Christ) by anointing with this shemen kadosh (sanctifying oil) we are about to apply. Let this shemen (oil), O YAHUWAH, be the shemen sason (oil of gladness), the shemen kidush (oil of sanctification), the shemen raphe (oil of healing), a royal garment, a breastplate of power, an averter of every operation of the devil, the seal that cannot be plotted against, the joy of heart, the eternal gladness. Thus will those who are anointed with this Shemen (Oil) of new birth terrify their adversaries, shine in the brightness of Your Kadoshiym (Saints), without spot or wrinkle, receive Your eternal rest, and accept the award of the high calling. For it is Yours to show mercy and save us, O our Elohim (God), and unto You we give glory: to the Father YAHUWAH, and to the Son Yah'shua (Jesus), ✠ and to the Ruach HaKodesh (Holy Spirit), now and ever and unto ages of ages.

PEOPLE: Amen.

THE SECOND EPISTLE READING

DEACON: Let us attend.

READER: YAHUWAH is my strength and my praise. YAHUWAH has disciplined me severely.

DEACON: Wisdom.

READER: The lesson is from the Epistle of Saint Paul to the Romans.

DEACON: Let us attend.

Romans 15:1-7

READER: Brethren, we then who are strong ought to bear with the weakness of the weak and not to please ourselves. Each of us must please his neighbor for the good purpose of building him up. For Messiah (Christ) did not please himself; but as it is written, "The insults of those who insult you fell on me." For whatever was written before was written for our instruction, so that we through patience and through the encouragement of the Scriptures might have hope. Now may the God of patience and encouragement grant you to be like-minded toward one another, according to the Messiah Yah'shuah (Christ Jesus), that you may with one mind and one mouth glorify the God and Father of our Lord Yah'shua the Mesiah (Jesus Christ). Therefore receive one another, just as the Messiah (Christ) also received us, to the glory of Elohim (God).

PRIEST: Shalom (Peace) be to you who has read.

PEOPLE: Halleluyah, Halleluyah, Halleluyah

THE SECOND GOSPEL READING

DEACON: Wisdom. Let us attend, let us hear the Holy Gospel.

PRIEST: Shalom (Peace) be to all.

PEOPLE: And to Your Spirit.

PRIEST: The reading from the Holy Gospel according to Saint Luke.

PEOPLE: Glory to You, O YAHUWAH, Glory to You.

DEACON: Let us attend.

Luke 19:1-10

DEACON: At that time, Yah'shua (Jesus) entered Jericho and was passing through. And there was a man named Zacchaeus; he was a chief tax collector, and rich. And he sought to see who Yah'shua (Jesus) was, but could not, on account of the crowd because he was small of stature. So he ran on ahead and climbed up into a sycamore tree to see Yah'shua (Jesus), for he was to pass that way. And when Yah'shua (Jesus) came to the place, he looked up and said to him, "Zacchaeus , make haste and come down, for I must stay at your house today." So he made haste and came down and received him joyfully. But when they saw it, they all murmured, "He has gone in to be a guest of a man who is a sinner." And Zacchaeus stood and said to the Lord, Behold, Lord, the half of my goods I give to the poor; and if I have defrauded any one of anything, I restore it fourfold." And Yah'shua (Jesus) said to him, "Today salvation has come to this house, since he also is a son of Abraham; for the Son of Man came to seek and to save the lost.

PEOPLE: Glory to You, O YAHUWAH, Glory to You.

DEACON: Have mercy on us, O Elohim (God), according to Your great goodness, we pray You, hearken and have mercy.

PEOPLE: YAHUWAH, have mercy.

PEOPLE: Yah'shua (Jesus), have mercy.

PEOPLE: Ruach HaKodesh (Holy Spirit), have mercy.

DEACON: Again we pray for mercy, life, peace, health, salvation, and visitation, remission and forgiveness of the sins of the servants of Elohim (God), all devout Messianic Yahudiym (Jews) and Christians who live and dwell in this community.

PEOPLE: YAHUWAH, have mercy.

PEOPLE: Yah'shua (Jesus), have mercy.

PEOPLE: Ruach HaKodesh (Holy Spirit), have mercy.

PRIEST: For You are a merciful God and love mankind, and unto You we give Glory: to the Father YAHUWAH, and to the Son Yah'shua (Jesus), ✠ and to the Ruach HaKodesh (Holy Spirit), now and ever and unto ages of ages.

PEOPLE: Amen.

THE SECOND PRAYER

DEACON: Let us pray to YAHUWAH.

PEOPLE: YAHUWAH, have mercy.

PRIEST: O El Elyon va'Gadol (Great and Most High God), adorned by all creation, source of wisdom, untraceable depth of goodness, and boundless ocean of tender mercy, O Master, lover of mankind, the El (God) of eternal and wondrous things whom no one can conceive or understand, look down favorably upon Your unworthy servants and hear us. Wherever in Your Shem Gadol (Great Name) we offer You this shemen (Oil), send down as Your free gift Your healing and forgiveness of sins and heal Your people in Your great mercy.

O YAHUWAH, You are easily reconcilable and alone are merciful and the lover of mankind. You did relent concerning terrible punishment for our evil deeds. You know that the inclination of the human heart is evil from youth. You desire not the death of a sinner, but rather yhat he might turn back and live. Though Elohim (God), You did become incarnate for the salvation of chata'iym (sinners), taking on the human form for Your creatures. You have said: "I have come to call not the tsadiyk'iym (righteous), but chata'iym (sinners)." You have looked for the lost sheep, You have searched carefully for the lost silver coin and You have found it. You have said: "Anyone who comes to me I will never drive away." You did not detest the sinful woman who bathed Your precious feet with her tears. You have said: "As often as you fall, arise, and you will be saved." You are he who said: "There will be joy in heaven over one sinner who repents." O merciful Master, look down favorably from the height of Your holy place; and in this hour overshadow us, Your sinful and unworthy servants, with the grace of Your Ruach HaKodesh (Holy Spirit); and dwell among Your servants who acknowledge their transgressions and approach You in faith. By Your love toward mankind, accept them and forgive them whatever they have done wrong, whether by word, or deed or thought; and cleanse them from every sin. Be present with them, and protect the remaining time of their life so that walking in Your chukiym (statutes), they may no longer become objects of the malignant joy of the devil. And may Your all-Holy name be glorified in them.

For it is Yours to show mercy and save us, O Messiah (Christ) our Elohim (God), and unto You we give glory together with Your Father who is from everlasting, and Your all-Holy good and life-giving Spirit: now and ever and unto ages of ages.

PEOPLE/CHOIR: Amen.

THE THIRD EPISTLE READING

DEACON: Let us attend.

READER: YAHUWAH is my light and my salvation. YAHUWAH is the stronghold of my life; Of whom shall I be afraid?

DEACON: Wisdom.

READER: The lesson is from the first epistle of Saint Paul to the Corinthians.

DEACON: Let us attend.

1 Cor.12:27-31;13:1-8

READER: Brethren, now you are the body of Messiah (Christ), and individually members of it. And Elohim (God) has appointed in the church, first Shaliych'iym (apostles), second Navi'iym (prophets), third me'lam'diym (teachers), after that gevurot (miracles), then matanot harephu'ot (gifts of healings), ta'miykot (helps, forms of assistance), hane'hagot (administrations, forms of leadership), miney lashonot (varieties of tongues). Are all Shaliych'iym (apostles)? Are all Navi'iym (prophets)? Are all me'lam'diym (teachers)? Are all osey gevurot (workers of miracles)? Do all have matanot rephu'ot (gifts of healings)? Do all devariym bi'lashonot (speak with tongues)? Do all ma'ab'arey lashonot (interpret)? But strive eagerly for the greater gifts. And yet I show you a more excellent way. If I speak with the tongues of anashiym (men) and of mal'akiym (angels), but have not ahava (love), I have become a noisy gong or a clanging cymbal. And if I have the gift of prophecy, and understand all mysteries and all knowledge, and if I have all faith so that I can remove mountains, but do not have love, I am nothing. And if I give away all my possessions, and if I give my body to be burned, but have not love, it profits me nothing. Love is patient; love is kind; love does not envy; love is not conceited, is not puffed up, does not behave rudely, does not seek its own, is not irritable, thinks no evil, does not rejoice in wrongdoing, but rejoices in the truth, bears all things, believes all things, hopes all things, endures all things. Love never comes to an end. But where there are prophecies, they will come to an end; where there are tongues, they will cease; whether there is knowledge, it will vanish away.

PRIEST: Shalom (Peace) be to you who has read.

PEOPLE: Halleluyah, Halleluyah, Halleluyah

THE THIRD GOSPEL READING

DEACON: Wisdom. Let us attend, let us hear the Holy Gospel.

PRIEST: Shalom (Peace) be to all.

PEOPLE: And to your Spirit.

PRIEST: The reading from the Holy Gospel according to Saint Matthew.

PEOPLE: Glory to You, O YAHUWAH, Glory to You.

DEACON: Let us attend.

Matthew 10:1, 5-8

DEACON: At that time, Yah'shua (Jesus) called to him his twelve disciples and gave them authority over ruchot ha'tumah (unclean spirits): to cast them out and to heal every disease and infirmity. These twelve Yah'shua (Jesus) sent out charging them: "Go nowhere among the Goyim (Gentiles), and enter no town of the Samaritans. But go rather to the lost sheep of the house of Israel. And preach as you go saying, 'The kingdom of heaven is at hand.' Heal the sick; cleanse the lepers; raise the dead; cast out shediym (demons). You received without pay, give without pay.

PEOPLE: Glory to You, O YAHUWAH, Glory to You.

DEACON: Have mercy on us, O Elohim (God), according to Your great goodness, we pray You, hearken, and have mercy.

PEOPLE: YAHUWAH, have mercy.

PEOPLE: Yah'shua (Jesus), have mercy.

PEOPLE: Ruach HaKodesh (Holy Spirit), have mercy.

DEACON: Again we pray for mercy, life, peace, health, salvation, visitation, remission and forgiveness of the sins of the servants of Elohim (God), all devout Messianic Yahuditm (Jews) and Christians who live and dwell in this community.

PEOPLE: YAHUWAH, have mercy.

PEOPLE: Yah'shua (Jesus), have mercy.

PEOPLE: Ruach HaKodesh (Holy Spirit), have mercy.

PRIEST: For You are a merciful God and love mankind, and unto You we give Glory: to the Father YAHUWAH, and to the Son Yah'shua (Jesus), ✠ and to the Ruach HaKodesh (Holy Spirit), now and ever and unto ages of ages.

PEOPLE: Amen.

THE THIRD PRAYER

DEACON: Let us pray to YAHUWAH.

PEOPLE: YAHUWAH, have mercy.

PRIEST: O El Shaddai (Almighty God), O Melek Kodesh (Holy King), You discipline yet do not put to death, You uphold all who are falling, and raise up all who are bowed down, You relieve the physical suffering of mankind. We implore You, O our Elohim (God), to send Your mercy upon this Shemen (Oil) and upon all those anointed with it in Your name. Let it be effectual for the healing of their souls and bodies and for cleansing and for relieving from every suffering, disease, sickness, and defilement, of both body and spirit. Yea, YAHUWAH, send down from heaven Your healing power. Touch the bodies, alleviate the fever, relieve the suffering, and expel every hidden sickness. Be the physician of Your servants; raise them up from the bed of their sickness and cruel suffering; and restore them to Your Church in safety and health to please You and to do Your will.

For it is Yours to show mercy and save us, O our Elohim (God), and unto You we give glory, to the Father YAHUWAH and to the Son Yah'shua (Jesus) ✠ and to the Ruach HaKodesh (Holy Spirit), now and ever and unto ages of ages.

PEOPLE/CHOIR: Amen.

THE FOURTH EPISTLE READING

DEACON: Let us attend.

READER: On the day when I called you answered me O YAHUWAH, hear my prayer. YAHUWAH is my light and my salvation.

DEACON: Wisdom.

READER: The lesson is from the second epistle of Saint Paul to the Corinthians.

DEACON: Let us attend.

2 Corinthians 6:14-7:1

READER: Brethren, Do not be unequally yoked together with lo-ma'amiyn (unbelievers). For what chev'rah (fellowship) has tsedakah (righteousness) with the av'lah (transgression of the law)? And what chavarut (communion) has light with darkness? And what accord has Messiah (Christ) with Beliya'al (Belial)? Or what part has a ma'amiyn (believer) with a lo-ma'amiyn (unbeliever)? And what agreement has the temple of Elohim (God) with eliyliym (idols)? For you are the temple of the Elohim Chayim (living God). As Elohim (God) has said: "I will dwell in them and walk among them. I will be their Elohim (God), and they shall be My people." Therefore "Come out from among them and be separate, says YAHUWAH. Do not touch what is tame (unclean), and I will receive you. I will be a Father to you, and you shall be My sons and daughters, Says YAHUWAH Shaddai (the Lord Almighty). Having these promises, beloved, let us cleanse ourselves from all defilement of the flesh and spirit and bring our holiness to perfection in the fear of Elohim (God)."

PRIEST: Shalom (Peace) be to you who has read.

PEOPLE: Halleluyah, Halleluyah, Halleluyah

THE FOURTH GOSPEL READING

DEACON: Wisdom. Let us attend, let us hear the Holy Gospel.

PRIEST: Shalom (Peace) be to all.

PEOPLE: And to Your Spirit.

PRIEST: The reading from the Holy Gospel according to Saint Matthew.

PEOPLE: Glory to You, O YAHUWAH, Glory to You.

DEACON: Let us attend.

Matthew 8:14-23

DEACON: At that time, Yah'shua (Jesus) entered Peter's house, and he saw Peter's mother-in-law lying sick with a fever; he touched her hand, and the fever left her, and she rose and served them. That evening they brought to him many who were possessed with shediym (demons); he cast out the ruchot (spirits) with a word, and healed all who were sick. This was to fulfill what was spoken by the prophet Isaiah, "He took our infirmities and bore our diseases." Now when Yah'shua (Jesus) saw great crowds around him, he gave orders to go over to the other side. And a scribe came up and said to him, "Teacher, I will follow you wherever you go." And Yah'shua (Jesus) said to him, "Foxes have holes and birds of heaven have nests, but the Son of Man has nowhere to lay his head." Another of his disciples said to him, "Lord, let me first go and bury my father." But Yah'shua (Jesus) said to him, "Follow me, and leave the dead to bury their own dead." And when he got into the boat, his disciples followed him.

PEOPLE: Glory to You, O YAHUWAH, Glory to You.

DEACON: Have mercy on us, O Elohim (God), according to Your great goodness, we pray You, hearken, and have mercy.

PEOPLE: YAHUWAH, have mercy.

PEOPLE: Yah'shua (Jesus), have mercy.

PEOPLE: Ruach HaKodesh (Holy Spirit), have mercy.

DEACON: Again we pray for mercy, life, peace, health, salvation, visitation, remission and forgiveness of the sins of the servants of Elohim (God), all devout Messianic Yahudiym (Jews) and Christians who live and dwell in this community.

PEOPLE: YAHUWAH, have mercy.

PEOPLE: Yah'shua (Jesus), have mercy.

PEOPLE: Ruach HaKodesh (Holy Spirit), have mercy.

PRIEST: For You are a merciful God and love mankind, and unto You we give Glory: to the Father YAHUWAH, and to the Son Yah'shua (Jesus), ✠ and to the Ruach HaKodesh (Holy Spirit), now and ever and unto ages of ages.

PEOPLE: Amen.

THE FOURTH PRAYER

DEACON: Let us pray to YAHUWAH.

PEOPLE: YAHUWAH, have mercy.

PRIEST: O Good and loving, compassionate and merciful Lord, You are plentiful in mercy, rich in benevolence, the Father of mercy and God of all comfort, who through Your holy

Disciples empowered us to heal the illness of Your people by Shemen (Oil) and prayer: Do Yourself confirm this Shemen (Oil) for the healing of those who will be anointed with it, for the relief from every sickness and malady and for the deliverance from the bodily illness of those who earnestly await deliverance from You. Yea, O El Shaddai (Almighty God), YAHUWAH our Elohim (God), we entreat You to save us. O only Physician of our souls and bodies, purify us all; heal Your servants, O healer of every malady. Raise them up from their sick-bed, through the mercies of Your goodness. Visit them with Your mercy and compassion. Expel by Your mighty hand every sickness and malady so that when they rise up, they may serve You with thanksgiving. We also, who now share in Your inexpressible love towards mankind, praise and glorify You who performs great, marvelous, glorious and splendid deeds.

For it is Yours to show mercy and save us, O our Elohim (God), and unto You we give glory, to the Father YAHUWAH and to the Son Yah'shua (Jesus) ✠ and to the Ruach HaKodesh (Holy Spirit), now and ever and unto ages of ages.

PEOPLE/CHOIR: Amen.

THE FIFTH EPISTLE READING

DEACON: Let us attend.

READER: You, O YAHUWAH, will protect us. Save me, O YAHUWAH, for the faithful have disappeared.

DEACON: Wisdom.

READER: The lesson is from the second epistle of Saint Paul to the Corinthians.

DEACON: Let us attend.

2 Corinthians 1:8-11

READER: Brethren, we do not want you to be uninformed of our affliction which came to us in Asia: we were burdened beyond measure and above strength so that we despaired of life itself. Indeed, we felt in ourselves that we received the sentence of death so that we should not rely on ourselves but on Elohim (God) who raises the dead, who delivered us from such terrible and deadly dangers and will continue to deliver us; on whom we have set our hope that he will still deliver us. You also join in helping us by your prayers that thanks may be given by many people on our behalf for the gift granted to us through many.

PRIEST: Shalom (Peace) be to you who has read.

PEOPLE: Halleluyah, Halleluyah, Halleluyah

THE FIFTH GOSPEL READING

DEACON: Wisdom. Let us attend, let us hear the Holy Gospel.

PRIEST: Shalom (Peace) be to all.

PEOPLE: And to Your Spirit.

PRIEST: The reading from the Holy Gospel according to Saint Matthew.

PEOPLE: Glory to You, O YAHUWAH, Glory to You.

DEACON: Let us attend.

(Matthew 25:1-13)

DEACON: "Then the kingdom of heaven shall be compared to ten virgins who took their lamps and went to meet the bridegroom. Five of them were wise, and five were foolish. When the foolish took their lamps, they took no oil with them; but the wise took flasks of oil with their lamps. As the bridegroom was delayed, they all slumbered and slept. And at midnight there was a cry, 'Behold, the bridegroom! Come out to meet him!' Then all the virgins rose and trimmed their lamps. And the foolish said to the wise, 'Give us some of your oil, for our lamps are going out.' But the wise replied, 'perhaps there will not be enough for us and for you; go rather to the dealers and buy for yourselves.' And while they went to buy, the bridegroom came, and those who were ready went in with him to the marriage feast; and the door was shut. Afterward, the other virgins came also saying, 'Lord, Lord, open to us!' But he replied, 'Truly, I say to you, I do not know you.' Watch therefore, for you know neither the day nor the hour when the Son of Man will come."

PEOPLE: Glory to You, O YAHUWAH, Glory to You.

DEACON: Have mercy on us, O Elohim (God), according to Your great goodness, we pray You, hearken, and have mercy.

PEOPLE: YAHUWAH, have mercy.

PEOPLE: Yah'shua (Jesus), have mercy.

PEOPLE: Ruach HaKodesh (Holy Spirit), have mercy.

DEACON: Again we pray for mercy, life, peace, health, salvation, visitation, remission and forgiveness of the sins of the servants of Elohim (God), all devout Messianic Yahudiym (Jews) and Christians who live and dwell in this community.

PEOPLE: YAHUWAH, have mercy.

PEOPLE: Yah'shua (Jesus), have mercy.

PEOPLE: Ruach HaKodesh (Holy Spirit), have mercy.

PRIEST: For You are a merciful God and love mankind, and unto You we give Glory: to the Father YAHUWAH, and to the Son Yah'shua (Jesus), ✠ and to the Ruach HaKodesh (Holy Spirit), now and ever and unto ages of ages.

PEOPLE: Amen.

THE FIFTH PRAYER

DEACON: Let us pray to YAHUWAH.

PEOPLE: YAHUWAH, have mercy.

PRIEST: O YAHUWAH our Elohim (God), You discipline, yet You heal; You raise the poor from the dust, and lift the needy from the ash heap. O Father of orphans, haven of the storm-tossed, and physician of the sick, You without weakness have borne our illness, and assumed our sickness, You show mercy with cheerfulness, and pass over our transgressions, pardoning our iniquity. You are quick to help and slow to anger. You did breath on Your holy Disciples and say to them: "Receive the Ruach HaKodesh (Holy Spirit). If you forgive the sins of any, they are forgiven them. You accept the repentance of sinners, and have authority to forgive numerous and grievous sins, bestowing healing upon all who have spent their life in sickness and chronic diseases; You have called me, also, Your humble, sinful and unworthy servant, entangled in heavy sins, and immersed in pleasures by my lustful passions, to the Holy and high degree of priesthood, and to enter the inner shrine behind the paroket (veil), into the Kadosh HaKadashiym (Holy of Holies), where the

Mal'akiym Kadoshiym (Holy Angels) desire to look, and to hear the voice of YAHUWAH which bears good news, and to see with their eyes the presence of the holy Oblation, and to enjoy the divine and sacred Liturgy. You have made me worthy to administer Your heavenly Mysteries, and to offer unto You gifts and sacrifices for our sins and the sins of the people, committed through ignorance, and to mediate for Your sheep which are endowed with reason, that, through Your great and inexpressible love toward mankind, You would wipe away their sins. O supremely good King, hear my prayer in this hour and this holy day and at every time and place; listen to the voice of my supplication. Grant healing to Your servants, who are sick both in soul and body, bestowing upon them forgiveness of sins and pardon for their transgressions, both voluntary and involuntary; heal their incurable diseases, every sickness and every malady. Give health to their souls, for You did touch the mother-in-law of Peter and the fever left her so that she rose and served them: Do Yourself, O Master, grant also healing to Your servants, relieving them from every pernicious disease. Be mindful of Your mercy, O YAHUWAH, and of Your steadfast love. Remember that every human mind inclines toward evil from his youth, and no one on the earth is found sinless; for You are alone without sin, having come down to save the human race and to set us free from the slavery to the enemy. If You enter into judgment with Your servants no one will be pure from stain, but every mouth will be sealed, having no defense; for all our righteousness is like filthy rags in Your presence. Therefore, remember not the sins of our youth. For You are the hope of the hopeless and the rest of those who are weary and are carrying heavy burdens, and unto You we give glory, together with Your Father, who is from everlasting, and Your all-holy and good and life-giving Spirit: now and ever and unto ages of ages.

PEOPLE/CHOIR: Amen.

THE SIXTH EPISTLE READING

DEACON: Let us attend.

READER: Have mercy on me, O Elohim (God), according to Your great mercy. Create in me a clean heart, O Elohim (God).

DEACON: Wisdom.

READER: The lesson is from the epistle of Saint Paul to the Galatians.

DEACON: Let us attend.

Galatians 5:22-6:2

READER: Brethren, the fruit of the Spirit is love, joy, peace, patience, kindness, goodness, faithfulness, gentleness, self-control. Against such things there is no law. And those who are Messiah's (Christ's) have crucified the flesh with its passions and desires. If we live in the Spirit, let us also walk in the Spirit. Let us not become conceited, irritating one another, envying one another. Brethren, if a man is caught in any sin, you who are spiritual restore such a one in a spirit of gentleness, taking care that you yourself are not tempted. Bear one another's burdens, and so fulfill the law of Messiah (Christ).

PRIEST: Shalom (Peace) be to you who has read.

PEOPLE: Halleluyah, Halleluyah, Halleluyah

THE SIXTH GOSPEL READING

DEACON: Wisdom. Let us attend, let us hear the Holy Gospel.

PRIEST: Shalom (Peace) be to all.

PEOPLE: And to Your Spirit.

PRIEST: The reading from the Holy Gospel according to Saint Matthew.

PEOPLE: Glory to You, O YAHUWAH, Glory to You.

DEACON: Let us attend.

Matthew 15:21-28

DEACON: At that time, Yah'shua (Jesus) went away to the district of Tyre and Sidon. And behold, a Canaanite woman from that region came and cried out, "Have mercy on me, O Lord, Son of David! My daughter is severely possessed by a shed (demon)." But Yah'shua (Jesus) did not answer her a word. And his disciples came and begged him, saying, "Send her away, for she is crying after us." Yah'shua (Jesus) answered "I was sent only to the lost sheep of the house of Israel." But she came and knelt before him saying, "Lord, help me!" And Yah'shua (Jesus) answered, "It is not right to take the children's bread and throw it to the dogs." She said, "Yes, Lord, yet even the dogs eat the crumbs that fall from their master's table." Then Yah'shua (Jesus) answered her, "O woman, great is your faith! Be it done to you as you desire." And her daughter was healed instantly.

PEOPLE: Glory to You, O YAHUWAH, Glory to You.

DEACON: Have mercy on us, O Elohim (God), according to Your great goodness, we pray You, hearken, and have mercy.

PEOPLE: YAHUWAH, have mercy.

PEOPLE: Yah'shua (Jesus), have mercy.

PEOPLE: Ruach HaKodesh (Holy Spirit), have mercy.

DEACON: Again we pray for mercy, life, peace, health, salvation, visitation, remission and forgiveness of the sins of the servants of Elohim (God), all devout Messianic Yahudiym (Jews) and Christians who live and dwell in this community.

PEOPLE: YAHUWAH, have mercy.

PEOPLE: Yah'shua (Jesus), have mercy.

PEOPLE: Ruach HaKodesh (Holy Spirit), have mercy.

PRIEST: For You are a merciful God and love mankind, and unto You we give Glory: to the Father YAHUWAH, and to the Son Yah'shua (Jesus), ✠ and to the Ruach HaKodesh (Holy Spirit), now and ever and unto ages of ages.

PEOPLE: Amen.

THE SIXTH PRAYER

DEACON: Let us pray to YAHUWAH.

PEOPLE: YAHUWAH, have mercy.

PRIEST: O YAHUWAH our Elohim (God), You who are loving, good, and the physician of our souls and bodies: we give thanks unto You, for You have easily borne our illness and by

Your wounds we have been healed. You did come in search of the sheep who went astray. You did encourage the faint-hearted and did give life to the oppressed. You did heal the woman who had been suffering from hemorrhages for twelve years. You did free the daughter of the Canaanite woman from a fierce shed (demon). You did forgive the debt of the two debtors and the sins of the sinful woman. You did heal the paralytic forgiving his sins. You did make the tax-collector righteous by one word and accepted the thief at his last confession. You take away the sin of the world, nailing it to the Cross. O Elohim (God), we pray and we implore You in Your goodness, pardon, remit and forgive the sins and iniquities of Your servants, both voluntary or involuntary, in knowledge or in ignorance, whether transgression or disobedience, at night or at day, whether they are under the ban of a priest, of a father or mother, whether through the pleasure of the eye or the weakness of the sense of smell, through the softness of the touch or the taste of adultery, or through any impulse of the flesh or of the spirit they have become alienated from Your will and from Your holiness. If we also have sinned in like manner forgive us: for You are a good, loving and forgiving El (God). Do not allow them or us to fall into an impure life, nor fall into destructive paths. Yea, O YAHUWAH, hear me, a sinner, in this hour on behalf of Your servants: overlook, as a forgiving El (God), all their sins. Set them free from the eternal punishment. Fill their mouths with Your praise; open their lips that they may glorify Your name; stretch forth their hands to do Your commandments; direct their feet in the way of Your Gospel, strengthening all their members and their minds by Your grace.

For You are our Elohim (God), who gave us a mitzvah (commandment) by Your holy Apostles saying: "Whatever you bind on earth will be bound in heaven, and whatever you loose on earth will be loosed in heaven," and "If you forgive the sins of any, they are forgiven them." And as You did listen to Ezekiel in the sorrow of his soul at the hour of his death and did not despise his supplications, so also, in like manner, hear me, Your humble and unworthy servant at this hour. For You are the Lord Yah'shua the Messiah (Jesus Christ), who through Your Goodness and love toward mankind commanded us to forgive those who fall in sins not even seven times, but seventy times seven. You forgive our wickedness and rejoice over the conversion of those who have gone astray. For as is Your majesty, so also is Your mercy, and unto You we give glory, with Your Father, who is from everlasting, and Your all-holy and good and life-giving Spirit: now and ever and unto ages of ages.

PEOPLE/CHOIR: Amen.

THE SEVENTH EPISTLE READING

DEACON: Let us attend.

READER: O YAHUWAH, do not rebuke me in Your anger, or discipline me in Your wrath. Have mercy on me, O YAHUWAH, for I am weak.

DEACON: Wisdom.

READER: The lesson is from the first epistle of the apostle Paul to the Thessalonians.

DEACON: Let us attend.

1 Thessalonians 5:14-23

READER: Brethren, we urge you, warn the idlers, comfort the fainthearted, uphold the weak, be patient with all. See that no one renders evil for evil to anyone, but always strive for what is good both for yourselves and for all. Rejoice always, pray without ceasing, in everything give thanks; for this is the will of Elohim (God) in Messiah Yah'shua (Christ Jesus) for you. Do not quench the Spirit. Do not despise prophecies. Test all things; hold fast to what is good. Abstain from every form of evil. Now may the Elohim Shalom (God of peace) himself sanctify you entirely; and may your whole spirit, soul, and body be preserved blameless at the coming of our Lord Yah'shua the Messiah (Jesus Christ).

PRIEST: Shalom (Peace) be to you who has read.

PEOPLE: Halleluyah, Halleluyah, Halleluyah

THE SEVENTH GOSPEL READING

DEACON: Wisdom. Let us attend, let us hear the Holy Gospel.

PRIEST: Shalom (Peace) be to all.

PEOPLE: And to Your Spirit.

PRIEST: The reading from the Holy Gospel according to Saint Matthew.

PEOPLE: Glory to You, O YAHUWAH, Glory to You.

DEACON: Let us attend.

Matthew 9:9-13

DEACON: At that time, as Yah'shua (Jesus) passed on from there, he saw a man named Matthew sitting at the tax office. And he said to him, "Follow me." And he arose and followed him. And as he sat at the table in the house, behold, many tax collectors and sinners came and sat down with him and his disciples. And when the Pharisees saw this, they said to his disciples, "Why does your Teacher eat with tax collectors and sinners?" When Yah'shua (Jesus) heard it, he said to them, "Those who are well have no need of a physician, but those who are sick. "Go and learn what this means: 'I desire mercy and not sacrifice.' For I came not to call the righteous, but sinners, to repentance."

PEOPLE: Glory to You, O YAHUWAH, Glory to You.

DEACON: Have mercy on us, O Elohim (God), according to Your great goodness, we pray You, hearken, and have mercy.

PEOPLE: YAHUWAH, have mercy.

PEOPLE: Yah'shua (Jesus), have mercy.

PEOPLE: Ruach HaKodesh (Holy Spirit), have mercy.

DEACON: Again we pray for mercy, life, peace, health, salvation, visitation, remission and forgiveness of the sins of the servants of Elohim (God), all devout Messianic Yahudiym (Jews) and Christians who live and dwell in this community.

PEOPLE: YAHUWAH, have mercy.

PEOPLE: Yah'shua (Jesus), have mercy.

PEOPLE: Ruach HaKodesh (Holy Spirit), have mercy.

PRIEST: For You are a merciful God and love mankind, and unto You we give Glory: to the Father YAHUWAH, and to the Son Yah'shua (Jesus), ✠ and to the Ruach HaKodesh (Holy Spirit), now and ever and unto ages of ages.

PEOPLE: Amen.

DEACON: Let us pray to YAHUWAH.

PEOPLE: YAHUWAH, have mercy.

THE SEVENTH PRAYER

PRIEST: O Master, YAHUWAH our Elohim (God), Physician of souls and bodies, You heal chronic sufferings and cure every infirmity and every sickness among the people. You desire every one to be saved, and to come to the knowledge of the truth. You desire not the death of a sinner, but that he should repent and live. In the ancient covenant, You did appoint repentance for sinners, for David, for the Ninevites, and for those both before and after them. When You have come in the flesh to dwell among Your people in the new dispensation, You did not call the righteous, but sinners, to repentance; You did accept through repentance the blasphemous and great persecutor Paul, as well as the tax-collector, the prostitute, and the thief. Through repentance You did accept the great Peter who denied You three times, promising and saying to him: "You are Peter, and on this rock I will build my Church, and the gates of Hades will not prevail against it. I will give You the keys of the kingdom of heaven." Therefore, O Good one, lover of mankind, according to Your trustworthy promise, we take courage to entreat You and implore You in this hour: Hear our supplication and receive it as incense offered unto You. Visit Your servants. If they have committed any sin whether by word or deed or thought, at night or during the day, or if they have fallen under the ban of a priest, or under self-binding oath, or have been provoked to commit a sin by an oath, or they have taken an oath, we entreat You and supplicate You: Pardon, remit, and forgive them, O Elohim (God), overlooking their sins and iniquities of knowledge or of ignorance. If they have transgressed Your commandments or have sinned because they bear flesh and dwell in the world, or by reason of the devil, do Yourself, as a Good and loving God, forgive them, for there is no one who lives and sins not. For You are sinless, and Your righteousness is to all eternity, and Your word is truth. For You have not created the human race to be destined to Hell, but to keep Your commandments and to inherit the incorruptible life: unto You we give glory, with Your Father, who is from everlasting, and Your all-holy and good and life-giving Spirit: now and ever and unto ages of ages.

PEOPLE: Amen.

THE PEOPLE KNEEL

Then the Rabbi/Kohen (Priest) takes the Book of the Holy Gospels, opened and with the printing facing down and raises it above the heads of the faithful attending and recites the following prayer aloud. If several priests take part in the service, they all shall hold the gospel Book and read the prayer silently.

THE PRAYER OF ANOINTING

PRIEST: O Holy Father, YAHUWAH, physician of our souls and bodies, You have sent Your Only-begotten Son, our Lord Yah'shua the Messiah (Jesus Christ), to heal every infirmity and deliver us from death: Heal also Your servants from the ills of the body and soul which are surrounding them and give them life by the Grace of Your Messiah (Christ), by the power of the mighty precious and life-giving cross; and by the protection of the honorable bodiless powers of heaven;

For You are the fountain of healing, O El (God), our Elohim (God), and unto You we give glory: to the Father YAHUWAH, and to the Son Yah'shua (Jesus), ✠ and to the Ruach HaKodesh (Holy Spirit), now and ever and unto ages of ages.

PEOPLE: Amen.

THE DISMISSAL

Then the Rabbi/Kohen (priest) concludes the office with the following dismissal:

DEACON: Wisdom!

PRIEST: Blessed is HE WHO IS, Messiah (Christ) our Elohim (God), always now and ever, and unto ages of ages.

PEOPLE: Amen. Preserve, O Elohim (God), the Holy Messianic Judaic Faith, and all Messianic Yahudiym (Jews) and Christians, now and ever and unto ages of ages. Amen.

PRIEST: O Most Holy Adonai (Lord) and Elohim (God), save us!

PRIEST: Glory to You, O Messiah (Christ), our Elohim (God) and our hope, glory to You.

PEOPLE: Glory to the Father YAHUWAH, and to the Son Yah'shua (Jesus), ✠ and to the Ruach HaKodesh (Holy Spirit): now and ever, and unto ages of ages, Amen.

YAHUWAH, have mercy.

Yah'shua (Jesus), have mercy.

Ruach HaKodesh (Holy Spirit), have mercy.

THE BENEDICTION

PRIEST: May Messiah (Christ) our true God, by the might of the precious and life-giving cross; by the protection of the honorable bodiless powers of heaven; have mercy upon us, and save us, for as much as he is good and love of mankind.

PRIEST: Through the prayers of our holy Fathers, Lord Yah'shua the Messiah (Jesus Christ) our Elohim (God), have mercy upon us and save us.

PEOPLE: Amen.

The Rabbi/Kohen (priests) anoint the forehead, chin, cheeks, hands, chest, back and feet of the faithful saying:

"The servant of Elohim (God) (N) is anointed with the Shemen Mishchat Kodesh (Holy Anointing Oil) for the healing of soul and body."

SHLOSHIM SHESH RAPHE MIZMOR'IYM
(36 Healing Psalms)

Prayer Before Reciting the Healing Psalms

YAHUWAH our Elohim (God) and God of our Fathers, the God and the Father of our Lord Yah'shua the Messiah (Jesus Christ), who chose King David and his descendants, and who favors songs and praises, please turn to me in mercy and accept the psalms I am going to say as if King David, himself, were saying them, and may his merit protect me. There is merit in every verse of the psalms, and in every word; in their letters, vowels, and notes, and in all the holy names they spell out. May this merit stand in my favor to atone for my sins and transgressions. Send down blessing from Your high and exalted place to my soul and spirit. Do not take me away from this world before my time. Give me a full measure of years and the strength to make full the measure of years allotted to me. Bless me from the treasury of Your generosity, as it is written, "I will be gracious to those to whom I will be gracious, and I will show mercy to those to whom I will show mercy." Just as I sing before You in this world, grant me the privilege to sing before You, O Elohim (God), in the world-to-come. Through my recital of the psalms, may pleasant song break forth with rejoicing and exultation. Let glory, splendor, and beauty be granted to the Household of Israel, speedily in our days. Amen.

Psalm 20

1 To the Chief Musician. A Psalm of David. May YAHUWAH answer you in the day of trouble; May the name of the Elohim (God) of Jacob defend you; 2 May He send you help from the sanctuary, and strengthen you out of Zion; 3 May He remember all your Minchot (offerings), and accept your Olat (burnt sacrifices). Selah. 4 May He grant you according to your heart's desire, and fulfill all your purpose. 5 We will rejoice in your salvation, and in the name of our Elohim (God) we will set up our banners! May YAHUWAH fulfill all your petitions. 6 Now I know that YAHUWAH saves His Mashiyach (anointed); He will answer him from His holy heaven with the saving strength of His right hand. 7 Some trust in chariots, and some in horses; But we will remember the name of YAHUWAH our Elohim (God). 8 They have bowed down and fallen; But we have risen and stand upright. 9 Save, YAHUWAH! May the King answer us when we call.

Psalm 6

1 To the Chief Musician. With stringed instruments. On an eight-stringed harp. A Psalm of David. YAHUWAH, rebuke me not in Your anger, nor chasten me in Your hot displeasure. 2 Have mercy on me, YAHUWAH, for I am weak; YAHUWAH, heal me, for my bones are troubled. 3 My soul also is greatly troubled; But You, YAHUWAH—how long? 4 Return, YAHUWAH, deliver me! Oh, save me for Your mercies' sake! 5 For in mavet (death) there is no remembrance of You; In Sheol (Hades, the grave, the underworld) who will give You thanks? 6 I am weary with my groaning; All night I make my bed swim; I drench my couch with my tears. 7 My eye wastes away because of grief; It grows old because of all my enemies. 8 Depart from me, all you polei aven (workers of iniquity); for YAHUWAH has heard the voice of my weeping. 9 YAHUWAH

has heard my supplication; YAHUWAH will receive my prayer. 10 Let all my oyev'iym (enemies) be ashamed and greatly troubled; Let them turn back and be ashamed suddenly.

Psalm 9

1 To the Chief Musician. To the tune of "Death of the Son." A Psalm of David. I will praise You, YAHUWAH, with my whole heart; I will tell of all Your marvelous works. 2 I will be glad and rejoice in You; I will sing praise to Your name, O Elyon (Most High). 3 When my oyev'iym (enemies) turn back, they shall fall and perish at Your presence. 4 For You have maintained my right and my cause; You sat on the throne judging in tsedekah (righteousness). 5 You have rebuked the Goyim (nations, heathens), You have destroyed the rasha (wicked); You have blotted out their name forever and ever. 6 O oyev (enemy), destructions are finished forever! And you have destroyed cities; Even their memory has perished. 7 But YAHUWAH shall endure forever; He has prepared His throne for mishpat (judgment). 8 He shall judge the world in tsedekah (righteousness), and He shall administer yadiyn (judgment) for the peoples in meyshar'iym (uprightness). 9 YAHUWAH also will be a refuge for the oppressed, a refuge in times of trouble. 10 And those who know Your name will put their trust in You; For You, YAHUWAH, have not forsaken those who seek You. 11 Sing praises to YAHUWAH, who dwells in Zion! Declare His deeds among the people. 12 When He doresh damiym (avenges blood), He remembers them; He does not forget the cry of the humble. 13 Have mercy on me, YAHUWAH! Consider my trouble from those who hate me, You who lift me up from the sha'ariym mavet (gates of death), 14 That I may tell of all Your praise in the gates of the daughter of Zion. I will rejoice in Your salvation. 15 The Goyim (nations) have sunk down in the pit which they made;

In the net which they hid, their own foot is caught. 16 YAHUWAH is known by the judgment He executes; The rasha (wicked) is snared in the work of his own hands. Haggaion (a Meditation). Selah. 17 The rasha'iym (wicked) shall be turned into Sheol (Hages, the grave, underworld), and all the Goyim (nations) that forget Elohim (God). 18 For the evyon (needy) shall not always be forgotten; The expectation of the aniyiym (poor) shall not perish forever. 19 Arise, YAHUWAH, Do not let man prevail; Let the Goy (heathen) be judged in Your sight. 20 Put them in fear, YAHUWAH, that the Goyim (nations) may know themselves to be but men. Selah.

Psalm 13

1 To the Chief Musician. A Psalm of David. How long, YAHUWAH? Will You forget me forever? How long will You hide Your face from me? How long shall I take counsel in my soul, having sorrow in my heart daily? 2 How long will my oyev (enemy) be exalted over me? 3 Consider and hear me, YAHUWAH Elohai (Lord my God); Enlighten my eyes, lest I sleep the sleep of mavet (death); 4 Lest my oyev (enemy) say, "I have prevailed against him;" Lest those who trouble me rejoice when I am moved. 5 But I have trusted in Your mercy; My heart shall rejoice in Your salvation. 6 I will sing to YAHUWAH, because He has dealt bountifully with me.

Psalm 16

1 A Michtam of David. Preserve me, O El (God), for in You I put my trust. 2 O my soul, you have said to YAHUWAH, "You are Adonai (my Lord), my goodness is nothing apart from You." 3 As for the kadoshiym (holy ones, saints, set apart ones) who are on the earth, "They are the addiyr'iym (excellent ones), in whom is all my delight." 4 Their sorrows shall be multiplied who hasten after another god; Their

nesek'iym (drink offerings, libations) of blood I will not offer, nor take up their names on my lips. 5 YAHUWAH, You are the portion of my inheritance and my cup; You maintain my lot. 6 The lines have fallen to me in pleasant places; Yes, I have a good inheritance. 7 I will bless YAHUWAH who has given me counsel; My heart also instructs me in the night seasons. 8 I have set YAHUWAH always before me; Because He is at my right hand I shall not be moved. 9 Therefore my heart is glad, and my glory rejoices; My flesh also will rest in hope. 10 For You will not leave my soul in Sheol (Hades, the grave, the underworld), nor will You allow Your Chasiyd (Holy One) to see corruption. 11 You will show me the path of life; In Your presence is fullness of joy; At Your right hand are pleasures forevermore.

Psalm 17

1 A Prayer of David. Hear a just cause, YAHUWAH, Attend to my cry; Give ear to my prayer which is not from deceitful lips. 2 Let my vindication come from Your presence; Let Your eyes look on the things that are upright. 3 You have tested my heart; You have visited me in the night; You have tried me and have found nothing; I have purposed that my mouth shall not transgress. 4 Concerning the works of men, By the word of Your lips, I have kept away from the paths of the Periyts (destroyer, violent one, robber). 5 Uphold my steps in Your paths, That my footsteps may not slip. 6 I have called upon You, for You will hear me, O El (God); Incline Your ear to me, and hear my speech. 7 Show Your marvelous lovingkindness by Your right hand, O You who save those who trust in You from those who rise up against them. 8 Keep me as the apple of Your eye; Hide me under the shadow of Your wings, 9 From the rasha'iym (wicked) who oppress me, from my oyev nephesh (enemies of my soul) who surround me. 10 They have closed up their fat hearts; With their mouths they speak

proudly. 11 They have now surrounded us in our steps; They have set their eyes, crouching down to the earth, 12 As a lion is eager to tear his prey, and like a young lion lurking in secret places. 13 Arise, YAHUWAH, confront him, cast him down; Deliver my life from the rasha (wicked) with Your sword, 14 With Your hand from men, YAHUWAH, from men of the world who have their portion in this life, and whose belly You fill with Your hidden treasure. They are satisfied with children, and leave the rest of their possession for their babes. 15 As for me, I will see Your face in tsedek (righteousness); I shall be satisfied when I awake in Your likeness.

Psalm 18

1 To the Chief Musician. A Psalm of David the servant of YAHUWAH, who spoke to YAHUWAH the words of this song on the day that YAHUWAH delivered him from the hand of all his enemies and from the hand of Saul. And he said: I will love You, YAHUWAH, my strength. 2 YAHUWAH is my rock and my fortress and my deliverer; My El (God), my strength, in whom I will trust; My shield and the horn of my salvation, my stronghold. 3 I will call upon YAHUWAH, who is worthy to be praised; So shall I be saved from my enemies. 4 The chevel mavet (pangs of death) surrounded me, and the floods of Beliya'al (Belial - worthlessness; a name of Satan, the enemy; an evil spirit) made me afraid. 5 The sorrows of Sheol (Hades, the grave, the underworld) surrounded me; The mokesh mavet (snares of death) confronted me. 6 In my distress I called upon YAHUWAH, and cried out to Elohai (my God); He heard my voice from His temple, and my cry came before Him, even to His ears. 7 Then the earth shook and trembled; The foundations of the hills also quaked and were shaken, because He was angry. 8 Smoke went up from His nostrils, and devouring fire from His mouth; Coals were kindled by it.

9 He bowed the heavens also, and came down with darkness under His feet. 10 And He rode upon a cherub, and flew; He flew upon the wings of the wind. 11 He made darkness His secret place; His canopy around Him was cheshkah mayim (dark waters) and thick clouds of the skies. 12 From the brightness before Him, His thick clouds passed with hailstones and coals of fire. 13 YAHUWAH thundered from heaven, and Elyon (the Most High) uttered His voice, Hailstones and coals of fire. 14 He sent out His arrows and scattered the foe, lightnings in abundance, and He vanquished them. 15 Then the channels of the sea were seen, the foundations of the world were uncovered at Your rebuke, YAHUWAH, at the blast of the breath of Your nostrils. 16 He sent from above, He took me; He drew me out of many waters. 17 He delivered me from my strong enemy, from those who hated me, for they were too strong for me. 18 They confronted me in the day of my calamity, but YAHUWAH was my support. 19 He also brought me out into a broad place; He delivered me because He delighted in me. 20 YAHUWAH rewarded me according to my tsedekah (righteousness); According to the cleanness of my hands He has recompensed me. 21 For I have kept the ways of YAHUWAH, and have not wickedly departed from my Elohim (God). 22 For all His mishpatiym (judgments) were before me, and I did not put away His chukkot (statutes) from me. 23 I was also tamiym (blameless) before Him, and I kept myself from my avon (iniquity). 24 Therefore YAHUWAH has recompensed me according to my tsedekah (righteousness), according to the cleanness of my hands in His sight. 25 With the chaciyd (godly) You will show Yourself chesed (merciful); With a tamiym (blameless) man You will show Yourself tamam (complete); 26 With the barar (pure) You will show Yourself barar (pure); And with the ikkesh (devious, twisted, perverse, distorted) You will show Yourself patal (twisted). 27 For You will save the aniy (poor, afflicted, humble) people, but will

bring down haughty looks. 28 For You will light my lamp; YAHUWAH Elohai (my God) will enlighten my darkness. 29 For by You I can run against a troop, by Elohai (my God) I can leap over a wall. 30 As for El (God), His way is perfect; The word of YAHUWAH is proven; He is a shield to all who trust in Him. 31 For who is Eloah (God), except YAHUWAH? And who is a rock, except our Elohim (God)? 32 It is El (God) who arms me with strength, and makes my way perfect. 33 He makes my feet like the feet of deer, and sets me on my high places. 34 He teaches my hands to make war, so that my arms can bend a bow of bronze. 35 You have also given me the shield of Your salvation; Your right hand has held me up, Your gentleness has made me great. 36 You enlarged my path under me, so my feet did not slip. 37 I have pursued my enemies and overtaken them; Neither did I turn back again till they were destroyed. 38 I have wounded them, so that they could not rise; They have fallen under my feet. 39 For You have armed me with strength for the battle; You have subdued under me those who rose up against me. 40 You have also given me the necks of my enemies, so that I destroyed those who hated me. 41 They cried out, but there was none to save; Even to YAHUWAH, but He did not answer them. 42 Then I beat them as fine as the dust before the wind; I cast them out like dirt in the streets. 43 You have delivered me from the strivings of the people; You have made me the head of the goyim (nations, Gentiles); A people I have not known shall serve me. 44 As soon as they hear of me they obey me; The Bnei Nekar (sons of foreigners) submit to me. 45 The Bnei Nekar (sons of foreigners) shall fade away, and come frightened from their hideouts. 46 YAHUWAH lives! Blessed be my Rock! Let the Elohim (God) of my salvation be exalted. 47 It is El (God) who avenges me, and subdues the peoples under me; 48 He delivers me from my oyev'iym (enemies). You also lift me up above those who rise against me; You have delivered me from the iysh chamas (violent man). 49 Therefore I will give thanks to You, YAHUWAH, among the Goyim (Gentiles), and sing praises to Your name. 50 Great deliverance He gives to His king, And shows mercy to His mashiyach (anointed), To David and his seed forevermore.

Psalm 22

1 To the Chief Musician. Set to "The Deer of the Dawn." A Psalm of David. Eli (My God), Eli (My God), why have You forsaken Me? Why are You so far from helping Me, and from the words of My groaning? 2 Elohai (My God), I cry in the daytime, but You do not hear; And in the night season, and am not silent. 3 But You are holy, Enthroned in the praises of Israel. 4 Our fathers trusted in You; They trusted, and You delivered them. 5 They cried to You, and were delivered; They trusted in You, and were not ashamed. 6 But I am a worm, and no man; A reproach of men, and despised by the people.7 All those who see Me ridicule Me; They shoot out the lip, they shake the head, saying, 8 "He trusted in YAHUWAH, let Him rescue Him; Let Him deliver Him, since He delights in Him!" 9 But You are He who took Me out of the womb; You made Me trust while on My mother's breasts. 10 I was cast upon You from birth. From My mother's womb You have been Eliy (my God). 11 Be not far from Me, for trouble is near; For there is none to help. 12 Many bulls have surrounded Me; Strong bulls of Bashan have encircled Me. 13 They gape at Me with their mouths, like a raging and roaring lion. 14 I am poured out like water, and all My bones are out of joint; My heart is like wax; It has melted within Me. 15 My strength is dried up like a potsherd, and My tongue clings to My jaws; You have brought Me to the dust of death. 16 For dogs have surrounded Me; The adat me're'iym (congregation of the wicked) has enclosed Me. They pierced My hands and My feet; 17 I can count all My bones. They look and stare at Me.

18 They divide My garments among them, and for My clothing they cast lots. 19 But You, YAHUWAH, do not be far from Me; O My Strength, hasten to help Me! 20 Deliver Me from the sword, my precious life from the power of the dog. 21 Save Me from the lion's mouth and from the horns of the re'emiym (unicorn)! You have answered Me. 22 I will declare Your name to My brethren; In the midst of the kahal (assembly) I will praise You. 23 You who fear YAHUWAH, praise Him! All you seed of Jacob, glorify Him, and fear Him, all you seed of Israel! 24 For He has not despised nor abhorred the enut (affliction) of the aniy (afflicted); Nor has He hidden His face from Him; But when He cried to Him, He heard. 25 My praise shall be of You in the kahal rav (great assembly); I will pay My neder'iym (vows) before those who fear Him. 26 The anaviym (humble, poor) shall eat and be satisfied; Those who seek Him will praise YAHUWAH. Let your heart live forever! 27 All the ends of the world shall remember and turn to YAHUWAH, and all the families of the Goyim (nations, Gentiles) shall worship before You. 28 For the kingdom is YAHUWAH's, and He rules over the Goyim (nations, Gentiles). 29 All the prosperous of the earth shall eat and worship; All those who go down to the dust shall bow before Him, even he who cannot keep himself alive. 30 A posterity shall serve Him. It will be recounted to Adonai (the Lord) to the next generation, 31 They will come and declare His tsedakah (righteousness) to a people who will be born, that He has done this.

Psalm 23

1 A Psalm of David. YAHUWAH is my Ro'iy (shepherd); I shall not want. 2 He makes me to lie down in green pastures; He leads me beside the still waters. 3 He restores my soul; He leads me in the paths of tsedek (righteousness) for His name's sake. 4 Yea, though I walk through the valley of the tsalmavet

(shadow of death), I will fear no ra (evil); for You are with me; Your rod and Your staff, they comfort me. 5 You prepare a table before me in the presence of my enemies; You anoint my head with oil; My cup runs over. 6 Surely goodness and mercy shall follow me all the days of my life; And I will dwell in the house of YAHUWAH forever.

Psalm 28

1 A Psalm of David. To You I will cry, YAHUWAH my Rock: Do not be silent to me, lest, if You are silent to me, I become like those who go down to the pit. 2 Hear the voice of my supplications when I cry to You, when I lift up my hands toward Your holy sanctuary. 3 Do not take me away with the rasha'iym (wicked) and with the polei aven (workers of iniquity), who speak peace to their neighbors, but ra'ah (evil) is in their hearts. 4 Give them according to their po'al'iym (deeds), and according to the roa (badness, evil) of their endeavors; Give them according to the ma'aseh yadeyhem (work of their hands); Render to them what they deserve. 5 Because they do not regard the works of YAHUWAH, nor the operation of His hands, He shall destroy them and not build them up. 6 Blessed be YAHUWAH, because He has heard the voice of my supplications! 7 YAHUWAH is my strength and my shield; My heart trusted in Him, and I am helped; Therefore my heart greatly rejoices, and with my song I will praise Him. 8 YAHUWAH is their strength, and He is the saving refuge of His mashiyach (anointed). 9 Save Your people, and bless Your inheritance; Ro'eh (Shepherd) them also, And bear them up forever.

Psalm 30

1 A Psalm. A Song at the dedication of the house of David. I will extol You, YAHUWAH, for You have lifted me up, and have

not let my foes rejoice over me. 2 YAHUWAH Elohai (my God), I cried out to You, and You healed me. 3 YAHUWAH, You brought my soul up from Sheol (Hades, the grave, the underworld); You have kept me alive, that I should not go down to the pit. 4 Sing praise to YAHUWAH, His chasiyd (godly ones), and give thanks at the remembrance of His Shem Kadosh (holy name). 5 For His anger is but for a moment, His favor is for life; Weeping may endure for a night, but joy comes in the morning. 6 Now in my prosperity I said, "I shall never be moved." 7 YAHUWAH, by Your favor You have made my mountain stand strong; You hid Your face, and I was troubled. 8 I cried out to You, YAHUWAH; And to YAHUWAH I made supplication: 9 "What profit is there in my blood, When I go down to shachat (the pit, destruction, corruption)? Will the dust praise You? Will it declare Your truth? 10 Hear, YAHUWAH, and have mercy on me; YAHUWAH, be my helper!" 11 You have turned for me my mispade (mourning) into machol (dancing); You have put off my sak (sackcloth) and clothed me with simchah (gladness), 12 To the end that my glory may sing praise to You and not be silent. YAHUWAH Elohai (my God), I will give thanks to You forever.

Psalm 31

1 To the Chief Musician. A Psalm of David. In You, YAHUWAH, I put my chasah (trust); Let me never be boshah (ashamed, disconnected); Deliver me in Your tsedakah (righteousness). 2 Bow down Your ear to me, deliver me speedily; Be my rock of refuge, a fortress of defense to save me. 3 For You are my rock and my fortress; Therefore, for Your name's sake, lead me and guide me. 4 Pull me out of the net which they have secretly laid for me, for You are my strength. 5 Into Your hand I commit my spirit; You have redeemed me, O YAHUWAH, the El Emet (god of truth). 6 I have hated those who regard empty

lies; But I trust in YAHUWAH. 7 I will be glad and rejoice in Your mercy, for You have considered my trouble; You have known my soul in adversities, 8 And have not shut me up into the hand of the oyev (enemy); You have set my feet in a wide place. 9 Have mercy on me, YAHUWAH, for I am in trouble; My eye wastes away with grief, Yes, my soul and my body! 10 For my life is spent with grief, and my years with sighing; My strength fails because of my iniquity, and my bones waste away. 11 I am a reproach among all my tsarar (foe), but especially among my neighbors, and am repulsive to my acquaintances; Those who see me outside flee from me. 12 I am forgotten like a dead man, out of mind; I am like a broken vessel. 13 For I hear the slander of many; Fear is on every side; While they take counsel together against me, they scheme to take away my life. 14 But as for me, I trust in You, YAHUWAH; I say, "You are Elohai (my God)." 15 My times are in Your hand; Deliver me from the hand of my oyev'iym (enemies), and from those who persecute me. 16 Make Your face shine upon Your servant; Save me for Your mercies' sake. 17 Do not let me be ashamed, YAHUWAH, for I have called upon You; Let the wicked be ashamed; Let them be silent in Sheol (Hades, the grave, the underworld). 18 Let the lying lips be put to silence, which speak insolent things proudly and contemptuously against the tsadiyk (righteous). 19 Oh, how great is Your goodness, which You have laid up for those who fear You, Which You have prepared for those who trust in You In the presence of the sons of men! 20 You shall hide them in the secret place of Your presence from the plots of man; You shall keep them secretly in a pavilion from the strife of tongues. 21 Blessed be YAHUWAH, for He has shown me His marvelous kindness in a strong city! 22 For I said in my haste, "I am cut off from before Your eyes"; Nevertheless You heard the voice of my supplications when I cried out to You. 23 Oh, love YAHUWAH, all His chasiyd (godly ones)! For YAHUWAH preserves the faithful, and fully repays the proud person. 24

Be of good courage, and He shall strengthen your heart, all you who hope in YAHUWAH.

Psalm 32

1 A Psalm of David. A Contemplation. Blessed is he whose pesha (transgression) is forgiven, whose chata'ah (sin) is covered. 2 Blessed is the man to whom YAHUWAH does not impute avon (iniquity), and in whose spirit there is no remiyah (deceit, slackness). 3 When I kept silent, my bones grew old through my groaning all the day long. 4 For day and night Your hand was heavy upon me; My vitality was turned into the drought of summer. Selah. 5 I acknowledged my sin to You, and my avon (iniquity) I have not hidden. I said, "I will Odeh (confess) my pesha (transgressions) to YAHUWAH," And You forgave the avon (iniquity) of my chata'ah (sin). Selah. 6 For this cause everyone who is chasiyd (godly) shall pray to You in a time when You may be found; Surely in a shetef mayim raviym (flood of great waters) they shall not come near him. 7 You are my hiding place; You shall preserve me from trouble; You shall surround me with ranei palet (songs/shouts of deliverance). Selah. 8 I will instruct you and teach you in the way you should go; I will guide you with My eye. 9 Do not be like the horse or like the mule, which have no understanding, which must be harnessed with bit and bridle, else they will not come near you. 10 Many mak'oviym (sorrows, pains, afflictions) shall be to the rasha (wicked); But he who batach (trusts, is bold) in YAHUWAH, mercy shall surround him. 11 Be glad in YAHUWAH and rejoice, you tsadiykiym (righteous); And shout for joy, all you yashariym lev (upright in heart)!

Psalm 33

1 Rejoice in YAHUWAH, O you tsadiykiym (righteous)! For praise from the yashariym (upright) is beautiful. 2 Praise YAHUWAH with the harp; Make melody to Him with an instrument of ten strings. 3 Sing to Him a new song; Play skillfully with a shout of joy. 4 For the word of YAHUWAH is right, and all His work is done in truth. 5 He loves tsedakah (righteousness) and mishpat (judgment); The earth is full of the goodness of YAHUWAH. 6 By the word of YAHUWAH the heavens were made, and all the host of them by the breath of His mouth. 7 He gathers the waters of the sea together as a heap; He lays up the deep in storehouses. 8 Let all the earth fear YAHUWAH; Let all the inhabitants of the world stand in awe of Him. 9 For He spoke, and it was done; He commanded, and it stood fast. 10 YAHUWAH brings the counsel of the Goyim (nations, Gentiles) to nothing; He makes the plans of the peoples of no effect. 11 The counsel of YAHUWAH stands forever, the plans of His heart to all generations. 12 Blessed is the Goy (nation, Gentile) whose Elohim (God) is YAHUWAH, the people He has chosen as His own inheritance. 13 YAHUWAH looks from heaven; He sees all the sons of men. 14 From the place of His dwelling He looks on all the inhabitants of the earth; 15 He fashions their hearts individually; He considers all their works. 16 No melek (king) is saved by the multitude of an army; A Gibor (mighty man) is not delivered by great strength. 17 A horse is a vain hope for safety; Neither shall it deliver any by its great strength. 18 Behold, the eye of YAHUWAH is on those who fear Him, on those who hope in His mercy, 19 To deliver their soul from mavet (death), and to keep them alive in famine. 20 Our soul waits for YAHUWAH; He is our help and our shield. 21 For our heart shall rejoice in Him, Because we have trusted in His Shem Kadosh (holy

name). 22 Let Your mercy, YAHUWAH, be upon us, Just as we hope in You.

Psalm 37

1 A Psalm of David. Do not fret because of ra'iym (evildoers), Nor be envious of the oseh avlah (workers of iniquity). 2 For they shall soon be cut down like the grass, and wither as the green herb. 3 Batach (Trust, be bold) in YAHUWAH, and do tov (good); Dwell in the land, and feed on His emunah (faithfulness). 4 Delight yourself also in YAHUWAH, and He shall give you the desires of your heart. 5 Commit your way to YAHUWAH, batach (trust, be bold) also in Him, and He shall bring it to pass. 6 He shall bring forth your tsedekah (righteousness) as the light, and your mishpat (judgment) as the noonday. 7 Rest in YAHUWAH, and wait patiently for Him; Do not fret because of him who prospers in his way, because of the man who brings mezimot (wicked schemes) to pass. 8 Cease from anger, and forsake wrath; Do not fret—it only causes harm. 9 For ra'iym (evildoers) shall be cut off; But those who wait on YAHUWAH, they shall inherit the earth. 10 For yet a little while and the rasha (wicked) shall be no more; Indeed, you will look carefully for his place, but it shall be no more. 11 But the meek shall inherit the earth, and shall delight themselves in the rov shalom (abundance of peace). 12 The rasha (wicked) plots against the tsadiyk (righteous), and gnashes at him with his teeth. 13 Adonai (The Lord) laughs at him, for He sees that his day is coming. 14 The rasha'iym (wicked) have drawn the sword and have bent their bow, to cast down the aniy (poor) and evyon (needy), to slay those who are of a yashar derek (upright way). 15 Their sword shall enter their own heart, and their bows shall be broken. 16 A little that a tsadiyk (righteous man) has is better than the riches of many rasha'iym (wicked). 17 For the arms of the rasha'iym (wicked) shall be broken, but YAHUWAH

upholds the tsadiykiym (righteous). 18 YAHUWAH knows the days of the tamiymim (blameless, upright), and their inheritance shall be forever. 19 They shall not be ashamed in the evil time, and in the days of famine they shall be satisfied. 20 But the rasha'iym (wicked) shall perish; And the oyev'iym YAHUWAH (enemies of the Lord), like the splendor of the meadows, shall vanish. Into smoke they shall vanish away. 21 The rasha (wicked) borrows and does not repay, but the tsadiyk (righteous) shows mercy and gives. 22 For those blessed by Him shall inherit the earth, but those cursed by Him shall be cut off. 23 The steps of a geber (warrior, good man) are ordered by YAHUWAH, and He delights in his way. 24 Though he fall, he shall not be utterly cast down; For YAHUWAH upholds him with His hand. 25 I have been young, and now am old; Yet I have not seen the tsadiyk (righteous) forsaken, nor his seed begging bread. 26 He is ever merciful, and lends; And his seed are blessed. 27 Depart from ra (evil), and do tov (good); And dwell forevermore. 28 For YAHUWAH loves mishpat (judgment, justice), and does not forsake His chaciyd'iym (godly ones); They are preserved forever, but the seed of the rasha'iym (wicked) shall be cut off. 29 The tsadiyk'iym (righteous) shall inherit the land, and dwell in it forever. 30 The mouth of the tsadiyk (righteous) speaks cholmah (wisdom), and his tongue talks of mishpat (judgment). 31 The torah (law) of his Elohim (God) is in his heart; None of his steps shall slide. 32 The rasha (wicked) watches the tsadiyk (righteous), and seeks to slay him. 33 YAHUWAH will not leave him in his hand, nor condemn him when he is judged. 34 Wait on YAHUWAH, and keep His way, and He shall exalt you to inherit the land; When the rasha'iym (wicked) are cut off, you shall see it. 35 I have seen the rasha (wicked) in great power, and spreading himself like a native green tree. 36 Yet he passed away, and behold, he was no more; Indeed I sought him, but he could not be found. 37 Mark the tam (blameless man), and observe the yashar (upright); For the future of that man is shalom (peace). 38 But the pasha'iym (transgressors, rebels) shall be destroyed together; The future of the rasha'iym (wicked) shall be cut off. 39 But the salvation of the tsadiyk'iym (righteous) is from YAHUWAH; He is their strength in the time of trouble. 40 And YAHUWAH shall help them and deliver them; He shall deliver them from the rasha'iym (wicked), and save them, because they trust in Him.

Psalm 38

1 A Psalm of David. To bring to remembrance. YAHUWAH, do not rebuke me in Your wrath, nor chasten me in Your hot displeasure! 2 For Your arrows pierce me deeply, and Your hand presses me down. 3 There is no soundness in my flesh because of Your anger, nor any shalom (peace, health) in my bones because of my chattat (sin; punishment for sin). 4 For my avonot (iniquities; punishment for iniquity) have gone over my head; Like a heavy burden they are too heavy for me. 5 My chavurot (wounds) are foul and festering because of my ivelet (foolishness, folly). 6 I am troubled, I am bowed down greatly; I go mourning all the day long. 7 For my loins are full of inflammation, and there is no soundness in my flesh. 8 I am feeble and severely broken; I groan because of the turmoil of my heart. 9 Adonai (Lord), all my desire is before You; And my sighing is not hidden from You. 10 My heart pants, my strength fails me; As for the light of my eyes, it also has gone from me. 11 My loved ones and my friends stand aloof from my nega (plague, disease), and my relatives stand afar off. 12 Those also who seek my life lay snares for me; Those who seek my hurt speak of destruction, and plan deception all the day long. 13 But I, like a deaf man, do not hear; And I am like a mute who does not open his mouth. 14 Thus I am like a man who does not hear, and in whose mouth is no response. 15 For in You, YAHUWAH, I hope; You will hear, O Adonai Elohai

(Lord my God). 16 For I said, "Hear me, lest they rejoice over me, lest, when my foot slips, they exalt themselves against me." 17 For I am ready to fall, and my sorrow is continually before me. 18 For I will declare my avon (iniquity; punishment for iniquity); I will be in anguish over my chattat (sin, punishment for sin). 19 But my oyev'iym (enemies) are vigorous, and they are strong; And those who hate me wrongfully have multiplied. 20 Those also who render ra (evil) for tov (good), they are my satan (adversaries), because I follow what is tov (good). 21 Do not forsake me, YAHUWAH; O Elohai (my God), be not far from me! 22 Make haste to help me, Adonai (Lord), my salvation!

Psalm 39

1 To the Chief Musician. To Jeduthun. A Psalm of David. I said, "I will guard my ways, lest I chata (sin) with my tongue; I will restrain my mouth with a muzzle, while the rasha (wicked) are before me." 2 I was mute with silence, I held my peace even from tov (good); And my sorrow was stirred up. 3 My heart was hot within me; While I was musing, the fire burned. Then I spoke with my tongue: 4 "YAHUWAH, make me to know my end, and what is the measure of my days, that I may know how frail I am. 5 Indeed, You have made my days as handbreadths, and my age is as nothing before You; Certainly every man at his best state is but vapor. Selah. 6 Surely every man walks about like a shadow; Surely they busy themselves in vain; He heaps up riches, and does not know who will gather them. 7 "And now, Adonai (Lord), what do I wait for? My hope is in You. 8 Deliver me from all my pesha'iym (transgressions); Do not make me the reproach of the nabal (foolish, stupid, vile). 9 I was mute, I did not open my mouth, Because it was You who did it. 10 Remove Your nega (plague) from me; I am consumed by the blow of Your hand. 11 When with rebukes You correct man for avon (iniquity), You make

his chamad (beauty, delight) melt away like a moth; Surely every man is vapor. Selah. 12 "Hear my tefillat (prayer), YAHUWAH, and give ear to my cry; Do not be silent at my tears; For I am a stranger with You, a sojourner, as all my fathers were. 13 Remove Your gaze from me, that I may regain strength, before I go away and am no more."

Psalm 41

1 To the Chief Musician. A Psalm of David. Blessed is he who considers the dal (poor, weak, lowly); YAHUWAH will deliver him in time of trouble. 2 YAHUWAH will preserve him and keep him chai (alive), and he will be blessed on the earth; You will not deliver him to the will of his oyev'iym (enemies). 3 YAHUWAH will strengthen him on his eres devai (bed of illness / languishing); You will sustain him in his choliy (sickness). 4 I said, "YAHUWAH, be merciful to me; Rafa'ah nafshiy (Heal my soul), for I have chatat (sinned) against You." 5 My oyev'iym (enemies) speak ra (evil) of me: "When will he die, and his name perish?" 6 And if he comes to see me, he speaks shav (lies, emptiness, falsehood); His heart gathers aven (iniquity, wickedness) to itself; When he goes out, he tells it. 7 All who hate me whisper together against me; Against me they devise my hurt. 8 "A Devar Beliya'al (thing of Belial - worthlessness; a name of Satan, the enemy; an evil spirit)," they say, "clings to him. And now that he lies down, he will rise up no more." 9 Even my own Shalom (peace, familiar friend) in whom I trusted, who ate my bread, has lifted up his heel against me. 10 But You, YAHUWAH, be merciful to me, and raise me up, that I may repay them. 11 By this I know that You are well pleased with me, because my oyev'iym (enemy) does not triumph over me. 12 As for me, You uphold me in my tom (integrity), and set me before Your face forever. 13 Blessed be YAHUWAH, the Elohim (God) of Israel from everlasting to everlasting! Amen and Amen.

Psalm 42

1 To the Chief Musician. A Contemplation of the sons of Korah. As the deer pants for the water brooks, so pants my soul for You, O Elohim (God). 2 My soul thirsts for Elohim (God), for the El Chai (living God). When shall I come and appear before Elohim (God)? 3 My tears have been my food day and night, while they continually say to me, "Where is your Elohim (God)?" 4 When I remember these things, I pour out my soul within me. For I used to go with the multitude; I went with them to the Bet Elohim (house of God), with the voice of rinah (cries of joy) and todah (praise, thanksgiving), with a multitude that kept a chagag (pilgrim feast). 5 Why are you cast down, O my soul? And why are you disquieted within me? Hope in Elohim (God), for I shall yet praise Him for the help of His countenance. 6 Elohai (my God), my soul is cast down within me; Therefore I will remember You from the land of the Jordan, and from the heights of Hermon, from the Hill Mizar. 7 Deep calls unto deep at the noise of Your tsinur'iym (waterspouts); All Your waves and billows have gone over me. 8 YAHUWAH will command Hischesed (lovingkindness, mercy) in the yomam (daytime), and in the lai'lah (night) His shiyr (song) shall be with me; A tefilla (prayer) to the El Chayai (God of my life). 9 I will say to El (God) my Rock, "Why have You forgotten me? Why do I go mourning because of the lachats oyev (oppression of the enemy)?" 10 As with a breaking of my bones, My tsarar'iym (enemies) reproach me, while they say to me all day long, "Where is your Elohim (God)?" 11 Why are you cast down, O my soul? And why are you disquieted within me? Hope in Elohim (God); For I shall yet praise Him, the help of my countenance and my Elohim (God).

Psalm 49

1 To the Chief Musician. A Psalm of the sons of Korah. Hear this, all amiym (peoples); Give ear, all yoshebei chaled (inhabitants of the world), 2 Both bnei adam (sons of humans) and bnei iysh (sons of man), ashiyr (rich) and evyon (poor) together. 3 My mouth shall speak chokmah (wisdom), and the hagut (meditation) of my heart shall give tevunot (understanding). 4 I will incline my ear to mashal (proverb, parable); I will disclose my chiydah (dark saying, riddle, puzzle) on the harp. 5 Why should I fear in the yom ra (days of evil), when the avon (iniquity) at my heels surrounds me? 6 Those who batach (trust) in their chayil (wealth) and halal (boast) in the multitude of their asheram (riches), 7 None of them can by any means redeem his brother, nor give to Elohim (God) a ransom for him. 8 For the redemption of their souls is costly, and it shall cease forever. 9 That he should continue to live eternally, and not see corruption. 10 For he sees chakamiym (wise men) die; Likewise the kesiyl (fool) and the ba'ar (brutish, stupid, senseless person) perish, and leave their chayil (wealth) to others. 11 Their inner thought is that their houses will last forever, their dwelling places to all generations; They call their lands after their own names. 12 Nevertheless man, though in honor, does not remain; He is like the beasts that perish. 13 This is the way of those who are kesel (stupid, folly), and of their achar'iym (posterity) who approve their sayings. Selah. 14 Like sheep they are laid in Sheol (Hades, the grave, the underworld); Mavet (Death) shall feed on them; The yashar'iym (upright) shall have dominion over them in the morning; And their beauty shall be consumed in Sheol (Hades, the grave, the underworld), far from their dwelling. 15 But Elohim (God) will redeem my soul from the power of Sheol (Hades, the grave, the underworld), for He shall receive me. Selah. 16 Do not be afraid when one

becomes ashar (rich), when the glory of his house is increased; 17 For when he dies he shall carry nothing away; His glory shall not descend after him. 18 Though while he lives he blesses himself (for men will praise you when you do well for yourself), 19 He shall go to the generation of his fathers; They shall never see light. 20 A man who is in honor, yet does not understand, is like the beasts that perish.

Psalm 55

1 To the Chief Musician. With stringed instruments. A Contemplation of David. Give ear to my tefilat (prayer), O Elohim (God), and do not hide Yourself from my supplication. 2 Attend to me, and hear me; I am restless in my complaint, and moan noisily, 3 Because of the voice of the oyev (enemy), because of the akat rasha (oppression of the wicked); For they bring down trouble upon me, and in wrath they hate me. 4 My heart is severely pained within me, and the eymot mavet (terrors of death) have fallen upon me. 5 Fearfulness and trembling have come upon me, and horror has overwhelmed me. 6 So I said, "Oh, that I had wings like a dove! I would fly away and be at rest. 7 Indeed, I would wander far off, and remain in the wilderness. Selah. 8 I would hasten my escape from the windy storm and tempest." 9 Destroy, Adonai (Lord), and divide their tongues, for I have seen violence and strife in the city. 10 Day and night they go around it on its walls; aven (Iniquity) and amal (trouble) are also in the midst of it. 11 Havah (Destruction, calamity) is in its midst; tok (Oppression) and mirmah (deceit) do not depart from its streets. 12 For it is not an oyev (enemy) who reproaches me; Then I could bear it. Nor is it one who hates me who has exalted himself against me; Then I could hide from him. 13 But it was you, a man my equal, My companion and my acquaintance. 14 We took sweet counsel together, and walked to the Bet Elohim (house of God) in the throng. 15

Let mavet (death) seize them; Let them go down alive into Sheol (Hades, the grave, the underworld), for ra'ot (wickedness) is in their dwellings and among them. 16 As for me, I will call upon Elohim (God), and YAHUWAH shall save me. 17 Erev (Evening) and boker (morning) and at tsohariym (noon) I will siyach (speak, talk), and ehameh (cry aloud), and He shall hear my voice. 18 He has redeemed my soul in shalom (peace) from the battle that was against me, for there were many against me. 19 El (God) will hear, and afflict them, even He who abides from of old. Selah. Because they do not chaliyfot (change), therefore they do not fear Elohim (God). 20 He has put forth his hands against those who were at shalom (peace) with him; He has broken his covenant. 21 The words of his mouth were smoother than butter, but kerav (war, hostile encounter) was in his heart; His words were softer than oil, yet they were drawn swords. 22 Cast your yehav (burden, lot –what is given) on YAHUWAH, and He shall sustain you; He shall never permit the tsadiyk (righteous) to be moved. 23 But You, O Elohim (God), shall bring them down to the be'er shachat (pit of destruction); Anshei damiym uv'mirmah (Bloodthirsty and deceitful men) shall not live out half their days; But I will batach (trust, be bold) in You.

Psalm 56

1 To the Chief Musician. Set to "The Silent Dove in Distant Lands." A Michtam of David when the Philistines captured him in Gath. Be merciful to me, Elohim (God), for man would swallow me up; Fighting all day he oppresses me. 2 My sharar'iym (enemies) would hound me all day, for there are many who fight against me maron (on high). 3 Whenever I am afraid, I will batach (trust, be bold) in You. 4 In Elohim (God) (I will praise His word), in Elohim (God) I have put my batach (trust); I will not fear. What can flesh do to me? 5 All day they

davar atsav (twist my words); All their machashavah (thoughts) are against me for ra (evil). 6 They gather together, they hide, they mark my steps, when they lie in wait for my life. 7 Shall they escape by aven (iniquity)? In anger cast down the peoples, O Elohim (God)! 8 You number my wanderings; Put my tears into Your bottle; Are they not in Your book? 9 When I cry out to You, then my oyev'iym (enemies) will turn back; This I know, because Elohim (God) is for me. 10 In Elohim (God) (I will praise His word), in YAHUWAH (I will praise His word), 11 In Elohim (God) I have put my batach (trust); I will not be afraid. What can adam (man, mankind, humans) do to me? 12 Nederiym (Vows) made to You are binding upon me, O Elohim (God); I will render praises to You, 13 For You have delivered my soul from mavet (death). Have You not kept my feet from falling, that I may walk before Elohim (God) in the light of the chayim (living)?

Psalm 69

1 To the Chief Musician. Set to "The Lilies." A Psalm of David. Save me, O Elohim (God)! For the waters have come in unto my soul. 2 I sink in deep mire, where there is no standing; I have come into deep waters, where the floods overflow me. 3 I am weary with my crying; My throat is dry; My eyes fail while I wait for Elohai (my God). 4 Those who hate me without a cause are more than the hairs of my head; They are mighty who would destroy me, being my oyev'iym sheker (enemies wrongfully); Though I have stolen nothing, I still must restore it. 5 O Elohim (God), You know my ivelet (foolishness, folly); And my ashmot (sins, guilt, wrong doing) are not hidden from You. 6 Let not those who wait for You, O Adonai YAHUWAH Tseva'ot (Lord GOD of hosts), be ashamed because of me; Let not those who seek You be confounded because of me, O Elohim (God) of Israel. 7 Because for Your

sake I have borne reproach; Shame has covered my face. 8 I have become a stranger to my brothers, and an alien to my mother's children; 9 Because zeal for Your house has eaten me up, and the reproaches of those who reproach You have fallen on me. 10 When I wept and chastened my soul with fasting, that became my reproach. 11 I also made sackcloth my garment; I became a byword to them. 12 Those who sit in the gate speak against me, and I am the song of the drunkards. 13 But as for me, my tefillah (prayer) is to You, YAHUWAH, in the acceptable time; O Elohim (God), in the multitude of Your chesed (mercy), hear me in the emet (truth) of Your yesha (salvation). 14 Deliver me out of the mire, and let me not sink; Let me be delivered from those who hate me, and out of the deep waters. 15 Let not the floodwater overflow me, nor let the deep swallow me up; And let not the pit shut its mouth on me. 16 Hear me, YAHUWAH, for Your chesed (mercy, lovingkindness) is tov (good); Turn to me according to the multitude of Your racham'iym (tender mercies). 17 And do not hide Your face from Your eved (servant), for I am in trouble; Hear me speedily. 18 Draw near to my soul, and redeem it; Deliver me because of my oyev'iym (enemies). 19 You know my reproach, my shame, and my dishonor; My tsarar'iym (adversaries) are all before You. 20 Reproach has broken my heart, and I am full of heaviness; I looked for someone to take pity, but there was none; And for comforters, but I found none. 21 They also gave me gall for my food, and for my thirst they gave me vinegar to drink. 22 Let their table become a snare before them, and their well-being a trap. 23 Let their eyes be darkened, so that they do not see; And make their loins shake continually. 24 Pour out Your indignation upon them, and let Your wrathful anger take hold of them. 25 Let their dwelling place be desolate; Let no one live in their tents. 26 For they persecute the ones You have struck, and talk of the grief of those You have wounded. 27 Add avon (iniquity, punishment for iniquity) to their avon (iniquity, punishment for iniquity), and let them not come into Your tsedakah (righteousness). 28 Let them be blotted out of the Sefer Chayim (book of the living), and not be written with the tsadiykiym (righteous). 29 But I am aniy (poor) and ka'av (sorrowful); Let Your yeshua (salvation), O Elohim (God), set me up on high. 30 I will praise the name of Elohim (God) with a shiyr (song), and will magnify Him with todah (thanksgiving). 31 This also shall please YAHUWAH better than an ox or bull, which has horns and hooves. 32 The humble shall see this and be glad; And you who seek Elohim (God), your hearts shall live. 33 For YAHUWAH hears the evyon'iym (poor, needy), and does not despise His asiyr'iym (prisoners). 34 Let heaven and earth praise Him, the seas and everything that moves in them. 35 For Elohim (God) will save Zion and build the cities of Judah, that they may dwell there and possess it. 36 Also, the seed of His servants shall inherit it, and those who love His name shall dwell in it.

Psalm 86

1 A Prayer of David. Bow down Your ear, YAHUWAH, hear me; For I am aniy (poor) and evyon (needy). 2 Preserve my life, for I am chasyd (godly); You are Elohai (my God); Save Your servant who batach (trusts, is bold) in You! 3 Be merciful to me, O Adonai (Lord), for I cry to You all day long. 4 Rejoice the soul of Your servant, for to You, Adonai (Lord), I lift up my soul. 5 For You, Adonai (Lord), are tov (good), and sallach (ready to forgive), and rav-chesed (abundant in mercy) to all those who call upon You. 6 Give ear, YAHUWAH, to my tefillah (prayer); and attend to the voice of my tachanun (supplications). 7 In the day of my trouble I will call upon You, for You will answer me. 8 Among the elohim (gods) there is none like You, O Adonai (Lord); Nor are there any works like Your works. 9 All goyim (nations) whom You have made shall come and worship before You, O Adonai (Lord),

and shall glorify Your name. 10 For You are great, and do wondrous things; You alone are Elohim (God). 11 Teach me Your way, YAHUWAH; I will halak (walk) in Your emet (truth); Unite my heart to fear Your name. 12 I will praise You, O Adonai Elohai (Lord my God), with all my heart, and I will glorify Your name forevermore. 13 For great is Your chesed (mercy) toward me, and You have delivered my soul from the depths of Sheol (Hades, the grave, the underworld). 14 O Elohim (God), the zediym (presumptious, proud) have risen against me, and a mob of ariyts'iym (violent men) have sought my soul, and have not set You before them. 15 But You, Adonai (Lord), are an El (God) full of rachum (compassion), and chanun (gracious), erek-apayim (longsuffering) and rav-chesed (abundant in mercy) and emet (truth). 16 Oh, turn to me, and have mercy on me! Give Your strength to Your servant, and save the son of Your maidservant. 17 Show me an ot (sign) for tov (good), that those who hate me may see it and be ashamed, because You, YAHUWAH, have helped me and comforted me.

Psalm 88

1 A Song. A Psalm of the sons of Korah. To the Chief Musician. Set to "Mahalath Leannoth." A Contemplation of Heman the Ezrahite. YAHUWAH, Elohim (God) of my salvation, I have cried out day and night before You. 2 Let my tefillah (prayer) come before You; Incline Your ear to my cry. 3 For my soul is full of troubles, and my soul draws near to Sheol (Hades, the grave, the underworld). 4 I am counted with those who go down to the pit; I am like a man who has no strength, 5 Chofdhiy (Adrift) among the metiym (dead), like the slain who lie in the kever (grave), whom You remember no more, and who are cut off from Your hand. 6 You have laid me in the lowest pit, in machashakiym (darkness), in the metsolah (depths, the deep, deep sea). 7 Your wrath lies heavy upon

me, And You have afflicted me with all Your waves. Selah. 8 You have put away my acquaintances far from me; You have made me a to'evah (abomination) to them; I am shut up, and I cannot get out; 9 My eye wastes away because of oniy (affliction). YAHUWAH, I have called daily upon You; I have stretched out my hands to You. 10 Will You work pele (wonders) for the metiym (dead)? Shall the rapha'iym (spirits of the dead; ghosts, shades, disembodied spirits) arise and praise You? Selah. 11 Shall Your chesed (mercy, lovingkindness) be declared in the kever (grave)? Or Your emunah (faithfulness) in the place of Aboddon (destruction)? 12 Shall Your pele (wonders) be known in the choshek (dark)? And Your tsedakah (righteousness) in the land of neshiyah (forgetfulness)? 13 But to You I have cried out, YAHUWAH, and in the morning my tefillah (prayer) comes before You. 14 YAHUWAH, why do You cast off my soul? Why do You hide Your face from me? 15 I have been aniy (afflicted) and ready to die from my youth; I suffer Your eymah (dread); I am distraught. 16 Your fierce wrath has gone over me; Your bi'uthiym (terrors) have cut me off. 17 They came around me all day long like mayim (water); They engulfed me altogether. 18 Loved one and friend You have put far from me, and my acquaintances into darkness.

Psalm 89

1 A Contemplationa of Ethan the Ezrahite. I will sing of the hesed (mercies) of YAHUWAH forever; With my mouth will I make known Your emunah (faithfulness) to all generations. 2 For I have said, "Chesed (Mercy) shall be built up forever; Your emuna (faithfulness) You shall establish in the very heavens." 3 "I have made a covenant with My bachiyr (chosen, elect), I have sworn to My servant David: 4 'Your seed I will establish forever, And build up your throne to all generations.'" Selah. 5 And the heavens will praise Your pele

(wonders), O YAHUWAH; Your emunah (faithfulness) also in the kehal (assembly) of the kadoshiym (holy ones, saints, set apart ones). 6 For who in the heavens can be compared to YAHUWAH? Who among the bnei eliym (sons of the gods) can be likened to YAHUWAH? 7 El (God) is greatly to be feared in the sod (assembly) of the kadoshiym (holy ones, saints, set apart ones), and to be held in reverence by all those around Him. 8 O YAHUWAH, Elohim Tseva'ot (God of hosts), who is chasiyn (mighty) like You, O YAH? Your emunah (faithfulness) also surrounds You. 9 You rule the raging of the sea; When its waves rise, You still them. 10 You have broken Rahab (a water demon, sea monster) in pieces, as one who is slain; You have scattered Your oyev'iym (enemies) with Your mighty arm. 11 The heavens are Yours, the earth also is Yours; The world and all its fullness, You have founded them. 12 The north and the south, You have created them; Tabor and Hermon rejoice in Your name. 13 You have a mighty arm; Strong is Your hand, and high is Your right hand.

14 Tsedek (Righteousness) and mishpat (judgment) are the foundation of Your throne; Chesed (Mercy) and emet (truth) go before Your face. 15 Blessed are the people who know the teru'ah (joyful sound)! They walk, YAHUWAH, in the light of Your countenance. 16 In Your name they rejoice all day long, and in Your tsedakah (righteousness) they are exalted. 17 For You are the glory of their strength, and in Your favor our horn is exalted. 18 For our shield belongs to YAHUWAH, and our Melek (king) to the Kadosh (Holy One) of Israel.

19 Then You spoke in a vision to Your chasiyd (Godly one), and said: "I have given help to one who is gibor (mighty); I have exalted one chosen from the people. 20 I have found My servant David; With My shemen kadosh (holy oil) I have anointed him, 21 With whom My hand shall be established; Also My arm shall strengthen him. 22 The oyev (enemy) shall

not outwit him, nor the ben avlah (son of unrighteousness, wickedness) afflict him. 23 I will beat down his foes before his face, and nagaf (plague, strike, smite) those who hate him. 24 "But My emunah (faithfulness) and My chesed (mercy) shall be with him, and in My name his horn shall be exalted. 25 Also I will set his hand over the sea, And his right hand over the rivers. 26 He shall cry to Me, 'You are my Father, Eli (My God), and the rock of my salvation.' 27 Also I will make him My bekor (firstborn), the highest of the melakiym (kings) of the earth. 28 My chesed (mercy) I will keep for him forever, and My brit (covenant) shall stand firm with him. 29 His seed also I will make to endure forever, and his throne as the days of heaven.

30 "If his baniym (sons, children) forsake My torah (law) and do not walk in My mishpatiym (judgments), 31 If they break My chuqot (statutes) and do not keep My mitzvot (commandments), 32 Then I will punish their pesha'iym (transgression) with the shevet (rod), and their avon (iniquity) with nega'iym (stripes, plagues, diseases).

33 Nevertheless My chesed (mercy, lovingkindness) I will not utterly take from him, nor allow My emunah (faithfulness) to fail. 34 My brit (covenant) I will not break, nor alter the word that has gone out of My lips. 35 Once I have sworn by My kodesh (holiness); I will not lie to David: 36 His seed shall endure forever, and his throne as the sun before Me; 37 It shall be established forever like the moon, even like the ed-ne'eman (faithful witness) in the sky." Selah.

38 But You have cast off and abhorred, You have been furious with Your mashiyach (anointed). 39 You have renounced the covenant of Your servant; You have profaned his crown by casting it to the ground. 40 You have broken down all his hedges; You have brought his strongholds to ruin. 41 All who

pass by the way plunder him; He is a reproach to his neighbors. 42 You have exalted the right hand of his adversaries; You have made all his tsariym (adversaries) rejoice. 43 You have also turned back the edge of his sword, and have not sustained him in the battle. 44 You have made his glory cease, and cast his throne down to the ground. 45 The days of his youth You have shortened; You have covered him with shame. Selah.

46 How long, YAHUWAH? Will You hide Yourself forever? Will Your wrath burn like fire? 47 Remember how short my time is; For what futility have You created all the children of men? 48 What man can live and not see death? Can he deliver his life from the power of Sheol (Hades, the grave, the underworld)? Selah. 49 Adonai (Lord), where are Your former chesed'iym (mercies, lovingkindnesses), Which You swore to David in Your emunah (faithfulness)? 50 Remember, Adonai (Lord), the reproach of Your servants; How I bear in my bosom the reproach of all the many peoples, 51 With which Your oyev'iym (enemies) have reproached, YAHUWAH, with which they have reproached the footsteps of Your mashiyach (anointed). 52 Blessed be YAHUWAH forevermore! Amen and Amen.

Psalm 90

1 A Prayer of Moses the man of Elohim (God). Adonai (Lord), You have been our dwelling place in all generations. 2 Before the mountains were brought forth, or ever You had formed the earth and the world, even from everlasting to everlasting, You are El (God). 3 You turn man to dakka (destruction), and say, "Return, O children of men." 4 For a thousand years in Your sight are like yesterday when it is past, and like a watch in the night. 5 You carry them away like a flood; They are like a sleep. In the morning they are like grass which grows up: 6

In the morning it flourishes and grows up; In the evening it is cut down and withers. 7 For we have been consumed by Your anger, and by Your wrath we are terrified. 8 You have set our avonot (iniquities) before You, our alum (secrets; secret sins) in the light of Your countenance. 9 For all our days have passed away in Your wrath; We finish our years like a sigh. 10 The days of our lives are seventy years; And if by reason of strength they are eighty years, yet their boast is only labor and sorrow; For it is soon cut off, and we fly away. 11 Who knows the power of Your anger? For as the fear of You, so is Your wrath. 12 So teach us to number our days, that we may gain a levav chokmah (heart of wisdom). 13 Return, YAHUWAH! How long? And have compassion on Your servants. 14 Oh, satisfy us early with Your chesed (mercy), that we may rejoice and be glad all our days! 15 Make us glad according to the days in which You have afflicted us, the years in which we have seen ra'ah (evil). 16 Let Your work appear to Your servants, and Your glory to their children. 17 And let the beauty of YAHUWAH our Elohim (God) be upon us, and establish the work of our hands for us; Yes, establish the work of our hands.

Psalm 91

1 He who dwells in the seter (secret place) of Elyon (the Most High) shall abide under the Tsel Shaddai (shadow of the Almighty). 2 I will say of YAHUWAH, "He is my refuge and my fortress; Elohai (My God), in Him I will batach (trust, be bold in)." 3 Surely He shall deliver you from the pach (snare; figuratively: calamity) and the yakush (fowler, trapper, bait layer) and from the dever havot (pestilence's destruction). 4 He shall cover you with His evrat (feathers), and under His kanaf'iym (wings) you shall take refuge; His emet (truth) shall be your shield and buckler. 5 You shall not be afraid of the pachad (terror) by laila (night), nor of the chets (arrow)

that flies by yomam (day), 6 Nor of the dever (pestilence) that walks in ophel (darkness, gloom; spiritual unreceptivity, calamity), nor of the ketev (destruction, destroying, ruin) that lays waste at tsohariym (noonday). 7 A thousand may fall at your side, and ten thousand at your right hand; But it shall not come near you. 8 Only with your eyes shall you look, and see the shilumat rasha'iym (reward of the wicked). 9 Because you have made YAHUWAH, who is my refuge, even Elyon (the Most High), your dwelling place, 10 No ra'ah (evil) shall befall you, nor shall any nega (plague) come near your ohel (tent, dwelling); 11 For He shall give His Mal'akiym (angels) charge over you, to keep you in all your derek (ways). 12 In their hands they shall bear you up, lest you dash your foot against a stone. 13 You shall tread upon the shachal (fierce lion) and the taniyn (dragon), the kephiyr (young lion) and the pethen (cobra) you shall trample underfoot. 14 "Because he has set his love upon Me, therefore I will deliver him; I will set him on high, because he has known My name. 15 He shall call upon Me, and I will answer him; I will be with him in trouble; I will deliver him and honor him. 16 With long life I will satisfy him, And show him My yeshua (salvation)."

Psalm 102

1 A tefillah le'aniy (Prayer of the afflicted), when he is overwhelmed and pours out his complaint before YAHUWAH. Hear my tefillah (prayer), YAHUWAH, and let my shav'ah (cry, cry for help) come to You. 2 Do not hide Your face from me in the day of my trouble; Incline Your ear to me; In the day that I call, answer me speedily. 3 For my days are consumed like smoke, and my bones are burned like a hearth. 4 My heart is stricken and withered like grass, so that I forget to eat my bread. 5 Because of the sound of my groaning my bones cling to my skin. 6 I am like a pelican of the wilderness; I am like an owl of the desert. 7 I lie awake, and am like a sparrow alone

on the housetop. 8 My oyev'iym (enemies) reproach me all day long; Those who deride me swear an oath against me. 9 For I have eaten ashes like bread, and mingled my drink with weeping, 10 Because of Your indignation and Your wrath; For You have lifted me up and cast me away. 11 My days are like a shadow that lengthens, and I wither away like grass. 12 But You, YAHUWAH, shall endure forever, and the remembrance of Your name to all generations. 13 You will arise and have racham (compassion, mercy) on Zion; For the time to favor her, yes, the set time, has come. 14 For Your servants take pleasure in her stones, and show favor to her dust. 15 So the goyim (nations, gentiles, heathens) shall fear the name of YAHUWAH, and all the kings of the earth Your glory. 16 For YAHUWAH shall build up Zion; He shall appear in His glory. 17 He shall regard the tefilat (prayers) of the ar'ar (destitute), and shall not despise their tefilat (prayers). 18 This will be written for the generation to come, that a people yet to be created may praise Yah. 19 For He looked down from the height of His kadosh (holy place, sanctuary); From heaven YAHUWAH viewed the earth, 20 To hear the groaning of the asiyr (prisoner), to release the bnei temuthah (sons of death), 21 To declare the name of YAHUWAH in Zion, and His praise in Jerusalem, 22 When the peoples are gathered together, and the kingdoms, to serve YAHUWAH. 23 He weakened my strength in the way; He shortened my days. 24 I said, "O Eli (my God), do not take me away in the midst of my days; Your years are throughout all generations. 25 Of old You laid the foundation of the earth, And the heavens are the work of Your hands. 26 They will perish, but You will endure; Yes, they will all grow old like a garment; Like a cloak You will change them, and they will be changed. 27 But You are the same, and Your years will have no end. 28 The children of Your servants will continue, and their seed will be established before You."

Psalm 103

1 A Psalm of David. Bless YAHUWAH, O my soul; And all that is within me, bless His holy name! 2 Bless YAHUWAH, O my soul, and forget not all His gemuliym (benefits): 3 Who forgives all your avoniym (iniquities), who rofe (heals) all your tachalu (diseases), 4 Who redeems your chai (life) from shachat (destruction), Who crowns you with chesed (mercy, lovingkindness) and rachamiym (tender mercies), 5 Who satisfies your mouth with tov (good things), so that your youth is renewed like the nesher (eagle's). 6 YAHUWAH executes tsedakah (righteousness) and mishpatiym (judgment) for all who are ashuk'iym (oppressed). 7 He made known His ways to Moses, His acts to the children of Israel. 8 YAHUWAH is rachum (merciful, full of compassion) and chanun (gracious), erek apayim (slow to anger), and rav chesed (abounding in mercy). 9 He will not always strive with us, nor will He keep His anger forever. 10 He has not dealt with us according to our chatat (sins), nor punished us according to our avonot (iniquities). 11 For as the heavens are high above the earth, so great is His chesed (mercy) toward those who fear Him; 12 As far as the east is from the west, so far has He removed our pesha'iym (transgressions) from us. 13 As a father pities his children, so YAHUWAH pities those who fear Him. 14 For He knows our frame; He remembers that we are dust. 15 As for man, his days are like grass; As a flower of the field, so he flourishes. 16 For the wind passes over it, and it is gone, and its place remembers it no more. 17 But the chesed (mercy) of YAHUWAH is from everlasting to everlasting on those who fear Him, and His tsedakah (righteousness) to children's children, 18 To such as keep His covenant, and to those who remember His pikudiym (precepts) to do them. 19 YAHUWAH has established His throne in heaven, and His kingdom rules over all. 20 Bless

YAHUWAH, you His Mal'akiym (angels), Who excel in strength, who do His word, heeding the voice of His word. 21 Bless YAHUWAH, all you His hosts, you sheret'iym (ministers) of His, who do His pleasure. 22 Bless YAHUWAH, all His works, in all places of His dominion. Bless YAHUWAH, O my soul!

Psalm 104

1 Bless YAHUWAH, O my soul! YAHUWAH Elohai (my God), You are very great: You are clothed with honor and majesty, 2 Who cover Yourself with light as with a garment, Who stretch out the heavens like a curtain. 3 He lays the beams of His upper chambers in the waters, Who makes the clouds His chariot, Who walks on the wings of the wind, 4 Who makes His Mal'akiym (angels) Ruchot (spirits), His sharatiym (ministers) a eish lohet (flame of fire). 5 You who laid the foundations of the earth, so that it should not be moved forever, 6 You covered it with the deep as with a garment; The waters stood above the mountains. 7 At Your rebuke they fled; At the voice of Your thunder they hastened away. 8 They went up over the mountains; They went down into the valleys, to the place which You founded for them. 9 You have set a boundary that they may not pass over, that they may not return to cover the earth. 10 He sends the springs into the valleys; They flow among the hills. 11 They give drink to every beast of the field; The wild donkeys quench their thirst. 12 By them the birds of the heavens have their home; They sing among the branches. 13 He waters the hills from His upper chambers; The earth is satisfied with the fruit of Your works. 14 He causes the grass to grow for the cattle, and vegetation for the service of man, that he may bring forth food from the earth, 15 And yayin (wine) that makes glad the heart of man, shemen (oil) to make his face shine, and lechem (bread) which strengthens man's heart. 16 The trees of

YAHUWAH are full of sap, the cedars of Lebanon which He planted, 17 Where the birds make their nests; The stork has her home in the fir trees. 18 The high hills are for the wild goats; The cliffs are a refuge for the rock badgers. 19 He appointed the moon for seasons; The sun knows its going down. 20 You make darkness, and it is night, in which all the beasts of the forest creep about. 21 The young lions roar after their prey, and seek their food from El (God). 22 When the sun rises, they gather together and lie down in their dens. 23 Man goes out to his work and to his labor until the evening. 24 YAHUWAH, how manifold are Your works! In wisdom You have made them all. The earth is full of Your possessions; 25 This great and wide sea, in which are innumerable teeming things, chayot (living things) both small and great. 26 There the ships sail about; There is that Livyatan (Leviathan) which You have made to play there. 27 These all wait for You, that You may give them their food in due season. 28 What You give them they gather in; You open Your hand, they are filled with good. 29 You hide Your face, they are troubled; You take away their breath, they die and return to their dust. 30 You send forth Your Ruach (Spirit), they are created; And You renew the face of the earth. 31 May the glory of YAHUWAH endure forever; May YAHUWAH rejoice in His works. 32 He looks on the earth, and it trembles; He touches the hills, and they smoke. 33 I will sing to YAHUWAH as long as I live; I will sing praise to Elohai (my God) while I have my being. 34 May my meditation be sweet to Him; I will be glad in YAHUWAH. 35 May chataiym (sinners) be consumed from the earth, and the rasha'iym (wicked) be no more. Bless YAHUWAH, O my soul! Halelu Yah (Praise YAHUWAH)!

Psalm 107

1 Oh, give thanks to YAHUWAH, for He is good! For His chesed (mercy) endures forever. 2 Let the redeemed of

YAHUWAH say so, whom He has redeemed from the hand of the tsar (adversary), 3 And gathered out of the lands, from the east and from the west, from the north and from the south. 4 They wandered in the wilderness in a desolate way; They found no city to dwell in. 5 Hungry and thirsty, their soul fainted in them. 6 Then they cried out to YAHUWAH in their batsar (trouble), and He delivered them out of their metsukah (distresses). 7 And He led them forth by the right way, that they might go to a city for a dwelling place. 8 Oh, that men would give thanks to YAHUWAH for His chesed (mercy, goodness), and for His nipla'ot (wonderful works) to the children of men!

9 For He satisfies the longing soul, and fills the hungry soul with tov (goodness). 10 Those who sat in choshek (darkness) and in the tsalmavet (shadow of death), asiyr (bound) in oniy (affliction) and barzel (irons); 11 Because they rebelled against the words of El (God), and despised the counsel of Elyon (the Most High), 12 Therefore He brought down their heart with labor; They fell down, and there was none to help. 13 Then they cried out to YAHUWAH in their batsar (trouble), nd He saved them out of their metsukah (distresses). 14 He brought them out of choshek (darkness) and the tsalmavet (shadow of death), and broke their moser'iym (chains) in pieces. 15 Oh, that men would give thanks to YAHUWAH for His chesed (mercy, goodness), and for His nipla'ot (wonderful works) to the children of men!

16 For He has broken the gates of bronze, and cut the bars of iron in two. 17 Eviyl'iym (Fools), because of their pesha'iym (transgression), and because of their avonot (iniquities), are yit'anu (afflicted). 18 Their soul abhors all manner of food, and they drew near to the sha'arei mavet (gates of death). 19 Then they cried out to YAHUWAH in their batsar (trouble), and He saved them out of their metsukah (distresses). 20 He

sent His davar (word) and healed them, and delivered them from their shechit'iym (destructions; pit). 21 Oh, that men would give thanks to YAHUWAH for His chesed (mercy, goodness), and for His nipla'ot (wonderful works) to the children of men! 22 Let them zabach (sacrifice) the zevach todah (sacrifices of thanksgiving), and declare His works with rejoicing.

23 Those who go down to the sea in ships, who do business on great waters, 24 They see the works of YAHUWAH, and His wonders in the deep. 25For He commands and raises the stormy wind, Which lifts up the waves of the sea. 26 They mount up to the heavens, they go down again to the depths; Their soul melts because of trouble. 27 They reel to and fro, and stagger like a drunken man, and are at their wits' end. 28 Then they cry out to YAHUWAH in their batsar (trouble), and He brings them out of their metsukah (distresses). 29 He calms the storm, so that its waves are still. 30 Then they are glad because they are quiet; So He guides them to their desired haven. 31 Oh, that men would give thanks to YAHUWAH for His chesed (mercy, goodness), and for His nipla'ot (wonderful works) to the children of men! 32 Let them exalt Him also in the kehal am (assembly of the people), and praise Him in the moshav zeken'iym (company of the elders).

33He turns rivers into a wilderness, and the watersprings into dry ground; 34 A fruitful land into barrenness, for the ra'at (wickedness) of those who dwell in it. 35 He turns a wilderness into pools of water, and dry land into watersprings. 36 There He makes the hungry dwell, that they may establish a city for a dwelling place, 37 And sow fields and plant vineyards, that they may yield a fruitful harvest. 38 He also blesses them, and they multiply greatly; And He does not let their cattle decrease. 39 When they are diminished and brought low through otser (oppression), ra'ah (affliction, evil), and yagon (sorrow), 40 He pours buz (contempt) on nadiyv'iym (nobles, princes), and causes them to wander in the wilderness where there is no way; 41 Yet He sets the evyon (needy) on high, far from oniy (affliction), and makes their families like a flock. 42 The yashar'iym (upright) see it and rejoice, and all avlah (unrighteousness) stops its mouth. 43 Whoever is chakam (wise) will observe these things, and they will understand the chesed (mercy, lovingkindness) of YAHUWAH.

Psalm 116

1 I love YAHUWAH, because He has heard my voice and my supplications. 2 Because He has inclined His ear to me, therefore I will call upon Him as long as I live. 3 The chevlei mavet (pains of death) surrounded me, and the pangs of Sheol (Hades, the grave, the underworld) laid hold of me; I found tsarah (trouble) and yagon (sorrow). 4 Then I called upon the name of YAHUWAH: "YAHUWAH, I implore You, deliver my soul!" 5 Chanun (Gracious) is YAHUWAH, and tsadiyk (righteous); Yes, our Elohim (God) is racham (merciful). 6 YAHUWAH preserves the simple; I was brought low, and He saved me. 7 Return to your rest, O my soul, for YAHUWAH has dealt bountifully with you. 8 For You have delivered my soul from mavet (death), my eyes from tears, and my feet from falling. 9 I will walk before YAHUWAH in the artsot hachayim (land of the living). 10 I believed, therefore I spoke, "I am aniy me'od (greatly afflicted)." 11 I said in my haste, "All men are kozev (liars)." 12 What shall I render to YAHUWAH for all His tagmuwl'iym (benefits) toward me? 13 I will take up the Kos Yeshu'ot (cup of salvation), and call upon the name of YAHUWAH. 14 I will pay my neder'iym (vows) to YAHUWAH now in the presence of all His people. 15 Precious in the sight of YAHUWAH is the mavet

(death) of His kadoshiym (holy ones, saints, set apart ones). 16 YAHUWAH, truly I am Your servant; I am Your servant, the son of Your maidservant; You have loosed my bonds. 17 I will offer to You the zevavh todah (sacrifice of thanksgiving), and will call upon the name of YAHUWAH. 18 I will pay my neder'iym (vows) to YAHUWAH now in the presence of all His people, 19 In the courts of YAHUWAH's house, in the midst of you, O Jerusalem. Halelu-Yah (Praise the Lord)!

Psalm 118

1 Oh, give thanks to YAHUWAH, for He is tov (good)! For His chesed (mercy) endures forever. 2 Let Israel now say, "His chesed (mercy) endures forever." 3 Let the house of Aaron now say, "His chesed (mercy) endures forever." 4 Let those who fear YAHUWAH now say, "His chesed (mercy) endures forever." 5 I called on Yah in metsar (distress); And Yah answered me and set me in a broad place. 6 YAHUWAH is on my side; I will not fear. What can man do to me? 7 YAHUWAH is for me among those who help me; Therefore I shall see my desire on those who hate me. 8 It is better to chasah (trust, hope) in YAHUWAH than to put batach (trust, confidence) in adam (man, human beings, mankind). 9 It is better to chasah (trust, hope) in YAHUWAH than to put batach (trust, confidence) in princes. 10 All goyim (nations) surrounded me, but in the name of YAHUWAH I will destroy them. 11 They surrounded me, Yes, they surrounded me; But in the name of YAHUWAH I will destroy them. 12 They surrounded me like bees; They were quenched like a fire of thorns; For in the name of YAHUWAH I will destroy them. 13 You pushed me violently, that I might fall, but YAHUWAH helped me. 14 Yah is my strength and song, and He has become my yeshua (salvation). 15 The voice of rejoicing and salvation is in the tents of the tsadiykiym (righteous); The right hand of YAHUWAH does valiantly. 16 The right hand of YAHUWAH is

exalted; The right hand of YAHUWAH does valiantly. 17 I shall not die, but live, and declare the works of Yah. 18 Yah has chastened me severely, but He has not given me over to mavet (death). 19 Open to me the sha'arei tsedek (gates of righteousness); I will go through them, and I will praise Yah. 20 This is the Sha'ar la'YAHUWAH (gate of the Lord), through which the tsadiykiym (righteous) shall enter. 21 I will praise You, for You have answered me, and have become my yeshua (salvation). 22 The stone which the builders rejected has become the chief cornerstone. 23 This was YAHUWAH's doing; It is marvelous in our eyes. 24 This is the day YAHUWAH has made; We will rejoice and be glad in it. 25 Save now, I pray, YAHUWAH; YAHUWAH, I pray, send now tsaleach (prosperity). 26 Blessed is he who comes in the name of YAHUWAH! We have blessed you from the house of YAHUWAH. 27 El (God) is YAHUWAH, and He has given us light; Bind the sacrifice with cords to the horns of the altar. 28 You are Eli (my God), and I will praise You; You are Elohai (my God), I will exalt You. 29 Oh, give thanks to YAHUWAH, for He is good! For His chesed (mercy) endures forever.

Psalm 142

1 A Contemplation of David. A Prayer when he was in the cave. I cry out to YAHUWAH with my voice; With my voice to YAHUWAH I make my supplication. 2 I pour out my siyach (meditation, complaint) before Him; I declare before Him my tsarah (trouble). 3 When my spirit was overwhelmed within me, then You knew my path. In the way in which I walk they have secretly set a snare for me. 4 Look on my right hand and see, for there is no one who acknowledges me; Refuge has failed me; No one cares for my soul. 5 I cried out to You, YAHUWAH: I said, "You are my refuge, My portion in the land of the chayim (living). 6 Attend to my cry, for I am brought very low; Deliver me from my radaph'iym (persecutors), for

they are stronger than I. 7 Bring my soul out of masger (prison), that I may praise Your name; The tsadiykiym (righteous) shall surround me, for You shall deal bountifully with me."

Psalm 143

1 A Psalm of David. Hear my tefillat (prayer), YAHUWAH, give ear to my tachanun (supplications)! In Your emunah (faithfulness) answer me, and in Your tsedakah (righteousness). 2 Do not enter into mishpat (judgment) with Your servant, for in Your sight no one chai (living) is tsadak (righteous). 3 For the oyev (enemy) has radaph (persecuted) my soul; He has crushed my chai (life) to the ground; He has made me dwell in machshak (darkness), like those who have long been met (dead). 4 Therefore my spirit is overwhelmed within me; My heart within me is distressed. 5 I remember the days of old; I hagah (muse) on all Your works; I siyach (meditate) on the work of Your hands. 6 I spread out my hands to You; My soul longs for You like a thirsty land. Selah. 7 Answer me speedily, YAHUWAH; My spirit fails! Do not hide Your face from me, lest I be like those who go down into the pit. 8 Cause me to hear Your chesed (mercy, lovingkindness) in the morning, for in You do I batach (trust); Cause me to know the way in which I should walk, for I lift up my soul to You. 9 Deliver me, YAHUWAH, from my oyev'iym (enemies); In You I take shelter. 10 Teach me to do Your will, for You are Elohai (my God); Your Ruach (Spirit) is tov (good). Lead me in the land of miyshor (uprightness). 11 Chayeniy (Quicken me, give me life), YAHUWAH, for Your name's sake! For Your tsedakah's (righteousness') sake bring my soul out of tsarah (trouble). 12 In Your chesed (mercy) cut off my oyev'iym (enemies), and destroy all those who tsarar (afflict) my soul; For I am Your servant.

Psalm 148

1 Halelu-Yah (Praise the Lord)! Praise YAHUWAH from the heavens; Praise Him in the heights! 2 Praise Him, all His Mal'akiym (angels); Praise Him, all His tseva'ot (hosts, armies)! 3 Praise Him, sun and moon; Praise Him, all you stars of light! 4 Praise Him, you heavens of heavens, and you waters above the heavens! 5 Let them praise the name of YAHUWAH, for He commanded and they were created. 6 He also established them forever and ever; He made a decree which shall not pass away. 7 Praise YAHUWAH from the earth, you great taniyn'iym (dragons) and all tehom'ot (the depths); 8 Fire and hail, snow and clouds; Stormy wind, fulfilling His word; 9 Mountains and all hills; Fruitful trees and all cedars; 10 Beasts and all cattle; Creeping things and flying fowl; 11 Kings of the earth and all peoples; Princes and all judges of the earth; 12 Both young men and maidens; Old men and children. 13 Let them praise the name of YAHUWAH, For His name alone is exalted; His glory is above the earth and heaven. 14 And He has exalted the horn of His people, The praise of all His kadoshiym (holy ones, saints, set apart ones); Of the children of Israel, a people near to Him. Halelu-Yah (Praise the Lord)!

After this, recite the stanzas from Psalm 119 that correspond to the letters of the ill individual's Jewish name(s). (Psalm 119 is an acrostic containing twenty-two stanzas, each stanza consisting of eight verses that begin with the same letter from the Hebrew alphabet. The first eight verses all start with the letter aleph, the next eight begin with bet, the next eight with gimel, etc.) E.g., if the person's name is Moshe (משה), recite the stanzas that begin with mem, shin, and hey. If the person's name is Rachel (רחל), recite the stanzas that begin with resh, chet and lamed.

Then recite the six stanzas that correspond to the words קְרַע שָׂטָן ("destroy the Prosecutor"): kuf, resh, ayin, shin, tet, and nun.

Psalm 119

ALEPH

1 Blessed are the tamiym'iym derek (undefiled in the way), who walk in the Torah YAHUWAH (Law of the Lord)! 2 Blessed are those who keep His edot (testimonies), who seek Him with the kol-lev (whole heart)! 3 They also do no avlah (unrighteousness, iniquity); They derek halakah (walk in His ways). 4 You have commanded us to shamar (keep) Your pikkudiym (precepts) me'od (diligently). 5 Oh, that my ways were directed to keep Your chukot (statutes)! 6 Then I would not be ashamed, when I look into all Your mitzvot (commandments). 7 I will praise You with yosher levav (uprightness of heart), when I learn Your mishpatiym tsedek (righteous judgments). 8 I will keep Your chukot (statutes); Oh, do not forsake me utterly!

BETH

9 How can a young man zakah (cleanse) his orach (way of living)? By taking heed according to Your davar (word). 10 With my kol levav (whole heart) I have sought You; Oh, let me not wander from Your mitzvot (commandments)! 11 Your word I have hidden in my heart, that I might not chata (sin) against You. 12 Blessed are You, YAHUWAH! Teach me Your chukot (statutes). 13 With my lips I have declared all the mishpat'iym (judgments) of Your mouth. 14 I have rejoiced in the derek (way) of Your edot (testimonies), as much as in all riches. 15 I will siyach (meditate) on Your pikudiym (precepts), and nabat (contemplate) Your orachot (ways of

life). 16 I will delight myself in Your chukot (statutes); I will not forget Your davar (word).

GIMEL

17 Deal bountifully with Your servant, that I may chayah (live) and keep Your davar (word). 18 Open my eyes, that I may see nipla'ot (wondrous things) from Your torah (law). 19 I am a ger (stranger) in the earth; Do not hide Your mitzvot (commandments) from me. 20 My soul breaks with longing for Your mishpatiym (judgments) at all times. 21 You rebuke the zediym (proud, presumptuous, arrogant, insolent) - the arur'iym (cursed), who stray from Your mitzvot (commandments). 22 Remove from me cherphah (reproach) and buz (contempt), for I have kept Your edot (testimonies). 23 Sar'iym (Princes) also sit and speak against me, but Your servant siyach (meditates) on Your chuk'iym (statutes). 24 Your edot (testimonies) also are my sha'shua (delight, enjoyment) and my counselors.

DALETH

25 My soul clings to the dust; Chayeniy (Quicken me, give me life) according to Your word. 26 I have declared my ways, and You answered me; Teach me Your chukot (statutes). 27 Make me understand the derek pikudiym (way of Your precepts); So shall I siyach (meditate) on Your nipla'ot (wonderful works). 28 My soul melts from heaviness; Strengthen me according to Your word. 29 Remove from me the derek sheker (way of lying), and grant me Your torah (law) graciously. 30 I have chosen the derek emunah (way of faith); Your mishpatiym (judgments) I have laid before me. 31 I cling to Your edot (testimonies); YAHUWAH, do not put me to shame! 32 I will run the course of Your mitzvot (commandments), for You shall enlarge my heart.

HE

33 Teach me, YAHUWAH, the derek chukiym (way of Your statutes), and I shall keep it to the end. 34 Give me understanding, and I shall keep Your torah (law); Indeed, I shall observe it with my kol-lev (whole heart). 35 Make me walk in the path of Your mitzvot (commandments), for I delight in it. 36 Incline my heart to Your edot (testimonies), and not to betsa (covetousness). 37 Turn away my einiym (eyes) from looking at shav (emptiness, vanity, falsehood, worthless things), and derek chayeniy (quicken me in Your way). 38 Establish Your imrah (word, speech) to Your servant, who is devoted to Your fear. 39 Turn away my reproach which I dread, for Your mishpatiym toviym (judgments are good). 40 Behold, I long for Your pikudiym (precepts); Chayeniy (Quicken me) in Your tsedakah (righteousness).

WAW

41 Let Your chesediym (mercies) come also to me, YAHUWAH; Your teshu'at (salvation) according to Your imrah (word). 42 So shall I have an answer for him who reproaches me, for I batach (trust) in Your davar (word). 43 And take not the devar emet (word of truth) utterly out of my mouth, for I have hoped in Your mishpatiym (judgments). 44 So shall I keep Your torah (law) continually, forever and ever. 45 And I will halakah ba'rachavah (walk at liberty), for I seek Your pikudiym (precepts). 46 I will speak of Your edot (testimonies) also before melekiym (kings), and will not be ashamed. 47 And I will delight myself in Your mitzvot (commandments), which I ahava (love). 48 My hands also I will lift up to Your mitzvot (commandments), which I ahava (love), and I will siyach (meditate) on Your chukot (statutes).

ZAYIN

49 Remember the word to Your servant, upon which You have caused me to hope. 50 This is my comfort in my oniy (affliction), for Your imrah (word) has chiyateniy (quickened me, given me life). 51 The zediym (proud) have me in great derision, yet I do not turn aside from Your torah (law). 52 I remembered Your mishpatiym (judgments) of old, YAHUWAH, and have comforted myself. 53 Zal'aphah (Indignation) has taken hold of me because of the rasha'iym (wicked), who azav (forsake, loose, leave behind, depart from) Your torah (law). 54 Your chukot (statutes) have been my songs in the house of my pilgrimage. 55 I remember Your name in the night, YAHUWAH, and I keep Your torah (law). 56 This has become mine, because I kept Your pikkudiym (precepts).

HETH

57 You are my portion, YAHUWAH; I have said that I would keep Your devariym (words). 58 I entreated Your favor with my whole heart; Be merciful to me according to Your word. 59 I thought about my ways, and turned my feet to Your edot (testimonies). 60 I made haste, and did not delay to keep Your mitzvot (commandments). 61 The chevel rasha'iym (cords of the wicked) have bound me, but I have not forgotten Your torah (law). 62 At chatsot (midnight) I will rise to give thanks to You, because of Your mishpatiym tsedek (righteous judgments). 63 I am a companion of all who fear You, and of those who keep Your pikudiym (precepts). 64 The earth, YAHUWAH, is full of Your chesed (mercy); Teach me Your chukidiym (statutes).

TETH

65 You have dealt well with Your servant, YAHUWAH, according to Your word. 66 Teach me good ta'am (judgment) and da'at (knowledge), for I believe Your mitzvot (commandments). 67 Before I was oniy (afflicted) I shagag (went astray), but now I keep Your imrah (word). 68 You are tov (good), and do tov (good); Teach me Your chukot (statutes). 69 The zediym (proud, presumpuous) have forged a sheker (lie) against me, but I will keep Your pikudiym (precepts) with my whole heart. 70 Their heart is as fat as grease, but I delight in Your torah (law). 71 It is good for me that I have been oniy (afflicted), that I may learn Your chuqiym (statutes). 72 The torah (law) of Your mouth is better to me than thousands of coins of gold and silver.

YOD

73 Your hands have made me and fashioned me; Give me understanding, that I may learn Your mitzvot (commandments). 74 Those who fear You will be glad when they see me, because I have hoped in Your word. 75 I know, YAHUWAH, that Your mishpatiym (judgments) are tsedek (righteous), and that in emunah (faithfulness) You have afflicted me. 76 Let, I pray, Your chesed (mercy) be for my comfort, according to Your word to Your servant. 77 Let Your racham (tender mercies) come to me, that I may live; For Your torah (law) is my delight. 78 Let the zediym (proud, presumpuous) be ashamed, for they treated me wrongfully with sheker (falsehood, lie); But I will siyach (meditate) on Your pikudiym (precepts). 79 Let those who fear You turn to me, those who know Your edot (testimonies). 80 Let my heart be blameless regarding Your chukot (statutes), that I may not be ashamed.

KAPH

81 My soul faints for Your salvation, but I hope in Your word. 82 My eyes fail from searching Your imrah (word), Saying, "When will You comfort me?" 83 For I have become like a wineskin in smoke, yet I do not forget Your Chukot (statutes). 84 How many are the days of Your servant? When will You execute mishpat (judgment) on those who persecute me? 85 The zediym (proud, presumptuous) have dug pits for me, which is not according to Your torah (law). 86 All Your mitzvot (commandments) are emunah (faithful); They persecute me wrongfully; Help me! 87 They almost made an end of me on earth, but I did not forsake Your pikudiym (precepts). 88 Chineniy (Quicken me, Give me life) according to Your chesed (mercy, lovingkindness), so that I may keep the edot (testimony) of Your mouth.

LAMED

89 Forever, YAHUWAH, your word is settled in heaven. 90 Your emunah (faithfulness) endures to all generations; You established the earth, and it abides. 91 They continue this day according to Your mishpatiym (judgments), for all are Your servants. 92 Unless Your torah (law) had been my sha'shua (delight), I would then have perished in my oniy (affliction). 93 I will never forget Your pikudiym (precepts), for by them You have chineniy (quickened me, given me life). 94 I am Yours, save me; For I have sought Your pikudiym (precepts). 95 The rasha'iym (wicked) wait for me to destroy me, but I will consider Your edot (testimonies). 96 I have seen the consummation of all perfection, but Your mitzvah (commandment) is exceedingly broad.

MEM

97 Oh, how I love Your torah (law)! It is my siyach (meditation) all the day. 98 You, through Your mitzvot (commandments), make me wiser than my oyev'iym (enemies); For they are ever with me. 99 I have more understanding than all my teachers, for Your edot (testimonies) are my siyach (meditation). 100 I understand more than the zekeniym (elders, ancients), because I keep Your pikudiym (precepts). 101 I have restrained my feet from every orach ra (evil way), that I may keep Your word. 102 I have not departed from Your mishpatiym (judgments), for You Yourself have taught me. 103 How sweet are Your words to my taste, sweeter than honey to my mouth! 104 Through Your pikudiym (precepts) I get understanding; Therefore I hate every orach sheker (false way).

NUN

105 Your word is a lamp to my feet and a light to my path. 106 I have sworn and confirmed That I will keep Your mishpatiym tsedek (righteous judgments). 107 I am oniy (afflicted) very much; Chayeniy (Quicken me, give me life), YAHUWAH, according to Your davar (word). 108 Accept, I pray, the nedavah (freewill offerings) of my mouth, YAHUWAH, and teach me Your mishpatiym (judgments). 109 My life is continually in my hand, Yet I do not forget Your torah (law). 110 The rasha'iym (wicked) have laid a snare for me, yet I have not strayed from Your pikudiym (precepts). 111 Your edot (testimonies) I have taken as a heritage forever, for they are the rejoicing of my heart. 112 I have inclined my heart to perform Your chukot (statutes) forever, to the very end.

SAMEK

113 I hate the Se'ephiym (double-minded, half-hearted), but I love Your torah (law). 114 You are my hiding place and my shield; I hope in Your word. 115 Depart from me, you re'iym (evildoers), for I will keep the mitzvot (commandments) of Elohai (my God)! 116 Uphold me according to Your word, that I may live; And do not let me be ashamed of my hope. 117 Hold me up, and I shall be safe, and I shall observe Your chukat (statutes) continually. 118 You reject all those who stray from Your chukat (statutes), for their tormah (deceitfulness, treachery) is sheker (a lie, falsehood). 119 You put away all the rasha (wicked) of the earth like dross; Therefore I love Your edot (testimonies). 120 My flesh trembles for fear of You, and I am afraid of Your mishpatiym (judgments).

AYIN

121 I have done mishpat (judgment) and tsedek (righteousness); Do not leave me to my ashak (oppressors). 122 Be surety for Your servant for good; Do not let the proud oppress me. 123 My eyes fail from seeking Your salvation and Your imrah tsedek (righteous word). 124 Deal with Your servant according to Your chesed (mercy), and teach me Your chukot (statutes). 125 I am Your servant; Give me understanding, that I may know Your edot (testimonies). 126 It is time for You to act, YAHUWAH, for they have made Your torah (law) void. 127 Therefore I love Your mitzvot (commandments) more than gold, yes, than fine gold! 128 Therefore all Your pikudiym (precepts) concerning all things I consider to be right; I hate every orach sheker (false way).

PE

129 Your edot (testimonies) are wonderful; Therefore my soul keeps them. 130 The entrance of Your words gives light; It gives understanding to the simple. 131 I opened my mouth and panted, for I longed for Your mitzvot (commandments). 132 Look upon me and be chanan (merciful, gracious) to me, as Your custom is toward those who love Your name. 133 Direct my steps by Your word, and let no aven (iniquity) have dominion over me. 134 Redeem me from the oppression of man, that I may keep Your pikudiym (precepts). 135 Make Your face shine upon Your servant, and teach me Your chukot (statutes). 136 Rivers of water run down from my eyes, because men do not keep Your torah (law).

TSADDE

137 Tsadiyk (Righteous) are You, YAHUWAH, and yashar (upright) are Your mishpatiym (judgments). 138 Your edot (testimonies), which You have commanded, are tsedek (righteous) and very emunah (faithful). 139 My zeal has consumed me, because my tsar'iym (adversaries) have forgotten Your words. 140 Your word is very pure; Therefore Your servant loves it. 141 I am small and despised, yet I do not forget Your pikudiym (precepts). 142 Your tsedakah (righteousness) is an tsedek olam (everlasting righteousness), and Your torah (law) is emet (truth). 143 Tsar (Trouble) and matsok (anguish) have overtaken me, yet Your mitzvot (commandments) are my sha'shua (delights). 144 The tsedek (righteousness) of Your edot (testimonies) is everlasting; Give me understanding, and I shall live.

QOPH

145 I cry out with my whole heart; Hear me, YAHUWAH! I will keep Your chukat (statutes). 146 I cry out to You; Save me, and I will keep Your edot (testimonies). 147 I rise before the dawning of the morning, and cry for help; I hope in Your word. 148 My eyes are awake through the night watches, that I may siyach (meditate) on Your word. 149 Hear my voice according to Your chesed (mercy); YAHUWAH, chayeniy (quicken me) according to Your mishpatiym (judgments). 150 They draw near who follow after zimah (mischief, wickedness); They are far from Your torah (law). 151 You are near, YAHUWAH, and all Your mitzvot (commandments) are emet (truth). 152 Concerning Your edot (testimonies), I have known of old that You have founded them forever.

RESH

153 Consider my aniy (affliction) and deliver me, for I do not forget Your torah (law). 154 Plead my cause and redeem me; chayeniy (Quicken me) according to Your word. 155 Salvation is far from the rasha'iym (wicked), for they do not seek Your chukat (statutes). 156 Great are Your rachamiym (tender mercies), YAHUWAH; chayeniy (quicken me) according to Your mishpatiym (judgments). 157 Many are my radaph (persecutors) and my tsar'iym (enemies), Yet I do not turn from Your edot (testimonies). 158 I see the bagadiym (transgressions), and am disgusted, because they do not keep Your word. 159 Consider how I love Your pikudiym (precepts); Chayeniy (Quicken me), YAHUWAH, according to Your chesed (mercy). 160 The entirety of Your davar (word) is emet (truth), and every one of Your mishpat tsedek (righteous judgments) endures forever.

SHIN

161 Princes persecute me without a cause, but my heart stands in awe of Your word. 162 I rejoice at Your word as one who finds great treasure. 163 I hate and abhor sheker (lying), but I love Your torah (law). 164 Seven times a day I praise You, because of Your mishpatiym tsedek (righteous judgments). 165 Shalom Rav (Great peace) have those who love Your torah (law), and nothing causes them to stumble. 166 YAHUWAH, I hope for Your salvation, and I do Your mitzvot (commandments). 167 My soul keeps Your edot (testimonies), and I love them exceedingly. 168 I keep Your pikudiym (precepts) and Your edot (testimonies), for all my ways are before You.

TAU

169 Let my cry come before You, YAHUWAH; Give me understanding according to Your word. 170 Let my supplication come before You; Deliver me according to Your word. 171 My lips shall utter praise, for You teach me Your chukot (statutes). 172 My tongue shall speak of Your word, for all Your mitzvot (commandments) are tsedek (righteousness). 173 Let Your hand become my help, for I have chosen Your pikudiym (precepts). 174 I long for Your salvation, YAHUWAH, and Your torah (law) is my delight. 175 Let my soul live, and it shall praise You; And let Your mishpatiym (judgments) help me. 176 I have gone astray like a lost sheep; Seek Your servant, for I do not forget Your mitzvot (commandments).

AVODAH YESHA
(Service For Deliverance)

SEALING PRAYER OF PROTECTION

The person anoints himself with Shemen Kodesh (Holy Oil):

YAHUWAH our Elohim (God) and Elohim (God) of our avot (fathers), I humbly ask of You in the name of Your only-begotten son, Yah'shua the Messiah (Jesus Christ) to seal me (my family, wife, children, animals, home, possessions, etc.) in His most Ahuv Dam (Precious Blood) against any and all plisha Hara (incursions of the evil one), in particular against any ruchot dibbuk (clinging spirits), ruach mishpachti (familial spirit), ruach mukar (familiar spirit) or ruchot nakam (retaliating spirits), in the Name of the Father YAHUWAH and of the Son Yah'shua (Jesus) ✠ and of the Ruach HaKodesh (Holy Spirit). Blessed are You YAHUWAH our Elohim (God), Melek Ha'Olam (King of the universe), who seals us in the most Ahuv Dam (Precious Blood) of Yah'shua (Jesus). Amen.

PRAYER OF COMMAND

In the Name of Yah'shua the Messiah (Jesus Christ) and by the power of His Tselav (Cross) and most Ahuv Dam (Precious Blood), I ask You YAHUWAH Elohai (Lord my God) to bind any ruchot ra'ah (evil spirits), ruchot ha'tumah (unclean spirits), ruchot rasha (wicked spirits), ruchot shediym (demonic spirits), Ayin Hara (Evil Eye), chayil'iym (forces) and ko'ach (powers) of the adama (earth), aviyr (air), esh (fire), or mayim (water), of the tachton-ha'olam (netherworld) and the chayil'iym Ha'Satani teva (satanic forces of nature). By the power of the Ruach HaKodesh (Holy Spirit) and by His rashut (authority), I ask Yah'shua the Messiah (Jesus Christ) to break any kelalot (curses), kishufiym (hexes), or kesimiym (spells) and send them back to where they came from. I beseech You Adonai Yah'shua the Messiah (Lord Jesus Christ) to protect us by pouring Your Ahuv Dam (Precious Blood) on us (my family, wife, children etc.), which You have shed for us and I ask You to command that any ruchot latset (departing spirits) leave quietly, without disturbance, and go straight to Yah'shua the Messiah (Jesus Christ) for Him to dispose of as He sees fit. I ask You to bind any demonic interaction, interplay or communications, I place N. (person, place or thing) under the protection of the Blood of Yah'shua the Messiah (Jesus Christ) which He shed for us. Blessed are You YAHUWAH our Elohim (God), Melek Ha'Olam (King of the universe), who binds and rebukes the chayil'iym ha'satan (forces of Satan). Amen.

PRAYER OF AUTHORITY

Adonai Yah'shua the Messiah (Lord Jesus Christ), in Your Name, I ask You to bind and silence all ko'ach (powers) and chayil'iym (forces) that do not accept You as Adon (Lord) and Melek (King), in the aviyr (air), in the mayim (water), in the adama (ground), the tachton ha'olam (netherworld) and teva (nature) and the aduk ha'olam (spiritual world). I ask You to bind all shedi ma'ase (demonic action) and shedi kesher (demonic communication). YAHUWAH, seal this whole place, all of us here and all our intentions in the Ahuv Dam (Precious Blood) of Yah'ahua the Messiah (Jesus Christ). Adonai YAHUWAH (Lord God), we ask you to surround us with your adderet chasut (mantle of protection) and crush the ko'ach ha'Satan (the power of Satan) in our lives. Kadosh Miyka'el Sar-Mal'ak (Saint Michael the Archangel), we ask you and all our Mal'akiym Apotropos (Guardian Angels) to defend us in battle against Satan and the ko'ach choshek (powers of darkness). Amen.

BINDING PRAYERS

Yah'shua the Messiah (Jesus Christ), our Adon (Lord) and Elohim (God), the Son of the Father, I ask You to render all ruchot (spirits) impotent, paralyzed and ineffective in attempting to take revenge against any one of us, our families, friends, communities, those who pray for us and their family members or anyone associated with us. I ask You to bind and sever and cut off all ruchot ra'ah (evil spirits), all ko'ach be-aviyr (powers in the air), the mayim (water), the adama (ground), the esh (fire), the machtarti (underground), the tachton ha'olam (netherworld), any chayil'iym satani teva (satanic forces in nature) and any and all emissaries of the satanic headquarters. I ask You to bind in Your Blood all of their attributes, aspects and characteristics, all of their interactions, communications and deceitful games. I break any and all bonds, ties and attachments in the Name of the Father YAHUWAH, and of the Son Yah'shua (Jesus) ✠ and of the Ruach HaKodesh (Holy Spirit). Amen.

In Your Name, Adonai Yah'shua the Messiah (Lord Jesus Christ), we pray that You would cover us, our families, and all of our possessions with Your ahava (love) and Your Most Ahuv Dam (Precious Blood) and surround us with Your heavenly mal'akiym (angels). Amen.

Yah'shua (Jesus), I ask You to bind and seal all power sources attached to any of us in the Most Ahuv Dam (Precious Blood) of Yah'shua (Jesus) and I ask You to render them all completely helpless, impotent, neutralized, paralyzed and ineffective, in the Name of the Father YAHUWAH and of the

Son Yah'shua (Jesus) ✠ and of the Ruach HaKodesh (Holy Spirit). Amen. (Three times).

PURIFICATION PRAYER

Yah'shua (Jesus) our Adon (Lord) and our Elohim (God), pour Your Ahuv Dam (Precious Blood) over me, my body, mind, soul, and spirit; my conscious and sub-conscious; my intellect and will; my feelings, thoughts, emotions and passions; my words and actions; my vocation, my relationships, family, friends and possessions. Protect with Your Ahuv Dam (Precious Blood) all other activities of my life. Adonai Yah'shua (Lord Jesus) I dedicate all of these things to You, and I acknowledge You as Adon (Lord) and Rav (Master) of all.

Adonai Yah'shua the Messiah (Lord Jesus Christ), I beg You for the grace to remain guarded beneath your adderet magen (protective mantle), surrounded by the holy briar from which was taken the Holy Crown of Thorns, and saturated with Your Ahuv Dam (Precious Blood) in the power of the Ruach HaKodesh (Holy Spirit), with our Mal'akiym Apotropos (Guardian Angels) for the greater glory of the Father YAHUWAH. Amen.

BINDING PRAYER

Spirit of (Name), I bind you in the Name of Yah'shua (Jesus), by the power of the Tselav Kadosh (Holy Cross), by the power of the most Ahuv Dam (Precious Blood) of Our Lord Yah'shua the Messiah (Jesus Christ), and I command you to leave N. *(Name of person or object)* and go to the foot of the Tselav Kadosh (Holy Cross) to receive your sentence, in the Name of the Father YAHUWAH, ✠ the Son Yah'shua (Jesus) ✠ and the Ruach HaKodesh ✠ (Holy Spirit). Amen.

LONGER FORM OF BINDING PRAYER

May it be Your will YAHUWAH our Elohim (God), and Elohim (God) of our avot (fathers) to grant us chofesh deror (complete freedom) from all avadiym (bondage), refuah shelema (complete healing) from every choli (illness), and yesha deror (complete deliverance) from every ruach ra'ah (evil spirit) and ruach ha'tumah (unclean spirit).

I ask you Adonai Yah'shua the Messiah (Lord Jesus Christ) to cover me with Your Blood, my hands, feet, arms, legs, head, tongue, mouth, saliva, lips, voice, throat, stomach, intestines, blood, the immune system, ears, eyes, and clothing, in the Name of the Father YAHUWAH and of the Son Yah'shua (Jesus), ✠ and of the Ruach HaKodesh (Holy Spirit).

I bind and render helpless all Ruchot (spirits) affecting me: the Ruach Heylel (spirit of Lucifer), Satan, Ba'al zebub (Beelzebub), Abaddon (Apollyon in Greek), Behemah (Beast), Beliya'al (Belial), Livyatan (Leviathan), the Taniyn (Dragon), the Nachash (Serpent), Kundalini, Piton (Python), Ach'av (Ahab), Ashtoreth, Asmodee, Ba'al, Baphomet, Dagon, Rach'av (Rahab), Iyzebel (Jezebel), Mamon (Mammon - wealth), Molech, Nebo, Pharmakeia; every Ruach Shediym (Demonic Spirit), Ruach Ra'ah (Evil Spirit), Ruach Ha'Tumah (Unclean spirit), Ruach Rasha (Wicked Spirit); every Ruach Adut (Religious spirit) and every Ruach Yami (Marine Spirit); the Tsiyiym (Desert Demon), the Sa'ariym (Goat Demon), the Iyiym (Howling Demon); Azazel, Semyaza, Samael, Lilith, the Bat Ya'anah (daughters of Lilith), and every succubus and incubus, every Siren, Alukah (vampire) Banshee and Jinn; the Mal'ak Ha'Mavet (Angel of Death) the Mashchiyt (destroyer), the Okel (devourer), the Arveh (locust) and the Yekek (cankerworm); every Ruach Choli (spirit of sickness), Ruach Chalah (spirit of infirmity), Ruach Machala (spirit of disease) and Ruach Nega (spirit of plague); every Ruach Shabar Shinayim (spirit of broken teeth), Machala Pe (mouth disease), Shemenut (obesity) and Machala Ayin (eye problem).

Spirits of never, communication, games, deceit, deception, ministering spirits, dissociation, unforgiving heart, abandonment, rejection, self-hatred, mocking, controlling, of capital sins, occult, spirits that cause hiccups, vomiting, fainting, falling, fear, panic, cowardliness, yelling, rage, explosions, defiance, amnesia, obscene gestures, tearing of clothing, reading of hearts, sudden movements, levitation, hot, cold, temperature fluctuation, upset stomach, bad odors, nausea, abandonment of state in life, of theft, murder, death, lies, brutality, trauma, resentment, terror, pride, arrogance, bitterness, confusion, cruelty, hatred, insecurity, adultery, fornication, masturbation, pornography, prostitution, unnatural sex, sexual perversions with all of their manifestations, contraception, sterilization, revenge, abortion, mutilation, suicide, blasphemy, sacrilege, heresy, schism, disobedience to authority, contempt for God, for His Name, for the Sabbath rest, eating disorders, involuntary vices (obsessive compulsive disorders), envy, jealousy, curiosity, coveting, stubbornness, perjury, drugs, drunkenness, lewd dancing, molestation, refusal to speak, false appearance of leaving, distraction, exaggeration, scrupulosity, presumption, slander, detraction, spirits that attack memory, imagination, mind, spirit, soul and body, the demons and spirits of freemasonry, the occult, wicca, covens, hexes, vexes, spells, charms, curses, snares, traps, obstacles, diversions, divisions, spiritual influences, evil wishes, evil desires, hereditary seals known and unknown, every dysfunction and disease, negative inherited DNA, blood sacrifices, Ruchot Ra'ah Dor (generational evil spirits), Ruchot Dibbuk (clinging spirits), and all others known to be present by Kadosh Miyka'el (Saint Michael) and the Mal'akiym Kadoshiym (Holy Angels).

I ask you Yah'shua (Jesus) to sever the transmission of any and all Satani Nederiym (satanic vows), heskem'iym (pacts), adut kesher (spiritual bonds), kesher nephesh (soul ties), and satani ma'aseh (satanic works).

I ask you Yah'shua (Jesus) to break and dissolve any and all links, and effects of links with: chartomiym (magicians), ashaphiym (astrologers), mekashefiym (witches), keshafiym (sorcerers), kosemitm (wizards), gazariyn (soothsayers), ovot (mediums; one who evokes the dead), yidoniym (spiritists: one who consults spirits), nafshiym (psychics, spiritualists), lahatutan (conjurers), kosem kesamiym (practioners of divination), nachashiym (diviners, enchanters), me'onen (observers of times), chover chaver (charm or spell workers), sho'el (consulter), doresh el hametiym (consulter of the dead: necromancers), tsachzan (clairvoyants), magid atidat (fortune tellers), bdoloch (crystals), bdoloch me'rafeiym (crystal healers), idan chadasha (New Age movement), magi choze (occult seers), kof kore (palm readers), te ale kore (tea leaf readers), ruach more derek (spirit guides), rofe elil (witch doctors), rav tsinak (dungeon masters), vudu (voodoo/ vodou), santeros (santeria), sataniym (satanism) or satani kat (satanic cults), heyleliym (luciferianism), chofshi be'niya (free-masonry), ruchot mukar (familiar spirits) and ruchot mishpachti (familial spirits).

I ask you Yah'shua (Jesus) to dissolve all effects of participation in si'ans (séances), nachash (divination), lu'ach siansim (ouija boards), horoskop (horoscopes), magi mischak (occult games) of all sorts, and any form of worship that does not offer true honor to Yah'shua the Messiah (Jesus Christ). In the Name of the Father YAHUWAH and of the Son Yah'shua (Jesus), ✠ and of the Ruach HaKodesh (Holy Spirit). Amen.

If Suitable, the person can make the following act of rejection:

I reject all these ruchot (spirits), pe'shi'a (vices) and resha (wickedness), in the Name of the Father YAHUWAH and of the Son Yah'shua (Jesus), ✠ and of the Ruach HaKodesh (Holy Spirit). Amen. (Thrice)

BINDING PRAYER TO BLIND THE DEMONS

Blessed are You YAHUWAH our Elohim (God), Melek Ha'olam (King of the Universe), the God and the Father of our Lord Yah'shua the Messiah (Jesus Christ), Who would crush the head of the nachash (serpent), protect us from the vengeance of the Hara (evil one). We offer our tefilat (prayers), techinot (supplications), sevel (sufferings) and ma'aseh tov (good works) to you so that you may purify them, sanctify them in the name of your Son Yah'shua the Messiah (Jesus Christ) as a korban tamiym (perfect offering). May this korban (offering) be given so that the shediym (demons) that influence us (could influence us or name the person) do not know the source of the expulsion and blindness. Blind them so they know not our ma'aseh tov (good works). Blind them so that they know not on whom to take vengeance. Blind them so that they may receive the just sentence for their works. Cover us with the Ahuv Dam (Precious Blood) of your Son Yah'shua the Messiah (Jesus Christ) so that we may enjoy the chasut (protection) which flows from His Teshuka (Passion) and Mavet (Death). We ask this through the same Messiah (Christ) Our Lord. Amen.

ACTS OF REJECTION

I renounce and reject any hakdasha (dedication), millu'iym (consecration), neder (vow), heskem (pact), havtacha (promise), choze (contract) or dam choze (blood contract), brit (covenant) or dam brit (blood covenant) to Satan of myself *(and insert names of others if you have made generational consecrations or included anyone else when making an offering to Satan)*, my heart, spirit, soul, body, mind, memory, imagination, intellect, will, dreams, inner thoughts, subliminal thoughts, touch, taste, smell, sight, hearing, stomach, blood, healthy bacteria, immune system, nervous system, and all other internal processes, especially through (insert list at this time) in the Name of the Father YAHUWAH and of the Son Yah'shua (Jesus), ✠ and of the Ruach HaKodesh (Holy Spirit). Amen. (Thrice)

I consecrate myself and my heart, spirit, soul, body, mind, memory, imagination, intellect, will, dreams, inner thoughts, subliminal thoughts, touch, taste, smell, sight, hearing, stomach, blood, healthy bacteria, immune system, nervous system, and all other internal processes, to YAHUWAH our Elohim (God) and to Yah'shua the Messiah (Jesus Christ) His only-begotten son, in the Name of the Father YAHUWAH and of the Son Yah'shua (Jesus), ✠ and of the Ruach HaKodesh (Holy Spirit). Amen.

After the person has made his rejection, he can then reconsecrate himself to the Trinity.

I completely and utterly reject, with the full force of my will N. *(insert any disorder one is experiencing or any evil one has committed)*. I do this in the Shem Kodesh (Holy Name) of Yah'shua the Messiah (Jesus Christ); and in the Name of the

Father YAHUWAH and of the Son Yah'shua (Jesus) and of the Ruach HaKodesh ✠ (Holy Spirit). Amen. (Thrice)

PRAYER FOR PROTECTION AGAINST CURSES, HARM, ACCIDENTS

Adonai Yah'shua (Lord Jesus), I ask You to protect our mishpacha (family) from all choli (sickness), from all nezek (harm) and from te'una (accidents). If any of us has been subjected to any kalala (curses), kishuf (hexes) or kesim (spells), I beg You to declare these kalala (curses), kishuf (hexes) or kesim (spells) null and void. If any ruchot ra'ah (evil spirits) have been sent against us, I ask Yah'shua the Messiah (Jesus Christ) to decommission you and I ask that you be sent to the foot of His Tselav (Cross) to deal with as He will. Then, Adonai (Lord), I ask You to send Your Mal'akiym Kadoshiym (holy Angels) to shomer (guard) and magen (protect) all of us. Amen.

PRAYERS FOR BREAKING CURSES OF THE OCCULT

I ask Yah'shua (Jesus) to bind in His Most Ahuv Dam (Precious Blood) any and all kalalot ra'ah (evil curses), heskem'iym (pacts), kesim'iym (spells), chatom'iym (seals), kishuf'iym (hexes), rogez'iym (vexes), hedek'iym (triggers), tar'demah (trances), neder'iym (vows), berachot shediym (demonic blessings), or any other avadiym shediym (demonic bondages) sent against N. or myself, or any of our loved ones or any of our possessions; I ask Him to bind them all and break them. In the Name of the Father YAHUWAH and of the Son Yah'shua (Jesus) ✠ and of the Ruach HaKodesh (Holy Spirit). (Thrice)

449

Yah'shua (Jesus), I ask You to bind any ruchot ra'ah (evil spirits) associated with any and all kalalot ra'ah (evil curses), heskem'iym (pacts), kesim'iym (spells), chatom'iym (seals), kishuf'iym (hexes), rogez'iym (vexes), hedek'iym (triggers), tar'demah (trances), neder'iym (vows), berechot shediym (demonic blessings), or any other avadiym shediym (demonic bondages) sent against N. or myself, or any of our loved ones or any of our possessions, and I ask You to bind all ruchot ra'ah (evil spirits) separately and individually and break all chatom'iym (seals). In the Name of the Father YAHUWAH and of the Son Yah'shua (Jesus) ✠ and of the Ruach HaKodesh (Holy Spirit). (Thrice)

BREAKING OCCULT TIES

In the Name of Our Adon Yah'shua the Messiah (Lord Jesus Christ), I ask you YAHUWAH Elohim (Lord God) the Father to break every magi zika (occult tie) of shachor kesem (black magic) (sorcery, curse, etc.) between the foul spirit N. (Name of demon) and N. (Name of person). I ask You to bind every ko'ach (power) of this ruach (spirit) and command him to leave N. and go to the foot of the Cross. Amen.

PRAYER TO REMOVE GENERATIONAL SPIRITS

Adonai Yah'shua the Messiah (Lord Jesus Christ), Son of Elohim Ha'Av (God the Father), You who have chosen to enter into human history by being carried in the womb of Your Blessed Mother Mary, grant, I beseech You, that any shediym (demons) that may have been introduced into my yichus dor (generational line) by any one of my rishoniym (ancestors) may be blocked from passing to the subsequent dorot (generations). I ask You that if the ruach ra'ah (evil spirit) entered the yichus dor (generational line) by the sin of one or more of my rishoniym (ancestors), that You would pardon the temporal punishment due to their sin and free us from the shediym's (demon's) involvement in our lives. Adonai Yah'shua (Lord Jesus), we ask you to grant your Precious Body, Blood, Soul and Divinity to Elohim (God) the Father in reparation for the sins of those rishoniym (ancestors) who may have introduced any ruchot ra'ah (evil spirits) into my yichus dor (generational line) as well as any subsequent sins that may have resulted from the ruchot ra'ah (evil spirits) affecting those of the yichus dor (generational line). If any ruach ra'ah (evil spirit) has been introduced into my yichus dor (generational line) as a result of a kalala (curse) or gevurah ra'ah (malefice) done by someone outside my mishpacha (family), I ask you to give me the grace to forgive them whole heartedly and I ask You Yah'shua (Jesus) to break the kalala (curse) or gevurah ra'ah (malefic), if it is still in place. YAHUWAH, I forgive them for any of the effects of their sin that they may have committed against my mishpacha yichus (family line) and for any damage it may have caused. Yah'shua (Jesus), I ask You to forgive me of any sins that may be the result of any ruchot dor (generational spirits) in my mishpacha (family) and I ask You to block any power the ruchot ra'ah (evil spirits) may have gained in my yichus dor (generational line) as a result of my own sin. Heal any damage in the lives of the members of my mishpacha (family) as a result of the ruach dor (generational spirit). I bind and completely and utterly reject, with the full force of my will any chet (sin) or ruchani migra'at (spiritual defect) of mine as well as any temptation, allurements or power that any ruach dor (generational spirit) may have over me as a result of my sin or the sin of any other person. I do this in the Shem Kadosh (Holy Name) of Yah'shua the Messiah (Jesus Christ) and in the Name of the Father YAHUWAH and of the Son

Yah'shua (Jesus) and of the Ruach HaKodesh ✠ (Holy Spirit). Amen.

It is highly recommended that one pray to Yah'shua (Jesus) to ask Him to reveal what the nature of the generational spirit is and how they may have entered the generational line so that specific binding prayers may be said against them and virtues may be developed to combat them.

ADJURATION

I adjure all you ruchot ra'ah (evil spirits), in the name of the spotless Lamb of Elohim (God), Yah'shua Ha'Natsri (Jesus of Nazareth) to depart from here. I cast you out, every ruach ha'tumah (unclean spirit), every pe'ri ha'dimyon (phantom), every encroachment of the shed (devil). Yield then to Elohim (God)! You are vanquished in your citadel, all you vile shediym (demons). The most Sovereign Melek Ha'Shamayim (King of Heaven), the Adon (Lord) and Moshiya (Savior) Yah'shua the Messiah (Jesus Christ), through His mighty Name drives you out; before His countenance you must flee. Give way, you ruchot ra'ah (evil spirits), to the Melek Ha'Shamayim (King of Heaven). He was destined by YAHUWAH El Shaddai (Lord God Almighty) to crush your head with His heel and to destroy all of the works of the shed (devil). Amen.

FOR CARDINAL AND OCCULT SPIRITS

One may either name the spirits or read from the list in appendix, then:

All you ruchot (spirits) just named and all your ruchot chaver (companion spirits): in the name of Yah'shua the Messiah

(Jesus Christ), by His Precious Blood and the authority of my kehuna (priesthood) [by the power of the Knesiya (Church)] I bind you separately and individually and break all chatam'iym (seals): you are bound and the chatam'iym (seals) are broken in the Name of the Father YAHUWAH and of the Son Yah'shua (Jesus) ✠ and of the Ruach HaKodesh (Holy Spirit). (Thrice)

I send you separately and individually to the foot of the Tselav (Cross) of Yah'shua the Messiah (Jesus Christ) to be held there and to be obedient to His Shem Kadosh (Holy Name) until He tells you to go elsewhere. In the Name of Yah'shua (Jesus), be gone! (Thrice)

You no longer have a rightful place in this child of Elohim (God) and in the Name of Yah'shua (Jesus), I command that you never return. In the Name of Yah'shua (Jesus), never return! (Thrice)

In the Name of Yah'shua (Jesus), be gone! Amen. (Thrice)

I come against your hooks, lines and tentacles, your roots, attachments and attenuations and I command in the Name of Yah'shua (Jesus) that you be me'kulal (cursed). In the Name of Yah'shua (Jesus), be me'kulal (cursed)! (Thrice)

You are me'kulal (cursed) because you do not bear good fruit in this child of YAHUWAH and you are like the fig tree that did not bear good fruit. In the Name of Yah'shua (Jesus) you must wither and die. (Thrice)

You must come forth from this child of YAHUWAH: you may not rend or tear, do harm or hurt of any kind as you come forth. In the Name of Yah'shua (Jesus), come forth. (Thrice)

In the power and authority of Yah'shua (Jesus), I command that you go directly to the foot of the Tselav (Cross), remain there and never return. In the Name of Yah'shua (Jesus) never return. (Thrice)

In the Name of Yah'shua (Jesus), be gone! (Thrice) Amen. (Thrice)

PRAYER AGAINST EVERY EVIL

El Shaddai (God Almighty), Father YAHUWAH, Son Yah'shua (Jesus), ✠ and Ruach HaKodesh (Holy Spirit), Hashilush Hakodesh (Most Holy Trinity), Mal'akiym (Angels), Sar Mal'akiym (Archangels), and Kadoshiym (Saints) of heaven, descend upon me. Please purify me, YAHUWAH, mold me, fill me with Yourself, and use me. Banish all the chayil'iym hara (forces of evil) from me, destroy them, vanquish them, so that I do Your Holy Will. Banish from me all kesim'iym (spells), mekashef'iym (witchcraft), shachor kesem (black magic), gevurot hara (malefice), zika (ties), kelalot (maledictions), and the Ayin Hara (evil eye); satani sheritsa (diabolic infestations), oshek (oppressions), chazaka (possessions); all that is evil and sinful; jealousy, perfidy, envy; physical, psychological, moral, spiritual, diabolical ailments. Cast into hell all shediym (demons) working these ra'ot (evils), that they may never again touch me or any other creature in the entire world. I command and bid all the powers who molest me by the power of El Shaddai (God Almighty), in the Name of Yah'shua the Messiah (Jesus Christ) our Savior to leave me forever, and to be consigned into the everlasting hell. Amen.

PRAYER OF DELIVERANCE

YAHUWAH, El Shaddai (Lord, God Almighty) the God and the Father of our Adon Yah'shua the Messiah (Lord Jesus Christ), we beg You through the intercession and help of the Sar Mal'akiym (Archangels) Kadoshiym (Saints) Miyka'el (Michael), Rapha'el (Raphael), and Gavriy'el (Gabriel) for the deliverance of our brothers and sisters who are enslaved by the Hara (evil one). All Kadoshiym Ha'Shamayim (Saints of Heaven), come to our aid.

From anxiety, sadness and obsessions – We implore You, YAHUWAH, deliver us.

From hatred, fornication, and envy – We implore You, YAHUWAH, deliver us.

From thoughts of jealousy, rage, and death – We implore You, YAHUWAH, deliver us.

From every thought of suicide and abortion – We implore You, YAHUWAH, deliver us.

From every form of sinful sexuality – We implore You, YAHUWAH, deliver us.

From every division in our family, and every harmful friendship – We implore You, YAHUWAH, deliver us.

From every sort of spell, malefice, witchcraft, and every form of the occult – We implore You, YAHUWAH, deliver us.

You who said, "Shalom (Peace) I leave with you, my shalom (peace) I give unto you." Grant that we may be liberated from every demonic influence and enjoy Your shalom (peace) always. In the Name of Yah'shua the Messiah (Jesus Christ) our Lord. Amen.

PRAYERS FOR TROUBLED SOULS

YAHUWAH, have mercy on us. El Shaddai (Almighty God), Adoneinu (Our Lord), King of Ages, You Who have made everything and Who transforms everything simply by Your Will. You who in Babylon changed into dew the flames of the "seven-times hotter" furnace and protected and saved the three holy children Shadrach, Meshach and Abed-Nego. You are the doctor and the physician of our souls. You are the salvation of those who turn to You. We beseech You to make powerless, banish, and drive out every satani ko'ach (diabolic power), presence, and machination; every evil influence, malefice, or Ayin Ra'ah (evil eye) and all evil actions aimed against Your servant N. Where there is envy and malice, grant to us goodness, endurance, victory, and charity. O YAHUWAH, You Who loves man, we beg You to reach out Your powerful hand and Your most high and mighty arm and come to our aid. Help us, who are made in Your image; send the Mal'ak Shalom (Angel of Peace) to us, to protect us body and soul. May he keep at bay and vanquish every ko'ach ra'ah (evil power), every poison or malice invoked against us by corrupt and envious people. Then, under the protection of Your authority may we sing, in gratitude, "YAHUWAH is my salvation; whom should I fear? I will not fear evil because You are with me, my Elohim (God), my strength, my powerful Lord, Adon Shalom (Lord of peace), Father of all ages."

Yes, YAHUWAH our Elohim (God), be merciful to us, Your image, and save Your servant N. from every threat or harm from the Hara (evil one), and protect him/her by raising him/her above all evil. We ask You this in the name of the blessed Lord Yah'shua the Messiah (Jesus Christ). Amen.

ANOTHER FORM

O Yah'shua (Jesus) our Moshiya (Savior), Adonai Elohai (My Lord and my God), Elohai (My God) and my all, With Your zevach (sacrifice) of the Tselav (Cross) You redeemed us and defeated the power of Satan. I beg You to deliver me from every noche'chut ra'ah (evil presence) and every hashpa'a ra'ah (evil influence).

I ask You in Your Name,

I ask You for the sake of Your wounds,

I ask You for the sake of Your Blood,

I ask You for the sake of Your Cross,

May the blood and the water that flowed from Your side wash over me to purify me, Deliver me, and heal me. Amen.

O YAHUWAH our Father, come and visit our home (shop, office, etc.) and protect us from the lures of the oyev (enemy); may Your mal'akiym Kadoshiym (holy angels) come to guard our shalom (peace) and may Your berachah (blessing) remain with us forever. In the name of Yah'shua the Messiah (Jesus Christ) Our Adon (Lord). Amen.

Adonai Yah'shua the Messiah (Lord Jesus Christ), who said to Your Shaliyachiym (Apostles), "In whatever home you enter, greet it, saying, 'Shalom (Peace) be in this bayit (home)", let this same shalom (peace), we pray, abide in this place. We beseech You to sanctify it by the merits of our trusting tefillah (prayer).

Pour Your berachot (blessings) on it and make it a place of shalom (peace). May salvation enter our abode as it entered the house of Zacheus, when You graced it with Your presence. Entrust Your mal'akiym (angels) to guard it and banish from it every ko'ach ra'ah (evil power).

Grant that all who live in it may please You with their ma'aseh tov (good works), and so receive from You, when their time comes, the reward of Your heavenly home. We ask this through Yah'shua the Mesiah (Jesus Christ) our Adon (Lord). Amen.

Yea, YAHUWAH our Elohim (God), spare Your creature(s), and deliver Your servant(s) from every harm and every influence caused by the Ayin Ra'ah (evil-eye) and preserve him (her, them) higher than every devar ra (evil thing). Amen.

PRAYERS AGAINST TEMPTATION

Adonai Yah'shua the Messiah (Lord Jesus Christ), Who was conducted as a criminal to the house of Annas, grant that I may never suffer myself to be led into sin by the temptations of the ruach ra'ah (evil spirit) or the evil suggestions of my fellow creatures, but that I may be securely guided by Your Ruach HaKodesh (Holy Spirit) in the perfect accomplishment of Your holy ordinances. Amen.

Come, O Ruach HaKodesh (Holy Spirit), and destroy in me, by Your sacred fire, every affection which cannot be referred to You or please You. Grant that I may be all Yours, that I may live and die ever true to You, my Love and my All. Amen.

PRAYER TO BE FREED FROM EVIL HABITS

Give me, I beseech You, O Ruach HaKodesh (Holy Spirit), Giver of all good gifts, that powerful grace which converts the stony hearts of mortals into burning furnaces of ahava (love).

By Your chen (grace), free my captive soul from the thraldom of every minhag ra (evil habit) and concupiscence, to restore to it the holy liberty of the children of Elohim (God). Give me to taste how sweet it is to serve Adonai (the Lord) and crucify the flesh with its vices and concupiscences. Enlarge my heart that I may ever cheerfully run the way of Your mitzvot (commandments) until I reach the goal of my aspirations, the joys and bliss of Your habitation in heaven. Amen.

PRAYER TO OVERCOME OUR SPIRITUAL ENEMIES

Chokmah Olam (Eternal Wisdom), come down into my soul, that all my oyev'iym (enemies) may be driven out; all my crimes melted away; all my chatat (sins) forgiven. Enlighten my understanding with the light of be'emet emunah (true faith); inflame my will with Your sweet ahava (love); clear up my mind with Your glad presence; and give virtue and perfection to all my powers. Watch over me especially at my death, that I may come to enjoy Your beatific vision in eternal bliss. Amen.

COMMISSION OF THE CARE OF SOUL AND BODY

May be prayed at any time, but especially before sleeping. For oneself:

Into Your hands, O YAHUWAH, I commend my body and my soul. I ask you to provide for them and to protect them. I ask you to protect them from the Hara (evil one). I ask you enlighten my mind, strengthen my will, and refrain my appetites by grace. Kadosh Miyka'el (St. Michael) call down from Heaven the legions of mal'akiym (angels) under your command to protect me; I ask of you all the things I ask of my Mal'ak Apotropos (Guardian Angel). My Mal'ak Apotropos (guardian angel), under your intellectual and volitional protection I place my body. I ask you to illumine my mind and refrain my appetites. I ask you to strengthen my cogitative power, my memory and my imagination. Help me to remember the things I should and not remember the things I should not. Help me to associate the things I should and not to associate the things I should not. Give me good clear images in my imagination. I ask you to drive away all the shediym (demons) that might affect me while I sleep (or throughout the course of the day). (Help me to sleep and, if you should deem it prudent, direct my dreams. Help me to arise refreshed). Amen.

For one other person:

Into your hands, YAHUWAH, I commend the body and soul of N. I ask you to provide for him (her) and to protect him (her). I ask you to protect him (her) from the Hara (evil one). I ask you to enlighten his (her) mind, strengthen his (her) will, and refrain his (her) appetites by grace. Kadosh Miyka'el (St. Michael), call down from Heaven the legions of mal'akiym (angels) under your command to protect him (her); I ask of you all the things I ask of his (her) Mal'ak Apotropos (guardian angel). Mal'ak Apotropos (Guardian angel) of N., under your intellectual and volitional protection I place his (her) body. I ask you to illumine his (her) mind and refrain his (her) appetites. I ask you to strengthen his (her) cogitative power, his (her) memory and his (her) imagination. Help him (her) to remember the things he (she) should and not remember the things he (she) should not. Help him (her) to associate the things he (she) should and not to associate the things he (she) should not. Give his (her) good clear images in his (her) imagination. I ask you to drive away all the shediym

460

(demons) that might affect him (her) while he (she) sleeps (or throughout the course of the day). (Help him (her) to sleep and, if you should deem it prudent, direct his (her) dreams. Help him (her) to arise refreshed). Amen.

For other people:

Into your hands, YAHUWAH, I commend the bodies and souls of NN. I ask you to provide for them and to protect them. I ask you to protect them from the Hara (evil one). I ask you to enlighten their minds, strengthen their wills, and refrain their appetites by grace. I also ask of you all the things I ask of their Mal'ak Apotropos (guardian angels). Kadosh Miyka'el (St. Michael), call down from Heaven the legions of mal'akiym (angels) to protect them; I ask all the things I ask of their Mal'ak Apotropos (guardian angels). Mal'ak Apotropos (Guardian angels) of NN., under your intellectual and volitional protection I place their bodies. I ask you to illumine their minds and refrain their appetites. I ask you to strengthen their cogitative powers, their memories and their imaginations. Help them to remember the things they should and not remember the things they should not. Help them to associate the things they should and not to associate the things they should not. Give them good clear images in their imagination. I ask you to drive away all the shediym (demons) that might affect them while they sleep (or throughout the course of the day). (Help them to sleep and, if you should deem it prudent, direct their dreams. Help them to arise refreshed). Amen.

PROTECTION PRAYER

May the Adon Yah'shua the Messiah (Lord Jesus Christ) be with me, that He may defend me; may He be within in me, that He may conserve me; may He be before, that He may lead me; may He be after me, so that He may guard me; may He be above me, that He may bless me, who with Elohim (God) the Father YAHUWAH and the Ruach HaKodesh (Holy Spirit) who lives and reigns forever and ever. Amen.

PRAYER TO PROTECT FACULTIES

Adonai Yah'shua the Messiah (Lord Jesus Christ) let your Ahuv Dam (Precious Blood) flowing from Your wounded Heart cover me, my cogitative power, memory, imagination, common sense power, sensitive appetites, my sight, hearing, taste, touch and smell, (and any part of your body they are affecting) driving the shediym (demons) to the foot of Your Tselav (Cross) where they may be judged by You. In the Name of the Father YAHUWAH, the Son Yah'shua (Jesus) ✠ and the Ruach HaKodesh (Holy Spirit). Amen.

PRAYER AGAINST RETALIATION

Adonai Yah'shua the Messiah (Lord Jesus Christ), in your ahava (love) and chesed (mercy), pour Your Ahuv Dam (Precious Blood) over me so that no shed (demon) or repha'iym (disembodied spirit) may retaliate against me. Surround me with the adderet (mantle), blocking any ruchot nakam (retaliating spirits) from having any authority over me. Kadosh Miyka'el (St. Michael), surround me with your magen (shield), so that no ruach ra'ah (evil spirit) may take revenge on me. Kadosh Miyka'el (St. Michael), send down the legions of mal'akiym (angels) under your command to fight off any ruchot (spirits) that would seek to harm me. All you kadoshiym ha'shamayim (saints of heaven), impede any ruchot nakam (retaliating spirit) from influencing me. YAHUWAH, You are the Just Judge, the avenger of the rasha'iym (wicked), the Advocate of the Just, we beg in Your chesed (mercy), that all we ask be also granted to all our loved ones, those whose prayer for us and their loved ones, that for Your Glory's sake, we may enjoy Your perfect protection. Amen.

SHORT-FORM DELIVERANCE

In the name of Adonai Yah'shua the Messiah (the Lord Jesus Christ), by the power of His Tselav (Cross), His Dam (Blood) and His Te'chiya Rresurrection), I bind you Satan, the ruchot (spirits), shaliytiym (powers) and chayil'iym ha'choshek (forces of darkness), the tachton ha'olam (nether world), and the chayil'iym ra'ah teva (evil forces of nature). I take authority over all kalalot (curses), kishuf'iym (hexes), shedi pe'ilut (demonic activity), and kesim'iym (spells) directed against me, my relationships, ministry, air space, finances, and the work of my hands; and I break them by the power and authority of Adonai Yah'shua the Messiah (the Lord Jesus Christ). I bind all shedi pe'ulat gomlin (demonic interaction), interplay, and communications between ruchot (spirits) sent against me, and send them directly to Yah'shua the Messiah (Jesus Christ) for Him to deal with as He wills. I ask forgiveness for, and denounce all negative inner nederiym (vows) that I have made with the oyev (enemy), willingly or unwillingly, and ask that Yah'shua the Messiah (Jesus Christ) release me from these nederiym (vows) and from any bondage they may have held in me. I claim the shed blood of Yah'shua the Messiah (Jesus Christ), the Son of Elohim Chayim (the living God), over every aspect of my life for my protection. I pray all these things in the precious name of my Adon (Lord) and Moshiya (Savior), Yah'shua the Messiah (Jesus Christ). Amen.

PERIMETER PRAYER

A. I adjure all you ruchot ra'ah (evil spirits), in the name of the spotless Lamb of Elohim (God), Yah'shua Ha'Natsri (Jesus of Nazareth) to depart from here. I cast you out, every ruach ha'tumah (unclean spirit), every pe'ri ha'dimyon (phantom), every encroachment of Satan (the devil). Yield then to Elohim (God)! You are vanquished in your citadel, all you vile shediym (demons). The most Sovereign Melek Ha'Shamayim (King of Heaven), Adonai Yah'shua the Messiah (the Lord Jesus Christ) drives you out; before His countenance you must flee. Give way, you ruchot ra'ah (evil spirits), to the Melek Ha'Shamayim (King of Heaven). He was destined by El Shaddai (God Almighty) to crush your head with His heel.

B. Adonai Yah'shua the Messiah (Lord Jesus Christ), in Your ahava (love) and chesed (mercy) establish a hekef ha'chasut (perimeter of protection) around N. and myself and all our loved ones, those who pray for us and their loved ones. May the mal'akiym Kadoshiym (Holy Angels) guard him/her/us and all our possessions, establishing a hekef ha'chasut (perimeter of protection) around N., rendering him/her/us immune from any kind of hashpa'a shed (demonic influence). I ask that no shi'abud shed (demonic bondage), delet shed (demonic door), yeshut shed (demonic entity), petach shed (demonic portal), kochavi hatala (astral projection), or resha'iym (disembodied spirit) may enter the space of 100 yards in all directions of him/her/us. I ask that any shediym (demons) within this vicinity or any that should try to enter here be rendered deaf, dumb and blind; that You would strip them of all weapons, armor, power, illusions, and authority; that You would bind, rebuke and disable them from communicating or interacting with each other in any way. Remove them, sending them directly to the foot of Your Tselav (Cross). Yah'shua (Jesus), Son of Elyon (the Most

High), I ask this in Your Glorious and Most Shem Kadosh (Holy Name). Amen.

PRAYER AGAINST RETALIATION

Adonai Yah'shua the Messiah (Lord Jesus Christ), in your ahava (love) and chesed (mercy), pour Your Ahuv Dam (Precious Blood) over N. so that no shed (demon) or rapha'iym (disembodied spirit) may retaliate against him (her). YAHUWAH, surround him (her) with Your mantle, blocking any ruchot nakam (retaliating spirits) from having any authority over him (her). Kadosh Miyka'el (St. Michael), surround him (her) with your magen (shield), so that no ruach ra'ah (evil spirit) may take revenge on him (her). Kadosh Miyka'el (St. Michael), send down the legions of mal'akiym (angels) under your command to fight off any ruchot (spirits) that would seek to harm him (her). All you kadoshiym hashamayim (saints of heaven), impede any ruchot nakam (retaliating spirit) from influencing him (her). YAHUWAH, You are the Just Judge, the avenger of the rasha'iym (wicked), the Advocate of the Just, we beg in Your chesed (mercy), that all we ask be also granted to all our loved ones, those who prayer for us and their loved ones, that for Your Glory's sake, we may enjoy Your perfect protection. Amen.

ANOTHER FORM

I bind in the Dam Yah'shua (Blood of Jesus) all of your hooks, lines and tentacles, your roots, attachments and attenuations and I command you in the Name of Yah'shua (Jesus) to remove them now completely and entirely: In the Name of Yah'shua (Jesus), remove them now. (Thrice).

FOR BREAKING THE WALL BUILT UP AROUND THE HEART

In order to break a wall that has a demonic cause, sometimes all that is necessary is to bind the wall that surrounds the heart in the Blood of Yah'shua (Jesus), and/or break it three times in these or similar words:

> I bind this wall that is around N.'s heart in the Blood of Yah'shua (Jesus) and I break it in the Name of the Father YAHUWAH and of the Son Yah'shua (Jesus) ✠ and of the Ruach HaKodesh (Holy Spirit).

At times severing the shediym's (demons) connection to the wall will help to begin the process of the wall coming down on the side of the person with the wall.

BREAKING THE SPIRIT OF DEATH

Offer a prayer such as this:

> Any ruchot hamavet (spirits of death) or anything connected with mavet (death), anything associated with the abortion, miscarriage, contraceptive use, etc., you and all of your ruchot chaver (companion spirits), I bind you separately and individually in the Blood of Yah'shua the Messiah (Jesus Christ) and break all chatamiym (seals), in the Name of the Father YAHUWAH, the Son Yah'shua (Jesus) ✠ and the Ruach HaKodesh (Holy Spirit).

> I send you directly and immediately to Yah'shua (Jesus). In the Name of Yah'shua (Jesus), begone. (Thrice)

> I command that you never return. In the name of Yah'shua (Jesus) never return. (Thrice)

In the Name of Yah'shua (Jesus), begone. (Thrice) Amen. (Thrice)

PRAYER TO REVERSE DECISIONS

To be said by the person:

Adonai Yah'shua the Messiah (Lord Jesus Christ), in Your Name and by the power of Your Ahuv Dam (Precious Blood), I retake the authority which was given to me by You in giving me freewill over the choices which I have made in the past as presented to me by Satan and his minions. I reject the choices I made N. *(here the person names the choices)*. I reclaim in Your name and for Your Glory, those things which I thought I had to abandon in order to preserve the things which I did choose. I beg You, in Your Chesed (Mercy), to reclaim those which I may have ceded control over to the shediym (demons). Protect all of those people and things which I may have relinquished, not knowing that choices laid before me were false. I rededicate myself to You by my free choice and by the authority of Your Name, I bind all haspa'a shed (demonic influence) which is the result of my choices and I command the shediym (demons) to go to the foot of Your Tselav (Cross) to receive their sentence. Adonai (Lord), I ask You to surround me, my family, my friends, all of those affected people and things affected by my choices with your adderet chasut (mantle of protection) and crush Satan's power in our lives. Kadosh Miyka'el Sar Mal'ak (Saint Michael the Archangel), we ask you and all our Mal'akiym Apotropos (Guardian Angels) to protect and defend us in battle against Satan and the powers of darkness. Amen. (Thrice, if necessary.)

The Priest then says, if present:

All you ruchot (spirits) which have sought to gain influence by presenting false choices to N. and all your ruchot chaver (companion spirits): in the name of Yah'shua the Messiah (Jesus Christ), by His Ahuv Dam (Precious Blood) and the authority of my Kehuna (priesthood) [with the authority granted to me by Yah'shua the Messiah (Jesus Christ) and His Knesiya (Church)] I le'garesh ruchot (exorcize) and bind you separately and individually and break all chatam'iyn (seals) and ko'ach (power) gained by you through these choices: I break all influence you have over those people and things as a result of N.'s choices. I bind you from ever seeking to gain power or influence over N., or anyone or anything associate with him(her). You are bound and the seals are broken in the Name of the Father YAHUWAH and of the Son Yah'shua (Jesus) ✠ and of the Ruach HaKodesh (Holy Spirit). (Thrice)

ADJURATION

I completely and utterly reject, with the full force of my will N.

I do this in the Shem Kadosh (Holy Name) of Yah'shua the Messiah (Jesus Christ) and in the Name of the Father YAHUWAH and of the Son Yah'shua (Jesus) ✠ and of the Ruach HaKodesh (Holy Spirit). Amen. (Thrice)

PRAYER AGAINST OPPRESSION

Most Blessed Hashilush Hakodesh (Holy Trinity), by the authority given to me by the natural law and by Your giving these things and rights to me, I claim authority, rights and power over my N. *(income, finances, possessions, etc.)* and anything else that pertains to the oshek (oppression). By the merits of Your Sacred Wounds, I reclaim the rights, powers and authority over anything which I may have lost or conceded to any shed (demon) and I ask You to remove any shediym's (demon's) ability to influence or affect anything in my life. YAHUWAH Elohim (God) the Father, humiliate the shediym (demons) that have sought to steal Your glory from You by oppressing Your creatures. We beseech You to show Your great glory and power over them and Your great generosity to me, Your unworthy creature, by answering all that I have asked of You. I bind all shediym (demons) of oppression, in the name of Yah'shua (Jesus), by the power of the Most Ahuv Dam (Precious Blood), the power of the humility with which Messiah (Christ) suffered His wounds, and I command you to leave and go to the foot of the Tselav Kadosh (Holy Cross) to receive your sentence, in the Name of the Father YAHUWAH, and of the Son Yah'shua (Jesus) ✠ and of the Ruach HaKodesh (Holy Spirit). Amen.

CONSECRATION OF ONE'S EXTERIOR GOODS TO THE LORD

This prayer is particularly useful for breaking various forms of oppression.

I, (Name), a faithless sinner, renew and ratify today in Your hands the nederiym (vows) of my te'vilah (Baptism); I renounce forever Satan, his pomps and works; and I give myself entirely to Yah'shua the Messiah (Jesus Christ), the Incarnate Wisdom, to carry my tselav (cross) after Him all the days of my life, and to be more faithful to Him than I have ever been before. In the presence of all the heavenly court, I choose you, O YAHUWAH, this day for my Av (Father) and Elohim (God). Knowing that I have received rights over all my exterior goods by the promulgation of the the Natural Law by the Divine Author, I deliver and consecrate to you, all of my exterior goods, past, present and future; I relinquish into your hands, my Av Shamayim (Heavenly Father), all rights over my exterior goods, including my health, finances, relationships, possessions, property, my job and my earthly success *(add any exterior good being oppressed)* and I retain for myself no right of disposing the goods that come to me but leave to you the entire and full right of disposing of all that belongs to me, without exception, according to your good pleasure, for the greater glory of Elohim (God) in time and in eternity. As I now interiorly relinquish what belongs to me exteriorly into your hands, I entrust to you the protection of those exterior goods against the Hara (evil one), so that, knowing that they now belong to you, he cannot touch them. Receive, O good and merciful Father, this little offering of what little is, in honor of, and in union with, that subjection which the Chokmah Olam (Eternal Wisdom) deigned to have to You; in homage to the power which both of you have over this poor sinner, and in thanksgiving for the privileges with which the Hashilush Hakodesh (Holy Trinity) has favored you. Trusting in the providential care of Elohim (God) the Father and your loving care, I have full confidence that you will take care of me as to the necessities of this life and will not leave me forsaken. Elohim Ha'Avi (God the Father), increase my trust in Your Son; Yah'shua the Messiah (Jesus Christ), give me perfect confidence in the providence of Your Shalom (Peace). Amen.

CONSECRATION PRAYER

To the Hashilush HaKodesh (Holy Trinity):

Abba Father, I love You. May I live and die within Your embrace, with grateful love, joyful hope, and child-like trust. May I lovingly drink from the chalice that You offer me today. Accomplish within me Your heart's desire, for You are my loving and good Father.

Adonai Yah'shua (Lord Jesus), through the faith that is in Your name, I consecrate myself to You, in union with the Zevach

Kadosh (Holy Sacrifice) of the Chavarut Aruchot Adonai (Communion of the Lord's Supper). Transform my heart, by allowing Your thoughts, Your will, and Your love, to be my life. Yah'shua (Jesus), take possession of my whole being, that You may love Your Father through me, with me and in me, for You are my faithful Spouse. (2 Cor. 11:2)

Ruach HaKodesh (Holy Spirit), I adore You. You are all Ahava (Love), Chokmah (Wisdom), Ko'ach (Power), Kedusha (Holiness), and Emet (Truth). Reveal the Father's will to me, that through Your strength and consolation, I may embrace His will with Love, accomplishing all that You ask of me today. Take possession of my mind, heart, soul, body, memory, and will. May I respond with joy, interior silence, and mortification, so as to be Your sacred dwelling place.

The Rabbi/Priest Consecrates the Person:

I offer to Elohim (God) the Dam Zevach (Blood Sacrifice) of Yah'shua the Messiah (Jesus Christ) and the piercing of the spear, and the nails and the thorns and the lash for N. I ask Yah'shua the Messiah (Jesus Christ) to take dominion of N. and his (her) heart, spirit, soul, body, mind, memory, imagination, intellect, will, dreams, inner thoughts, subliminal thoughts, touch, taste, smell, sight, hearing, stomach, blood, healthy bacteria, immune system, nervous system, and all other internal processes, in the Name of the Father YAHUWAH and of the Son Yah'shua (Jesus), ✠ and of the Ruach HaKodesh (Holy Spirit). Amen. (Thrice)

After the re-consecration to Yah'shua (Jesus) the Rabbi/Priest may anoint the person with the sign of the cross (with exorcized oil): the top of the head, bottom of both feet, forehead, eyelids, ears, back of the neck, upper sternum, palms of both hands and shoulders.

BINDING EVIL SPIRITS

In the name of the Lord Yah'shua the Messiah (Jesus Christ), I stand with the power of YAHUWAH, El Shadai (God Almighty), to bind Satan and all his ruchot ra'ah (evil spirits), chayil shediym (demonic forces), satani he'atiyd (satanic powers), sararot (principalities), along with all melekiym (kings) and sariym (princes) of eymah (terrors), from the ayir (air), mayim (water), esh (fire), adama (ground), tachton ha'olam (netherworld), and the chayil ra'ah teva (evil forces of nature).

I take authority over all matala shediym (demonic assignments) and functions of destruction sent against me, my wife (husband), my children, my family and my house, and I expose all chayil shediym (demonic forces) as weakened, defeated oyev'iym (enemies) of Yah'shua the Messiah (Jesus Christ).

I stand with the power of YAHUWAH, El Shaddai (God Almighty), to bind all oyev'iym (enemies) of Messiah (Christ) present together, all shediym yeshut (demonic entities) under their one and highest authority, and I command these ruchot (spirits) into the tehom (abyss) to never again return. Their assignments and influences are over.

In the name of Yah'shua the Messiah (Jesus Christ), I bind, reject, rebuke, and cast out the ruach heylel (spirit of Lucifer), Satan, Ba'al Zebub (Beelzebub), Abaddon, Apollyon, Behemah (Beast) and Beliya'al (Belial).

In the name of Yah'shua (Jesus), I bind, reject, rebuke, and cast out the ruach Livyatan (spirit of Leviathan), the Taniyn (Dragon), the Nachash (Serpent), Kundalini, and Piton (Python).

In the name of Yah'shua (Jesus), I bind, reject, rebuke, and cast out the spirit of Ahab, Ashtoreth, Asmodee, Baal, Baphomet, Dagon, Iyzebel (Jezebel), Mammon, Molech, Nebo, and Pharmakeia.

In the name of Yah'shua (Jesus), I bind, reject, rebuke, and cast out every ruach aduk (Religious spirit) and every ruach nekat (Marine Spirit).

In the name of Yah'shua (Jesus), I bind, reject, rebuke, and cast out the Tsiyiym (Desert Demon), the Sa'ariym (Goat Demon), the Iyiym (Howling Demon); Azazel, Semyaza, Samael, Lilith, the Bat Ya'anah (daughters of Lilith), and every succubus and incubus.

In the name of Yah'shua (Jesus), I bind, reject, rebuke, and cast out every Siren, Alukah (vampire) Banshee and Shed (Jinn or Genie).

In the name of Yah'shua (Jesus), I bind, reject, rebuke, and cast out the Okel (devourer), the arveh (locust) and the yelek (cankerworm).

In the name of Yah'shua (Jesus), I bind, reject, rebuke, and cast out the Dibbuk (clinging spirit), and the Repha'iym (disembodied spirit).

In the name of Yah'shua (Jesus), I bind, reject, rebuke, and cast out every ruach choli (spirit of sickness), ruach chalah (spirit of infirmity), ruach mechala (spirit of disease), ruach dever (spirit of pestilance) and ruach nega (spirit of plague).

In the name of Yah'shua (Jesus), I bind, reject, rebuke, and cast out every ruach shabar shinayim (spirit of broken teeth), ruach mechala pe (spirit of mouth disease), ruach shemenut (spirit of obesity) and ruach mechala ayin (spirit eye disease).

473

In the name of Yah'shua (Jesus), I bind, reject, rebuke, and cast out every ruach mechosh (spirit of ache) and ruach ke'ev (spirit of pain).

In the name of Yah'shua (Jesus), I bind, reject, rebuke, and cast out every ruach oniy (spirit of poverty), choser (lack) and tsorech (want /need).

In the name of Yah'shua (Jesus), I bind, reject, rebuke, and cast out every ruach me'kulkal (spirit of brokenness), ruach rakav (decay, rot), and ruach ovesh (mildew, mold).

I arise today with the power of YAHUWAH, El Shaddai (God Almighty), in the name of Yah'shua the Messiah (Jesus Christ) and by the power and authority that is in his name, to call forth the heavenly host, the mal'akiym kadoshiym (holy angels) of Elohim (God), to surround and protect, and cleanse with Elohim's (God's) Kadosh Or (holy light) all areas vacated by the chayil'iym ha'ra (forces of evil).

I ask the Ruach HaKodesh (Holy Spirit) to permeate my mind, heart, body, soul and spirit, creating a hunger and thirst for Elohim's (God's) holy Word, and to fill me with the life and love of my Lord, Yah'shua the Messiah (Jesus Christ). Amen.

LOOSING THE BOND OF SATAN

In the name of Yah'shua (Jesus), I am loosed, released and set free from the bond of Satan.

In the name of Yah'shua (Jesus), I am loosed, released and set free from the bond of choli (sickness), chala (infirmity), me'chala (disease) and nega (plague).

In the name of Yah'shua (Jesus), I am loosed, released and set free from the bond of broken teeth and mouth disease.

In the name of Yah'shua (Jesus), I am loosed, released and set free from the bond of stomach illness and intestinal disorder.

In the name of Yah'shua (Jesus), I am loosed, released and set free from the bond of sinusitis and sinus problems.

In the name of Yah'shua (Jesus), I am loosed, released and set free from the bond of boils, cysts, acne and stinky sores.

In the name of Yah'shua (Jesus), I am loosed, released and set free from the bond of obesity.

In the name of Yah'shua (Jesus), I am loosed, released and set free from the bond of tiredness.

In the name of Yah'shua (Jesus), I am loosed, released and set free from the bond of scars and stretchmarks.

In the name of Yah'shua (Jesus), I am loosed, released and set free from the bond of eye problems.

In the name of Yah'shua (Jesus), I am loosed, released and set free from the bond of ache and pain.

In the name of Yah'shua (Jesus), I am loosed, released and set free from the bond of poverty, lack and want.

In the name of Yah'shua (Jesus), I am loosed, released and set free from the bond of weakness.

RELEASING POWER AND HEALING

I call upon, loose and release the Ruach Elohim (Spirit of God) the Father in my body, my wife (husband), my children, my house and every aspect of my life.

I call upon, loose and release the Ruach Yah'shua the Messiah (Spirit of Jesus Christ), the Son of the Father, in my body, my wife (husband), my children, my house and every aspect of my life.

I call upon, loose and release the Ruach HaKodesh (Spirit of Holiness) in my body, my wife (husband), my children, my house and every aspect of my life.

I call upon, loose and release the power of the Blood of Yah'shua the Messiah (Jesus Christ) in my body, my wife (husband), my children, my house and every aspect of my life.

I call upon, loose and release complete, sound and perfect healing in my body, in my wife (husband), my children, my house and every aspect of my life.

I call upon, loose and release complete, sound and perfect healing in my body, my bones, my teeth, my mouth, and my eyes.

I call upon, loose and release complete and perfect health and fitness in my body, in my wife (husband), my children, and my animals.

I call upon, loose and release complete, sound and perfect healing in my prosperity, finances and blessings.

I call upon, loose and release complete, sound and perfect healing and restoration to my house, possessions, my pets and all that Elohim (God) has given to me.

I call upon, loose and release complete and perfect love, joy and peace in my body, in my wife (husband), my children, my animals, my house and every aspect of my life.

I call upon, loose and release the complete and perfect blessings of Elohim (God) in my body, in my wife (husband), my children, my animals, my house and every aspect of my life.

I call upon, loose and release the miraculous and healing power of the Ruach HaKodesh (Holy Spirit) in me.

In the name of Yah'shua the Messiah (Jesus Christ). Amen.

SPIRITUAL WARFARE PRAYERS

PRAYER OF ST. MICHAEL THE ARCHANGEL

Kadosh Miyka'el Sar-Mal'ak (St. Michael the Archangel), defend us in battle, be our protection against the rasha (wickedness) and snares of Satan (the devil). May Elohim (God) rebuke him, we humbly pray; and do you, O Sar HaShamayim Tseva'ot (Prince of the heavenly host), by the power of Elohim (God), cast into hell Satan and all the ruach ra'ah (evil spirits) who prowl about the world seeking the ruin of souls. Amen.

BREAKING CURSES

In the name of Adonai Yah'shua the Messiah Ha'Natsriy (the Lord Jesus Christ of Nazareth), by the power of his Tselav (Cross), his Dam (Blood) and his Te'chiya (Resurrection, I take authority over all kalalot (curses), kishuf'iym (hexes), kesim'iym (spells), vudu minhag (voodoo practices), kishufiym matala (witchcraft assignments), pulchan satani (satanic rituals), le'haksim (incantations) and lirtsot ra (evil wishes) that have been sent my way, or have passed down the dorot kirvat dam (generational bloodline). I break their influence over my life by the power of the risen Lord Yah'shua the Messiah (Jesus Christ), and I command these kalalot (curses) to go back to where they came from and be replaced with a beracha (blessing).

I ask forgiveness for and renounce all negative inner nederiym (vows) and agreements that I have made with the oyev (enemy), and I ask you Adonai Yah'shua (Lord Jesus) to release me from any bondage they may have held in me. I claim your shed blood over all aspects of my life, relationships, ministry endeavors and finances. I thank you for your enduring love, your mal'achi chasut (angelic protection), and for the fullness of your abundant blessings. In the name of the Father YAHUWAH, and of the Son Yah'shua (Jesus), ✠ and of the Ruach HaKodesh (Holy Spirit). Amen.

PRAYER AGAINST EVIL

Ruach Elohim (Spirit of God), Father YAHUWAH, Son Yah'shua (Jesus) and Ruach HaKodesh (Holy Spirit), Most Hashilush HaKodesh (Holy Trinity), descend upon me. Please purify me, mold me, fill me with yourself, and use me. Banish all the chayil'iym ra (forces of evil) from me; destroy them, vanquish them so that I can be healthy and do good deeds.

Banish from me all kalalot (curses), kishuf'iym (hexes), kesim'iym (spells), kishuf (witchcraft), shakor kesem (black magic), shediym matala (demonic assignments), gevurot ra'ah (malefic) and the ayin hara (evil eye); diabolic infestations, oppressions, possessions; all that is evil and sinful; jealousy, treachery, envy; all physical, psychological, moral, spiritual and diabolical ailments; as well as all ruchot pitui (enticing spirits), deaf, dumb, blind, mute and sleeping spirits, ruchot idan chadasha (new-age spirits), ruchot magi (occult spirits), ruchot aduk (religious spirits), ruchot anti-mashiyach (antichrist spirits), and any other ruchot (spirits) of mavet (death) and choshek (darkness).

I command and bid all the powers who molest me—by the power of El Shaddai (God Almighty), in the name of Yah'shua the Messiah (Jesus Christ) my Moshiya (Savior)—to leave me forever, and to be consigned into the everlasting lake of fire,

479

that they may never again touch me or any other creature in the entire world. Amen.

DENOUNCING THE OCCULT

Heavenly Father, YAHUWAH, in the name of your only begotten Son, Yah'shua the Messiah (Jesus Christ), I denounce Satan and all his works, all forms of kishef (witchcraft), the use of nachash (divination), the practice of keshafiym (sorcery), dealing with Ovot (mediums), channeling with ruach more derek (spirit guides), the la'ach siansim (Ouija board), ashaphiym (astrology), Reiki, hipnoza (hypnosis), otomati ketuv (automatic writing), horoskop (horoscopes), gimatria (numerology), all types of magid atidot (fortune telling), kof kore (palm readings), richuf (levitation), and anything else associated with the magi (occult) or Satan. I denounce and forsake my involvement in all of them in the name of Yah'shua the Messiah (Jesus Christ) who came in the flesh, and by the power of his Tselav (Cross), his dam (blood) and his te'chiya (resurrection), I break their hold over my life.

I confess all these sins before you and ask you to cleanse and forgive me. I forgive myself and ask you Adonai Yah'shua (Lord Jesus) to enter my heart and create in me the kind of person you have intended me to be. I ask you to send forth the gifts of your Ruach HaKodesh (Holy Spirit) to baptize me, just as you baptized your talmiydiym (disciples) on the day of Shavuot (Pentecost).

I thank you heavenly Father for strengthening my inner spirit with the power of your Ruach HaKodesh (Holy Spirit), so that the Messiah (Christ) may dwell in my heart. Through faith, rooted and grounded in love, may I be able to comprehend with all the kadoshiym (saints), the breadth, length, height and depth of the Messiah's (Christ's) love which surpasses all understanding. Amen.

STANDARD DELIVERANCE

In the name of Adonai Yah'shua the Messiah (the Lord Jesus Christ) of Nazareth, by the power of his Tselav (Cross), his dam (blood) and his te'chiya (resurrection), I bind you Satan, the ruchot (spirits), ko'ach (powers) and chayil choshek (forces of darkness), the tachton ha'olam (nether world), and the chayil ra teva (evil forces of nature).

I take authority over all kalalot (curses), kishuf'iym (hexes), pe'ilut shediym (demonic activity) and kesim'iym (spells) directed against me, my relationships, ministry endeavors, finances, and the work of my hands; and I break them by the power and authority of the risen Lord Yah'shua the Messiah (Jesus Christ). I stand with the power of Adonai El Shaddai (the Lord God Almighty) to bind all demonic interaction, interplay and communications between spirits sent against me, and send them directly to Yah'shua the Messiah (Jesus Christ) for him to deal with as he wills.

I ask forgiveness for and renounce all negative inner nederiym (vows) that I have made with the oyev (enemy), and ask that Yah'shua the Messiah (Jesus Christ) release me from these nederiym (vows) and from any bondage they may have held in me. I claim the shed blood of Yah'shua the Messiah (Jesus Christ), the Son of the El Chai (living God), over every aspect of my life for my protection. Amen.

PRAYER AGAINST MALEFICE

YAHUWAH, our Elohim (God), King of ages, All-powerful and Almighty, you who made everything and who transform everything simply by your will; you who changed into dew the flames of the seven-times hotter furnace and protected and saved your three holy children Shadrach, Mishach and Abed-Nego.

You are the doctor and physician of my soul. You are the salvation of those who turn to you. I beseech you to make powerless, banish, and drive out every satani ko'ach (diabolic power) and noche'chut (presence); every hashpa'a ra (evil influence), gevurot ra (malefice) or ayin hara (evil eye) and all ma'ase ra (evil actions) aimed against me.

Where there is kina (envy) and ro'a (malice), give me an abundance of goodness, endurance, victory and charity. O Adonai (Lord), you who love man, I beg you to reach out your powerful hands and your most high and mighty arms and come to my aid.

Send your Mal'ak Shalom (angel of peace) over me, to protect my body and soul. May he keep at bay and vanquish every ko'ach ra (evil power), every eres (poison) or ro'a (malice) invoked against me by corrupt and envious people.

Then under the protection of your authority may I sing with gratitude, "YAHUWAH is my yeshu'ah (salvation); whom should I fear?" I will not fear evil because you are with me, Elohai (my God), my strength, my powerful Lord, Adon Shalom (Lord of peace), Father of all ages. Amen.

PRAYER FOR A SPIRITUAL CANOPY

Adonai Yah'shua (Lord Jesus), please forgive me for all the times I have not submitted to your will in my life. Please forgive me for all my sinful actions, making agreements with the oyev (enemy), and for believing the devil's lies. I now submit to you as my Lord, Yah'shua (Jesus). Now I break every agreement that I have made with the oyev (enemy).

Adonai Yah'shua (Lord Jesus), please send an assignment of mal'akiym (angels) to remove and bind to the abyss all shediym (demons) and their devices that had access to me because I believed their lies. I now ask you to establish a me'sucha chasut (hedge of protection) around me, over me and under me, and seal it with your blood, Lord Yah'shua the Messiah (Jesus Christ).

I now choose to put on the full shiryon (armor) of Elohim (God) and ask that you cleanse me and seal me, body, mind, soul and spirit, with your blood, Adonai Yah'shua the Messiah (Lord Jesus Christ). Please have your mal'achi tsava (angelic army) bind up and remove all shediym (demons), their devices, and all their power from within this me'sucha chasut (protective hedge) and have them sent to the abyss.

Please have your mal'akiym (angels) destroy all satani (demonic), magi (occult) or kishuf matala (witchcraft assignments) directed against me. Please have your mal'akiym (angels) stand guard over me and protect me from all hatkafa oyev (attacks of the enemy). I thank you for establishing an impenetrable magen chasut (shield of protection) around me, in Yah'shua's (Jesus') name. Amen.

PRAYER AGAINST TRAFFICKING WITCHES

Adonai Yah'shua (Lord Jesus), please send a special assignment of nilcham mal'akiym (warring angels) to remove all trafficking people from me. Please have your warriors strip these mekashephiym (witches) of nafshi ko'ach (psychic powers), shediym ko'ach (demonic powers) and magi ko'ach (occult powers). Please strip them of kesem kame'a (magic charms), nafshi re'iya (psychic vision) and nachash ko'ach (powers of divination). Please have all their powers and devices destroyed and cast into the abyss. I ask you to bring these people before your throne and bless them with the revelation of who you are and your love and plans of salvation for them. Please show them how they are being deceived by Satan. I take authority over all kochavi matala (astral assignments) directed against me, and I ask you to establish an impenetrable magen chasut (shield of protection) between me and all those who traffic on me, in Yah'shua's (Jesus') name, Amen.

BINDING EVIL SPIRITS

In the name of Adonai Yah'shua the Messiah (the Lord Jesus Christ) of Nazareth, I stand with the power of YAHUWAH El Shaddai (the Lord God Almighty) to bind Satan and all his ruchot ra'ah (evil spirits), chayil shediym (demonic forces), ko'ach satani (satanic powers), ne'sichut (principalities), along with all melekiym (kings) and sariym (princes) of mora'iym (terrors), from the ayir (air), mayim (water), esh (fire), adama (ground), tachton ha'olam (netherworld), and the chayil ra teva (evil forces of nature).

I take authority over all shediym metala (demonic assignments) and functions of destruction sent against me, and I expose all chayil shediym (demonic forces) as weakened, defeated oyev'iym (enemies) of Yah'shua the Messiah (Jesus Christ). I stand with the power of YAHUWAH El Shaddai (the Lord God Almighty) to bind all oyev'iym (enemies) of Messiah (Christ) present together, all shediym yeshutiym (demonic entities) under their one and highest authority, and I command these ruchot (spirits) into the tehom (abyss) to never again return.

I arise today with the power of YAHUWAH El Shaddai (the Lord God Almighty) to call forth the shamayim tsava'ot (heavenly host), the mal'akiym kadoshiym (holy angels) of Elohim (God), to surround and protect, and cleanse with Elohim's (God's) holy light all areas vacated by the chayil'iym ra'ah (forces of evil). I ask the Ruach HaKodesh (Holy Spirit) to permeate my mind, heart, body, soul and spirit, creating a hunger and thirst for Elohim's (God's) devar kadosh (holy Word), and to fill me with the life and love of Adonai Yah'shua the Messiah (my Lord Jesus Christ).

REMOVING DEMONIC INFLUENCE

Adonai Yah'shua the Messiah (Lord Jesus Christ), please send a special assignment of nilcham mal'akiym (warring angels) to remove and bind to the abyss every hashpa'a shediym (demonic influence) that has contributed to my sinful behaviors of criticism, impatience, resentment, pride, rebellion, stubbornness, unforgiveness, gossip, disobedience, strife, violence, divorce, accusation, anger, manipulation, jealousy, greed, laziness, revenge, coveting, possessiveness, control, retaliation, selfishness, deceitfulness, deception, dishonesty, unbelief, seduction, lust, pornography, masturbation, idolatry and witchcraft.

May your mal'achi lochem (angelic warriors) remove and bind to the abyss every hashpa'a shediym (demonic influence) that has contributed to my physical, psychological or spiritual infirmities of nerve disorder, lung disorder, brain disorder or dysfunction, AIDS, cancer, hypochondria, hyperactivity, depression, schizophrenia, fatigue, anorexia, bulimia, addictions, gluttony, perfectionism, alcoholism, sexual addictions, sexual perversions, attempted suicide, incest, pedophilia, lesbianism, homosexuality, adultery, confusion, procrastination, self-hatred, isolation, paranoia, nervousness, passivity, indecision, doubt, oppression, rejection, poor self-image, anxiety, shame and fear.

I arise today through the power of Adonai Yah'shua the Messiah (the Lord Jesus Christ) and ask to be filled with the Ruach HaKodesh's (Holy Spirit's) gifts of peace, patience, love, joy, kindness, generosity, faithfulness, gentleness, self-control, humility, forgiveness, goodness, fortitude, discipline, truth, relinquishment, good self-image, prosperity, charity, obedience, a sound mind, fulfillment in the Messiah (Christ), acceptance of self, acceptance of others, trust, freedom from addictions, freedom of having-to-control, freedom from shame, wholeness, wellness, health, wisdom, knowledge, understanding, and the light and life of Adonai Yah'shua the Messiah (the Lord Jesus Christ). Amen.

PRAYER FOR INNER HEALING

Adonai Yah'shua (Lord Jesus), please come and heal my wounded and troubled heart. I beg you to heal the torments that are causing anxiety in my life. I beg you, in a particular way, to heal the underlying source of my sinfulness. I beg you to come into my life and heal the psychological harms that struck me in my childhood and from the injuries they have caused throughout my life.

Adonai Yah'shua (Lord Jesus), you know my burdens. I lay them on your Good Shepherd's Heart. I beseech you—by the merits of the great open wound in your heart—to heal the small wounds that are in mine. Heal my memories, so that nothing that has happened to me will cause me to remain in pain and anguish, filled with anxiety.

Heal, O YAHUWAH, all those wounds that have been the cause of ra (evil) that is rooted in my life. I want to forgive all those who have offended me. Look to those inner sores that make me unable to forgive. You who came to forgive the afflicted of heart, please, heal my wounded and troubled heart.

Heal, O Adonai Yah'shua (LordJesus), all those intimate wounds that are the root cause of my gufani choli (physical illness). I offer you my heart. Accept it, YAHUWAH, purify it and give me the sentiments of your Divine Heart.

Heal me, O YAHUWAH, from the pain caused by the death of my loved ones. Grant me to regain shalom (peace) and simchah (joy) in the knowledge that you are the Te'chiya (Resurrection) and the Chai (Life). Make me an authentic witness to your te'chiya (resurrection), your victory over sin and death, and your loving presence among all men. Amen.

HEALING YOUR FAMILY LINEAGE

YAHUWAH, Heavenly Father, I come before you as your child, in great need of your help. I have physical health needs, emotional needs, spiritual needs and interpersonal needs. Many of my problems have been caused by my own failures, neglect and sinfulness, for which I humbly beg your forgiveness, Adonai (Lord). I also ask you to forgive the sins of my riyshoniym (ancestors) whose failures may have left their effects on me in the form of unwanted tendencies, negative behavior patterns and a predisposition toward sin. Heal me, Adonai (Lord), of all these disorders.

With your help I sincerely forgive everyone, living or dead members of my family lineage, who have directly offended me or my loved ones in any way, or those whose sins have resulted in our present sufferings and disorders. In the name of your divine Son Yah'shua (Jesus), by the power of the

Ruach HaKodesh (Holy Spirit), I ask you Father, to deliver me and my entire family from the haspa'a ra (influence of evil).

Free all members of my family tree, including those in adoptive relationships, and those in extended family relationships, from every contaminating form of bondage. By your loving concern for us, heavenly Father, and by the shed blood of your precious Son Yah'shua (Jesus), I beg you to extend your blessing upon me and my entire family lineage. Heal every negative effect transmitted through all past generations, and prevent such negative effects in all future generations.

I symbolically place the Tselav (Cross) of the Messiah (Christ) over the head of every person in my family lineage and I ask you to let the cleansing blood of Yah'shua (Jesus) purify every aspect of my family. Send magen mal'akiym (protective angels) to encamp around us and administer to us your divine healing power, even in areas of genetic disability. Give special power to our family members' mal'akiym apotropos (guardian angels) to heal, protect, guide and encourage each of us in all our needs. Let your healing power be released at this very moment, and let it continue as long as your sovereignty permits.

Replace all bondage in our family lineage with a bonding of holy family love. May there be an ever-deeper bonding with you, Heavenly Father, through the power of your Ruach HaKodesh (Holy Spirit), to your Son, Yah'shua the Messiah (Jesus Christ). Let the family of the Hashilush HaKodesh (Holy Trinity) pervade our family with its tender, warm, loving presence, so that our family may recognize and manifest that love in all our relationships; in the precious name of Yah'shua the Messiah (Jesus Christ). Amen.

DENOUNCING LODGES & SECRET SOCIETIES

Adonai Yah'shua (Lord Jesus), I come to you as a sinner seeking forgiveness and healing from all sins committed against you by my family lineage. I honor my earthly av (father), em (mother) and riyshoniym (ancestors), but I utterly turn away from and denounce all their sins, especially those that have exposed me to any kind of harmful influence. I forgive all my riyshoniym (ancestors) for the effects of their sins and ask to be washed clean of their destructive consequences.

I denounce and rebuke Satan and every ko'ach ra'ah (evil power) that has affected my family lineage. I denounce and forsake my involvement in all bitan (lodges), sod chevra (secret societies) and any other me'lachara (evil craft) practiced by my riyshonim (ancestors). I denounce all shevu'at (oaths) and pulchan (rituals) in every level and degree. I denounce keshef (witchcraft), the ruach anti-mashiyach (spirit of the antichrist) and the curse of any torah shediym (demonic doctrine). I denounce avoda zara (idolatry), giduph (blasphemy) and all destructive forms of sodiyut (secrecy) and sibun (deception). I denounce the love of power, the love of money, and any fears that have held me in bondage.

I denounce all spiritually binding oaths taken in Freemasonry, Mormonism, the Order of Amaranth, Oddfellows, Buffalos, Druids and Foresters Lodges, the Ku Klux Klan, The Grange, the Woodmen of the World, Riders of the Red Robe, the Knights of Pythias, the Mystic Order of the Veiled Prophets of the Enchanted Realm, the women's Orders of the Eastern Star and of the White Shrine of Jerusalem, the Daughters of the Eastern Star, the International Orders of Job's Daughters, the

489

Rainbow Girls and the boys' Order of De Molay and any other secret society along with their destructive effects on me and my family.

I denounce the blindfold and hoodwink, and any effects they had on my emotions and eyes, including all confusion and fears. I denounce the noose around the neck, the fear of choking and any spirit that causes difficulty in breathing. I denounce the effects of all pagan objects and symbolism, aprons, books of rituals, rings and jewelry. I denounce the entrapping of others, and observing the helplessness of others during rituals. I denounce false communion, all mockery of the redemptive work of Yah'shua the Messiah (Jesus Christ) on the cross, all unbelief, confusion and deception, and all worship of Heylel (Lucifer) as a elohim (god).

I humbly ask for your forgiveness, Adonai Yah'shua (Lord Jesus), and for your blood to cleanse me of all the sins I have committed. Please purify my spirit, soul, mind, emotions and every other part of my body. Please destroy any ruchot ra'ah (evil spirits) that have attached themselves to me, or my family, because of these sins and cleanse us with the fire of your Ruach HaKodesh (Holy Spirit). I invite you into my heart, Adonai Yah'shua (Lord Jesus), and enthrone you as Adonai (my Lord) and Moshiya (Savior) for all eternity.

CLOSING OF DELIVERANCE PRAYERS

Thank you, Adonai Yah'shua (Lord Jesus), for awakening my sleeping spirit and bringing me into your light. Thank you, YAHUWAH, for transforming me by the renewing of my mind. Thank you, YAHUWAH, for pouring out your Spirit on me, and revealing your Word to me. Thank you, YAHUWAH, for giving your mal'akiym (angels) charge over me in all my ways.

Thank you for my emunah (faith) in you and that from my innermost being shall flow rivers of mayim chayim (living water). Thank you for directing my mind and heart into the love of the Father and the steadfastness of all your ways. Fill me to overflowing with your life and love, Adonai (my Lord) and Melek (King), Yah'shua the Messiah (Jesus Christ). Amen.

PRAYER FOR PROTECTION

Adonai Yah'shua (Lord Jesus), thank you for sharing with me your wonderful ministry of healing and deliverance. Thank you for the healings that I have experienced today. I realize that the sickness of evil is more than my humanity can bear, so I ask you to cleanse me of any sadness, negative thinking or despair that I may have picked up while interceding for others.

If I have been tempted to anger, impatience or lust, cleanse me of those temptations, and replace them with your ahava (love), simchah (joy) and shalom (peace). If any ruchot ra'ah (evil spirits) have attached themselves to me or oppressed me in any way, I command you, ruchot adama (spirits of earth), esh (fire), mayim (water), the tachton ha'olam (netherworld), or the chayil ra teva (evil forces of nature), to depart now and go straight to Yah'shua the Messiah (Jesus Christ), for him to deal with you as he wills.

Come Ruach HaKodesh (Holy Spirit), renew me, fill me with your ahava (love), shalom (peace) and simchah (joy). Strengthen me where I feel weak and clothe me with your light. Fill me with your life. Adonai Yah'shua (Lord Jesus), please send your mal'akiym kadoshiym (holy angels) to minister to me and protect me from all forms of sickness, harm and accidents. I thank you and praise you Adonai (my Lord), Elohai (my God) and Malkiy (my King).

Psalm 91

1 He who dwells in the seter (secret place) of Elyon (the Most High) shall abide under the Tsel Shaddai (shadow of the Almighty). 2 I will say of YAHUWAH, "He is my refuge and my fortress; Elohai (My God), in Him I will batach (trust, be bold in)." 3 Surely He shall deliver you from the pach (snare; figuratively: calamity) and the yakush (fowler, trapper, bait layer) and from the dever havot (pestilence's destruction). 4 He shall cover you with His evrat (feathers), and under His kanaf'iym (wings) you shall take refuge; His emet (truth) shall be your shield and buckler. 5 You shall not be afraid of the pachad (terror) by laila (night), nor of the chets (arrow) that flies by yomam (day), 6 Nor of the dever (pestilence) that walks in ophel (darkness, gloom; spiritual unreceptivity, calamity), nor of the ketev (destruction, destroying, ruin) that lays waste at tsohariym (noonday). 7 A thousand may fall at your side, and ten thousand at your right hand; But it shall not come near you. 8 Only with your eyes shall you look, and see the shilumat rasha'iym (reward of the wicked). 9 Because you have made YAHUWAH, who is my refuge, even Elyon (the Most High), your dwelling place, 10 No ra'ah (evil) shall befall you, nor shall any nega (plague) come near your ohel (tent, dwelling); 11 For He shall give His Mal'akiym (angels) charge over you, to keep you in all your derek (ways). 12 In their hands they shall bear you up, lest you dash your foot against a stone. 13 You shall tread upon the shachal (fierce lion) and the taniyn (dragon), the kephiyr (young lion) and the pethen (cobra) you shall trample underfoot. 14 "Because he has set his love upon Me, therefore I will deliver him; I will set him on high, because he has known My name. 15 He shall call upon Me, and I will answer him; I will be with him in trouble; I will deliver him and honor him. 16 With long life I will satisfy him, And show him My yeshua (salvation)."

PRAYER TO RENOUNCE THE POSSESSION OF CURSED OBJECTS

YAHUWAH, I come to you about me'kulal davariym (cursed objects), cherem (accursed thing) and any shed sheritsa (demon infestation) in my possessions and home. I ask your forgiveness for having any such items in the precious name of Yah'shua (Jesus). I understand that this is avoda zara (idolatry).

I forgive my riyshoniym (ancestors), tse'etsa'iym (descendants) and others who have had spiritual influence over me. I ask you to forgive and bless them, especially with salvation in the name of Yah'shua (Jesus). Please forgive me and I forgive myself for ruchani ni'uf (spiritual adultery).

I forgive those who have me'kulal (cursed) me; forgive me for kalala (cursing) others. I break the kalalot (curses) and shediym kesher nephesh (demonic soul ties) including ov (medium), yidoni (spiritism), nafshi (psychic) and magi tefilot (occultic prayers), in the name of Yah'shua (Jesus).

I will clean out my home and workplace of any me'kulal davariym (cursed objects) or simliyut (symbols). I will drive the ruchot ra'ah (evil spirits) out of the house in the name of Yah'shua (Jesus). Please show me me'kulal davariym (cursed objects), or simliyut (symbols), or shediym sheritsa (demon infestation) and ruchot (spirits) that need to be cast out. In the precious name of your son, Yah'shua the Messiah (Jesus Christ). In the Name of the Father YAHUWAH and of the Son Yah'shua (Jesus) ✠ and of the Ruach HaKodesh (Holy Spirit). Amen.

Go through your home, garden, garage, workplace, and car, carefully checking for items and symbols against a

493

comprehensive cursed objects list such as the one available in this book. Generally it's a good idea to go through things several times over a period of time, as it is easy to miss them and usually more will be found each time as your knowledge and perception increases.

PRAYER FOR PROTECTION

Heavenly and Holy Father (Matthew 6:9), we look to you as the Almighty one (Genesis 17:1). We boldly come before the throne of grace (Hebrews 4:16) claiming our position in heavenly places in Messiah Yah'shua (Christ Jesus) (Ephesians 1:20-21).

By faith I pull down every stronghold (2 Corinthians 10:4) I have yielded unto Satan and claim by faith it is null and void and covered under the blood of the Lord Yah'shua the Messiah (Jesus Christ) (Revelation 12:11). Thank you for forgiving me of my sins (Matthew 6:14) when Messiah (Christ) died on the cross and I thank you that you have cleansed me of all my sins (1 John 1:9).

I claim by faith that all that I am outside of Messiah (Christ) was nailed to the cross (Galatians 2:20). I reckon self, sin, Satan, the law, and the world to be nailed to the cross (Luke 9:23; Galatians 5:24). By faith, I claim the resurrected and ascended life of Messiah (Christ) living in me and through me (2 Corinthians 4:11).

By faith, I put on the helmet of salvation (Ephesians 6:17), the breastplate of righteousness (Ephesians 6:14), my loins gird about with truth, my feet shod with the preparation of the gospel of peace (Ephesians 6:15), the shield of faith to quench all the fiery darts of the wicked one, and the sword of the Spirit (Ephesians 6:16).

494

I submit myself under the authority of the Lord Yah'shua the Messiah (Jesus Christ) (James 4:6-7; 1 Peter 5:6-9) and I bind all demonic forces by the blood of Yah'shua the Messiah (Jesus Christ) that are trying to hinder me (Matthew 16:19) from obeying the will of Elohim (God) today in the north, south, east, and west (Revelation 7:1). I claim by faith that I am surrounded by a hedge of protection (Hosea 2:6), a wall of fire (Zechariah 2:5), and a huge wall of faith all covered under the blood of the Lord Yah'shua the Messiah (Jesus Christ).

I bind all demonic forces by the blood of the Lamb and pray that Messiah (Christ) would send holy angels to stop any evil assignment against me (Hebrews 1:14). By faith I release the working of the power of the resurrected Lord (Romans 6:4) and the energizing power of the Holy Spirit in my life (Ephesians 5:18). By faith I claim that this has already been bound in heaven (Matthew 18:18) and thank you that you will guide me into the center of your will (John 16:13) and show me the works you have planned for me today.

I pray that you will cause confusion in the camp of all mine enemies (Psalm 35:4, 26) so that I may have victory over them. Thank you in advance for victory over ever trial this day (1 Corinthians 15:57). Send your messengers that I need to accomplish your will this day (Luke 6:38). Give me the knowledge and wisdom to know and do your will (Ephesians 1:17-19). Fill me with the power of the Holy Spirit and give me the fruit of the Spirit I need today to accomplish your will (Galatians 5:22-23).

Surround me with your holy angels to strengthen me and protect me from any evil force that may come against me (Psalm 34:7). Thank You for your presence and power that will empower and guide me this day (Hebrews 13:5). In the name of Yah'shua (Jesus) I pray, AMEN (John 14:13-14).

AVODAH GERUSH RUCHOT
(Service For Exorcism)

EXORCISM PRAYER

✠ In the name of the Father YAHUWAH, and of the Son Yah'shua (Jesus), and of the Ruach HaKodesh (Holy Spirit). Amen.

Let YAHUWAH arise and let His enemies be scattered, and let them that hate Him flee from before His face! As smoke vanishes, so let them vanish away; as wax melts before the fire, so let the rasha (wicked) perish at the presence of YAHUWAH. (Ps. 67:2-3)

Judge you, O YAHUWAH, them that wrong me; overthrow them that fight against me. Let them be confounded and ashamed that seek after my soul. Let them be turned back and be confounded that devise evil against me. Let them become as dust before the wind, and let the Mal'ak YAHUWAH (Angel of the Lord) straighten them. Let their way become dark and slippery, and let the Mal'ak YAHUWAH (Angel of the Lord) pursue them. For without cause they have hidden their net for me unto destruction, without cause they have upbraided my soul. Let the snare which he knows not, come upon him; and let the net which he has hidden catch him; and into that very snare let him fall. But my soul shall rejoice in the Lord and shall be delighted in His salvation. (Ps. 34:1, 4-9)

V. Glory be to the Father YAHUWAH, and to the Son Yah'shua (Jesus), ✠ and to the Ruach HaKodesh (Holy Spirit).

R. As it was in the beginning, is now and ever shall be, forever and ever. Amen.

O most glorious Prince of the heavenly armies, Kadosh Miyka'el Sar-Mal'ak (St. Michael the Archangel), defend us in the battle and in our wrestling against Sariym (Principalities) and Shaliytiym (Powers), against the hamsheliym b'cheshkot ha'olam hazeh (rulers of the world of this darkness), against the ruchot hara'ot (spirits of wickedness) ba'me'romiym (in the high places). (Eph. 6:12) Come to the aid of men, whom Elohim (God) created incorruptible and to the image of His own likeness He made him (Wis. 2:23); and from the tyranny of the Mal'shiyn (devil) He bought him at a great price. (Cor. 7:23) Fight the battles of YAHUWAH today with the army of the blessed mal'akiym (angels), as once you did fight against Heylel (Lucifer), the leader of pride, and his apostate mal'akiym (angels), and they prevailed not, neither was their place found anymore in heaven. But that HaTaniyn HaGadol (great dragon) was cast out, the HaNachash HaKad'moniy (serpent of old), who is called Mal'shiyn (the devil) and HaSatan (Satan), who seduces the whole world. And he was cast unto the earth, and his mal'akiym (angels) were thrown down with him. (Apoc. 12:8-9)

Behold, the kadmon oyev (ancient enemy) and murderer strongly raises his head! Transformed into an Mal'ak Ha'Or (angel of light), with the entire horde of ruchot rasha'iym (wicked spirits) he goes about everywhere and takes possession of the earth so that therein he may blot out the name of YAHUWAH and of His Messiah (Christ) and steal away, afflict, and ruin into everlasting destruction the souls destined for a crown of eternal glory.

On men depraved in mind and corrupt in heart, the Rasha Taniyn (wicked dragon) pours out like a most foul river the poison of his villainy, a spirit of lying, impiety, and blasphemy, and the deadly breath of lust and of all iniquities and vices. Her most crafty enemies have engulfed the Church,

497

the Spouse of the Immaculate Lamb; with sorrows they have drenched Her with wormwood, on all Her desirable things they have laid their wicked hands.

Where the Chair of Truth has been set up for the light of the Goyim (Gentiles), there they have placed the throne of the abomination of their wickedness so that, the Pastor having been struck, they may also be able to scatter the flock. Therefore, O you unconquerable leader, be present with the people of YAHUWAH and against the spiritual wickedness which is bursting in upon them, and bring them the victory.

The Kadosh Knesiya (Holy Church) venerates you as its guardian and patron, and it glories in the fact that you are its defender against the wicked powers of earth and hell. To you YAHUWAH has assigned the souls of the redeemed to be placed in heavenly bliss. Beseech the El Shalom (God of Peace) to crush Satan under our feet, that he may no more be able to hold men captive and to harm the Church.

Offer our prayers in the sight of the Elyon (Most High) so that the mercies of YAHUWAH may quickly come to our aid, that you may seize the Taniyn (dragon), the Nachash Kadmon (ancient serpent), who is the Mal'shiyn (devil) and HaSatan (Satan), and that having bound him you may cast him into the bottomless pit so that he may no more seduce the nations. (Apoc. 20:3)

Hence confiding in your protection and guardianship, [say the following only if you are an authorized minister: by the sacred authority of our ministry,] we confidently and securely begin the task, in the name of Yah'shua the Messiah (Jesus Christ) our Elohim (God) and Adon (Lord), of driving away the attacks of diabolical deceit.

V. Behold the Tselasv Adonai (cross of the Lord); flee away, you hostile forces.

R. The Lion of the tribe of Judah, the Root of David, has conquered.

V. May your mercy, O Adonai (Lord), be upon us.

R. Since we have hoped in you.

V. O YAHUWAH, hear my prayer.

R. And let my cry come unto you.

LET US PRAY:

O God and Father of our Lord Yah'shua the Messiah (Jesus Christ), we invoke your Shem Kadosh (holy name) and we humbly implore your chesed (mercy), that you would deign to afford us help against Satan and all the other ruchot ha'tumah (unclean spirits) and against whatever wanders throughout the world to do harm to the human race and to ruin souls. Through the same Messiah (Christ) our Lord. Amen.

THE EXORCISM PRAYER

We exorcize you, O every ruach ha'tumah (unclean spirit), ko'ach satani (Satanic power), infernal invader, wicked legion, assembly and sect; in the name and by the power of Adonai Yah'shua the Messiah (the Lord Jesus Christ) ✠ may you be snatched away and driven from the Knesiya Elohim (Church of God) and from the souls made to the image of Elohim (God) and redeemed by the precious blood of the Divine Lamb ✠. Most cunning nachash (serpent), you shall no more dare to deceive the human race, persecute the Knesiya

(Church), torment Elohim's (God's) elect, and sift them as wheat ✠. YAHUWAH El Elyon (The Lord God Most High) commands you ✠, He with whom in your great insolence you still claims to be equal, He who wants all men to be saved and to come to the knowledge of the truth. (1 Tim. 2:4)

Elohim (God) the Father YAHUWAH commands you ✠; Elohim (God) the Son Yah'shua (Jesus) commands you ✠; Elohim (God) the Ruach HaKodesh (Holy Spirit) commands you ✠. The majesty of the Messiah (Christ), the Eternal Word of Elohim (God) made flesh, commands you ✠; He who to save our race, outdone through your envy, "humbled Himself, becoming obedient even unto mavet (death)" (Phil. 2:8); He who has built His Knesiya (Church) on the firm rock and declared that the gates of hell shall never prevail against Her because He will dwell with Her "all days even to the end of the world." (Mt. 28:20) The sacred sign of the cross commands you ✠, as does also the power of the Mysteries of the Messianic Faith ✠.

Thus, Me'kulal Taniyn (cursed dragon) and you diabolical legion, we adjure you by Elohim Chayim (the Living God) ✠, by the El Emeth (True God) ✠, by the El Kadosh (Holy God) ✠, by the Elohim (God) "who so loved the world that He gave up His only Son, that every soul believing in Him might not perish but have life everlasting" (Jn. 3:16), stop deceiving human creatures and pouring out to them the poison of eternal damnation. Stop harming the Knesiya (Church) and ensnaring Her liberty. Begone, Satan, inventor and master of all deceit, enemy of man's salvation. Give place to Messiah (Christ) in whom you have found none of your works. Give place to the one, holy, Universal and Apostolic Church, acquired by Messiah (Christ) at the price of His blood. Stoop beneath the powerful hand of YAHUWAH. Tremble and flee when we invoke the holy and terrible name of YAH'SHUA

(JESUS); this name which causes hell to tremble; this name to which the Virtues, Powers, and Dominations of heaven are humbly submissive; this name which the Cherubim and Seraphim praise unceasingly, repeating: Holy, holy, holy is YAHUWAH Tzeva'ot (the Lord, the God of armies)!

V. O YAHUWAH, hear my prayer.

R. And let my cry come unto you.

LET US PRAY:

Elohei Ha'Shamayim (God of Heaven), Elohei Ha'Arets (God of Earth), Elohei Mal'akiym (God of Angels), Elohei Sar-Mal'akiym (God of Archangels), Elohei Patriarchiym (God of Patriarchs), Elohei Navi'iym (God of Prophets), Elohei Shalichiym (God of Apostles), Elohei Kadosh Me'un'e (God of Martyrs), Elohei mitvade (God of Confessors), Elohei betulot (God of Virgins), Elohim (God) who has power to give life after death and rest after work, because there is no other El (God) than you and there can be no other, for you are the Bore (Creator) of all things visible and invisible, of whose reign there shall be no end. We humbly prostrate ourselves before your glorious majesty; and we beseech you to deliver us by your power from all the tyranny of the infernal spirits, from their snares, their lies, and their furious wickedness. Deign, O YAHUWAH, to grant us your powerful protection and to keep us safe and sound. We beseech you through Yah'shua the Messiah (Jesus Christ) our Lord. Amen.

V. From the snares of the Mal'shiyn (devil).

R. Deliver us, O YAHUWAH.

V. Grant that your Knesiya (Church) may serve you in secure liberty.

R. We beseech you, hear us.

V. Deign to crush down the enemies of the Kadosh Knesiya (Holy Church).

R. We beseech you, hear us.

While reciting the Exorcism Prayer of St. Michael the Archangel, holy water is sprinkled on the persons present and in the place where the exorcism is done, usually the home and property.

Then repeat 3 times:

V. Adonai Yah'shua (Lord Jesus).

R. Have mercy on us.

EXORCISM PRAYER OF ST. MICHAEL THE ARCHANGEL

Kadosh Miyka'el Sar-Mal'ak (St. Michael the Archangel), defend us in milchamah (battle), be our protection against the wickedness and snares of the Mal'shiyn (devil). May Elohim (God) rebuke him, we humbly pray; and do you, O Prince of the heavenly host, by the power of Elohim (God), cast into hell Satan and all the ruchot ra'ah (evil spirits) who prowl about the world seeking the ruin of souls. Amen.

EXORCISM PRAYERS

O YAHUWAH, El Olam (Eternal God), Who has redeemed the race of men from the captivity of mal'shiyn (the devil), deliver us Your avadiym (servants) from all the workings of ruchot ra'ah (evil spirits) and ruchot ha'tumah (unclean spirits).

Command the ruchot ra'ah (evil spirits), ruchot ha'tumah (unclean spirits), ruchot me'zoham (impure spirits) and shediym (demons) to depart from the soul and body of us your avadiym (servants) and not to remain nor hide in us.

Let them be banished from this the creation of Your hands in Your own Shem Kadosh (holy name) YAHUWAH and that of Your only begotten Son Yah'shua the Messiah (Jesus Christ), and of Your life-creating Spirit, so that, after being cleansed from all demonic influence, we may live holy, godly, justly and righteously and may be counted worthy to receive the Holy Mysteries of Your only-begotten Son and our Elohim (God) Yah'shua the Messiah (Jesus Christ) with Whom You are blessed and glorified together with the all holy and good and life-creating Spirit now and ever and unto the ages of ages. Amen.

In the name of Yah'shua the Messiah (Jesus Christ), the only-begotten Son of the Father, bind, reject, rebuke and cast out every ruach ra'ah (evil spirit) and ruach ha'tumah (unclean spirit).

In His name and by the faith that is in His name, bind, reject, rebuke, and cast out every ruach chalah (spirit of infirmity), ruach choliy (spirit of sickness), ruach mechalah (spirit of disease) and ruach nega (spirit of plague).

In the name of Yah'shua the Messiah (Jesus Christ), the only-begotten Son of the Father, bind, reject, rebuke and cast out every Ruach Shabar Shinayim (spirit of broken teeth), Mechala Pe (mouth disease), Shemenut (obesity), beten choliy (stomach illness) and Mechala Ayin (eye problem).

You, YAHUWAH, Who has rebuked every ruach ra'ah (evil spirit) and ruach ha'tumah (unclean spirit) and by the power of Your Word has banished the legion, come now, through Your only begotten Son Yah'shua the Messiah (Jesus Christ), upon us Your creatures, which You have fashioned in Your own image and deliver us from the adversary that holds us in bondage, so that, receiving Your chesed (mercy) and becoming purified, we might join the ranks of Your holy flock and be preserved as a heykal chayim (living temple) of the Ruach HaKodesh (Holy Spirit) and might receive the divine and holy Mysteries through the grace and compassion and loving kindness of Your only-begotten Son Yah'shua the Messiah (Jesus Christ) with Whom You are blessed together with Your all-holy and good and life-creating Spirit now and ever and unto the ages of ages. Amen.

We beseech You, O YAHUWAH Elohim (Lord God), El Shadai (Almighty God), El Elyon (God Most High), El Chai (God of the living), untempted, peaceful King, have mercy on us and heal us, in the name of Yah'shua the Messiah (Jesus Christ), for You are YAHUWAH who heals us.

We beseech You YAHUWAH, Who has created the heaven and the earth, have mercy on us for out of You has issued the Alpha and the Omega, the beginning and the end.

You Who has ordained that the four-footed and irrational beasts be under subjection to man, for You have subjected them, have mercy on us.

YAHUWAH Elohim (Lord God), stretch out Your mighty hand and Your sublime and holy arm and in Your watchful care look down upon us Your creatures and send down upon us a Mal'ak Shalom (peaceful angel), a Mal'ak Chazak (mighty angel), a guardian of soul and body, that will rebuke and drive away every shed ra (evil demon) and shed ha'tumah (unclean demon) from us, for You alone are Adonai Elyon (Lord Most

High), almighty and blessed forever and ever and unto ages of ages. Amen.

Do You Yourself, therefore, O YAHUWAH Elohim (Lord God), the Confirmation of those who have set their hope on You and the wall of strength for those whose expectation is in You, bind, reject, rebuke, renounce, drive away, cast out and put to flight every ruach ra'ah (evil spirit) and ruach ha'tumah (unclean spirit), in the name of Yah'shua the Messiah (Jesus Christ).

O YAHUWAH, bind, reject, rebuke, and cast out the ruach Heylel (spirit of Lucifer), Satan, Ba'al Zebub (Beelzebub), Abaddon, Apollyon, Behemah (Beast) and Beliya'al (Belial) in the name of Yah'shua the Messiah (Jesus Christ).

O YAHUWAH, bind, reject, rebuke, and cast out the ruach Levyitan (spirit of Leviathan), the Taniyn (Dragon), the Nachash (Serpent), Kundalini, and Piton (Python), in the name of Yah'shua the Messiah (Jesus Christ).

O YAHUWAH, bind, reject, rebuke, and cast out the ruach Ach'av (spirit of Ahab), Ashtoreth, Asmodee, Baal, Baphomet, Dagon, Iyzebel (Jezebel), Rachav (Rahab), Mammon, Molech, Nebo, and Pharmakeia, in the name of Yah'shua the Messiah (Jesus Christ).

O YAHUWAH, bind, reject, rebuke, and cast out every ruach aduk (religious spirit) and every ruach yami (Marine Spirit), in the name of Yah'shua the Messiah (Jesus Christ).

O YAHUWAH, bind, reject, rebuke, and cast out the tsiyiym (Desert Demon), the sa'ariym (Goat Demon), the iyiym (Howling Demon); Azazel, Semyaza, Samael, Lilith, the bat ya'anah (daughters of Lilith), and every succubus and incubus, in the name of Yah'shua the Messiah (Jesus Christ).

O YAHUWAH, bind, reject, rebuke, and cast out every Siren, Alukah (vampire) Banshee and Jinn, in the name of Yah'shua the Messiah (Jesus Christ).

O YAHUWAH, bind, reject, rebuke, and cast out every ruach choli (spirit of sickness), ruach chalah (spirit of infirmity), ruach mechala (spirit of disease) and ruach nega (spirit of plague), in the name of Yah'shua the Messiah (Jesus Christ).

O YAHUWAH, bind, reject, rebuke, and cast out every Ruach Shabar Shinayim (spirit of broken teeth), Machala Pe (mouth disease), Shemenut (obesity) and Machala Ayin (eye problem), in the name of Yah'shua the Messiah (Jesus Christ).

O YAHUWAH, bind, reject, rebuke, and cast out every ruach oni (spirit of poverty), choser (lack) and tsorech (want), in the name of Yah'shua the Messiah (Jesus Christ).

O YAHUWAH, bind, reject, rebuke, and cast out every ruach me'kulkal (spirit of brokenness), ruach rakav (decay, rot), and ruach ovesh (mildew, mold), in the name of Yah'shua the Messiah (Jesus Christ).

O YAHUWAH, bind, reject, rebuke, and cast out every satani ma'ase (diabolical action), every satani pelisha (satanic invasion), every lashon hara (evil tongue; slander) and ko'ach kontra (contrary power), from those who have been seized by them, and from those who walk about bearing Your Tselav (Cross), the sign of victory, dreadful against shediym (demons), and calling upon Your Tov Shem Kadosh (good and Holy Name) through your only begotten Son, Yah'shua the Messiah (Jesus Christ). Amen.

INVOCATION FOR THE DEVILS EXPULSION

We make this great, divine, holy and awesome invocation and plea, O Satan (Devil), for your expulsion, as well as this rebuke for your utter annihilation, O apostate! YAHUWAH Rebukes you Satan (Devil)!

Elohim (God) Who is holy, beginningless, frightful, invisible in essence, infinite in power and incomprehensible in divinity, the Melek HaKavod (King of glory) and Adon Shaddai (Lord Almighty), YAHUWAH Rebukes you Satan (Devil)!

He Who composed all things well by his Word from nothingness into being; He Who walks upon the wings of the air. YAHUWAH rebukes you, Satan (devil)!

He Who calls forth the water of the sea and pours it upon the face of all the earth. YAHUWAH TZEVA'OT (Lord of Hosts) is His name. Satan (Devil): YAHUWAH rebukes you!

He Who is ministered to and praised by numberless heavenly orders and adored and glorified in fear by multitudes of angelic and archangelic hosts. Satan: YAHUWAH rebukes you!

He Who is honored by the encircling Powers, the awesome six-winged and many-eyed Cherubim and Seraphim that cover their faces with two wings because of His inscrutable and unseen divinity and with two wings cover their feet, lest they be seared by His unutterable glory and incomprehensible majesty, and with two wings do fly and fill the heavens with their shouts of "Holy, holy, holy, YAHUWAH Tseva'ot (Lord of Hosts), heaven and earth are full of Your glory!" Satan (Devil): YAHUWAH rebukes you!

He Who came down from the Father's bosom and, through the holy, inexpressible, immaculate and adorable Incarnation from the Virgin, appeared ineffably in the world to save it and cast you down from heaven in His authoritative power and showed you to be an outcast to every man. Satan (Devil), Adonai Yah'shua the Messiah (the Lord Jesus Christ) rebukes you!

He Who said to the sea, be silent, be still, and instantly it was calmed at His command. Satan (Devil), Adonai Yah'shua the Messiah (the Lord Jesus Christ) rebukes you!

He Who made clay with His immaculate spittle and refashioned the wanting member of the man blind from birth and gave him his sight. Satan (Devil): Adonai Yah'shua the Messiah (the Lord Jesus Christ) rebukes you!

He Who by His word restored to life the daughter of the ruler of the bet kneset (synagogue) and snatched the son of the almanah (widow) out from the mouth of death and gave him whole and sound to his own mother. Satan (Devil): Adonai Yah'shua the Messiah (the Lord Jesus Christ) rebukes you!

The Adon (Lord) Who raised Lazarus the four-days dead from the dead, undecayed, as if not having died, and unblemished to the astonishment of many. Satan (Devil): Adonai Yah'shua the Messiah (the Lord Jesus Christ) rebukes you!

The Adon (Lord) Who loosed the woman bent over for eighteen years, whom you had bound with chains of chalah (infirmity): Adonai Yah'shua the Messiah (the Lord Jesus Christ) rebukes you Satan (Devil).

He Who destroyed the kalalah (curse) by the blow on His face and by the lance in His immaculate side lifted the flaming sword that guarded Paradise. Satan (Devil): Adonai Yah'shua the Messiah (the Lord Jesus Christ) rebukes you!

He Who dried all tears from every face by the spitting upon His precious expressed image. Satan (Devil): Adonai Yah'shua the Messiah (the Lord Jesus Christ) rebukes you!

He Who set His Tselav (Cross) as a support, the salvation of the world, to your fall and the fall of all the mal'akiym (angels) under you. Satan (Devil): Adonai Yah'shua the Messiah (the Lord Jesus Christ) rebukes you!

He Who spoke from His Tselav (Cross) and the paroket heykal (curtain of the temple) was torn in two, and the rocks were split and the tombs were opened and those who were dead from the ages were raised up. Satan (Devil): Adonai Yah'shua the Messiah (the Lord Jesus Christ) rebukes you!

He Who by death put death to death and by His rising granted life to all men. May Adonai Yah'shua the Messiah (the Lord Jesus Christ) rebuke you, Satan (Devil)!

That is, He Who descended into Sheol (Hades) and opened its tombs and set free those held prisoner in it, calling them to Himself; before Whom the gatekeepers of Sheol (Hades) shuddered when they saw Him and, hiding themselves, vanished in the anguish of Sheol Sheol (Hades). May Adonai Yah'shua the Messiah (the Lord Jesus Christ) rebuke you, Satan (devil)!

That is, Messiah (Christ) our Elohim (God) Who arose from the dead and granted His Te'chiya (Resurrection) to all men. May Adonai Yah'shua the Messiah (the Lord Jesus Christ) rebuke you, Satan (Devil)!

He Who in glory ascended into heaven to His Father YAHUWAH, sitting on the right hand of majesty upon the throne of glory. Satan (Devil): May Adonai Yah'shua the Messiah (the Lord Jesus Christ) rebuke you!

He Who shall come again with glory upon the clouds of heaven with His mal'akiym kadoshiym (holy angels) to judge the living and the dead. Satan (Devil): May Adonai Yah'shua the Messiah (the Lord Jesus Christ) rebuke you!

He Who has prepared for you unquenchable fire, the unsleeping worm and the outer darkness unto eternal punishment. Satan (Devil): May Adonai Yah'shua the Messiah (the Lord Jesus Christ) rebuke you!

For before Him all things shudder and tremble from the face of His power and the wrath of His warning upon you is uncontainable. Satan (Devil): Adonai Yah'shua the Messiah (the Lord Jesus Christ) rebukes you by His frightful name!

Shudder, tremble, be afraid, depart, be utterly destroyed, be banished! You who fell from hasahamayim (heaven) and together with you every ruach ra'ah (evil spirit) and ruach ha'tumah (unclean spiri)t: every ruach ra'ah ta'ava (evil spirit of lust), the ruach ra'ah (spirit of evil), a ruach yom (spirit of the day) and ruach leili (nocturnal spirit), a ruach tsohorayim (noonday spirit) and ruach erev (evening spirit), a ruach chatsot (midnight spirit), a ruach ba'al dimyon pore (imaginative spirit), a ruach hitaklut (encountering spirit), either of the yabasha (dry land) or of the mayim (water), or one in a ya'ar (forest), or among the kane (reeds), or in machporet (trenches), or in a derek (road) or a hitstalvut (crossroad), in a yama (lake), or a nachal (stream), in a bayit (house), or one sprinkling in the ambat (baths) and cheder (chambers), or one altering the mind of man. Depart swiftly from us the creatures of the Bore Messiah (Creator Christ) our Elohim (God)! And be gone from us the avadiym Elohim (servants of God), from our mind, from our soul, from our heart, from our reins, from our senses, from all our members, that we might become whole and sound and free, knowing Elohim (God), our own Adon (Master) and Bore (Creator) of all things, He Who gathers together those who have gone astray and Who gives them the seal of salvation through the rebirth and restoration of divine Tevilah (Baptism), so that he may be counted worthy of His immaculate, heavenly and awesome Mysteries and be united to His true fold, dwelling in a place of pasture and nourished on the waters of repose, guided pastorally and safely by the staff of the Tselav (Cross) unto the forgiveness of sins and life everlasting. For unto Him belong all glory, honor, adoration and majesty together with Your beginningless Father YAHUWAH and His all-holy, good and life-giving Spirit, the Ruach HaKodesh (Holy Spirit), now and ever, and unto ages of ages. Amen.

FIRST EXORCISM

Adonai Yah'shua the Messiah (the Lord Jesus Christ) rebukes you, O Satan (Devil), for he came into the world and dwelt among men in order to shatter your tyranny and free mankind; hanging on the Tselav (Cross), he triumphed over all the hostile powers, when the sun was darkened and the earth was shaken, when the kevariym (graves) were opened and the bodies of the kadoshiym (Saints) arose; he destroyed death by death and conquered you, O Satan (Devil), who had the power of mavet (death).

I adjure you in the name of YAHUWAH, the God and the Father of our Lord Yah'shua the Messiah (Jesus Christ), who revealed the Ets HaChayim (tree of life) and appointed the

511

Cherubim and the fiery sword that turns each way to guard it. Be rebuked and depart Satan (devil);

I adjure you in the name of him who walked on the water as if it were dry land, and calmed the tempest, whose look dries up the tehom (abyss) and whose threatening makes the mountains melt away, Adonai Yah'shua the Messiah (the Lord Jesus Christ) rebuke you Satan (Devil).

It is this same Adon (Lord) who now commands you, through us. Fear, come out and depart from us Adam (human beings), and never return, nor hide in us, neither meet nor act upon us, not by laila (night) or by yom (day), not at shachar (dawn) or at tsohorayim (noontime), but depart to your own choshek (darkness) until the appointed day of judgment.

Fear Elohim (God) who sits upon the Cherubim and looks down into the tehom (abyss); before whom tremble Mal'akiym (Angels), Sar-Mal'akiym (Archangels), Kisot (Thrones), Mem'shalot (Dominions), Sariym (Principalities), Rashuyot (Authorities), Shaliytiym (Powers), the many-eyed Cherubim and the six-winged Seraphim; before whom tremble the heavens and the earth, the sea and all that is in them. Yah'shua the Messiah (Jesus Christ) rebukes you Satan (Devil)!

Come out and depart from these chayaliym (soldiers) of Messiah (Christ) our Elohim (God), for we have been marked with the Ot Ha'Tselav (sign of the Cross) and newly enlisted. For it is in His name and by the faith that is in His name that I adjure you, the name of Adonai (the Lord) who walks upon the wings of the wind, who makes his Mal'akiym (Angels) ruchot (spirits) and his Sharatiym (ministers) a esh lohet (flame of fire), In the name of Yah'shua the Messiah (Jesus Christ).

Come out and depart from us Adam (human beings), with all your power and your mal'akiym (angels). For the name of the Father YAHUWAH and of the Son Yah'shua (Jesus) and of the Ruach HaKodesh (Holy Spirit) is glorified, now and ever, and to the ages of ages. Amen.

SECOND EXORCISM

YAHUWAH Elohim Kadosh (The Lord God, the holy), the fearful, the glorious, incomprehensible and inscrutable in all his works and all his might, who ordained for you, O Satan (Devil), the punishment of eternal torment, through us his unworthy avadiym (servants), orders you, and all the powers that work with you, to depart from us who have been sealed in the name of our Adon Yah'shua the Messiah (Lord Jesus Christ), our true Elohim (God).

Therefore, I adjure you, most wicked, impure, abominable, loathsome and alien spirit: Come out of us and never again enter into us. In the name of Yah'shua the Messiah (Jesus Christ).

Depart, admit the vanity of your power which could not even control the swine. Remember him who, at your own request, commanded you to enter into the herd of the swine.

Fear Elohim (God), by whose command the earth was made firm upon the waters; who made the heaven, who weighted the mountains in a balance and the valleys on a pair of scales who placed the sand as a boundary to the sea and a safe path in the raging waters; who makes the mountains smoke at his touch; who clothes himself with light as a garment; who covers over his lofty dwellings with waters; who laid the foundations of the earth so secure that it should never be shaken from them; who lifts up the water and the sea and returns it as rain upon the face of all the earth.

Come out and depart from us who are the servants of Elohim Ha'Av (God the Father) and Yah'shua the Messiah (Jesus Christ), the Son of the Father.

I adjure you by the saving Passion of our Adon Yah'shua the Messiah (Lord Jesus Christ) and his sacred Body and Blood and his awesome return; for he shall come without delay to judge all the earth, and shall assign you, and all the powers working with you, to the fire of hell, having delivered you to the outer darkness, where the worm constantly devours, and the fire is never extinguished. For the power belongs to Messiah (Christ) our Elohim (God), together with the Father YAHUWAH and the Ruach HaKodesh (Holy Spirit), now and ever unto the ages of ages Amen.

THIRD EXORCISM

O Elohim (God), YAHUWAH Tzeva'ot (Lord of hosts), the God of Israel, the God and the Father of our Lord Yah'shua the Messiah (Jesus Christ), who heals every illness, every infirmity, look upon us your servants; seek out examine and expel from us all the workings of Satan (the Devil). Rebuke the ruchot ra'ah (evil spirits) , ruchot ha'tumah (unclean spirits) and ruchot me'zoham (impure spirits) and banish them, and cleanse the works of your hands; by your swift action crush Satan under our feet, and grant to us victory over the Mel'shiyn (Devil) and his ruchot ra'ah (evil spirits), ruchot ha'tumah (unclean spirits) and ruchot me'zoham (impure spirits); so that, having received your chesed (mercy), we may become worthy of your immortal and heavenly mysteries and may give glory to you, Father YAHUWAH, Son

Yah'shua (Jesus) and Ruach HaKodesh (Holy Spirit), now and ever, and to ages of ages. Amen.

FOURTH EXORCISM

O YAHUWAH, Elohei Ha'Elohim (God of gods) and Adonei Ha'Adoniym (Lord of lords), Bore (Creator) of the Saraphiym (fiery spirits) and Artificer of the eino-nir'e (invisible powers), of all things heavenly and earthly: You Who no man has seen, nor is able to see; You Whom all creation fears and before Whom it trembles; You Who did cast into the choshek tehom (darkness of the abyss) of Tartarus the mal'akiym (angels) who did fall away with him who once was commander of the mal'achi tseva'ot (angelic host), who disobeyed You and haughtily refused to serve You, do You expel by the terror of Your name the Hara (evil one) and his legions loose upon the earth, Heylel (Lucifer) and those with him who fell from above. Set him to flight and command him and his shediym (demons) to depart completely. Let no harm come to them who are sealed in Your image and let those who are sealed receive dominion, "to tread on nachashiym (serpents) and akraviym (scorpions) and all the power of the oyev (enemy)." For You do we hymn and magnify and with every breath do we glorify Your all-holy name of the Father YAHUWAH and of the Son Yah'shua (Jesus) and of the Ruach HaKodesh (Holy Spirit) now and ever and unto ages of ages. Amen.

FIFTH EXORCISM

I expel you, primal source of giduph (blasphemy), Sar mored tsava (prince of the rebel host), yotser ha'ra (originator of evil). In the name of Yah'shua the Messiah (Jesus Christ).

I expel you, Heylel (Lucifer), who was cast from the brilliance on high into the darkness of the abyss on account of your arrogance: In the name of Yah'shua the Messiah (Jesus Christ).

I expel you and all the fallen hosts which followed your will: In the name of Yah'shua the Messiah (Jesus Christ).

I expel you, ruach ha'tumah (spirit of uncleanness), who revolted against YAHUWAH Elohim (the Lord God), the Kol Yachol Elohim Tseva'ot (omnipotent God of Hosts) and the tsava mal'akav (army of His angels). In the name of Yah'shua the Messiah (Jesus Christ).

Be gone and depart from us the avadiym Elohim (servants of God).

I expel you in the name of YAHUWAH, Who created all things by His Word, His Only-Begotten Son, our Adon Yah'shua the Messiah (Lord Jesus Christ), Who was ineffably and dispassionately born before all the ages; by Whom was formed all things visible and invisible, Who made man after His Image: Who guarded him by the mal'akiym (angels), Who trained him in the Torah (Law), Who drowned sin in the flood of waters from above and Who shut up the tehomiym (abysses) under the heaven, Who demolished the impious race of Nephiliym (giants), Who shook down the tower of Babel, Who reduced Sodom and Gomorrah to ashes by sulfur and fire, a fact to which the unceasing vapors testify; and Who by the staff of Moses separated the waters of the Red Sea, opening a waterless path for the people while the tyrannical Pharaoh and his God-fighting army were drowned forever in its waves for his wicked persecution of them; and Who in these last days was inexplicably incarnate of a pure Betulah (Virgin) who preserved the seal of her chastity intact; and

Who was pleased to purge our ancient defilement in the baptismal cleansing.

I expel you, Satan, by virtue of Messiah's (Christ's) baptism in the Jordan, which for us is a type of our inheritance of incorruption through grace and sanctified waters: the same One Who astounded the mal'akiym (angels) and all the heavenly powers when they beheld Elohim (God) incarnate in the flesh and also revealed at the Jordan His beginningless Father YAHUWAH and the Ruach HaKodesh (Holy Spirit) with Whom He shares the unity of the Hashilush Hakodesh (Trinity).

I expel you, Hara (evil one), in the name of Yah'shua the Messiah (Jesus Christ) Who rebuked the winds and stilled the turbulent sea; Who banished the legion of shediym (demons) and opened the eyes of him who was born blind from his mother's womb; and Who from clay fashioned sight for him, whereby He re-enacted the ancient refashioning of our face; Who restored the speech of the speechless, purged the stigma of leprosy, raised the dead from the grave and Who Himself despoiled Hades by His mavet (death) and Te'chiya (Resurrection) thereby rendering mankind impervious to death.

I expel you, in the name of YAHUWAH, the El Shaddai (Almighty God) Who filled men with the inbreathing of a divinely inspired voice and Who wrought together with the Shaliyachiym (Apostles) the piety, which has filled the universe. Fear and flee, run, leave, ruach ha'tumah (unclean spirit) and ruach me'kulal (accursed spirit), deceitful and unseemly creature of the infernal depths, visible through deceit, hidden by pretense.

Depart wherever you may appear, Ba'al zebub (Beelzebub), vanish as smoke and heat, bestial and serpentine thing, whether disguised as male or female, whether beast or crawling thing or flying, whether garrulous, mute or speechless, whether bringing fear of being trampled, or rending apart, conniving, whether oppressing us in sleep, by some display of weakness, by distracting laughter, or taking pleasure in false tears whether by lechery or stench of carnal lust, pleasure, addiction to drugs, divination or astrology, whether dwelling in a house, whether possessed by audacity, or contentiousness or instability, whether striking us with lunacy, or returning to us after the passage of time, whether you be of the morning, noonday, midnight or night, indefinite time or daybreak, whether spontaneously or sent to someone or coming upon us unawares, whether from the sea, a river, from beneath the earth, from a well, a ravine, a hollow, a lake, a thicket of reeds, from matter, land, refuse, whether from a grove, a tree, a thicket, from a fowl, or thunder, whether from the precincts of a bath, a pool of water or from a pagan sepulcher or from any place where you may lurk; whether by knowledge or ignorance or any place not mentioned.

Depart, separate yourself from us, be ashamed before him who was made in the image of Elohim (God) and shaped by His hand. Fear the likeness of the incarnate Elohim (God) and no longer hide in us His servants; rather await the rod of iron, the fiery furnace of Tartarus, the gnashing of teeth as reprisal for disobedience. Be afraid, be still, flee, neither return nor hide in him some other kind of ruach ra'ah (evil spirit) or ruach ha'tumah (unclean spirit).

Depart into the uncultivated, waterless waste of the desert where no man dwells, where Elohim (God) alone vigilantly watches, Who shall bind you that dares with envy to plot against His image and Who, with chains of darkness shall hold

518

you in Tartarus, Who by day and night and for a great length of time has devised all manner of ra'ah (evils), O Satan (devil); for great is your fear of Elohim (God) and great is the glory of the Father YAHUWAH, of the Son Yah'shua(Jesus) and of the Ruach HaKodesh (Holy Spirit). Amen.

SIXTH EXORCISM

O YAHUWAH, Elohei HaShamayim (God of the heavens), Elohei Ha'Arets (God of Earth), Elohei Or (God of Light), Elohei Mal'akiym (God of the Angels) and Elohei Sar-Mal'akiym (God of Archangels) obedient to Your Authority and Power; O Elohim (God) Who are glorified in Your kadoshiym (Saints), the God and the Father of our Lord Yah'shua the Messiah (Jesus Christ), Your Only-begotten Son, Who delivered the souls which were bound to mavet (death) and Who enlightened them that dwelt in choshek (darkness); He Who released us from all our misery and pain and Who has protected us from the assaults of the oyev (enemy). And You, O Son and Word of Elohim (God), has purposed us for immortality by Your death and glorified us with Your glory; You Who loosed us from the fetters of our sins through Your Tselav (Cross), rendering us pleasing to Yourself and uniting us with Elohim (God); You Who did rescue us from destruction and cured all our diseases; You Who set us on the path to heaven and changed our corruption to incorruption. Hear me who cry unto You with longing and fear, You before Whom the mountains and the firmament under the heavens do shrink; You Who makes the physical elements to tremble, keeping them within their own limits; and because of Whom the fires of retribution dare not overstep the boundary set for them but must await the decision of Your Will; and for Whom all creation sighs with great sighs awaiting deliverance; by Whom all adverse natures have been put to flight and the legion of the oyev (enemy) has been subdued, Satan (the devil) is affrighted, the nachash (serpent) trampled underfoot and the Taniyn (dragon) slain; You Who has enlightened the nations which confess and welcome Your rule, O YAHUWAH; You through Whom life has appeared, hope has prevailed, through Whom the man of the earth was recreated by belief in You. For Who is like unto You, El Shaddai (Almighty God)? Wherefore we beseech You, O Father, Lord of mercies, Who existed before the ages and surpasses all good, calling upon Your Shem Kadosh (holy name), through the love of Your Child, Yah'shua the Messiah (Jesus Christ), the Kadosh (Holy One), and Your All-powerful Spirit.

Cast away from our soul every malady, all disbelief, spare us from the furious attacks of unclean, infernal, fiery, evil-serving, lustful spirits, the love of money, gold and silver, conceit, fornication, every shameless, unseemly, dark and profane shed (demon). Indeed, O Elohim (God), expel from us Your servants every energy of Satan (the devil), every enchantment and delusion; all idolatry, lunacy, astrology, necromancy, every bird of omen, the love of luxury and the flesh, all greed, drunkenness, carnality, adultery, licentiousness, shamelessness, anger, contentiousness, confusion and all evil suspicion. Yea, YAHUWAH our Elohim (God), breathe upon us the Spirit of Your Shalom (Peace), watch over us and produce thereby the fruits of faith, virtue, wisdom, chastity, self-control, love, uprightness, hope, meekness, longsuffering, patience, prudence and understanding in us Your servants that we may be welcomed by You in the name of Yah'shua the Messiah (Jesus Christ), believing in the coessential Hashilush Hakodesh (Trinity), giving witness and glorifying Your dominion, along with the Mal'akiym (Angels) and Sar-Mal'akiym (Archangels) and all the heavenly host, guarding our hearts by them; for all things are possible to You, O YAHUWAH Elohim (Lord God). Therefore, we ascribe glory to the Father YAHUWAH, and to the Son Yah'shua (Jesus) and to the Ruach HaKodesh (Holy Spirit), now and ever and unto the ages of ages. Amen.

SEVENTH EXORCISM

In the name of Adonai Yah'shua the Messiah (the Lord Jesus Christ) and by His power, we cast you out Satan, every ruach ra'ah (evil spirit), every ruach ha'tumah (unclean spirit), every ruach shediym (demonic spirit), every ruach satani (devilish spirit), every satani ko'ach (devilish power), every assault of the infernal adversary, every legion, every diabolical group and sect, Lilith and the bat ya'anah (daughters of Lilith), every tsiyiym (desert demon), every iyiym (howling demon), every sa'ariym (goat demon); begone and stay far from the Church of Elohim (God), from all who are made in the image of Elohim (God) and redeemed by the precious blood of the divine Lamb.

Never again dare, you cunning nachash (serpent), to deceive the human race, to persecute the Knesiya Elohim (Church of God), nor to strike the chosen of Elohim (God) and to sift them as wheat. For it is El Elyon (the God Most High) who commands you, He to whom you heretofore in your great pride considered yourself equal; He who desires that all men might be saved and come to the knowledge of truth.

Elohim (God) the Father YAHUWAH commands you. Elohim (God) the Son Yah'shua (Jesus) commands you. Elohim (God) the Ruach Hakodesh (Holy Spirit) commands you. The majesty of Messiah (Christ), the eternal Word of Elohim (God) made flesh commands you; He who for the salvation of our race, the race that was lost through your envy, humbled Himself and became obedient even unto death; He who built His Knesiya (Church) upon a solid rock, and proclaimed that the gates of hell should never prevail against her, and that He

521

would remain with her for all days, even to the end of the world.

The sacred mystery of the tselav (cross) commands you, as well as the power of all the mysteries of faith. The exalted Lord Yah'shua the Messiah (Jesus Christ) commands you, who in his lowliness crushed your proud head from the first moment of his Conception. The faith of the holy apostles Peter and Paul and the other apostles commands you. The blood of the martyrs and the devout intercession of all holy men and women commands you.

Therefore, accursed Taniyn (dragon) and every diabolical legion, we adjure you by YAHUWAH, Elohim Chayim (the living God), by the El Emet (true God), by the El Kadosh (holy God), by the Elohim (God) who so loved the world that He gave His only-begotten Son, that whoever believes in Him shall not perish but shall have life everlasting; cease your deception of the human race and your giving them to drink of the poison of everlasting damnation; desist from harming the Knesiya (Church) and fettering her freedom.

Be gone Satan, you father and teacher of lies and oyev ha'adam (enemy of mankind). Give place to Messiah (Christ) in whom you found none of your works; give place to the one, holy, Universal Church, which Messiah (Christ) Himself purchased with His blood. May you be brought low under Elohim's (God's) mighty hand. May you tremble and flee as we call upon the holy and awesome name of Yah'shua (Jesus), before whom hell quakes, and to whom the virtues, powers, and dominations are subject; whom the cherubim and seraphim praise with unwearied voices, saying: Holy, holy, holy, YAHUWAH Elohim Tzeva'ot (Lord God of hosts)!

PULCHAN GERUSH RUCHOT
(THE RITE OF EXORCISM)

The Litany

YAHUWAH, have mercy.

Messiah (Christ), have mercy.

Ruach HaKodesh (Holy Spirit), have mercy.

Messiah (Christ), hear us.

Messiah (Christ), graciously hear us.

Elohim (God), the Father in heaven, YAHUWAH, Have mercy on us.

Elohim (God), the Son, Redeemer of the world, Yah'shua (Jesus), Have mercy on us.

Elohim (God), the Ruach HaKodesh (Holy Spirit), Have mercy on us.

Hashiulush Hakodesh (Holy Trinity), El Echad (one God), Have mercy on us.

Kadosh Miyka'el (St. Michael), Pray for us.

Kadosh Gavriy'el (St. Gabriel), Pray for us.

Kadosh Rapha'el (St. Raphael), Pray for us.

Kadosh Uriy'el (St. Uriel), Pray for us.

Kadosh Mal'akiym Apotropos (Holy Guardian Angels), Pray for us.

All Kadoshiym Mal'akiym Va'Sar-Mal'akiym (holy angels and archangels), Pray for us.

All holy orders of blessed spirits, Pray for us.

Adonai be merciful, Spare us, O YAHUWAH.

Adonai be merciful, Graciously hear us, O YAHUWAH.

From all evil, Deliver us, O Adonai.

From all sin, Deliver us, O Adonai.

From your wrath, Deliver us, O Adonai.

From sudden and unprovided death, Deliver us, O Adonai.

From the snares of Satan (the devil), Deliver us, O Adonai.

From anger, hatred, and all ill will, Deliver us, O Adonai.

From all lewdness, Deliver us, O Adonai.

From lightning and tempest, Deliver us, O Adonai.

From the scourge of earthquakes, Deliver us, O Adonai.

From illness, plague, famine, and war, Deliver us, O Adonai.

From everlasting death, Deliver us, O Adonai.

By the mystery of your holy incarnation, Deliver us, O Adonai.

By your coming, Deliver us, O Adonai.

By your birth, Deliver us, O Adonai.

By your baptism and holy fasting, Deliver us, O Adonai.

By your cross and passion, Deliver us, O Adonai.

By your death and burial, Deliver us, O Adonai.

By your holy resurrection, Deliver us, O Adonai.

By your wondrous ascension, Deliver us, O Adonai.

By the coming of the Ruach HaKodesh (Holy Spirit), the Advocate, Deliver us, O Adonai.

On the day of judgment, Deliver us, O Adonai.

We are chata'iym (sinners), We beg you to hear us.

That you spare us, We beg you to hear us.

That you pardon us, We beg you to hear us.

That you bring us to true repentance, We beg you to hear us.

That you govern and preserve your holy Church, We beg you to hear us.

That you humble the enemies of holy Church, We beg you to hear us.

That you give shalom (peace) and true concord to all Messianic and Christian rulers, We beg you to hear us.

That you give shalom (peace) and unity to the whole Messianic and Christian world, We beg you to hear us.

That you restore to the unity of the Church all who have strayed from the truth, and lead all unbelievers to the light of the Gospel, We beg you to hear us.

That you confirm and preserve us in your holy service, We beg you to hear us.

That you lift up our minds to heavenly desires, We beg you to hear us.

That you grant everlasting blessings to all our benefactors, We beg you to hear us.

That you deliver our souls and the souls of our brethren, relatives, and benefactors from everlasting damnation, We beg you to hear us.

That you give and preserve the fruits of the earth, We beg you to hear us.

That you grant eternal rest to all the faithful departed, We beg you to hear us.

That you graciously hear us, We beg you to hear us.

Son of Elohim (God), We beg you to hear us.

At the end of the litany the priest adds the following:

Antiphon: Do not keep in mind, O YAHUWAH, our offenses or those of our parents, nor take vengeance on our sins.

Avinu / Tefillat Talmid
(Our Father / The disciple's prayer)

Avinu (Our Father), Who is in heaven, hallowed be Your Name. Your Kingdom come. Your will be done, on earth as it is in heaven. Give us this day our daily bread; and forgive us our trespasses, as we forgive those who trespass against us; and lead us not into temptation, but deliver us from the Hara (evil one). For Yours is the kingdom, and the power, and the glory, for ever. Amen.

Psalm 53

1 To the Chief Musician. Set to "Mahalat." A Contemplation of David. The nabal (fool) has said in his heart, "There is no Elohim (God)." They are shachat (corrupt, destroyed), and have done ta'av avel (abominable iniquity); There is none who does tov (good). 2 Elohim (God) looks down from heaven upon the children of men, to see if there are any who understand, who seek Elohim (God). 3 Every one of them has turned aside; They have together become alach (filthy); There is none who does tov (good), no, not one. 4 Have the polei aven (workers of iniquity) no knowledge, who eat up my people as they eat bread, and do not call upon Elohim (God)? 5 There they are in great fear where no fear was, for Elohim (God) has scattered the bones of him who encamps against you; You have put them to shame, because Elohim (God) has despised them. 6 Oh, that the salvation of Israel would come out of Zion! When Elohim (God) brings back the captivity of His people, let Jacob rejoice and Israel be glad.

Psalm 91

1 He who dwells in the seter (secret place) of Elyon (the Most High) shall abide under the Tsel Shaddai (shadow of the Almighty). 2 I will say of YAHUWAH, "He is my refuge and my fortress; Elohai (My God), in Him I will batach (trust, be bold in)." 3 Surely He shall deliver you from the pach (snare; figuratively: calamity) and the yakush (fowler, trapper, bait layer) and from the dever havot (pestilence's destruction). 4 He shall cover you with His evrat (feathers), and under His kanaf'iym (wings) you shall take refuge; His emet (truth) shall be your shield and buckler. 5 You shall not be afraid of the pachad (terror) by laila (night), nor of the chets (arrow) that flies by yomam (day), 6 Nor of the dever (pestilence) that walks in ophel (darkness, gloom; spiritual unreceptivity, calamity), nor of the ketev (destruction, destroying, ruin) that lays waste at tsohariym (noonday). 7 A thousand may fall at your side, and ten thousand at your right hand; But it shall not come near you. 8 Only with your eyes shall you look, and see the shilumat rasha'iym (reward of the wicked). 9 Because you have made YAHUWAH, who is my refuge, even Elyon (the Most High), your dwelling place, 10 No ra'ah (evil) shall befall you, nor shall any nega (plague) come near your ohel (tent, dwelling); 11 For He shall give His Mal'akiym (angels) charge over you, to keep you in all your derek (ways). 12 In their hands they shall bear you up, lest you dash your foot against a stone. 13 You shall tread upon the shachal (fierce lion) and the taniyn (dragon), the kephiyr (young lion) and the pethen (cobra) you shall trample underfoot. 14 "Because he has set his love upon Me, therefore I will deliver him; I will set him on high, because he has known My name. 15 He shall call upon Me, and I will answer him; I will be with him in trouble; I will deliver him and honor him. 16 With long life I will satisfy him, And show him My yeshua (salvation)."

Let us pray.

Elohim (God), whose nature is ever merciful and forgiving, accept our prayer that this servant of yours, bound by the fetters of sin, may be pardoned by your loving kindness. Adonai Kadosh (Holy Lord), Avi Shaddai (almighty Father), El Olam (everlasting God) and God and Father of our Adon Yah'shua the Messiah (Lord Jesus Christ), who once and for all consigned that fallen and apostate tyrant to the flames of hell, who sent your only-begotten Son into the world to crush that roaring lion; hasten to our call for help and snatch from ruination and from the clutches of the noonday devil this human being made in your image and likeness. Strike terror, YAHUWAH, into the beast now laying waste your vineyard. Fill your servants with courage to fight manfully against that reprobate taniyn (dragon), lest he despise those who put their trust in you, and say with Pharaoh of old: "I know not Elohim (God), nor will I set Israel free." Let your mighty hand cast him out of your servant, (Name), ✠ so he may no longer hold captive this person whom it pleased you to make in your image, and to redeem through your Son Yah'shua the Messiah (Jesus Christ); who lives and reigns with you, in the unity of the Ruach HaKodesh (Holy Spirit), Elohim (God), forever and ever.

All: Amen.

Then he commands the demon as follows:

I command you, ruach ra'ah (unclean spirit), whoever you are, along with all your minions now attacking this servant of Elohim (God), by the mysteries of the incarnation, passion, resurrection, and ascension of our Lord Yah'shua the Messiah (Jesus Christ), by the descent of the Ruach HaKodesh (Holy Spirit), by the coming of our Lord for judgment, that you tell me by some sign your name, and the day and hour of your departure. I command you, moreover, to obey me to the letter, I who am a sheret Elohim (minister of God) despite my unworthiness; nor shall you be emboldened to harm in any way this creature of Elohim (God), or the bystanders, or any of their possessions.

The priest lays his hand on the head of the sick person, saying:

They shall lay their hands upon the sick and all will be well with them. May Yah'shua (Jesus), Son of the Father, Lord and Savior of the world, show you favor and mercy.

All: Amen.

Next he reads over the possessed person these selections from the Gospel, or at least one of them.

The beginning of the holy Gospel according to St. John.

Glory to you, O YAHUWAH, Glory to You.

A Lesson from the holy Gospel according to St. John

John 1:1-14

As he says these opening words he signs himself and the possessed with the cross on the brow, lips, and breast.

1 In the beginning was the Word, and the Word was with Elohim (God), and the Word was Elohim (God). 2 He was in the beginning with Elohim (God). 3 All things were made through Him, and without Him nothing was made that was made. 4 In Him was life, and the life was the light of men. 5 And the light shines in the darkness, and the darkness did not

comprehend it. 6 There was a man sent from Elohim (God), whose name was John. 7 This man came for a witness, to bear witness of the Light, that all through him might believe. 8 He was not that Light, but was sent to bear witness of that Light. 9 That was the true Light which gives light to every man coming into the world. 10 He was in the world, and the world was made through Him, and the world did not know Him. 11 He came to His own, and His own did not receive Him. 12 But as many as received Him, to them He gave the right to become children of Elohim (God), to those who believe in His name: 13 who were born, not of blood, nor of the will of the flesh, nor of the will of man, but of Elohim (God). 14 And the Word became flesh and dwelt among us, and we beheld His glory, the glory as of the only begotten of the Father, full of grace and truth.

All:Thanks be to Elohim (God).

Lastly he blesses the sick person, saying:

May the blessing of YAHUWAH El Shaddai (the Lord God Almighty), Father YAHUWAH, Son Yah'shua (Jesus), ✠ and Ruach HaKodesh (Holy Spirit), come upon you and remain with you forever.

All:Amen.

Then he sprinkles the person with holy water.

A Lesson from the holy Gospel according to St. Mark

Mark 16:15-18

15 And He said to them, "Go into all the world and preach the gospel to every creature. 16 He who believes and is baptized will be saved; but he who does not believe will be

condemned. 17 And these signs will follow those who believe: In My name they will cast out shediym (demons); they will speak with new tongues; 18 they will take up nachash (serpents); and if they drink anything deadly, it will by no means hurt them; they will lay hands on the sick, and they will recover."

A Lesson from the holy Gospel according to St. Luke

Luke 10:17-20

17 Then the seventy returned with joy, saying, "Lord, even the shediym (demons) are subject to us in Your name." 18 And He said to them, "I saw Satan fall like lightning from heaven. 19 Behold, I give you the authority to trample on nachash (serpents) and Akrav (scorpions), and over all the power of the oyev (enemy), and nothing shall by any means hurt you. 20 Nevertheless do not rejoice in this, that the ruchot (spirits) are subject to you, but rather rejoice because your names are written in heaven."

A Lesson from the holy Gospel according to St. Luke

Luke 11:14-22

And He was casting out a shed (demon), and it was mute. So it was, when the shed (demon) had gone out, that the mute spoke; and the multitudes marveled. 15 But some of them said, "He casts out shediym (demons) by Beelzebub, the ruler of the demons." 16 Others, testing Him, sought from Him a sign from heaven. 17 But He, knowing their thoughts, said to them: "Every malchut (kingdom) divided against itself is brought to desolation, and a bayit (house) divided against a bayit (house) falls. 18 If Satan also is divided against himself, how will his kingdom stand? Because you say I cast out shediym (demons) by Beelzebub. 19 And if I cast out shediym (demons) by Beelzebub, by whom do your sons cast them out? Therefore they will be your judges. 20 But if I cast out shediym (demons) with the finger of Elohim (God), surely the Malchut Elohim (kingdom of God) has come upon you. 21 When a strong man, fully armed, guards his own palace, his goods are in peace. 22 But when a stronger than he comes upon him and overcomes him, he takes from him all his armor in which he trusted, and divides his spoils."

YAHUWAH, heed my prayer.

And let my cry be heard by you.

Let us pray.

Adon Shaddai (Almighty Lord), Word of God the Father, Yah'shua the Messiah (Jesus Christ), God and Lord of all creation; who gave to your Kadosh Shaliyach'iym (holy apostles) the power to tramp underfoot nachash (serpents) and akrav (scorpions); who along with the other mandates to work miracles was pleased to grant them the authority to say: "Depart, you devils!" and by whose might Satan was made to fall from heaven like lightning; I humbly call on your holy name in fear and trembling, asking that you grant me, your unworthy servant, pardon for all my sins, steadfast faith, and the power - supported by your mighty arm - to confront with confidence and resolution this cruel shed (demon). I ask this through you, Yah'shua the Messiah (Jesus Christ), our Lord and God, who are coming to judge both the living and the dead and the world by fire.

All:Amen.

Next he makes the sign of the cross over himself and the one possessed, places the end of the stole/prayer shawl on the latter's neck, and, putting his right hand on the latter's head, he says the following in accents filled with confidence and faith:

> See the Tselav Adonai (cross of the Lord); begone, you hostile powers!

> The stem of David, the lion of the tribe of Juda has conquered.

> Lord, heed my prayer.

> And let my cry be heard by you.

> Let us pray.

> YAHUWAH, God and Father of our Lord Yah'shua the Messiah (Jesus Christ), I appeal to your holy name, humbly begging your kindness, that you graciously grant me help against this and every ruach ha'tumah (unclean spirit) now tormenting this creature of yours; through Messiah (Christ) our Lord.

> All: Amen.

Exorcism

I cast you out, ruach ha'tumah (unclean spirit), along with every Ko'ach Satani Ha'Oyev (Satanic power of the enemy), every repha'iym (spectre) from hell, and all your fell companions; in the name of our Lord Yah'shua the Messiah (Jesus Christ) ✠. Begone and stay far from this creature of Elohim (God). ✠ For it is He who commands you, Yah'shua the Messiah (Jesus Christ) who flung you headlong from the heights of heaven into the depths of hell. It is He who commands you, Yah'shua the Messiah (Jesus Christ) who once stilled the sea and the wind and the storm. Hearken, therefore, and tremble in fear, Satan, you enemy of the faith, you foe of the human race, you begetter of death, you robber of life, you corrupter of justice, you root of all evil andvice; seducer of men, betrayer of the nations, instigator of envy, font of avarice, fomentor of discord, author of pain and sorrow. Why, then, do you stand and resist, knowing as you must that Messiah (Christ) the Lord brings your plans to nothing? Fear Him, who in Isaac was offered in sacrifice, in Joseph sold into bondage, slain as the paschal lamb, crucified as man, yet triumphed over the powers of hell. *(The three signs of the cross which follow are traced on the brow of the possessed person)*. Begone, then, in the name of the Father YAHUWAH, ✠ and of the Son Yah'shua (Jesus), ✠ and of the Ruach HaKodesh (Holy Spirit) ✠. Give place to the Ruach HaKodesh (Holy Spirit) by this sign of the Kadosh Tselav (holy cross) ✠ of our Lord Yah'shua the Messiah (Jesus Christ), who lives and reigns with the Father and the Ruach HaKodesh (Holy Spirit), Elohim (God), forever and ever.

All: Amen.

YAHUWAH, heed my prayer.

And let my cry be heard by you.

Let us pray.

Elohim (God), Bore (Creator) and defender of the human race, who made man in your own image, look down in pity on this your servant, (Name), now in the toils of the ruach ha'tumah (unclean spirit), now caught up in the fearsome threats of man's ancient enemy, sworn foe of our race, who befuddles and stupefies the human mind, throws it into terror, overwhelms it with fear and panic. Repel, O YAHUWAH, the devil's power, break asunder his snares and traps, put the unholy tempter to flight. By the sign ✠ *(on the brow)*of your name, let your servant be protected in mind and body. *(The three crosses which follow are traced on the breast of the possessed person).* Keep watch over the inmost recesses of his (her) ✠ heart; rule over his (her) ✠ emotions; strengthen his (her) ✠ will. Let vanish from his (her) soul the temptings of the mighty adversary. Graciously grant, O YAHUWAH, as we call on your Shem Kadosh (holy name), that the ruach ra'ah (evil spirit), who hitherto terrorized over us, may himself retreat in terror and defeat, so that this servant of yours may sincerely and steadfastly render you the service which is your due; through Yah'shua the Messiah (Jesus Christ) our Lord.

All:Amen.

Exorcism

I adjure you, kadmon nachash (ancient serpent), by the judge of the living and the dead, by your Bore (Creator), by the Bore (Creator) of the whole universe, by Him who has the power to consign you to hell, to depart forthwith in fear, along with your savage minions, from this servant of Elohim (God), (Name), who seeks refuge in the fold of the Knesiya (Church). I adjure you again, ✠ *(on the brow)* not by my weakness but by the might of the Ruach HaKodesh (Holy Spirit), to depart from this servant of Elohim (God), (Name), whom El Shaddai (almighty God) has made in His image. Yield, therefore, yield not to my own person but to the Sharet Ha'Mashiyach (minister of Christ). For it is the power of Messiah (Christ) that compels you, who brought you low by His cross. Tremble before that mighty arm that broke asunder the dark prison walls and led souls forth to light. May the trembling that afflicts this human frame, ✠ *(on the breast)* the fear that afflicts this image ✠ *(on the brow)* of Elohim (God), descend on you. Make no resistance nor delay in departing from this man, for it has pleased Messiah (Christ) to dwell in man. Do not think of despising my command because you know me to be a great sinner. It is Elohim (God) ✠ Himself who commands you; the majestic Messiah (Christ) ✠ who commands you. Elohim (God) the Father: YAHUWAH ✠ commands you; Elohim (God) the Son: Yah'shua (Jesus) ✠ commands you; Elohim (God) the Ruach HaKodesh (Holy Spirit) ✠ commands you. The mystery of the Tselav (cross) ✠ commands you. The faith of the holy apostles Peter and Paul and of all the kadoshiym (saints) ✠ commands you. The blood of the martyrs ✠ commands you. The continence of the confessors ✠ commands you. The devout prayers of all holy men and women ✠ commands you. The saving mysteries of our Christian faith ✠ command you. Depart, then, transgressor. Depart, seducer, full of lies and cunning, foe of virtue, persecutor of the innocent. Give place, abominable creature, give way, you monster, give way to Messiah (Christ), in whom you found none of your works. For He has already stripped you of your powers and laid waste your kingdom, bound you prisoner and plundered your weapons. He has cast you forth into the outer darkness, where everlasting ruin awaits you and your abettors. To what purpose do you insolently resist? To what purpose do you brazenly refuse? For you are guilty before El Shaddai (almighty God), whose laws you have transgressed. You are guilty before His Son, our Lord Yah'shua the Messiah (Jesus Christ), whom you presumed to tempt, whom you dared to nail to the cross. You are guilty before the whole human race, to whom you proferred by your enticements the poisoned cup of death. Therefore, I adjure you, profligate taniyn (dragon), in the name of the spotless ✠ Lamb, who has trodden down the ef'e (asp) and the basilisk, and overcome the arye (lion) and the taniyn (dragon), to depart from this man (woman) ✠ *(on the brow)*, to depart from the Knesiya Ha'Elohim (Church of God) ✠ *(signing the bystanders)*. Tremble and flee, as we call on the name of Adonai (the Lord), before whom the denizens of hell cower, to whom the heavenly Virtues and Powers and Dominations are subject, whom the Cherubim and Seraphim praise with unending cries as they sing: Holy, holy, holy, YAHUWAH Elohim Tseva'ot (Lord God of Hosts). The Word made flesh ✠ commands you; the Virgin's Son ✠ commands you; Yah'shua (Jesus) ✠ of Nazareth commands you, who once, when you despised His disciples, forced you to flee in shameful defeat from a man; and when He had cast you out you did not even dare, except by His leave, to enter into a herd of swine. And now as I adjure you in His ✠ name, begone from this man (woman) who is His creature. It is futile to resist His ✠ will. It is hard for you to kick against the ✠ goad. The longer you delay, the heavier your punishment shall be; for it is not men you are condemning, but rather Him who rules the living and the dead, who is coming to judge both the living and the dead and the world by fire.

All: Amen.

Lord, heed my prayer.

And let my cry be heard by you.

Let us pray.

Elohei HaShamayim Va'Arets (God of heaven and earth), Elohei Mal'akiym va'Sar-Mal'akiym (God of the angels and archangels), Elohei Navi'iym va'Shaliyachiym (God of the prophets and apostles), Elohei Kadosh Me'un'e Ve'Betulot (God of the martyrs and virgins), Elohim (God) who has power to bestow life after death and rest after toil; for there is no other El (God) than you, nor can there be another true El (God) beside you, the Bore (Creator) of heaven and earth, who are truly a Melek (King), whose kingdom is without end; I humbly entreat your glorious majesty to deliver this servant of yours from the ruach ha'tumah (unclean spirits); through Yah'shua the Messiah (Jesus Christ) our Lord.

All: Amen.

Exorcism

Therefore, I adjure you every ruach ha'tumah (unclean spirit), every repha'iym (spectre) from hell, every ko'ach satani (satanic power), in the name of Yah'shua the Messiah (Jesus Christ) ✠ of Nazareth, who was led into the desert after His baptism by John to vanquish you in your citadel, to cease your assaults against the creature whom He has, formed from the slime of the earth for His own honor and glory; to quail before wretched man, seeing in him the image of El Shaddai (almighty God), rather than his state of human frailty. Yield then to Elohim (God), ✠ who by His servant, Moses, cast you and your malice, in the person of Pharaoh and his army, into the depths of the sea. Yield to Elohim (God), ✠ who, by the singing of holy canticles on the part of David, His faithful servant, banished you from the heart of King Saul. Yield to Elohim (God), ✠ who condemned you in the person of Judas Iscariot, the traitor. For He now flails you with His divine scourges, ✠ He in whose sight you and your legions once cried out: "What have we to do with you, Yah'shua (Jesus), Son of El Elyon (the Most High God)? Have you come to torture us before the time?" Now He is driving you back into the everlasting fire, He who at the end of time will say to the rashaiym (wicked): "Depart from me, you accursed, into the everlasting fire which has been prepared for Satan (the devil) and his Mal'akiym (angels)." For you, O Hara (evil one), and for your followers there will be worms that never die. An unquenchable fire stands ready for you and for your minions, you prince of accursed murderers, father of lechery, instigator of sacrileges, model of vileness, promoter of heresies, inventor of every obscenity. Depart, then, ✠ impious one, depart, ✠ accursed one, depart with all your deceits, for Elohim (God) has willed that man should be His Heykal (temple). Why do you still linger here? Give honor to Elohim Ha'Avi Shaddai (God the Father almighty) ✠, before whom every knee must bow. Give place to Adonai Yah'shua the Messiah (the Lord Jesus Christ) ✠, who shed His most precious blood for man. Give place to the Ruach HaKodesh (Holy Spirit), who by His blessed apostle Peter openly struck you down in the person of Simon Magus; who cursed your lies in Annas and Saphira; who smote you in King Herod because he had not given honor to Elohim (God); who by His apostle Paul afflicted you with the night of blindness in the magician Elyma, and by the mouth of the same apostle bade you to go out of Pythonissa, the soothsayer. Begone, ✠ now! Begone, ✠ seducer! Your place is in solitude; your abode is in the nest of nachashiym (serpents); get down and crawl with them. This matter brooks no delay; for see, Adonai (the Lord), the ruler comes quickly, kindling fire before Him, and it will run on ahead of Him and encompass His oyeviym (enemies) in flames. You might delude man, but Elohim (God) you cannot mock. It is He who casts you out, from whose sight nothing is hidden. It is He who repels you, to whose might all things are subject. It is He who expels you, He who has prepared everlasting hellfire for you and your mal'akiym (angels), from whose mouth shall come a sharp sword, who is coming to judge both the living and the dead and the world by fire.

All:Amen.

All the above may be repeated as long as necessary, until the one possessed has been fully freed.

Here follow a number of psalms which may be used at the exorcist's discretion as part of the rite. Some of them occur in other parts of the Ritual and are so indicated; the others may be taken from the Psalms: Psalm 90; psalm 91; psalm 67; psalm 69; psalm 53; psalm 117; psalm 34; psalm 30; psalm 21; psalm 3; psalm 10; psalm 12.

Psalm 90

1 A Prayer of Moses the man of Elohim (God). Adonai (Lord), You have been our dwelling place in all generations. 2 Before the mountains were brought forth, or ever You had formed the earth and the world, even from everlasting to everlasting, You are El (God). 3 You turn man to dakka (destruction), and say, "Return, O children of men." 4 For a thousand years in Your sight are like yesterday when it is past, and like a watch in the night. 5 You carry them away like a flood; They are like a sleep. In the morning they are like grass which grows up: 6 In the morning it flourishes and grows up; In the evening it is cut down and withers. 7 For we have been consumed by Your anger, and by Your wrath we are terrified. 8 You have set our avonot (iniquities) before You, our alum (secrets; secret sins) in the light of Your countenance. 9 For all our days have passed away in Your wrath; We finish our years like a sigh. 10 The days of our lives are seventy years; And if by reason of strength they are eighty years, yet their boast is only labor and sorrow; For it is soon cut off, and we fly away. 11 Who knows the power of Your anger? For as the fear of You, so is Your wrath. 12 So teach us to number our days, that we may gain a levav chokmah (heart of wisdom). 13 Return, YAHUWAH! How long? And have compassion on Your servants. 14 Oh, satisfy us early with Your chesed (mercy), that we may rejoice and be glad all our days! 15 Make us glad according to the days in which You have afflicted us, the years in which we have seen ra'ah (evil). 16 Let Your work appear to Your servants, and Your glory to their children. 17 And let

the beauty of YAHUWAH our Elohim (God) be upon us, and establish the work of our hands for us; Yes, establish the work of our hands.

Psalm 91

1 He who dwells in the seter (secret place) of Elyon (the Most High) shall abide under the Tsel Shaddai (shadow of the Almighty). 2 I will say of YAHUWAH, "He is my refuge and my fortress; Elohai (My God), in Him I will batach (trust, be bold in)." 3 Surely He shall deliver you from the pach (snare; figuratively: calamity) and the yakush (fowler, trapper, bait layer) and from the dever havot (pestilence's destruction). 4 He shall cover you with His evrat (feathers), and under His kanaf'iym (wings) you shall take refuge; His emet (truth) shall be your shield and buckler. 5 You shall not be afraid of the pachad (terror) by laila (night), nor of the chets (arrow) that flies by yomam (day), 6 Nor of the dever (pestilence) that walks in ophel (darkness, gloom; spiritual unreceptivity, calamity), nor of the ketev (destruction, destroying, ruin) that lays waste at tsohariym (noonday). 7 A thousand may fall at your side, and ten thousand at your right hand; But it shall not come near you. 8 Only with your eyes shall you look, and see the shilumat rasha'iym (reward of the wicked). 9 Because you have made YAHUWAH, who is my refuge, even Elyon (the Most High), your dwelling place, 10 No ra'ah (evil) shall befall you, nor shall any nega (plague) come near your ohel (tent, dwelling); 11 For He shall give His Mal'akiym (angels) charge over you, to keep you in all your derek (ways). 12 In their hands they shall bear you up, lest you dash your foot against a stone. 13 You shall tread upon the shachal (fierce lion) and the taniyn (dragon), the kephiyr (young lion) and the pethen (cobra) you shall trample underfoot. 14 "Because he has set his love upon Me, therefore I will deliver him; I will set him on high, because he has known My name. 15 He shall call

upon Me, and I will answer him; I will be with him in trouble; I will deliver him and honor him. 16 With long life I will satisfy him, And show him My yeshua (salvation)."

Psalm 67

1 To the Chief Musician. On stringed instruments. A Psalm. A Song. Elohim (God) be merciful to us and bless us, and cause His face to shine upon us, Selah. 2 That Your way may be known on earth, Your salvation among all Goyim (Gentiles, nations). 3 Let the peoples praise You, O Elohim (God); Let all the peoples praise You. 4 Oh, let the leumiym (nations) be glad and sing for joy! For You shall judge the people miyshor (righteously), and govern the le'umiym (nations) on earth. Selah. 5 Let the peoples praise You, O Elohim (God); Let all the peoples praise You. 6 Then the earth shall yield her increase; Elohim (God), our own Elohim (God), shall bless us. 7 Elohim (God) shall bless us, and all the ends of the earth shall fear Him.

Psalm 69

1 To the Chief Musician. Set to "The Lilies." A Psalm of David. Save me, O Elohim (God)! For the waters have come in unto my soul. 2 I sink in deep mire, where there is no standing; I have come into deep waters, where the floods overflow me. 3 I am weary with my crying; My throat is dry; My eyes fail while I wait for Elohai (my God). 4 Those who hate me without a cause are more than the hairs of my head; They are mighty who would destroy me, being my oyev'iym sheker (enemies wrongfully); Though I have stolen nothing, I still must restore it. 5 O Elohim (God), You know my ivelet (foolishness, folly); And my ashmot (sins, guilt, wrong doing) are not hidden from You. 6 Let not those who wait for You, O Adonai YAHUWAH Tseva'ot (Lord GOD of hosts), be ashamed

because of me; Let not those who seek You be confounded because of me, O Elohim (God) of Israel. 7 Because for Your sake I have borne reproach; Shame has covered my face. 8 I have become a stranger to my brothers, and an alien to my mother's children; 9 Because zeal for Your house has eaten me up, and the reproaches of those who reproach You have fallen on me. 10 When I wept and chastened my soul with fasting, that became my reproach. 11 I also made sackcloth my garment; I became a byword to them. 12 Those who sit in the gate speak against me, and I am the song of the drunkards. 13 But as for me, my tefillah (prayer) is to You, YAHUWAH, in the acceptable time; O Elohim (God), in the multitude of Your chesed (mercy), hear me in the emet (truth) of Your yesha (salvation). 14 Deliver me out of the mire, and let me not sink; Let me be delivered from those who hate me, and out of the deep waters. 15 Let not the floodwater overflow me, nor let the deep swallow me up; And let not the pit shut its mouth on me. 16 Hear me, YAHUWAH, for Your chesed (mercy, lovingkindness) is tov (good); Turn to me according to the multitude of Your racham'iym (tender mercies). 17 And do not hide Your face from Your eved (servant), for I am in trouble; Hear me speedily. 18 Draw near to my soul, and redeem it; Deliver me because of my oyev'iym (enemies). 19 You know my reproach, my shame, and my dishonor; My tsarar'iym (adversaries) are all before You. 20 Reproach has broken my heart, and I am full of heaviness; I looked for someone to take pity, but there was none; And for comforters, but I found none. 21 They also gave me gall for my food, and for my thirst they gave me vinegar to drink. 22 Let their table become a snare before them, and their well-being a trap. 23 Let their eyes be darkened, so that they do not see; And make their loins shake continually. 24 Pour out Your indignation upon them, and let Your wrathful anger take hold of them. 25 Let their dwelling place be desolate; Let no one live in their tents. 26 For they persecute the ones You have struck, and talk of the grief of those You have wounded. 27 Add avon (iniquity, punishment for iniquity) to their avon (iniquity, punishment for iniquity), and let them not come into Your tsedakah (righteousness). 28 Let them be blotted out of the Sefer Chayim (book of the living), and not be written with the tsadiykiym (righteous). 29 But I am aniy (poor) and ka'av (sorrowful); Let Your yeshua (salvation), O Elohim (God), set me up on high. 30 I will praise the name of Elohim (God) with a shiyr (song), and will magnify Him with todah (thanksgiving). 31 This also shall please YAHUWAH better than an ox or bull, which has horns and hooves. 32 The humble shall see this and be glad; And you who seek Elohim (God), your hearts shall live. 33 For YAHUWAH hears the evyon'iym (poor, needy), and does not despise His asiyr'iym (prisoners). 34 Let heaven and earth praise Him, the seas and everything that moves in them. 35 For Elohim (God) will save Zion and build the cities of Judah, that they may dwell there and possess it. 36 Also, the seed of His servants shall inherit it, and those who love His name shall dwell in it.

Psalm 53

1 To the Chief Musician. Set to "Mahalat." A Contemplation of David. The nabal (fool) has said in his heart, "There is no Elohim (God)." They are shachat (corrupt, destroyed), and have done ta'av avel (abominable iniquity); There is none who does tov (good). 2 Elohim (God) looks down from heaven upon the children of men, to see if there are any who understand, who seek Elohim (God). 3 Every one of them has turned aside; They have together become alach (filthy); There is none who does tov (good), no, not one. 4 Have the polei aven (workers of iniquity) no knowledge, who eat up my people as they eat bread, and do not call upon Elohim (God)? 5 There they are in great fear where no fear was, for Elohim (God) has scattered the bones of him who encamps against

you; You have put them to shame, because Elohim (God) has despised them. 6 Oh, that the salvation of Israel would come out of Zion! When Elohim (God) brings back the captivity of His people, let Jacob rejoice and Israel be glad.

Psalm 117

1 Praise YAHUWAH, all you goyim (Gentiles, nations)! Laud Him, all you peoples! 2 For His chesed (mercy) is great toward us, and the emet (truth) of YAHUWAH endures forever. Halelu-Yah (Praise the Lord)!

Psalm 34

1 A Psalm of David when he pretended madness before Abimelech, who drove him away, and he departed. I will bless YAHUWAH at all times; His praise shall continually be in my mouth. 2 My soul shall make its boast in YAHUWAH; The humble shall hear of it and be glad. 3 Oh, magnify YAHUWAH with me, and let us exalt His name together. 4 I sought YAHUWAH, and He heard me, and delivered me from all my fears. 5 They looked to Him and were radiant, and their faces were not ashamed. 6 This aniy (poor/humble/afflicted man) cried out, and YAHUWAH heard him, and saved him out of all his troubles. 7 The Mal'ak YAHUWAH (Angel of the Existing One) encamps all around those who fear Him, and delivers them. 8 Oh, taste and see that YAHUWAH is good; Blessed is the man who trusts in Him! 9 Oh, fear YAHUWAH, you His kadoshiym (holy ones, saints, set apart ones)! There is no want to those who fear Him. 10 The young lions lack and suffer hunger; But those who seek YAHUWAH shall not lack any good thing. 11 Come, you children, listen to me; I will teach you the fear of YAHUWAH. 12 Who is the man who desires life, and loves many days, that he may see good? 13 Keep your tongue from ra (evil), and your lips from speaking

mirmah (deceit). 14 Depart from ra (evil) and do tov (good); Seek shalom (peace) and pursue it. 15 The eyes of YAHUWAH are on the tsadiykiym (righteous), and His ears are open to their cry. 16 The face of YAHUWAH is against those who do ra (evil), to cut off the remembrance of them from the earth. 17 The tsadiykiym (righteous) cry out, and YAHUWAH hears, and delivers them out of all their troubles. 18 YAHUWAH is near to those who have a shavar lev (broken heart), and saves such as have a dakka ruach (contrite spirit). 19 Many are the ra'ot (evils, afflictions) of the tsadiyk (righteous), but YAHUWAH delivers him out of them all. 20 He guards all his bones; Not one of them is broken. 21 Ra'ah (Evil) shall slay the rasha (wicked), and those who hate the tsadiyk (righteous) shall be asham (guilty, condemned, desolate). 22 YAHUWAH redeems the soul of His servants, and none of those who chasiym (trust) in Him shall be asham (guilty, condemned, desolate).

Psalm 30

1 A Psalm. A Song at the dedication of the house of David. I will extol You, YAHUWAH, for You have lifted me up, and have not let my foes rejoice over me. 2 YAHUWAH Elohai (my God), I cried out to You, and You healed me. 3 YAHUWAH, You brought my soul up from Sheol (Hades, the grave, the underworld); You have kept me alive, that I should not go down to the pit. 4 Sing praise to YAHUWAH, His chasiyd (godly ones), and give thanks at the remembrance of His Shem Kadosh (holy name). 5 For His anger is but for a moment, His favor is for life; Weeping may endure for a night, but joy comes in the morning. 6 Now in my prosperity I said, "I shall never be moved." 7 YAHUWAH, by Your favor You have made my mountain stand strong; You hid Your face, and I was troubled. 8 I cried out to You, YAHUWAH; And to YAHUWAH I made supplication: 9 "What profit is there in my

blood, When I go down to shachat (the pit, destruction, corruption)? Will the dust praise You? Will it declare Your truth? 10 Hear, YAHUWAH, and have mercy on me; YAHUWAH, be my helper!" 11 You have turned for me my mispade (mourning) into machol (dancing); You have put off my sak (sackcloth) and clothed me with simchah (gladness), 12 To the end that my glory may sing praise to You and not be silent. YAHUWAH Elohai (my God), I will give thanks to You forever.

Psalm 21

1 To the Chief Musician. A Psalm of David. The king shall have joy in Your strength, YAHUWAH; And in Your salvation how greatly shall he rejoice! 2 You have given him his heart's desire, and have not withheld the request of his lips. Selah. 3 For You meet him with the blessings of goodness; You set a crown of pure gold upon his head. 4 He asked life from You, and You gave it to him— Length of days forever and ever. 5 His glory is great in Your salvation; Honor and majesty You have placed upon him. 6 For You have made him most blessed forever; You have made him exceedingly glad with Your presence. 7 For the king trusts in YAHUWAH, and through the mercy of Elyon (the Most High) he shall not be moved. 8 Your hand will find all Your enemies; Your right hand will find those who hate You. 9 You shall make them as a fiery oven in the time of Your anger; YAHUWAH shall swallow them up in His wrath, and the fire shall devour them. 10 Their offspring You shall destroy from the earth, and their seed from among the sons of men. 11 For they intended evil against You; They devised a plot which they are not able to perform. 12 Therefore You will make them turn their back; You will make ready Your arrows on Your string toward their faces. 13 Be exalted, YAHUWAH, in Your own strength! We will sing and praise Your power.

Psalm 3

1 A Psalm of David when he fled from Absalom his son. YAHUWAH, how they have increased who trouble me! Many are they who rise up against me. 2 Many are they who say of me, "There is no help for him in Elohim (God)." Selah. 3 But You, YAHUWAH, are a shield for me, My glory and the One who lifts up my head. 4 I cried to YAHUWAH with my voice, and He heard me from His holy hill. Selah. 5 I lay down and slept; I awoke, for YAHUWAH sustained me. 6 I will not be afraid of ten thousands of people who have set themselves against me all around. 7 Arise, YAHUWAH; Save me, O my Elohim (God)! For You have struck all my oyev'iym (enemies) on the cheekbone; You have broken the teeth of the rasha'iym (ungodly). 8 Salvation belongs to YAHUWAH. Your blessing is upon Your people. Selah.

Psalm 10

1 Why do You stand afar off, YAHUWAH? Why do You hide in times of trouble? 2 The rasha (wicked) in his ga'avah (pride) persecutes the aniy (poor); Let them be caught in the plots which they have devised. 3 For the rasha (wicked) boasts of his heart's desire; He blesses the betsa (greedy, covetous) and renounces YAHUWAH. 4 The rasha (wicked) in his proud countenance does not seek Elohim (God); Elohim (God) is in none of his thoughts. 5 His ways are always prospering; Your mishpat'iym (judgments) are far above, out of his sight; As for all his enemies, he sneers at them. 6 He has said in his heart, "I shall not be moved; I shall never be in adversity." 7 His mouth is full of alah (cursing) and mirmot (deceit) and tok (oppression); Under his tongue is amal (trouble) and aven (iniquity). 8 He sits in the lurking places of the villages; In the secret places he murders the innocent; His eyes are secretly fixed on the nakiy (helpless, innocent). 9 He lies in wait

secretly, as a lion in his den; He lies in wait to catch the aniy (poor); He catches the aniy (poor) when he draws him into his net. 10 So he crouches, he lies low, that the chelekah (helpless, unfortunate person) may fall by his strength. 11 He has said in his heart, "El (God) has forgotten; He hides His face; He will never see." 12 Arise, YAHUWAH! O El (God), lift up Your hand! Do not forget the anav'iym (humble). 13 Why do the rasha (wicked) renounce Elohim (God)? He has said in his heart, "You will not require an account." 14 But You have seen, for You observe trouble and grief, to repay it by Your hand. The chelekah (helpless) commits himself to You; You are the helper of the yatom (fatherless, orphan). 15 Break the arm of the rasha (wicked) and the ra (evil man); Seek out his resha (wickedness) until You find none. 16 YAHUWAH is Melek (King) forever and ever; The Goyim (nations, heathens, Gentiles) have perished out of His land. 17 YAHUWAH, You have heard the desire of the anav'iym (humble); You will prepare their heart; You will cause Your ear to hear, 18 to do justice to the yatom (fatherless, orphan) and the dak (oppressed, afflicted), That the man of the earth may oppress no more.

Psalm 12

1 To the Chief Musician. On an eight-stringed harp. A Psalm of David. Help, YAHUWAH, for the chasiyd (godly man) ceases! For the amuniym (faithful) disappear from among the benei adam (sons of men). 2 They speak idly everyone with his neighbor; with flattering lips and a double heart they speak. 3 May YAHUWAH cut off all flattering lips, and the tongue that speaks proud things, 4 Who have said, "With our tongue we will prevail; Our lips are our own; Who is lord over us?" 5 "For the oppression of the aniy'iym (poor), for the sighing of the evyon'iym (needy), Now I will arise," says YAHUWAH; "I will set him in the safety for which he yearns." 6 The words of

YAHUWAH are pure words, like silver tried in a furnace of earth, purified seven times. 7 You shall keep them, YAHUWAH, You shall preserve them from this generation forever. 8 The rasha'iym (wicked) prowl on every side, when vileness is exalted among the benei adam (sons of men).

Prayer Following Deliverance

YAHUWAH El Shaddai (Lord God Almighty), we beg you to keep theruach ra'ah (evil spirit) from further molesting this servant of yours, and to keep him far away, never to return. At your command, O YAHUWAH, may the goodness and peace of our Lord Yah'shua the Messiah (Jesus Christ), our Redeemer, take possession of this man (woman). May we no longer fear any evil since YAHUWAH is with us; who lives and reigns with you, in the unity of the Ruach HaKodesh (Holy Spirit), Elohim (God), forever and ever.

All: Amen.

Exorcism of Satan and the Fallen Angels

Whereas the **preceding rite** of gerush ruchot (exorcism) is designated for a particular person, the present one is for general use - to combat the power of the ruchot ra'ah (evil spirits) over a **community or locality**.

In the name of the Father YAHUWAH, and of the Son Yah'shua (Jesus), ✠ and of the Ruach HaKodesh (Holy Spirit). Amen.

Prayer to St. Michael the Archangel

Kadosh Miyka'el Sar-Mal'ak (St. Michael the Archangel), illustrious leader of the heavenly army, defend us in the battle against principalities and powers, against the rulers of the world of darkness and the ruach rasha (spirit of wickedness) in high places. Come to the rescue of mankind, whom Elohim (God) has made in His own image and likeness, and purchased from Satan's tyranny at so great a price. The Kadosh Knesiya (Holy Church) venerates you as her patron and apotropos (guardian). YAHUWAH has entrusted to you the task of leading the souls of the redeemed to heavenly blessedness. Entreat the Adon Shalom (Lord of peace) to cast Satan down under our feet, so as to keep him from further holding man captive and doing harm to the Knesiya (Church). Carry our prayers up to Elohim's (God's) throne, that the mercy of YAHUWAH may quickly come and lay hold of the behemah (beast), the nachash (serpent) of old, Satan and his shediym (demons), casting him in chains into the abyss, so that he can no longer seduce the goyim (nations).

Exorcism

In the name of Yah'shua the Messiah (Jesus Chris)t, our Adon (Lord) and Elohim (God), by the intercession of Mary, spotless Virgin and Mother of God, of Kadosh Miyka'el Sar-Mal'ak (St. Michael the Archangel), of the blessed shaliyachiym (apostles) Peter and Paul, and of all the kadoshiym (saints), and by the authority residing in our holy ministry, we steadfastly proceed to combat the onslaught of the wily enemy.

Psalm 68

1 To the Chief Musician. A Psalm of David. A Song. Let Elohim (God) arise, let His oyev'iym (enemies) be scattered; Let those also who hate Him flee before Him. 2 As smoke is driven away, so drive them away; As wax melts before the fire, so let the rasha'iym (wicked) perish at the presence of Elohim (God). 3 But let the tsadakiym (righteous) be glad; Let them rejoice before Elohim (God); Yes, let them rejoice exceedingly. 4 Sing to Elohim (God), sing praises to His name; Extol Him who rides on the clouds, by His name YAH, and rejoice before Him. 5 An avi (father) of the yatom'iym (fatherless, orphans), a dayan (judge, defender) of almanot (widows), is Elohim (God) in His ma'on kadosh (holy habitation). 6 Elohim (God) sets the yachiyd'iym (solitary) in bayit (houses, families); He brings out the asiyr'iym (those who are bound, prisoners, captives) into kosharah (prosperity); But the sarar'iym (rebellious, stubborn) dwell in a tsechiychah (dry land). 7 O Elohim (God), when You went out before Your people, when You marched through the wilderness, Selah. 8 The earth shook; The heavens also dropped rain at the presence of Elohim (God); Sinai itself was moved at the presence of Elohim (God), the Elohim (God) of Israel. 9 You, O Elohim (God), sent a plentiful rain, whereby

You confirmed Your inheritance, when it was weary. 10 Your congregation dwelt in it; You, O Elohim (God), provided from Your tovat (goodness) for the aniy (poor). 11 Adonai (The Lord) gave the omer (word); Great was the company of those who proclaimed it: 12 "Kings of armies flee, they flee, and she who remains at home divides the spoil. 13 Though you lie down among the sheepfolds, You will be like the wings of a dove covered with silver, and her feathers with yellow gold." 14 When the Shaddai (Almighty) scattered kings in it, it was white as snow in Zalmon. 15 A mountain of Elohim (God) is the mountain of Bashan; A mountain of many peaks is the mountain of Bashan. 16 Why do you fume with envy, you mountains of many peaks? This is the mountain which Elohim (God) desires to dwell in; Yes, YAHUWAH will dwell in it forever. 17 The chariots of Elohim (God) are twenty thousand, Even thousands of thousands; Adonai (the Lord) is among them as in Sinai, in the Kodesh (Holy Place). 18 You have aliyah (ascended) on marom (high), You have led sheviy (captivity) shavah (captive); You have received matanot (gifts) among men, even from the sorar'iym (rebellious, stubborn), That Yah Elohim (the Lord God) might dwell there. 19 Blessed be Adonai (the Lord), who daily loads us with benefits, the El yeshu'at (God of our salvation)! Selah. 20 Our El (God) is the El Mosha'ot (God of salvation); And to YAHUWAH Adonai (the Lord) belong escapes from mavet (death). 21 But Elohim (God) will wound the head of His oyev'iym (enemies), the hairy scalp of the one who still goes on in his asham (guiltiness, trespasses, offences). 22 Adonai (the Lord) said, "I will bring back from Bashan, I will bring them back from the depths of the sea, 23 That your foot may crush them in blood, and the tongues of your kelev'iym (dogs) may have their portion from your oyev'iym (enemies)." 24 They have seen Your procession, O Elohim (God), the procession of Eli (my God), Malki (my King), into the Kodesh (Holy Place, sanctuary). 25 The shariym (singers) went before, the noganiym (players on instruments) followed after; Among them were the maidens playing timbrels. 26 Bless Elohim (God) in the makhelot (congregations), YAHUWAH, from the fountain of Israel. 27 There is little Benjamin, their leader, the princes of Judah and their company, the princes of Zebulun and the princes of Naphtali. 28 Your Elohim (God) has commanded your strength; Strengthen, O Elohim (God), what You have done for us. 29 Because of Your Heykal (Temple) at Jerusalem, Melekiym (Kings) will bring presents to You. 30 Rebuke the chayat (living things) of the reeds, the herd of bulls with the calves of the peoples, till everyone submits himself with pieces of silver. Scatter the peoples who delight in war. 31 Envoys will come out of Egypt; Ethiopia will quickly stretch out her hands to Elohim (God). 32 Sing to Elohim (God), you kingdoms of the earth; Oh, sing praises to Adonai (the Lord), Selah. 33 To Him who rides on the heaven of heavens, which were of old! Indeed, He sends out His voice, a mighty voice. 34 Ascribe strength to Elohim (God); His excellence is over Israel, and His strength is in the clouds. 35 O Elohim (God), You are more awesome than Your Mikdash'iym (holy places). The Elohim (God) of Israel is He who gives strength and power to His people. Blessed be Elohim (God)!

See the Tselav Adonai (cross of the Lord); begone, you hostile powers!

The stem of David, the lion of the tribe of Judah has conquered.

May your mercy, YAHUWAH, remain with us always.

For we put our whole trust in you.

We cast you out, every ruach ha'tumah (unclean spirit), every ko'ach satani (satanic power), every onslaught of the infernal adversary, every legion, every diabolical group and sect, in the name and by the power of our Lord Yah'shua the Messiah (Jesus Christ) ✠. We command you, begone and fly far from the Knesiya Ha'Elohim (Church of God), from the souls made by Elohim (God) in His image and redeemed by the precious blood of the divine Lamb. ✠ No longer dare, armumi nachash (cunning serpent), to deceive the human race, to persecute Knesiya Ha'Elohim (Church of God), to strike the bachiyr Elohim (elect of God) and to sift them as wheat. ✠ For the YAHUWAH El Elyon (Most High God) commands you, ✠ He to whom you once proudly presumed yourself equal; YAHUWAH who wills all men to be saved and come to the knowledge of truth. Elohim Ha'Avi: YAHUWAH (God the Father: the Lord) ✠ commands you. Elohim Ha'Ben: Yah'shua (God the Son: Jesus) ✠ commands you. Elohim Ha'Ruach HaKodesh (God the Holy Spirit) ✠ commands you. Messiah (Christ), the eternal Word of Elohim (God) made flesh, ✠ commands you, who humbled Himself, becoming obedient even unto death, to save our race from the perdition wrought by your envy; who founded His Knesiya (Church) upon a firm rock, declaring that the gates of hell should never prevail against her, and that He would remain with her all days, even to the end of the world. The sacred mystery of the Tselav (cross) ✠ commands you, along with the power of all mysteries of Christian faith.

Therefore, Me'kulal Taniyn (accursed dragon) and every diabolical legion, we adjure you by the Elohim Chayim (living God) ✠, by the El Emet (true God) ✠, by the El Kadosh (holy God) ✠, by Elohim (God), who so loved the world that He gave His only-begotten Son, that whoever believes in Him might not perish but have everlasting life; to cease deluding human creatures and filling them with the poison of everlasting damnation; to desist from harming the Knesiya

(Church) and hampering her freedom. Begone, Satan, father and master of lies, enemy of man's welfare. Give place to Messiah (Christ), in whom you found none of your works. Give way to the one, holy, universal, and apostolic Church, which Messiah (Christ) Himself purchased with His blood. Bow down before Elohim's (God's) mighty hand, tremble and flee as we call on the holy and awesome name of Yah'shua (Jesus), before whom the denizens of hell cower, to whom the heavenly Virtues and Powers and Dominations are subject, whom the Cherubim and Seraphim praise with unending cries as they sing: Holy, holy, holy, YAHUWAH Elohim Tseva'ot (Lord God of Hosts).

YAHUWAH, hear my prayer.

And let my cry be heard by you.

Let us pray.

Elohei HaShamayim Va'Arets (God of heaven and earth), Elohei Mal'akiym Va'Sar-Mal'akiym (God of the angels and archangels), Elohei Patriarch'iym Va'Navi'iym (God of the patriarchs and prophets), Elohei Shaliyachiym Va'Kadosh Me'un'e (God of the apostles and martyrs), Elohei Mitvade Va'Betulot (God of the confessors and virgins), Elohim (God) who have power to bestow life after death and rest after toil; for there is no other Elohim (God) than you, nor can there be another true Elohim (God) beside you, the Bore (Creator) of all things visible and invisible, whose kingdom is without end; we humbly entreat your glorious majesty to deliver us by your might from every influence of the ruchot me'kulal (accursed spirits), from their every evil snare and deception, and to keep us from all harm; through Yah'shua the Messiah (Jesus Christ) our Lord.

All: Amen.

From the snares of the devil.

YAHUWAH, deliver us.

That you help your Church to serve you in security and freedom.

We beg you to hear us.

That you humble the enemies of the Holy Church.

We beg you to hear us.

The surroundings are sprinkled with holy water.

HOME BLESSING

PRAYERS FOR BREAKING

CURSES, SPELLS, AND INCANTATIONS

You can pray all of these at once or just 1 a week.

Avi Ba'Shamayim (Heavenly Father), I come to You as Your child, born again, redeemed and washed in the blood of Yah'shua (Jesus). I declare that You, Yah'shua the Messiah (Jesus Christ), have redeemed me from the kalalah (curse) of the Torah (law) having been made a kalalah (curse) for me at Calvary. I proclaim that I am a partaker of the inheritance of the kadoshiym Elohim (saints of God). I give thanks unto You, Father, for delivering me from all the powers of darkness and translating me into the kingdom of your dear Son. Amen.

As one who is covered with the blood of Yah'shua the Messiah (Jesus Christ), I here and now renounce, reject and disown all the chatot (sins), heskem'iym (pacts), hakdasha (dedications), kalalot (curses) and magi bechira (occult selections) of my av kadmon (ancestors) or any ke'rov mishpacha (relatives), which has been passed on to me intentionally or unintentionally. Amen.

In the Name of Yah'shua (Jesus), YAHUWAH El Shaddai (Lord God Almighty), I ask to be redeemed and cleansed from all kalaot ra (evil curses), lahatutan (incantations), hakdasha (dedications), kesim'iym (spells), heskem'iym (pacts), and ruchot mukar (familiar spirits) passed on to me from my hore (parents), saba (grandparents), saba gadol (great-grandparents), av kadmon (ancestors), ke'rov mishpacha (relatives), or any other person. Amen.

In the name of the Lord Yah'shua the Messiah (Jesus Christ), I renounce, reject and rebuke all spells, kishuf'iym (hexes), kalalot (curses), vudu (voodoo practices), kishuf (witchcraft), pulchan satani (satanic rituals), lahatutan (incantations) and ma'avayim hara (evil wishes) that have been sent my (_____'s) way, or have passed down the generational bloodline. I take authority over all of them and command that they go back where they came from and be replaced with a berachah (blessing). Amen.

In the name of the Lord Yah'shua the Messiah (Jesus Christ), and powerful in the holy authority of His Precious and Wondrous Name, We ask, O YAHUWAH our Elohim (God), that you break and dissolve any and all kalaot (curses), kishuf'iym (hexes), kesim'iym (spells), chatom'iym (seals), satani nederiym (satanic vows) and heskim'iym (pacts), ruchani kesher (spiritual bondings) and kesher nephesh (soul ties) with satani chayil'iym (satanic forces), ma'avayim hara (evil wishes), ta'ava hara (evil desires), torashti chatom'iym (hereditary seals), malkoldet (snares, traps), sheker (lies), michshol (obstacles), sibun (deceptions), hasacha (diversions), ruchani hashpa'a (spiritual influences), and every tikfud lakui (dysfunction) and mechala (disease) from any source. Amen.

BLESSING YOUR HOME PRAYER

(should be done at least once a week)

Protection Prayers in Preparation

(anoint each person with Holy Oil)

O YAHUWAH, have mercy on me, a sinner.

O Yah'shua (Jesus), have mercy on me, a sinner.

O Ruach HaKodesh (Holy Spirit), have mercy on me, a sinner.

O Adonai Yah'shua the Messiah (Lord Jesus Christ), Son of Elohim (God), have mercy on us. Amen.

Glory to You, YAHUWAH our Elohim (God); glory to You.

O Melek HaShamayim (Heavenly King), Me'nachem (Comforter), Ruach Ha-Emet (Spirit of Truth), Who are everywhere and fills all things, Treasury of Blessings, and Giver of Life: Come and abide in us, and cleanse us from every impurity, and save our souls, O HaTov (Good One).

✠ El Kadosh (Holy God), Abiyr Kadosh (Holy Mighty), Almavet Kadosh (Holy Immortal One), have mercy on us.

✠ El Kadosh (Holy God), Abiyr Kadosh (Holy Mighty), Almavet Kadosh (Holy Immortal One), have mercy on us.

✠ El Kadosh (Holy God), Abiyr Kadosh (Holy Mighty), Almavet Kadosh (Holy Immortal One), have mercy on us.

✠ Glory to the Father YAHUWAH, and to the Son Yah'shua (Jesus), and to the Ruach HaKodesh (Holy Spirit), now and ever, and unto ages of ages. Amen.

O Hashilush HaKodesh (Most Holy Trinity), have mercy on us; Adonai (Lord), cleanse our sins; Adon (Master), pardon our transgressions; Kadosh (Holy One), visit and heal our infirmities for Your Name's sake.

YAHUWAH, have mercy.

Yah'shua (Jesus), have mercy

Ruach HaKodesh (Holy Spirit), have mercy.

✠ Glory to the Father YAHUWAH, and to the Son Yah'shua (Jesus), and to the Ruach HaKodesh (Holy Spirit), now and ever, and unto ages of ages. Amen.

Avinu / Tefillat Talmid
(Our Father / The disciple's prayer)

Avinu (Our Father), Who is in heaven, hallowed be Your Name. Your Kingdom come. Your will be done, on earth as it is in heaven. Give us this day our daily bread; and forgive us our trespasses, as we forgive those who trespass against us; and lead us not into temptation, but deliver us from the Hara (evil one). For Yours is the kingdom, and the power, and the glory, for ever. Amen.

GLORY BE

✠ Glory be to the Father YAHUWAH, and to the Son Yah'shua (Jesus), and to the Ruach HaKodesh (Holy Spirit). As it was in the beginning, is now, and ever shall be, world without end. Amen.

We ask the Light of Your presence, YAHUWAH our Elohim (God), to surround us as a shield.

We ask the Blood of Yah'shua the Messiah (Jesus Christ) to cover us and defend us against the attacks of all ruchot ra'ah (evil spirits) and ruchot ha'tumah (unclean spirits).

We ask the Kadosh Mal'akiym (Holy Angels) to be with us and join us in our battle against the powers of choshek (darkness).

Kadosh Miyka'el Sar-Mal'ak (St. Michael the Archangel), defend us in battle. Be our protection against the wickedness and snares of the Devil. May Elohim (God) rebuke him, we humbly pray, and do you, O Prince of the heavenly hosts, by the power of Elohim (God), cast into hell Satan, and all the ruchot ra'ah (evil spirits), who prowl about the world seeking the ruin of souls. Amen.

INTRODUCTION

✠ In the Name of the Father YAHUWAH, and of the Son Yah'shua (Jesus), and of the Ruach HaKodesh (Holy Spirit). Amen.

O Elohim (God), come to our assistance.

O YAHUWAH make haste to help us.

✠ Glory be to the Father YAHUWAH and to the Son Yah'shua (Jesus) and to the Ruach HaKodesh (Holy Spirit); as it was in the beginning is now and ever shall be, world without end. Amen.

O YAHUWAH, Hear my prayer

and let my cry come unto You.

(Tracing the sign of the Cross over the main door way of house)

✠ In the name of Yah'shua the Messiah (Jesus Christ), please bless this house.

O Elohim (God) of our yeshu'ah (salvation), Son of the El Chai (living God), who are borne on the Cherubim, above all Sararot (Principalities), Rashuyot (Authorities), Shaliytiym (Powers) and Mem'shalot (Dominions): You are great and dreadful to all that are round about You; You have set heaven

563

as a vault, and have made the earth in Your might; You did order the universe in Your wisdom; You cause that which is under the heavens to shake from its very foundations, yet its pillars are unshaken; You speak to the sun and it does not shine, You seal the stars; You do interdict the seas and dry them up; Rashuyot (Authorities) and Shaliytiym (Powers) hide at Your wrath, and the rocks tremble before You. You have shattered the gates of brass and have broken the iron bars. You have bound the mighty one and smashed his vessels; You have cast down the tyrant by Your Tselav (Cross) and have drawn out the nachash (serpent) with the hook of Your Humanity; having cast him down, You have bound him with chains in the gloom of Tartarus.

Do You Yourself, therefore, O Adonai (Lord), the Confirmation of those who have set their hope on You and the wall of strength for those whose expectation is in You, renounce, drive away, and put to flight every ruach ra'ah (evil spirit) and ruach ha'tumah (unclean spirit); the Ruach Heylel (spirit of Lucifer), Satan, Ba'al zebub (Beelzebub), Abaddon (Apollyon in Greek), Behemah (Beast), Beliya'al (Belial), Livyatan (Leviathan), the Taniyn (Dragon), the Nachash (Serpent), Kundalini, Piton (Python), Ach'av (Ahab), Ashtoreth, Asmodee, Ba'al, Baphomet, Dagon, Rach'av (Rahab), Iyzebel (Jezebel), Mamon (Mammon - wealth), Molech, Nebo, Pharmakeia; every Ruach Shediym (Demonic Spirit), Ruach Ra'ah (Evil Spirit), Ruach Ha'Tumah (Unclean spirit), Ruach Rasha (Wicked Spirit); every Ruach Adut (Religious spirit) and every Ruach Yami (Marine Spirit); the Tsiyiym (Desert Demon), the Sa'ariym (Goat Demon), the Iyiym (Howling Demon); Azazel, Semyaza, Samael, Lilith, the Bat Ya'anah (daughters of Lilith), and every succubus and incubus, every Siren, Alukah (vampire) Banshee and Jinn; the Mal'ak Ha'Mavet (Angel of Death) the Mashchiyt (destroyer), the Okel (devourer), the Arveh (locust) and the Yelek (cankerworm); every Ruach Choli (spirit of sickness), Ruach Chalah (spirit of infirmity), Ruach Machala (spirit of disease) and Ruach Nega (spirit of plague); every Ruach Shabar Shinayim (spirit of broken teeth), Machala Pe (mouth disease), Shemenut (obesity) and Machala Ayin (eye problem), every satani ma'ase (diabolical action), every satani plisha (satanic invasion), every lashon hara (evil tongue; slander) and ko'ach keriy (contrary power) lying under this roof, from those who have been seized by them, and from those who walk about under it, bearing Your Tselav (Cross), the sign of victory, dreadful against shediym (demons), and calling upon Your Shem Tov Kadosh (good and Holy Name).

Yea, O Adonai Yah'shua the Messiah (Lord Jesus Christ), who did drive away a legion of shediym (demons), and who, having restrained the dumb and deaf shed (demon) and the ruach ha'tumah (unclean spirit), did command it to depart from the man and never to return again; who did utterly destroy the army of our invisible oyeviym (enemies), and did depart wisdom unto the faithful who have known You, saying, 'Behold, I give unto you power to tread on nachashiym (serpents) and akraviym (scorpions), and over all the power of the oyev (enemy):' Do You Yourself, O Master, keep everyone in this house beyond every harm and temptation, delivering them from the terror of the night, from the arrow that flies by day, from that which walks about in the darkness, and from the calamity and shed (demon) of noonday.

Let Your servants, Your handmaidens, and infants, delighting in Your help, and protected by the angelic hosts, cry out in faith, with one accord, 'YAHUWAH is my helper, and I will not fear; what can man do unto me?' And again, 'I will fear no evil, for You are with me.' For You, O Elohim (God), are my confirmation, the mighty Master, the Sar Shalom (Prince of

Peace), the Father of the age to come, and Your kingdom is an eternal kingdom. And Yours alone is the kingdom, and the power, and the glory, together with the Father YAHUWAH, and the Ruach HaKodesh (Holy Spirit), now and ever, and unto ages of ages. Amen.

PRAYERS IN EACH ROOM

(Say these prayers as the rooms are sprinkled with Holy Water, Salt and Incense.)

Visit, we beseech You, O YAHUWAH, this place (our home), and drive away all the snares of the enemy; let Your Mal'akiym Kadoshiym (holy angels) dwell herein to preserve us in peace; and may Your blessing be upon us evermore; through Yah'shua the Messiah (Jesus Christ) our Lord. Amen.

We Seal this place in the most Precious Blood of Yah'shua the Messiah (Jesus Christ) and command all evil spirits to be gone never to return.

I command you, in the Name of Yah'shua the Messiah (Jesus Christ), to go to the feet of Yah'shua (Jesus) for judgment.

I now close, through the power of Yah'shua the Messiah (Jesus Christ), any ruchani sha'ariym (spiritual portals) in this place so that ruchot ra'ah (evil spirits) may no longer enter into our realm.

Holy Father, in the name of Yah'shua the Messiah (Jesus Christ), crush the power of evil in this place with the light of your grace. Amen and Amen.

CLOSING PRAYERS AGAINST RETALIATION

Kadosh Miyka'el Sar-Mal'ak (St. Michael the Archangel), protect us, both body and soul from the Hara (Evil One), his followers and anyone who would approach us with malicious intent.

Protect us, our bodies, and our vehicles, as we travel about in our daily activities.

Protect our home, our property, our family and possessions from all shedi nakam (demonic retaliation).

O glorious Kadosh Miyka'el Sar-Mal'ak (St. Michael the Archangel), I beseech you to fight against those who fight us and who make war upon us.

Take up your sword and shield and rise up in our defense. BLOCK THE WAY OF OUR DEMONIC PURSUERS.

Let those be turned back who plot evil against us! We cover ourselves in the Most precious Blood of Yah'shua (Jesus) for protection against any spiritual retaliation.

Avinu (Our Father), Who is in heaven, hallowed be Your Name. Your Kingdom come. Your will be done, on earth as it is in heaven. Give us this day our daily bread; and forgive us our trespasses, as we forgive those who trespass against us; and lead us not into temptation, but deliver us from the Hara (evil one). For Yours is the kingdom, and the power, and the glory, for ever. Amen.

PRAYER FOR A HOME TROUBLED BY EVIL SPIRITS

O Adonai (Lord), the Elohei Yishenu (God of our salvation), Yah'shua the Messiah (Jesus Christ) Son of the Elohim Chayim (Living God), Who is borne by the Cherubim, being above all dominions, principalities, authorities and powers: You are great and fearsome to all around You. You are the One Who set the heavens like a vault and made the earth in Your might; Who directs the universe in Your wisdom. When earthquakes occur under heaven from the foundations, its pillars are unshaken. You speak and the sun does not shine. You sealed the stars. You forbade the seas and dried them up. Authorities and dominions hide from Your wrath, and the rock trembles before You. You obliterated the gates of brass and demolished the bars of iron. You bound the Mighty One and smashed his vessels. By Your Cross You cast down tyrants and drew in the Nachash (Serpent) with the hook of Your humanity. Having cast him down, You bound him with hooks in the gloom of Tartarus. As the same Lord, the Hope of those who place their confirmation on You, and the Wall of might for those whose expectation is in You, anathematize, drive away and transform all diabolical actions and all satanic indictments, all slanders of the Adversary, and of the powers lying under this roof. Free those bearing the Sign which is awesome against shediym (demons): the Cross of Your victory, and calling upon Your gracious Name, from possession by him and from those wandering about under this roof.

Yea, Adonai Yah'shua (Lord Jesus), You drove away legions of shediym (demons), and the shediym (demons) and ruchot ha'tumah (unclean spirits) by which the deaf and dumb were held. These You commanded to depart and not to return again. You have consumed all the chayil (armies) of our eino nir'e oyeviym (invisible enemies), and have made wise the faithful who have known You. For You said, "Behold, I give you power to trample underfoot nachashiym (snakes) and akraviym (scorpions), and all the ko'ach oyeviym (power of enemies)" (Luke 10:19). Preserve, O Master, all who live in this house from all harm and every temptation from below, delivering them from fear of the feeble one and the arrows that fly by day, from things proceeding from the darkness and attacks by shediym (demons) at midday. Let Your servants and Your children, delighting in Your help, and preserved by chayiliym mal'akiym (armies of angels), faithfully sing with one accord: "YAHUWAH is my Helper and I will not be afraid; what can man do to me?" and again, "I will fear no evil, for You are with me."

As You are our Confirmation, O Elohim (God), Mighty Master, Prince of Peace, and Father of the age to come, for Your kingdom is an eternal Kingdom, to you alone is the Kingdom, and the Power, and the Glory, with the Father YAHUWAH and the Ruach HaKodesh (Holy Spirit), now and ever and unto ages of ages. Amen.

PRAYER AGAINST
THE AYIN HARA (EVIL EYE)

O YAHUWAH our Elohim (God), the King of the ages, almighty and all powerful, who create and alter all things by your will alone; who changed into dew the flames of the furnace in Babylon that had been heated seven times more than usual, and preserved in safety your three holy youths Shadrach, Meshach and Abed-Nego; the physician and healer of our souls; the security of those who hope in you; we pray you and beseech you: Remove, drive away and banish every diabolical activity, every satanic attack and every plot, evil curiosity and injury, and the Ayin Hara (evil eye) of mischievous and anashiym ha'rashaiym (wicked men) from us your avadiym (servants) (Names);

And whether it was brought about by beauty, or bravery, or happiness, or jealousy and envy, or Ayin Hara (evil eye), do you yourself, O YAHUWAH who love mankind, stretch out your mighty hand and your powerful and lofty arm, look down upon us your creatures and watch over us, and send us a Mal'ak Shalom (angel of peace), a mighty guardian of soul and body, who will rebuke and banish from us every wicked intention, every spell and Ayin Hara (evil eye) of destructive and envious men; so that, guarded by you, your supplicant may sing to you with thanksgiving: 'YAHUWAH is my helper, and I shall not be afraid; what can man do to me?' And again: 'I shall fear no evil because you are with me.'

For you are El (God) my strength, the powerful ruler, the Sar Shalom (Prince of Peace), the Father of the age to come. Yes, YAHUWAH our Elohim (God), spare your creatures and save your servants (Names) from every injury brought about by the Ayin Hara (evil eye), and keep us safe above every ill.

For you are our Melek (King) and all things are possible to You, O YAHUWAH. Therefore, we ascribe glory to the Father YAHUWAH, and to the Son Yah'shua (Jesus) and to the Ruach HaKodesh (Holy Spirit), now and ever and unto the ages of ages. Amen.

PRAYER AGAINST EVIL

Ruach Elohim (Spirit of God), Father YAHUWAH, Son Yah'shua (Jesus) and Ruach HaKodesh (Holy Spirit), Hashilush Hakodesh (Most Holy Trinity), descend upon us. Please purify us, mold us, fill us with yourself, and use us.

Banish all the forces of evil from this home and family; destroy them and vanquish them, so that we can be healthy and do good deeds, walking in the fear of YAHUWAH and rejoicing in your salvation all the day long.

Banish from us all spells, witchcraft, black magic, demonic assignments, malefice, and the evil eye; diabolic infestations, oppressions, possessions; all that is evil and sinful; jealousy, treachery, envy; all physical, psychological, moral, spiritual and diabolical ailments, and any other spirits of death and darkness.

I command and bid all the powers who molest this family—by the power of YAHUWAH, El Shaddai (God Almighty), the El Chai (God of Life), El Elyon (God Most High), the Elohim Chayim (God of the Living), in the name of Yah'shua the Messiah (Jesus Christ) our Moshiya (Savior)—to leave this home forever, and to be consigned into the everlasting lake of fire, that they may never again return. Amen.

PRAYER AND SANCTIFICATION

YAHUWAH, Father Almighty, I ask that You would sanctify and put Your seal of ownership upon this home, upon this property and upon each article that is in this home and on this property for they are Yours to govern over.

O YAHUWAH, as Your Son Yah'shua the Messiah (Jesus Christ) had cleared Your temple from those who had been spiritually tainting the holiness of that building (Matthew 21:12,13) I ask for You Yah'shua (Jesus) to come and spiritually purge our home, property and its possessions from anything that spiritually taints the holiness of our home, property and possessions.

In the powerful name of Yah'shua the Messiah (Jesus Christ), I claim this home and property for the Kingdom of Elohim (God).

I renounce every work of iniquity that has ever been perpetrated in this home, or on its property.

I plead the blood of Yah'shua the Messiah (Jesus Christ) to rectify and forgive every unrepented sin that has been committed here by a previous owner, renter, or guest who had ever stayed here.

In the name of Yah'shua the Messiah (Jesus Christ), I command broken off of this home and property all decay, rot, mold and mildew, every chain of bondage, every curse, every ungodly vow, every dark spirit and every legal right Satan has had to this home and property. By whatever person, whatever opportunity, whatever legal right, or whatever sin perpetrated, I command every possible work Satan has put onto, or against this property rescinded and declared null and void.

I command every demonic influence to relinquish its position and be purged from this home and property and sent to dry and arid places.

Holy Father send a cleansing fire throughout our home and property and burn up the remnants of sin and darkness that has covered this home and property and fill this home and property up with Your Ruach HaKodesh (Holy Spirit).

In the name of Yah'shua the Messiah (Jesus Christ). Amen and Amen.

PRAYER AGAINST DEMONIC INFLUENCE

O YAHUWAH, Who delivered Your people from the bondage of the adversary, and through Your Son Yah'shua the Messiah (Jesus Christ), cast down Satan like lightning, deliver me also from every influence of ruchot ha'tumah (unclean spirits).

Command Satan to depart far from me, (from my family, my wife (husband), my children, my home, and my possessions) by the power of Your only begotten Son Yah'shua the Messiah (Jesus Christ).

Rescue me from demonic imaginings and darkness. Fill me with the light of the Ruach HaKodesh (Holy Spirit) that I may be guarded against all snares of crafty shediym (demons).

Grant that a Mal'ak (angel) will always go before me and lead me to the path of tsedakah (righteousness) all the days of my life, to the honor of Your glorious Name, In the Name of the Father YAHUWAH and of the Son Yah'shua (Jesus) and of the Ruach HaKodesh (Holy Spirit) ✠. Amen.

FOR THE CHOLE (SICK)

O Adonai Yah'shua the Messiah (Lord Jesus Christ), Who alone are our Defender: Visit and heal Your suffering servants, delivering us from every sickness, disease, illness, and plague. Deliver us from broken teeth, mouth disease, obesity, stomach illness, eye problem and grievous pain. Raise us up that we may sing to You and praise You without ceasing, O You Who alone loves mankind. In the Name of the Father YAHUWAH and of the Son Yah'shua (Jesus) and of the Ruach HaKOdesh (Holy Spirit) ✠. Amen.

HEDGE PRAYER FOR PROTECTION OF HOUSEHOLD

The "Hedge Prayer of Protection" is one of the most powerful prayers in the arsenal of spiritual warfare. We learn from Job that God has placed a "hedge of protection" around his children that Satan cannot cross except that God allows it (or as we allow it).

It should be noted, as it is with all prayer, the Hedge Prayer of Protection is not a magic bullet. There are no guarantees that the Hedge surrounding us cannot be breached. We can allow Satan and his shediym (demons) to breach the Hedge by our carelessness of leaving the gate open, through direct or indirect invitation to the shediym (demons), through sins of commission and omission, through holes left unrepaired after sins are confessed and forgiven, through ancestral afflictions, etc. Even if there are no other reasons, Elohim (God) may allow shediym (demons) to breach the hedge, as He did with Job, for purposes of testing, learning, or other Divine Reasons that only Elohim (God) may know.

And YAHUWAH said to Satan, "Have you considered my servant Job, that there is none like him on the earth, a blameless and upright man, who fears Elohim (God) and turns away from evil?" Then Satan answered YAHUWAH, "Does Job fear Elohim (God) for naught? Have You not put a hedge about him and his house and all that he has, on every side? You have blessed the work of his hands, and his possessions have increased in the land. —Job 1:8-10

577

Submit yourselves therefore to Elohim (God). Resist the devil and he will flee from you. Draw near to Elohim (God) and he will draw near to you. Cleanse your hands, you sinners, and purify your hearts, you men of double mind. — James 4:7-8

Trusting in the promise that whatever we ask the Father YAHUWAH in Yah'shua's (Jesus') name He will do, I (we) now approach You Father with confidence in Our Lord's words and in Your infinite power and love for me (us) and for my (our) household and family, and with the intercession of the Blessed Sar-Mal'akiym Miyka'el (Archangel Michael), my (our) mal'ak apotropos (guardian angel(s)) and the mal'ak apotropos (guardian angels) of my (our) household and family, with all the kadoshiym (saints) and mal'akiym (angels) of heaven, and Holy in the power of His blessed Name, ask you Father to protect my (our) household and its members and keep us from the harassment of the devil and his minions.

Father YAHUWAH I (we) ask in desire to serve You and adore You and to live our lives for You that You build a me'sucha chasut (hedge of protection) around my (our) household, like that which surrounded Job, and to help us to keep that hedge repaired and the gate locked so that the devil and his minions have no access or means to breach the hedge except by your expressed will. I (we) specifically ask for protection for

_____.

Father, I am (we are) powerless against the spiritual forces of evil and recognize my (our) utter dependence on You and Your power. Look with mercy upon me (us) and upon my (our) household and family. Do not look upon our sins, O YAHUWAH; rather, look at the sufferings of your Beloved Son and see the Victim who's bitter passion and death has reconciled us to You. By the victory of the cross, protect us from all evil and rebuke any ruchot ra'ah (evil spirits) who wish to attack, influence, or breach Your me'sucha chasut (hedge of protection) in any way. Send them immediately back to Hell and fortify Your Me'sucha (Hedge) for our chasut (protection) by the blood of Your Son, Yah'shua (Jesus). Send your Mal'akiym Kadoshiym (Holy Angels) to watch over us and protect us.

Father, all of these things I (we) ask in the most Shem Kadosh (holy name) of Yah'shua the Messiah (Jesus Christ), Your Son. Thank you, Father, for hearing my (our) prayer. I (we) love You, I(we) worship You, I (we) thank You and I (we) trust in You. Amen.

HEDGE PRAYER
FOR PROTECTION OF SELF

Trusting in the promise that whatever we ask the Father in Yah'shua's (Jesus') name He will do, I now approach You Father with confidence in Our Lord's words and in Your infinite power and love for me. With the intercession of the Blessed Sar-Mal'ak Miyka'el (Archangel Michael), my mal'ak apotropos (guardian angel), with all the kadoshiym (saints) and mal'akiym (angels) of heaven, and Holy in the power of His blessed Name, I ask you Father to protect me and keep me from the harassment of the devil and his minions.

Father I ask that You build a me'sucha chasut (hedge of protection) around me, like that which surrounded Job, and help me to keep that hedge repaired and the gate locked so that the devil and his minions have no access or means to breach the hedge except by your expressed will. I specifically ask for protection for {Special needs}.

Father, I know that I am powerless against the spiritual forces of evil and recognize my utter dependence on You and Your power. Look with mercy upon me. Do not look upon my sins, O YAHUWAH; rather, look at the sufferings of your Beloved Son and see the Victim whose bitter passion and death has reconciled me to You. By the victory of the cross, protect me from all evil and rebuke any ruchot ra'ah (evil spirits) who wish to attack, influence, or breach Your me'sucha chasut (hedge of protection) in any way. Send them immediately and quietly back to Hell and fortify Your Hedge for my protection by the blood of Your Son, Yah'shua (Jesus). Send your mal'akiym kadoshiym (Holy Angels) to watch over me and protect me.

Father, all of these things I ask in the most Shem Kadosh (holy name) of Yah'shua the Messiah (Jesus Christ), Your Son. Thank you, Father, for hearing my prayer. I love You, I worship You, I thank You and I trust in You. Amen.

HEDGE PRAYER FOR PROTECTION OF OTHERS

Trusting in the promise that whatever we ask the Father in Yah'shua's (Jesus') name He will do, I now approach You Father with confidence in Our Lord's words and in Your infinite power and love for me and for [person's name] , and with the intercession of the Blessed Sar-Mal'ak Miyka'el (Archangel Michael), my mal'ak apotropos (guardian angel) and the mal'ak apotropos (guardian angel) of [person's name], with all the kadoshiym (saints) and mal'akiym (angels) of heaven, and Holy in the power of His blessed Name, as ask you Father to protect [person's name] and keep him/her from the harassment of the devil and his minions.

Father I ask on behalf of [person's name] that You build a me'sucha chasut (hedge of protection) around him/her, like that which surrounded Job, and to help [person's name] to keep that hedge repaired and the gate locked so that the devil and his minions have no access or means to breach the hedge except by your expressed will. I specifically ask for protection for [person's name] for _____.

Father, I know that we are powerless against the spiritual forces of evil and recognize our utter dependence on You and Your power. Look with mercy upon [person's name]. Do not look upon his/her sins, O YAHUWAH; rather, look at the sufferings of your Beloved Son and see the Victim whose bitter passion and death has reconciled us to You. By the victory of the cross, protect [person's name] from all evil and rebuke any ruchot ra'ah (evil spirits) who wish to attack, influence, or breach Your me'sucha chasut (hedge of protection) in any way. Send them immediately and quietly back to Hell and fortify Your Hedge for his/her protection by the blood of Your Son, Yah'shua (Jesus). Send your Holy Angels to watch over and protect him/her.

Father, all of these things I ask in the most Shem Kadosh (holy name) of Yah'shua the Messiah (Jesus Christ), Your Son. Thank you, Father, for hearing my prayer. I love You, I worship You, I thank You and I trust in You. Amen.

REBUKING PARTICULAR SPIRITS AFFECTING THE HOUSEHOLD

It is important to rebuke ruchot pigu'at (attacking spirits) each and every time they attack. So if one is attacked fifty times a day one must rebuke the spirit fifty time each and every time it attacks. The long prayer below may be said in the morning and evening for example, but it not practical when rebuking a ruach ra'ah (evil spirit) many times throughout the day. Thus, the smaller prayer may be said. In situation when saying the prayer cannot be out loud, then say it under your breath or in your mind, but do say it each time you are attacked. Here is the smaller prayer:

> "By my authority as head of this household, I (we) rebuke you spirit(s) of ____. Father in heaven please remove this spirit from our household and family never to return, and instead give our household and family a spirit of _(the opposite spirit*)_."

*Example: The opposite of fear may be peace, the opposite of lust is purity, the opposite of depression may be joy, etc. Whatever you feel is the opposite of the spirit that is attacking.

HERE IS THE LONGER PRAYER:

In the name of the Lord Yah'shua the Messiah (Jesus Christ), strengthened by the intercession of Blessed Miyka'el Sar-Mal'ak (Michael the Archangel), of the Blessed Shaliyachiym

(Apostles) and all the Kadoshiym (Saints) and Mal'akiym (Angels) of Heaven, and powerful in the holy authority of His name, (and by my authority as head of this household) I (we) ask of the heavenly Father YAHUWAH to rebuke this spirit of _____ and to command it in the name of the Lord Yah'shua the Messiah (Jesus Christ) to depart from (me, family member) and from this household, immediately, quietly, and without harm to anyone never to return.

I (we) bring the power and the protection of the blood of our Lord Yah'shua the Messiah (Jesus Christ) over this household, (*and over particular family member*). Satan has no part in this household or with any member of my (our) family. This family and household is sealed with the saving blood of the Lord Yah'shua the Messiah (Jesus Christ).

Heavenly Father, forgive me (us) and my (our) family for not being all we should be in Your eyes. Let the cleansing, healing waters of our tevilah (baptism) wash over me (us) and this household, and cleanse us from all avel (unrighteousness).

Lord Yah'shua the Messiah (Jesus Christ), fill me (us) (*and a particular family member*) with Your (*attribute opposite to that of the spirit being rebuked*) to replace the (*attribute of the spirit being rebuked*). [*e.g. the spirit of peace to replace the spirit of anxiety; spirit of purity to replace the spirit of lust; etc*]

Lord Yah'shua (Jesus), bring to bear all the mal'akiym apotropos (guardian angels) of this family, and all the mal'akiym hashamayim (angels of heaven), against the forces of evil that seek to cause trouble for me (us) and my (our) household.

Kadosh Miyka'el (Saint Michael), be our protection against the wickedness and snares of the devil.

Thank You, Heavenly Father, for setting us free. We praise You, we bless You, we worship You. Thank You for the wisdom and light of the Ruach HaKodesh (Holy Spirit).

Thank You for enabling me (us) (and/or "me" as head of the household) to be aggressive against the works of the enemy. Thank You for Your hope, that takes away discouragement; thank You for ongoing victory. "...in all these things we are more than conquerors through Him who loved us" (Rom. 8:37). Amen.

RESISTING SATAN'S ATTACK AGAINST OUR HOUSEHOLD

In the name of the Lord Yah'shua the Messiah (Jesus Christ), strengthened by the intercession of the Blessed Miyka'el Sar-Ma'lak (Michael the Archangel), of the Blessed Shaliyachiym (Apostles), and all the Kadoshiym (Saints) and Mal'akiym HaShamayim (Angels of Heaven), and powerful in the holy authority of His name (and by my authority as head of the household), I (we) come before You Heavenly Father to ask you to come against the ko'ach choshek (powers of darkness) causing (name whatever symptom). Come against these powers, O YAHUWAH, because of the power of my (our) union with the Lord Yah'shua the Messiah (Jesus Christ). According to Your Word, O YAHUWAH, and through His precious blood I (we) resist the devil and his minions.

I (we) resist the devil and all of his workers by the Person and power of the Lord Yah'shua the Messiah (Jesus Christ). I (we) submit (and submit this household) to the Lordship and control of the Lord Yah'shua (Jesus), and I (we) ask you Father to bring the power of my (our) Lord's incarnation, His crucifixion, His resurrection, His ascension, His glorification, and His second coming directly to focus against all evil forces and all of the evil work against _____. (By the authority of my position as head of the household), I (we) claim my (our) union with the Lord Yah'shua the Messiah (Jesus Christ), and I (we) resist the devil; I (we) resist the devil and all his minions, and I (we) ask You heavenly Father to force these hara'iym (evil ones) to flee from before the truth of Elohim (God).

Further, O YAHUWAH, I (we) ask You to bind together the whole kingdom of the Hara (evil one) and to bind them from working, and finally to command all evil forces and their kingdom to leave _____ and to go immediately and quietly wherever the Lord Yah'shua the Messiah (Jesus Christ) may send them. Amen.

BREAKING PERSONAL CURSES AND SPELLS

In the name of the Lord Yah'shua the Messiah (Jesus Christ), strengthened by the intercession of the Blessed Miyka'el Sar-Mal'ak (Michael the Archangel), of the Blessed Shaliyachiym (Apostles), and all the Kadoshiym (Saints), and powerful in the holy authority of His Precious and Wondrous Name, I ask, O YAHUWAH Elohim (Lord God), that you break and dissolve any and all kalalot (curses), kishuf'iym (hexes), kesim'iym (spells), chatom'iym (seals), satani nederiym (satanic vows) and heskem'iym (pacts), ruchani kesher (spiritual bondings) and nephesh kesher (soul ties) with satani chayil'iym (satanic forces), ma'avayim hara (evil wishes), ta'ava hara (evil desires), torashti chatom'iym (hereditary seals), malkoldet (snares, traps), sheker (lies), michshol (obstacles), sibun (deceptions), hasacha (diversions), ruchani hashpa'a (spiritual influences), and every tikfud lakui (dysfunction) and mechala (disease) from any source whatsoever, that have been placed upon me.

Father in Heaven, please rebuke these ruchot ra'ah (evil spirits) and their effects and cast them away from me so that I may continue to do Your Will and fulfill the mission you have for me to Your Greater Glory.

Thank you, Father, for hearing my prayer. I praise Your Shem Kadosh (Holy Name) and worship You and Love You. Thank You for the wisdom and light of Your Ruach HaKodesh (Holy Spirit). Thank You for enabling me through Your Ruach HaKodesh (Holy Spirit) to be aggressive against the works of the oyev (enemy). Thank You for Your Hope, that takes away discouragement; thank You for ongoing victory. "...in all these things we are more than conquerors through Him who loved us" (Rom. 8:37).

Father, I now place my oyeviym (enemies) into your hands. Look with mercy upon them, and do not hold their sins against them. Anyone who has cursed me, I now bless. Anyone who has hurt me, I now forgive. For those who have persecuted me, I now pray

Avinu (Our Father), Who is in heaven, hallowed be Your Name. Your Kingdom come. Your will be done, on earth as it is in heaven. Give us this day our daily bread; and forgive us our trespasses, as we forgive those who trespass against us; and lead us not into temptation, but deliver us from the Hara (evil one). For Yours is the kingdom, and the power, and the glory, for ever. Amen.

Glory to the Father YAHUWAH, and to the Son Yah'shua (Jesus), and to the Ruach HaKodesh (Holy Spirit), now and ever, and unto ages of ages. Amen.

O Yah'shua (Jesus), forgive us our sins and save us from the fires of Hell. Lead all souls to Heaven, and help especially those who are most in need of Your Mercy.

Kadosh Miyka'el Sar-Mal'ak (Holy Michael the Archangel), defend us in battle. Be our protection against the wickedness and snares of the devil. May Elohim (God) rebuke him, we humbly pray; and do You, O prince of the heavenly hosts, by the power of Elohim (God), thrust into hell Satan and all the other ruchot ra'ah (evil spirits) who prowl through the world seeking the ruin of souls. Amen and Amen.

PRAYER TO BREAK ADDICTIONS

Dear Heavenly Father. You have told us in Your Word that those who set their minds on things of the flesh cannot please Elohim (God), are hostile to Elohim (God), and leads to death (Ro. 8:5-8). I acknowledge that my mind has been set on things of the flesh, in the form of addiction to _____, _____, _____ *[drugs, alcohol, tobacco, food, gossip, judgmentalism, sex, etc.]* that wage war against my soul (1 Pet. 2:11). I have transgressed Your holy torah (law) and given the enemy an opportunity to wage war in my members (Eph. 4:27; Ja. 4:1; 1 Pet. 5:8). Indeed You have said that it is better to cut out our eye if it makes us stumble than to burn in hell (Matt. 5:29-30).

I come before Your presence to acknowledge these sins and to seek Your cleansing (1 Jn. 1:9) that I may be freed from the bondage of sin (Gal. 5:1). I thank You that in Messiah (Christ) my sins are forgiven. I now ask You to reveal to my mind the ways that I have brought myself to this addiction and therefore grieved the Ruach HaKodesh (Holy Spirit). So that I may find healing and freedom I ask You YAHUWAH that all ground gained by ruchot ra'ah (evil spirits) because of my addictions be canceled and taken back and that all bonds and bondages the devil has placed upon me be broken forever (Gal. 5:1). I pray that You will shed light on all my ways that I may know the full extent of my addiction. I claim my body and mind for the Lord Yah'shua the Messiah (Jesus Christ), and in His Name, and with His authority, declare freedom from my addictions of _____, _____, _____ and to all attachments, bondages, and involvements with the enemies of the Lord Yah'shua the Messiah (Jesus Christ). By faith and by the Sacraments of the Church I have received You into my life and am now seated with Messiah (Christ) in the heavenlies (Eph.

2:6). I now choose to adopt a ruach chofesh (spirit of freedom) from addictions and a heart given over to You. In the name of Messiah Yah'shua (Christ Jesus) I pray. Amen.

PRAYER FOR OUR CHILDREN

We bow humbly before You, heavenly Father, to pray for our children, [names of children], and for our whole family. We bring our children and our family before You in the name of the Lord Yah'shua the Messiah (Jesus Christ).

We thank You, YAHUWAH, that You love [names of children] and our entire family with the love of Calvary. We thank You that You have given [names of children] to us to love and nurture in Messiah (Christ).

We ask You to forgive us together as parents, and each of us alone in our roles as father and mother, for all our failures to guide our children in the way they ought to go. Help us YAHUWAH to be the parents You want us to be; that we may train [names of children] in Your ways, that we may model the Christ-life before them, so that when they grow-up they will love You and live for You.

Accepting our position through You of having "divine power to demolish strongholds" (2 Cor. 10:4) that come into our family, we ask You Father to bring all the work of the Lord Yah'shua (Jesus), strengthened by the intercession of the Blessed Miyka'el Sar-Mal'ak (Michael the Archangel), of the Blessed Shaliyachiym (Apostles), and all the Kadoshiym (Saints) and Mal'akiym (Angels) of Heaven, and powerful in the holy authority of His Name, to focus directly against the powers of darkness that do now or may later bother, influence, and bind [names of children] and our family in any way; and specifically against (name specific areas of troubles or problems).

We pray that You shall bring the victory of our Lord's incarnation, crucifixion, resurrection, ascension, and glorification directly against all of Satan's power brought against us in our family and specifically in the lives of [names of children] . We ask You heavenly Father to bind up all power of darkness set to destroy [names of children], or our family, and we loose [names of children], and this family from the influence and harassment of Satan and his Shediym (demons), in the name of the Lord Yah'shua the Messiah (Jesus Christ).

We invite the blessed Ruach HaKodesh (Holy Spirit) to move in the hearts of [names of children] that they may know the truth as they are able at their age. We invite the blessed Ruach HaKodesh (Holy Spirit) to move in our hearts and to convict us of sin, of righteousness, and of our responsibility as parents to raise [names of children] in Your name.

We plead the blood of Messiah (Christ) over [names of children] and this family. We claim for us a life yielded to serve the true and Elohim Chayim (living God) in the name of the Lord Yah'shua the Messiah (Jesus Christ). Amen.

TYPES OF BERACHOT

(Types of Blessings)

"I will bless YAHUWAH at all times;
his praise shall continually be in my mouth."
(Psalm 34:2)

A BLESSING (berakha, pl. berachot) is meant to help us become more aware of the all-encompassing Presence of Elohim (God) in our lives.

1. By pausing,

2. By reflecting,

3. By practicing kavanah (intention)

4. and finding gratitude

When we take the time to focus our minds and recite a blessing in response to a life event (no matter how seemingly insignificant), we transform the knee-jerk habits of our mundane experience to moments of profound sanctity. We translate the profane moments to those of the sacred. We come to see and understand that life is a gift to us.

Moreover, reciting blessings is a way of practicing the simple virtue of gratitude. If you want pleasure in this life, you must learn to focus on the good.

Engaging the mind with the awareness that Elohim (God) is the Source of all that is good is a means, then, of increasing your joy in this life.

In early Jewish history, the berachot were not standardized. However, after the Babylonian conquest, the Men of the Great Assembly (Anshei Knesset

HaGedolah) codified the berachot in order to help unify the Jewish experience. In the Jewish tradition it is generally considered bad form to spontaneously compose your own berakha.

The Anshei Knesset HaGedolah (Men of the Great Assembly) identified three general types of berachot:

1. **Birkhot hanehenim** - Recited before enjoying a material pleasure (such as eating, drinking, smelling something pleasant, etc.) For example, "Blessed are You, YAHUWAH our Elohim (God), King of the universe, Who brings forth bread from the earth," recited when partaking of bread.

2. **Birkhot ha-mitzvot** - Recited in gratitude for the privilege of being given a commandment (mitzvah) to perform (for example, "Blessed are You, YAHUWAH our Elohim (God), King of the universe, Who has sanctified us with His commandments, and has commanded us to hear the sound of the Shofar").

3. **Birkhot hoda'ah** - Blessings of praise and gratitude, usually recited at special times and events.

As followers of Yah'shua the Messiah, blessed be He, we are not constrained to follow rabbinic halakhah (rules), but rather Apostolic Halakhah as set forth by the Apostles in the Brit Chadasha (New Testament). We are free to spontaneously offer up praise and thanks to YAHUWAH for all things, regardless of time or place. And such will be our practice if we are living in genuine emunah (faithfulness) before YAHUWAH, for we will be given the Ruach Hakodesh (Holy Spirit) with "joy unspeakable and full of glory" as we dwell within His Presence.

The Jewish tradition has a lot to teach most Christians about gratitude. How many times have you consciously thanked YAHUWAH for all His kindness given to you this day?

Apostolic tradition and teaching requires that we personally bless YAHUWAH for each detail of our daily experience. Such a requirement "if not practiced legalistically" surely points to a deep inward appreciation for the good things Elohim (God) personally provides for us throughout each day. These sample blessings vocalize our gratitude to Elohim (God) for His daily provision and care:

"In all things give thanks, this thing indeed is the will of Elohim (God) in Yah'shua the Messiah (Jesus Christ) for you." (1 Thess. 5:18)

"And obscenity, and foolish talk, or coarse joking, which are not proper, but rather thanksgiving." (Eph. 5:4)

"Through him, therefore, let us offer the sacrifice of praise through all things to Elohim (God), that thing is the fruit of our lips confessing his name." (Heb. 13:15)

"Otherwise, when you bless with the spirit, those filling the place that do not understand, how will they say 'Amen' at your giving of thanks? .... For truly you rightly give thanks, but the others are not edified." (1 Co. 14:16-17)

"And do not be drunk with wine where in is dissipation, but be filled with the Spirit, speaking to yourselves with psalms, and hymns, and songs that are spiritual, singing and praising in your hearts to the YAHUWAH, giving thanks always for all things in the name of our LORD Yah'shua the Messiah (Jesus Christ) to God and the Father." (Eph. 5:18-20)

"Giving thanks to the Father that has qualified us for the partaking of the inheritance of the saints in light, who delivered us from the authority of darkness, and has transferred us into the kingdom of the Son of his love, in whom we have redemption, the forgiveness of sins." (Col. 1:12-14)

"Let the word of Messiah (Christ) dwell in you richly in all wisdom, teaching and admonishing one another in psalms, hymns, spiritual songs, with grace singing in your hearts to Elohim (God). And everything whatsoever you do in word or in deed, do all in the name of the LORD Yah'shua (Jesus), giving thanks to God the Father through him." (Col 3:16-17)

"Because every creature of God is good and nothing to be rejected if it is received with thanksgiving. For it is sanctified by the word of Elohim (God) and intercession." (1 Tim. 4:4-5)

The traditional blessing set forth by the the Men of the Great Assembly (Anshei Knesset HaGedolah) is "Blessed are you, YAHUWAH our Elohim (God), king of the universe.....," but the Apostles did the blessings through Yah'shua the Messiah (Jesus Christ). We have three examples in the Brit Chadasha (New Testament) given by the Apostles, 2 Corinthians 1:3, Ephesians 1:3, and 1 Peter 1:3, which is "Blessed be the God and the Father of our Lord Yah'shua the Messiah.........." Therefore, we see three ways to render the blessings, 1) the traditional Judaic way, 2) the Messianic or Apostolic way, 3) mixing the two together.

1. Berakah (gk. Eulogetos) - Bless (plural: Berachot)

2. Todah (gk. Eucharist) - Thanksgiving (plural: Todat)

3. Tehillah (gk. Epainos) - Praise (plural: Tehillim)

4. Tefillah (gk. Prosueche) - Prayer (plural: Tefillat)

GRACE BEFORE MEALS

Berikat Netilat Yedaliym
(Blessing for Washing the Hands)

On washing the hands, previous to partaking of a Meal, say:—

Blessed be YAHUWAH our Elohim (God), Melek Ha'Olam (King of the universe), the God and the Father of our Lord Yah'shua the Messiah (Jesus Christ), who has sanctified us by Your commandments, and has given us command concerning the washing of the hands.

The following Blessing is said over the Bread:—

Blessed be YAHUWAH our Elohim (God), Melek Ha'Olam (King of the universe), the God and the Father of our Lord Yah'shua the Messiah (Jesus Christ), who brings forth bread from the earth.

The Grace

Hear, O Israel; YAHUWAH our Elohim (God), YAHUWAH is one: And You will love YAHUWAH Your Elohim (God) with all Your heart, and with all Your soul, and with all Your mind, and with all Your strength: this is the first mitzvah (commandment). And the second is like it, You will love Your neighbour as yourself. There is no other mitzvah (commandment) greater than these. (Mark 12:29-31)

Now the Spirit expressly says that in latter times some will depart from the faith, giving heed to ruchot me'rame (deceiving spirits) and torah Ha'shediym (doctrines of demons), speaking lies in hypocrisy, having their own conscience seared with a hot iron, forbidding to marry, and commanding to abstain from foods which Elohim (God) created to be received with thanksgiving by those who believe and know the truth. For every creature of Elohim (God) is good, and nothing is to be refused if it is received with thanksgiving; for it is sanctified by the word of Elohim (God) and prayer. If you instruct the brethren in these things, you will be a good minister of Yah'shua the Messiah (Jesus Christ), nourished in the words of faith and of the good doctrine which you have carefully followed. (1 Timothy 4:1-6)

Blessed be YAHUWAH our Elohim (God), Melek Ha'Olam (King of the universe), the God and the Father of our Lord Yah'shua the Messiah (Jesus Christ), who gives food to all flesh, and nourishes every creature, for His mercy endures for ever. Amen

Blessed be YAHUWAH our Elohim (God), Melek Ha'Olam (King of the universe), the God and the Father of our Lord Yah'shua the Messiah (Jesus Christ), who has made all things clean. Amen.

The poor shall eat and be satisfied, and those who seek YAHUWAH shall praise Him; their hearts shall live forever. Amen.

Bless us, YAHUWAH, and these Your gifts which we are about to receive from Your bounty. Through Yah'shua the Messiah (Jesus Christ) our Lord. Amen.

O YAHUWAH our Elohim (God), bless the food and drink of Your servants, for You are holy, always, now and forever, and unto the ages of ages. Amen.

Blessed are you, O Merciful One, Provider of this food. Amen.

May the Merciful One send abundant blessing upon this dwelling and the table at which we are about to eat. Amen.

GRACE AFTER MEALS

On Weekdays

Blessed be YAHUWAH our Elohim (God), Melek Ha'Olam (King of the universe), the God and the Father of our Lord Yah'shua the Messiah (Jesus Christ), for these benefits which we have received from His bounty. We thank You, YAHUWAH our Elohim (God), for You have satisfied us with Your earthly gifts.

We thank you YAHUWAH, who has had mercy on us and fed us from His rich gifts, through His Grace and love for mankind, You, YAHUWAH, have made us glad by Your works; in the works of Your hands shall we rejoice. Lift up the Light of Your countenance upon us, YAHUWAH! You have put joy in my heart. With the fruit of wheat, wine and oil have we been satisfied. In peace I will both lie down and sleep; for You alone make me to dwell in hope.

Blessed be YAHUWAH our Elohim (God), Melek Ha'Olam (King of the universe), the God and the Father of our Lord Yah'shua the Messiah (Jesus Christ), who in mercy feeds all people and fills every soul with good things. Amen.

On Shabbat (Sabbath)

On Sabbaths and Holy days, and on those days when Tachanun is not said, Psalm 126 is said:—

Psalm 126

1 A Song of Ascents. When YAHUWAH brought back the captivity of Zion, we were like those who dream. 2 Then our mouth was filled with laughter, and our tongue with singing.

Then they said among the goyim (nations, gentiles), "YAHUWAH has done great things for them." 3 YAHUWAH has done great things for us, and we are glad. 4 Bring back our captivity, YAHUWAH, as the streams in the South. 5 Those who sow in tears shall reap in joy. 6 He who continually goes forth weeping, bearing seed for sowing, shall doubtless come again with rejoicing, bringing his sheaves with him.

The following Introduction is customary if three or more Males, above the age of thirteen, have eaten at table together:

He who says Grace commences thus:—

Let us say grace.

The others respond:—

Blessed be the name of YAHUWAH from this time forth and for ever.

He who says Grace proceeds:—

With the sanction of those present,

If there be present ten or more Males above the age of thirteen, the words "our God" are added:—

We will bless YAHUWAH (our God) of whose bounty we have partaken.

The others respond:—

Blessed be YAHUWAH (our God), he of whose bounty we have partaken, and through whose goodness we live.

Persons present who have not partaken of the Meal, say the following:—

Blessed be his name, yes, continually to be blessed for ever and ever.

He who says Grace replies:—

Blessed be YAHUWAH of whose bounty we have partaken, and through whose goodness we live. Blessed be he, and blessed be his name.

If less than three Males above the age of thirteen be present, begin here:—

Blessed be YAHUWAH our Elohim (God), Melek Ha'Olam (King of the universe), the God and the Father of our Lord Yah'shua the Messiah (Jesus Christ), who feeds the whole world with Your goodness, with grace, with lovingkindness and tender mercy; You give food to all flesh, for Your lovingkindness endures for ever. Through Your great goodness food has never failed us: O may it not fail us for ever and ever for Your great name's sake, since You nourish and sustain all beings and do good unto all, and provide food for all Your creatures whom You have created. Blessed are You, YAHUWAH, who gives food unto all.

We thank You, YAHUWAH our Elohim (God), because You did give as an heritage unto our fathers a desirable, good and ample land, and because You did bring us forth, YAHUWAH our Elohim (God), from the land of Egypt (the land of bondage), and did deliver us from the house of bondage; as well as for Your covenant which You have sealed in our flesh, Your Torah (Law) which You have taught us, Your chukot (statutes) which You have made known unto us, the life, grace and lovingkindness which You have vouchsafed unto us, and for the food wherewith You do constantly feed and sustain us on every day, in every season, at every hour.

On Chanukah and Purim add, "We thank thee also for the miracles," etc.,

For all this, YAHUWAH our Elohim (God), we thank and bless You, blessed be Your name by the mouth of all living continually and for ever, even as it is written, And you shall eat and be satisfied, and you shall bless YAHUWAH Your Elohim (God) for the good land which he has given You. Blessed are You, YAHUWAH, for the land and for the food.

Have mercy, YAHUWAH our Elohim (God), upon Israel Your people, upon Jerusalem Your city, upon Zion the abiding place of Your glory, upon the kingdom of the house of David Your anointed, and upon the great and holy house that was called by Your name. O our Elohim (God), our Father, feed us, nourish us, sustain, support and relieve us, and speedily YAHUWAH our Elohim (God), grant us relief from all our troubles. We beseech You, YAHUWAH our Elohim (God), let us not be in need either of the gifts of flesh and blood or of their loans, but only of Your helping hand, which is full, open, holy and ample, so that we may not be ashamed nor confounded for ever and ever.

On Sabbath say:—

Be pleased, YAHUWAH our Elohim (God), to fortify us by Your mitzvot (commandments), and especially by the mitzvah (commandment) of the seventh day, this great and holy Shabbat (Sabbath), since this day is great and holy before You, that we may rest and repose thereon in love in accordance with the precept of Your will. In Your favor, YAHUWAH our Elohim (God), grant us such repose that there be no trouble, grief or lamenting on the day of our rest. Let us, YAHUWAH our Elohim (God), behold the consolation of Zion Your city, and the rebuilding of Jerusalem Your holy city, for You are the LORD of salvation and of consolation.

On New Moons and Festivals add:—

Our God and God of our fathers! May our remembrance rise and come and be accepted before You, with the remembrance of our fathers, of Messiah the son of David Your servant, of Jerusalem Your holy city, and of all Your people the house of Israel, bringing deliverance and well-being, grace, lovingkindness and mercy, life and Shalom (peace) on this day of

On new Moon say—

The New Moon.

On New Year—

Memorial.

On Tabernacles—

The Feast of Tabernacles.

On Shemini Atseret (the Eighth Day of Solemn Assembly) and on the Simchat Torah (Rejoicing of the Law)—

The Eighth Day Feast of Solemn Assembly.

On Passover.—

The Feast of Unleavened Bread.

On Pentecost—

The Feast of Weeks.

Remember us, YAHUWAH our Elohim (God), thereon for our wellbeing; be mindful of us for blessing, and save us unto life: by Your promise of salvation and mercy, spare us and be gracious unto us; have mercy upon us and save us; for our eyes are bent upon You, because You are a gracious and merciful God and King.

And rebuild Jerusalem the holy city speedily in our days. Blessed are You, YAHUWAH, who in Your compassion rebuilds Jerusalem. Amen.

Blessed are You, YAHUWAH our Elohim (God), King of the universe, the God and the Father of our LORD Yah'shua the Messiah (Jesus Christ), O God, our Father, our King, our Mighty One, our Creator, our Redeemer, our Maker, our Holy One, the Holy One of Jacob, our Shepherd, the Shepherd of Israel, O King, who are kind and deals kindly with all, day by day You have dealt kindly, do deal kindly, and will deal kindly with us: You have bestowed, You do bestow, You will ever bestow benefits upon us, yielding us grace, lovingkindness, mercy and relief, health, deliverance and prosperity, blessing and salvation, consolation, sustenance and supports mercy, life, peace and all good: of no manner of good let us be in want.

The All-merciful shall reign over us for ever and ever. The All-merciful shall be blessed in heaven and on earth. The All-merciful shall be praised throughout all generations, glorified among us to all eternity, and honored among us for everlasting. May the All-merciful grant us an honorable livelihood. May the All-merciful break the yoke from off our neck, and lead us upright to our land. May the All-merciful send a plentiful blessing upon this house, and upon this table at which we have eaten. The All-merciful has sent us Elijah the prophet (let him be remembered for good), who has given us good tidings, salvation and consolation.

The following has to be varied according to circumstances:—

May the All-merciful bless my honored father, the master of this house, and my honored mother, the mistress of this house, them, their household, their seed and all that is theirs, us also and all that is ours, as our fathers Abraham, Isaac and Jacob were blessed each with his own comprehensive blessing; even thus may he bless all of us together with a perfect blessing, and let us say Amen.

Both on their and on our behalf may there be such advocacy on high as shall lead to enduring peace; and may we receive a blessing from YAHUWAH, and righteousness from the God of our salvation; and may we find grace and good understanding in the sight of God and man.

On Sabbath:—

May the All-merciful let us inherit the day which shall be wholly a Sabbath and rest in the life everlasting.

On New Moon:—

May the All-merciful renew unto us this month for good and for blessing.

On Festivals:—

May the All-merciful let us inherit the day which is altogether good.

On New Year:—

May the All-merciful renew unto us this year for good and for blessing.

On the Intermediate Days of Tabernacles:—

May the All-merciful allow us to honor him with our bodies, which are the Temple of the Ruach HaKodesh (Holy Spirit).

May the All-merciful make us worthy of Yah'shua the Messiah (Jesus Christ), and of the life of the world to come.

On Week-days:—

Great salvation gives he to his king.

On Sabbaths, Festivals, and New Moons:—

He is a tower of salvation to his king;

And shows lovingkindness to his anointed, to David and to his seed, for evermore. He who makes peace in his high places, may he make peace for us and for all Israel, and say, Amen.

O fear YAHUWAH, you his holy ones; for there is no want to them that fear him. Young lions do lack and suffer hunger: but they that seek YAHUWAH shall not want any good. O give thanks unto YAHUWAH, for he is good: for his lovingkindness endures for ever. You open Your hand, and satisfy every living thing with favor. Blessed is the man that trusts in YAHUWAH, and whose trust YAHUWAH is. I have been young and now I am old; yet have I not seen. the righteous forsaken, nor his seed begging for bread. YAHUWAH will give strength unto his people; YAHUWAH will bless his people with peace.

BLESSINGS ON VARIOUS OCCASIONS

BLESSING OVER WINE

Blessed be YAHUWAH our Elohim (God), Melek Ha'Olam (King of the universe), the God and the Father of our Lord Yah'shua the Messiah (Jesus Christ), who creates the fruit of the vine.

Blessing before partaking of Food, other than Bread, prepared from any of "the five species of Grain" (wheat, barley, rye, oats and spelt)

Blessed be YAHUWAH our Elohim (God), Melek Ha'Olam (King of the universe), the God and the Father of our Lord Yah'shua the Messiah (Jesus Christ), who creates various kinds of food.

Blessing after Wine

Blessed be YAHUWAH our Elohim (God), Melek Ha'Olam (King of the universe), the God and the Father of our Lord Yah'shua the Messiah (Jesus Christ), for the vine and the fruit of the vine;

Blessing after partaking of Grapes, Figs, Pomegranates, Olives or Dates

Blessed be YAHUWAH our Elohim (God), Melek Ha'Olam (King of the universe), the God and the Father of our Lord

Yah'shua the Messiah (Jesus Christ), for the tree and the fruit of the tree;

Blessing after Food prepared as above

Blessed be YAHUWAH our Elohim (God), Melek Ha'Olam (King of the universe), the God and the Father of our Lord Yah'shua the Messiah (Jesus Christ), for the sustenance and the nourishment;

After Food prepared as above and Wine

Blessed be YAHUWAH our Elohim (God), Melek Ha'Olam (King of the universe), the God and the Father of our Lord Yah'shua the Messiah (Jesus Christ), for the sustenance and the nourishment, the vine and the fruit of the vine;

Blessed be YAHUWAH our Elohim (God), Melek Ha'Olam (King of the universe), the God and the Father of our Lord Yah'shua the Messiah (Jesus Christ), for the produce of the field; for the desirable, good and ample land which You was pleased to give as a heritage unto our fathers, that they might eat of its fruits and be satisfied with its goodness. Have mercy, YAHUWAH our Elohim (God), upon Israel Your people, upon Jerusalem Your city, upon Zion the abiding place of Your glory, upon Your altar and Your temple. Rebuild Jerusalem, the holy city, speedily in our days; lead us up there and make us rejoice in its rebuilding. May we eat of the fruits of the land, and be satisfied with its goodness, and bless You for it in holiness and purity.

On Sabbath say:—

Be pleased to fortify us on this Sabbath day.

On New Moon:—

Be mindful of us on this day of the New Moon.

On Festivals:—

Make us rejoice

On Passover:—

On this Feast of Unleavened Bread.

On Pentecost:—

On this Feast of Weeks.

On Tabernacles:—

On this Feast of Tabernacles.

On the Eighth Day of Solemn Assembly and on the Rejoicing of the Law:—

On this Eighth-day Feast of Solemn Assembly.

On New Year:—

Be mindful of us for good on this Day of Memorial. For You, YAHUWAH, are good and beneficent unto all; and we will give You thanks for the land,

After Wine:—

—and for the fruit of the vine. Blessed are You, YAHUWAH, for the land and for the fruit of the vine.

After Fruit:—

—and for the fruits. Blessed are You, YAHUWAH, for the land and for the fruits.

After Food prepared from any of "the five species of Grain":—

—and for the sustenance. Blessed are You, YAHUWAH, for the land and for the sustenance.

After Food prepared as above and Wine:—

—for the sustenance and for the fruit of the vine. Blessed are You, YAHUWAH, for the land, the sustenance and the fruit of the vine.

If Wine and Fruit are partaken of at the same time, begin the Blessing thus:—

—for the vine and the fruit of the vine, the tree and the fruit of the tree.

and conclude:—

—for the land, the vine and the fruits. Blessed are You, YAHUWAH, for the land, the vine and the fruits.

If Food prepared from any of "the five species of Grain," and Fruit are partaken of at the same time, begin:—

—for the sustenance and the nourishment, the tree and the fruit of the tree.

and conclude:—

—for the land, the sustenance and the fruits. Blessed are You, YAHUWAH, for the land, the sustenance and the fruits.

If Food prepared from any of "the five species of Grain," Fruit and Wine are partaken of at the same time, begin:—

—for the sustenance and the nourishment, for the vine and the fruit of the vine, for the tree and the fruit of the tree.

And conclude:—

Blessed are You, YAHUWAH, for the sustenance and the nourishment, for the vine and the fruit of the vine, for the tree and the fruit of the tree.

OTHER BLESSINGS:

On eating Fruit which grows on trees

Blessed be YAHUWAH our Elohim (God), Melek Ha'Olam (King of the universe), the God and the Father of our Lord Yah'shua the Messiah (Jesus Christ), who creates the fruit of the tree.

On eating Fruit which grows on the Ground, Herbage, etc.

Blessed be YAHUWAH our Elohim (God), Melek Ha'Olam (King of the universe), the God and the Father of our Lord Yah'shua the Messiah (Jesus Christ), who creates the fruit of the earth.

On partaking of Flesh, Fish, Eggs, Cheese, etc., or drinking any Liquor except Wine

Blessed be YAHUWAH our Elohim (God), Melek Ha'Olam (King of the universe), the God and the Father of our Lord Yah'shua the Messiah (Jesus Christ), by whose word all things exist.

After partaking of any of the Aliments referred to in the three preceding Blessings

Blessed be YAHUWAH our Elohim (God), Melek Ha'Olam (King of the universe), the God and the Father of our Lord Yah'shua the Messiah (Jesus Christ), who creates many living beings with their wants, for all the means You have created wherewith to sustain the life of each of them. Blessed be he who is the life of all worlds.

On smelling Fragrant Woods or Barks

Blessed be YAHUWAH our Elohim (God), Melek Ha'Olam (King of the universe), the God and the Father of our Lord Yah'shua the Messiah (Jesus Christ), who creates fragrant woods.

On smelling Odorous Plants

Blessed be YAHUWAH our Elohim (God), Melek Ha'Olam (King of the universe), the God and the Father of our Lord Yah'shua the Messiah (Jesus Christ), who creates odorous plants.

On smelling Odorous Fruits

Blessed be YAHUWAH our Elohim (God), Melek Ha'Olam (King of the universe), the God and the Father of our Lord

Yah'shua the Messiah (Jesus Christ), who gives a goodly scent to fruits.

On smelling Fragrant Spices

Blessed be YAHUWAH our Elohim (God), Melek Ha'Olam (King of the universe), the God and the Father of our Lord Yah'shua the Messiah (Jesus Christ), who creates divers kinds of spices.

On smelling Fragrant Oils

Blessed be YAHUWAH our Elohim (God), Melek Ha'Olam (King of the universe), the God and the Father of our Lord Yah'shua the Messiah (Jesus Christ), who creates fragrant oil.

On witnessing Lightning, or on seeing Falling Stars, Lofty Mountains, or Great Deserts

Blessed be YAHUWAH our Elohim (God), Melek Ha'Olam (King of the universe), the God and the Father of our Lord Yah'shua the Messiah (Jesus Christ), who has made the creation.

On hearing Thunder

Blessed be YAHUWAH our Elohim (God), Melek Ha'Olam (King of the universe), the God and the Father of our Lord Yah'shua the Messiah (Jesus Christ), whose strength and might fill the world.

At the sight of the Sea

Blessed be YAHUWAH our Elohim (God), Melek Ha'Olam (King of the universe), the God and the Father of our Lord Yah'shua the Messiah (Jesus Christ), who has made the great sea.

On seeing beautiful Trees or Animals

Blessed be YAHUWAH our Elohim (God), Melek Ha'Olam (King of the universe), the God and the Father of our Lord Yah'shua the Messiah (Jesus Christ), who has such as these in Your world.

On seeing the Rainbow

Blessed be YAHUWAH our Elohim (God), Melek Ha'Olam (King of the universe), the God and the Father of our Lord Yah'shua the Messiah (Jesus Christ), who remembers the covenant, are faithful to Your covenant, and keeps Your promise.

On seeing Trees blossoming the first time in the Year

Blessed be YAHUWAH our Elohim (God), Melek Ha'Olam (King of the universe), the God and the Father of our Lord Yah'shua the Messiah (Jesus Christ), who has made Your world lacking in nothing, but has produced therein goodly creatures and goodly trees wherewith to give delight unto the children of men.

On seeing a Sage distinguished for his knowledge of the Law

Blessed be YAHUWAH our Elohim (God), Melek Ha'Olam (King of the universe), the God and the Father of our Lord

Yah'shua the Messiah (Jesus Christ), who has imparted of Your wisdom to them that fear You.

On seeing Wise Men distinguished for other than Sacred Knowledge

Blessed be YAHUWAH our Elohim (God), Melek Ha'Olam (King of the universe), the God and the Father of our Lord Yah'shua the Messiah (Jesus Christ), who has given of Your wisdom to flesh and blood.

On seeing a King and his Court

Blessed be YAHUWAH our Elohim (God), Melek Ha'Olam (King of the universe), the God and the Father of our Lord Yah'shua the Messiah (Jesus Christ), who has given of Your glory to flesh and blood.

On seeing strangely formed Persons, such as Giants or Dwarfs

Blessed be YAHUWAH our Elohim (God), Melek Ha'Olam (King of the universe), the God and the Father of our Lord Yah'shua the Messiah (Jesus Christ), who varies the forms of Your creatures.

On fixing a Mezuzah

Blessed be YAHUWAH our Elohim (God), Melek Ha'Olam (King of the universe), the God and the Father of our Lord Yah'shua the Messiah (Jesus Christ), who has sanctified us by Your commandments, and commanded us to affix the Mezuzah.

On tasting any Fruit for the first time in the season; on entering into possession of a new House or Land; or on using new Raiment for the first time

Blessed be YAHUWAH our Elohim (God), Melek Ha'Olam (King of the universe), the God and the Father of our Lord Yah'shua the Messiah (Jesus Christ), who hast kept us in life and hast preserved us, and has enabled us to reach this season.

On hearing Good Tidings

Blessed be YAHUWAH our Elohim (God), Melek Ha'Olam (King of the universe), the God and the Father of our Lord Yah'shua the Messiah (Jesus Christ), who are good, and does good.

On hearing Evil Tidings

Blessed be YAHUWAH our Elohim (God), Melek Ha'Olam (King of the universe), the God and the Father of our Lord Yah'shua the Messiah (Jesus Christ), the true Judge.

The following is said on the Appearance of the New Moon

Blessed be YAHUWAH our Elohim (God), Melek Ha'Olam (King of the universe), the God and the Father of our Lord Yah'shua the Messiah (Jesus Christ), by whose word the heavens were created, and by the breath of whose mouth all their host. You did assign them a statute and a season, that they should not change their appointed charge. They are glad and rejoice to do the will of their Master, the truthful Worker whose work is truth, who bade the moon renew itself, a crown of glory unto those that have been upborne by him from the womb, who in the time to come will themselves be renewed like it, to honor their Creator for his glorious kingdom's sake. Blessed are You, YAHUWAH, who renew the months.

HALLEL

The Hallel is recited on New Moon [Rosh Chodesh], the first two days of Passover [Pesach], and Pentecost [Shavuot]; each of the nine days of the Feast of Tabernacles [Sukkot], and the eight days of the Feast of Lights and Dedication [Chanukah].

On the Intermediate Days of Festivals the Tephillin are removed before Hallel; on New Moon, before the Additional Service.

Blessed are You YAHUWAH our Elohim (God), Melek Ha'Olam (King of the Universe), the God and the Father of our Lord Yah'shua the Messiah (Jesus Christ), who has sanctified us by Your mitzvot (commandments), and has commanded us to read the Hallel.

Psalm 113

1 Halelu-Yah (Praise the Lord)! Praise, O servants of YAHUWAH, Praise the name of YAHUWAH! 2 Blessed be the name of YAHUWAH from this time forth and forevermore! 3 From the rising of the sun to its going down YAHUWAH's name is to be praised. 4 YAHUWAH is high above all goyim (nations), His glory above the heavens. 5 Who is like YAHUWAH our Elohim (God), Who dwells on high, 6 Who humbles Himself to behold the things that are in the heavens and in the earth? 7 He raises the dal (poor, lowly) out of the dust, and lifts the evyon (needy) out of the ash heap, 8 That He may seat him with princes, with the princes of His people. 9 He grants the akaret (barren woman) a home, like a joyful mother of children. Halelu-Yah (Praise the Lord)!

Psalm 114

1 When Israel went out of Egypt, the house of Jacob from a people of strange language, 2 Judah became His kadosh (holy place, sanctuary), and Israel His dominion. 3 The sea saw it and fled; Jordan turned back. 4 The mountains skipped like rams, the little hills like lambs. 5 What ails you, O sea, that you fled? O Jordan, that you turned back? 6 O mountains, that you skipped like rams? O little hills, like lambs? 7 Tremble, O earth, at the presence of Adon (the Lord), at the presence of the Eloah (God) of Jacob, 8 Who turned the rock into a pool of water, the flint into a fountain of waters.

Psalm 115

1 Not unto us, YAHUWAH, not unto us, but to Your name give glory, because of Your chesed (mercy), because of Your emet (truth). 2 Why should the goyim (Gentiles, heathens) say, "So where is their Elohim (God)?" 3 But our Elohim (God) is in heaven; He does whatever He pleases. 4 Their atsabiym (idols) are silver and gold, the work of men's hands. 5 They have mouths, but they do not speak; Eyes they have, but they do not see; 6 They have ears, but they do not hear; Noses they have, but they do not smell; 7 They have hands, but they do not handle; Feet they have, but they do not walk; Nor do they mutter through their throat. 8 Those who make them are like them; So is everyone who trusts in them. 9 O Israel, trust in YAHUWAH; He is their help and their shield. 10 O house of Aaron, batach (trust) in YAHUWAH; He is their help and their shield. 11 You who fear YAHUWAH, batach (trust) in YAHUWAH; He is their help and their shield. 12 YAHUWAH has been mindful of us; He will bless us; He will bless the house of Israel; He will bless the house of Aaron. 13 He will bless those who fear YAHUWAH, both small and great. 14 May YAHUWAH give you increase more and more, you and your children. 15 May you be blessed by YAHUWAH, who made heaven and earth. 16 The heaven, even the heavens, are

YAHUWAH's; But the earth He has given to the children of men. 17 The metiym (dead) do not praise Yah, nor any who go down into dumah (silence). 18 But we will bless Yah, from this time forth and forevermore. Halelu-Yah (Praise the Lord)!

Psalm 116

1 I love YAHUWAH, because He has heard my voice and my supplications. 2 Because He has inclined His ear to me, therefore I will call upon Him as long as I live. 3 The chevlei mavet (pains of death) surrounded me, and the pangs of Sheol (Hades, the grave, the underworld) laid hold of me; I found tsarah (trouble) and yagon (sorrow). 4 Then I called upon the name of YAHUWAH: "YAHUWAH, I implore You, deliver my soul!" 5 Chanun (Gracious) is YAHUWAH, and tsadiyk (righteous); Yes, our Elohim (God) is racham (merciful). 6 YAHUWAH preserves the simple; I was brought low, and He saved me. 7 Return to your rest, O my soul, for YAHUWAH has dealt bountifully with you. 8 For You have delivered my soul from mavet (death), my eyes from tears, and my feet from falling. 9 I will walk before YAHUWAH in the artsot hachayim (land of the living). 10 I believed, therefore I spoke, "I am aniy me'od (greatly afflicted)." 11 I said in my haste, "All men are kozev (liars)." 12 What shall I render to YAHUWAH for all His tagmuwl'iym (benefits) toward me? 13 I will take up the Kos Yeshu'ot (cup of salvation), and call upon the name of YAHUWAH. 14 I will pay my neder'iym (vows) to YAHUWAH now in the presence of all His people. 15 Precious in the sight of YAHUWAH is the mavet (death) of His kadoshiym (holy ones, saints, set apart ones). 16 YAHUWAH, truly I am Your servant; I am Your servant, the son of Your maidservant; You have loosed my bonds. 17 I will offer to You the zevavh todah (sacrifice of thanksgiving), and will call upon the name of YAHUWAH. 18 I will pay my

neder'iym (vows) to YAHUWAH now in the presence of all His people, 19 In the courts of YAHUWAH's house, in the midst of you, O Jerusalem. Halelu-Yah (Praise the Lord)!

Psalm 117

1 Praise YAHUWAH, all you goyim (Gentiles, nations)! Laud Him, all you peoples! 2 For His chesed (mercy) is great toward us, and the emet (truth) of YAHUWAH endures forever. Halelu-Yah (Praise the Lord)!

Psalm 118

1 Oh, give thanks to YAHUWAH, for He is tov (good)! For His chesed (mercy) endures forever. 2 Let Israel now say, "His chesed (mercy) endures forever." 3 Let the house of Aaron now say, "His chesed (mercy) endures forever." 4 Let those who fear YAHUWAH now say, "His chesed (mercy) endures forever." 5 I called on Yah in metsar (distress); And Yah answered me and set me in a broad place. 6 YAHUWAH is on my side; I will not fear. What can man do to me? 7 YAHUWAH is for me among those who help me; Therefore I shall see my desire on those who hate me. 8 It is better to chasah (trust, hope) in YAHUWAH than to put batach (trust, confidence) in adam (man, human beings, mankind). 9 It is better to chasah (trust, hope) in YAHUWAH than to put batach (trust, confidence) in princes. 10 All goyim (nations) surrounded me, but in the name of YAHUWAH I will destroy them. 11 They surrounded me, Yes, they surrounded me; But in the name of YAHUWAH I will destroy them. 12 They surrounded me like bees; They were quenched like a fire of thorns; For in the name of YAHUWAH I will destroy them. 13 You pushed me violently, that I might fall, but YAHUWAH helped me. 14 Yah is my strength and song, and He has become my yeshua (salvation). 15 The voice of rejoicing and salvation is in the

tents of the tsadiykiym (righteous); The right hand of YAHUWAH does valiantly. 16 The right hand of YAHUWAH is exalted; The right hand of YAHUWAH does valiantly. 17 I shall not die, but live, and declare the works of Yah. 18 Yah has chastened me severely, but He has not given me over to mavet (death). 19 Open to me the sha'arei tsedek (gates of righteousness); I will go through them, and I will praise Yah. 20 This is the Sha'ar la'YAHUWAH (gate of the Lord), through which the tsadiykiym (righteous) shall enter. 21 I will praise You, for You have answered me, and have become my yeshua (salvation). 22 The stone which the builders rejected has become the chief cornerstone. 23 This was YAHUWAH's doing; It is marvelous in our eyes. 24 This is the day YAHUWAH has made; We will rejoice and be glad in it. 25 Save now, I pray, YAHUWAH; YAHUWAH, I pray, send now tsaleach (prosperity). 26 Blessed is he who comes in the name of YAHUWAH! We have blessed you from the house of YAHUWAH. 27 El (God) is YAHUWAH, and He has given us light; Bind the sacrifice with cords to the horns of the altar. 28 You are Eli (my God), and I will praise You; You are Elohai (my God), I will exalt You. 29 Oh, give thanks to YAHUWAH, for He is good! For His chesed (mercy) endures forever.

All Your works shall praise You, YAHUWAH our Elohim (God), and Your pious ones, the just who do Your will, together with all Your people, the house of Israel, shall with exultation thank, bless, praise, glorify, exalt, reverence, sanctify and ascribe sovereignty unto Your name, O our King; for it is good to give thanks unto You, and becoming to sing praises unto Your name, because from everlasting to everlasting You are Elohim (God). Blessed are You, YAHUWAH, a King extolled with praises.

Psalm 146

1 Halelu-Yah (Praise the Lord)! Praise YAHUWAH, O my soul! 2 While I live I will praise YAHUWAH; I will sing praises to Elohai (my God) while I have my being. 3 Do not put your batach (trust) in nadiyv'iym (nobles), nor in a ben adam (son of man), in whom there is no help. 4 His spirit departs, he returns to his earth; In that very day his plans perish. 5 Happy is he who has the El (God) of Jacob for his help, whose hope is in YAHUWAH his Elohim (God), 6 Who made heaven and earth, the sea, and all that is in them; Who keeps emet (truth) forever, 7 Who executes mishpat (judgment) for the ashak'iym (oppressed), Who gives food to the hungry. YAHUWAH matiyr (looses; gives freedom to) the asar'iym (prisoners). 8 YAHUWAH opens the eyes of the blind; YAHUWAH raises those who are bowed down; YAHUWAH loves the tsadiyk'iym (righteous). 9 YAHUWAH shomer (keeps) the geriym (strangers); He relieves the yatom (fatherless, orphan) and almanah (widow); But the derek rasha'iym (way of the wicked) He turns upside down. 10 YAHUWAH shall reign forever; Your Elohim (God), O Zion, to all generations. Halelu-Yah (Praise the Lord)!

Psalm 148

1 Halelu-Yah (Praise the Lord)! Praise YAHUWAH from the heavens; Praise Him in the heights! 2 Praise Him, all His Mal'akiym (angels); Praise Him, all His tseva'ot (hosts, armies)! 3 Praise Him, sun and moon; Praise Him, all you stars of light! 4 Praise Him, you heavens of heavens, and you waters above the heavens! 5 Let them praise the name of YAHUWAH, for He commanded and they were created. 6 He also established them forever and ever; He made a decree which shall not pass away. 7 Praise YAHUWAH from the earth, you great taniyn'iym (dragons) and all tehom'ot (the

depths); 8 Fire and hail, snow and clouds; Stormy wind, fulfilling His word; 9 Mountains and all hills; Fruitful trees and all cedars; 10 Beasts and all cattle; Creeping things and flying fowl; 11 Kings of the earth and all peoples; Princes and all judges of the earth; 12 Both young men and maidens; Old men and children. 13 Let them praise the name of YAHUWAH, For His name alone is exalted; His glory is above the earth and heaven. 14 And He has exalted the horn of His people, The praise of all His kadoshiym (holy ones, saints, set apart ones); Of the children of Israel, a people near to Him. Halelu-Yah (Praise the Lord)!

Psalm 149

1 Halelu-Yah (Praise the Lord)! Sing to YAHUWAH a new song, and His praise in the assembly of kadoshiym (holy ones, saints, set apart ones). 2 Let Israel rejoice in their Maker; Let the children of Zion be joyful in their Melek (King). 3 Let them praise His name with the dance; Let them sing praises to Him with the timbrel and harp. 4 For YAHUWAH takes pleasure in His people; He will beautify the avaniym (humble, meek) with yshu'ah (salvation). 5 Let the kadoshiym (holy ones, saints, set apart ones) be joyful in glory; Let them sing aloud on their beds. 6 Let the high praises of El (God) be in their mouth, and a two-edged sword in their hand, 7 To execute nekamah (vengeance) on the goyim (nations, gentiles, heathen), and tokechot (punishments) on the umiym (peoples); 8 To asar (bind) their melek'iym (kings) with zikiym (chains), and their kavod'iym (nobles, great ones, glorious ones) with kevel barzel (fetters of iron); 9 To asot (execute) on them the mishpat ketuv (written judgment); This hadar (honor, ornament, majesty, glory) have all His kadoshiym (holy ones, saints, set apart ones). Halelu-Yah (Praise the Lord)!

Psalm 150

1 Halelu-Yah (Praise the Lord)! Praise El (God) in His kadosh (holy place, sanctuary); Praise Him in His mighty firmament! 2 Praise Him for His gevurot (mighty acts); Praise Him according to His rov godel (excellent greatness)! 3 Praise Him with the sound of the shofar (rams horn); Praise Him with the lute and harp! 4 Praise Him with the timbrel and dance; Praise Him with stringed instruments and flutes! 5 Praise Him with loud cymbals; Praise Him with clashing cymbals! 6 Let everything that has breath praise Yah. Halelu-Yah (Praise the Lord)!-Yah!

BIRKOT MAYIM KADOSHIYM (BLESSING OF HOLY WATER)

Mayim Kadoshiym (Holy water) is mentioned in Numbers 5:17. This was regular water that was blessed by the koheniym (priests) and was used for washing, immersing, sprinking and purification.

In Numbers 19:1-22 we see the Torot Tohora (Laws of Purification) which was the ritual for making the Mey Niddah (Waters of Separation) used for Chattat (Purification for sin). This was to take the Epher (ashes) of the Para Aduma (red heifer) for Chattat (Purification for sin) and put it into a keliy (vessel), and then add Mayim Chayim (Living Water, i.e. running water). This was then sprinkled upon the unclean person and he was made clean. This was declared a Chukat Olam (perpetual or everlasting statute) in verse 21. This was used for purifying other objects as well in Numbers 31:23.

This is also refered to In the book of Hebrews:

> "For if the blood of bulls and goats and the ashes of a heifer, sprinkling the unclean, sanctifies for the purifying of the flesh, how much more shall the blood of Messiah (Christ), who through the eternal Spirit offered Himself without spot to Elohim (God), cleanse your conscience from dead works to serve the Elohim Chayim (living God)?" (Hebrews 9:13-15)

Mayim Kadoshiym (Holy Water) is still used for sprinkling the unclean for Chattat (purification for sin). Which is to say that this Mey Niddah (Water of Separation) for Chattat (purification of sin) is still used today only without the sacrifice of the Para Adumah (red heifer) and its Epher (ashes). Yah'shua's (Jesus') sacrifice on the cross replaced all of the Old Testament animal sacrifices. The blood of Yah'shua (Jesus) is represented by two elements in the Brit Chadasha (New Testament), both Yayin (Wine) and Mayim (Water). For this reasons, John says:

> "For there are three that bear witness in heaven: Ha'Av (the Father), Ha'Davar (the Word), and the Ruach HaKodesh (Holy Spirit); and these three are one. And there are three that bear witness on earth: the Ruach (Spirit), the Mayim (water), and the Dam (blood); and these three agree as one." (1 John 5:7-8)

This can also be seen in Numbers 8:7, when YAHUWAH told Moshe (Moses) to cleanse the Levites by sprinkling Mey Chattat (the water of purification for sin) upon them. This injunction was given way before the commandment to put the ashes of a heifer into the water. Therefore, the book of Hebrews says,

> "let us draw near with a true heart in full assurance of faith, having our hearts sprinkled from an evil conscience and our bodies washed with the Mey Chattat (Waters of Purification for sin)." (Hebrews 10:22)

Thus the Brit Chafasha (New Testament) uses the Mayim Kadoshiym (Holy Water) as the Dam Yah'shua (Blood of Jesus) which is used for all of the Old Testament purposes all in one.

1. Mayim Kadoshiym (Holy Water).
2. Mayim Tahoriym (Water of Purification).
3. Mey Niddah (Waters of Separation from uncleanness).
4. Mey Chattat (Waters of Purification from sin).

This water can be used to immerse in, or it can be sprinkled upon the person. It can be sprinkled upon objects, in houses, on animals and can be used in exorcisms and to drive away shediym (demons) etc.

Pulchan Mayim Kadoshiym
(The Rite of Holy Water)

Blessed are You YAHUWAH our Elohim (God), Melek Ha'Olam (King of the universe), the God and the father of our Lord Yah'shua the Messiah (Jesus Christ), Who sanctified us with His mitzvot (commandments), and commanded us concerning Mayim Kadoshiym (Holy Water).

O YAHUWAH, Borey (Creator) unconquerable, invincible King, Victor ever-glorious, Who did hold in check the forces bent on dominating us, Who did overcome the cruelty of the za'aph oyev (raging enemy), Who did in Your power beat down the rasha oyev (wicked foe): Humbly and fearfully do we pray to You, O YAHUWAH, and we ask You to look with favor on this Melach (salt) and Mayim (water) which You have created. Shine on it with the light of Your mercy and lovingkindness. Sanctify it by the dew of Your Ahava (love), so that, through the invocation of Your Shem Kadosh (holy name), wherever this Mayim (water) and Melach (salt) is sprinkled it may turn aside, rebuke, drive away and banish every attack of Satan (the adversary): Heylel (Lucifer), Samael, Semyaza, Azazel, Liyliyt (Lilith; night demon), Na'amah, Rahab (Water Demon), Iyzebel (Jezebel), Livyatan (Leviathan), Behemah (beast), Beliya'al (Belial), the Mal'ak HaMavet (angel of death), the Mashchiyt (destroyer), the Taniyn (dragon), the Nachash (serpent), the Piton (python), the Shediym (demons), the Sa'iyriym (goat demon), the Bat Ya'anah (daughters of Lilith), the Tsiyiym (desert demon), the Iyiym (howling demon), the Alukah (vampire spirit) the

Siren, the Ruach Ha'Tumah (unclean spirit), Ruach Ra'ah (evil spirit), Ruach Rasha'iym (spirit of wickedness), Ruach Chalah (spirit of infirmity), Aluka (vampire spirit) Rapha'iym (disembodied spirit; ghost) and Dybbuk (dibbuk me ruach ra'ah – a clinging of an evil spirit) and dispel the terror of the arsi nachash (poisonous serpent).

And wherever we may be, make the Ruach HaKodesh (Holy Spirit) present to us who now implore Your mercy. Through our Lord Yah'shua the Messiah (Jesus Christ), Your Son, Who lives and reigns with You in the unity of the Ruach HaKodesh (Holy Spirit), Elohim (God), forever and ever. Amen.

Our help is in the name of YAHUWAH.

Who made heaven and earth.

EXORCISM OF SALT (if not done in advance)

Elohim's (God's) creature, Melach (salt), I cast out the shed (demon) from you by the Elohim Chayim ✠ (living God), by the El Emet ✠ (true God), by the Elohim Kadoshiym ✠ (holy God), by Elohim (God) who ordered you to be thrown into the water-spring by Eliysha Ha-Navi (Elisha the Prophet) to heal it of its barrenness. May you be a Melach Me'tohar (purified salt), a means of health and purification for those who believe, a medicine for body and soul for all who make use of you. May all evil fancies of the foul fiend, his malice and cunning, be driven afar from the place where you are sprinkled. And let every Ruach Ha'Tumah (unclean spirit), every Ruach Ra'ah (evil spirit), and every Shed (demon) be repulsed by Him who is coming to judge both the living and the dead and the world by fire. Amen.

Let us pray.

YAHUWAH, El Shaddai Olam (Lord, Almighty Everlasting God), we humbly appeal to your mercy and goodness to graciously bless ✠ this creature, Melach (salt), which you have given for mankind's use. May all who use it find in it a remedy for body, soul, and mind. And may everything that it touches or sprinkles be freed from uncleanness and any influence of the ruach ra'ah (evil spirit); through Messiah (Christ) our Lord. Amen.

EXORCISM OF THE WATER

Elohim's (God's) creature, Mayim (water), I cast out the Shed (demon) from you in the name of Elohim (God) ✠ the Avi SHaddai (Father almighty), in the name of Yah'shua (Jesus) ✠ the Messiah (Christ), His Son, our Lord, and in the power of the Ruach HaKodesh ✠ (Holy Spirit). May you be a purified water, empowered to drive far away all power of the enemy, in fact, to root out and banish the enemy Satan himself, along with his Mal'akiym Naful (fallen angels). We ask this through the power of our Lord Yah'shua the Messiah (Jesus Christ), who is coming to judge both the living and the dead and the world by fire. Amen.

Let us pray.

O Elohim (God), who for man's welfare established the most wonderful mysteries in the substance of Mayim (water), hearken to our tefillah (prayer), and pour forth your blessing ✠ on this element now being prepared with various purifying rites. May this creature of yours, when used in your mysteries and endowed with your grace, serve to cast out Shediym (demons) and to banish all sickness and disease. May everything that this Mayim (water) sprinkles in the homes and gatherings of the faithful be delivered from all that is unclean, evil and hurtful; let no breath of contagion hover there, no taint of corruption; let all the wiles and attacks of the lurking enemy come to nothing. By the sprinkling of this Mayim (water) may everything opposed to the safety and peace of the occupants of these homes be banished, so that in calling on your holy name they may know the well-being and healing they desire, and be protected from every peril; through Yah'shua the Messiah (Jesus Christ) our Lord. Amen.

Now the Kohen (priest) pours the Melach (salt) into the Mayim (water) in the form of a cross, saying:

May this Melach (salt) and Mayim (water) be mixed together; in the name of the Father YAHUWAH, and of the Son Yah'shua (Jesus), ✠ and of the Ruach HaKodesh (Holy Spirit). Amen.

Let us pray.

YAHUWAH Elohim (Lord God), source of irresistible might and king of an invincible realm, the ever-glorious conqueror; who restrain the force of the oyev (adversary), silencing the uproar of his rage, and valiantly subduing his wickedness; in awe and humility we beg you, YAHUWAH, to regard with favor this creature thing of Melach (salt) and Mayim (water), to let the light of your kindness shine upon it, and to hallow it with the dew of your mercy; so that wherever it is sprinkled and your holy name is invoked, every assault of Satan, the Ruach Ha'Tumah (unclean spirit), and the Ruach Ra'ah (evil spirit) may be banished, baffled, and all dread of the Nachash Eres (serpent's venom) be cast out. To us who entreat your mercy grant that the Ruach HaKodesh (Holy Spirit) may be with us wherever we may be; through Yah'shua the Messiah (Jesus Christ) our Lord. Amen.

BIRKAT MELACH KADOSHIYM (BLESSING OF HOLY SALT)

This Rite of Blessing of Melach (Salt) is used outside of the Rite of Blessing of Mayim Kadoshiym (Holy Water) which incorporates the blessing of Melach (salt) in preparation for the blessing of Mayim (water).

Pulchan Melach Kadoshiym (The Rite of Holy Salt)

Blessed are You YAHUWAH our Elohim (God), Melek Ha'Olam (King of the universe), the God and the father of our Lord Yah'shua the Messiah (Jesus Christ), Who sanctified us with His mitzvot (commandments), and commanded us concerning Melach Kadoshiym (Holy Salt).

O YAHUWAH, Borey (Creator) unconquerable, invincible King, Victor ever-glorious, Who did hold in check the forces bent on dominating us, Who did overcome the cruelty of the za'aph oyev (raging enemy), Who did in Your power beat down the rasha oyev (wicked foe): Humbly and fearfully do we pray to You, O YAHUWAH, and we ask You to look with favor on this Melach (salt) which You have created. Shine on it with the light of Your mercy and lovingkindness. Sanctify it by the dew of Your Ahava (love), so that, through the invocation of Your Shem Kadosh (holy name), wherever this Melach (salt) is sprinkled it may turn aside, rebuke, drive away and banish every attack of Satan (the adversary): Heylel (Lucifer), Samael, Semyaza, Azazel, Liyliyt (Lilith; night demon), Na'amah, Rahab (Water Demon), Iyzebel (Jezebel), Livyatan (Leviathan), Behemah (beast), Beliya'al (Belial), the Mal'ak HaMavet (angel of death), the Mashchiyt (destroyer), the Taniyn (dragon), the Nachash (serpent), the Piton (python), the Shediym (demons), the Sa'iyriym (goat demon), the Bat Ya'anah (daughters of Lilith), the Tsiyiym (desert demon), the Iyiym (howling demon), the Alukah (vampire spirit) the Siren, the Ruach Ha'Tumah (unclean spirit), Ruach Ra'ah (evil spirit), Ruach Rasha'iym (spirit of wickedness), Ruach Chalah (spirit of infirmity), Aluka (vampire spirit) Rapha'iym (disembodied spirit; ghost) and Dybbuk (dibbuk me ruach ra'ah – a clinging of an evil spirit) and dispel the terror of the arsi nachash (poisonous serpent).

And wherever we may be, make the Ruach HaKodesh (Holy Spirit) present to us who now implore Your mercy. Through our Lord Yah'shua the Messiah (Jesus Christ), Your Son, Who lives and reigns with You in the unity of the Ruach HaKodesh (Holy Spirit), Elohim (God), forever and ever. Amen.

Our help is in the name of YAHUWAH.

Who made heaven and earth.

EXORCISM

Elohim's (God's) creature, Melach (salt), I cast out the shed (demon) from you by the Elohim Chayim ✠ (living God), by the El Emet ✠ (true God), by the Elohim Kadoshiym ✠ (holy God), by Elohim (God) who ordered you to be thrown into the water-spring by Eliysha Ha-Navi (Elisha the Prophet) to heal it of its barrenness. May you be a Melach Me'tohar (purified salt), a means of health and purification for those who believe, a medicine for body and soul for all who make use of you. May all evil fancies of the foul fiend, his malice and cunning, be driven afar from the place where you are sprinkled. And let every Ruach Ha'Tumah (unclean spirit), every Ruach Ra'ah (evil spirit), and every Shed (demon) be repulsed by Him who is coming to judge both the living and the dead and the world by fire. Amen.

Let us pray.

El Shaddai Olam (Almighty everlasting God), we humbly appeal to your mercy and goodness to graciously bless ✠ this creature, Melach (salt), which you have given for mankind's use. May all who use it find in it a remedy for body and mind. And may everything that it touches or sprinkles be freed from uncleanness and any influence of the Ruach Ra'ah (evil spirit); through Yah'shua the Messiah (Jesus Christ) our Lord. Amen.

Let us pray.

YAHUWAH Elohim (Lord God), source of irresistible might and king of an invincible realm, the ever-glorious conqueror; who restrain the force of the adversary, silencing the uproar of his rage, and valiantly subduing his wickedness; in awe and humility we beg you, YAHUWAH, to regard with favor this creature thing of Melach (salt), to let the light of your kindness shine upon it, and to hallow it with the dew of your mercy; so that wherever it is sprinkled and your holy name is invoked, every assault of Satan, the Ruach Ha'Tumah (unclean spirit), and the Ruach Ra'ah (evil spirit) may be banished, baffled, and all dread of the Nachash Eres (serpent's venom) be cast out. To us who entreat your mercy grant that the Ruach HaKodesh (Holy Spirit) may be with us wherever we may be; through Yah'shua the Messiah (Jesus Christ) our Lord. Amen.

BIRKAT SHEMEN HA-MISCHAH (BLESSING OF ANOINTING OIL)

Blessed are You, YAHUWAH our Elohim (God), Melek Ha-Olam (King of the Universe), Who sanctified us with His mitzvot (commandments), and commanded us concerning the Shemen Mishchat Kodesh (Holy anointing oil).

Our help is in the name of YAHUWAH.

Who made heaven and earth.

EXORCISM

Elohim's (God's) creature, Shemen (oil), I cast out the Shed (demon) from you by YAHUWAH the Father ✠ almighty, who made heaven and earth and sea, and all that they contain. Let the adversary's power, the devil's legions, and all Satan's attacks and machinations be dispelled and driven afar from this creature, Shemen (oil). Let it bring health in body, soul and mind to all who use it, in the name of YAHUWAH ✠ the Father almighty, and of our Lord Yah'shua ✠ the Messiah (Jesus Christ), His Son, and of the Ruach HaKodesh ✠ (Holy Spirit), the Advocate, as well as in the love of the same Yah'shua the Messiah (Jesus Christ) our Lord, who is coming to judge both the living and the dead and the world by fire. Amen.

YAHUWAH, hear my prayer, and let my cry be heard by you.

Let us pray.

YAHUWAH El Shaddai (Lord God almighty), before whom the hosts of Mal'akiym (angels) stand in awe, and whose heavenly service we acknowledge; may it please you to regard favorably and to bless ✠ and hallow ✠ this creature, Shemen (oil), which by your power has been pressed from the juice of olives. You have ordained it for anointing the sick, so that, when they are made well, they may give thanks to you, the living and true Elohim (God). Grant, we pray, that those who will use this Shemen (oil), which we are blessing ✠ in your name, may be delivered from all suffering, all infirmity, and all wiles of the enemy. Let it be a means of averting any kind of adversity from man, made in your image and redeemed by the precious blood of your Son, so that he may never again suffer the sting of the ancient serpent; through Yah'shua the Messiah (Jesus Christ) our Lord. Amen.

The oil is then sprinkled with holy water.

BIRKAT KETORET HAKODESH (BLESSED HOLY INCENSE)

[A mixture of frankincense and myrrh is preferred. In the story of the Magi who came to honor the Christ child, brought three gifts for Him. The first gift was gold, which is a gift given to a king. The second gift was frankincense, which is a gift given to a god. The third gift was myrrh, which is a spice used in burial. Thus, these gift were given to a King, who is God, and who will die for His people. Thus, this mixture of frankincense and myrrh represents a God who died for us. This fact of the sacrifice of Messiah (Christ) on the Cross and His Resurrection is of particularly powerful against demons as this even represents they total defeat.

Ketoret Kodesh (Holy Incense) can be used to bless a house or person using a censer with a handle to be able to walk around to incense each room. The censer may also be used to burned incense in a stationary place for regular use to fill the house with the fragrance and the blessing.

> Blessed are You, YAHUWAH our Elohim (God), Melek Ha-Olam (King of the Universe), Who sanctified us with His mitzvot (commandments), and commanded us concerning the Ketoret Kodesh (Holy Incense).

> Our help is in the name of YAHUWAH.

> Who made heaven and earth.

EXORCISM

Elohim's (God's) creature, Ketoret (incense), I cast out the Shed (demon) from you by YAHUWAH, the Father ✠ almighty, who made heaven and earth and sea, and all that they contain. Let the adversary's power, the devil's legions, and all Satan's attacks and machinations be dispelled and driven far away from this creature, Ketoret (incense). Let it bring health in body, soul and mind to all who use it, stopping every illness and plague, in the name of YAHUWAH ✠ the Father almighty, and of our Lord Yah'shua ✠ the Messiah (Jesus Christ), His Son, and of the Ruach HaKodesh ✠ (Holy Spirit), the Advocate, as well as in the love of the same Yah'shua the Messiah (Jesus Christ) our Lord, who is coming to judge both the living and the dead and the world by fire. Amen.

YAHUWAH, heed my prayer.

And let my cry be heard by you.

Let us pray.

YAHUWAH El Shaddai (Lord God almighty), before whom the hosts of Mal'akiym (angels) stand in awe, and whose heavenly service we acknowledge; may it please you to regard favorably and to bless ✠ and hallow ✠ this creature, Ketoret (incense), which by your power has been prepared from aromatic plant materials. You have ordained it as a fragrant offering to glorify You and to bless people and things, they may give thanks to you, the living and true Elohim (God). Grant, we pray, that those who will use this incense, which we are blessing ✠ in your name, may be delivered from all suffering, all infirmity, and all wiles of the enemy. Let it be a means of averting any kind of adversity from man, made in

643

your image and redeemed by the precious blood of your Son, so that he may never again suffer the sting of the ancient serpent; through Yah'shua Messiah (Jesus Christ) our Lord. Amen.

The incense is then sprinkled with holy water.

Made in the USA
Las Vegas, NV
22 November 2023

81362923R00374